The Field Guide to Parenting

A Comprehensive Handbook of
Great Ideas, Advice, Tips,
and Solutions for Parenting Children
Ages One to Five

By Shelley Butler & Deb Kratz

CHANDLER
HOUSE
PRESS

Worcester, Massachusetts
1999

The Field Guide to Parenting:
A Comprehensive Handbook of Great Ideas, Advice, Tips
and Solutions for Parenting Children Ages One to Five

ISBN 1-886284-21-0
Library of Congress Catalog Card Number: 99-067458

First Edition
A B C D E F G H I J K

Published by
Chandler House Press
335 Chandler Street
Worcester, MA 01602
USA

President
Lawrence J. Abramoff

Editorial/Production Manager
James A. Karis II

Book Design
Anna B. Type & Graphics

Cover Design
Marshall Henrichs

Author Photo
Larry Callahan, Callahan & Co., Minneapolis

Chandler House Press books are available at special discounts for bulk purchases. For more information about how to arrange such purchases, please contact Chandler House Press, 335 Chandler Street, Worcester, MA 01602, or call (800) 642-6657, or fax (508) 756-9425, or find us on the World Wide Web at www.chandlerhousepress.com.

Chandler House Press books are distributed to the trade by
National Book Network, Inc.
4720 Boston Way
Lanham, MD 20706
(800) 462-6420

To John, Jakob, and Joey,
for believing in and making dreams come true everyday.
Love, Shelley/Mom

To Tim, Kate, and Will,
with whom the fire and the rose are one.
Love, Deb/Mom

Acknowledgements

The authors gratefully acknowledge the following:

Our husbands for their belief, advice, and many levels of support throughout.

Shelley's circle of family. Thank you to my mother, Betty, for inspiring a love of books, an awe of what's in them, and the pride in creating one, and to my late father, Ray, for passing on the amazing value of putting words on the page. Thanks to Mary and Ted, for always being there to help, for keeping me warm on the outside with wool and down, and for keeping me warm on the inside with immeasurable love and support. Much love and gratitude to my extended group of sisters and their families, Cid, Steph, Anita and Ann, Gary, Steve, not only for their generous time in working on the book itself, but also for their unwavering enthusiasm, optimism, affection, pride, and support.

Deb's circle of family. Thank you to my mother, Carol, my late father, Al, and my brother, Greg for always being there, and for providing me with a family and community to grow within as a child. Thanks to Barb, Tim and Jenny for adding new and wonderful dimensions to that family. Thanks to my late grandmother, Margaret Tuttle for showing me unconditional love always. Thanks to Rich, Sue, Kevin, Brendan, and Chris Kramp for inspiring me to believe that consistent and committed parenting can lead to great children and young adults.

Our agent, Pat Snell, and our publishers, Dick Staron and Larry Abramoff for taking on a couple of eager new writers and for sticking with us until we met the goal of publishing this book. Thank you to Jennifer Goguen, Claire Cousineau Smith and everyone at Chandler House Press for their hard work in the making of the book and for helping us plod through what was new territory for us.

All who generously contributed pieces, voices, or art. Special thanks to:

Authors Jean Illsley Clarke, Laura Davis and Janis Keyser, Michael Gurian, Vicki Lansky, Jane Nelsen, Mary Nelsen, Elizabeth Pantley, Nancy Samalin, and Linda Ziedrich.

The Early Childhood and Family Education sites in MN, the Parenthood Web, and Kidsource Online for helping us collect parent voices.

The wise parents who contributed great ideas.

The children who contributed art: Maddie Baker, Elise Bremer, Maura Bremer, Jakob Butler, Joey Butler, Evan Coppock, Rachel Holle, Laura Macke, Kara Maki, Tennae Maki, Rachel McNamee, Hannah McNamee, Jennifer Meunier, Brian Novak, Jason Novak, Matt Novak, August Ogren-Dehn, Sophia Ogren-Dehn, Kate Scott, Will Scott, Joe Sellwood, Tom Sellwood, Connor Slawson, Reed Thompson, and Rustin Thompson.

The Bloomington Early Childhood Family Education site and to Anita Witta, for their work in collecting children's art from the special education program.

Jodie Spirer for her artwork in the early stages and her support throughout.

Photographer Larry Callahan of Callahan & Co., Minneapolis.

Our team of professional and parent reviewers who made sure that we were on the mark by offering valuable insights based on their practice and wisdom:

Katie Arvesen, OTR
Kimberly Ball, RD, LD
Patty Bartlett
Cheryl Bauer, MS, Licensed Early Childhood Special Education Teacher
Barbara Brandt, MEd., Licensed Elementary Teacher
Becky Casper
Tammy Clow
Elizabeth G. Dewyre, BSW
Linda Evans, MA, Licensed Early Childhood Special Education Teacher
Debbie Flick, MSW, LGSW
Maria Gerar
Lori Gersch
Linnea Grey, MS
Melissa Haugen
Joan Henderson, MEd.
Jeffry Jeanetta-Wark, MA., LICSW
Waid Johnson, MSEd.
Ann Kragenbring, MSW, LICSW
Karen Kramer, RNC
Barbara J. Kratz, MS, CPNP
Denise Lanoux, BS, Licensed Early Childhood Teacher
Joyce E. Lindgren, PHN, MPH
Laurie Masanz, MPH, LN
Sue McCarthy, MA, Licensed Early Childhood Teacher
Nancy Melquist, BS, Licensed Parent Educator and Elementary Teacher
Tiana Meyers
Kathy Morris, BS, Licensed Parent Educator
Beth Melin Nelson, BS, MS in progress, Licensed Music Educator
Gail Nordstrom, MLIS
Cecile M. Penna, BS, AMI
Nicole Poirier, MST CCC
Angela Reichel
Lydia Roehl
Mary Rudeen, OTR
Kathryn Schwister, BME, MME in progress, Licensed Music Educator
Cherylee Sherry, MPH, CHES
Jean Shulte, MEd., AMI
Hilary Pert Stecklein, MD
Anne Vanic, MS, CPNP, IBCLC
Margie Walsh, RN, LSW, MEd., Licensed Parent Educator
Christina Woods, MA, Licensed Elementary Teacher

Shelley's friends, mentors, and caring community. Thanks to my supportive friends and neighbors in Minneapolis and Shoreview from whom I continue to learn so much about being a parent, and who offered to care for my children while I was glued to work (that's you Cindy, Beth, Luanne, and Rïse, among others). Special thanks to Chris Langseth for the long distance love and support. Thanks to Stephanie Langenkamp, for mentoring in the practice of public librarianship at it's best. Thanks to the many fine teachers and professors from Mpls. Urban Arts to the University of Minnesota who helped me believe that I could be a writer.

Deb's friends, mentors, and caring community. Thanks to Meg Emmett Farrell, Donna Mienk, and Judy Jackson for your long-standing, deep support, and your belief in my creativity and writing. Thanks to Merrie Dahlgren for noticing and telling me that I was a writer way back in fourth grade. Thanks to Virginia Jacobson for keeping me firmly planted in the values of social work practice. Thanks to the women that I share day-to-day mothering with, Patrice Bremer, Jennifer Ogren Dehn, Barb Brandt, Lori Baker, Katie Macke, and Deb Kulinski. Special thanks to them for kindly helping me to get myself and my kids to the right places at the right time and for giving Kate and Will extra care when the last many months of writing the book created a wave of chaos.

The many children in our lives who helped create and celebrate this book, and who served as constant reminders of why we were writing it in the first place. Special thanks to:

- Joey and Jake Butler, and Kate and Will Scott for being you, the children we most admire, and for all the great help with the book: reading and reviewing countless books for little kids, locating books at the library, photocopying, stapling, assembling, and other important jobs.

- Terra Alvarez for her tireless and skilled copying.

- Alex Alvarez, and Laura Macke for eagerly inquiring about the book progress many afternoons after school.

- Sarah Boike, Sean and Rian Denich, Becky and David Kreps, and Tim O'Brien for being the great kids that you are.

The Minnesota Early Childhood Family Education Program for giving us support and education when we were parenting our young children, and for the inspiration for writing the book.

The Early Childhood Family Education sites in Stillwater and Mahtomedi, for sharing their parenting information resources, both in printed form and through the collective wisdom of the program staff and families that has been passed through discussions over time. A special thanks to supervisors, Nancy Melquist and Mary Harcey, for being so genuinely excited about the book, when in fact, the time it took to write it created extra challenges for them.

Susan Perry, because we took an oath in her class to thank her if we ever got this book published from the proposal she helped us write.

The VORT Corporation, producers of *HELP: The Hawaii Early Learning Profile* (650-322-8282, www.vort.com), and *Family Information Services* (800-852-8112, www.familyinfoserv.com) for their wealth of sound child development and child rearing information that we used heavily, though not exclusively, in the research for this book.

Public libraries all over Minnesota and the U.S., without which the preparation of this book would not have been possible. Special thanks to the professional, supportive staffs at the Shoreview and White Bear Lake Branches of the Ramsey County Library, the Wildwood and Stillwater Branches of the Washington County Library, and the Nokomis Branch of the Minneapolis Public Library.

Last but not least, we gratefully acknowledge each other, for believing in one another enough to create a book together and remain good friends.

This book is designed to provide a wide variety of ideas on many topics. It does not offer legal, medical, or psychological advice and should not be used as a substitute for seeking competent medical or legal help. The book is not meant as a substitute for the reader's personal consultation with a qualified professional regarding any topic presented.

Every attempt has been made to accurately paraphrase and represent the ideas that have been found in the work of the many fine authors and experts credited in this book, and to obtain copyright permission when direct quotes were used. Since only brief descriptions of ideas are typically given, we urge readers to seek out the whole book or work when they find an idea presented that interests them.

Sources cited do not necessarily endorse other sources.

Authors' reference to the review team in the acknowledgment section of the book pertains to a general endorsement of the whole book and should not be construed as specific advice or opinion on any particular topic.

Table of Contents

Table of Contents

Part II – Great Ideas, Advice, Tips, and Solutions for Parenting Children Ages One to Five 177

Table of Contents

Table of Contents

The Field Guide to Parenting

Parenting Everyday

Six o'clock. A small, dark-haired, curious two-year-old and his mother rush into the house from a busy day of play, work, and errands. It is dinnertime now, and still there are groceries to put away and food to cook. The little boy reaches for a bag of cookies from a grocery bag. The mother takes a deep breath, and then, jumps in: "Hey, thanks for helping. You can be my delivery person and deliver those to the cupboard. Can you show me where we keep the cookies?" The boy is eager to show that he can do this and completes the assignment.

As the mother reaches to give him a hug, the boy becomes fascinated with his mother's earrings. "Green ear-ring," the mother says slowly. Just then, a bag of groceries falls off the table, and the boy runs to see what he can find. He tries to help by picking up and dropping several boxes, cans, and bags of food. Another deep breath for the mother.

"Ball!" the boy says as he struggles to open a box of cereal. The mother stops to look and sure enough, on the cereal box a sports star holds a football high in the air, ready to throw. "You're right! It's a ball!" She picks him up, believing he is the most clever and beautiful child, as he gives her a proud and satisfied smile. Turning challenging situations into golden opportunities to listen and interact with a child is an everyday occurrence for most parents.

Taking advantage of those opportunities, like most things to do with raising a child, requires patience, energy, and knowledge. Parents need the humility to make mistakes and the courage to try again. Every day offers the opportunity to start fresh and begin something new. But where should parents begin?

First, children have a right to expect that their basic needs will be met. Children deserve each and every day:

- Food and clothes
- Shelter and safety
- Good health care
- Love, smiles, and affection
- Time and attention
- Someone to talk to who listens
- Someone who understands what he is able to do and what he is still struggling to master
- A confident, healthy parent or caregiver

Parenting involves getting to know your child, his personality, his temperament, his likes and dislikes, and taking pleasure in his company. Then, it's necessary to get to know your child again and again as he grows and changes. Looking at the world from your child's point of view, and slowing down to let him move and grow at his own pace is also an important part of raising a child.

Parenting requires acting from a thoughtful place. Before making a decision, trying an approach to a problem, or teaching your child something new, ask yourself, "Does this help my child? Does this harm my child?"

Young children grow best in the love and shelter of family, but they need others too. The fact is, no one can raise a child alone. Close by is a community of friends, family, neighbors, and family professionals who care and want to give your family the support you need to succeed. To seek outside help, assistance, and resources is one way of showing both love to your child and a healthy respect for all family members.

Parenting everyday is full of joys and concerns, and there is no one right way to handle any one of them. There are no magic bullets or quick fixes to get your child to sleep through the night or to get along with his sibling. There are, however, many solutions, and help is available to sort them out. *The Field Guide to Parenting* offers tools to help parents make positive choices for their families.

The Field Guide Tools For Parenting Everyday

The Growing Child Year-By-Year

Children learn and master many new skills in the early years. This part of *The Field Guide to Parenting* is a year-by-year guide to the skills that young children typically develop between ages one and five, that includes suggestions for fostering that development.

Great Ideas, Advice, Tips, and Solutions for Parenting Children Ages One to Five

From everyday challenges like dawdling to more special circumstances like death and grief, a wide range of topics, concerns, and problems arise in parenting a young child. *The Field Guide to Parenting* presents a variety of information, advice, tips, and solutions from people in specialized fields, parenting experts, and even parents themselves, on each topic.

DESCRIPTION

The description starts at the beginning, defining the topic and discussing it in relation to children from one to five years of age.

REALISTIC EXPECTATIONS

REALISTIC EXPECTATIONS provides information on the topic that may affect parenting decisions: what is typical to expect of children regarding the topic, the possible reasons for children's behavior, what else may be going on with children, some things to think about in approaching this topic with children, and how this topic may affect the growth and development of young children.

APPROACHES

For every challenge, concern or topic, there is a variety of information, credible advice and practical ideas about respectfully guiding your child's behavior and your own. One particular tip, solution, or piece of advice will not work for every child or for every family. The APPROACHES section within each topic provides a variety of sound information, which, although possibly conflicting, equips parents to make choices and decisions that fit their family. There is no advice in *The Field Guide to Parenting* that punishes, treats children harshly, or causes physical harm. Instead, the emphasis is on nurturing development, promoting positive values, preventing and guiding undesirable behaviors, setting limits, and using play and children's literature to understand and teach.

WHEN TO GET MORE HELP

Even though the range of typical behavior is wide, parents often wonder if their child may fall outside of that range. WHEN TO GET MORE HELP offers guidelines to help a parent decide whether they or their child may need professional help.

MORE HELP & INFORMATION

This part of each topic gives parents ideas on where they can look outside of *The Field Guide to Parenting* for books, articles, brochures, pamphlets, web sites, videos, hotlines, national organizations, government agencies, videos, and resources in their community when, good useful tools were found. For every resource listed in this section, there are many, many more good ones out there. Ask your local library or bookstore for help in finding more great parenting resources.

FINDING HELP IN YOUR COMMUNITY GUIDE

There is help available for every parent and child in every community. An information and referral telephone help-line, the Government and Community pages of your telephone book, the telephone information operator, or your public library are good starting points to find the helping people in your community. Finding help may take several phone calls to get to just the right person or agency, but remember that help is there! Be patient and keep trying until you find the help, support, or advice that you need and want. Some of the people who may be able to help:

Early Childhood Intervention

WHO THEY ARE: Typically, a team of teachers, social workers, physical therapists, occupational therapists, psychologists, and speech therapists provide a free assessment of your child to identify any special needs when you have concerns about behavior, growth and development, and/or the speech and language of your child. They can also guide you to other services that may be useful to you.

WHERE TO FIND THEM:

- To request an evaluation for children birth to five years, talk to your health care provider, county, city, or state public health department, or local school district to find out which agency performs evaluations in your area.
- To find out about services for your child in your area, contact the National Information Center for Children and Youth with Disabilities (NICHCY) at 800-695-0285 or visit their web site: www.nichcy.org.

Health Care Providers

WHO THEY ARE: Your local health care providers include pediatricians, doctors, nurses, and nurse practitioners who provide services that prevent and treat illness. If related services are needed, such as medical specialists for specific medical needs, speech therapy, occupational therapy, physical therapy, behavior management, play therapy, or psychotherapy, these providers will be able to refer you to someone on their own team of professionals, or to someone in another agency.

WHERE TO FIND THEM:

- Call your county, city, or state public health department and ask what services they provide, and what services they can help you locate in your area.
- Call a local hospital and ask if they have a referral service or can help you locate health care providers in your area.
- Send a stamped self-addressed envelope with your request for a list of pediatricians in your area to: American Academy of Pediatrics, P.O. Box 927, Elk Grove, IL 60009.

- Visit the American Medical Association web site at www.ama-assn.org for information about local physicians in your area.
- If you need help paying for health care, call the main or general information number in your local social service or human service office and ask for your local medical assistance program telephone number.

Mental Health Professionals

WHO THEY ARE: Your local mental health professionals may include social workers with special training, psychologists, nurses, or psychiatrists. The services they can provide include a wide range of assistance, including behavioral, learning, and mental health assessments, help with solving problem behaviors, support groups, counseling, and individual, group, or family therapy. Services can be as short as a telephone call or a one-hour session, or may include many sessions continuing over many years.

WHERE TO FIND THEM:

- Talk to your health care provider about what services are offered under your health plan.
- Call your county, city, or state public health department or a community mental health center and ask what services they provide, and what services they can help you locate in your area.
- Contact a local Mental Health Association or The National Mental Health Association at 800-969-NMHA or online at: www.nmha.org, for names of mental health service providers in your community.
- Contact The American Academy of Child and Adolescent Psychiatry at 800-333-7636 or on-line: www.aacap.org, for names of mental health service providers in your community.

Parent Educators and Consultants

WHO THEY ARE: Parenting information and support is offered by many different professionals including parent educators, social workers, nurses, and psychologists. Sometimes, parent education is performed by trained volunteers. Typically these people offer information on child development, parenting tips and ideas, and a chance to talk over problems and plan solutions. The services may be provided individually in your home or at an agency. They may be offered in a group with other parents to give you the opportunity to share similar joys and concerns with each other, and a time to reflect upon your parenting.

WHERE TO FIND THEM: Contact public schools, community education, health care clinics, churches, hospitals, community mental health clinics, and local public health departments. Ask if they offer parenting classes or if they know of anyone in your community who does. Look in the community pages of your city, neighborhood, or parenting newspaper for listings of groups and classes that meet near you.

Telephone Help-Line Staff

WHO THEY ARE: Staff on telephone help-lines typically offer free information and advice on many topics. Some help-lines are set up to answer specific types of questions like medical or mental health concerns, while other help-lines will offer help on any child development or parenting issue. Various help-lines are set up so that you can hear recorded information on a topic of your choice, while some other help-lines offer you the opportunity to have a conversation with a trained staff member.

WHERE TO FIND THEM:

- Contact United Way at 1-800-411-UWAY (8929), or visit its web site: www.unitedway.org/localway/iandr.html, to help you find a variety of help-lines and other services in your community.

- Look in your phone book under Helpline, Information and Referral, Warmline, or First Call for Help©.

- Call your local public library or your local social services or human services department and ask for telephone numbers for local help-lines.

More Help and Information

BOOKS FOR PARENTS

- *Guide To Your Child's Symptoms: The Official, Complete Home Reference, Birth Through Adolescence,* (American Academy of Pediatrics). Villard, 1997.

- *Becoming The Parent You Want To Be: A Source Book of Strategies for the First Five Years* by Laura Davis and Janis Keyser. Broadway Books, 1997.

- *Caring for Your Baby and Young Child: Birth to Age 5,* (American Academy of Pediatrics, revised edition). Bantam, 1998.

- *Every Parent's Guide to the Law* by Deborah L. Forman. Harcourt Brace, 1998.

- *Positive Discipline A-Z: From Toddlers to Teens - 1001 Solutions to Everyday Parenting Problems* (revised and expanded 2nd edition) by Jane Nelsen, Lynn Lott, and H. Stephen Glen. Prima, 1999. Web site: www.positivediscipline.com

- *Positive Parenting From A to Z* by Karen Renshaw Joslin. Fawcett Columbine: Ballantine Books, 1994. Web site: www.becomingtheparent.com

- *Touchpoints: Your Child's Emotional and Behavioral Development* by T. Berry Brazelton. Addison-Wesley, 1992.

- *What to Expect the Toddler Years* by Arlene Eisenberg, Heidi E. Murkoff, and Sandee E. Hathaway. Workman Pub., 1994. Web site: www.whattoexpect.com
- *The Yale Guide to Children's Nutrition*, (William V. Tamborlane, MD, editor). Yale University Press, 1997.
- *Your Baby & Child: From Birth to Age Five* (3rd edition) by Penelope Leach. Alfred A. Knopf, 1997.

ARTICLES, PAMPHLETS, & BOOKLETS

"Children's Mental Health—What Every Child Needs for Good Mental Health."
Call, write or read online:

The National Mental Health Association
1021 Prince Street, Alexandria, VA 22314
800-433-5959
Web site: www.nmha.org

COMMUNITY RESOURCES

When looking for services in your community, call your local county social services agency, your local school district, or your local public library for information.

MAGAZINES & NEWSLETTERS

- *Child*. Gruner & Jahr.
- *Family Life*. Hachette Fillipacchi Magazines.
- *Parents*. Gruner & Jahr USA.
- *Parenting*. Time Publishing Ventures, Inc.

NATIONAL ORGANIZATIONS

- National Parent Information Network (NPIN)
  ERIC Clearinghouse on Elementary and Early Childhood Education
  (800) 583-4135 (voice/TTY)
  E-mail: ericeece@uiuc.edu
  Web site: http://npin.org

  NPIN offers a service called Parents Ask ERIC: submit a question or request for information and NPIN staff will search for information for you.

- The National Parenting Center
  800-753-6667
  E-mail: ParentCtr@tnpc.com
  Web site: www.tnpc.com

WEB SITES

- ABC's of Parenting: www.abcparenting.com

- Family.com. Web site: www.family.com

- Kidsource Online. Web site: www.kidsource.com

- Parenthood Web. Web site: www.parenthoodweb.com

- Parent Soup. Web site: www.parentsoup.com

- ParentsPlace. Web site: www.parentsplace.com

All of these web sites have experts' advice, discussion forums, links to other good parenting sites on the web, and most have a panel of experts that will accept questions from parents.

PART ONE

The Growing Child Year-by-Year

Understanding the Growing Child

Children change quickly and constantly as they grow. What children learn and how much they develop in the first five years is nothing short of amazing. Children typically learn key skills in common patterns, within certain age ranges, and in a usual order. These common patterns form the body of knowledge called *child development*.

Child development information is based on averages that describe how *most* children *often* behave. Each child is unique. Within any group of children of the same age, there will be wide variations in abilities. If your child does not fall within the averages given, he or she may still be developing within the normal range. You can use this information to encourage your child to develop skills. Have realistic expectations about your child's behavior and abilities, but seek help or advice if you are concerned.

The Growing Child Year-by-Year is a tool to understand child development and how it applies to raising your child. Within each year of this guide, you will find:

✔ Five subject areas or domains that describe the skills children typically develop during that year:

💜 *Feelings and Relationships*, sometimes called social and emotional development, includes the skills that allow children to manage their full range of feelings and to have peaceful and meaningful relationships with others.

☝ *Hand and Body Movement*, which is also referred to as fine-motor and gross-motor development, includes the skills that allow children to develop hand-eye coordination, to balance, and to coordinate their arms, legs, and all other body parts and their movements.

👕 *Self-Help Skills* includes the skills that allow children to take care of their own physical needs and to become responsible: dressing, doing household chores, eating, using the toilet, bathing, following rules, and sleeping.

! *Talking*, also called speech and language development, includes the skills that allow your child to communicate and to appreciate reading and music.

✱ *Thinking*, often called cognitive development, includes the skills that allow your child to explore and experiment, to concentrate, to imitate and play make-believe, to understand cause and effect, to notice details, to develop problem-solving, and to understand concepts.

✔ *Common Concerns* outlines common behaviors of young children that parents typically worry about, but that usually pass with time and some guidance from parents and caregivers.

✔ *When to Get More Help* suggests at what point children may fall outside the norm of typically developing children, when they have fallen behind in developing one particular skill or a combination of skills. When parents have questions or doubts about their child's development, they may need professional advice.

Although the child development information here is arranged by year, children develop skills in their own time. Consider reading the years before and after your child's current age to gain a greater understanding of the range of typical patterns of development. Notice that some ideas to help your child learn skills are repeated in more than one year or in all years. That's because some things, such as giving your child attention and affection, are worth continuing in each and every year of your child's life.

In the activity section of **The Growing Child Year-by-Year**, you will find a wealth of practical, simple ideas to spend positive time with your child. These fun activities will help your child develop his or her full potential while bringing the two of you closer together.

Learn about, watch for, enjoy, and accept your child's stages of development. Treasure and celebrate each step along his or her way!

The Growing Child at 12 Months

Your child has grown in remarkable ways during his first year of life, gaining many new skills. Children typically grow and learn new skills in their own time and at their own pace within the wide range of what is normal.

By twelve months of age, your child SHOULD BE ABLE TO DO the following:

❒ Creep or crawl.

❒ Stand when supported.

❒ Search for something hidden after he watches you hide it.

❒ Use gestures like waving or shaking his head.

❒ Blink at or look at bright or moving objects.

❒ Watch, point to, or reach for pictures or desired things.

❒ Turn to sounds and imitate sounds.

❒ Say a single word like "mama" or "dada."

❒ Seem attached to parent or caregiver: attached children will typically look for, touch, or return to you in strange places.

❒ Demonstrate knowing the difference between strangers and familiar people.

❒ Soothe or comfort easily.

❒ Settle into a pattern of sleeping and eating.

❒ Feed self by picking up finger foods and holding own bottle or cup.

If your child DOES NOT demonstrate most of the skills listed above by one year, consider seeking advice about whether or not your child needs help in developing delayed or missing skills. You are the expert when it comes to your child. If you have a concern, trust your instinct and find someone trained to help you: health care providers, teachers, social workers, parent educators, mental health workers, or telephone help-line staff. Consider talking it over with friends and family, too. You don't need to worry alone! Turn to "Finding Help in Your Community," on page 4, to learn about finding help near you.

♥ Feelings & Relationships ～ ♥ ～ ♥ ～ ♥ ～

5 yrs.

DEVELOPING SKILL	DESCRIPTION
Ability to Relate to Others	One-year-olds are usually friendly toward others, and naturally curious about them. They need lots of adult attention and interaction, and they need to know that an adult is nearby at all times. Security grows from a strong relationship with at least one responsive, caring adult. This security gives children the confidence and courage to explore their world as they grow. If they are loved and cared for generously now, they will learn how to show love in return. Children may experience separation anxiety, or difficulty leaving the adult that they are most attached to.
Increasing Self-Esteem	Children are so wrapped up in a new sense of ME that they cannot think beyond themselves. They need to be self-centered to learn that they are separate people. What may look like selfishness is really a discovery process of learning that "self" exists. They have a strong sense of self-importance: they enjoy being the center of attention, may love to perform, and can recognize and may admire themselves in photographs and in the mirror.
Growing Independence	As children are beginning to learn that they are separate from the adult they are most attached to, they experiment with the possibilities of their power: they say, "NO!", they may resist getting dressed or eating, they want to do things without help, they want to decide for themselves, and they have tantrums when things don't go their way.
Expression of Emotions	Emotions are blooming. Children are experiencing the range of emotions: fear, anger, jealousy, joy, and excitement. In their short lifetime, these are relatively new forces to reckon with.
Ability to Cope with Change and Transitions	Moving from one activity to the next or taking directions may be difficult. Children have clear desires and ideas. They also have a limited understanding of the world and limited language skills. As a result, they are frequently and easily frustrated when those around them do not understand or agree with their decisions. They may want to wear shorts outside on a snowy day, or want to use the red cup instead of the blue one but not have the words to ask. Tantrums are often the result when adults disagree.

4 yrs.

3 yrs.

2 yrs.

1 yr.

Birth

～ ♥ ～ ♥ ～ ♥ ～ ♥ ～ ♥ ～ ♥ ～ ♥ ～ ♥

Feelings & Relationships ♥

DEVELOPING SKILL	DESCRIPTION
Ability to Play Near Other Children and Alone	Children prefer to be in the company of adults or much older children. They may play *near* other children their own age, but they usually are not interested in playing *with* them. They will play alone briefly.
Ability to Share	"Mine!" Children are fiercely possessive of things, from something they love, like a prized teddy bear, to something they see someone else looking at from across the room, like a table leg.
	They may share a toy, but are more likely to offer to show it while they clutch it. They may go through a phase of needing to possess things. Once they have experienced holding onto and owning things, they can begin to share them. Sharing freely may not happen until four years of age.
Conquering Fears	As children learn that they are separate people, they realize how small and powerless they really are in the world. Many fears emerge: strange places, the dark, thunder, lightning, large animals, water, and loud noises. Children are largely dependent on adults to help them with their fears.
Awareness of Sexuality	Children receive powerful messages about their bodies and relationships from the adults who give them care. If the adults are positive, children learn to like their bodies and to believe that close relationships can be safe and loving.
	They may experience pleasure as they explore their own genitals.

5 yrs.

4 yrs.

3 yrs.

2 yrs.

1 yr.

♥

Birth

♥ Feelings & Relationships ~ ♥ ~ ♥ ~ ♥ ~

5 yrs.

HELP YOUR CHILD LEARN ABOUT:

Relating to Others

- Give your child lots of time, care, attention, and love: pats, hugs, kisses, cuddles, conversations, comforting words, gentle tickles, and verbal expressions of love.

- Eat meals together and talk with each other as often as you can as a family.

4 yrs.

- Introduce your child to people outside of the immediate family: friends, extended family, neighbors, or other communities you belong to.

Feeling Good about Herself

- Listen to your child and respect her. Don't use sarcasm or words that ridicule—like stupid, dumb, little monster, little devil, or brat.

- Encourage and allow your child to explore the things that interest her.

3 yrs.

Becoming Independent

- Eliminate unnecessary frustrations for your child and child-proof your home.

- Compliment your child's efforts to learn and her achievements.

- Set reasonable limits for your child and enforce them.

Expressing Emotions

- Remain calm and steady in the face of your child's emotional outbursts; neither give in nor overpower.

2 yrs.

- Help your child to name her feelings. Accept all feelings, positive or negative. Teach options for expressing them to prevent your child from hitting or biting.

- Encourage your child to begin to think about her own feelings, and the feelings of others.

1 yr.

Birth

~ ♥ ~ ♥ ~ ♥ ~ ♥ ~ ♥ ~ ♥ ~ ♥ ~ ♥ ~ ♥ ~ ♥

~ ♥ ~ ♥ ~ ♥ ~ Feelings & Relationships ♥

5 yrs.

Coping with Change and Transitions

- Establish routines and order in your child's day to help prevent some frustrations that come from not understanding what is going to happen.

- Give your child a warning before changing activities: "In a few minutes, after the table is set, we will eat and you will need to stop playing."

4 yrs.

- Make positive suggestions instead of giving orders: "It's time to wash our hands in the water," instead of "Go wash your hands."

- Make a game of tasks, like beating the timer: "See if you can pick up all the toys with me before the timer goes off!"

Playing with Other Children and Alone

- Give your child opportunities to play *near* (she probably won't play *with*) other children: playing in a sandbox, drawing, working with play dough, or playing with toys.

3 yrs.

Sharing

- Allow your child to keep some of her special toys just for her. Encourage her to take turns with the others, but don't expect her to freely share her things until she is four years of age.

Conquering Fears

- Take her fears seriously and comfort her: tell her, "I see you are afraid!" as you cuddle her.

Exploring Sexuality

- Allow her to look at and touch all the parts of her body, including her genitals. Be careful not to make her feel bad about herself for this normal exploration.

2 yrs.

1 yr.

♥

Birth

Hand & Body Movement

5 yrs.

4 yrs.

3 yrs.

2 yrs.

1 yr.

Birth

DEVELOPING SKILL	DESCRIPTION
Ability to Walk	Children usually take their first independent steps around their first birthday, and then spend several months learning to walk alone smoothly.
	First they totter from side to side with stiff legs that are spread wide apart, while holding their arms up and out for balance. As they gain control of their movements, they loosen up, pull their feet in, and relax their arms.
	They may continue to crawl or creep, along with walking.
	Once children learn to walk smoothly, they can pull a toy behind them, carry something large as they walk, and walk backwards and sideways.
Ability to Run	Children first "run" with a fast walk—one foot always on the ground.
	As balance and coordination improve, they run with eyes ahead, their arms and legs alternating, and both feet momentarily off of the ground. Steering and stopping quickly are still difficult.
Ability to Climb Up and Down Stairs	Children vary widely in their ability to climb stairs. They learn to climb stairs in stages in the following order:
	1. Crawl up stairs on all fours.
	2. Back down stairs on all fours.
	3. Walk up stairs with one hand held or holding rails, with both feet on each step.
	4. Walk down stairs holding someone's hand for support, with both feet on each step.

Hand & Body Movement

DEVELOPING SKILL	DESCRIPTION
Ability to Pick Things Up and to Throw Them	Often times children first roll and throw while sitting down. As they gain more balance, children throw while standing. First, children throw "underhand," then "overhand."
	Aim is poor; children may even throw a ball behind them when trying to throw forward. Later this year, they may be able to throw a ball close to a target placed a few feet from them.
Ability to Use a Riding Toy Without Pedals	Children can make a riding toy go by sitting on it and pushing it with their feet. They usually learn to push backward before forward.
	Learning to use pedals typically doesn't happen until after two years of age.
Ability to Make Random Marks on a Page, to Scribble	Children grasp a large crayon or marker with their whole fist to scribble. Simply making marks gives them great pleasure.
Ability to Coordinate Eyes and Hands to Work with Materials	Children develop strength and control of fingers, eyes, and hands that gives them the ability to:
	• Pile blocks or lay them out on the floor, and then stack four or more block-like objects to make a tower.
	• Put objects in a container and turn the container over to empty it.
	• Turn pages of a book.
	• Pick up a variety of different-sized materials or toys and carry them around.
	• Tear paper.

5 yrs.

4 yrs.

3 yrs.

2 yrs.

1 yr.

Birth

Hand & Body Movement

5 yrs.

HELP YOUR CHILD LEARN ABOUT:

Walking and Running

- Allow your child to walk barefoot on warm smooth surfaces, which are the best when learning to walk. Consider buying shoes with flexible, soft rubber soles like moccasins or soft tennis shoes, or socks with non-skid material.

4 yrs.

- As your child is learning to walk, give him many chances to practice on a smooth floor that is free from clutter. Encourage him to push small chairs, his own stroller, boxes with some weight in the bottom, or store-bought push toys that don't tip easily or go too fast.

- Encourage your child to pull a wagon, a box with a string attached to it loaded with toys, store-bought pull toys, or noisy things that you have attached to a short string—like bells, canning jar lids, or pie tins. **Supervise your child with string at all times.**

3 yrs.

- Create reasons for your child to practice walking by asking him to do errands: "Please bring me a book to read," or "Please put the toilet paper in the bathroom," or "Please throw away this napkin."

- Chase and catch your child, let him chase and catch you, and encourage him to chase balls, wind-up toys, or bubbles.

Climbing Stairs

- Make practice steps for your child to climb by placing cushions against the sofa.

2 yrs.

- Spend time helping your child practice climbing stairs. Stand behind him as he crawls up. When he has mastered crawling up, show him how to crawl down: turn him on his tummy with feet pointing down the stairs, and gently pull him down over the step to the next one down. Do it a few times, making a game of it, and he will quickly learn to do it on his own. **Supervise your child at all times on stairs; place a gate over the stairs when not climbing them together.**

- Visit local playgrounds often to provide many opportunities for your child to climb, run, and jump. **Supervise your child at all times on playground equipment!**

1 yr.

Birth

Throwing

- Give your child lots of soft things to practice throwing: rolled-up socks, bean bags, yarn balls, sponges, stuffed animals, crumpled paper, or balls.

Using Riding Toys

- Make sure your child has the opportunity to use a riding toy that is sturdy, will not tip over easily, and that fits him. Begin to teach him safety: never ride in the street or down steep hills. **Supervise your child at all times on riding toys.**

4 yrs.

Making Art/Making Marks

- Make sure your child has many opportunities to experience making marks and art. Find a place in your home where he can draw, paint, scribble, color, and be messy. Stock it with supplies that he can use independently. **Only use art supplies that have been certified as Non-Toxic.**

- Direct your child to keep his marks on paper or a tabletop. Beyond that, allow him freedom in his artwork. Value and comment on the process, not the product: "You sure are enjoying yourself," instead of, "What is it?" He usually won't know or care what his marks represent yet.

3 yrs.

Working with Eyes and Hands

- Provide your child with containers to fill and small objects to dump. Containers: jars, boxes, plastic milk bottles, bowls, buckets, pots, coffee cans, or oatmeal boxes. Things to drop in containers: plastic hair rollers, blocks, beanbags, o-shaped cereal, cars, small stuffed animals, jar lids, or juice can lids.

- Give your child opportunities to stack block-like things: wooden or cardboard blocks, cereal boxes, fabric blocks, or plastic containers.

- Save old magazines, colored paper, wrapping paper, or newspaper, and let your child tear them into small pieces. He may enjoy pasting the pieces onto a large piece of paper. **Supervise your child so he doesn't eat paper or paste.**

2 yrs.

1 yr.

Birth

Self-Help Skills

5 yrs.

DEVELOPING SKILL	DESCRIPTION
Understanding and Following Rules	One-year-olds begin to learn that they cannot always behave as they please, but they cannot easily understand and follow rules. Knowing the difference between right and wrong is an abstract concept that is learned throughout childhood. Children need consistent structure from adults, including an environment that protects them, and firm but loving limits to guide them.
Household Responsibilities	Children imitate actions that they see: sweeping, dusting, cleaning up spills, and stirring food. Their efforts are far from helpful, but these are the first steps to independence and responsibility.
Ability to Feed Self	Children are able to lift a cup with handles using one hand, or a small glass using two hands. Now that they are able to take liquids well from a cup, they do not need to drink from a bottle. Many experts agree that the bottle should be given up entirely by age one, or by 18 months at the latest. They eat with their fingers and begin to use a spoon.
Healthy Eating Habits	Children's appetites decrease this year because their growth is less intense. They may go through "food jags" in which they ask for a particular food over and over for days.
Mealtime Manners	Expect children to spill and be messy as they eat. Their exploration of food is an important part of the process of learning to feed themselves and enjoy eating. Children can understand a few simple manners: it's not OK to throw food, we sit down when we eat, and we eat the food on our own plate.

4 yrs.

3 yrs.

2 yrs.

1 yr.

Birth

DEVELOPING SKILL	DESCRIPTION
Sound Sleep	Children sleep an average of approximately 11.5 hours at night and 2 hours during the day. The sleep needs of one-year-olds vary widely.
	Difficulty going to bed is common. Children stall bedtime as they become more curious about what's going on in their home after they go to bed.
	Teething and fears may awaken children.
Body Care	Children require an adult to wash their hands, body, and hair, and to brush their teeth, but they like to help with the job.
Dressing	Children are able to remove their hats, socks, shoes, and shirts. They may want to dress themselves, but still need help. They can assist by putting their arms in sleeves, and their legs in pants.
Toilet Learning	Children may tell an adult when their diaper is wet or messy. Most experts agree that children are not ready to be toilet trained until after their second birthday. There is no exact timetable for deciding when a child is ready to be toilet trained, but there are signs of readiness to watch for.
	Toilet learning is more difficult and less effective when begun too early.

5 yrs.

4 yrs.

3 yrs.

2 yrs.

1 yr.

Birth

Self-Help Skills

HELP YOUR CHILD LEARN ABOUT:

Understanding and Following Rules and Routines

- Childproof the home to protect your child from harm.

- Set reasonable limits and enforce them. Provide structure and guidance as your child's understanding of rules develops. Start teaching a few rules related to safety and taking care of property: "don't touch the hot cup," "be gentle with the cat," and "walk instead of running near the table."

- Since her language is limited, it may be helpful to communicate with your child through touch and words: as you take her hand to guide her, tell her, "It is time to leave the park now."

- Set routines or flexible schedules for eating, sleeping, dressing, and playing.

Becoming Responsible for Household Jobs

- Let your child help you with jobs around the home or yard. Praise her for her effort, focusing more on the process than the outcome: when she tries to sweep, compliment her even though she misses much of the dirt.

Eating Well

- At mealtimes, take advantage of her desire for independence: encourage her to feed herself as much as she can, and to drink from a cup. Expect her to make a mess and understand that a certain amount of what looks like "playing with her food" is one more way that she explores her world.

- Don't battle over food. Your job is to provide nutritious foods for regular meal and snack times. Your child's job is to decide how much to eat. Plan three nutritious meals and two snacks in between meals and stick to that. As long as you don't allow constant nibbling, sweets, and junk food, you can trust her to eat what she needs.

- Strike a balance between food likes and dislikes. Consider your child's likes and dislikes when you plan a meal or snack. Include one food that she likes at each meal, but don't prepare the whole meal according to her preferences. Once the meal is on the table, don't get up and fix something else if she doesn't like what's there. Encourage her to eat until her stomach feels full and then allow her to leave the table. Remind her that there will not be more food available until the next meal or routine snack time.

- Direct your child, who may be in a hurry to eat, to take her time and chew food well. **Avoid foods that need a grinding motion to chew and round foods that are common choking hazards until at least after the age of four years: hot dogs, popcorn, hard candy, peanuts, grapes, raw carrot sticks, and raw celery. Don't let her eat while she runs.**

Sleeping Well

- To help your child sleep well, make sure she gets plenty of exercise during the day, avoids caffeine, shares a calming bedtime routine with you, and stays on a fairly regular sleep schedule. Always respond to her nighttime fears with care and comfort. She may prefer a night-light, having the door open, or some soft music.

Taking Care of Her Body

- Assist her with caring for her body, talking to her about how to do each step as you clean her. **Supervise your child in the bathtub at all times! Set your water heater to less than 120 degrees Fahrenheit to avoid burns.**

Dressing

- Buy loose-fitting clothes and dress your child slowly so that she can help.

Using the Toilet

- Talk about the joys of using the toilet, let her watch you, read potty books, put a child's potty chair in the bathroom, and occasionally encourage her to sit on it with her clothes on. Watch and wait for toilet training readiness signs that usually happen after two years of age.

♫ Talking ! ? ! ♫ ! ? ! ♫ ! ? ! ♫ ! ? !

5 yrs.

4 yrs.

3 yrs.

2 yrs.

1 yr.

! ?
Birth

DEVELOPING SKILL	DESCRIPTION
Understanding and Using Words	Children typically say "dada" or "mama" with an understanding of the meaning sometime between about eleven and fourteen months of age.
	The rate that children learn words varies widely! Most children speak at least 50 words by two years.
	Children understand more words than they can speak. They show understanding by pointing, picking up objects when asked, or obeying directions.
	If children learn two languages at the same time, they typically mix the two and progress more slowly. This is not cause for concern; by age three or four, most will separate the two languages.
Ability to Produce Sounds of Speech	Throughout this year, children master many, but not all, of the sounds needed to produce language. Children move from babbling, to imitating and experimenting with sounds, to forming words by putting the sounds together.
	Refining the ability to make sounds, or articulation, takes time.
Ability to Imitate Sounds in the Environment	Children experiment with sounds by imitating what they hear: "mauw-mauw" for cat, "room-room" for car, "beep-beep" for horn.
Ability to Speak in Phrases	Early this year, children use one word to express a thought: "Ball!" probably means, "I want the ball!"
	Gradually, children put more words together, using two- to three-word sentences by age two. The sentences are not grammatically correct yet: "me ball," "more juice," or "me go park."
Ability to Have a Conversation	Children chatter, trying to imitate conversations they hear around them.
	Children respond directly to someone when spoken to.
	A slight melody, or inflection, begins to appear in a one-year-old's voice: "UH-oh!" or, "NO-No!"

! ? ! ♫ ! ? ! ♫ ! ? ! ♫ ! ? ! *Talking* ♫

DEVELOPING SKILL	DESCRIPTION
Ability to Understand and Follow Simple Instructions	Children understand and are likely to follow a simple one-step direction: "Please pick up your doll."
Capacity to Listen to Books or Spoken Stories	Children typically listen to one picture book or story in a sitting. They may prefer looking at and pointing to the pictures that they recognize. They also enjoy listening to an adult talk about or tell a story instead of reading it. Children can help turn the pages, but will probably turn several at once.
Ability to Explore and Appreciate Music	Early singing may sound like talking loudly. Children show enjoyment of music and rhythm by: • Listening to all kinds of music. • Imitating voice tones and pitch. • Humming and exploring their vocal range with all kinds of sounds. • Trying to sing the words to simple songs. • Experimenting with rhythm by hitting objects together or clapping hands to music, though often not with the beat.

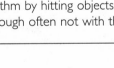

! ♫ ! ? ! ♫ ! ? ! ♫ ! ? ! ♫ ! ? !

The Growing Child at Age One

♫ Talking ! ? ! ♫ ! ? ! ♫ ! ? ! ♫ ! ? !

HELP YOUR CHILD LEARN ABOUT:

Language

- Talk to your child throughout the day. Tell him the names of things as he looks at them, touches them, or plays with them. Visit familiar and unfamiliar places, and talk about what you see: parks, neighborhoods, backyards, museums.

- Listen attentively and respond promptly to any of his efforts to babble or say words: "Really? Tell me more!" Give him plenty of time to say more.

- Speak slowly and clearly in fairly short sentences. Get face to face with your child. Exaggerate your inflections sometimes to show him how to add expression to his voice. Sometimes, repeat the main words or ideas several times: "Bath. It is time for your bath. I took my bath. Time to take your bath."

- Ask your child questions and answer his.

- Instead of correcting his mispronounced words and incomplete sentences, repeat an expanded, accurate version:

  - If he says, "Baby," you could say, "Yes, I see the baby sitting on her mama's lap."

  - If he says, "Dahee!" you could say, "Yes, what a beautiful dog!"

- Point out sounds in the environment by telling him what they are and imitating the sound: "The bird says, 'chirp-chirp,' the clock says, 'tick-tock.'" Invite him to make sounds with you.

- Recite and read rhymes to your child: "Hey diddle diddle, the cat and the fiddle, the cow jumped over the moon!"

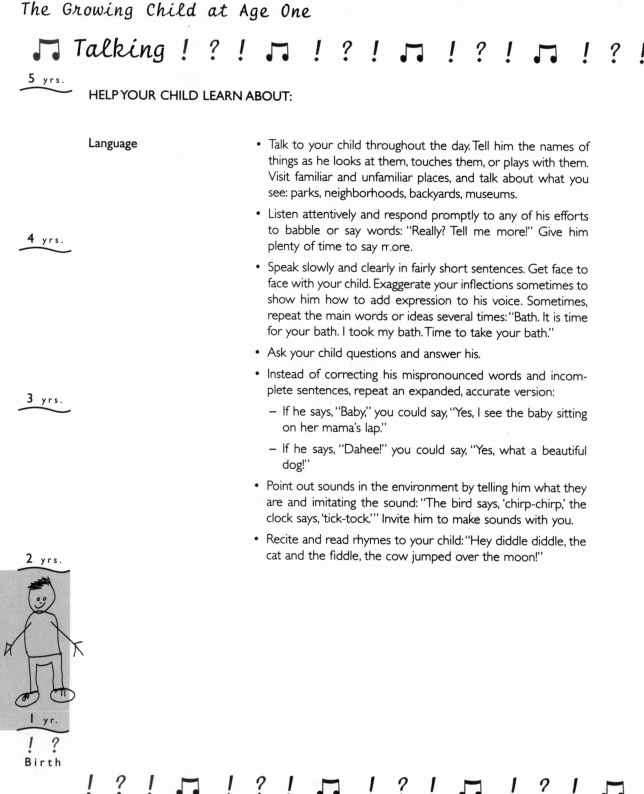

4 yrs.

3 yrs.

2 yrs.

1 yr.

! ?
Birth

! ? ! ♫ ! ? ! ♫ ! ? ! ♫ ! ? ! ♫ !

! ♪ ! ? ! ♫ ! ? ! ♫ ! ? ! ♫ ! ? ! Talking ♫

<u>5 yrs.</u>

Following Directions

- Ask your child to do simple tasks throughout the day: "Get your doll, please," "Find your shoes, please," or "Please, put your cup in the sink."

Listening to Books or Spoken Stories

- Tell stories and read short, simple, colorful books with few words, moving toward more complicated stories as his attention span grows. Aim for at least 20 minutes a day in several sittings.

<u>4 yrs.</u>

Making Music

- Explore music with your child: sing simple songs, listen and dance to different types of music, bounce him to rhythms on your hip or knee, and let him play simple rhythm instruments.

<u>3 yrs.</u>

<u>2 yrs.</u>

<u>1 yr.</u>

! ?
Birth

! ♫ ! ? ! ♫ ! ? ! ♫ ! ? ! ♫ ! ? !

Thinking

DEVELOPING SKILL	DESCRIPTION
Ability to Actively Explore and Experiment	One-year-olds are curious and learn by doing. They use their mouths less to explore things now. You may see them filling and emptying drawers or cupboards, putting things in and pulling them out of wastebaskets, or playing with water in the sink. They use all of their senses to interact with the world.
Ability to Imitate	Children copy the actions and gestures of those around them and learn a great deal from their observations and imitation. Children may sweep the floor, hug a doll, or wrinkle their nose after watching someone do the same.
Ability to Focus and Concentrate	Children appear to be in constant motion and typically run around the room, stopping only briefly to explore things. They usually don't attend to a task for more than a few minutes at a time, though attention span varies between children of the same age.
Ability to Understand Relationships between Objects	One-year-olds begin to understand that objects have particular functions: spoons go with bowls for eating, radios play music, and bathtubs are for bathing.

5 yrs.

4 yrs.

3 yrs.

2 yrs.

1 yr.

Birth

Thinking (

DEVELOPING SKILL	DESCRIPTION
Capacity for Simple Problem Solving	Children learn that they have the power to make things go or that there is a means to an end: they wind up an action toy to see it move, and turn a doorknob to intentionally make the door open and close, open and close.
	They learn that when something is out of sight, it still exists: if a ball rolls around a corner, they know that it does not disappear, but that it is just out of sight.
Ability to Match Objects and Shapes	Children learn how objects are similar and different. When given a circle, square, or triangle shape, they match it with another, or put it in the hole of a shape-sorter game.
Understanding the Concept of Size	One-year-olds just begin to explore size. They may experiment by nesting a set of bowls or measuring cups together or stacking graduated rings in order of size on a stacking toy.

5 yrs.

4 yrs.

3 yrs.

2 yrs.

1 yr.

Birth

☾ Thinking ☾ ✦ 🌎 ✦ ☾ ✦ 🌎 ✦ ☾ ✦ 🌎 ✦

__5 yrs.__

HELP YOUR CHILD LEARN ABOUT:

Exploring

- Encourage your child to taste, touch, smell, listen and look at the many things around her.

- Allow her to get messy and dirty as she explores, and get messy with her.

- Childproof your home as much as possible so your child does not have to hear "no" very often.

__4 yrs.__

- In rooms where she spends a lot of time, try to give her at least one low drawer or shelf that she can explore freely. (Fill it with non-breakables or some of her own things.)

- Encourage your child to experiment with making things happen: winding up action toys, turning on and off light switches, opening and closing drawers, turning on and off faucets, and making the volume go loud or soft on a radio.

__3 yrs.__ ### Imitating

- Let your child watch you complete tasks and help you with simple chores: sweeping, doing dishes, or cleaning up spills.

- Let her practice using things from real life in real situations or through make-believe with toys: stir with a real spoon in a bowl while you cook, pretend to call you on her toy phone, feed her doll and put it to bed, or dig a hole in the garden with a hand shovel.

Paying Attention

- Encourage her to do a variety of interesting things; sit with her and participate. Follow her lead; if she is ready to move on let her do so.

__2 yrs.__

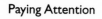

__I yr.__

🌎
Birth

☾ ✦ 🌎 ✦ ☾ ✦ 🌎 ✦ ☾ ✦ 🌎 ✦ ☾ ✦

Thinking (

5 yrs.

Solving Problems

- Play peek-a-boo with your child by covering your face with your hands, a scarf, or a towel, and then pull them away from your face and say "Peek-a-boo!" Try playing by covering her face or popping up from behind a chair. Puppets, dolls, and stuffed animals can play, too.

- Hide an object under a cloth or a box as your child watches, and ask her to find it.

4 yrs.

Matching

- Have your child practice matching during everyday activities:

  - While dressing her, hold up one shoe or one sock, and ask her to find the other.

  - While you are putting groceries away, hold up a can or box, and ask her to find another.

  - Make a pile of pairs of toys and have her match them: cars, trucks, balls, etc.

3 yrs.

Size

- Give your child a few things of the same size to fit together: cups, bowls, or plastic containers. Once she has figured out how to stack those, give her sets of different-sized things to fit together: plastic bowl sets, cooking pot sets, measuring cups, canisters, or aerosol can covers.

2 yrs.

1 yr.

Birth

<u>5 yrs.</u>

Common Concerns

The following are common behaviors in children this age that typically concern or frustrate parents. The child:

<u>4 yrs.</u>

- Is in constant motion.
- Is inflexible or wants things "just so."
- Makes messes and gets into things.
- Jabbers.
- Whines.
- Is aggressive: bites, hits, or throws.
- Clings to parent in new situations and cries when left.
- Shows off.
- Dawdles.

<u>3 yrs.</u>

- Has difficulty sharing and is possessive: "Mine!"
- Is negative or stubborn: "No!"
- Is quickly frustrated.
- Has tantrums.
- Resists bedtime.

Be assured that these behaviors will usually pass with time and appropriate guidance from you, but if you have any questions, ask for help.

<u>2 yrs.</u>

<u>1 yr.</u>

When to Get More Help <u>5 yrs.</u>

Children typically grow and learn new skills in their own time and at their own pace within the wide range of what is normal. Sometimes, however, children need a bit of extra help to keep their development on track, or to stay healthy and happy.

By two years of age, in addition to all of the skills typically mastered by one year (listed on page 13), your child SHOULD BE ABLE TO DO the following:

<u>4 yrs.</u>

- ❐ Walk (by 16 months).
- ❐ Speak at least 15 words (by 18 months).
- ❐ Point to pictures of familiar things or something desired (by 18 months).
- ❐ Pay attention to the ring of a telephone, doorbell, or someone entering the room.
- ❐ Answer simple questions with a "yes" or "no."
- ❐ Try to use words instead of gestures to express needs.
- ❐ Use two-word sentences.

<u>3 yrs.</u>

- ❐ Show a range of emotions: anger, delight, fear.
- ❐ Respond to comforting when irritable, fearful, or anxious.
- ❐ Become increasingly independent, little by little.
- ❐ Imitate actions.
- ❐ Push a toy with wheels.
- ❐ Follow simple instructions.
- ❐ Know the function of some common things (by 15 months).

<u>2 yrs.</u>

- ❐ Learn to walk with a heel-toe pattern after walking for a few months (not on toes).

If your child DOES NOT demonstrate most of the skills listed above by two years, consider seeking advice about whether or not your child needs help in developing delayed or missing skills. You are the expert when it comes to your child. If you have a concern, trust your instinct and find someone trained to help you: health care providers, teachers, social workers, parent educators, mental health workers, or telephone help-line staff. Consider talking it over with friends and family, too. You don't need to worry alone! Turn to "Finding Help in Your Community," on page 4, to learn about finding help near you.

<u>I yr.</u>

♥ Feelings & Relationships ～ ♥ ～ ♥ ～ ♥ ～

5 yrs.

DEVELOPING SKILL	DESCRIPTION
Ability to Relate to Others	Two-year-olds use the adult who has cared for them the most as a secure base from which to explore the world. They want to go beyond the adult's arms, yet be able to come back to them when they want. They will move away from adults to play but look at or go near the adults now and then to feel safe. They are learning that they can separate from the adults they are attached to—and still be loved. Children may have trouble with separation as they try to become more independent.
Increasing Self-Esteem	Children develop a sense of pride in themselves. They love to hear compliments about how smart they are, the great things they do, how hard they try, their clothes, their looks, and the things they do to help out.
Growing Independence	Two-year-olds declare their independence with "No!" and "Do it myself!" They experiment with a new sense of power by trying out being bossy and negative with those around them. Little by little, they learn acceptable ways to get their needs met while getting along with others and following the rules.
Expression of Emotions	Control of emotions is difficult. Two-year-olds may: • Have extreme mood swings. • Express a wide range of emotions: fear, anger, joy, concern. • Be quick to hit, bite, or push to get their point across when they can't find the words quickly enough. Learning about emotions is confusing, frustrating and takes time. Tantrums are common, frequent, and can be fiercely intense in two-year-olds. Still, shortly after a tantrum, you may see them make a quick shift to being very affectionate and compassionate.
Ability to Cope with Change and Transitions	Children are easily frustrated when asked to stop one activity and start another, or when asked to do something that is out of their usual routine. They sometimes dawdle when it is time to change activities.

4 yrs.

3 yrs.

2 yrs.

1 yr.

♥

Birth

～ ♥ ～ ♥ ～ ♥ ～ ♥ ～ ♥ ～ ♥ ～ ♥ ～ ♥

~ ❤ ~ ❤ ~ ❤ ~ Feelings & Relationships ❤

DEVELOPING SKILL	DESCRIPTION
Change and Transitions (cont.)	Children are seeking routine and order in their world to help them make sense of it. Sometimes this causes them to resist change and to want things in their world to be "just so."
	They find new choices and options confusing, so they often have difficulty making decisions. This can slow them down when acting on even simple requests. They might wonder: "Should I finish making the play dough snake or should I do what Dad says and go to dinner right now?"
Ability to Play Near Other Children and Alone	Children prefer playing alone or near other children, rather than playing with them. They learn to get along with other children by watching and imitating each other. When children do begin to play with other children—late this year or next year—they will usually do best playing with just one child at a time.
Ability to Share	Children may take toys away from each other, even when they are happy with what they have. If they see another child looking at a toy, they may grab it.
Capacity for Imaginary Friends	Children play with dolls and stuffed animals as if they were real friends. They may have an imaginary friend. They share thoughts, problems, feelings, frustrations, secrets, and humor with these friends. They may communicate to you their innermost thoughts through these friends. If a child is comforting his doll or imaginary friend on the way to a new child care center, he is communicating to you that he is afraid.
	These relationships are also a non-threatening way of imitating adults, and experimenting with conversation and feelings.
Conquering Fears	Children are afraid of many different things, both real and imagined: the dark, monsters, large animals, vacuum cleaners, bodies breaking, and getting sucked down the bathtub drain. These fears are very real to them; they can't always tell the difference between fantasy and reality.
Awareness of Sexuality	Children at this age begin to understand which sex they are. They are curious about their bodies and they naturally explore them. Masturbation may be a part of this exploration.

5 yrs.

4 yrs.

3 yrs.

2 yrs.

1 yr.

❤

Birth

❤ ~ ❤ ~ ❤ ~ ❤ ~ ❤ ~ ❤ ~ ❤ ~ ❤ ~

♥ Feelings & Relationships ～ ♥ ～ ♥ ～ ♥ ～

HELP YOUR CHILD LEARN ABOUT:

Relating to Others

- Give your child time, attention, and many expressions of love: pats, hugs, and tickles. Tell him often how much you love him.

- Eat meals together and talk together as often as you can as a family.

- Introduce your child to people outside of your immediate family: aunts, uncles, grandparents, cousins, neighbors, or people in the community.

Feeling Good about Himself

- Listen to your child. Respect him. Don't use sarcasm or words that ridicule: stupid, dumb, brat, etc.

- Let your child explore the things, ideas, and other people that interest him.

Becoming Independent

- Help your child to become independent by allowing him to do the things that he can safely do by himself: getting spoons out for breakfast, choosing what color shirt to wear, putting on his pants by himself.

- Remove sources of frustration from your child's reach: irresistible breakables or small appliances like the blender. Look at your home from his new level and childproof it accordingly.

- Praise your child for all his work in learning new things and comment on the skills he has mastered.

- Make sure that your child knows the limits and rules, and the consequences for not following them. Notice and praise him when he follows the rules and stays within the limits.

Expressing Emotions

- Accept that tantrums are a fact of life and stay calm. Don't give in to your child's demands but don't overpower him either.

- Accept all of his feelings and teach many ways to express them to prevent him from hitting or biting.

- Help him to name his feelings. Remind him to think about his own feelings and the feelings of others.

Coping with Change and Transitions

- Keep life predictable by setting and following routines. Transitions are easier for him if he knows what to expect.

- When it is just about time for your child to switch activities, give him fair warning: "In five minutes, it will be time to stop playing and go in the car."

♥

～ ♥ ～ ♥ ～ ♥ ～ ♥ ～ ♥ ～ ♥ ～ ♥ ～ ♥

Feelings & Relationships ♥

- Be positive when suggesting something to your child instead of giving orders: "It's time to get ready for a bath," instead of "Go get ready for a bath!"

- Make a game out of switching activities: "Let's try to pick up all the toys before the timer goes off and it's time for dinner."

Playing with Other Children and Alone

- Give your child opportunities to play *near* (he probably won't play *with*) other children: playing in a sandbox, drawing, playing with play dough, or playing with toys.

- Allow and observe his relationships with his imaginary friends. You can learn what he's thinking or feeling and communicate with him through the "friend."

Sharing

- Allow your child to have things of his own that he does not have to share. This may make it easier for him to take turns with other things.

- Encourage your child to take turns with others, but don't expect him to freely share his things until he is at least four years of age.

- Show your child what sharing looks like by sharing some of your things with him: give him a piece of your fruit or let him look at your book with you.

Conquering Fears

- Believe your child when he tells you that he is afraid and don't make him feel bad about it. Comfort him with hugs and understanding. Consider ways to help him deal with the fear instead of making it go away.

Becoming Aware of Sexuality

- Respond matter-of-factly and accurately to your child's curiosity about the human body and the differences between boys and girls. Allow him to look at and touch all of the parts of his body, including his genitals. Avoid making him feel ashamed of looking at or touching his body. Give him the correct names of his body parts.

Hand & Body Movement

5 yrs.

4 yrs.

3 yrs.

2 yrs.

1 yr.

Birth

DEVELOPING SKILL	DESCRIPTION
Ability to Run	Children begin this year running with little control. They gradually learn to make sharp turns around corners, to steer around objects, and to stop quickly.
Ability to Jump and Hop	Children jump up and down in one place with both feet, hop on one foot a few times, jump sideways, and jump backward a few steps.
Ability to Walk Up and Down Stairs	Children vary widely in their ability to climb stairs. They usually learn to walk up and down stairs without help in the following order: 1. Walk up stairs one step at a time, stopping with both feet on each step. 2. Walk down stairs one step at a time, stopping with both feet on each step. 3. Walk up stairs one step at a time, alternating feet. 4. Walk down stairs one step at a time, alternating feet.
Ability to Climb Ladders	Children climb up short ladders on slides and playground equipment. They are able to climb up before they can climb down.
Ability to Catch and Throw	Children catch a large, lightweight ball when it is thrown gently from a few feet away.
Ability to Kick	Children can kick balls that are not moving. They first sit down while learning to kick, then they may hold on to someone's hand, a tree, or a table for balance.
Ability to Pedal a Tricycle or Ride a Toy with Pedals	Children first sit on a tricycle or riding toy and push it with their feet. Gradually, they learn to use the pedals to propel themselves.

Hand & Body Movement

DEVELOPING SKILL	DESCRIPTION
Ability to Scribble, Draw, and Reproduce Lines	Children hold a thick marker or crayon between thumb and all other fingers in the hand to scribble. They take pleasure in simply making marks on the page rather than trying to make a picture that represents something. The typical progression of drawing is to: 1. Scribble randomly. 2. Copy someone drawing lines, then circles, then horizontal lines. 3. Try to draw a picture that represents something: "See my dog?" two-year-olds may ask about a mass of circles scribbled on their page. Children may start to show a preference for using one hand over the other; a clear preference is usually made by age five.
Ability to Coordinate Eyes and Hands to Work with Materials	The developing strength and control of fingers, eyes, and hands gives children the ability to: • Stack more than six blocks in a tower, knock them down, and re-stack them, and build roads with blocks. • Complete simple three- to four-piece puzzles. • String large beads and lace a shoestring in large holes. • Snip in small bits with child-sized blunt-edged scissors. • Glue two things together.

5 yrs.

4 yrs.

3 yrs.

2 yrs.

1 yr.

Birth

Hand & Body Movement

5 yrs.

HELP YOUR CHILD LEARN ABOUT:

Running, Jumping, and Hopping

- Show your child that exercise is important—by your own example.
- Play running games with your child.
- Create an indoor space for jumping and hopping using pillows or an old mattress. Play hopping and jumping games.

4 yrs.

Climbing Stairs

- Provide opportunities for your child to practice climbing on playground equipment at a park, school, or community center. **Supervise your child on playground equipment at all times.**
- Take time to help your child practice climbing stairs. Stand right behind her as she walks up and down, encouraging her to use a handrail or hold your hand. **Supervise your child on stairs at all times, and put a gate in front of all stairways when not climbing them together.**

3 yrs.

Catching, Throwing and Kicking

- Play ball with your child so she can practice throwing and catching with a large, slightly deflated beach ball, bean bag, or hollow plastic ball.
- Provide opportunities for your child to practice kicking a large, lightweight ball back and forth between you and her. Let her practice kicking the ball into a box or basket that is lying on its side.

2 yrs.

Riding a Tricycle or Riding Toy

- Provide your child with the opportunity to practice pedaling a sturdy tricycle or riding toy that fits her and that does not tip over easily. Push the tricycle or riding toy while she has her feet on the pedals so that she can see how they move. Teach her to stay out of the street and off of steep hills and stairways. **Supervise your child on riding toys or tricycles at all times.**

1 yr.

Birth

Making Art/Making a Mark

- Provide supplies for scribbling, drawing, and various art projects, as well as a place to work where your child can be messy. **Use only art supplies that have been certified as Non-Toxic.**

- Comment on the effort, not the end product: "I love the colors that you are using," or "Look at the big strokes you made," instead of "What is it?" As she moves into the stage of representing things in her work, a respectful way to ask about her picture is to say, "Tell me about your picture."

Working with Eyes and Hands

- Give your child lots of opportunities to work with her hands, eyes, and small muscles:

  - Use glue or glue sticks.

  - Put together puzzles.

  - Lace and string beads.

  - Snip with scissors.

  - Play with play dough.

  - Help with chores at home like setting the table, taking laundry out of the washer and putting it into the dryer, or unloading the dishwasher.

Supervise your child with scissors and small objects at all times.

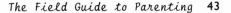

Self-Help Skills

5 yrs.

4 yrs.

3 yrs.

2 yrs.

1 yr.

Birth

DEVELOPING SKILL	DESCRIPTION
Understanding and Following Rules	Children follow simple rules, though not consistently. They are more interested in gaining your approval than they are in doing the right thing. Knowing right from wrong is a concept that develops slowly over time. As children grapple with the idea of order and rules, they focus on routines. If things are out of order, they remind the people around them. They may appear inflexible and resistant to change: If you forget to turn on the night-light as usual, they may refuse to go to bed: "Can't go to bed. Light on!"
Household Responsibilities	Children help put things away with encouragement when the home is set up so they can manage the job. They can hang up a jacket when hooks are placed low enough for them to reach, put books away on low shelves, and put toys away in containers that are labeled with pictures. Children imitate adult activities: sweeping, washing dishes, wiping tables, or pulling weeds in the garden. This is the beginning step of learning to do these chores.
Ability to Feed Self	Children feed themselves though it can be messy and there are spills. They first learn to use a spoon, then a fork, and next, a dull knife for spreading. They can hold a small cup in one hand. Children are still developing and coordinating their chewing and swallowing skills.
Healthy Eating Habits	Children have smaller appetites this year because growth slows down. They may have little interest in eating because they are not hungry or are too busy. It is common for two-year-olds to be fussy or picky about eating. They may go through "food jags" in which they ask for a particular food over and over for days. They usually like food to be separated on the plate and not mixed.
Mealtime Manners	Children sit at the table for a meal just long enough to eat it and don't sit still for very long. Children try to follow simple table manners: we sit while we eat, we don't throw food, and we wipe hands and face with a napkin.

DEVELOPING SKILL	DESCRIPTION
Healthy Sleep Patterns	Children sleep an average of approximately 11.5 hours at night and 1.5 hours during the day. Some children give up their nap this year, but most still need it. Sleep needs vary widely. Children typically: • Dawdle or resist bedtime because they don't want to stop playing. • Have difficulty unwinding and settling down to sleep. • Bounce, rock, sing, or talk themselves to sleep. • Experience nightmares and nighttime fears.
Body Care	Children wash and dry their hands independently. At bathtime, children need an adult to wash their body and hair. They need assistance with teeth and hair brushing, but they are learning how to do these jobs.
Dressing	Children can completely undress themselves. They may be able to button and unbutton large buttons, and can usually pull pants up and down. Typically, children want to dress themselves, but still need help.
Toilet Learning	Most children learn to use the toilet with some assistance between two and three years of age, and then use it regularly without being asked between about three and a half and four years of age. There is no exact timetable that dictates when children are ready to learn. They are ready to learn to use the toilet when they show interest and physical signs of readiness. Children show signs of interest when they: • Help their doll or animal to use the toilet. • Sit on the toilet for a few minutes. • Watch other children and adults go to the toilet. • Say, "I have to go potty." Children show physical signs of readiness when they: • Stay dry for two hours or more. • Wake up dry from naps. • Feel the urge to go to the bathroom and tell you. • Are able to pull pants up and down. Training too early is more difficult and less effective.

Self-Help Skills

HELP YOUR CHILD LEARN ABOUT:

Understanding and Following Rules and Routines

- Help your child to be as independent as he can in his daily routines. Leave extra time in your schedule each day for him to slowly practice new skills without rushing, and make things easy to reach in your home.

- Model responsible behavior, good eating habits, good sleeping habits, good grooming habits, and a positive attitude about work.

- Set a few rules related to safety, respect for things and people, bedtime, and mealtimes.

- Provide structure and guidance as his own understanding of rules develops.

- Set routines about eating, sleeping, dressing, playing, and doing chores: in the morning when we wake up, we eat breakfast, get dressed, brush our teeth, and then play.

Becoming Responsible about Household Jobs

- Give your child opportunities to participate in household tasks. Teach him a task by showing him each step separately: go to the closet, get out the broom, sweep all around the floor, use the dustpan, and throw the dirt away in the garbage can.

Eating Well

- At mealtimes, your child will naturally want to get back to play as quickly as he can. It is not reasonable to expect him to sit at the table long after he is finished eating with nothing to do. Allow him to sit just long enough to finish eating all he wants, and then excuse him. Remind him to eat until his stomach feels full, and that there will not be more food until the next meal or planned snack.

- When your child spills, clean it up with little comment. Consider having him help you clean up, as long you are doing so with kindness to teach him responsibility, and not to punish him.

- Avoid battling over food. Your job is to put nutritious foods out at regular meal and snack times. Your child's job is to decide how much to eat. Plan three nutritious meals and two snacks in between meals; stick to that. As long as you don't allow constant nibbling, sweets, and junk food, you can trust him to eat what he needs.

Self-Help Skills

- Strike a balance about food likes and dislikes. Consider every family member's food preferences when you plan a meal or snack. A good rule of thumb is to include one food that your two-year-old likes at each meal, but don't prepare the whole meal according to his preferences. Once the meal is on the table, don't get up and fix him something else if he doesn't like what's there.

- Decide on the rules for mealtime manners and model them. Over time he will learn by example.

- Direct your child, who may be in a hurry to eat, to take his time and chew food well. **Avoid foods that need a grinding motion to chew and round foods that are common choking hazards until at least after the age of four years: hot dogs, popcorn, hard candy, peanuts, grapes, raw carrot sticks, and raw celery. Don't let him eat while he runs.**

Sleeping Well

- To help your child sleep well, make sure he gets plenty of exercise in the day, avoids caffeine, shares a calming bedtime routine with you, and stays on a fairly regular sleep schedule. Always respond to his nighttime fears with care and comfort. He may prefer a night-light, having the door open, or some soft music.

Taking Care of His Body

- Teach your child how to wash his hands and about the dangers of burns from hot water. At bathtime, give him a washcloth to practice washing his body and let him rub shampoo into his hair—you'll need to finish the jobs! Let him practice on dolls. Brush his teeth for him at least twice a day, but allow him to practice, too. **Supervise your child in the tub at all times. Set your water heater temperature to less than 120 Fahrenheit degrees to avoid burns.**

Dressing

- Select clothing that is easy to put on and take off: elastic-waist pants, T-shirts, sweatshirts, and shirts or sweaters with large buttons or snaps. Take the time to let your child do as much as he can. Help him finish dressing, and talk about what you are doing: "The tag goes in the back. One arm, then the other." Let him practice dressing his dolls.

Using the Toilet

- Wait for clear signs before you begin toilet training. When your child seems ready to begin, find a one-week period of time when you can give the job plenty of attention.

♫ Talking ! ? ! ♫ ! ? ! ♫ ! ? ! ♫ ! ? !

5 yrs.

4 yrs.

3 yrs.

2 yrs.

DEVELOPING SKILL	DESCRIPTION
Understanding and Using Words	Most children speak at least 50 words at two years, and 300 or more by age three. The rate that children learn words varies widely!
	Children understand many more words than they can say.
	Children are frequently misunderstood due to their limited ability to use language.
	Children who learn two languages at the same time typically mix the two languages until three or four years of age, when they separate the two languages. Their progress learning each language will move more slowly.
Ability to Produce Sounds of Speech	Children sometimes make words more simple to say:
	• Cat becomes "ca," as they leave off the final letter of the word.
	• Plane becomes "pane," or ring becomes "wing," as they substitute an easier sound to make.
	• Water becomes "wa," as they repeat one part of the word.
	• Telephone becomes "tephone," as they drop one of the syllables.
	Children say many sounds clearly. It will take many children until eight years of age to complete the task of learning to articulate the sounds of speech.
Ability to Speak in Sentences	Around age two, most children begin to form simple, two- to three-word sentences: "More juice." "No want." "Go home."
	By three, they may be combining four or five words.
Ability to Answer Questions	Children answer questions with more than a "yes" or "no."
	Children give their first and last names, sex, and age, when asked.

1 yr.

! ?

Birth

! ? ! ♫ ! ? ! ♫ ! ? ! ♫ ! ? ! *Talking* ♫

DEVELOPING SKILL	DESCRIPTION
Understanding the Rules of Language	Children begin to learn the complicated rules of language and make many mistakes: "foots" instead of "feet," "doed" instead of "did," and "me do" instead of "I do" or "I will." As they listen and talk, children eventually learn correct usage naturally and effortlessly.
Ability to Have a Conversation	Children listen and respond while having conversations with others.
Ability to Understand and Follow Directions	Children first follow two related directions: "Please take off your mittens, then take off your coat." Next, children follow two unrelated directions: "Please give me a hug, then put on your shoes."
Capacity to Listen to Books or Spoken Stories	Children listen attentively to a brief story being told or read. They remember many parts of the story and retell them. They may look at books independently. With practice, they can turn pages one at a time.
Ability to Explore and Appreciate Music and Rhythm	Children listen to all kinds of music and: • Imitate tunes and do vocal exploration. • Learn to sing words to simple songs, especially action songs. • Dance and move their body spontaneously to music or rhymes. • Experiment with rhythm using simple instruments or improvising with their hands or toys. • Repeat brief rhymes and enjoy the predictability of them.

! ♫ ! ? ! ♫ ! ? ! ♫ ! ? ! ♫ ! ? !

♫ Talking ! ? ! ♫ ! ? ! ♫ ! ? ! ♫ ! ? !

5 yrs.

HELP YOUR CHILD LEARN ABOUT:

Learning about Language

4 yrs.

3 yrs.

- Talk to your child about everything you do throughout the day. Continue to visit familiar places and new places: the library, city buildings, other people's homes, parks, or a farm. Talk about where she goes and what she sees.

- Listen attentively when your child speaks to you. Encourage her to talk often.

- Speak clearly, keeping your sentences short and simple. Repeat the main ideas several times in different ways: "Time to go home. We will go home in ten minutes. It will be good to get home to eat lunch."

- Name things and say new words over and over. Have fun with words: "Look – there's a skyscraper. A skyscraper is a building that is so tall, it looks like it is scraping or touching the sky!"

- Ask your child simple questions to get her thinking and talking. Give her plenty of time to think of and state her answer. Answer her questions.

- Avoid correcting or criticizing her speech. Instead of correcting her mispronounced words and incomplete sentences, repeat an expanded, accurate version: If she says, "In car," you could say, "That's right, your doll is in the car."

- Recite and read rhymes to your child, teaching her some of the lines:

  See, see! What shall I see?
  A horse's head where his tail should be. —Mother Goose

2 yrs.

1 yr.

! ?

Birth

! ? ! ♫ ! ? ! ♫ ! ? ! ♫ ! ? ! Talking ♫

Following Directions

- Have your child practice by asking her a few times each day to do two things that are related: "Please, get your doll, and then find her coat." "Get your socks out of your drawer and then find some shoes."

- Once she is able to do two related things, a few times each day, ask her to do two unrelated things: "Feed your fish and then get the crayons out." "Eat your desert and then pick out a book."

Listening to Books or Spoken Stories

- Tell stories and read simple, colorful, books with familiar pictures that encourage touching and pointing. Move toward more complicated stories as your child's attention grows. Aim for reading together at least twenty minutes a day in several sittings.

Making Music

- Sing simple songs and teach them to your child. Listen and dance to different types of music. Let her explore simple rhythm instruments. To help her learn the difference between high and low notes, have her move her body to the notes of simple songs: touch the floor when you sing low notes in a song, and stretch to the high notes.

! ♫ ! ? ! ♫ ! ? ! ♫ ! ? ! ♫ ! ? !

Thinking

DEVELOPING SKILL	DESCRIPTION
Ability to Actively Explore and Experiment	Children are curious explorers. They touch, taste, smell, watch, and listen to things around them. When they pour, scoop, measure, and dump sand, they are experimenting with their ideas and learning about how things work.
Ability to Pretend and Play Make-Believe	Children make sense of the real world by creating small imaginary worlds. In these fantasy worlds, they are in charge and have the freedom to take control over things that are bigger, confusing, or forbidden to them in real life: "I'm going to drive the car now," or "I'm going to make that big mean dog get small." They imitate actions that they see adults doing in real life, books, or movies: playing house, doctor, grocery store, or library.
Capacity to Focus and Concentrate	Children move most of the time, occasionally stopping long enough to complete a simple puzzle, to draw a picture, to look at a short picture book, or to play something engaging. Attention span varies among children, and typically grows over time—usually, the older the child, the longer the attention span.
Ability to Notice Details	Children's awareness of details is keen. They notice and comment on things like the sound of a passing airplane, the smell of smoke, the sour taste of a lemon, or the color and softness of a rose. In picture books, they point to things like a partially hidden mouse, a bird in a tree, or buttons on a dress.
Ability to Name and Describe Functions of Common Things	Children name at least six parts of the body, and state their function: "Ear is for hearing," they say as they point to their ear. They state the use of familiar objects: "phone is for talking," or "a jacket is to keep warm."
Understanding Cause and Effect	Children develop a broad understanding that they have the power to make things happen instead of thinking that things happen outside of their control. They learn this through repetition and investigation: flipping the light switch teaches them that pushing the switch up makes the light go on.

4 yrs.

3 yrs.

2 yrs.

1 yr.

Birth

DEVELOPING SKILL	DESCRIPTION
Ability to Match Colors and Shapes	Children's understanding of colors and shapes follows a pattern: 1. First, they match a color or shape when it is shown to them. If shown an apple and asked to find something the same color, they find something red. 2. Once children are able to match colors and shapes, they point to the color or shape when it is named for them. If they are asked to find a circle, they will point to a circle. 3. Next, children name colors or shapes, though usually after three years of age.
Ability to Sort Objects	Children sort by one characteristic: they find all the socks in a group of socks and shoes, or all the animals in a pile of animals and blocks.
Understanding the Concept of Size	Children point out the smaller and larger of two objects, or the shorter or longer line. They begin to use words that reflect size: "I am little, you are big."
Understanding the Concept of Numbers and Counting	Children begin to show awareness of an order in counting, and that there is a word for the number of objects in a group. They can count up to three objects. Next, they understand the concept of taking one or two things from a group: when children are asked to bring two bananas from a bunch, they bring two.
Understanding the Concept of Time	Children have a vague sense of time. They begin to understand time by relating it to the order of events in the day: Sleep comes after story, or Mom comes home after nap.

5 yrs.

4 yrs.

3 yrs.

2 yrs.

1 yr.

Birth

Thinking (✦ 🌐 ✦ (✦ 🌐 ✦ (✦ 🌐 ✦

5 yrs.

HELP YOUR CHILD LEARN ABOUT:

Exploring

- Talk your way through your time with your child, explaining things as you go.

- Point out details while visiting familiar and unfamiliar places.

- Encourage your child to explore with all of his senses, allowing him to get dirty and messy.

4 yrs.

- Childproof your home as much as possible so he can freely explore without hearing "no" too often.

Imitating and Pretending

- Let your child help you with simple chores. Teach him the steps of a task: "First, we put the eggs and milk in the bowl, then we beat them with a whisk."

- Encourage your child to play make-believe and join him yourself sometimes.

- Provide your child with dress-up clothes, play dishes, sets of animals, dolls, or stuffed animals for him to use in pretend play.

3 yrs.

Paying Attention

Encourage your child's focus and attention:

- Keep a variety of things available for him to do.

- Match activities to his ability level.

- Play alongside him.

- After he completes an activity that requires concentration, comment on his ability to stay focused.

2 yrs.

- Sometimes encourage him to stick with an activity a little bit longer, but typically, follow his lead: if he is ready to move on, let him do so.

Experimenting

- Encourage your child to experiment with making things happen like turning a tape player on and off, rolling a ball down a ramp, or pouring water into different-sized containers.

1 yr.

🌐

Birth

(✦ 🌐 ✦ (✦ 🌐 ✦ (✦ 🌐 ✦ (✦

Thinking (

Matching Colors and Shapes
- Point out colors and shapes all around. Hold up a color or shape and ask your child to find one that matches: "Look at this red sock; can you find something else red in the room?" "Look at this circle; can you find another circle on this page?"

Sorting
- Include your child in sorting during everyday tasks: putting the silverware away in compartments in the drawer, separating laundry into different-colored piles, or sorting the food from the grocery bags.

Understanding Size
- Provide opportunities for your child to feel and see size: hand him a large and small potato, or long and short sticks. Talk about sizes and ask him if he can tell which things are larger or smaller and which are longer or shorter.

Counting and Using Numbers
- Count the objects for your child that he uses throughout the day: "You are playing with one, two, three, four cars," or "One, two—you have two hands!" Ask him to count familiar objects up to two or three: "Can you tell me how many socks you are wearing?"
- Include picture books about matching, shapes, numbers, and counting among the many other books you read.

Exploring Time
- Set a routine that gives order to your child's day to give him a sense of when things happen. Talk about activities or events that are attached to certain times of the day, or days of the week: "Every Wednesday, we go to the library for storytime," or "After nap, I pick you up from Grandma's."

5 yrs. # Common Concerns

The following are common behaviors in children this age that typically concern or frustrate parents. The child:

4 yrs.

- Is in constant motion.
- Is inflexible or wants things "just so."
- Makes messes and gets into things.
- Jabbers.
- Whines.
- Stutters.
- Mispronounces words.
- Is aggressive: bites, hits, throws.
- Dawdles.
- Has difficulty sharing and is possessive: "Mine!"
- Is negative or stubborn: "No!"
- Has emotional ups and downs.
- Is easily frustrated.
- Has tantrums.
- Appears unreasonable, selfish, contrary, or bossy.
- Has picky eating habits.
- Resists bedtime.

3 yrs.

2 yrs.

Be assured that these behaviors will usually pass with time and appropriate guidance from you, but if you have any questions, ask for help.

1 yr.

When to Get More Help <u>5 yrs.</u>

Children typically grow and learn new skills in their own time and at their own pace within the wide range of what is normal. Sometimes, however, children need a bit of extra help to keep their development on track, or to stay healthy and happy.

By three years of age, in addition to all of the skills typically mastered by one year and two years (listed on pages 13 and 35), your child SHOULD BE ABLE TO DO the following:

<u>4 yrs.</u>

- ❏ Walk smoothly without falling or bumping into things.
- ❏ Pick up and handle small objects.
- ❏ Copy a circle.
- ❏ Build a tower of more than four blocks.
- ❏ Speak clearly, and be easy to understand.
- ❏ Use two-word sentences.
- ❏ Separate from parent without extreme difficulty.
- ❏ Show interest in other children.

<u>3 yrs.</u>

- ❏ Behave less aggressively toward other people and things.
- ❏ Name familiar objects.
- ❏ Enjoy listening to stories being read.
- ❏ Manage stairs without difficulty.
- ❏ Participate in pretend play.

If your child DOES NOT demonstrate most of the skills listed by three years, consider seeking advice about whether or not your child needs help in developing delayed or missing skills. You are the expert when it comes to your child. If you have a concern, trust your instinct and find someone trained to help you: health care providers, teachers, social workers, parent educators, mental health workers, or telephone help-line staff. Consider talking it over with friends and family, too. You don't need to worry alone! Turn to "Finding Help in Your Community," on page 4, to learn about finding help near you.

<u>2 yrs.</u>

<u>1 yr.</u>

Feelings & Relationships

5 yrs.

DEVELOPING SKILL	DESCRIPTION
Ability to Relate to Others	Children are typically friendly, agreeable, better able to understand another's point of view, and eager to please.
	Little by little, they move away from the adult that they are most attached to with ease; separation anxiety lessens.
Increasing Self-Esteem	Children are increasingly aware of themselves as whole and separate people.
Growing Independence	Children are more fully viewing themselves as separate from others, and realizing that they are the boss of themselves. They must grapple with how to use their newfound power.
	They are developing some self-reliance and self-restraint.
Expression of Emotions	Children are learning to name and express feelings. They have fewer tantrums and more frequently use words to express frustration. They may have sudden bouts of anger and jealousy.
Ability to Cope with Change and Transitions	Children accept change and move from one activity to another with a bit more ease than last year.
Ability to Play with Other Children and Alone	Children like to play with other children, though they prefer one or two at a time. They begin to cooperate with other children with less adult supervision.

4 yrs.

3 yrs.

2 yrs.

1 yr.

Birth

Feelings & Relationships ♥

DEVELOPING SKILL	DESCRIPTION
Ability to Share and Take Turns	Children begin to understand taking turns even though they aren't always willing to do so. They play simple games with adults and other children. Typically, children freely share toys at around four years of age.
Capacity for Imaginary Friends	Children may have an imaginary friend. They share thoughts, problems, fears, feelings, frustrations, secrets, and humor with that friend, and may talk to the friend to communicate their feelings to others.
Conquering Fears	Children have many fears: the dark, strange places, monsters, fire, blood, and getting hurt or breaking their body. They have difficulty telling the difference between what's real and what's not real, so these fears are very real to them.
Awareness of Sexuality	Children know the gender of other children and adults.
	They are curious about bodies. They may play "doctor" or "mommy and daddy" with same-age children as a way to explore genitals; this exploration is quite natural.
	They continue to be curious about their own bodies, and they may masturbate.

5 yrs.

4 yrs.

3 yrs.

2 yrs.

1 yr.

♥

Birth

♥ Feelings & Relationships ～ ♥ ～ ♥ ～ ♥ ～

HELP YOUR CHILD LEARN ABOUT:

Relating to Others

- Give your child lots of your time, care, attention, and love: pats, hugs, kisses, cuddles, conversations, comforting words, tickles, and verbal expressions of love.

- Eat meals and talk together as often as you can as a family.

- Introduce your child to people outside of your immediate and extended family: neighbors, community members, and other children in preschool or playgroups.

Feeling Good about Herself

- Listen to your child and respect her. Don't use sarcasm or words that ridicule: stupid, dumb, brat, etc.

- Encourage and allow your child to explore the things, ideas, and other people that interest her.

Becoming Independent

- Eliminate unnecessary frustrations and childproof your home.

- Compliment your child's achievements and her efforts to learn.

- Set reasonable limits and enforce them. Provide appropriate positive or negative consequences for her actions.

Expressing Emotions

- Remain constant in the face of your child's outbursts; remind her that she can be powerful and ask for help at the same time.

- Help her to name her feelings. Accept positive and negative feelings and teach options for expressing them to prevent her from hitting or biting.

- Expect her to express her feelings, and to connect feelings and thinking.

1 yr.

♥

Birth

～ ♥ ～ ♥ ～ ♥ ～ ♥ ～ ♥ ～ ♥ ～ ♥ ～ ♥

❤ ~ ❤ ~ ❤ ~ *Feelings & Relationships* ❤

Coping with Change and Transitions

- Keep things predictable to help prevent some of the inevitable frustrations at this age.
- Give her five-minute warnings before changing activities.
- She may benefit from a teddy bear or a security blanket to help her through the rough emotional spots.
- Make positive suggestions instead of giving orders: "It's time to go home from the park and make lunch. What should we make for dessert?" instead of, "Get out of the park."

Playing with Other Children and Alone

- Provide opportunities for your child to play with other children. Now that she enjoys other children, preschool, a class, or a playgroup could offer her opportunities to make new friends.
- Allow and observe her relationships with her imaginary friends. You can learn what she's thinking and feeling, and communicate with her through the "friend."

Sharing

- Encourage your child to take turns and share with others by sharing things with your child: give her a bite of your fruit or let her look at your book.
- Play games with rules. Practice taking turns.

Conquering Fears

- Take your child's fears seriously and comfort her.

Awareness of Sexuality

- Respond matter-of-factly and accurately to your child's curiosity about the human body and the differences between boys and girls. Teach her rules about privacy and appropriate touch. Allow her to look at and touch all of the parts of her body, including her genitals. Give her the correct names of her body parts.

❤ ~ ❤ ~ ❤ ~ ❤ ~ ❤ ~ ❤ ~ ❤ ~ ❤ ~ ❤ ~ ❤ ~ ❤

Hand & Body Movement

5 yrs.

4 yrs.

3 yrs.

DEVELOPING SKILL	DESCRIPTION
Ability to Run	Children master running; they move smoothly with the coordination needed to turn and stop.
Ability to Jump and Hop	Without falling, children jump forward one or two feet and jump from a bottom step without falling. They take a few steps on tiptoe.
Ability to Walk Up and Down Stairs	Children walk up and down stairs by themselves, alternating one foot per step.
Ability to Climb Ladders	Children climb ladders, if they have had opportunities to practice.
Ability to Catch and Throw	Children bounce and catch a large ball without losing balance. Their underhand and overhand throws can move the ball several feet forward.
Ability to Kick	Children walk up to a ball that is not moving and kick it. Later this year, they will kick a ball that is rolled to them.
Ability to Ride a Tricycle or Riding Toy	Children pedal or propel tricycles and riding toys with the coordination to turn, steer, and stop.
Ability to Balance	Children walk along a wide straight line for several feet without losing balance.

2 yrs.

1 yr.

Birth

Hand & Body Movement

DEVELOPING SKILL	DESCRIPTION
Ability to Draw and Copy Marks	Children copy circles, crosses, and squares. They draw pictures that represent something: "This is a big eagle flying." Their pictures become increasingly complicated over time, with more actions and parts.
Ability to Coordinate Eyes and Hands to Work with Materials, and to Solve Simple Problems	Children show the strength and control of fingers, eyes, and hands necessary to: • Build simple towers, towns and buildings with blocks. • String half-inch beads and lace a shoestring in large holes. • Twist open a toothpaste tube. • Operate door knobs. • Cut on a line with child-sized blunt-edged scissors. • Glue things together.

4 yrs.

3 yrs.

2 yrs.

1 yr.

Birth

✋ Hand & Body Movement

5 yrs.

HELP YOUR CHILD LEARN ABOUT:

Running, Jumping, Hopping, Climbing, Catching, Throwing, Kicking, and Balancing

- Show your child that exercise is important by your own example.
- Provide opportunities for him that encourage and allow him to explore the movement of his body. Backyards and local playgrounds are great places to do so! **Supervise your child on playground equipment at all times.**

4 yrs.

Riding a Tricycle or Riding Toy •

- Provide your child with many opportunities to ride a sturdy tricycle or riding toy that does not tip over easily and that fits him. Teach him to stay out of the street and off of steep hills and stairways. **Supervise your child on a tricycle or riding toy at all times. Do not allow your child to ride in the street until at least eight years of age.**

Making Art/Making a Mark

- Provide your child with writing materials. Talk about how useful writing is, and point out the many ways you use it each day: making lists, writing notes, copying recipes, writing letters, making notes on the calendar, and writing checks.

3 yrs.

- Provide him with a place in your home to be messy and stock it with art materials.
- Concerning his creative projects, comment on effort, not the end product: "I love the colors that you are using," or "Look at the big strokes you made," instead of, "What is it?" As he moves into the stage of representing things in his work, a respectful way to ask about his art is to say, "Tell me about your picture."

2 yrs.

1 yr.

Birth

**Working with
Eyes and Hands**

• Give your child lots of opportunities to work with his hands, eyes, and small muscles:

— Stack block-like objects.

— Put together puzzles.

— Lace cards and string beads.

— Cut with scissors.

— Use glue.

— Play with play dough.

Always supervise your child with scissors and small objects.

4 yrs.

3 yrs.

2 yrs.

1 yr.

Birth

Self-Help Skills

5 yrs.

4 yrs.

3 yrs.

2 yrs.

DEVELOPING SKILL	DESCRIPTION
Understanding and Following Rules	At this age, children follow rules to avoid consequences and danger, and to gain approval and rewards. They are developing some self-control, but need structure, routines, order, and guidance. Their sense of right and wrong develops over many years. Typically, children can: • Avoid some forbidden things and dangers like a hot stove, the street, fire, or fragile things (though not reliably yet). • Obey an authority figure. • Come when called. • Wait for their turn. • Begin to care for some things with respect.
Household Responsibilities	Children do simple household chores, if taught: set the table, put things away, make a bed, feed the pet, or clean up spills.
Ability to Feed Self	Children skillfully use a spoon and fork without much spilling and pour from a pitcher into a cup. They can fix a simple snack: pour a bowl of cereal, scoop ice cream, or wash a piece of fruit.
Healthy Eating Habits	Their appetites are fairly good, and they like an increasing variety of foods.
Mealtime Manners	Children sit at the meal table for brief periods only. Their increase in language skills allows for more conversation. They work on learning table manners: asking for food with "please" and "thank you," passing food when asked, using a napkin to wipe hands and mouth during or after the meal, and asking to be excused from the table.

1 yr.

Birth

DEVELOPING SKILL	DESCRIPTION
Healthy Sleep Habits	Children sleep approximately 11 hours per night, and one hour during the day. Some children give up their nap, but benefit from a quiet hour alone to rest, look at books, draw, or listen to calm music. Sleep needs vary widely.
	Nighttime fears and nightmares may awaken children.
Body Care	Children wash hands, brush teeth, and bathe themselves with supervision and encouragement. They need an adult to wash and comb hair.
Dressing	Children dress with very little help: button, snap, put on a shirt, pants, socks, and shoes. They typically need help with small buttons, zippers, and tying shoelaces.
Toilet Learning	Most children learn to use the toilet or potty-chair with some reminders between two and three years of age. They typically use the toilet independently and regularly, without being asked, between ages of about three and a half and four.
	Three-year-olds are typically dry during the day, but accidents are common. Nighttime bedwetting often occurs until age six.

Self-Help Skills

HELP YOUR CHILD LEARN ABOUT:

Understanding and Following Rules and Routines

- Model responsible behavior, a positive attitude about work, and good exercise, eating, and grooming habits.
- Set routines about eating, sleeping, dressing, playing, and doing chores.
- Help your child to be as independent as she can in her daily routines by making things easy to reach and by moving at a pace slow enough for her to take the time she needs to complete tasks.
- Make a few rules, make sure she understands them, and stick to them. For example: no hurting people with words or actions, no leaving the yard without an adult, and no breaking things on purpose.

Becoming Responsible for Household Jobs

- Communicate your expectations about household responsibilities clearly. Teach your child by showing, telling, and doing each task needed to get the job done. Make it clear what chores should be done, when they should be done, and what being done means: "You need to make your bed each morning. That means clearing the toys off of it and pulling the sheet and blankets up." Show her. Encourage and compliment her efforts. A job chart or list with pictures of her jobs and the order in which she should do them may help to organize and motivate her.

Eating Well

- Involve your child in preparing the meal: cutting, washing, rolling, stirring, mixing, and baking.
- Set up foods and utensils so that she can prepare the planned snack for herself and practice her skills: fruit in a bowl to be washed; or cereal, milk in a small pitcher, and sugar in a bowl with a spoon.
- Put out nutritious foods at regular meal and snack times—don't allow constant nibbling, sweets, and junk food—then trust your child to make good decisions about what she eats and how much she eats. Remind her to eat just until her stomach feels full, and that there will be no food until the next meal or planned snack. Don't try to force her to eat!
- Strike a balance about food likes and dislikes. Consider every family member's food preferences when you plan a meal or snack. Once the meal is on the table, if she doesn't like what's being served, don't get up and fix her something else. Serve old favorites with new foods at meals, asking her to try at least 1/2 teaspoon of the new one. If she doesn't want to eat more, try again another day.

- Keep the atmosphere pleasant at mealtimes and take your time eating. Adopt a "no arguing at the table" policy. Decide on your family's rules for mealtime manners and conversation and model them; over time, she will learn by example.

- Direct your child, who may be in a hurry to eat, to take her time and chew food well. **Avoid foods that need a grinding motion to chew and round foods that are common choking hazards until at least after the age of four years: hot dogs, popcorn, hard candy, peanuts, grapes, raw carrot sticks, and raw celery. Don't let her eat while running.**

Sleeping Well

- To foster healthy sleep, make sure your child gets plenty of exercise in the day, avoids caffeine, follows a calming bedtime routine with you, and stays on a fairly regular sleep schedule. Always respond to her nighttime fears and nightmares with care and comfort. She may prefer a night-light, having the door open, or some soft music.

Taking Care of Her Body

- Give her reminders to wash her hands, brush her teeth, and take a bath when she should. Show her the steps of combing and washing her hair: wet hair, measure the right amount of shampoo, lather, rinse with a plastic pitcher, wring water out, towel dry, and comb. **Supervise your child in the tub at all times. Set your water heater temperature to less than 120 Fahrenheit degrees to avoid burns.**

- Your child should visit the dentist by three years, and then every six months. A trip with an older sibling or adult first might help to prepare her.

Dressing

- Allow your child to begin to make some choices about dressing on her own: "Do you want the blue shirt or the white one?" Let her pick an outfit for you one day, as a reminder of how it feels to have no control over selecting the clothes you will wear all day!

Using the Toilet

- If she is not trained yet, wait for clear signs of readiness before you begin toilet training. When she seems ready to begin, select a one-week period of time in which you can give the job plenty of attention. If she is trained, work with her on remembering to wipe, flush and wash her hands, and on finding the bathroom in time away from home. **Never leave your child unattended in a public restroom.**

♫ Talking ! ? ! ♫ ! ? ! ♫ ! ? ! ♫ ! ? !

5 yrs.

DEVELOPING SKILL	DESCRIPTION
Understanding and Using Words	Children speak between 300 and 1,000 words. The rate that they learn words varies widely.
	Children who learn two languages at once usually separate the two languages by age three or four years. By the time they go to school, they will be speaking as well as children their own age in both languages.
Ability to Produce Sounds of Speech	Children typically speak clearly enough for anyone to understand them. They work to produce the sounds of speech, which are usually mastered by age eight.
	Stuttering is common in children and typically passes after a few months.
Ability to Speak in Sentences	By four years, children are likely to use five- to six-word sentences. They use "or," "and," or "but" to connect thoughts:
	"I go and read book."
	"Go home or to Grandma's?"
	"I eat bread but not carrots."
Ability to Answer and Ask Simple Questions	Children ask and answer simple questions such as who, what, and where about the world and events around them.
Understanding the Rules of Language	Children use parts of speech correctly:
	• Action verbs: I <u>dance</u>.
	• Plurals: I like <u>kitties</u>.
	• Adjectives: I am a <u>big</u> girl.
	• Pronouns: <u>He</u> is using <u>her</u> chair, but <u>she</u> can use <u>his</u>.
Ability to Have a Conversation	Children understand and participate in common social give and take: hello/goodbye, please/thank you, excuse me.
	They love to talk, make conversation, and use language to get what they want.

4 yrs.

3 yrs.

2 yrs.

1 yr.

! ?
Birth

! ? ! ♫ ! ? ! ♫ ! ? ! ♫ ! ? ! ♫ !

! ? ! ♫ ! ? ! ♫ ! ? ! ♫ ! ? ! ♫ ! ? ! *Talking* ♫

5 yrs.

DEVELOPING SKILL	DESCRIPTION
Ability to Understand and Follow Directions	Children follow three related directions: "Put on your coat, then your boots, then your mittens."
	They follow two to three unrelated directions: "Put down your milk, then, find your blocks."
Capacity to Listen to Books or Spoken Stories	Children will: • Listen to a story. • Remember and comment on some details. • Enjoy looking at books independently. • Sometimes pretend to read to others. • Tell you when you have skipped a part of a favorite story.
Ability to Explore and Appreciate Music and Rhythm	Children listen to all kinds of music and: • Sing many simple songs. • Begin to distinguish high notes from low notes. • Dance and move to the rhythm of music or rhymes. • Create rhythm with hands or percussion instruments. • Make simple tunes on simple instruments. • Play rhyming or word games. • Recite simple rhymes.

4 yrs.

3 yrs.

2 yrs.

1 yr.

! ?

Birth

! ♫ ! ? ! ♫ ! ? ! ♫ ! ? ! ♫ ! ? !

♫ Talking ! ? ! ♫ ! ? ! ♫ ! ? ! ♫ ! ? !

5 yrs.

HELP YOUR CHILD LEARN ABOUT:

4 yrs.

3 yrs.

Learning about Language

- Talk *with* your child, not *at* him.

- Listen to him carefully when he speaks—and let him know that you are listening. Look at him, smile, nod, and talk to him about what he said.

- Speak slowly and clearly. If he is consistently having difficulty pronouncing certain sounds, emphasize those sounds when you speak, but don't draw attention to him when he mispronounces them.

- Have him describe things: groceries as you put them away, the yard, and the food on his plate.

- Ask your child lots of questions. That is the way he learns to ask and answer them himself. Answer his questions.

- Avoid pressure, and don't draw attention to or correct his speech. This is especially important if he is stuttering.

- Instead of correcting his mispronounced words and incomplete sentences, repeat an expanded, accurate version: If he says, "I w-w-wuv you so much," you could say, "Yes, I know you love me so much!"

- Visit new and old places and talk about what you see: shopping malls, beaches, pools, bus rides.

- Recite and read rhymes to your child. Teach him some rhymes, and make up some rhymes together.

2 yrs.

1 yr.

! ?
Birth

! ? ! ♫ ! ? ! ♫ ! ? ! ♫ ! ? ! ♫ !

! ? ! ♫ ! ? ! ♫ ! ? ! ♫ ! ? ! Talking ♫

Following Directions

- Ask your child to do three related tasks periodically throughout the day: "Get your doll, and then find her coat, and put her in her stroller."
- Once he is able to do three related things, ask him to do three unrelated things throughout the day: "Feed your fish, then get the crayons and paper out, then call Grandpa."

4 yrs.

Listening to Books or Spoken Stories

- Tell stories and read many kinds of books to your child. Aim to read for at least 20 minutes a day—in more than one sitting if he can't sit still for 20 minutes at a time.
- Point out how useful reading is in everyday life by reading to your child words, phrases, and text from many places: recipes, magazines, bus schedules, street signs, menus, and the mail.

Making Music

- Sing simple songs and teach them to your child. Listen and dance to different types of music. Let him explore simple rhythm instruments.

3 yrs.

2 yrs.

1 yr.

! ?

Birth

! ♫ ! ? ! ♫ ! ? ! ♫ ! ? ! ♫ ! ? !

Thinking

DEVELOPING SKILL	DESCRIPTION
Ability to Actively Explore and Experiment	Children are on a mission to understand the world. They actively interact with things to learn about them.
Ability to Pretend and Play Make-Believe	Children create complicated stories or themes, and use more props to play make-believe: they gather animals, blocks, pillows, and blankets to construct and play zoo, or they bathe, dress, feed, and put to bed a baby doll.
	They may pretend to be many characters: mother, father, baby, grandma, construction worker, mail carrier, or doctor.
Capacity to Focus and Concentrate	Children are improving their ability to complete and work on tasks. Attention span varies between children, and typically grows over time—usually, the older the child, the longer the attention span. Some children may not be able to attend to a task for five to 10 minutes until four or five years of age.
Ability to Notice Details	Children notice when details are wrong or out of order: pictures of an elephant in a kitchen, or a toaster in a tree. They can put three pictures in order that tell a familiar story.
Ability to Understand Opposites, and Concepts about Place	Children begin to understand ideas about where something is in space: up, down, top, bottom, under, over, next to, beside, around, in front of, behind, between, high, and low. They begin to understand opposites: fast/slow, empty/full, and tall/short.
Ability to Name Colors and Shapes	Children name at least the primary colors when shown: red, blue, and yellow.
	They can point to at least four common shapes: square, circle, triangle, and rectangle.

4 yrs.

3 yrs.

2 yrs.

1 yr.

Birth

Thinking

DEVELOPING SKILL	DESCRIPTION
Ability to Sort Objects	Children sort objects according to their color, shape, function, or physical characteristic. When shown a pile of animals and cars, they would be able to sort the living things from the machines. When shown a pile of blocks of three different colors, they could sort them into three piles of different colors.
Understanding the Concept of Size	Children pick out the smaller and larger objects from a group of two: a marble is smaller, an apple is bigger.
Understanding the Concept of Numbers and Counting	Children count out loud four or more objects.

When they are shown a set of one, two, three or four objects, they say the right number that represents the group. |
| Understanding the Concept of Time | Children's sense of time is inexact, fuzzy, or vague. They understand that certain events happen at particular times of the day: breakfast is in the morning and bedtime is at night. They begin to talk about time, though not always accurately: "I eat lunch all day" or "I went to sleep for two days." |

Thinking

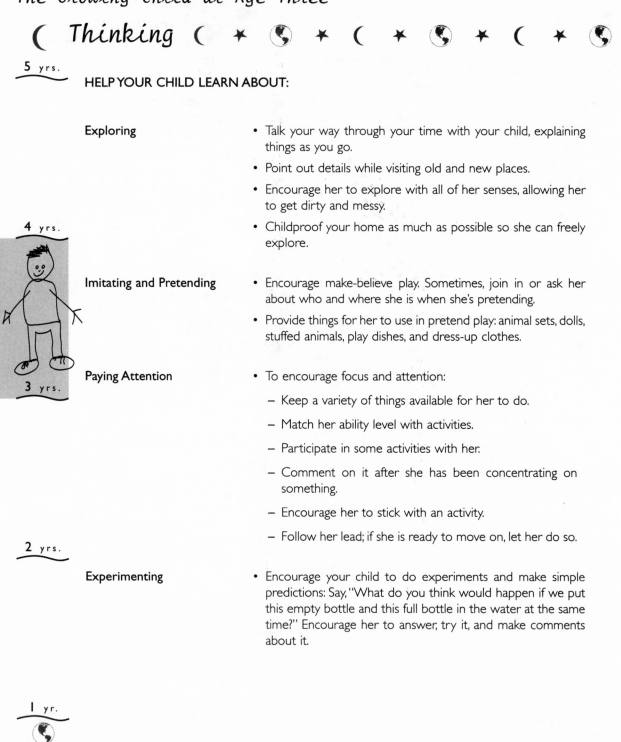

HELP YOUR CHILD LEARN ABOUT:

Exploring

- Talk your way through your time with your child, explaining things as you go.
- Point out details while visiting old and new places.
- Encourage her to explore with all of her senses, allowing her to get dirty and messy.
- Childproof your home as much as possible so she can freely explore.

Imitating and Pretending

- Encourage make-believe play. Sometimes, join in or ask her about who and where she is when she's pretending.
- Provide things for her to use in pretend play: animal sets, dolls, stuffed animals, play dishes, and dress-up clothes.

Paying Attention

- To encourage focus and attention:
  - Keep a variety of things available for her to do.
  - Match her ability level with activities.
  - Participate in some activities with her.
  - Comment on it after she has been concentrating on something.
  - Encourage her to stick with an activity.
  - Follow her lead; if she is ready to move on, let her do so.

Experimenting

- Encourage your child to do experiments and make simple predictions: Say, "What do you think would happen if we put this empty bottle and this full bottle in the water at the same time?" Encourage her to answer, try it, and make comments about it.

* ☽ * (* ☽ * (* ☽ * (*Thinking* (

Naming Colors and Shapes

• Point out colors and shapes wherever you go, and help your child to name them.

Sorting

• Include your child in sorting tasks during everyday routines: putting the silverware away in compartments in the drawer, separating laundry into different-colored piles, or sorting the food from the grocery bags.

Understanding Size

• Let your child feel and touch size in different ways: hand her things of different sizes or lengths and ask her to pick the biggest or longest.

Counting and Using Numbers

• Count things frequently throughout the day, especially those your child is interested in or that are useful: forks, pennies, or stamps for letters.

• Play board games that involve matching, colors, concepts, shapes, and counting.

• Read books that illustrate matching, colors, concepts, shapes, letters, and numbers.

Time

• Give your child's day a sense of order by setting a routine that helps her get a sense of when things happen in the day. Talk about how certain things are attached to certain days of the week or times of the day.

* (* ☽ * (* ☽ * (* ☽ * (*

5 yrs. # Common Concerns

The following are common behaviors in children this age that typically concern or frustrate parents. The child:

4 yrs.

3 yrs.

- Sucks thumb.
- Whines.
- Interrupts.
- Stutters.
- Talks back.
- Teases, tattles, and calls names.
- Dawdles.
- Is loud and demanding.
- Is aggressive: hitting, kicking.
- Has some difficulty sharing.
- Ignores requests.
- Is fearful.
- Has nervous habits: nose picking, nail biting, or grimacing.
- Has intense emotions.
- Is insecure, shy, and fearful.
- Uses bathroom language or swearing.
- Lies or stretches the truth.
- Has picky eating habits.
- Resists bedtime.

2 yrs.

Be assured that these behaviors will usually pass with time and appropriate guidance from you, but if you have any questions, ask for help.

1 yr.

When to Get More Help

Children typically grow and learn new skills in their own time and at their own pace within the wide range of what is normal. Sometimes, however, children need a bit of extra help to keep their development on track, or to stay healthy and happy.

By four years of age, in addition to all of the skills typically mastered by one year, two years, and three years (listed on pages 13, 35, and 57), your child SHOULD BE ABLE TO DO the following:

- ❑ Throw a ball in an overhand manner.
- ❑ Jump in place.
- ❑ Ride a tricycle.
- ❑ Balance briefly on one foot.
- ❑ Grasp a crayon between thumb and fingers.
- ❑ Scribble, or show any interest in it.
- ❑ Play simple board games with adult assistance.
- ❑ Use sentences of more than three words.
- ❑ Ask questions.
- ❑ Use "me" and "you" accurately.
- ❑ Say name and age.
- ❑ Speak clearly.
- ❑ Show interest in other children and adults outside of the family.
- ❑ Show some self-control of aggressive behavior when angry or upset.
- ❑ Show steady progress in dressing (though may need help with difficult fasteners) and using the toilet.
- ❑ Build a tower of ten blocks and copy simple block designs.

If your child DOES NOT demonstrate most of the skills listed above by four years, consider seeking advice about whether or not your child needs help in developing delayed or missing skills. You are the expert when it comes to your child. If you have a concern, trust your instinct and find someone trained to help you: health care providers, teachers, social workers, parent educators, mental health workers, or telephone help-line staff. Consider talking it over with friends and family, too. You don't need to worry alone! Turn to "Finding Help in Your Community," on page 4, to learn about finding help near you.

Feelings & Relationships

5 yrs.

4 yrs.

3 yrs.

2 yrs.

DEVELOPING SKILL	DESCRIPTION
Ability to Relate to Others	Children are typically outgoing, eager, enthusiastic, and cooperative. They also typically brag, boast, exaggerate, and demand.
Increasing Self-Esteem	Children take great pride in their accomplishments and seek adult approval often. They are typically sensitive to praise, blame, and criticism.
Growing Independence	Children demand the opportunity to do things by themselves. Many times, they succeed, but often they don't; they get frustrated quickly when faced with problems in accomplishing something independently.
Expression of Emotions	Children are better able to rely on words to express emotions and resolve conflicts. Their moods may change suddenly, without warning.
Ability to Cope with Change and Transitions	Most children handle transitions and changes in plans more calmly at this age.
Ability to Play with Other Children and Alone	Children cooperate well with other children. They participate in group activities. Children begin to choose to play with other children over adults, and they may have a best friend. Conflicts such as name-calling, tattling, and teasing are common, and require adult help or supervision.
Ability to Share and Take Turns	Children wait their turn and follow simple rules in board, card, or playground games. Competition may arise. Sharing is usually not a problem.

1 yr.

Birth

~ ❤ ~ ❤ ~ ❤ ~ *Feelings & Relationships* ❤

DEVELOPING SKILL	DESCRIPTION
Capacity for Imaginary Friends	Children may have an imaginary friend with whom they share thoughts, problems, feelings, frustrations, secrets, and humor. They may use their imaginary friend to communicate their innermost thoughts to you.
Conquering Fears	Children typically have many fears: the dark, monsters, fire, blood, their body "being broken," "what if" disasters, and strange places. Their active imaginations contribute to their fears. They sometimes can't tell the difference between what's real and what's not real—between fantasy and reality.
Awareness of Sexuality	As children explore sexuality and differences between boys and girls, men and women, they: • May be curious about where babies come from. A small amount of information is usually all that they want. Typically, children will not ask how the baby got into the womb until age six or seven. • May want to marry the opposite sex parent (boys may want to marry their mother, and girls may want to marry their father). • May masturbate. • May seek privacy for their naked bodies.

5 yrs.

4 yrs.

3 yrs.

2 yrs.

1 yr.

❤

Birth

❤ ~ ❤ ~ ❤ ~ ❤ ~ ❤ ~ ❤ ~ ❤ ~ ❤ ~ ❤ ~ ❤ ~ ❤ ~

Feelings & Relationships

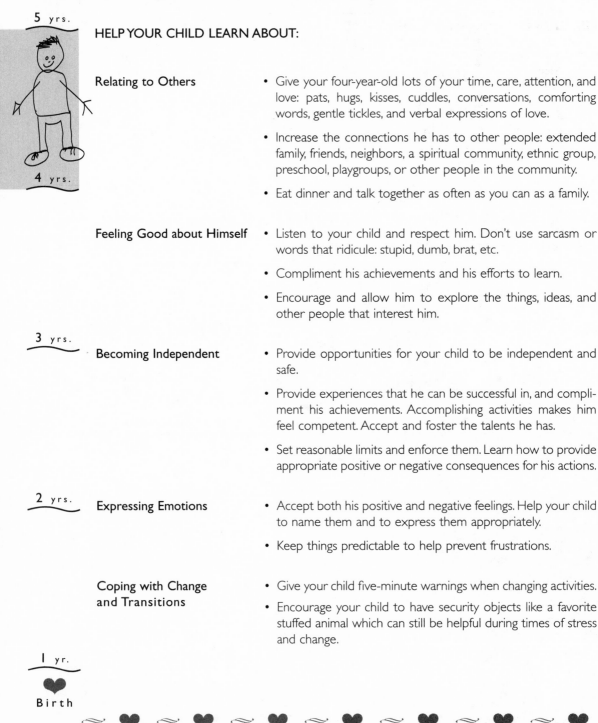

5 yrs.

4 yrs.

3 yrs.

2 yrs.

1 yr.

Birth

HELP YOUR CHILD LEARN ABOUT:

Relating to Others

- Give your four-year-old lots of your time, care, attention, and love: pats, hugs, kisses, cuddles, conversations, comforting words, gentle tickles, and verbal expressions of love.

- Increase the connections he has to other people: extended family, friends, neighbors, a spiritual community, ethnic group, preschool, playgroups, or other people in the community.

- Eat dinner and talk together as often as you can as a family.

Feeling Good about Himself

- Listen to your child and respect him. Don't use sarcasm or words that ridicule: stupid, dumb, brat, etc.

- Compliment his achievements and his efforts to learn.

- Encourage and allow him to explore the things, ideas, and other people that interest him.

Becoming Independent

- Provide opportunities for your child to be independent and safe.

- Provide experiences that he can be successful in, and compliment his achievements. Accomplishing activities makes him feel competent. Accept and foster the talents he has.

- Set reasonable limits and enforce them. Learn how to provide appropriate positive or negative consequences for his actions.

Expressing Emotions

- Accept both his positive and negative feelings. Help your child to name them and to express them appropriately.

- Keep things predictable to help prevent frustrations.

Coping with Change and Transitions

- Give your child five-minute warnings when changing activities.

- Encourage your child to have security objects like a favorite stuffed animal which can still be helpful during times of stress and change.

Feelings & Relationships ❤

5 yrs.

4 yrs.

Playing with Other Children and Alone

- Give your child opportunities to play and learn with other children and adults. Preschool, playgroups, or other organized group settings provide a good opportunity to transition smoothly into kindergarten next year.

- Allow and observe his relationships with his imaginary friends. You can learn about his thoughts and feelings and communicate with him through the "friend."

Sharing and Taking Turns

- Play games with rules with your child. Practice taking turns, and winning and losing gracefully.

Conquering Fears

- Take his fears seriously and comfort him.

Becoming Aware of Sexuality

- If your child is attached to the opposite sex parent, accept it for the normal stage of development that it is, instead of seeing it as a rejection.

3 yrs.

- Respond calmly and accurately to his curiosity about the human body and the differences between boys and girls. Give him the correct names of body parts. Children usually don't ask how the baby got into the mother's womb until age six or seven. Set a pattern of responding with simple, matter-of-fact answers which will serve you well in the future when questions inevitably become more complicated.

- Teach your child rules about privacy and appropriate touch. If he is asking for privacy when he is naked, give it to him, and assume he would like you to cover up, too.

2 yrs.

- Allow him to look at and touch all of the parts of his body, including his genitals.

1 yr.

❤

Birth

🖐 Hand & Body Movement 👣 ～ ✋ ～ 👣 ～ ✋ ～

5 yrs.

4 yrs.

3 yrs.

2 yrs.

1 yr.

Birth

DEVELOPING SKILL	DESCRIPTION
Ability to Run	Children run easily—moving around obstacles, turning sharp corners, changing directions without stopping, and stopping with skill.
Ability to Jump and Hop	Children jump or hop forward on either foot a few steps.
Ability to Climb	Children climb ladders, stairs, and playground equipment skillfully.
Ability to Catch and Throw	Children throw a small ball with one hand in an overhand manner. When they catch a ball, they watch it, judge where it may land, and move toward it with open hands.
Ability to Kick	Children kick a moving ball that is rolled to them.
Ability to Ride a Tricycle, Riding Toy, or Bicycle with Training Wheels	The age that children are ready to ride two-wheel bicycles varies. However, most children are not physically able to ride a bicycle with training wheels until they are six years of age. They are ready to ride when they have physical dexterity, balance, concentration, confidence, and the ability to listen and follow rules.
Ability to Balance	Children typically walk a few feet on a low, wide balance beam that is a few inches from the floor.

DEVELOPING SKILL	DESCRIPTION
Ability to Draw and Print	Children draw or paint pictures that represent things: cars, houses, people, or animals.
	Children draw a person that has three to six body parts, usually a head, body, arms, and legs.
	Children copy some shapes and letters, and can trace the letters of their own name or print them.
Ability to Coordinate Eyes and Hands to Work with Materials, and to Solve Simple Problems	Children refine control of fingers, eyes and hands. They can:
	• Build more complicated buildings and structures with blocks.
	• Complete puzzles with at least 12 to 18 pieces.
	• String small beads.
	• Cut on a line with child-sized, blunt-edged scissors.
	• Use glue with good aim and control.
	• Mold objects out of play dough: cookies, snakes, animals.

5 yrs.

4 yrs.

3 yrs.

2 yrs.

1 yr.

Birth

Hand & Body Movement

5 yrs.

4 yrs.

3 yrs.

2 yrs.

1 yr.

Birth

HELP YOUR CHILD LEARN ABOUT:

Running, Jumping, Hopping, Climbing, Catching, Throwing, Kicking, and Balancing

- Show your child that exercise is important by your own example.

- Provide opportunities for her that encourage and allow her to explore the movement of her body. Backyards and local playgrounds are great places to do so! **Supervise your child on playground equipment at all times.**

Riding a Tricycle

- Provide your child with many opportunities to ride a sturdy tricycle that does not tip over easily and that fits her. Teach her basic tricycle/bicycle safety skills: stay out of the street, stay off of steep hills and stairways, maintain your "bike," keep clothing and shoelaces out of spokes, watch with your eyes for trouble, and be ready to stop. **Supervise your child on a tricycle or riding toy at all times. Do not allow your child to ride in the street until at least eight years of age.**

Making Art/Writing

- Provide your child with writing materials: paper, notebooks, calendars, note pads, markers, and large pencils. Talk about how useful writing is and point out the many ways you use it each day: copying recipes, making lists, writing notes, writing letters, making notes on the calendar, or writing checks.

- Provide her with a place to be messy and and give her materials for drawing and other types of art.

Hand & Body Movement

5 yrs.

4 yrs.

- Ask your child to tell you about her work. Compliment her efforts, no matter what the outcome: "I love the way you made the girl in the picture smile."

- Show her how to print her first name and encourage her to write it on her "work" whenever she has the chance. Expect it to take lots of practice and time. Compliment her efforts and don't push her.

Working with Eyes and Hands

- Give your child lots of opportunities to work with her hands, eyes, and small muscles:

  – Stack and build with block-like objects.

  – Put together puzzles.

  – Lace shoes and string small beads.

  – Cut with scissors.

  – Play with play dough.

  – Use glue.

Supervise your child with scissors and small objects at all times.

3 yrs.

2 yrs.

1 yr.

Birth

Self-Help Skills

5 yrs.

4 yrs.

3 yrs.

2 yrs.

DEVELOPING SKILL	DESCRIPTION
Understanding and Following Rules	At four, children follow rules to avoid consequences or danger, or to gain rewards or approval. They do not fully understand the abstract concept of right and wrong. Throughout childhood, structure, routines, order, and guidance will help them to learn right from wrong. Their increasing ability to follow rules shows in many ways. They: • Avoid known dangerous situations (though not reliably yet). • Obey an authority figure. • Come when called. • Wait in line and wait for a turn. • Respond to a request for quiet. • Stay in an area when asked to. • Play games and follow the rules. • Return things to their place without being asked. • Treat things with care and respect.
Household Responsibilities	Once taught, four-year-olds can do many household chores: make the bed, sort and fold clean clothes, put things where they belong, clean up spills, feed the pet, water plants, or set the table.
Ability to Feed Self	Children take pride in their skillful use of spoon and fork, and in their ability to spread with a knife. They can fix a simple snack: prepare cheese and crackers, wash a piece of fruit, make a sandwich.
Healthy Eating Habits	Children's appetites fluctuate during this year. They may have very specific tastes, but their refusals and preferences are usually not as strong as last year.

1 yr.

Birth

DEVELOPING SKILL	DESCRIPTION
Mealtime Manners	Children enjoy being part of family mealtimes, and can strike a balance between eating and participating in conversation. They demonstrate manners: ask for food with "please" and "thank you," pass food when asked, use a napkin, and ask to be excused from the table.
Healthy Sleep Habits	Children sleep an average of approximately 11.5 hours in the night. Children have probably given up their nap. Children's sleep needs vary widely.
Body Care	Children are able to independently set their bath water temperature, take a bath, brush their teeth, and brush their hair, but they still need an adult to do spot checks regularly. They may be able to wash their own hair but will probably still need help.
Dressing	Children can dress and undress independently. Color and style combinations may be interesting. Children may be able to tie their shoes if taught, but many children do not learn until after five years of age.
Toilet Learning	Most children learn to use the toilet regularly without being asked between ages three and a half and four. Four-year-olds are usually dry during the day, but some accidents do occur. Nighttime bedwetting may happen until six years of age. Children use the toilet independently and often begin to demand privacy in the bathroom. After becoming reliable about using the toilet, they refine their skills: wiping, washing hands, flushing, anticipating the need to go to the bathroom and getting there on time, learning to find a toilet away from home, and using the real toilet instead of a child-sized one.

5 yrs.

4 yrs.

3 yrs.

2 yrs.

1 yr.

Birth

The Growing Child at Age Four
Self-Help Skills

5 yrs.

4 yrs.

3 yrs.

2 yrs.

1 yr.

Birth

HELP YOUR CHILD LEARN ABOUT:

Understanding and Following Rules and Routines

- Model responsible behavior, good eating habits, good sleeping habits, good grooming habits, and a positive attitude about work.
- Set a schedule for eating, sleeping, dressing, playing, and doing chores. You don't need to follow it perfectly, but some sense of order is reassuring to your child. Cues from objects are usually more acceptable reminders to do tasks than an adult's request: clock hands on a certain number, after the bedtime snack, after *Sesame Street*, or when the timer goes off.
- Set a few rules, make sure he understands them, and stick to them. For example: no hurting people with words or actions, stay in the yard and leave only with an adult, and be gentle with things.
- Communicate your expectations about household responsibilities clearly. Teach him by showing, telling, and doing each task needed to get the job done. Make it clear what chores should be done, when they should be done, and what being done means: "You need to clean your room each Saturday, and a clean room means everything off of the floor and table/dresser tops, and a bed that is made." Show him. Encourage and compliment his efforts. A job chart or list, with pictures to remind him of his jobs and the order he should do them in, may help to organize and motivate him.

Becoming Independent

- Help your child to be as independent as he can in his daily routines by making things easy to reach, and by moving at a pace slow enough for him to take the time he needs to complete tasks.
- Involve him in preparing the meal: cutting, washing, stirring, or baking. Set up foods and utensils so that he can prepare the planned snack for himself and practice using utensils:
  - Bread, peanut butter, and a dull knife
  - A small pitcher of juice and a small cup
  - An apple slicer and apples to core and slice
  - An egg slicer and boiled eggs to peel and slice

Eating Well

- If you provide nutritious foods at regular meal and snack times—and don't allow constant nibbling, sweets, and junk food—you can trust your child to make good decisions about what he eats and how much he eats. Encourage him to eat until he is full, not until all the food is gone from his plate.

Self-Help Skills

5 yrs.

4 yrs.

- Strike a balance about food likes and dislikes. Consider every family member's food preferences when you plan a meal or snack. Once the meal is on the table, if he doesn't like what's being served, don't get up and fix him something else. Keep asking him to try small bites of new foods. If he doesn't want to eat more, try again another day.
- Keep the atmosphere pleasant at mealtimes and take your time eating. Adopt a "no arguing at the table" policy. Turn the television off. Encourage him to practice his manners, and tell him that they are important in getting along in the world. Compliment him when he uses his manners.
- Direct your child, who may in a hurry to eat, to take his time and chew food well. **Avoid foods that need a grinding motion to chew and round foods that are common choking hazards until at least after the age of four years: hot dogs, popcorn, hard candy, peanuts, grapes, raw carrot sticks, and raw celery. Don't let him eat while he runs.**

Sleeping Well

- To foster healthy sleep, make sure your child gets plenty of exercise during the day, avoids caffeine, has a calming bedtime routine with you, and stays on a fairly regular sleep schedule. Always respond to his nighttime fears and nightmares with care and comfort. He may prefer a night-light, having the door open, or some soft music.

3 yrs.

Taking Care of His Body

- Remind your child to wash his hands, comb his hair, brush his teeth, and take a bath. Continue to help him wash his hair. Check frequently on his teeth-brushing and bathing to make sure he is doing a good job. He should visit the dentist every six months. **Supervise your child in the tub at all times. Set your water heater temperature to less than 120 Fahrenheit degrees to avoid burns.**

Dressing

- Compliment your child's independence and allow mistakes in his color and style choices as he is learning to pick his clothes. You could help him to lay out clothes the night before and use this time as an opportunity to teach him how to put clothing together: plaids and stripes don't match, coordinate colors, and match the outside temperature to the clothing. Teach him how to tie his shoelaces.

2 yrs.

Using the Toilet

- If your child asks for privacy in the bathroom, respect his wishes. Remind him to wipe himself, flush the toilet, and wash his hands every time he goes to the bathroom. Remind him to think about whether he needs to use the toilet if he is engrossed in play for a long time. If you will be out somewhere, remind him to go before he leaves home. **Never leave your child unattended in a public restroom.**

1 yr.

Birth

♫ Talking ! ? ! ♫ ! ? ! ♫ ! ? ! ♫ ! ? !

	DEVELOPING SKILL	DESCRIPTION
5 yrs.	**Understanding and Using Words**	Children typically have a vocabulary of 1,500 to 2,500 words.
		They love to play with words, tell jokes, and use silly language. They ask about word meanings often.
		Children who learn two languages at once have usually separated the two by four years, and will speak as well as children their own age in both languages by the time they go to school.
4 yrs.	**Ability to Produce Sounds of Speech Clearly**	By four, children speak clearly enough to be understood even by people that don't know them. Some children don't produce all sounds until age eight.
	Ability to Speak in Sentences	Children speak with increasing complexity. Their sentences are more than five words long: "I saw a blue bird fly by."
	Ability to Answer and Ask Questions	Children ask and answer questions with increasing detail.
3 yrs.	**Understanding the Rules of Language**	Children use many parts of speech correctly:
		• Plurals: one dog, many <u>cats</u>.
		• The past tense of verbs. The bird <u>sang</u>.
		• Possessives: <u>hers</u>, <u>mine</u>, <u>theirs</u>, and <u>baby's</u>.
	Ability to Have a Conversation	Children can carry on a conversation.
2 yrs.		They change the way they speak according to who they are talking to. To a baby, they might say, "Cookie all gone?" To an adult they might say, "Did Dominic eat all of his cookie?"

1 yr.

! ?

Birth

! ? ! ♫ ! ? ! ♫ ! ? ! ♫ ! ? ! ♫

! ? ! ♫ ! ? ! ♫ ! ? ! ♫ ! ? ! *Talking* ♫

DEVELOPING SKILL	DESCRIPTION
Ability to Understand and Follow Directions	Children understand and follow four simple, related directions: "Please go to the bathroom, and brush your hair, brush your teeth, and wash your hands."
Capacity to Listen to Books or Spoken Stories	Children can listen to a story and can recount what happened in the story.
Ability to Explore and Appreciate Music and Rhythm	Children show enjoyment of music and rhythm; they: • Listen to all kinds of music. • Sing many simple songs. • Identify high and low pitches, and sing them with their voices. • March and dance to music with the beat. • Tap, clap, or play rhythm instruments with the beat of songs or rhymes. • Recite simple rhymes and play word games. Some children may be ready for formal instrument lessons. For most children, the appropriate "training" is exposure to and interaction with music: listening, singing, dancing, and playing simple rhythm instruments.

5 yrs.

4 yrs.

3 yrs.

2 yrs.

1 yr.

! ?

Birth

! ♫ ! ? ! ♫ ! ? ! ♫ ! ? ! ♫ ! ? !

♫ Talking ! ? ! ♫ ! ? ! ♫ ! ? ! ♫ ! ? !

5 yrs.

4 yrs.

3 yrs.

2 yrs.

1 yr.

! ?

Birth

HELP YOUR CHILD LEARN ABOUT:

Language

- Share riddles, jokes, and puns.

- Talk to your child and model good speech. Show pleasure when conversing with her. Remind her to do the same with you and others.

- Ask her lots of questions and answer her questions.

- Give her lots of encouragement and praise about speaking. Don't criticize her.

- Instead of correcting her mispronounced words and incomplete sentences, repeat an expanded, accurate version: if she says, "I like mine kitty," you could say, "I know you like your kitty."

- Visit familiar and unfamiliar places: a corner of your backyard, the fire station, a community gym, or a restaurant. Talk about what you see.

- Recite and read rhymes to her and teach her to say some rhymes. Clap syllables of words with her: Al-li-ga-tor, Twid-dle-dee-dee.

Paying Attention

- Several times a day, ask your child to do a series of unrelated tasks: "Please put your book away now, water the flowers by the door outside, and then, you may eat some ice cream."

! ? ! ♫ ! ? ! ♫ ! ? ! ♫ ! ? ! ♫ !

? ! ♫ ! ? ! ♫ ! ? ! ♫ ! ? ! Talking ♫

5 yrs.

Listening to Books and Spoken Stories

- Tell stories and read different kinds of books with your child. Aim for at least 20 minutes a day. Point out how useful reading can be and read all kinds of written language to your child: brochures, signs, advertisements, T-shirts, games, mail, cereal boxes, and TV listings. Get her a library card if you haven't yet done so, and visit often.

- Introduce her to interactive books and programs on the computer.

4 yrs.

Making Music

- Help your child explore music:

  – Sing songs to her and teach her simple ones.

  – Listen to different types of music.

  – Encourage her to dance to different types of music.

  – Let her play simple rhythm instruments and clap to music with her.

  3 yrs.

  – Talk about high and low notes, showing her with your hand, or have her move her body to the music.

2 yrs.

1 yr.

! ?

Birth

! ♫ ! ? ! ♫ ! ? ! ♫ ! ? ! ♫ ! ? !

(Thinking (

5 yrs.

4 yrs.

3 yrs.

2 yrs.

DEVELOPING SKILL	DESCRIPTION
Ability to Actively Explore and Experiment	Children's curiosity runs wild! They ask and answer "Why?" constantly. They can think of many solutions to a simple problem. Exploring and experimenting become more complicated and independent.
Ability to Pretend and Play Make-Believe	Children enjoy complicated play and make-believe with other children and adults. They take on roles that include clothes, voice, speech, and physical actions. Sometimes, they plan out the play ahead of time: As a "dad" organizing a pretend camping trip in the yeard, they collect friends to take on the journey and pack clothes, blankets, food, a tent, a map, and a flashlight.
Capacity to Focus and Concentrate	Most children can work on a task for at least five to 10 minutes. Attention span varies between children, and typically grows over time—usually, the older the child, the longer the attention span.
Ability to Understand Opposites, and Concepts about Place	Children understand opposites such as fast/slow, empty/full, tall/short, more/less, light/dark, and pretty/ugly.
Letter Recognition	If shown letters, children may name many upper or lower case letters. Some four-year-olds recognize their name and some common words. Some children begin to read simple books this year. Most children do not read until six years of age.
Ability to Name Colors and Shapes	Children correctly name at least four colors and a few simple shapes.

1 yr.

Birth

DEVELOPING SKILL	DESCRIPTION
Ability to Sort Objects	Children sort objects in many categories: color, shape, function, size, feel, and physical characteristics. If you show them a pile of plastic dogs, fish, and birds, they could sort them into piles of different sizes, colors, or kinds of animals.
Understanding the Concept of Size	Children put three objects in order by size: • Big, bigger, biggest: marble, apple, basketball. • Short, shorter, shortest: yard stick, one-foot ruler, pencil.
Understanding Numbers and the Concept of Counting	Children count aloud to 10 while pointing to one object at a time. They count to 20 or more from memory. They recognize the numerals 1, 2, 3, 4, 5, and show the number of objects each numeral represents.
Understanding the Concept of Money	Children match and name a penny, nickel, dime, and quarter if they have been taught using real coins.
Understanding the Concept of Time	Children's sense of time is clearer. They begin to accurately use phrases such as "in a minute," "a minute ago," "just a few more minutes," "some other week," "next month," "early in the morning," "next summer," "last summer," or "this winter." Typically, children learn to accurately read a clock and calendar after age seven.

5 yrs.

4 yrs.

3 yrs.

2 yrs.

1 yr.

Birth

Thinking (✦ 🌓 ✦ (✦ 🌓 ✦ (✦ 🌓 ✦

5 yrs.

HELP YOUR CHILD LEARN ABOUT:

4 yrs.

Exploring

- Talk your way through your time with your child, explaining things as you go, asking questions, and encouraging him to think.
- Point out details while visiting familiar and unfamiliar places.
- Encourage him to explore with all of his senses, allowing him to get dirty and messy.

Experimenting

- Encourage your child to perform experiments and make simple predictions.

Pretending

- Encourage make-believe play:
    - Join in, sometimes.
    - Ask him about who and where he is, sometimes.
    - Provide "props" for him to use in pretend play.
    - Provide opportunities for him to play with other children.

3 yrs.

Paying Attention

- Encourage focus and attention:
    - Keep a variety of things available for him to do.
    - Match his ability level with activities.
    - Participate in some activities with him.
    - Comment on it after he has been concentrating on something.
    - Encourage him to stick with an activity, but follow his lead; if he is ready to move on, let him do so.

2 yrs.

1 yr.

🌐

Birth

(✦ 🌓 ✦ (✦ 🌓 ✦ (✦ 🌓 ✦ (✦

5 yrs.

Colors and Shapes

- Point out colors and shapes wherever you go. Have your child name them.

Sorting

- Include your child in sorting tasks during everyday routines: putting the silverware away in compartments in the drawer, separating laundry into different-colored piles, or sorting the food from the grocery bags.

4 yrs.

Size

- Let your child feel and touch size in different ways: hand him things that are three different sizes or lengths, and ask him to put them in order—biggest to smallest.

Counting and Using Numbers

- Count things with your child frequently throughout the day, especially things that he is interested in or that are useful.
- Play board games that involve matching, colors, shapes, opposites, numbers, letters, and counting.

3 yrs.

- Include picture books about matching, colors, shapes, opposites, numbers, letters, and counting among the many other books you read.

Time

- Give your child's day a sense of order by setting a routine that helps him get a sense of when things happen in the day. Talk about how certain things are attached to certain days of the week or times of the day. Each day, find the day on the calendar. Mark important dates on the calendar and count the days until the event.

2 yrs.

1 yr.

Birth

5 yrs.

4 yrs.

3 yrs.

2 yrs.

1 yr.

Common Concerns

The following are common behaviors in children this age that typically concern or frustrate parents. The child:

- Sucks thumb.

- Whines.

- Interrupts.

- Talks back.

- Teases, tattles, and calls others names.

- Dawdles.

- Is loud and demanding.

- Is aggressive: hitting, kicking.

- Has some difficulty sharing.

- Ignores requests.

- Is fearful.

- Has nervous habits: nose picking, nail biting, or grimacing.

- Has intense emotions.

- Uses bathroom language or swearing.

- Lies or stretches the truth.

- Resists doing chores.

- Resists bedtime.

Be assured that these behaviors will usually pass with time and appropriate guidance from you, but if you have any questions, ask for help.

When to Get More Help

5 yrs.

Children typically grow and learn new skills in their own time and at their own pace within the wide range of what is normal. Sometimes, however, children need a bit of extra help to keep their development on track, or to stay healthy and happy.

By five years of age, in addition to mastering all of the skills typical of one year, two years, three years, and four years (listed on pages 13, 35, 57, and 79), your child SHOULD BE ABLE TO DO the following:

- ❐ Catch a large bounced ball.
- ❐ Show interest in crayons, scissors, and in gluing projects.
- ❐ Identify some colors and simple shapes, compare objects, identify same or different, and develop some knowledge of the alphabet and numbers.
- ❐ Show an interest in listening to children's books and stories, remember part of the story, and understand it.
- ❐ Know the difference between fantasy and reality most of the time.
- ❐ Concentrate on any single activity for more than five minutes.
- ❐ Dress and undress, wash and dry hands, brush teeth, and use the toilet independently.
- ❐ Talk about everyday experiences.
- ❐ Play in a variety of ways, with a variety of tools.
- ❐ Speak clearly enough to be understood even by strangers.
- ❐ Understand two-part commands using prepositions: "Put the doll on the bed," "Get the book that is under the chair."
- ❐ Use plurals or past tense properly.
- ❐ Show interest in connecting with adults.
- ❐ Play with other children.
- ❐ Move beyond being extremely fearful, timid, or anxious.
- ❐ Seem happy or joyful much of the time.

4 yrs.

3 yrs.

2 yrs.

   If your child DOES NOT demonstrate most of the skills listed above by five years, consider seeking advice about whether or not your child needs help in developing delayed or missing skills. You are the expert when it comes to your child. If you have a concern, trust your instinct and find someone trained to help you: health care providers, teachers, social workers, parent educators, mental health workers, or telephone help-line staff. Consider talking it over with friends and family, too. You don't need to worry alone! Turn to "Finding Help in Your Community," on page 4, to learn about finding help near you.

1 yr.

Thanks to the VORT Corporation, producers of *HELP: The Hawaii Early Learning Profile*, and to the American Academy of Pediatrics, for their wealth of sound child development information, which we used extensively, but not exclusively, in researching this chapter.

Child Development at a Glance

YOUR BABY IS

Becoming a Person

(Babies begin to do things between these months)

	0	3	6	9	12	18	24

m o n t h s

Looks at parents.............................

Smiles in response to seeing parent.......

Smiles to get you to smile....................

Impossible to wait to have needs met...........

Can wait a few minutes for feeding.....................

Will tug at object you're
holding or pulling.................................

Feeds self cracker....................................

Works to get toy that's out of reach........

Shy at first with anyone but parent..........

Plays peek-a-boo......................................

Plays pat-a-cake.......................................

Most cry when parent leaves...................

May wake up at night due to
teething, fears...

Rolls ball back..

Drinks from cup..

Indicates wants without crying...................

Frustration causes outbursts
of anger/tantrums.....................................

Imitates housework..................................

Uses spoon...

Takes off clothes – helps with
simple tasks..

Washes, dries own hands....................

Plays with others....................................

Developed by MELD. To order copies, call 612-332-7563.

Child Development at a Glance

YOUR CHILD IS

Becoming a Person

(Children begin to do things between these years)

3   4   5   6

y   e   a   r   s

Plays next to other children....

Deals with anger and frustration with words..........

Buttons clothes...................

Separates from parent easily....

Dresses without supervision....

Understands and names feelings...................

Uses toilet with little or no help.........

Controls behavior – waits, won't touch, if asked.............

Plays with other children.........

Afraid of the dark, strangers, unknown.................

Takes turns, plays cooperatively............

Recognizes that others have feelings.................

Tolerates frustration better – fewer tantrums.................

Interested in where babies come from.............

Starts to be able to delay activities...............

Knows different settings require different behavior.........

Zips clothes.................

Washes face and hands without getting wet.............

Uses simple manners, if taught.....

Ties shoes.................

Starts to know "right" from "wrong"...............

Developed by MELD. To order copies, call 612-332-7563.

Child Development at a Glance

YOUR BABY IS

Growing Strong

(Babies begin to do things between these months)

	0	3	6	9	12	18	24
	m	o	n	t	h	s	

Lifts head when on tummy.................

Lifts head back when on tummy............

Holds head steady when
sitting – supported.............................

Lifts chest up off surface
when on tummy...................................

Rolls over: tummy to back.....................

Rolls over: back to tummy......................

Sits alone...

Stands, holding onto something.............

Pulls self to stand...............................

Gets to sitting position by self..............

Crawling – already scooting on tummy...

Walks, holding onto furniture.................

Stands alone – steadily.........................

Stoops to pick up a toy –
then stands again.................................

Walks well..

Walks up steps......................................

Can kick ball..

Throws ball overhand............................

Jumps in place......................................

Peddles trike..

Developed by MELD. To order copies, call 612-332-7563.

Child Development at a Glance

YOUR CHILD IS

Growing Strong

(Children begin to do things between these years)

	3	4	5	6
	y	e a r	s	

Rides trike or foot-powered toy

Runs with few falls

Walks up steps holding on

Jumps over low object

Catches ball with arms stiff

Carries objects on tray without dropping

Throws ball overhand six to ten feet

Hops on one foot; plays hopscotch

Walks up steps without holding on

Rides trike with speed and accurate steering

Catches bounced ball

Walks down steps using alternate feet on stairs

Catches ball with arms bent at elbows

Carries cup of water without spilling

Throws ball overhand twelve or more feet

Walks easily along low wall or curb

Plays running games

Tries to jump rope

Rides bicycle

Runs and kicks ball without stopping

Developed by MELD. To order copies, call 612-332-7563.

YOUR BABY IS
Learning to Play
BY USING HANDS AND EYES

(Babies begin to do things between these months)

	0	3	6	9	12	18	24
	m	o	n	t	h	s	

Looks at parent.............................

Eyes follow parent..........................

Eyes follow – baby moves head, too........

Holds hands together.........................

Grasps rattle................................

Reaches for toy...............................

Eyes follow object that's moving out of sight................

Passes toy or object from hand to hand................

Holds onto two things, bangs together................

Can pick up object using only thumb & finger................

Can scribble with pencil................

Build tower of two blocks................

Pours, rather than reaches in – dumps things out................

Builds tower of four blocks................

Can draw lines................

Developed by MELD. To order copies, call 612-332-7563.

Child Development at a Glance

YOUR CHILD IS

Learning to Play

(Children begin to do things between these years)

	3	4	5	6

y e a r s

	3	4	5	6
Builds tower with eight blocks	▨			
Prefers one hand to write and draw	▨▨▨			
Holds fork with fist	▨▨▨			
Cuts paper in half with scissors	▨▨▨▨▨			
Imitates drawings	▨▨▨▨▨▨			
Copies circle shapes	▨			
Holds crayon with three fingers, not fist	▨▨			
Turns pages of book one at a time	▨▨			
Copies cross shapes	▨▨▨			
Pours from pitcher to cup	▨▨▨▨			
Forms letters	▨▨▨▨▨			
Draws person with three parts		▨▨▨▨		
Can string large beads		▨		
Cuts straight line with scissors		▨▨		
Holds fork with three fingers, not fist		▨▨		
Copies square shapes		▨▨▨▨		
Builds more elaborate structures with blocks		▨▨▨		
Draws person with six parts			▨▨	
Prints name and numbers			▨▨	

Developed by MELD. To order copies, call 612-332-7563.

Child Development at a Glance

YOUR BABY IS

Learning to Talk

(Babies begin to do things between these months)

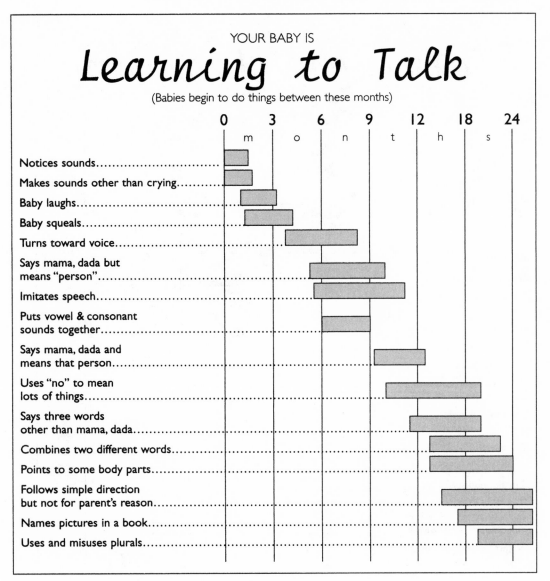

Developed by MELD. To order copies, call 612-332-7563.

Child Development at a Glance

YOUR CHILD IS

Talking & Learning

(Children begin to do things between these years)

	3	4	5	6

y e a r s

Gives first and last name.........

Knows whether boy or girl......

Can put objects on, under,
behind and in front of...........

Recognizes and names colors...

Follows three-step directions...

Knows general times, like
bedtime, lunchtime, etc......................

Sorts things by either
color, size, or shape......................

Easily understood when talking.............

Likes to rhyme and make up
silly words......................

Asks many questions —
why, where, and what.........................

Understands opposites —
cold/hot, big/little, etc........................

Counts from 1 to 10....................

Has vocabulary of 1,500 words......................

Can sit and listen to story
for 10 minutes......................

Recites and sings familiar
songs and nursery rhymes......................

Defines word by its use
or group — balls roll...........................

Matches related pictures
such as sock and shoe......................

Puts events in order —
get up, get dressed, etc..........................

Puts 3 to 4 things
in order by size.............................

Uses regular plurals
correctly — ball/balls.............

Developed by MELD. To order copies, call 612-332-7563.

Speech Sounds at a Glance

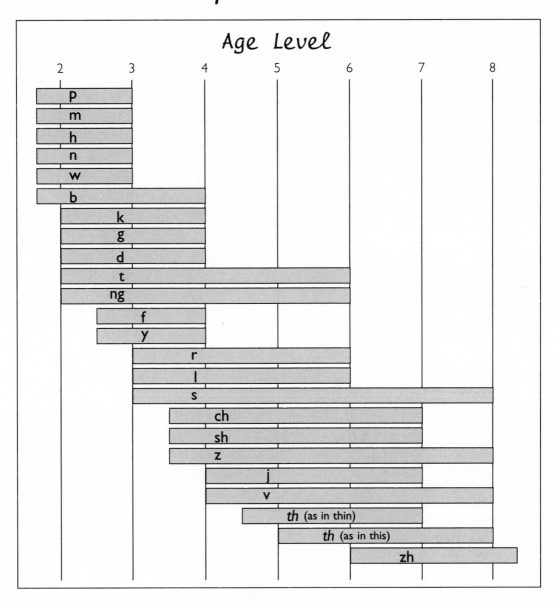

Age ranges of normal consonant development. Average age estimates and upper age limits of customary consonant production. The bar corresponding to each sound starts at the median age of customary articulation; it stops at an age level at which 90% of all children are customarily producing the sound.

© American Speech-Language-Hearing Association. Reprinted by permission.

Activities for the Growing Child

Each activity here provides an opportunity to share time with your child, to have fun, and to learn something together, too. Some of the activities can be done between busy moments throughout the day or while you are doing everyday tasks; others may require setting aside some time, generally no more than half an hour. Most use inexpensive supplies, props, tools, or equipment, or things you already have around your home.

When doing the activities, meet your child at his own pace and stage of development. If an activity seems like it matches your child's abilities, holds his attention, and he is enjoying it, continue. If he doesn't seem quite ready for it, put it away and try again when he is a little older, and perhaps choose a different activity. Have fun, play, and work hard!

Art and Making a Mark

"It's a horse but it's missing it's feet. The horse's name is Jennifer."

by Jennifer, age 3

Freedom to Express

Allow your child freedom in her work—to be natural and not self-conscious. Aside from instructing her to keep her marks on the paper or tabletop, *do not* try to control, correct, guide, or direct her scribbling, painting, drawing, sculpting, or experimenting with making marks.

Focus on the Process

Notice and comment positively on your child's effort, and her choice of colors/materials, *not* her end product:

"You sure are enjoying yourself!"

"I love the colors that you are using."

"You are making so many green lines!"

Don't ask, "What is it?" A respectful way to ask about her pictures is, "Tell me about your picture." Listen to her story and sometimes, write it down on the back of the paper to save it.

Create an Art Space

Find a place in your home where your child can do art without worrying about being messy. Put art supplies on a low shelf, drawer, or in a box. Allow her to have free access to some art supplies that she can use any time and by herself: crayons, paper, glue sticks, and other safe supplies. Find time to work with your child on projects and with materials that require supervision and help.

Showing Art

Display art on the refrigerator, a wall, a bulletin board, shelf, table, or bookcase. Hang 3-D pieces from the ceiling, or photograph them and put the photos in a book or on display. Date, label, and save some of your child's best pieces and store them in a box or portfolio. Look through them from time to time to re-mind both of you of her progress.

The Field Guide Art Kit		
Paints and Drawing Tools	• Finger paint	• Non-toxic washable markers
	• Shaving cream	• Crayons
	• Non-toxic, washable tempera, poster, or children's paint	• Colored glue
	• Chalk	• Soap crayons
Canvases	• Newsprint	• Waxed paper
	• White paper: computer, typing, copy, drawing, painting, or finger-paint paper	• Aluminum foil
		• Sidewalks
	• Construction paper	• Cookie sheet
	• Grocery bags	• Tabletop
	• Used manila envelopes or folders	• Shower or bathtub walls
Brushes	• Paint brushes: various thickness'	• Piece of sponge clipped to the end of a spring clothespin
	• Feathers	• New foam toilet brushes
	• Cotton-tipped swabs	• Painters' trim brushes
	• Toothbrushes	• Fingers
Palettes	• Egg cartons	• Shallow plastic food containers
	• Muffin tins	• Pie tins

! **WARNING!** Check the labels of markers, crayons, glue, chalk, soap crayons and paints to make sure that they are certified as **NON-TOXIC**.

Rubbings

Allow your child to place paper over leaves, coins, or anything with a pattern or texture. Have her rub crayons, chalk, or markers on the paper to make an impression "magically" appear.

Tile Paintings

Buy a 12" × 12" square of 1" × 1" or 2" × 2" of plain white ceramic tile squares from a tile store. Leave them joined together with the backing material that holds them together. Give your child the primary colors in a palette, and have her mix colors on the tiles, covering each tile with paint. Press a blank piece of paper on top of the tiles when she has painted each one, peel it back off carefully, and find repeated prints in a pattern of squares, each with different colors and designs.

Art and Making a Mark

Double Image Paintings Help your child fold a piece of paper in half. Open it, allow your child to place many drops of two or three different colors of paint on one side. Have her close the paper, press it together, and open it up to find a mirror image.

Stencils Buy or make your own stencil. Show your child how to color or paint over the stencil on paper; then remove the stencil to see an image.

Spin Painting Have your child place a paper plate in the bottom of a salad spinner. Allow her to place many drops of different-colored paint on the bottom. Show her how to spin the spinner, and see what happens. Mention to her that centrifugal force (moving away from the center) is at work here.

Pounded Leaves Pick fresh flowers and leaves with your child. Ask her to lay them on an old cutting board or piece of scrap wood. Cover them with a plain white piece of muslin or fabric. Help her pound with a hammer to make a leaf or flower print.

Fruit or Vegetable Prints Cut a fruit or vegetable in half. Show your child how to dip it in paint and press it on paper or fabric to create a beautiful print.

Water Painting Outside, give your child a bucket of plain water and a large paintbrush. Have her "paint" the house, sidewalk, fence, car, or other places that she can think of to "paint."

Beautiful Books Help your child understand more about art by reading about it together:

Art Dog by Thatcher Hurd

A Child's Book of Art: Great Pictures First Words by Lucy Micklethwait

Harold and the Purple Crayon; Harold's Fairy Tale: Further Adventures With the Purple Crayon by Crockett Johnson

Paintings (A First Discovery Art Book) by Claude Delafosse

Balancing and Swinging

"Evan" by Evan

Walking a Line

- With chalk or masking tape, mark a wide straight line on the sidewalk, or at a playground. Ask your child to walk the line.

- Walk in the sand to create footprints and ask your child to follow in your footsteps.

- Play follow the leader with your child and have him walk on a line.

Balancing on an Edge

Encourage your child to walk along a curb or a sandbox edge while you hold his hand.

Balance Beam

Find a low balance beam to play on, or make one by setting a smooth board on top of bricks—no more than a few inches off the ground. Allow your child to walk the beam. Always spot him and hold his hand if needed.

Balancing and Swinging

Swinging!

Give your child the wonderful and important experience of swinging. Swinging enhances the body's vestibular system and encourages a sense of balance and rhythm.

- Push your baby gently in an infant or toddler swing for short periods of time.

- Push your two-year-old on a child swing with a safety belt or gate.

- Push your three and a half-year-old to four and a half-year-old on a regular child-sized swing.

- Let your four and a half- to five-year-old try to pump on his own.

- Get on a swing yourself! It is healthy for the body to continue swinging throughout life!

Balancing with a Book

Help your child understand more about balancing by reading about it together:

 Circus: Funny Fingers by Karin Blume

 D.W. Flips! By Marc Brown

Balls: Catching, Kicking, and Throwing

"Dad throwing a football"
by Tom, age 5

Play Ball

Provide your child with many opportunities to play with balls. Encourage her to use smaller and harder balls as she gets better at throwing, catching, and kicking. Use a variety of everyday soft objects as balls for throwing or kicking:

- Rolled-up socks
- Yarn balls
- Sponges
- Stuffed animals
- Crumpled paper
- Bean bags

- Beach balls
- Large plastic balls
- Wiffle balls
- Foam balls
- Tennis balls
- Soft balls

Target Practice

Provide your child with upright targets for throwing into, or place on their side for kicking into. Use a variety of targets and baskets to throw or kick into:

- Clothes basket
- Corner of a room
- Cardboard box
- Child's swimming pool
- Trash can

- Stacked blocks
- Picture taped to a wall
- Hula-hoop
- Your hands

Bath Time and Brushing Fun!

by Matt, age 5

Washing Up Time

Make washing up more fun:

- Wash your child with sponges, bath mittens with faces or characters on them, or attractive washcloths.

- Let your child wash with fancy soaps, children's soaps, foam soap, or special hotel soaps.

- Talk about the parts of your child's body as you wash: "Now we wash the shoulder, down to the elbow, and scrub down the arm to the pinky on your hand!"

- Sing songs together and make up your own about washing and baths. Sing to the tune of *Mary Had a Little Lamb*:

    Joey had a big wet bath, big wet bath, big wet bath,
    Joey had a big wet bath, that washed him clean all over.

- Tell stories and make up your own. Encourage your child to help you: "Once upon a time there was a diver and his name was [add your child's name]. What do you think he saw when he went down in the ocean?"

- Let your child try taking a shower if he wants to.

- Blow soapy bubbles.

- Use foam soap for shaving and washing. Put foam soap on your child's face and let your child shave it off with a pretend razor: his finger, a toy razor, or a blunt, real razor with the blade removed. Then put foam on other parts of his body and shave it off there, too.

! **WARNING!** Supervise children in the tub at all times. Set your water heater temperature to less than 120 degrees Fahrenheit to avoid burns.

Shampoo to You

Make shampooing more tolerable and maybe even fun:

- Let your child wear a visor, swimming goggles, or a diving mask to keep the shampoo out of his eyes while you wash his hair.

- Rinse hair with a hand held shower or hose that attaches to the tub spigot.

- Design new soapy hairstyles or sculptures while shampooing.

Bath Play

- Allow your child to put a few special toys in the tub:
  - A doll to wash its hair and play hair salon.
  - A few plastic cars or trucks and put them through the car wash.
  - Some plastic animals to play washing time at the zoo.

- Gather some empty plastic containers, pitchers, or bottles and allow your child to use a kitchen ladle, large spoon, non-glass measuring cup, and measuring spoons to play with in the bath: filling and dumping, mixing magic potions, and measuring secret ingredients.

- Allow your child to create bath art by drawing or painting on the sides on the tub or tiles with shaving cream, soap, finger paints, or soap crayons.

Tooth Time

- Give your child two fun and attractive toothbrushes to choose from: "Should we brush with Big Bird or the squiggles brush tonight?"

- Start a sticker chart and let him put one sticker on the chart each time he brushes his teeth.

- Let your child brush your teeth, sometimes.

- Use a tooth dye or stain disclosing agent that turns the dirty teeth a different color, and ask your child to brush all the color off.

- Set a timer for the amount of time you need to brush his teeth.

- Play "I See Your Breakfast/Lunch/Dinner." As you look in your child's mouth and brush his teeth, name the food he ate at the last meal: "I see the pasta you ate over there, and there's some of that cookie on this side."

- To encourage your child to open wide for brushing, ask him if you can search for characters or wild animals in his mouth: "Is Mickey Mouse in there? How about a lion?"

Bath Time and Brushing Fun!

**Bathing and
Brushing Reading**

Help your child understand more about bathing and brushing by reading about them together:

 *Brush Your Teeth, Please* by Leslie McGuire

Dad's Car Wash by Harry A. Sutherland

Do You Brush With A Llama? By Viki Woodworth

Dragon Teeth and Parrot Beaks: Even Creatures Brush Their Teeth by Almute Grohmann

Franklin and the Tooth Fairy by Paulette Bourgeois

King Bidgood's in the Bathtub by Audrey Wood

"Baby bird with hair"
by Will, age 3

Blocks

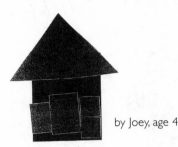

by Joey, age 4

Blocks of All Kinds

Blocks are great tools for learning. Give your child a clear, flat space to build on. Provide plenty of store-bought or homemade blocks, or block-like objects:

- Sponges
- Diaper wipe boxes
- Books
- Cereal boxes
- Milk cartons: wash, fold the top down, and tape into a block shape

- Grocery bags: fill with crushed newspaper, cover the open end, and tape closed
- Tissue boxes
- Cans
- Scraps of wood: sand the surfaces smooth

Stack and Knock

Show her how to stack a few blocks and ask her to copy you. Let her knock the tower down and do it all over again. Encourage her to build taller towers with smaller blocks as she gets older and develops more coordination. Sometimes, count the blocks as you stack them.

Create Play Scenes

- Use blocks to create towns, zoos, castles, skyscrapers, farms, construction sites, or houses that can be used for dramatic play. Add animals, toy figures, cars, trucks, or decorations as needed.

- Encourage her to talk about the things she builds: "Tell me about your building. Do you think you could make a ramp for the car? How did you get that block to stay up there?"

- Take pictures of some of her buildings to keep and display.

Colors and Shapes

by Laura, age 5

Pointing Out Colors and Shapes

Point to colors and talk to your child about colors in everyday activities: while you dress him, while you eat, or when you go for walks.

Matching Colors and Shapes

- Hold up a sample of something red and ask your child: "Find all of the red things in the room." Point to a circle on a page of a picture book and ask, "Find all of the circles on this page."

- Take a color or shape walk: pick a color or a shape, and walk around the room, home, school, block, and neighborhood to find all the things with that color or shape.

Go Fishin' for Colors and Shapes

What You Need:

- Colored paper
- Glue
- Scissors
- Paper clips
- Stick
- String
- Magnet

What You Do:

1. Cut paper of various colors into different shapes.

2. Glue paper clips to the cut pieces of paper.

3. Make a fishing pole by tying a string to the stick, and attaching a magnet to the end of the string.

4. As you name different shapes and colors, have your child "fish" for them. The magnet on the string should attract the paper clip on the shapes, allowing him to "catch" the fish.

**Making Colors
and Shapes**

- Show your child how to mix paint to make new colors. Let him experiment with making his own colors. Talk about and name the colors that you make and the colors you used to make the new ones.

- Make colors with food coloring. Fill each compartment in a muffin tin or styrofoam egg carton with water. Add food coloring to make red, blue, and yellow water in three compartments. Give him an eyedropper and let him mix colors in the compartments with clear water.

- Fold napkins into shapes: triangles, squares, and rectangles.

**Colors and
Shapes Games**

Look for and play games that encourage play and learning with colors and shapes: dominoes, *Candyland*, and *Memory*.

Colorful Books

Help a child understand more about colors and shapes by reading about them together:

 Brown Rabbit's Shape Book by Alan Baker

 Colors (A First Discovery Book) by Pascale De Bourgoing

 Red, Blue, Yellow Shoe by Tana Hoban

 What Shape? by Debbie MacKinnon

 Mouse Paint by Ellen Stoll Walsh

Cutting

by Brian, age 4

Pre-Cutting or Tearing for Your Toddler

Before your child is ready to use scissors, introduce her to cutting by letting her tear paper, old magazines, catalogs, or paper bags. **Supervise your child to be sure she does not put the paper in her mouth.**

Snipping for Your Toddler and Preschooler

Provide good quality, blunt-edged, child-sized safety scissors. Teach your child how to snip, following these steps:

1. Show her how to hold the scissors, and how to open and close them.
2. Cut a 1-inch wide strip of paper and let her snip pieces off of it.
3. Show her how to make fringe by snipping around the edge of paper.
4. Provide opportunities for her to use her skill: snipping food packaging to open it, a ribbon for a package, or a flower.

Cutting on a Line for Your Preschooler

Teach your child how to cut on a line, following these steps:

1. With a thick marker, draw lines one or two inches apart around the edges of a piece of paper. Allow your child to cut on the lines to make a fringe.
2. Make a thick line the length of the paper and ask her to cut along it.

Cutting Shapes for Your Preschooler

- Draw circles, squares, and triangles with a thick marker on paper and ask your child to cut out the shape following the outline.
- Provide opportunities for her to practice her skill by cutting out coupons or other simple shapes.

! **WARNING!** Supervise children with scissors at all times.

Experiments!

by Laura, age 5

Hide and Find

What You Need:

- Objects/Toys: stuffed animals, car, trucks, blocks, spoons, or anything that fits under the cloth or box
- A piece of cloth or a box: shirt, scarf, small towel, cloth napkin, cardboard box, or shoe box

What You Do:

1. Pick one toy or object and hide it under the cloth or box as your child watches.
2. Ask him to find it.
3. Experiment with hiding different objects under a cloth or box.

Tubes and Balls

Tape or tie a wrapping paper tube to a stairway banister. Or hold it diagonally. Show him how to put the small ball in the top of the tube and watch it come out the other end.

Experiments!

Pop Bottle Shaker

What You Need:

- A small, plastic pop bottle
- Baby or mineral oil
- Glitter, sequins, beads, or other tiny substances
- Permanent glue

What You Do:

1. Fill the bottle with oil and glitter or other interesting objects.
2. Glue the bottle cap on and let dry overnight.
3. Let your child shake it, roll it, and move it gently to see what happens to the glitter inside.

What Floats?

What You Need:

- A large bowl, sink, wading pool, or tub
- A variety of small objects of varying weights: soap, toy car, a cork, an empty plastic container, an unopened can

What You Do:

1. Fill the sink, pool, or tub with water.
2. Have your child pick out something to test. Before he puts it in the water, ask him to guess what will happen, or to make a prediction: Will it float?
3. Have him drop it in and see if he was right.
4. Repeat the experiment as many times as he likes using as many objects as you and he can think of.

Colors Rising!

What You Need:

- A long piece of celery or a white flower with a stem
- Food coloring
- Clear glass filled with water
- Knife

What You Do:

1. Allow your child to put 10 drops of food coloring in the glass of water.
2. Cut the celery or flower stem at a slant.
3. Have your child put the celery or flower in the glass and ask him to guess what will happen next.
4. Throughout the day, watch the color rise!

**Taking It Apart/
Putting It Together**

- Let your child take apart and put back together a flashlight to see how it works. **Supervise him with this project.**

**Experiment
with Reading**

Help your child understand more about experimenting by reading about it together. Also, provide pop-up books, lift-the-flap books, and books with textures to experiment with how books work:

 Alpha Bugs by David Carter

 *The Carrot Seed* by Ruth Krauss

 Fuzzy Yellow Ducklings: Fold-Out Fun With Textures, Colors, Shapes, Animals by Matthew Van Fleet

Pat the Bunny by Dorothy Kunhardt

The Please Touch Cookbook from the Please Touch Museum, Edited by Bonnie Brook

Explore!

by Maddie, age 4

Question! Question! Question!

- Encourage your child to ask questions. When she asks, "Why?" answer with an open-ended question that encourages more thinking:

  "What do you think is going on?"

  "What do you think will happen next?"

  "What would happen if...?"

  Give her time to think and answer. Focus on encouraging her to explore her thoughts rather than being concerned about correct answers.

- Play "What If": Encourage your child to use her imagination by asking questions that stretch her thinking and help her consider new possibilities:

  "What if a butterfly landed on your nose?"

  "What if you could fly?"

  "What would happen if I left a tray of ice outside on a hot day?"

  "What would happen if all the cars were gone?"

  Listen to your child and compliment her ideas. Share some of your ideas with her.

The Way Things Work Take time to explain some of the many things that you do and the machines that you use in a day: washing clothes in a washing machine, driving a car, or preparing food. Think out loud and explore the way things work with your child:

- Explain what, why, and how:

  "The washing machine does many things: it agitates, rinses, and spins to clean the clothes."

- Ask her questions:

  "Why do we add soap? What happens to the water inside?"

- Help her answer the questions in simple terms:

  "The soap rubs against the dirt and helps the dirt come off the clothes."

- Allow her to safely try to make some things work: add the soap, turn the dial to select the wash cycle, and pull or push the knob on the washer to make it start.

Exploring a Child's World Dress your child and yourself in clothes you can get dirty. Grab your sense of wonder and playfulness and explore.

- Take her to many places: a backyard, parks, shorelines, streams, gardens, woods, or other outdoor sites.

- Bring a pail for her to collect treasures along the way: rocks, flowers, leaves, sticks, bugs, or anything of interest to her.

- Talk about where you go, what you see, what you do, and the things you hear, smell, and feel.

- Allow her to go at her own speed, get dirty, and explore whatever is safe for her. The idea is not to get somewhere or fill up the pail, but to look, listen, feel, smell, and notice all the small and wonderful things around you.

- Explore with your child the many places and things to do in your community or city: ride a bus or subway, visit local landmarks, watch a building or road being built, go to a zoo or aquarium, check out books at the library. Attend storytimes, programs, and book events for children at libraries, toy stores, and bookstores. Take your child to museums of all kinds: art, science, children's air and space, history, natural history, etc. Many have free days, family days, or special events for children.

Explore!

Explore Through Reading Help a child understand more about exploring the nature of things by reading about it together:

 *Can You Guess?* by Margaret Miller

Everybody Needs a Rock by Byrd Baylor

Sheep Take a Hike by Nancy Shaw

What's Inside? Trucks and other books in the What's Inside series

What's It Like to Be a Fish? and other books in the Let's-Read-and-Find-Out-Science series

The Universe and other books in the First Discovery Books series

Zoo Animals and other books in the Eye Openers series

"This is the Science Museum!"
by Will, age 4

Feelings

by Rustin, age 5

**Make a Face or
Paint a Face**

While looking in a mirror, make faces and encourage your child to do the same. Talk about what different faces mean: happy, sad, angry, scared, etc. Use face paints to make expressive faces on your child. **Use lotion on your child's face first to protect his skin and make removing the paints easier.**

Dance a Feeling

Play different kinds of music. Ask your child how different music makes him feel. Ask him to show the emotion with his whole body.

Feeling Face Matching

What you need:

- Magazines
- Scissors

What you do:

1. Cut out pairs of faces that have obvious matching feelings, talking about the feelings as you do.
2. Lay four to six faces on the table or floor.
3. Shuffle their pairs.
4. Hold up faces one by one and have your child match the feelings on the face.
5. Next, make a game of it. Give four faces to each player and see who matches all four pairs first. The person with the first full set of matching faces will be the leader of the next game.

People Watch

Go to a mall, zoo, restaurant, park, grocery store, or anywhere there are people. Sit on a bench for a few minutes and watch the people with your child, talking about the passersby expressions.

Feelings

Feelings and Books

Help a child understand more about feelings by reading about them together and talking about the emotions and expressions explored in the books:

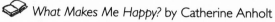 *A is for Angry* by Sandra Boynton

Sometimes I Feel Like a Mouse: A Book About Feelings by Jeanne Modesitt

Today I Feel Silly & Other Moods That Make My Day by Jamie Lee Curtis

What Makes Me Happy? by Catherine Anholt

by Reed, age 5

Gluing

Create Masterpieces with Glue

Provide opportunities and materials for your child to create pictures, sculptures, and decorated boxes with glue.

The Field Guide Glue Art Kit		
Non-Toxic Glues	• White school glue • Paste	• Glue sticks • Colored glue
Tools for Applying Glue	• Paint brush • Cotton swab • Craft stick	• Any stick • Dull knife
Gluing Backgrounds	• Paper plates • Paper • Old cardboard • Wood scraps	• Aluminum foil • Disposable pie tins • Boxes
Things to Glue	• Macaroni • Beans • Seeds • Ribbon • Cotton balls • Fabric scraps • Leaves • Sticks	• Cut or torn paper scraps • Buttons • Lace • Sequins • Beads • Small wood scraps • Feathers • Buttons

! **WARNING!** Check the label to see that all glue and art supplies are certified as **NON-TOXIC**.

Gluing

Early Gluing

When your child is more interested in playing with the glue than using it to glue with, allow her to experiment with pouring it. Consider letting her make pictures with colored glue.

Sticky Paper Pictures

What You Need:

- Pre-glued paper, such as contact paper
- Light things to "glue": leaves, feathers, ribbons, paper scraps, etc.
- Scissors

What You Do:

1. Cut pre-glued paper into a shape: cat, bunny, leaf, or whatever you like.
2. Help your child to peel the paper off the pre-glued paper.
3. With sticky side up, staple the pre-glued paper onto a paper plate.
4. Ask her to "glue" things onto the sticky paper to create a picture.
5. Proudly display her masterpiece!

! **WARNING!** Always supervise the use of small objects to prevent choking!

by Joey, age 4

Jumping and Hopping

by Tennae

Indoor Jumping

Adapt indoor spaces for jumping and hopping by clearing an area and putting a mattress or several pillows on the floor. Let your child practice his jumping skills on rainy or winter days.

Bubble Jumping

Tape a sheet of bubble-wrap packing material to the floor. See if your child can jump or hop on the bubbles to make them pop!

Simon Says, "JUMP!"

Play Simon Says:

- Choose a person to be Simon.

- When Simon says, "Simon says, 'jump'" everyone must jump. Simon can choose any command that he wants: jump, hop, take a big step, take a baby step, or any kind of action.

- If Simon gives a command without first saying "Simon says," no one should do it.

- Take turns being Simon and giving the commands. Occasionally, omit "Simon says" from the command.

Jumping and Hopping

Jump over a Crack

Encourage your child to jump over cracks in the sidewalk, puddles, lines drawn in the sand, or lines in the carpet. Jump to a jingle: "*Jack be nimble, Jack be quick, Jack jump over the candlestick!*"

Circle Jumping

1. Mark circles on the ground by drawing with chalk, marking with tape, drawing in the sand, or making circles with rope.

2. Next, put different objects or shapes inside the circles: soft toys, socks, pictures of animals, or other soft items.

3. Then, ask your child to jump in the different circles: "Jump in the circle with the red sock," or "Jump in the hoop with Winnie the Pooh!"

Hurdles

- Make hurdles for jumping by placing a yardstick on two stacks of books, about 12" high. Or, make hurdles by stacking large, cardboard blocks or empty, clean milk cartons.

- Lower or raise the "hurdles" by adding/taking away blocks or raising/lowering the yardstick. Create two or three hurdles in a row for jumping. **Supervise your child as you allow him to jump the hurdles.**

Standing and Running Jumps

Show your child how to jump:

- Mark a starting line. Ask your child to stand behind the line and jump as far as he can.

- Mark the spot where he lands and ask him to jump again. Compare the distances.

- Show him how to swing his arms to help him jump farther.

- Demonstrate how to take a running start and jump. Compare the distances between the standing and running jumps.

Preschool Jump Rope

Show your child how to play jump rope:

- Tie one end of a long jump rope to a tree.

- Hold the other end and move it slowly from side to side.

- Encourage your child to jump over the rope with both feet together, or with first one foot and then the other.

Stepping Stones

- Look for real stepping stones and encourage your child to try hopping from one to another: large, flat stones in a very shallow stream or bricks laid out in a garden or a walkway. Spot him as he hops.

- Create stepping stones 12" apart by spreading out carpet squares, pillows, or small piles of leaves in mounds. Ask him to jump from one to the other.

Jump into Books!

Help your child understand more about jumping and exercise by reading about it together:

 *Bounce, Tigger, Bounce* by Isabel Gaines

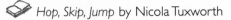 *D.W. Flips!* By Marc Brown

Hello Toes! Hello Feet! by Ann Whitford Paul

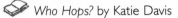 *Hop on Pop* by Dr. Seuss

Hop, Skip, Jump by Nicola Tuxworth

One Gaping Wide-Mouthed Hopping Frog by Leslie Tryon

Who Hops? by Katie Davis

Letters and Writing

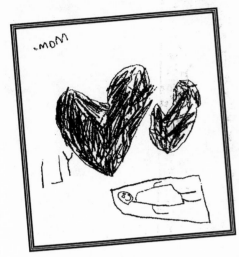

"I Love You"
a get well card from Jakob, age 4

Many Uses of Writing

Talk to your child about and show her the many uses of writing: making lists, writing checks, marking important dates on the calendar, jotting down notes, leaving messages for other people, copying recipes, and writing letters.

Copying Lines and Shapes

If your child is interested, draw lines on a page and ask her to copy them. Typically, as she grows, she will be able to copy lines in this order:

1. Vertical (up-down) lines
2. Circles
3. Horizontal (side-side) lines
4. Crosses
5. Squares

**Sandpaper and
Bean Letters**

To make letters that your child can feel:

- Cut out letters from sandpaper and glue them on cardboard or index cards.
- Glue dried beans in the shape of letters to cardboard.

Introduce your child to letters in this sequence:

1. Let her trace a letter with her finger as you tell her the name and sound of it. Put the letter aside and try another.

2. Put both letters in front of her and ask, "Which one is W?" Then ask, "Which one is D?"

3. If she answers correctly, point to the W and ask, "What is this?" Then point to the D and ask the same question.

Cheer all of her efforts, and keep the task fun. If she is frustrated, quit and try another time.

by Kate

by Jakob

Copying Letters

Put sand, colored salt, or shaving cream in a cake pan. Show your child how to trace letters in the pan.

Letters and Writing

Writing Letters

Show your child how to print her name:

- Draw her name in dots (like a dot to dot without the numbers) on a piece of paper and ask her to connect the dots with a crayon to form the letters. Make the letters large enough to fill a sheet of paper.

KATE

- Draw or design on the computer an outline of her name:

Kate

Ask her to follow or write the letters on the inside with a crayon. Make the outline of the letters large enough to fill a sheet of paper.

I Spy With My Little Eye

Play "I Spy With My Little Eye" with your child:

- Pick out an object that is in clear view of your child.

- Ask her if she can guess what it is by giving her the beginning sound: "I spy with my little eye something that begins with the sound 'D.'"

- Consider adding more clues if she gets stuck: "I spy something that wags it's tail and begins with the sound 'D.'"

- Ask her to spy something else that begins with the same sound. Take turns spying and guessing.

Letter Sounds

Introduce your child to letter sounds:

- Pick out four to six objects that begin with the same letter and sound: box, ball, book, block, and banana.

- Point to them one at a time as you say the name of the object, emphasizing the beginning sound.

- Add a few more objects that begin with a different letter and sound. Point to them and say their names.

- Ask your child to pick up an object that starts with "B." If she gives the wrong letter, try saying the word but substitute the wrong letter for the beginning letter: "Is this a *pox* or is it a *box*?" Have fun with sounds and don't criticize wrong answers.

Your Child the Author

When your child wants to tell you a story, ask her if you can write it down, or ask her to tell you a story so you can make a book together:

1. Place a few sentences from the story on each page.

2. Encourage her to illustrate it, or help her if she prefers.

3. Help her to add a title and make a cover.

4. Staple it together, or put it in a folder to keep and read!

Alphabet Books   Provide alphabet books for her to look at and that you can read together:

- *ABC I Like Me* by Nancy Carlson
- *Dr. Seuss's ABC* by Dr. Seuss
- *Eating the Alphabet* by Lois Ehlert
- *Miss Spider's ABC* by David Kirk
- *My Little House ABC* by Laura Ingalls Wilder
- *Paddington's ABC* by Michael Bond
- *Sign Language ABC* by Linda Bove
- *The ABC Book* by C.B. Falls
- *The ABC Bunny* by Wanda Gag
- *Tomorrow's Alphabet* by George Shannon

Make-Believe!

by Kara

Let the Imagination Soar! Encourage pretend or make-believe play:

- Provide a collection of toys and props.
- Give your child the space in which to set up a fantasy world.
- Allow time for your child to drift into his imagination and dramatic play. Avoid over-structuring your days with too many planned activities and events.
- Provide opportunities to play make-believe with other children.
- Join him in playing make-believe, sometimes: "Could I buy some apples from your store?" "Doctor, would you fix my broken arm?"
- Provide your child with opportunities to play alone, without any imposition from you, so he can let his imagination fly!

The Field Guide Make-Believe Play Box

Clothes/Accessories	• Purses and briefcases • Hats • Ties and scarves • Jewelry (not sharp or breakable)	• Clothes: shirts, pants, skirts, dresses, jackets • Shoes and boots • Billfolds, wallets, and small bags
Tools and Props	• Dishes, pots, and pans (play or real) • Big spoons, ladles, and spatulas • Food (play or real): food cans, empty food boxes, clean food containers • Baby bottle • Play tools: hammer, pliers, screwdriver, nuts, and bolts • Phone (play or real) • Suitcase • Play or child flashlight	• Small broom and shovel • Print material from real life: recipes, magazines, order pads, menus, newspapers, phone books, maps, greeting cards, mail order catalogs, old mail, tickets, and calendars • Calculator • Checkbook register • Play money • Musical instruments
People/Animals/Vehicles	• Dolls, doll bed, and blanket (a box and towel will do) • Job-related kits: doctor, firefighter, dancer, clown • Play animal sets and stuffed animals	• Cars, trucks, and trains • Buildings and fences • Blocks to make towns, zoos, houses, or other places for dolls, people and animals to visit

! **WARNING!** Supervise children at all times with small objects and materials that could be choking hazards. Don't allow young children to work with small objects until they are beyond the stage of putting things in their mouths.

Make-Believe!

Imaginary Reading

Help a child understand more about imagination and make-believe by reading about it together:

📖 *From Head to Toe* by Eric Carle

📖 *Harold and the Purple Crayon* by Crockett Johnson

📖 *Let's Pretend!* by Margaret Miller

📖 *What Am I?* by Debbie MacKinnon

📖 *Where The Wild Things Are* by Maurice Sendak

Rachel, age 4½

Matching and Sorting

Everyday Matching

- During dressing time: hold up one sock or shoe and ask your child to find the other.

- While putting groceries away: hold up a can or box and ask her to find another can or box.

- At mealtime: hold up a piece of food and ask her to find the same food on her plate.

- While folding clothes: lay out one sock and ask her to find its match in the pile of socks.

Trace and Match

What You Need:

- Paper
- Dark crayon or marker
- Three or four objects of various shapes: jar lids, small boxes, a wedge of cheese, a cup, a plate, a small book, cookie cutters, or any small object in the shape of a circle, square, rectangle, or triangle

What You Do:

1. Place an object on a piece of paper and trace a dark line around it. Pick two or three more objects and trace the outline on paper.
2. Lay out the tracings and mix up the objects.
3. Ask your child to match the object to the traced outline.

Everyday Sorting

Include your child in sorting everyday household items. Allow your child to:

- Put the silverware away in compartments in the drawer after washing it.
- Separate laundry into different-colored piles.
- Sort the food from the grocery bags as you organize it to put it away.

The Button Sort

What You Need:

- Three bowls
- Three sets of matching buttons of various sizes and colors

What You Do:

1. Place the buttons in a pile and lay out the bowls nearby.
2. Ask your child to sort the buttons into separate dishes.
3. For a greater challenge, ask her if she would like to try sorting by size with her eyes closed or with a blindfold on.

Matching and Sorting

The Bag of Pairs

What You Need:

- Several pairs of various objects: clothespins, crayons, buttons, coins, rocks, shells, or two of any safe and small object
- Bag large enough to hold the collection of pairs

What You Do:

1. Put the pairs in the bag and mix them up.
2. Ask your child to dump out the contents of the bag and sort the objects into pairs.

Mix and Sort by Two and Three

- Put together in one pile several objects of two different kinds: red apples/ green apples, balls/blocks, forks/spoons, animals/ dolls, any other combination of small objects. Ask your child to sort them into two piles.
- After she has mastered sorting by two, put together in one pile several objects of three different kinds: apples/pears/oranges, cars/balls/blocks, forks/knives/ spoons, animals/dolls/ cars, any other combination of three kinds of objects. Ask her to sort the objects into three piles.

The Layered Jar

What You Need:

- Several varieties of large dried beans: pinto, red, black, pea, navy
- Small clear jar with lid
- Glue

What You Do:

1. Mix the beans in one bowl.
2. Ask your child to sort the beans into piles.
3. Allow her to layer the piles of beans in the jar in any order she chooses.
4. Glue the cover on and enjoy her fine work!

! WARNING! Supervise children at all times with small objects and materials that could be choking hazards. Don't allow young children to work with small objects until they are beyond the stage of putting things in their mouths.

Sorting Books

Help a child understand more about sorting by reading about it together:

Disney's Beauty and the Beast Teacup Mix-Up: A Sorting Book by Zoe Lewis

A Pair of Socks: Matching (Mathstart series) by Stuart J. Murphy

Measuring

"Me with one long arm and one big foot"
by Will, age 3

Bigger or Smaller?
Heavier or Lighter?
Longer or Shorter?

- Provide your child with opportunities to feel and handle items of different sizes: cans, socks, potatoes, cats, flowers, cars, dolls, rocks, boxes, tools, blocks, shirts, or apples. Compare the items and talk about which is bigger and which is smaller. Then, talk about which is heavier and which is lighter.

- Play with lines. Cut two different lengths of the same material: ribbon, yarn, carrots, bananas, sandwiches, or straws. Or, draw two different lines in the sand or dirt outside, or in the shaving cream on the bathtub. Ask your child to point to the longer and shorter line.

Big, Bigger, Biggest?
Heavy, Heavier, Heaviest?
Long, Longer, Longest?

- Give your child three similar things that are different sizes: marble, golf ball, and tennis ball. Ask him to put them in order: smallest to biggest, then lightest to heaviest.

- Cut three different lengths of the same material, or draw three lines in the sand or dirt. Ask him to put them in order: shortest to longest.

Measure-Up Reading

Help your child understand more about size and measuring by reading about it together:

 The Best Bug Parade: Comparing Sizes (Mathstart series) by Stuart J. Murphy

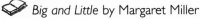 *Big and Little* by Margaret Miller

 Bigger by Daniel Kirk

The NBA Book of Big and Little by James Preller

Money

Naming Coins

- Show and name for your preschool child: penny, nickel, dime, quarter, and dollar.

- Put an assortment of coins in a pile and ask her to sort them by kind of coin.

- Let her watch you make change when you shop together, and make a point of counting coins for her. **Supervise your child with coins — they are a choking hazard.**

Play Store

What You Need:

- Variety of objects: shirts, dolls, cars, trucks, cans/boxes of food, tools, or anything that your child wants in the play store.
- Tape and pen.
- Purse with 50 cents or so in pennies.

What You Do:

1. Put a piece of tape on each item in the store and mark a price between 1 cent and 10 cents on it.
2. Ask your child to pick out what she wants to buy and count out the number of pennies needed to match the number on the price tag.
3. Take a turn being the shopper and let your child tell you how many pennies you need to make your purchase. Ask her to help you count out the right number. **Supervise children with coins — they are a choking hazard.**

Money Books

Help your child understand more about money by reading about it together:

📖 *26 Letters and 99 Cents* by Tana Hoban

📖 *Jelly Beans for Sale* by Bruce McMillan

Music Making!

by Maura, age 5

Sing! Sing! Sing!

- Even if you think you can't sing, sing to your child! Sing anytime, anywhere: in the car, while making breakfast or walking to the store, at the park, or anytime you feel the spirit. Make up your own songs, or make up words to songs if you don't know them all. Sing simple songs and songs with repeating phrases: *Mary Had a Little Lamb; Twinkle, Twinkle Little Star; The Wheels on the Bus.*

- Teach your child to sing simple songs. Sing one phrase and ask him to repeat it. Then sing two phrases and ask him to repeat them, and so on. Encourage all attempts at singing, and show your enjoyment. Add finger movements to some of the songs.

- Tape your child singing and play it back for him. Save the tape and add to it now and then, or mail it to a loved one far away.

Music Making!

Listen to the Music

- Expose your child to many kinds of music and to a variety of rhythms, tempos, and moods. Listen to music of many cultures, times, and styles: Jamaican reggae, American jazz, Italian opera, baroque, folk music from all over the world, rock, country, or any kind of music that you enjoy.

- Talk about basic musical concepts such as loud and soft, fast and slow, and high and low. As you sing or listen to a song, move your hand up and down to show how the notes would follow, or ask him to put his arms in the air or on the floor when he hears high or low notes.

- Provide opportunities for you and your child to listen and dance to a variety of music for children on tape, video, or CD:

  ♫ *Baby Songs; More Baby Songs: Featuring the Songs of Hap Palmer*

  ♫ *A Child's Celebration of Song* (Music for Little People)

  ♫ *A Child's Celebration of the World* (Music for Little People)

  ♫ *Dance Along With the Daise Family* (A Gullah Gullah Island video)

  ♫ *Ella Jenkins Live at the Smithsonian* (video)

  ♫ *Get Up and Dance* (A Sesame Street video)

  ♫ *Kids Classics Series*

  ♫ *My Favorite Opera for Children* (Pavarotti)

  ♫ *Papa's Dream* (Featuring Los Lobos and Lalo Guerrero)

  ♫ *The Wee Sing Train* (video)

Dancing and Moving to Music

- As you sing or listen to music, dance with your child. Carry him as you dance, or hold hands and dance together.

- As you listen to or play different types of music, encourage your child to move to the rhythms and express feelings through movement and dance.

- Ask your child to dance like an elephant, the wind, a gentle breeze, a thunderstorm, and a mouse. Ask him for ideas to dance.

The Field Guide Music-Making Box

Toy, Real, or Homemade	• Flute, horn, harmonica, or fife	• Tambourine, shakers, or maracas
	• Triangle	• Kazoo
	• Drums	• Bells
	• Rhythm or rain sticks	• Xylophone or keyboard
	• Guitar or banjo	• Whistle

Making Music

• Create your own simple instruments to play with your child:

Bells: Sew cow bells or jingle bells on a 1" elastic strip and sew ends of strip together to form a wrist or ankle band.

Drums: Beat the lid on a coffee can or upside-down pots and pans with a wooden spoon.

Rhythm Sticks: Tap together two wooden dowels, wooden rulers, or wooden spoons.

Kazoos: Stretch wax paper over the end of a toilet paper tube and secure with rubber band. Blow out a tune on your kazoo.

Tambourines/Shakers: Fill plastic eggs, film canisters, or aluminum pie tins with rice, beans, sand, bolts, marbles, or another small substance and glue together. Shake out a rhythm.

Chimes: Fill clear glasses or glass jars with different amounts of water. Tap lightly with a spoon to make different notes.

• Play orchestra or marching band: get out your instruments and make music together. Allow your child to be the orchestra leader or leader of the marching band. Don't worry about the sound—it will be music to your child's ears!

• Clap or tap to rhythms with your hand and various instruments. Ask him to copy you.

Sophia, age 5

Music Making!

Rhythm and Rhyme

- Find the rhythm in words by clapping or tapping out the beat to each syllable: Jon-a-thon, Lil-y, the ver-y hun-gry cat-er-pil-lar. For variation, as you clap, ask your child to jump, step, or hop to the beat.

- Read and recite rhymes to your child.

  At early morn the spiders spin,
  And by and by the flies drop in;
  And when they call, the spiders say,
  Take off your things, and stay all day!

  —Mother Goose

- Have fun with your child and have him say simple rhymes with you:
  "I love you. Yes, I do."

- Make up your own rhymes, sometimes using your child as the hero:
  "Sammy Lee Famood
  is such a handsome dude."

Musical Books

Help your child understand more about music and rhyme by reading about it together:

📖 *Finger Rhymes* by Marc Brown

📖 *Humpty Dumpty & Other Nursery Rhymes* by Lucy Cousins

📖 *Mother Goose Magic* by Kay Chorao

📖 *My First Music Book: A Lifesize Guide to Making and Playing Simple Musical Instruments* by Helen Drew

📖 *My First Songs* by Jane Manning

📖 *Read-Aloud Rhymes for the Very Young*, selected by Jack Prelutsky

📖 *Rise and Shine (Raffi Songs to Read)* by Raffi

📖 *Watch Me Dance* by Andrea Davis Pinkney

📖 *You Be Good & I'll Be Night: Jump on the Bed Poems* by Eve Merriam

📖 *Zin! Zin! Zin! A Violin* by Lloyd Moss

Numbers and Counting

Numbers Are Useful

- Point out numbers in everyday life to your child: elevator buttons, recipes, speedometers, house numbers, phone numbers, the numbers on basketball players' jerseys, or television channels.

- Talk about how useful numbers are: "Since we know the number of your new friend's apartment, # 505, we should be able to find her easily." "We can look in the newspaper to see what time *Sesame Street* comes on."

Counting Everyday

Point out items to count as you go through the day with your child: the number of steps to climb, red cars you see on a walk to the park, how many times a clock chimes, windows in a room, cereal boxes on the shelf, forks on the table, or toys that she is playing with. Count out loud, and as she learns to count, encourage her to count with you: "Let's count the number of steps to climb. There are one, two, three, four, five, six steps."

Collection Counting

Give your child some baskets, bags, or boxes to start some collections: pennies, shells, rocks, leaves, bottle caps, toy animals, toy people, pencils, pencil sharpeners, trading cards, or anything of interest to her. From time to time, encourage her to lay out her collections and count them with her.

Sandpaper and Bean Numbers

To make numbers that your child can feel:

- Cut out numbers from sandpaper and glue them on cardboard or index cards. Or glue beans on cardboard or index cards in the shape of numbers.

- By the side of the sandpaper or bean number, glue the same number of dried beans.

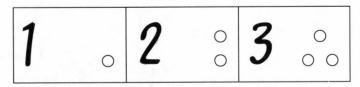

Then, introduce her to numbers in this sequence:

1. Let her run her fingers over the numbers as you say them. Put the number aside and try another.

2. Let her count the number of beans by the number on each card and say the number.

3. If she answers correctly, point to the 1 and say, "What is this?" Then point to the 2 and ask the same question.

Applaud all of her efforts, and have fun with the activity. If she gets frustrated, stop and try it another time.

Numbers and Counting

Copying Numbers   Put sand, colored salt, or shaving cream in a cake pan. Show your child how to trace numbers in the pan.

Writing Numbers   Show your child how to print numbers:

- Draw a number in dots (like a dot to dot) on a piece of paper and ask her to connect the dots with a crayon to form the numbers. Make the numbers large enough to fill a sheet of paper.

2

- Draw or design by hand or on the computer an outline of a number:

1

Ask her to follow or write the number on the inside of the outline with a crayon. Make the outline of the number large enough to fill a sheet of paper.

Counting Games
- Play board games like *Chutes & Ladders* and *The Uncle Wiggly Game* that have dice, a spinner, or number cards, and that require counting spaces.

- Make up your own counting games, using real objects: Put ten crayons on the table. Take some away and help your child count what's left. Add some back in and help your child count the total.

Number Reading   Help a child understand more about numbers by reading about them together:

📖 *How Many Bugs in a Box* by David A. Carter

📖 *The Lifesize Animal Counting Book*

📖 *Fish Eyes* by Lois Ehlert

K 34. 56789

by Will

Opposites and Directions

Opposite Talk

- Find opportunities to show him opposites: hot/cold, front/ back, old/new, open/shut, wet/dry, soft/hard, full/empty, happy/ sad, high/low, asleep/awake, and more.

- Talk about opposites: "Look, my shoes are wet, but yours are dry. They are the opposite of each other."

- When your child knows some opposites, say a word and ask him to tell you its opposite: "What's the opposite of hot?"

Opposite Charades

- Act out a word and have your child guess what it is: you could pretend to cry for "sad," pretend to fall asleep, or pretend to carry something heavy.

- Next, have him act out the opposite: he could pretend to laugh for happy, open his eyes wide for awake, or pretend to carry something small.

Where Is It?

Using words that show a relationship between things and describe where things appear (in, under, over, near, below, beside, between, among, across) point out to your child where things familiar to him are located:

"The book is *on* the table."

"The dog is *under* the chair."

"Hercules is *behind* the box."

Toy Hide and Seek

Pick a small toy and hide it from your child. Give him clues and ask him to find it:

"The elephant is *next to* something big."

"The ice cream truck is *on top of* something in your room.

Opposites and Directions

Treasure Hunt

What You Need:

- paper or index cards
- pictures from magazines or catalogs of things similar to what you have in your home
- crayon or marker
- glue or tape

What You Do:

1. Glue or tape a picture of something that you have in your home to a piece of paper or a card. Make six to 10 of these clues.

2. Draw on each clue a directional arrow to indicate on top of, under, beside, etc.

3. Keep the first card to give to him as the first clue. Hide the second clue near the item pictured on the first card. Hide the third clue near the item pictured on the second card, and so on, until all the clues are hidden. Make sure to hide the treasure/prize (a coin, small toy, food treat) near the final item.

4. Give him the first clue and send him on the hunt!

Read High and Low, Fast and Slow, Loud and Soft

Help your child understand more about opposites by reading about them together:

The Lifesize Animal Opposites Book by Lee Davis

Paddington's Opposites by Michael Bond

Popposites: A Lift, Pull, and Pop Book of Opposites by Roger Culbertson

by Jason, age 5

Pegboards and Puzzles

Provide opportunities to play with toys that fit together. Buy pegboards and puzzles or make your own fit-together toys:

- Cut a slot in the cover of an oatmeal box or coffee can and let your child drop in juice can lids.
- Find a box with dividers (used to pack bottles or jars) and have your child fit paper towel tubes into the slots.
- Ask her to practice fitting straws into a covered cup with a straw hole.
- Turn a strainer upside down and let her fit pieces of spaghetti through the holes.
- Glue a large picture on a piece of cardboard or find a used greeting card. Cut the picture up in large pieces that can be fit together. Give your child the pieces and ask her to put together the puzzle, offering help if she needs it.

Play Dough

Buy or make play dough for your child to squeeze, poke, roll, and pound.

The Field Guide Play Dough Kit

Play Dough Recipe

2 cups flour	Mix flour, salt, and cream of tartar.
1 cup salt	Mix boiling water, and oil.
4 teaspoons cream of tartar	Mix the two together.
2 cups boiling water (add food coloring)	Knead the dough until it cools.
2 tablespoons oil	Store in a covered airtight container.

Tools to Work the Dough

- Small rolling pin
- Cookie cutters
- Golf tees
- Plastic or wooden mallet
- Scissors

- Dull pie fluting tool
- Plastic animals
- Straws
- Plastic hair rollers
- Garlic press

Glurch recipe:

Mix: 2 parts school glue and 1 part liquid starch with your hands for about 10 to 15 minutes; for most of that time, expect it to look like it is not working — hang in there, it will!
If it seems very sticky, add more starch. If it seems very runny, add more glue. You are aiming for a slightly sticky, putty-like mixture that you and your child can pull, stretch, roll, cut, and bounce!

Goop recipe:

Place one 16 oz. box of cornstarch in a bowl and add enough water to make a thick paste.
For colored Goop, add food coloring.
The mixture should be "scoopable" with hands or fingers.
When squeezed it melts, then it becomes more solid again.
Allow your child to explore the gooey mess between his fingers! Join in!

! **WARNING!** Supervise children at all times with small objects and materials that could be choking hazards. Don't allow young children to work with small objects until they are beyond the stage of putting things in their mouths.

Running

Running Wild

- Provide opportunities for your child to experience running on several different, safe, soft surfaces: sand, soft and bug-free grass, carpet, a blanket, tile floors, wood floors.

- Let her run in different places: a park, baseball diamond, a gym during open-gym time, soccer field, or playground.

- **Chase:** Play chase by running after your child and catching her. Take turns chasing and being chased. Be sure to let her catch you, too.

- **Bubble Chase:** Blow bubbles and ask her to catch them. Also, try chasing and catching wind-up toys or a willing family dog.

- **Kites:** Fly a kite — ask her to run and follow it as you move it through the air.

- **Sprinklers:** Turn on a sprinkler and see how fast she can run through it.

- **Race:** Run a race with your child. Give her the opportunity to win some and lose some.

Obstacle Courses

- **Indoor:** Set up a course for your child to follow with pillows to jump on, soft chairs to run around, boxes to jump in and out of, cushions to run over, or large toys to run past.

- **Outdoor:** Set a course for her to follow around trees, around bushes, under lawn furniture, past the park bench, down the slide, around the baseball diamond, or anywhere outside that you can mark a path for her to follow while running.

Red Light, Green Light

Be the stoplight and say "Red light" to cue your child to stop and "Green light" to make her run. Choose a beginning and ending point; play indoors or out. Alternate saying "Red light" and "Green light" several times as she makes her way from start to finish.

I Challenge You to Run

Be the challenger and direct your child to run in many directions: around you, forward, backward, sideways, in circles, in giant steps, in baby steps, in zigzags, around corners, or under objects. Say, "I challenge you to run in circles." After a few circles, change the directions.

Running

Duck, Duck, Grey Duck
(a.k.a. Duck, Duck, Goose)

1. Ask four or more people to sit in a circle.

2. The person who is Grey Duck walks around the outside of the circle saying "Duck" as she touches each person's head. After circling once or twice, she picks a person in the circle to be "IT" by saying "Grey Duck" (or "Goose") as she touches their head.

3. That person becomes Grey Duck (or Goose), jumps up, and chases her around the circle. The new Grey Duck/Goose must try to tag her before she runs around the circle once and sits down in the spot where Grey Duck was sitting. If she gets caught, she is IT again. If not, the new Grey Duck begins the game again.

You Can't Cross

1. Choose someone to be IT. This child stands in the middle of the yard, field, or playground.

2. Line up two or more people on one side of a yard or playground.

3. The person who is IT begins by calling out, "You can't cross my yard unless you are wearing the color red!" Anyone wearing red may safely pass to the other side. Anyone not wearing red must run past the person who is IT without being tagged by her.

4. When someone is tagged, she becomes IT and begins the call to run by changing the condition of who may safely pass: blue pants, black shoes, brown hair, shorts, long sleeves, jackets, hats, or anything on or about a person that you can easily see.

Senses

by Maddie, age 4

Name That Sound

- Help your child notice and identify a wide variety of sounds throughout the day:

  "What a noisy bus!"

  "Who is crying? Is it your brother?"

  "The kitty is meowing outside."

- Together with your child, sit very still and quietly for a minute, and listen for sounds. Help him name them: dog barking, a siren, airplanes, the furnace, a bird, the refrigerator hum, the door closing.

- Together with your child, take a walk inside or outside and look for things that make sound: water running, toilet flushing, brushing teeth, vacuum cleaner, TV, horn honking, bus driving by, doorbell, telephone, or any sound you hear. Talk about them. Tape record some sounds, then play the tape, and ask him to identify the sound.

- Ask your child to cover his eyes. Make a sound: open a jack-in-the-box, close a door, crumple paper, open a can of pop, play notes on an instrument, turn on the water, flush the toilet, knock down a stack of blocks, imitate an animal, or make any sound with which the child is familiar. See if he can guess what sound was made.

Match the Sounds

Find plastic eggs that open. Gather small things that could be shaken inside the eggs: sand, rice, beans, nuts, or coins. Open two eggs and fill them with the same shaking material. Glue the egg halves together. Make several sets of shakers. Let him shake the eggs and try to match the pairs by how they sound.

Senses

Listen to the Heartbeat

- Place a stethoscope near your heart or the heart of a pet, and let your child listen to the heartbeats.

- Place the stethoscope on a tabletop and let him listen while you scratch the table with different objects: keys, dishcloth, a pencil, your fingernails, a cup.

Listen to the Voices

Tape record the voices of your child, parents, friends, neighbors, or anyone close to him. He will delight in hearing his own voice, as well as those he loves.

Can You Remember?

- Line up four toys or household objects: spoon, toy car, soap, keys, or any objects familiar to your child. Ask him to look at the line-up and then close his eyes. Remove one of the objects from his sight. Ask your child to open his eyes and look at the line-up. Can he identify the missing object?

- Arrange the four objects in a line-up. Have him look at them and then ask him to close his eyes. While his eyes are closed, rearrange the objects in a new order. Ask him to open his eyes and see if he can put them back in the original order.

- When four objects are no longer challenging enough for him, add more objects to the line-up.

Magnifying!

What You Need:
- A magnifying glass
- Tweezers (caution the child about the sharp end)
- A clear plastic bag (approximately one gallon size)

What You Do:
1. Choose an area to explore: backyard, park, or neighborhood. Go exploring.
2. Show your child how to use the tweezers to pick up small objects and place in the bag.
3. After he collects a bagful of things, lay out the collection and look at each item under the magnifying glass. Talk about and compare the qualities: tiny, sharp, round, bumpy, smooth, spotted, etc.

Night Watch

Together with your child, explore nighttime by taking a walk in a safe place, or by turning off the lights and looking out an open window. Look at the stars and moon. Listen to night sounds. Talk about what you see, hear, and feel. Compare this experience to daytime. Have a tea party under the stars.

Name That Scent

- Help your child notice, locate, and identify a wide range of smells: soap, shaving cream, flowers, people, pets, shoes, trees, grass, cooking, baking, smoke, the doctor's office, the dentist's office, Grandma's room, a bus, spices, herbs, perfume, pine needles, fruits, vegetables, or anything with an identifiable scent.

- Ask him to close his eyes, give him something familiar to smell, and see if he can identify it.

- Pick an object with a clear scent: onion, scented candle, a jar of spice, and soap. Hide it and ask him to find it!

Name That Taste

- Help him to notice and identify tastes: sweet, sour, salty, bitter, hot (spicy), tart.

- Ask him to cover or close his eyes. Give him a taste of several familiar foods, one at a time, and see if he can name them.

Another Way to Slice It

Talk to and ask your child about the differences between one food that is prepared in two different ways: peanuts/peanut butter, potato chips/mashed potatoes, milk/ice cream, or apples/ apple pie.

Match the Smell and Taste

- Pick out two things that have distinctly different smells or tastes but similar textures: salt/sugar, juice/water, oranges/lemons, yogurt/ice cream. Ask your child to cover or close his eyes.

- Take three bowls and put some of one food in each of two bowls, and put the other food in the remaining bowl. Let him smell and taste what is in each of the bowls. Ask him to match the two that are the same and identify the one that is different.

Name the Texture

- Help your child notice, locate, and identify textures and surfaces.

- Locate items with varying degrees of wetness, dryness, and sliminess: water, milk, yogurt, a raw egg, pudding, cooked and cooled spaghetti, dirt, shampoo, shaving cream, a piece of bread, uncooked rice, or any items he may not usually feel with his fingers. Put one item in each bowl, shallow container, or pan and allow him to feel them. Ask him to talk about and describe them: "Is it wet? Does the yogurt feel different from shampoo? How?"

- Help your child to make a texture collection: silk, burlap, feathers, rope, seashells, mirrors, balls, driftwood, beads, furry slippers, or anything with an interesting texture. Allow him to proudly display his texture collection.

Senses

Noisy, Slimy, Stinky, Eye-Catching Books

Help a child understand more about the senses by reading about them together:

📖 *The Ear Book* by Al Perkins

📖 *The Eye Book* by Theodore LeSieg

📖 *Fuzzy Yellow Ducklings: Fold-Out Fun With Textures, Colors, Shapes, Animals* by Matthew Van Fleet

📖 *My Five Senses* by Aliki

Stringing and Lacing

Stringing

Provide materials and opportunities for your child to have fun with stringing. With simple materials, he can make necklaces, bracelets, or just experience the joy of stringing.

The Field Guide Stringing Kit		
Strings to Use	• Yarn with end taped or dipped in glue to create a needle	• Shoestrings • Pipe cleaners
First Beads to String	• Large one-inch beads • Washers	• Large uncooked tube-shaped colored pasta
Beads for More Experienced Stringers	• O-shaped cereal • Plastic straws cut into pieces	• Smaller uncooked tube-shaped colored pasta • Smaller beads

Lacing

Provide inexpensive kits, shoes, or homemade lacing cards for your child to enjoy lacing. To make lacing cards, punch holes around the edge of an old greeting card. Tie the end of a shoestring in one of the holes, and show your child how to weave it in and out of the holes to make an edge around the card.

! **WARNING!** Supervise children at all times with small objects and materials that could be choking hazards. Don't allow young children to work with small objects until they are beyond the stage of putting things in their mouths.

Talk, Talk, Talk!

by Brian, age 4

Everything under the Sun

- Talk your way through your time with your child. Talk with her about everything! Include her in your conversation whenever and wherever you can. It's better to talk too much than too little.

- Describe what you are doing, seeing, feeling, smelling, tasting, and hearing—using lots of descriptive words:

  "I'll get a clean diaper and we'll change your wet diaper."

  "I'm calling Grandma to see if she wants to come over today."

  "We're driving to the store to buy a hat. A hat will keep the sun out of your eyes."

- Describe what she is doing, seeing, feeling, smelling, tasting, and hearing—using lots of descriptive words:

  "I see you looking at the black cat outside the window!"

  "You seem sad that you can't go outside today because of the rain."

  "Do you hear the city bus? Can you make that sound? Whoosh!"

- Name things for her and give her the words for things that she doesn't know. Say the name many times:

  "Look at that *watermelon*. That *watermelon* is so red. Would you like some *watermelon*?"

- Ask yourself questions and answer them in her presence:

  "Where did I leave my keys? Here they are, I left them on the table."

  "I wonder if the sun is shining today. Yes, it's shining bright!"

- Model good speech and language. Speak slowly and clearly. Often, get face to face with her and look her in the eye so that she can see your lips, tongue, and expressions.

Listen Up

- Be a good listener. Pay attention and look at your child as she speaks. Let her take her time. Show her that you understand what she said by answering, smiling, or nodding. If she has trouble getting her point across, patiently and matter-of-factly encourage her to try again instead of talking for her. If she can't find the words, offer suggestions.

- Allow her to make mistakes in her speech without criticism or correction.

Conversation Starters

- Find time to give your child some undivided attention each day and invite her to have a conversation with you:

  "What is that?"

  "Tell me about it!"

  "Tell me something important that happened today."

  Encourage her to take her time and give many details.

- Ask her many questions about things that are happening around her and stories that you read. Include many questions that are open-ended and require more than a "yes" or "no" answer:

  "Which leaves are the same? Which are different?"

  "Why do you like going to visit Grandpa?"

  "What are all of the things you can think of that grow on trees?"

  "What happened in the story after Arthur got the chicken pox? Did he get to go to the circus after all?"

- Repeat what your child says in an expanded, accurate version instead of correcting her:

  If she says, "Me want duice" for "I want juice," you say, "You would like more juice, I will get you some."

  If she says, "I it" for "I want to sit," you say, "Yes, you may sit down now."

  If she says, "I wuv you so much" you say, "Yes, I know you love me so much!"

- Encourage her to ask questions. Answer her questions patiently and help her to find the answers if you don't know them.

- Create opportunities to practice conversation throughout the day: direct her to give messages to family members: "Tell your sister that dinner is ready," or allow her to order her own ice cream cone at the store.

Kidding Around

Tell jokes, riddles, and tongue twisters. If you don't know any, make them up—children will think they are hilarious! Ask your friends for ideas, or go to the library and ask for joke and riddle books.

Talk, Talk, Talk!

Practice Talk

- Practice the art of conversation through play. Hold a pretend tea party and invite puppets, dolls, and stuffed animals. Encourage your child to talk to all the guests. Invite yourself to some of the parties but encourage your child to throw parties without you, too.

- Provide or make a toy telephone so your child can practice talking to her stuffed animals, dolls, puppets, and to you on the phone.

Read, Read, and Talk

Help a child understand more about words and talking by reading about them together:

📖 *Bennet Cerf's Book of Riddles* by Bennet Cerf

📖 *I Love You So Much* by Carl Norac

📖 *My First Word Book* by Angela Wilkes

📖 *Spot's Big Book of Words* by Eric Hill

📖 *Quick as a Cricket* by Audrey Wood

Encourage her to point things out in the book, ask questions, and learn new words.

by Rachel, age 3

Time

Time Talk

Talk about times of the day, days of the week, and which activities are attached to the times and days:

"On Wednesday, we do laundry."

"On Thursday, we go grocery shopping."

"At eight o'clock, we read bedtime stories."

Timelines

- Together with your child, create a timeline of your child's typical day.

    What You Need:
    - Paper
    - Tape and glue
    - Magazines with pictures (optional)
    - Scissors

    What You Do:
    1. Take a long piece of paper or tape many sheets together.
    2. Draw, help him draw, or cut pictures from magazines to represent the main activities of his day: waking up, getting dressed, brushing teeth, eating breakfast, playing outside, eating lunch, resting, more playing, eating supper, reading bedtime stories, going to bed.
    3. Help him glue the pictures on the paper in the order that they happen.
    4. Write the time that they usually occur next to the picture and talk about it:

        "At 7 A.M., we wake up."

        "At 1 P.M., we have rest time for an hour, until 2 P.M."

- Create a timeline of your child's week. Write the days of the week on the paper next to the pictures of your child's main activities: preschool, day care, routine visits with family or friends, grocery shopping, cleaning, laundry, or anything that happens regularly on the same day of each week.

- Create a timeline of seasons and events that happen during your child's year: spring, summer, fall, winter, birthdays, holidays, school, vacation, or special events. Next to the pictures of the events, write the month or months that the season or events occur. Add a date for birthdays and holidays.

Time

Telling Time

Expose your child to the clock but keep in mind that children don't typically learn to tell time until after they are seven years old. When your child can recognize numbers, begin pointing out how to tell time, either by showing the position of the hands on the clock or what the numbers on a digital clock mean. Point out what time on a clock looks like at key points in your child's day:

"When both hands point to the twelve, it is time to eat lunch."

"When the clock says "8:00," it's time for school."

Reading Time

Help your child understand more about time by reading about it together:

All About Time (A First Discovery Book) by Andre Verdet

Brown Rabbit's Day by Alan Baker

My First Book of Time by Claire Llewellyn

My First Look at Time by Toni Rann

Richard Scarry's Pop-Up Time by Richard Scarry

Tomorrow's Alphabet by George Shannon

Tricycles, Riding Toys, and Bicycles

Practice, Practice, Practice

Provide opportunities for your child to, first ride on a riding toy, then a tricycle, and then a small bike with training wheels. Give her opportunities to practice so she can improve her skills, endurance, balance, agility, and understanding of safety issues:

- Create a track in your yard, basement, or garage.
- Allow her to ride on city sidewalks, park paths, off road trails, or in a yard.
- Set up an obstacle course: place cones, yard furniture, or coffee cans with flags in a path that encourages steering and stopping practice.

Anticipate the day when she is older and will be riding alone, and begin to talk about safety rules of the road.

! WARNING:
- Always supervise children when they are riding.
- Do not let children ride in the road until at least eight years of age.
- Wait to buy a tricycle until children are ready for one: usually around three years.
- Wait to buy a bicycle until children are ready for one: usually around six years with training wheels.
- Make sure everyone in the family wears properly fitting helmets approved by the American National Standards Institute or the Snell Memorial Foundation when riding a bicycle.

by Joey, age 5

Water, Sand, and Other Stuff, too

Scoop, Shovel, and Pour Provide opportunities for your child to play with tools and materials for measuring, scooping, sifting, shoveling, and pouring. Place a box on an old plastic shower curtain or tablecloth, fill with materials, and let your child have a great time! Supervise this activity to avoid a mess. Encourage your child to talk about what she is doing by asking questions: "Why do you think that sinks/floats? Why does that sand stay molded? How does the birdseed feel between your fingers?"

The Field Guide Scoop, Shovel, and Pour Kit		
Things to Pour, Sift, and Scoop	• Sand • Water (in the tub works!) • Dried beans or peas • Birdseed	• Ice cubes • Rice • Foam packing peanuts
Toys and Things to Add	• Plastic animals • Cars and trucks • Toy people • Rocks • Shells	• Wood • Plastic flowers and leaves • Rubber fishing bait without hooks
Tools	• Ladles • Small fish nets or scoops • Cups • Funnels • Spoons • Shovels • Pails • Small pitchers	• Plastic or metal measuring cups • Measuring spoons • Small pots and pans • Pie tins • Sand or gelatin molds • Turkey baster • Egg beater (with dish soap!)

! **WARNING!** Supervise children at all times with small objects and materials that could be choking hazards. Don't allow young children to work with small objects until they are beyond the stage of putting things in their mouths.

The Growing Child Year-by-Year

More Help and Information

Books for Parents

- *Developmental Profiles: Pre-Birth Through Eight*, 3rd Edition, by K. Eileen Allen and Lynn R. Marotz. Delmar Publishers, 1999.

- *The Early Childhood Years: The 2-to-6-Year Old* by Theresa and Frank Caplan. Putnam, 1983.

- The Gesell Institute of Child Development series by Louise Bates Ames and Frances L. Ilg, et al., Delacorte Press:

    Your One-Year-Old: The Fun-Loving, Fussy 12-24-Month-Old. 1982.

    Your Two-Year-Old: Terrible or Tender. 1976.

    Your Three-Year-Old: Friend or Enemy. 1976.

    Your Four-Year-Old: Wild and Wonderful. 1976.

- *How Babies Talk: The Magic and Mystery of Language in the First Three Years of Life* by Kathryn Hirsh-Pasek and Roberta Michnick Golinkoff. E.P. Dutton, 1999.

- *Magic Trees of the Mind: How to Nurture Your Child's Intelligence, Creativity and Healthy Emotions From Birth Through Adolescence* by Marian Diamond and Janet Hopson. Dutton, 1998.

- *Touchpoints* by T. Berry Brazelton. Addison-Wesley, 1992.

- *The Second Twelve Months of Life: A Kaleidoscope of Growth: Includes a Mini-Course in Infant and Toddler Development* by Frank and Theresa Caplan. Grossett & Dunlap, 1977.

- *Your Baby & Child: From Birth to Age Five* by Penelope Leach. Alfred A. Knopf, 1997.

- *Your Child: What Every Parent Needs to Know About Childhood Development From Birth to Preadolescence* by David Pruitt (Editor). HarperCollins, 1998.

Community Resources

To find classes or support groups near you concerning parenting, early childhood education, or family life education, ask you friends, neighbors, or pediatrician, or consult your local school district, library, or your county's social services agency.

Magazines

- *Newsweek*, "Special Edition: Your Child From Birth to Three." Spring/Summer 1997. Available in most libraries.

- *Parenting*, look for feature articles under "Development" and at the monthly department: "Ages & Stages."

- *Parents*, look at the monthly department: "As They Grow: An Age-By-Age Guide to Your Child's Development."

National Organizations

- ZERO TO THREE: National Center for Infants, Toddlers, and Families
  734 15th St. NW, Suite 1000,
  Washington, D.C. 20005
  800-899-4301
  E-mail: 0to3@zerotothree.org
  Web site: www.zerotothree.org

Resources for Family Professionals

- *Family Information Services*
  12565 Jefferson St. NE, Suite 102,
  Minneapolis, MN 55434
  800-852-8112, fax: 612-755-7355
  E-mail: services@familyinfoserv.com
  Web site: www.familyinfoserv.com

- *HELP: The Hawaii Early Learning Profile*
  VORT Corporation
  P.O. Box 60132, Palo Alto, CA 94306
  650-332-8282, fax: 650-327-0747
  E-mail: sales@vort.com
  Web site: www.vort.com

Videos for Parents

- *The First Years Last Forever*, a Johnson & Johnson
  presentation. Reiner Foundation, 1997. Available
  to borrow free of charge from public libraries
  and Blockbuster Video, or call 1-888-447-3400 for
  information about ordering.

- *Touchpoints: The Brazelton Study, v. 3 One Year Through
  Toddlerhood*. GoodTimes Home Video, 1991.

Web Sites

- Family.com, choose "Parenting" from the home page
  menu, then "Development" for a list of articles. Web
  site: www.family.com

- Kidsource, choose "Toddlers" or "Preschoolers" from
  the home page menu, then "Growth & Development"
  for a list of articles. Web site: www.kidsource.com

- Parenting Me. Web site: www.parentingme.com

- ParenthoodWeb, choose "Development" from
  the topics menu for a list of articles. Web site:
  www.parenthoodweb.com

- I Am Your Child, information about development of
  children, from prenatal to age three. Web site:
  www.iamyourchild.org

PART TWO

Great Ideas, Advice, Tips, and Solutions for Parenting Children Ages One to Five

Anger

"Lion who ate another animal"

by Will, age 4

Description

Anger is a normal and healthy human emotion expressed by both children and adults. Anger signals that something isn't right, gives energy, releases tension, and encourages action. It can also cause problems if it is not handled well.

Realistic Expectations

- Children are capable of showing anger clearly and directly beginning at infancy.
- Children typically become angry when they are:
  - Frustrated that they can't do or have something immediately.
  - Struggling to learn a new skill.
  - Frustrated because they are having difficulty expressing their needs and desires.
  - Hurt emotionally.
  - In physical pain.
  - Disappointed.
  - Misunderstood.
  - Feeling helpless or powerless.
  - Feeling rushed.

- Burying or denying anger can cause physical and emotional problems in both children and adults.
- Anger—both their own anger and anger expressed by others—can be very frightening to young children.
- When children overhear adults arguing in angry voices, they may not understand what the argument is about and worry that they are the cause.
- Spanking, shaking, or hitting children, especially when angry, can lead to injury or abuse.
- Preschoolers believe that thinking something can make it so; they may worry that their angry thoughts about you or someone else could come true, or that something bad happened because they had angry thoughts.
- Learning to experience and express anger in positive ways is a lifelong task; children with practice during childhood are more likely to carry those skills with them into adulthood.

Approaches

Find ways to express your anger without hurting or insulting your child. Express your anger in ways that enrich your relationship with your child rather than aggravate it:

- Exit or wait. The two most important four-letter words to remember when you are angry are "exit" and "wait." When you are so angry that you are about to lose control, leaving the situation or calling an adult time-out can give you a breather so that you are not at the mercy of your emotions. Attacks that occur in the heat of anger are usually met with a return of anger.

- Say "I" not "you." When your child does something that makes you angry, your automatic response may be to shout an accusation: "Why are you behaving like such a brat?" "What kind of slob are you—throwing your jacket on the floor?" The message you communicate is that the child is unacceptable, not the action. "You" statements have the ability to wound. "I" statements make the point much more effectively, without damaging your child's self-esteem. When you're angry, it is better to say (or even shout), "I'm mad!" than to say or shout, "You're bad!"

- Stay in the present. Don't use the incident as a springboard for gloomy forecasts or as an opportunity to dredge up ancient history. Say, "I'm disappointed in this mess," not, "Your room is always a mess!"

- Avoid physical force and threats. When you've won by asserting your physical power as a big person over a small person, you have won nothing.

- Stay short and to the point. Be specific. It's pointless to tell a four-year-old to clean up his room. If you expect results, you might wait forever. Give him specific instructions about how to do it, and not too many.

- Restore good feelings. Your child and you both want and need to share good feelings most of the time, even when the battles become fierce. Time and distance heal many wounds, and a simple apology can go a long way toward feeling positive again.

> —From "Eight Weapons in the War on Anger" by Nancy Samalin, author of *Love and Anger*, Penguin, 1992, in *Family Information Services*, 1998.

! WARNING! Never shake a child and never harm a child with physical punishment.

Shaking a baby or child under the age of three can cause brain damage, blindness, paralysis, seizures, or death. Even a small amount of shaking or a less vigorous shaking can severely harm a young child.

The American Academy of Pediatrics (AAP) warns that children who are routinely disciplined with spanking and other physical forms of punishment are more likely to become aggressive and to learn that aggressive behavior is the way to solve problems. Spanking or hitting can also lead to injury and abuse, especially when it is done in anger.

Consider whether or not you are mishandling your anger with your child. Coping with a certain amount of anger at home is part of every child's life. But when anger is out of control, it can leave your child feeling threatened. Ask yourself the following questions:

- Do I shout when a child interrupts my train of thought?
- Am I particularly riled by even minor changes in our schedule?

- Does a child's expression of emotion—excitement or distress—arouse extreme irritation?
- Do all the child's requests suddenly seem excessive?
- Do I get very angry at behavior that is really only inconvenient, rather than objectionable?
- Do I frequently shout when helping my child learn something or complete a task?

If the answer to several of these questions is "yes," then stress and anger are probably interfering with your ability to respond positively to your child.

> —From *The Confident Child* by Terri Apter. Copyright © 1997 by Terri Apter.
> Reprinted by permission of W.W. Norton & Company, Inc.

When you feel like you are going to blow up at your child, STOP! When everyday pressures build up:

- Take a deep breath. And another. Remember, *you* are the adult.
- Close your eyes. Pretend you're hearing what your child is about to hear from you.
- Press your lips together and count to ten. Better yet, count to twenty.
- Put your child in a time-out chair (one minute for each year of age).
- Put *yourself* in a time-out chair. Think about why you are angry. Is it your child, or is your child simply a convenient target for your anger?
- Phone a friend.
- If someone can watch your child, go outside and take a walk.
- Take a hot bath.
- Splash water on your face.
- Hug a pillow.
- Turn on some music. Maybe even dance or sing along.
- Write down as many helpful words as you can think of. Save the list.

You'll feel better when you are in control of your anger. So will your child.

> —Information provided by the National Committee to Prevent Child Abuse.

Have realistic expectations about your child's abilities and behaviors to keep your anger level low. When your expectations are too high, and far from reality, there is great potential for your anger level to rise easily. When your expectations are realistic, typical child misbehavior and the many calamities of childhood will be much easier to handle. Learn about child development to make sure your expectations are appropriate for the child's age and stage of development. Focus on the big picture: you have his entire childhood to help him become a competent, independent, and loving adult.

Also think about the reality of the situation. Is the problem really as bad as you are making it? Many of the things that anger us are unimportant and will be forgotten in a few weeks or years.

> —Ideas found in *Kid Cooperation: How to Stop Yelling, Nagging and Pleading and Get Kids to Cooperate* by Elizabeth Pantley, New Harbinger Publications, Inc., 1996.

Consider the ways that *you* may be making your child angry. Most parents mean well, but at one time or another, all of us will cause anger in our families. Sometimes, even though we have good intentions, we cause the child to feel helpless and angry. When this happens occasionally, the anger passes quickly. However, if a pattern develops, it can lead to ongoing anger in your child.

Consider ways that you may unknowingly fuel anger in your child: treating him unfairly, making him feel unwanted, breaking promises, disciplining him inconsistently, making him feel guilty, teasing him, sending mixed messages about what you expect, overprotecting him, being pessimistic, allowing him to continually fail without helping him, making too many demands, comparing him to others, and intimidating, humiliating, or bullying him.

You can never *not* make others angry, and that should not be your goal. However, take an honest look at yourself. If you are caught in a daily pattern of anger between you and your child, think about ways to change it.

> —Ideas found in *When Kids Are Mad, Not Bad: A Guide to Recognizing and Handling Children's Anger* by Henry A. Paul, Berkley Books, 1995.

Show your child positive ways to handle anger:

- Stay calm when facing your child's anger. Anger has a way of creating more anger; if you can stay calm, he will be able to control himself better.

- Hold him or stay near him to let him know that it is safe for him to lose control and that he will not lose you if he does.

- Talk calmly to him, telling him that you see he is angry. Say, "You are very angry."

- Model respect for yourself and everyone in your family. He's watching you to learn how to handle his strong emotions. If you are angry as well, take time to cool off before trying to talk to your child. When you are arguing with another adult, cool off; then listen to the person, avoid blaming, focus on solutions, and do not try to talk the person into doing anything.

- If you accidentally lose your temper, say you're sorry and explain. Say, "I am sorry that I was mean to dad. You don't like to see that. Our fight is not your fault. We all make mistakes; I'll try not to do it again. I was angry because dad was late. I love him but I do not like his being late."

When you are in the heat of a battle, stop and imagine that your child is one of your friends. If you wouldn't have the argument in front of a good friend, you probably shouldn't have it in front of your child.

> —Ideas found in *Positive Parenting A-Z* by Karen Renshaw Joslin, Fawcett Columbine: Ballantine Books, 1994.

Treat angry outbursts with respect and teach your child to be angry in positive ways. The goal is not to repress or destroy angry feelings in your child, but to accept the feelings and to help direct them to helpful, non-harmful actions. Allow your child to experience all of his feelings. Show him acceptable ways of expressing them. Help your child deal with angry feelings:

- Use closeness and touching. Move physically closer to your child to calm his angry impulse; sometimes just having an adult nearby helps. For another child, a sudden hug can help him regain control.

- Express interest in his activities. Young children need adult involvement in their interests. A child about to use a toy or tool in a destructive way is sometimes easily stopped by an adult who expresses interest in having it shown to him.

- Use humor. Playfully kidding your child out of an angry outburst offers him an opportunity to "save face." However, it is important neither to tease or ridicule him nor to respond with sarcasm.

- Ask your child to consider your feelings. Tell him how you feel, and ask him to be helpful to you: "I know that noise you're making doesn't usually bother me, but today I've got a headache, so could you find a quieter way to be angry."

- Explain difficult situations. Help your child understand the cause of a stressful situation. We often fail to realize how easily young children can begin to react properly once they understand the cause of their frustration.

- Remove your child from the scene to prevent him from hurting himself or others and as a means to tell him, "You can't do that." When your child is having an angry outburst, you cannot afford to lose your temper. Unfriendly remarks by other children should not be tolerated.

- Encourage your child to see his strengths as well as his weaknesses. Tell him that he can reach his goals and help him to do so.

- Show your child acceptable ways to express angry feelings without using hurting: punching pillows, stomping feet, or drawing an angry picture. Also encourage him to use words: "I don't like it when you take my doll. I don't want to share right now."

- Say, "No!" Set clear limits with your child, explain them, and enforce them. Then give him the freedom to function within these limits.

- Build a positive self-image. Encourage him to see himself as valued and valuable.

- Model appropriate behavior. Adults' actions have a very powerful influence on the child. Show him how to handle anger in positive ways through your own reactions.

- Change the surroundings. Sometimes the situation is just too tempting for your child. Stop a "problem" activity and substitute a more desirable one.

- Ignore inappropriate behavior that can be tolerated. If your child is not in danger, not hurting anyone, or not being destructive, ignore him. For this to work, you need to be very consistent and not give him any attention.

- Make sure your child gets plenty of physical exercise. Movement can help the body release tension.

- Catch your child being good. Tell him what behaviors please you many times throughout the day: "I like the way you come in for dinner without being reminded," or "I am so glad you shared your snack with your sister."

Strong feelings cannot be denied, and angry outbursts should not always be viewed as a sign of serious problems; they should be recognized and treated with respect.

—Ideas found in "Plain Talk About Dealing with the Angry Child,"
U.S. Department of Health and Human Services, 1992.

Create a space where it is OK for your child to be angry in your home. Give your child a place to release the tension caused by anger before it leads to hitting, fighting, kicking, screaming, or other inappropriate means of expression. Tell him to go to this place whenever he likes. In this "mad corner," put some tension relievers:

- Things to punch: large pillows, punching balls, or punching clowns.

- Things to do with his hands: clay, play dough, sand, water, shaving cream on a cookie sheet, soft balls to squeeze or squish bags made by squirting shaving cream or hair gel into a sandwich-size zip-close bag, adding a bit of glitter and food color, zipping the bag closed and sealing it with duct tape for extra security, and letting the child squeeze the bag to mix the colors.

- Things to pound: wooden mallets for pounding play dough or golf tees to pound into Styrofoam.

- Painting, scribbling, or drawing materials: paper with bold, dark-colored markers, crayons, and paints.

- Things to destroy: old junk to take apart, old sheets, newspapers, or magazines to rip.

- Noise makers: cookie sheets or pots to pound, maracas, shakers, or whistles.

- A target with beanbags to throw at it.

- Teddy bears to hug or to whom he can tell his problems.

- A yelling box: take a large appliance box and cut a door in it, decorate it, and tell him to go inside and yell or roar like a lion when he is angry.

None of these activities are meant to get rid of anger or other emotions. Instead they are meant to help acknowledge it, express it, and learn to deal with it in positive ways. Doing these activities will make him feel better!

—Ideas found in *The Crisis Manual for Early Childhood Teachers*
by Karen Miller, Gryphon House, 1996.

Help your child calm down when he is becoming angry, and begin to encourage him to do so on his own. At the first signs of anger, help your child learn to relax:

- Hum or sing with him when a task is frustrating your child. This might encourage the child to try again more calmly.
- Give him suggestions when he gets stuck trying to do something. Don't do it for him, but help him see new ways to approach the project.
- Stay calm yourself. Speak to him in a calm voice. This gives him something to imitate in the heat of the moment.
- Try distracting him with another activity. This gives him a chance to refocus and calm himself: read a favorite book, draw, or play a game.
- Avoid using treats to coax him out of his anger. This can backfire and actually encourage him to continue expressing his anger inappropriately to get more treats.

Different children find different things helpful; find the solutions that work for you and your child.

—Ideas found in *Taming the Dragon in Your Child: Solutions for Breaking the Cycle of Family Anger* by Meg Eastman, John Wiley & Sons, 1994.

Help your child understand more about anger by reading about it together:

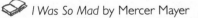 *Andrew's Angry Words* by Dorothea Lachner

The Grouchy Ladybug by Eric Carle

I Was So Mad by Mercer Mayer

I'll Fix Anthony by Judith Viorst

Mean Soup by Betsy Everitt

No! No! No! by Anne Rockwell

When Mom Turned into a Monster by Joanna Harrison

Where the Wild Things Are by Maurice Sendak

When to Get More Help

Children typically grow and learn new skills in their own time and at their own pace within the wide range of what is normal. Sometimes, children need a bit of extra help to keep their development on track or to stay healthy and happy. Sometimes, parents need help providing for a child's needs or sorting out the best approaches to parenting.

Consider getting help for your child if he:

- Stands out as a lot more angry than other children his own age.
- Often overreacts to situations or events in anger and does not respond to comfort.
- Is very impulsive and acts without thinking about safety while angry.
- Does not show a range of emotions: joy, anger, sorrow, grief, enthusiasm, excitement, frustration, love, and affection.
- Frequently is cruel toward other children or animals, threatens others, plays with fire, harms property, or engages in play that has violent themes.

Consider getting help for yourself if you:

- Feel angry much of the time: you find yourself often being rude, punishing, vindictive, or sullen.
- Frequently yell at your child.
- Use shaking, hitting, spanking, or other physical punishment, especially when you are very angry or while under the influence of drugs or alcohol.
- Find that your anger disrupts your relationships with others or interferes with your work.
- Have physical symptoms related to your anger like headaches or a tense stomach.
- Emotionally, verbally, sexually, or physically abuse others.
- Find yourself in power struggles that escalate into hitting or shouting.

You are the expert when it comes to your family and child. If you have a concern, trust your instinct and find someone trained to help you: health care providers, early intervention teams, mental health professionals, parent educators and consultants, or telephone help-line staff. Consider talking it over with friends and family, too. You don't need to worry alone! Turn to "Finding Help in Your Community" on page 4 to learn about finding help near you.

More Help and Information

Books for Parents

- *Love and Anger: The Parental Dilemma (reissue edition)* by Nancy Samalin and Catherine Whitney. Penguin, 1995.

- *Taming the Dragon in Your Child: Solutions for Breaking the Cycle of Family Anger* by Meg Eastman. John Wiley & Sons, 1994.

- *When Anger Hurts Your Kids: A Parent's Guide* by Matthew McKay, Patrick Fanning, Kim Paleg, and Donna Landis. New Harbinger Publications, Inc., 1996.

- *When Kids Are Mad, Not Bad: A Guide to Recognizing and Handling Children's Anger* by Henry A. Paul. Berkley Books, 1995.

National Organizations

- Parents Anonymous (PA)
  909-621-6184, Fax: 909-625-6304
  Web site: www.parentsanonymous-natl.org

  Request or view online information about PA in your area.

Bad Habits

Description

A habit is a behavior that is repeated so often that it becomes a regular practice; often it is unconscious and automatic. Examples of good habits include buckling a seat belt before every car ride or brushing your teeth every night. Habits that are neither good nor bad include foot wiggling or quiet humming. Bad habits—like nose picking and nail biting—are the ones that embarrass the child, cause the child physical discomfort or injury, are annoying or embarrassing to others, or get in the child's way of doing other things.

Realistic Expectations

- The more a behavior is repeated, the more likely it is to become a strongly established habit.
- Bad habits are very common in young children; they are annoying, but usually harmless.
- Children may start a habit as a result of being bored, tired, or stressed; having too much stimulation or too little attention; or repeating a behavior they saw someone else do.
- Sometimes habits provide tension relief and/or stimulation.
- Children outgrow most habits without any outside help; however, they may need help breaking a habit if they do not outgrow it.

Approaches

Accept some behaviors and habits as a normal part of childhood exploration. Your child may rock back and forth, bite her nails, or pick her nose as a way to ease tension. These normal explorations typically are short-lived, and the child tries out a variety of them, not fixing on one. As long a you don't make a fuss and your child is able to find other ways to comfort herself, the behavior usually passes and the child moves on to experimenting with a different one.

Any of these behaviors can get fixed into a pattern or habit *that is a problem*. There are things a parent can do to help prevent bad habits from forming:

- Don't overreact to the behavior by showing disapproval or trying to stop it, and remind other adults and older children to do the same.
- Look for and deal with any underlying reasons for the behavior: Is she stressed? Is there too much excitement around her? Is she overtired much of the time?
- Help her find ways to comfort herself, such as a rubbing a security blanket or hugging a teddy bear.

Talk to her health care provider if you have any concerns about her habits.

—Ideas found in *Touchpoints* by T. Berry Brazelton, Addison-Wesley, 1992.

Help your child stop a bad habit if it causes her physical discomfort, embarrasses her, keeps her from doing other activities, or changes her appearance. For habits like nose picking, nail biting, or hair twisting, take several steps:

- Try to notice a pattern of when and why she does the behavior: while watching television, on the way to day care, when playing with a certain child, when she's bored, or when she's nervous.
- Talk to your child about the habit. Describe it to her because she may not even know she is doing it, and explain why it is a problem.
- Remind her respectfully, quietly, and gently when she is doing the behavior.
- Praise her for trying to quit, and give her positive attention when she is not doing the behavior.
- If the ideas listed above don't work, try a reward system: at the end of each day she shows progress, give her a free or inexpensive reward like a sticker or time with you playing a special game. Begin with a goal of reducing the number of times she does the behavior, and then move day by day toward stopping it entirely.
- Don't emphasize success too much, and don't criticize her when she slips; she may feel pressured. It's best to focus on praising her efforts in trying to quit.

> —Ideas found in *A to Z Guide to Your Child's Behavior*, (Children's National Medical Center) Putnam, 1993.

Consider ignoring a bad habit, but if ignoring it doesn't work quickly, make a plan to help your child stop it. Strike a balance: many times just ignoring a bad habit in its beginning stages works well to stop it; however, the more a behavior is repeated, the stronger the habit becomes, and the more difficult it will be for the child to quit. Once a habit is strongly ingrained, ignoring it won't work well because you are allowing her to repeat it and allowing it to become even more ingrained. Most habits can be weakened if you catch them early and work to reduce their frequency.

> —Ideas found in *Good Kids/Bad Habits* by Charles E. Schaefer and Theresa Foy DiGeronimo, Prince Paperbacks, 1993.

Help your child understand more about bad habits by reading about them together:

📖 *The Berenstain Bears and the Bad Habit* by Stan and Jan Berenstain

📖 *The Nose Book* by Al Perkins

When to Get More Help

Children typically grow and learn new skills in their own time and at their own pace within the wide range of what is normal. Sometimes, children need a bit of extra help to keep their development on track or to stay healthy and happy. Sometimes, parents need help providing for a child's needs or sorting out the best approaches to parenting.

Consider getting help for your child if she:

- Holds her breath.
- Bangs her head.
- Has tics: sudden, non-purposeful body movements like shrugging, blinking, squinting, shoulder or head jerking, grimacing, head shaking, nodding, or nose wrinkling.
- Grinds, grits, or gnashes her teeth.

*Note: All of the above behaviors are somewhat common and usually harmless when done individually; but any of them may be a sign that the child needs medical attention. Your health care provider can quickly help you tell the difference between a harmless habit that will probably pass with time and a medical concern. Even if they are harmless, these behaviors often concern and frustrate parents, so some support may be useful.

- Stutters to the point that it causes her embarrassment, causes her to avoid speaking, or causes her to have great difficulty getting words out; or if she stutters for more than several months.
- Causes physical harm to herself with the habit: she bites her nails so much that she bleeds.
- Will not interrupt the habit to respond to you: she prefers masturbating to being comforted and cuddled by you.
- Frequently breaks away from an activity to do the habit: she stops playing a game to go bite her nails.
- Prefers the habit to being with people: she prefers biting her nails to playing with you or her friends.
- Can't seem to stop a bad habit even after you have tried to help her stop.

Consider getting help for yourself if you:

- Have any bad habits that you would like to quit.
- Feel excessive frustration or anger over her bad habits.

You are the expert when it comes to your family and child. If you have a concern, trust your instinct and find someone trained to help you: health care providers, early intervention teams, mental health professionals, parent educators and consultants, or telephone help-line staff. Consider talking it over with friends and family, too. You don't need to worry alone! Turn to "Finding Help in Your Community" on page 4 to learn about finding help near you.

More Help and Information

Books for Parents

- *Good Kids/Bad Habits* by Charles E. Schaefer and Theresa Foy DiGeronimo. Prince Paperbacks, 1993.

Birthdays

by Elise

Description

A birthday is the anniversary of a person's birth and marks the passage of time in a life. Different cultures, countries, families, and religions honor birthdays in different ways, but most people around the world and throughout modern history recognize birthdays as a celebration of life.

Realistic Expectations

- At ages one and two, children don't have expectations for their birthdays because they haven't had experience with them.
- By age three, children may have definite ideas, opinions, and expectations about their birthdays and celebrations.
- Too many people, gifts, noise, or fuss can be overwhelming to young children, and they may lose control because of it.
- Don't assume that twins or multiples will want to share a birthday celebration or receive identical or shared gifts. Each child is unique and wants to be recognized as such on their special day.
- Children may experience post-holiday let down after a birthday and may need more help in general and in finding things to do.
- The amount of money spent on birthdays is not what makes them special or what creates lasting memories; what matters is how happy and honored children feel and how much fun they have.

Approaches

Plan a small, simple, short party for your child:

- Allow your child to help plan his party and, when you can, respect his choices about who to invite, what party theme to have, which games to play, and what food to serve.
- Generally, invite the same number of guests as your child's age.
- Keep decorations simple.
- Aim for a party that lasts an hour to an hour and a half.
- Prepare food that the children can eat with their hands.
- Choose simple games and activities that don't have a lot of rules or complicated steps.
- Allow your child to open a gift as soon as he gets it or ask your child to wait until a special time during the party when the guests can open their party favors, too.

> —Ideas found in *The Penny Whistle Birthday Party Book* by Meredith Brokaw and Annie Gilbar, Simon & Schuster, 1992.

Birthdays

Pick a time of day for your child's celebration when he is likely to be feeling his best. Keep him on schedule with naps, bedtimes, and mealtimes. Plan a short celebration when he is usually not tired, hungry, or fussy.

—Ideas found in *What to Expect the Toddler Years* by Arlene Eisenberg, Heidi E. Murkoff, and Sandee E. Hathaway, Workman Pub., 1994.

Consider planning a birthday celebration for your child where his only guests are he and his parents. If your child doesn't like celebrating his special day with many other people, consider giving him the gift of your special time and attention. Take him out for a meal and let him know that you appreciate him as an individual, not just part of an active family. Make it a tradition.

—Ideas found in *New Traditions* by Susan Abel Lieberman, Noonday Press, 1990.

Mark your child's first birthday by making a keepsake record:

1. Make his hand and foot prints by drawing an outline of his hand and foot on a piece of paper.
2. Write down interesting thoughts, ideas, and milestones: how tall he is; what sounds or words he can say; when he started to walk, crawl, or pull himself up; when he started to eat favorite foods; what his favorite books or toys are; what was happening in the world or to people in your family; popular movies, songs, and books; and the weather of the day.

Your child may not remember his first birthday, but you both will enjoy looking at this keepsake when he is older.

—Ideas found in *Kid-Tastic Birthday Parties: The Complete Party Planner for Today's Kids* by Jane Chase, Brighton Publications, 1995.

> *I use birthdays, half-birthdays, and quarter-birthdays to encourage my daughter to try new things: "You're three and a half today! That means you can start getting dressed all by yourself!"*
>
> —Mike from Columbus, MN

Tell your birthday child the story of his coming into the world and into your family. Share the positives of the story and tell it on a level that he can understand. Include the joy and wonder of a child's birth, and how special it was when he came into your life.

—Ideas inspired by *On the Day You Were Born* by Debra Frasier, Harcourt Brace Jovanovich, 1991.

Be reasonable in what you give your child for his birthday. To your small child, anything wrapped up is an exciting present. You don't need to spend a lot of money on gifts. Consider giving as gifts some of the things that you would provide for him anyway: hats, mittens, books. Consider wrapping up a ticket to a fun time with just you, to do whatever the child wants.

What's more important than the number of gifts is how well the gifts match a child's interest, age, and developmental level, and how well they hold up to long use. Expect that he will be most excited about the bigger gifts, but if he uses the smaller ones in time, then you have chosen well.

—Ideas found in *Mom, Can I Have That?* by Janet Bodnar, Kiplinger Times Business, 1996.

Start a birthday custom for your child that will help him mark the passage of years. It may become more meaningful as the child grows older, when, hopefully, he will appreciate the effort you made in the early years. Consider these ideas:

- Each year, add a tree or perennial plant to the yard or garden that you and your child can watch grow together.
- Start a birthday box for your child and add the same thing(s) each year. Choose:
  - The birthday newspaper
  - Photographs of your child throughout the year
  - A report on your child's progress and family events throughout the year (can be written as a letter)
  - Birthday cards your receives
  - Photographs of your child's birthday celebration
- Give your child an object for a collection that you can add to each year.

> —Ideas found in *Practical Parenting Tips (revised and updated edition)* by Vicki Lansky, Meadowbrook Press, 1992.

Explore birthday traditions, foods, and celebrations from all over the world with your child, and learn about the origins of present-day customs:

- Noisemakers on birthdays may have originated in ancient times as a way to scare away evil spirits.
- Many people in China don't have birthday celebrations on their day of birth. Instead, they celebrate Chinese New Year together. On that day, everyone turns a year older.
- Seaweed soup is often served at birthday parties in Korea because it is believed to give strength.
- Australian children eat Fairy Bread, which you can make by shaking sprinkles or nonpareils on buttered bread and cutting it into triangles.

Read more about customs and traditions together to give your child a perspective on his place in the world and in time. It may make his birthday feel even more special because he is part of a bigger tradition.

> —Ideas found in *Happy Birthday, Everywhere* by Arlene Erlbach, Millbrook Press, 1997; and *Birthdays! Celebrating Life Around the World* by Eve B. Feldman, Bridge Water, 1996.

Help the sibling who isn't having the birthday enjoy the celebration, too:

- Talk with him about the birthday plans before the celebration, and ask him how it may feel to watch someone else have a special day.
- Encourage him to think of ideas to help make the celebration a success for his sibling.
- Ask him to think about how he would like people to act at his birthday party so he can consider how he should behave at another child's party.
- Ask him to take on an important role at the celebration such as announcing when it is cake time or giving out party favors.
- Give him a lot of attention at the celebration.

> —Ideas found in *Positive Discipline A-Z (revised and expanded 2nd edition)* by Jane Nelsen, Lynn Lott, and H. Stephen Glenn. Prima Pub., 1999.

Birthdays

Help your child deal with the birthday let down that can occur after the stimulation, excitement, expectations, and gifts are over. Give him time to get used to everyday life again. Help a child understand that a birthday is one celebration among many throughout the year. On a calendar, point out upcoming special days and fill in any that your family is looking forward to.

> —Ideas found in "Post-Holiday Blahs" by Ron Pitzer and Sue Meyer, Online, Children Youth and Family Consortium, Available: www.cyfc.umn.edu

Help your child understand more about birthdays by reading about them together:

- *A Birthday for Frances* by Russell Hoban
- *A Birthday Basket for Tia* and *Pablo's Tree* by Pat Mora
- *Birthdays! Celebrating Life Around the World* by Eve B. Feldman
- *Happy Birthday, Everywhere* by Arlene Erlbach
- *Max's Birthday* by Rosemary Wells
- *On the Day You Were Born* by Debra Frasier
- *There Goes Lowell's Party* by Esther Hersherhorn

When to Get More Help

When deciding whether children need some extra help, usually it is best to look for patterns in behavior and skills that remain constant over a period of time. Birthdays are isolated and stressful events in the life of your child, and therefore not a good time to make general judgments about how he is developing and whether or not he needs more help.

More Help and Information

Books for Parents

- *Birthday Parties for Kids! Creative Party Ideas Your Kids and Their Friends Will Love* by Penny Warner. Prima Pub., 1998.
- *Child Magazine's Book of Children's Parties* by Angela Wilkes. Dorling Kindersley, 1996.
- *Kid-Tastic Birthday Parties: The Complete Party Planner for Today's Kids* by Jane Chase. Brighton Publications, 1995.
- *The Only Kid's Part Book You'll Ever Need: Hundreds of Great Ideas Plus a Unique Mix-and-Match Planner* by Gill Dickinson. Reader's Digest, 1998.

- *The Penny Whistle Birthday Party Book* by Meredith Brokaw and Annie Gilbar. Simon & Schuster, 1992.
- "Traditions: Birthday Specials" in *Practical Parenting Tips: Over 1,500 Helpful Hints for the First Five Years* by Vicki Lansky. Meadowbrook Press, 1992.

Boredom

Description

Boredom is the condition of feeling weary and dull as a result of performing uninteresting or repetitive tasks or due to a lack of stimulation. When children say, "There is nothing to do," they may be bored.

Realistic Expectations

- An activity or object that is ordinary or boring to you may not be to young children: an ordinary trip to the store for milk may be an adventure full of new sights and sounds for toddlers, or changing play to another room may be interesting to one-year-olds who haven't learned to walk yet.
- Young children have a limited ability to play by themselves for long periods of time. Most of the time, young children need help and attention.
- When activities are not challenging to children, expect boredom.
- Children who spend many hours a day passively entertained by television, video games, or computer games may have difficulty actively entertaining themselves.
- Boredom happens more often when children are sick, tired, or have played alone for what feels to them like a long period of time.
- When children are quiet or appear to be doing nothing, it doesn't mean necessarily that they are bored; it may mean they are involved in valuable pursuits: actively using their imagination, dreaming, or thinking.
- Many young children may not understand the meaning of the word "bored" even though they use it. They may be repeating something that they have heard but don't yet understand.
- Young children imitate what they see and hear and will complain of boredom if those around them complain of it often.
- Children who are used to adults doing or fixing things for them most of the time may be more prone to boredom and may need help learning how to play independently.
- Learning to be responsible for your own unstructured time takes many years to master.

Approaches

Set up your home to encourage independence and safe play. Make sure that your home is as safe as possible for your child to explore, and teach her rules about safety. Supply her with toys and materials that are safe and appropriate for her age. Consider choosing toys that she can use in many different ways: blocks can be used to make a house for her to play in, or to make a road for toy cars and trucks to drive on. When scheduling your child's day, be sure to leave free time for her to do whatever she wants: draw, look at books, play in any way she chooses, lay on the grass and watch the clouds, or just sit, think, and dream.

> —Ideas found in *The Parent's Journal Guide to Raising Great Kids* by Bobbi Conner,
> Bantam Books, 1997.

Boredom

Help your child learn how to handle unstructured time by naming what she is feeling and reflecting with her on possible solutions. Offer just enough help so that she can find her own initiative. This help may entail sharing your observations about what kind of activity (active or quiet) she appears to be ready for. Spark her interest with things she enjoys and if need be, help her begin: "What could you build with your blocks?" or "Where could you do some jumping?" With your support, your child can rediscover the pleasures of free time.

—Ideas found in *Becoming the Parent You Want to Be* by Laura Davis and Janis Keyser, Broadway Books, 1997.

Help your child learn to solve the problem of boredom for herself by first asking her if she has any ideas about what she could do. A child does not need an adult to fix every problem for her. Show that you are listening to her and support her feelings without offering your own suggestions for what to do. She will get the message that you are not going to tell her what to do and she will probably find something to do on her own.

—Ideas found in *Positive Discipline A-Z*, (revised and expanded 2nd edition), by Jane Nelsen, Lynn Lott, and H. Stephen Glenn, Prima Pub., 1993.

Allow your child time to daydream; she may be exercising a great imagination. Don't insist that your child who appears to be doing nothing should do something. Help her use her imagination and look inside herself for answers. Point out some of the things that you wonder about and show her how you find things to do in your free time. Limit passive activities like watching television, and build creativity and imagination skills to help prevent boredom from setting in so often.

—Ideas found in "I'm Bored," by Sophia Dembling, *McCall's*, July 1997.

Create a log of at least twenty activities that your child can do all alone. Get input from your child when making the log. Then, when she complains about having nothing to do, you can pull out the log and show her all that she can do on her own.

—Ideas found in *It Works for Us!*, contributed by Rebecca Robinson, Pocket Books, 1993.

To relieve or prevent boredom in waiting rooms:
- Carry paper, crayons, and pencils to draw with.
- Create a bag with special toys to be used only while out of the house.
- Bring a book of rhymes, a touch-and-feel book, a pop-up book, lift-the-flap book, or any book that invites participation.
- Bring snacks.
- Use the time to play games like "I Spy" or practice naming things familiar to your child.

—Ideas found in *Help! For Parents of Children from Birth to Five*, HarperSanFrancisco, 1993.

Help a child understand more about boredom and imagination by reading about it together:

 All by Myself by Mercer Mayer

 Harold and the Purple Crayon by Crockett Johnson

When to Get More Help

Children typically grow and learn new skills in their own time and at their own pace within the wide range of what is normal. Sometimes, children need a bit of extra help to keep their development on track, or to stay healthy and happy. Sometimes, parents need help providing for a child's needs or sorting out the best approaches to parenting.

Consider getting help for your child if she:

- Seems bored more often than other children of her age.

Consider getting help for yourself if you:

- Need help finding activity ideas and supplies for your child.

You are the expert when it comes to your family and child. If you have a concern, trust your instinct and find someone trained to help you: health care providers, early intervention teams, mental health professionals, parent educators and consultants, or telephone help-line staff. Consider talking it over with friends and family, too. You don't need to worry alone! Turn to "Finding Help in Your Community" on page 4 to learn about finding help near you.

More Help and Information

Books for Parents

- *The Little Hands Big Fun Craft Book: Creative Fun For 2- to 6-Year-Olds* by Judy Press. Williamson Pub., 1996.
- *Turn off the TV and—* by Anne Rogovin. Abingdon Press, 1995.

Articles

- "10 Ways to Get Your Kids to Entertain Themselves" by Mary Arrigo. *Redbook*, November 1997.

Boys and Girls, Gender Identity

"Mom and Dad"

by Tennae, age 5

Description

Children are classified by sex as male or female — boys or girls. Gender identity is the awareness of being male or female that grows over time. It develops from a variety of influences including how children feel about their sex, and the attitudes, ideas, stereotypes, behavior, characteristics that are attributed to a sex by parents, other people in the lives of children, books, television, movies, advertising, and other sources of culture.

Realistic Expectations

- No one can predict how children will behave or grow solely on the basis of gender. Despite differences between boys and girls, children typically have similar capabilities, behavior, and potential, no matter which gender they are.

- Boys and girls typically are not treated the same, even though they have equal potential to be caring, smart, kind, peaceful, independent, capable, responsible, resilient, and self-reliant.

- Stereotypes (general, simplified ideas about what boys and girls can do or how they behave) promote the false idea that boys and girls have different and predictable behavior and feelings based on their gender. Stereotypes limit the expectations that children come to have for themselves.

- Children start noticing gender differences at age two.

- Around age three, children begin to figure out what it means to be a boy or girl. They may prefer one adult for a period of time, ignore another, and then switch focus as they work to understand how they are alike and different from the adults of different genders around them.

- It is common for toddlers and preschoolers to prefer to play with children of the same gender.

- At ages three and four, children know whether they are boys and girls, but they don't know why nor understand that they will remain the same gender. A girl may think that by cutting her hair short or by wearing blue, she will turn into a boy. A boy may think that by wearing dresses, he may turn into a girl.

- Children between the ages of three and five are experimenting with and reinforcing their ideas about what it means to be a boy or girl. At this age, some girls may insist on wearing only dresses and jewelry, while some boys may resist crying and carry toy guns.

- Around age five, when children more fully understand what is typical behavior for boys and girls, children may become rigid in their thinking about boys and girls. If their experience has been that only boys play basketball, they may firmly believe that basketball is for boys only.

- Children learn attitudes about boys and girls from television, advertising, friends, society, teachers, and from what parents say and do. These can influence a child's play preferences, self-esteem, independence, and self-reliance.

- Research shows that there are differences between the brains and hormones of boys and girls, such as: girls are born with more nerve cells, girls hear equally well in both ears while boys tend to hear better in one ear, and girls understand visual information equally well with both eyes while boys tend to interpret it better with the left eye. Researchers don't agree on how these differences affect behavior.

- Different tendencies have been identified in boys and girls. They may be linked to physical differences, but are also affected by the environment and the way children are raised: girls tend to have better language and verbal skills, and boys tend to do better at tasks that require spatial reasoning.

- By looking ahead at some of the facts related to boys or girls as they grow from childhood into adolescence, parents may be able to take action in the early years to avoid some common problems. Reported facts:

  - A large number of girls experience a drop in self-esteem between the ages of nine and sixteen.

  - Girls learn early about the importance of body image for women in our culture: many girls feel dissatisfied with their weight by age six, and in 1996, The Council on Size and Weight Discrimination reported that 80 percent of ten-year-old girls had dieted already.

  - Peak onset times for anorexia nervosa are between ages twelve and thirteen, and at seventeen. This eating disorder, which affects far more girls than boys, has the highest mortality rate of any psychiatric disorder: 20 percent of those afflicted.

  - Boys are twice as likely to get hurt as girls, and their injuries tend to be worse.

  - Twice as many teenage boys die as teenage girls.

  - Twice as many boys are diagnosed as learning disabled, four times as many boys are diagnosed as emotionally disturbed, and boys with ADHD (attention deficit hyperactivity disorder) outnumber girls by six to one.

- Children need both male and female positive role models because they learn positive values from both genders.

- Boys and girls are individuals with individual strengths and challenges. When caring adults value children as individuals and are sensitive to the needs of their gender, children—boys and girls—grow up feeling that they are great and can accomplish anything!

Approaches

Respond to your child's questions about physical differences between boys and girls, and men and women, with honest, matter-of-fact answers. There is no need to explain everything to your young child who asks a simple question like "What do you call it?" Answer questions with language appropriate for his age, but be correct in the information that you give him: "They are called breasts."

—Ideas found in *Your Baby & Child: From Birth to Age Five* (third edition)
by Penelope Leach, Alfred A. Knopf, 1997.

Boys and Girls, Gender Identity

Raise your child to have positive values and traits regardless of gender:

- Show your child that jobs and roles are not gender-bound: Mothers can repair toys and fathers can be nurses.

- Provide toys, activities, and responsibilities based on the child and not on the basis of gender: boys can help sort laundry as successfully as girls can pick up sticks in the yard; girls can construct a building toy structure as easily as boys can play make-believe house.

- Help a child to notice and question when gender does influence the world around them: if a day care provider organizes activities where the girls are asked to participate in one activity and the boys are asked to participate in another, question it with your child; if a movie, TV show, advertisement, or book shows roles assigned by gender, point it out to your child and question it.

> —Ideas found in *Children and Their Development* by Robert V. Kail, Prentice Hall, 1998.

Create similar expectations for boys and girls regarding rules, behavior, and feelings. It is as common to allow boys to get away with being aggressive because they are boys as it is to expect girls to be passive about their wants and needs. Both boys and girls need to know that feelings are different from actions, and neither are related to gender. Allow children to have feelings without criticism but also help them understand that acting on those feelings needs to be done in a respectful way.

> —Ideas found in *Positive Discipline A-Z* (revised and expanded 2nd edition) by Jane Nelsen Lynn Lott, and H. Stephen Glenn, Prima Pub., 1999.

Consider the traits and accomplishments that you praise and value in girls and those you praise and value in boys. Are they different? For example, a girl may be complimented for how quietly she plays while a boy is praised for his ability to jump high. Some adults compliment boys and girls for different things related to the same activity. A boy who makes a modeling dough sculpture may be complimented for his achievement, while the girl may be complimented for how neatly she created her sculpture. Praise accomplishments when you see them.

> —Ideas found in *How to Mother a Successful Daughter: A Practical Guide to Empowering Girls from Birth to Eighteen*, by Nicky Marone, Random House, 1998.

Talk and play with children in an equal way, regardless of gender:

- Allow both boys and girls to express feelings. Talk to them about the feeling: avoid relating feelings to gender: "I can see that you look unhappy," instead of "Don't cry—you're a boy!" or "I'm sorry you fell, you unlucky girl."

- Dress all children in comfortable clothes to play in. Avoid fancy dresses and suits for play.

- Talk to both boys and girls about how they look and what they can do: "Gina, you can climb so high. Can you see Mike from there, he looks so dressed up in his costume!"

- Show children that men and women do lots of different jobs and have many different talents.

- Talk to boys about their nurturing side: "Carl, you're being so caring with that doll. I liked they way you gently put a bandage on its arm."

- Allow girls to be loud, too, sometimes, and celebrate it.

Make sure that your young child feels good about himself or herself; avoid boxing them into preset ideas of what they should be or do because of their gender.

> —Ideas found in *1,2,3—The Toddler Years* by Irene Van der Zande with Santa Cruz Toddler Care Center Staff, The Center, 1986.

Encourage your child through play to understand that gender does not limit who he or she is. Provide toys and activities that are not gender-specific: art supplies, music toys, building toys, etc. Provide toys that seem gender specific, like dishes or tools, to both boys and girls. Avoid limiting the kind of play you encourage in your child based on gender. Instead encourage both girls and boys to participate in a wide variety of activities that include everything from running and jumping to looking at books. Then, let your child choose and explore lots of different toys and experiences. Children may realize early on that they don't need to be limited by gender, but that they can choose, play, and eventually become anything they want to be.

—Ideas found in *The Parents Answer Book*, (Parents Magazine), Golden Books, 1998.

Begin to help a young girl develop the skills that she needs to become independent:

- Allow her to grow and develop in whatever time frame she needs. Talk to her and play with her on whatever level she is at.
- Encourage her to speak for herself. Teach her to ask for exactly what she wants instead of beating around the bush. Show her that she can ask for what she needs and still be loved.
- Let her express whatever she may be feeling. Avoid giving the message that it's not OK to feel certain things or that she shouldn't feel the way she does. She may learn that she can't depend on her feelings to tell her what's happening.
- Help her spirit grow and develop by exposing her to the natural world, by feeding her mind with the richness of story and myth, and by encouraging her to dream.
- Assume that she is strong and capable, and let her know that you think she can master many things. Encourage her to use her body and be active. Allow her to fall and fail, sometimes, and let her get up on her own so she can learn that she has the power to help herself. Don't treat her as breakable or helpless—she's not.

—Ideas found in *Raising a Daughter: Parents and the Awakening of a Healthy Woman*
by Jeanne Elium and Don Elium, Celestial Arts, 1994.

Let girls be girls by celebrating their individuality. Help her find meaning and magic in being a girl by creating a home where she can:

- Learn to recognize and be guided by her own authority and experiences.
- Declare her independence: test, explore, risk, and find answers on her own terms.
- See herself as the author of her accomplishments.
- Gain an understanding of her culture—how its theories of sex differences and emphasis on female beauty and body can limit her opportunities.
- Blossom as a learner and discover her unique style and strengths of mind.
- Find comfort and joy in a rich, expansive definition of femininity. Try out many interests and roles.
- Stay connected to loved ones—especially when she dances away.

Letting girls be girls requires a passionate belief that a girl knows herself best. This means making room at the table for a whole range of behaviors and experiences. We can champion her behavior as an *individual*—without devaluing any of her qualities, believing she was born to have them, or elevating them to sexual superiority.

—From *Growing a Girl: Seven Strategies for Raising a Strong, Spirited Daughter*
by Barbara Mackoff. © 1996 by Dr. Barbara Mackoff. Used by permission of
Dell Books, a division of Bantam Doubleday Dell Publishing Group, Inc.

Boys and Girls, Gender Identity

Boys, if nurtured properly, provide the world with indomitable spirits, humble hopes, courageous love, and un-flagging energy. What a boy needs to grow from a boy into healthy manhood is:

- Nurturing parents/caregivers.
- A clan or tribe—family including friends, teachers, caregivers, mentors, and a culture/community consisting of responsible media, church groups, help from the government, and other institutions and influential community figures.
- Spiritual life and inner life.
- Important work.
- Mentors and role models.
- To know the rules.
- To learn how to lead and how to follow.
- An adventure, and a best friend to have it with.
- Lots of games.
- An important role in life.

This list is a starting point in learning how to guide boys in a more positive, inspiring way to discover their masculinity, one of life's most nurturing and creative forces.

> —Reprinted by permission of G.P. Putnam's Sons, a division of Penguin Putnam Inc.
> from *The Wonder of Boys* by Michael Gurian. Copyright © 1996 by Michael Gurian.

Try to get behind the mask of feelings that boys learn to put on at an early age. Boys learn early to hide or bury sadness because our culture does not approve of nor expect boys to be sad. So it can be hard to tell when a boy needs help. To try to get in touch with a boy's emotions:

- Know that boys often say that everything is OK, when it isn't, or that they just don't say anything at all—this is masking.
- Allow a boy to talk to you about what is wrong without making him feel bad about himself or being scared to come to you.
- Help a boy to unmask his feelings through some kind of action rather than insisting he talk about his feelings; join him in his play or his task and allow him to tell you what is going on in his own time.
- Tell a boy your stories of times when you were young and got in trouble, or felt lonely, or share any other emotion that he might be feeling.

> —From *Real Boys: Rescuing Our Sons from the Myths of Boyhood* by William Pollack, Random House, 1998.

I have two boys, ages six and three, and I feel that by being an at-home dad they can see that mommies work and mommies stay home and daddies work and daddies stay home. So when they get older, they will be less likely to stereotype moms and dads and peg them as having a certain life choice.

—Peter Baylies, Publisher, At-Home-Dad Network

Help your child understand more about what it means to be a boy and a girl by reading stories that explore positive images of gender:

- *Abuela* by Arthur Dorros

- *Alexander and the Terrible, Horrible, No-Good, Very Bad Day* by Judith Viorst

- *Free to Be...You and Me* by Marlo Thomas, Carol Hart, and others

- *George and Martha: The Complete Stories of Two Best Friends* by James Marshall

- *Gina* by Bernard Waber

- *Imogene's Antlers* by David Small

- *Is That Josie* by Keiko Narahashi

- *The Trek* by Ann Jonas

- *William's Doll* by Charlotte Zolotow

When to Get More Help

Children typically grow and learn new skills in their own time and at their own pace within the wide range of what is normal. Sometimes, children need a bit of extra help to keep their development on track, or to stay healthy and happy. Sometimes, parents need help providing for a child's needs or sorting out the best approaches to parenting.

Consider getting help for your child if he or she:

- Does not know his or her own gender by four years, or refers to himself with the wrong gender.
- Seems overly curious about body parts of the opposite gender for his or her age.
- Acts out sexual scenarios.

Consider getting help for yourself if you:

- Feel confused, embarrassed, anxious, or shameful when your child asks questions about his or her anatomy or yours.

You are the expert when it comes to your family and child. If you have a concern, trust your instinct and find help from someone trained to help you: health care providers, early intervention teams, mental health professionals, parent educators and consultants, or telephone help-line staff. Consider talking it over with friends and family, too. You don't need to worry alone! Turn to "Finding Help in Your Community" on page 4 to learn about finding help near you.

More Help and Information

Books for Parents

- *Beyond Dolls and Guns: 101 Ways to Help Children Avoid Gender Bias* by Susan Hoy Crawford. Heinemann, 1996.

- *Great Books for Boys: More than 600 Books for Boys 2 to 14* by Kathleen Odean. Ballantine Books, 1998.

- *Great Books for Girls: More than 600 Books to Inspire Today's Girls and Tomorrow's Women* by Kathleen Odean. Ballantine Books, 1997.

- *Growing a Girl: Seven Strategies for Raising a Strong, Spirited Daughter* by Barbara Mackoff. Dell Pub., 1996.

- *Let's Hear It for the Girls: 375 Great Books for Readers 2-14* by Erica Bauermeister and Holly Smith. Penguin Books, 1997.

- *Things Will Be Different for My Daughter: A Practical Guide to Building Her Self-Esteem and Self-Reliance* by Mindy Bingham and Sandy Stryker with Susan Allstetter Neufeldt. Penguin Books, 1995.

- *Raising a Daughter: Parents and the Awakening of a Healthy Woman* by Jeanne Elium and Don Elium. Celestial Arts, 1994.

- *Raising a Son: Parents and the Making of a Healthy Man* by Jeanne Elium and Don Elium. Celestial Arts, 1996.

- *Real Boys: Rescuing Our Sons from the Myth of Boyhood* by William Pollack. Random House, 1998.

- *The Wonder of Boys: What Parents, Mentors and Educators Can Do to Shape Boys into Exceptional Men* by Michael Gurian. Putnam, 1996.

Breastfeeding and Weaning

"Mama pig with mamas to suck"
by Will, age 4

Description

Breastfeeding means feeding the child milk from the mother's breast. Weaning is the process of helping a child learn to eat without suckling from a breast or bottle, an activity that they have been enjoying their whole life.

Realistic Expectations

- Babies and young children like to breastfeed for comfort, closeness, and security, as well as for nourishment. Sometimes, they may ask to breastfeed out of boredom.

- Most children in the US are weaned from breastfeeding by six months, but the American Academy of Pediatrics recommends that babies breastfeed at least until their first birthday. The World Health Organization recommends breastfeeding for two years or longer, when complimented by other food.

- Breast milk continues to provide good nutrients and antibodies for children as long as they breastfeed.

- It may not be safe for a child to breastfeed if the mother is taking certain prescribed medications, has an infectious disease, or is using illegal drugs. A health care provider will be able to assess the safety of breast-feeding in these situations.

- Many experts agree that children are ready to eat and should be gradually introduced to a variety of solid foods by the time they are one year old.

- It is common for children who have given up breastfeeding to ask to start again when a new baby sibling is breastfeeding.

- Weaning from the breast or bottle is one step toward independence. The time at which children are ready to wean from the breast varies from child to child. Most pediatricians recommend weaning from the bottle between age one and 18 months.

- Weaning children before they are ready may cause them to start a behavior that they have already given up, like thumbsucking.

- Young children who are weaned suddenly and all at once may show anger or sadness; they may refuse meals or drinks.

- Weaning is a major transition in children's lives. Though it can be emotional and stressful for children, it may be a source of self-esteem. Children may take pride in mastering a new skill and growing out of something that they were dependent on as a baby.

- Weaning during a time free of other stresses such as moving, divorce, or the addition of a new baby to the family is usually more successful.

- When children receive the same amount of attention during weaning as when they were breastfeeding, they may learn that it is not just the breast that comforts them. They can see that though they may lose the breast, they won't lose their source of love and comfort, which is a warm relationship with the parents.

Approaches

Consider the many benefits of breastfeeding your child if he continues to ask for it, and make your own decision about what's right for you and your child. Breastfeeding can:

- Help meet a toddler's continuing need for comfort and security.
- Help calm a tired child who is having trouble settling down to sleep.
- Comfort a child who is hurt or frustrated.
- Ease the stress of traveling for a child who finds the comfort of home in breastfeeding.
- Provide nutrition and immunities for good health.

Breastfeeding children beyond one year is common in many parts of the world and throughout history and does not result in overly-dependent children. Consider your own needs and the needs of your child and your family. Try to ignore pressure from others when making a decision about breastfeeding.

> —Ideas found in *The Womanly Art of Breastfeeding*, (6th edition),
> La Leche League International, 1997.

Consider the language that you use for breastfeeding and teach your now verbal child words that you are comfortable with in public. Inevitably, your child will ask to breastfeed in public. To avoid embarrassing situations, teach him a word to use when he wants to breastfeed that you wouldn't mind hearing screamed across a parking lot full of people.

> —Ideas found in *So That's What They're For: Breastfeeding Basics* by Janet Tamaro,
> Adams Media, 1996.

Wean your child from the bottle at age one, or at the latest, by 18 months. It may not be easy. Start by substituting a cup for the midday bottle. Then stop giving the other daytime or evening feedings, giving up the bedtime feeding last. Don't give your child a bottle during the night or allow him to use the bottle as a comfort object to help him get to sleep. A drink or snack before sleeping may help your child, but be sure he brushes his teeth before falling asleep.

> —Ideas found in *Caring for Your Baby and Young Child: Birth to Age 5*
> (American Academy of Pediatrics, revised edition.) Bantam Books, 1998.

Wean your child from a bottle to a cup. When weaning off of a bottle, teach your child how to use a cup by tilting and bringing it up to his mouth. Use a cup without a lid and gradually increase its use. Avoid using a bottle as a pacifier. If your child is used to a bottle at naptime, substitute water for milk. Offer a cup of milk before bedtime, and try offering a story or rocking the child instead of giving him a bottle. If your child is sick during weaning, let him have the bottle and continue to wean to the cup when he is well again. Once he is off the bottle, put all the bottles away; out of sight, out of mind!

> —Ideas found in "Weaning From the Bottle: Help Your Baby Give Up The Bottle Between
> 12-15 Months" US Department of Agriculture.

Before weaning your child from breastfeeding, note the breastfeeding routine: when, where, why, and how interested he seems to be at each feeding. Identifying the reasons a child wants to breastfeed will help you decide how to wean. For example, if the child is asking to breastfeed mid-morning after he has had a snack and played alone for a while, he may be bored and want your company more than your breast. If he does not seem interested in the feeding itself, consider giving him time and attention instead.

—Ideas found in *The Nursing Mother's Companion* (revised edition) by Kathleen Huggins, Harvard Common Press, 1990.

When weaning your child from breastfeeding, try a gradual approach:

- Come to an understanding with him about where breastfeeding can and can't take place. Talk to him about the fact that breastfeeding will end sometime soon. Set a date in the future, such as the next time you visit Grandma. It's alright if you can't meet the goal, as long as the child starts thinking in terms of stopping. During weaning, be sure to continue to breastfeed if he needs it for comfort when he is sick or hurt.

- Talk about how your child is growing up and point out all the things that he can now do that he couldn't when he was a baby. Tell him that breastfeeding is important for babies, but not for bigger kids.

- Consider the places that you usually breastfeed. If it's in a certain chair, try moving it out of your home until weaning is over. If breastfeeding usually takes place in his room at bedtime or when he wakes up in the night, consider asking your partner to put him to bed or answer his night callings.

- Shorten the time spent nursing and eliminate one feeding at a time.

- Give him something to eat right before the time of day that he would ask to breastfeed.

- Rearrange your day so that at the times when he would usually ask to breastfeed, he is busy with something else: an outing, a visit from a friend, or a new activity.

- Keep your breasts covered in front of him—if he sees them, he may ask to breastfeed.

- Stay away from weaning advice that will make breastfeeding unpleasant for him, like putting pepper, dirt, or other awful-tasting things on your breasts.

Expect that both you and your child may feel sad, even if you have initiated weaning. Expect to give him lots of love and attention during this time, and look forward to a continuing close relationship.

—Ideas found in *The Complete Book of Breastfeeding* by Marvin S. Eiger and Sally Wendkos Olds, Workman Pub., 1987.

If postponing nursing, substituting foods and toys, and distracting your child with other activities just isn't working for you, consider putting off weaning for a while, and try again later. In a few months your child may wean much more easily, particularly if he'll then be almost three years old or older. Try asking your child to give up nursing on a particular date, such as his third birthday, or consider whether he will give up nursing in exchange for something else, like a new kitten.

If your child shows signs of anxiety after weaning, give him extra cuddling and plenty of time with new bedtime and naptime rituals. He may be satisfied to have a back rub as he falls off to sleep.

—Linda Ziedrich, co-author with Kathleen Huggins of *The Nursing Mother's Guide to Weaning*, and mother of three successfully nursed and weaned children.

Make the cup more desirable than the bottle when weaning your child off the bottle. Consider putting only water in the bottle. Offer milk or your child's favorite drink in a cup. Offer him drinks in a fun cup with pictures on it or with a straw. He may think the cup tastes better than the bottle and give it up more easily.

—Ideas found in *Help! For Parents of Children from Birth to Five*, a collection of ideas from parents edited by Jean Illsley Clarke, et al. HarperSanFrancisco, 1993.

Help your child understand more about breastfeeding and weaning by reading about it together:

- *Contemplating Your Bellybutton* by Jun Nanao (shows breastfeeding)
- *Crinkleroot's 25 Mammals Every Child Should Know* by Jim Aronsky (shows breastfeeding)
- *Eat Up, Gemma* by Sarah Hayes
- *Let's Eat!* By Ana Zamorano
- *Michele, The Nursing Toddler—A Story About Sharing Love* by Jane Pinczuic

When to Get More Help

Children typically grow and learn new skills in their own time and at their own pace within the wide range of what is normal. Sometimes, children need extra help to keep their development on track, or to stay healthy and happy. Sometimes, parents need help providing for a child's needs or sorting out the best approaches to parenting.

Consider getting help for your child if he:

- Shows any signs of tooth decay.
- Is having a hard time giving up his bottle after eighteen months.
- Is one year old or older and does not show interest in eating solid food.

Consider getting help for yourself if you:

- Would like to continue breastfeeding your young child, but are feeling ambivalent about it, are getting pressured to quit, or are receiving mixed messages about it.
- Are breastfeeding and use alcohol or drugs.
- Are breastfeeding and need advice about your illness or medication.

You are the expert when it comes to your family and child. If you have a concern, trust your instinct, and find someone trained to help you: registered dietitians, lactation specialists, health care providers, early intervention teams, parent educators and consultants, mental health professionals, or telephone help-line staff. Consider talking it over with friends and family, too. You don't need to worry alone! Turn to "Finding Help in Your Community" on page 4 to learn about finding help near you.

More Help and Information

Books for Parents

- *Mothering Your Nursing Toddler* (revised edition) by Norma J. Baumgarner. La Leche League, International, 1982.
- *The Nursing Mother's Guide to Weaning* by Kathleen Huggins and Linda Ziedrich. Harvard Common Press, 1994.
- *The Womanly Art of Breastfeeding* (6th edition), from La Leche League International. Plume, 1997.

Articles

- "Banishing the Bottle: Ways to Make the Transition Easy on Everyone" by Ellen Alcorn, *Parents*, October 1997.

National Organizations

- La Leche League International
  800-LA LECHE

  Web site: www.lalecheleague.org

  Call, write or visit the web site for information on a LLL group near you, and information on breastfeeding.

Web Sites

- Moms Online: choose the "Ask the Pros" menu to submit a question to the lactation expert.

  Web site: www.momsonline.com/pros

- ABC's of Parenting: enter "breastfeeding" in the search box to find a list of links to sites with breastfeeding information.

  Web site: www.abcparenting.com

- Parents Place: choose "Lactation Expert" from the "Ask Our Expert" menu.

  Web site: www.parentsplace.com

Child Abuse, Neglect, and Strangers

Description

There are four types of child abuse: physical abuse, sexual abuse, emotional abuse, and neglect. Children often experience more than one form of abuse at a time. Every state in the United States has a law against abusing and neglecting children, but the legal definitions of what constitutes abuse and neglect differ from state to state. Some definitions are common to all states.

Physical abuse includes the infliction of physical injury. It can include injuries from punching, beating, kicking, biting, choking, burning, shaking, or otherwise physically harming a child. The parent or caretaker may or may not have intended to hurt the child; rather the injury may have resulted from over-discipline or physical punishment.

Emotional abuse is treating a child in such a way that causes or could cause serious behavioral, emotional, or mental disorders. It can include constantly criticizing, terrorizing, belittling, insulting, and rejecting, and providing little or no love, support, or guidance.

Sexual abuse includes any sexual act with a child by an adult or older child. It can include fondling a child's genitals, anal or vaginal penetration, rubbing the child's genitals, making the child fondle genitals, any mouth to genital contact, showing the child genitals, or using the child for prostitution or the production of pornographic materials.

Child neglect is failing to provide for the child's basic needs for food, clothing, shelter, supervision, medical care, or education.

Realistic Expectations

- According to United States Department of Health and Human Services statistics, almost one million children were confirmed victims of child abuse in 1996. Of this one million:
  - Neglect was the most common form of child abuse: approximately 52 percent of the victims suffered neglect, 24 percent physical abuse, 12 percent sexual abuse, 6 percent emotional maltreatment, and 3 percent medical neglect.
  - It was estimated that over 1,000 children died as the result of neglect and abuse, and about 75 percent of them were under three years of age.
  - The children were abused and neglected by their parents in approximately 77 percent of the cases, other relatives in 11 percent of the cases, and other caretakers in 2 percent of the cases (10 percent were unknown).
- The American Academy of Pediatrics warns that spanking, hitting, shaking, and physically punishing children can lead to injury and abuse, especially when done in anger.
- Domestic violence, or violence between adult couples, often includes child abuse:
  - Children may be victimized and threatened as a way of punishing and controlling the adult victim of domestic violence.
  - Children may be injured unintentionally when acts of violence occur in their presence.
  - Often domestic violence escalates to include attacks on children.

- Alcohol or drug abuse in the home increases the risk of child abuse: The National Clearinghouse on Child Abuse and Neglect Information estimates that 50 percent to 80 percent of all child abuse cases proven by child protection services also reveal some degree of drug and alcohol abuse by the child abuser.

- Having been physically, sexually, or emotionally abused as a child can lead to:

  - Fears
  - Poor self-image
  - Feelings of shame, betrayal, and guilt
  - Aggressive and disruptive behavior
  - Passive and withdrawn behavior
  - School failures later in life
  - Drug and alcohol abuse later in life
  - Inability to trust or love others

- Children under five do not yet understand what's safe and what is not.

- Even very young children are aware of touch that makes them comfortable and uncomfortable, and usually try to express their feelings about it.

- Children can start naming their body parts around age three and can learn which ones are private.

- Preschoolers are not consistent about not talking to, taking treats from, or helping strangers, because they are still easily deceived and have a difficult time understanding the concept of who a stranger is and is not.

- There are many ways you can help prevent child abuse and neglect in your family and help any family who is experiencing it to stop the cycle.

Approaches

Prevent child abuse in your home. Make your home safe and work to foster trust, independence, and self-esteem in your child:

- Establish house rules. Make simple rules for your child. Start with a few "things we do and don't do." Discuss them with her.

- Discipline with short time-outs. If a rule is broken, discipline with a short time-out: a few minutes of quiet time alone, without play.

- Take five. When tensions and anger rise—in you or your child—take five minutes to cool down and ask yourself, "Where is my anger coming from?" Identify the real problem, then find the right solution.

- Interview your baby-sitters. Check out every one. Meet them before you hire them. Let your child meet them, too. If she is uncomfortable, don't hire that person. Set clear rules for bedtime and discipline. Do not permit baby-sitters to bathe your child.

- Never strike in anger. Hitting your child never helps and always does more damage. Never strike her in anger.

- Do not yell. Words hurt, too. Never yell at your child in anger. Do not put her down. If she breaks a rule, tell her what she did wrong and why that makes you angry. Be angry at what she did, NOT at who she is.

- Get away. When you feel frustrated, angry, or overwhelmed, vent your feelings positively—away from your child. Call a friend or leave your child with someone trustworthy. Get out. Exercise. Do not stay alone with your child when you are overwhelmed. Get help.

- Call a counselor if you have ever been abused. Many people who abuse children were once victims of abuse themselves and have never worked through their feelings about being abused. Have you ever been abused? If so, consider calling a professional counselor about it if you have never done so. The more you understand about yourself, the better you'll be able to help your child.

- Listen up. Let your child talk. Ask, "How does that make you feel?" Allow her to openly express ideas, feelings, and worries. Listen. Do not lecture. Be available. Encourage her to express feelings creatively by drawing a picture.

- Be consistent. Establish a reliable routine. A clear and consistent routine will help your child feel safe and secure.

- Let your "no" be no. If you say "no" to your child, make sure she understands the rule. Then act firmly and safely when the rule is challenged. She wants to know that your "no" means no.

- Do not keep secrets. Tell your child it is never good to keep a secret that feels bad or confusing.

- Use the right words for body parts. Help your child talk comfortably about her body. Use the proper words for sex organs: penis and vagina.

- Say "no" to drugs in your home. Forbid the use of illegal substances in your home. Alcohol and drug abuse increase child abuse dramatically. If you, a relative, or a friend are dependent on chemical substances, get help today—for your sake and the safety of your child.

- Take a stress check. Make an agreement with a close friend to check your stress regularly. Agree to watch each other's children when you need a break.

- Say "yes" to no. Give your child permission to say "no" to anyone who asks her to do something she knows or feels is wrong. Teach her to say "no" emphatically and then go tell another adult.

- Establish a private space. Give your child a place to be alone and call her own. Respect her privacy, particularly her physical privacy.

- Teach respect. Teach your child to respect the rights, bodies, and property of other people.

- Ask yourself some key questions. Take an honest look in the mirror and ask yourself: "Am I in constant battle with my child? Do I find myself wanting to hit my child? Do I think my child is acting out to spite me? Do I sometimes have sexual thoughts about my child or any child?" If you answer "yes" to any of these questions, talk to someone. Call a minister, a friend, or a professional counselor. Help is available.

- Speak love. Say, "I love you" and "You're important and special to me." Praise talents. Don't use sarcasm or kidding around to point out weaknesses. Be positive and affirming.

- Give a hug a day. Your child needs to feel your love through positive physical touch: handholding, an arm around the shoulder, or a simple hug.

- Know that quality time is quantity time. Love is something you do—so do more with your child. Spend more time doing things your child enjoys. Turn off the television. Do activities as a family. Eat dinner together at least three times a week.

- Take your child's place. Put yourself in her place and ask: "Is what I've said or done building my child up or putting my child down? Is what I've said or done really for my needs or the needs of my child?"

- Go with your gut. If someone or something makes you feel uncomfortable, go with your gut. Teach your child to trust her instincts by listening to her and respecting what she feels.

> —From "24 Ways You Can Prevent Child Abuse," Online, KidsPeace,
> Available: www.kidspeace.org.

! **WARNING!** Never shake a child and never harm a child with physical punishment. Shaking a baby or child under the age of three can cause brain damage, blindness, paralysis, seizures, or death. Even a small amount of shaking or a less vigorous shaking can severely harm a young child.

The American Academy of Pediatrics (AAP) warns that children who are routinely disciplined with spanking and other physical forms of punishment are more likely to become aggressive and to learn that aggressive behavior is the way to solve problems. Spanking or hitting can also lead to injury and abuse, especially when it is done in anger.

Teach your preschool child personal safety skills. She is still too young to be left alone and is dependent on adults to keep her safe. However, she is not too young to begin to learn some lessons about personal safety. Teach your preschooler to:

- Always tell the adult who's in charge where she is going before she goes into the house to go to the bathroom or before she moves to another sandbox in the playground. Your child wants to be near you at this age and know where you are; use her natural tendency to teach her the habit of always letting someone know where she is.

- Know the difference between good touches and bad touches, and to say no to the bad ones. Good touches include a tickle or hug when she wants, holding hands, an arm placed around her shoulder, a kiss on the cheek, or rocking. Bad touches are any forced or unwanted touches, including being kissed, tickled, or hugged too hard or for too long, hitting, kicking, punching, touching private parts, or being forced to touch or kiss someone. Children who have practiced saying no from an early age are more likely to say no in an abusive situation.

- Notice details when something in her environment is out of place and compliment her when she does. If your child is ever abused, being a good observer helps her to give accurate information to help catch and convict an abuser.

- Know the correct names for body parts and understand that genitals are private and only to be touched by parents or a doctor to clean her or check her medically. If a child is molested, knowing the correct body parts helps her to give an accurate and credible report.

- Recite her full name, address, and phone number. Explain to her what an emergency is and to dial 9-1-1 to get help during an emergency. She may not be reliable about calling 9-1-1 during an emergency, but if you teach her, there is a chance that she will be able to make an emergency call when necessary.

- Ask permission from you before accepting candy, gifts, or rides from anyone. She may have a hard time understanding the concept of "a stranger," but she should be able to follow the simple rule of asking for permission.

- Tell you if an older child or adult is asking her to keep a secret. Tell her that adults should never ask children to keep a secret. Be aware that many abusers use very ugly measures to get the child to keep secrets.

> —Ideas found in *On the Safe Side: Teach Your Child to Be Safe, Strong, and Street-Smart* by Paula Statman, HarperCollins, 1995.

Teach your child the difference between telling and tattling. Telling isn't tattling. However, many children and adults have trouble knowing the difference:

Children are *telling* when they:

- Want protection for themselves or someone else.
- Want protection for their property or someone else's.
- Are scared.
- Are in danger.

Children *tattle* when they want to:

- Get someone in trouble.
- Look good in someone else's eyes.
- Get attention.
- Have an adult solve their problem.

> —From *Telling Isn't Tattling* by Kathryn M. Hammerseng, Parenting Press, Inc., 1995. For more information, call 800-992-6657.

Child Abuse, Neglect, and Strangers

Prevent child abduction:

- Don't EVER leave your child alone or unattended in public places (in a car, in a store, in a public rest room). Learn to work around or just put up with the inconvenience. Children have often been abducted when they were left alone for just a minute.

- Check the references and qualifications of baby-sitters, preschool staff, or day care staff before leaving your child in their care.

- Become involved in your child's activities (attend and volunteer).

- Listen to your child and let her know you take her concerns seriously. Don't ignore her fears or make her feel bad for having them.

Protecting your child from a possible abductor is like preparing for a natural disaster. You hope it will never happen, but good preparation can prevent tragedy. Keep current records and identification of your child in a safe and accessible place (photo, video, physical description including height, weight, hair color, eye color, and unusual features like moles, pierced ears or braces). Know how to obtain her up-to-date dental x-rays and medical records. Always know where your child is, who she is with, and how she will get home.

> —From "Child Safety Tips," Online, Polly Klaas Foundation, Available: www.pollyklaas.org

Select and monitor child care situations carefully. Your child may tell you with changes in her behavior that there is a problem at child care, but she may not. Also, she may be unable to tell you in words. In addition to watching for clues from your child, check up on the child care situation now and then.

If you have concerns, stop and think about them calmly and carefully; it is easy to overreact. However, if you have specific reasons to suspect abuse or neglect, call the child abuse referral center in your community, and they can investigate your concerns.

> —Ideas found in *Touchpoints* by T. Berry Brazelton. Addison-Wesley, 1992.

Learn about child abuse and neglect laws in your state and county. Parents have a constitutional right to raise their children without interference from the state government, as long as they don't abuse or neglect them. However, the state also has the right and responsibility to step in and protect children who are in danger. The challenge of the law is finding a balance between respecting family privacy and preventing harm to children. In all states, child abuse and neglect are criminal offenses, but every state has its own particular statutes that define criminal abuse and neglect. Check with your local child protective service for more information about the laws in your area.

> —Ideas found in *Every Parent's Guide to the Law* by Deborah L. Forman, Harcourt Brace & Company, 1998.

Learn about the symptoms of child abuse and watch for them in *ALL* of the children you know. Any child at any age may experience any type of child abuse. None of these signs alone prove that child abuse is present in a family. Any of the signs may be found in any child at one time or another. But when these signs appear repeatedly or in combination, they should cause an adult to take a closer look at the situation and to consider the possibility of child abuse.

Generally consider the possibility of abuse when a child:

- Shows sudden changes in behavior: is fearful, has trouble sleeping, has a change in appetite, wets the bed, withdraws, is restless, shows regression in any area, or is aggressive.

- Has not received help for physical or medical problems brought to the parents' attention.

- Has learning problems that cannot be attributed to specific physical or psychological causes.

- Is always watchful, as though preparing for something bad to happen.
- Lacks adult supervision.
- Is overly compliant, an overachiever, or too responsible.
- Comes to school early, stays late, and does not want to go home.

Consider the possibility of physical abuse when a child:

- Has unexplained burns, bites, bruises, broken bones, or black eyes.
- Has fading bruises or other marks noticeable after an absence from school or day care.
- Seems frightened of the parents and protests or cries when it is time to go home from school or day care.
- Shrinks at the approach of adults.
- Reports injury by a parent or another adult caregiver.

Consider the possibility of neglect when a child:

- Is frequently absent from school or day care.
- Begs or steals food or money from classmates.
- Lacks needed medical or dental care, immunizations, or glasses.
- Is consistently dirty and has severe body odor.
- Lacks sufficient clothing for the weather.
- Abuses alcohol or other drugs.
- States there is no one at home to provide care.

Consider the possibility of sexual abuse when a child:

- Has difficulty walking or sitting.
- Suddenly is reluctant to undress or to participate in physical activities.
- Demonstrates bizarre, sophisticated, or unusual sexual knowledge or behavior.
- Becomes pregnant or contracts a venereal disease, particularly if under age fourteen.
- Runs away.
- Reports sexual abuse by a parent or another adult caregiver.

Consider the possibility of emotional maltreatment when a child:

- Shows extremes in behavior, such as overly compliant or demanding behavior, extreme passivity, or aggression.
- Is either inappropriately adult (parenting other children, for example) or inappropriately infantile (frequently rocking or head banging, for example).
- Is delayed in physical or emotional development.
- Has attempted suicide.
- Reports a lack of attachment to the parent.

If you know of a child who is in immediate danger of being abused or who has been physically hurt, take them to the doctor immediately and/or call the police. If you suspect that a child from another family is being abused or neglected, report your concern to someone who can help the family. Contact your local child protective services agency, the police, or call your state or national hotline number.

> —Reprinted with permission from "Educators, Schools, and Child Abuse"
> by Diane D. Broadhurst, copyright 1994, by permission of the publisher,
> the National Committee to Prevent Child Abuse, Chicago, Illinois.

Child Abuse, Neglect, and Strangers

! **WARNING!** If you are abusing a child, or worry that you might, ask for help immediately. You can get help to break the cycle of abuse. One good place to start is by calling Parents Anonymous at 909-621-6184.

If you see a situation between another parent and child that is getting out of control, don't just ignore it, do something:

- Strike up a conversation with the parent to divert attention away from the child and to offer support. You could say, "She seems to be trying your patience," or "It looks like it has been a long day for both of you," or "My child used to get upset like that."
- Divert the misbehaving child's attention by talking to the child.
- Praise the child and parent at the first opportunity.
- If you know the parent, offer to watch the child while he/she takes a break.

All parents get upset with their children, and sometimes a supportive gesture from another adult is enough to prevent a situation from getting out of hand. However, if you are concerned that the child is in danger, call the police immediately.

—From "Shopping with Children," Prevent Child Abuse Minnesota.

Respond quickly if your child is missing. Stay calm. Most likely, your child is safe, preoccupied in an activity, and has no clue you are worried. If your young child is missing at home, you should check closets, piles of laundry, in and under beds, inside old refrigerators—wherever a child could crawl into or hide and possibly be asleep or not able to get out. If elementary age children or teens are missing, check with your child's friends, with neighbors, or at other hangouts. If you still cannot find your child, call the police immediately.

If your child disappears when you are shopping, notify the manager of the store or the security office and ask for assistance finding your child. Then telephone the police. When speaking with the police, identify yourself and your location and say, "Please send an officer. I want to report a missing child." When an officer arrives to take your report:

- Give your child's name, date of birth, height, weight, and any unique identifiers.
- Tell when you noticed the disappearance and where you last saw your child.
- Describe the clothing your child was wearing when she disappeared.
- Tell the officer if your child has any unique problems.
- Listen to instructions and answer any questions as completely as you can.
- Provide police with a recent photograph.
- Write down the officer's name, badge number, telephone number, and the police report number.
- Keep a record of all information about the investigation.
- Tell the police that you want your child immediately entered into the National Crime Information Center (NCIC) Missing Person File. This ensures that any law enforcement agency in the country will be able to identify your child if found in another community. There is NO mandatory waiting period for reporting a missing child to the police or for entry into NCIC.
- Call the National Center for Missing and Exploited Children at 800-843-5678 and the National Runaway Switchboard at 800-621-4000.
- Don't panic or lose sight of the immediate task at hand, locating your child.

—From "About Protecting Your Child," Metropolitan Life Insurance Company.

Get help immediately if your child has been physically or sexually abused. First get your own emotions under control. Many parents feel rage toward the abuser and guilt that they were unable to protect their child. Right now focus on your child and get help for yourself later. It is very common for child victims to initially deny that they have been molested; talking about it may take time. Most experts recommend that a specially trained professional interview a possible child victim of sexual molestation. You should get enough information about what has happened so that you can decide whether it is a medical emergency. Beyond that, if your child wants to talk about what happened to her, listen, but don't interrogate her.

1. Be supportive and reassuring to your child. Tell her that: she is now surrounded by people who love her and will protect her; you will always love her no matter what; if someone has done something wrong to her it is not her fault; you understand that some things are hard to talk about; and there should be no secrets between you.

2. If you believe your child may have suffered pain, physical injury, or penetration, take her to the doctor or emergency room immediately.

3. Call the police. Be prepared to explain why you think your child has been molested and whom you suspect. They will assign an investigator to the case, probably an officer of the sex crimes unit or crimes-against-children unit of your local police department. Sometimes a specially trained psychologist or counselor will be available to interview child victims and work with parents.

4. Arrange therapy sessions by a trained professional for your child and for your family. Ask the police officer or the pediatrician for a referral to someone specially trained to work with child victims and their families. This is an extremely stressful situation for everyone. Therapy and support for the victim and her family help reduce trauma and improve your child's recovery rate.

> —From *Stranger Danger: How to Keep Your Child Safe* by Carol Soret Cope, Cader Books, 1997.

If you think you know someone involved in molesting or abducting children, call the police—*NOW!* There is nothing in the world more important than the safety of our children. *Nothing!* Molesters and abductors are dangerous people. It is impossible for the local police to watch over every child. Make a personal commitment to help protect all children.

- If there's a suspicious person hanging around places where children are, get a description of the person, their car, and their license plate. Then call the police. Molesters and abductors are out there, and they usually study their victims before they strike.

- If you know of a relationship between an adult and child that seems suspicious, report it to law enforcement.

- If you see anything suspicious, report it to the police. Don't wait. Don't talk yourself out of it. Your concern for children and your instincts could save a child's life.

- Watch for legislation on local, state, and federal levels. Be an advocate for tougher laws and sentences for pedophiles and child molesters.

> —From "What You Can Do to Help," Jacob Wetterling Foundation.

Help your child understand more about keeping safe by reading about it together:

 Beware of Boys by Tony Blundell

 Franklin Is Lost by Paulette Bourgeois

 I Like You to Make Jokes with Me, But I Don't Want You to Touch Me / Me Gusta Que Bromees Conmigo, Pero No Quiero Que Me Toques by / *Escrito por* Ellen Bass

 Telling Isn't Tattling by Kathryn M. Hammerseng

The Berenstain Bears Learn About Strangers by Stan and Jan Berenstain

The Better Safe Than Sorry Book: a Family Guide for Sexual Assault Prevention by Sol and Judith Gordon

There's No Such Thing As a Dragon by Jack Kent

Your Body Belongs to You by Cornelia Spelman

When to Get More Help

Children typically grow and learn new skills in their own time and at their own pace within the wide range of what is normal. Sometimes, children need a bit of extra help to keep their development on track, or to stay healthy and happy. Sometimes, parents need help providing for a child's needs or sorting out the best approaches to parenting.

Consider getting help for your child if she:

- Reports or shows signs of abuse or neglect as outlined by the National Committee to Prevent Child abuse on pages 212 and 213.

Consider getting help for yourself if you:

- Find yourself in power struggles that escalate into hitting or shouting.
- Have been abused or neglected as a child and feel confusion about how to respond to your child in the loving way you would like to.
- Suspect a family member, friend, or child care provider of abuse or neglect (reported information can be confidential).
- Worry that you might abuse or neglect your child, even though you have not done so in the past.

You are the expert when it comes to your family and child. If you have a concern, trust your instinct and find someone trained to help you: child protective services, health care providers, early intervention teams, mental health professionals, parent educators and consultants, or telephone help-line staff. Consider talking it over with friends and family, too. You don't need to worry alone! Turn to "Finding Help in Your Community" on page 4 to learn about finding help near you.

More Help and Information

Books for Parents

- *Every Parent's Guide to the Law* by Deborah L. Forman. Harcourt Brace, 1998.

- *Safe and Sound: Protecting Your Child in an Unpredictable World* by Vanessa L. Ochs. Penguin Books, 1995.

- *Safe, Smart and Self-Reliant: Personal Safety for Women and Children* (Foundation for Crime Prevention Education) edited by Gerri M. Dyer. Safety Press, 1996.

- *Stranger Danger: How to Keep Your Child Safe* by Carol Soret Cope. Andrews and McMeel, 1997.

- *Telling Isn't Tattling* by Kathryn M. Hammerseng. Parenting Press, 1995.

Articles, Pamphlets, and Books

- "About Protecting Your Child." Metropolitan Life Insurance Company. Request: 800-METLIFE. Web site: www.metlife.com.

- "It Shouldn't Hurt to Be a Child," and "Help the Hurt Go Away." Prevent Child Abuse America (see National Organizations).

- "A Street-Smart Guide: When to Teach Safety Skills." *Parenting*, September 1997.

- "Suggestions for Recovery of Missing Children." The Polly Klaas Foundation. (see National Organizations).

Hotlines

- Child Find of America: 800-I-AM-LOST (800-426-5678)

- Childhelp USA—National Child Abuse Hotline: 800-4-A-CHILD (800-422-4453)

- National Center for Missing and Exploited Children: 800-THE-LOST (800-843-5678)

National Organizations

- The Jacob Wetterling Foundation 800-325-HOPE

- KidsPeace For emergency help, call 800-334-4KID Web site: www.kidspeace.org

- National Clearinghouse on Child Abuse and Neglect Information 800-FYI-3366 (800-394-3366) E-mail: nccanch@calib.com Web site: www.calib.com/nccanch

- Prevent Child Abuse America 312-663-3520 Fax: 312-939-8962 E-mail: ncpca@childabuse.org Web site: www.childabuse.org

- Parents Anonymous (PA) 909-621-6184, Fax: 909-625-6304 Web site: www.parentsanonymous-natl.org Request or view online information about PA in your area.

- The Polly Klaas Foundation 800-587-HELP Web site: www.pollyklaas.org Request or view online articles, safety tips, and free safety kit.

Web Sites

- American Bar Association, Center for Children and the Law. www.abanet.org/child/home.html

- Missing Children Web Page. www.missingkids.org

- Safe-Child Handbook. www.kidsuccess.com/safechld.htm

Child Care

Description

Child care is when people other than parents or primary caregivers take care of children: day care providers, baby-sitters, nannies, neighbors, friends, or relatives. Although nothing can replace the parent-child relationship, good caregivers provide some of the important nurturing that children get at home: support, stimulation, love, security, and a safe place to play, eat, sleep, and grow.

Realistic Expectations

- According to the Children's Defense Fund, in 1998, thirteen million pre-kindergarten children were in child care each day in the United States.

- Regulation or licensing of day care does not necessarily ensure quality. Forty states don't require training for child care workers providing service in their homes. Most child care workers earn slightly more than minimum wage and there is often a high turnover in child care jobs. Training and adequate pay may contribute to a higher level of child care quality.

- Entering or switching child care programs can be difficult for young children. They may show stress: fussiness, crying, having more accidents if they've been potty trained, changes in eating or sleeping habits, not wanting to separate from you, having tantrums, or showing anger at parents, the child care provider, or other children.

- Young children have a very limited sense of time and need help understanding what will happen and when you will come and go: "After we get dressed, Sandy will come to baby-sit and I will go to work. After lunch, I will come home."

- The transition times of separating and reconnecting may be difficult for children. Children may cry or hang on to a caregiver when parents pick them up from child care, not because they are unhappy to see parents, but as a release of emotion after a long day away from them.

- It is common for parents to feel sad when leaving a young child in someone else's care and jealous when the child connects to a caregiver. Becoming attached to a caregiver is positive for children and may be a sign that the caregiver is doing a good job.

- It is never safe to leave a child under the age of five home alone, not even for a few minutes. Guidelines regarding how old is old enough for a child to stay home alone vary from community to community.

- The age at which siblings or other children are ready to baby-sit younger children varies. A child of one age may be responsible and ready to baby-sit, while another of the same age may not. Guidelines regarding how old is old enough for a sibling or other child to baby-sit vary from community to community.

- Children watch and imitate adults: if parents are positive about leaving the child at child care, children will more likely be positive.

Approaches

Choosing child care first requires making a decision about what type of full-time or part-time child care you need:

- Child care center or day care center
- Family child care from a single provider or a group provider in a home
- Care by a relative outside the home: grandparent, aunt, uncle, cousin, older sibling
- In-home care: parent, relative, baby-sitter, friend, neighbor
- Au pair in-home care: a foreign student living with the family, helping with child care
- Nanny, living in or out
- Employer-sponsored, on-site child care
- Nursery school, preschool, pre-kindergarten programs, extended day kindergarten, Head Start
- Combination of more than one kind of child care

—Ideas found in *Child Care That Works* by Eva and Mon Cochran, Houghton Mifflin, 1997.

Four Steps to Selecting a Child Care Provider

INTERVIEW
CHECK REFERENCES
MAKE THE DECISION
STAY INVOLVED

1. INTERVIEW CAREGIVERS

CALL FIRST

Ask...

✓ Is there an opening for my child?

✓ What hours and days are you open and where are you located?

✓ How much does care cost? Is financial assistance available?

✓ How many children are in your care? What age groups do you serve?

✓ Do you provide transportation?

✓ Do you provide meals (breakfast, lunch, dinner, snacks)?

✓ Do you have a license, accreditation, or other certification?

✓ When can I come to visit?

VISIT NEXT (Visit more than once, stay as long as you can!)

Look for...

✓ Responsive, nurturing, warm interactions between caregiver and children.

✓ Children who are happily involved in daily activities and comfortable with their caregiver.

✓ A clean, safe, and healthy indoor and outdoor environment, especially napping, eating and toileting areas.

✓ A variety of toys and learning materials, such as books, puzzles, blocks, and climbing equipment, that your child will find interesting and which will contribute to their growth and development.

✓ Children getting individual attention.

Ask...

✓ Can I visit at any time?

✓ How do you handle discipline?

✓ What do you do if a child is sick?

✓ What would you do in case of an emergency?

✓ Are all children and staff required to be immunized?

✓ Do you have a substitute or back-up caregiver?

✓ Where do children nap? Do you know that babies should go to sleep on their backs?

✓ What training have you (and other staff/substitutes) had?

✓ May I see a copy of your license or other certification?

✓ May I have a list of parents (current and former) who have used your care?

2. CHECK REFERENCES

Ask other parents...

✓ Was the caregiver reliable on a daily basis?

✓ How did the caregiver discipline your child?

✓ Did your child enjoy the child care experience?

✓ How did the caregiver respond to you as a parent?

✓ Was the caregiver respectful of your values and culture?

✓ Would you recommend the caregiver without reservation?

✓ If your child is no longer with the caregiver, why did you leave?

Ask the local child care resources and referral program or licensing office...

✓ What regulations should child care providers meet in my area?

✓ Is there a record of complaints about the child care provider I am considering and how do I find out about it?

3. MAKE THE DECISION FOR QUALITY CARE

From what you heard and saw, ask yourself...

✓ Which child care should I choose so that my child will be happy and grow?

✓ Which caregiver can meet the special needs of my child?

✓ Are the caregiver's values compatible with my family's values?

✓ Is the child care available and affordable according to my family's needs and resources?

✓ Do I feel good about my decision?

4. STAY INVOLVED

Ask yourself...

✓ How can I arrange my schedule so that I can...
 – talk to my caregiver every day?
 – talk to my child every day about how the day went?
 – visit and observe my child in care at different times of the day?
 – be involved in my child's activities?

✓ How can I work with my caregiver to resolve issues and concerns that may arise?

✓ How do I keep informed about my child's growth and development while in care?

✓ How can I promote good working conditions for my child care provider?

✓ How can I network with other parents?

—From "Four Steps to Selecting a Child Care Provider," Child Care Bureau, Administration for Children and Families, U.S. Department of Health and Human Services.

Child Care

Consider group size when evaluating child care; The American Public Health Association & the American Academy of Pediatrics recommend the following group size and child-to-staff ratios:

Age	Maximum Group Size	Child-to-Staff Ratio
0-24 months	6	3:1
25-30 months	8	4:1
31-35 months	10	5:1
3 years	14	7:1
4-6 years	16	8:1

The legal requirements for child care vary from state to state. Choose a small group size if you can. Smaller groups can impact the quality of care that your child receives. Also, associated with smaller group size: more cooperation from the children, a greater chance of a child becoming involved in an activity, a greater likelihood of a child talking without being asked, and a more positive outcome on a child's development.

> —Ideas found in *The ABC's of Safe and Healthy Child Care* by Cynthia Hale, Centers for Disease Control & Prevention.

Check out safety when visiting a program for toddlers; look for safety precautions:

1. Covered electrical outlets and wires kept out of children's reach.
2. A first-aid kit handy and well-stocked.
3. Non-slip carpet; sturdy and low furniture so children can pull themselves up.
4. Children always kept in sight; objects that might trip them removed.
5. Sanitized non-toxic toys without breakable parts or any parts that can be easily swallowed.
6. Fire extinguishers located on every floor and near the kitchen stove.
7. Smoke detectors located outside all sleeping areas and at the top of any stairway.
8. Posted evacuation plans and up-to-date safety plans readily accessible.
9. Enclosed outdoor play areas separate from those of older children; equipment safe for toddlers.
10. Adult equipment areas (garages, tool sheds, balconies, and the like) securely off-limits to children.

> —From "A Caring Place for Your Toddler." Reprinted with permission from the National Association for the Education of Young Children.

Allow your child to bring a toy, blanket, or something of yours to help him feel more secure in a new child care setting. A new place may seem less strange if your child has something familiar and comforting to look at, touch, and smell during the day. Ask your child if he wants to bring a piece of an article of your clothing or a picture of you. Consider calling the caregiver and talking to your child during the day.

> —Ideas found in *The Working Parents Handbook* by June S. Sale, Simon & Schuster, 1996.

Create a ritual for saying good-bye when you leave your child and a process for reuniting with him when you come back. A routine made into a ritual will make the transition from being with you to child care easier for your child. His knowing and understanding what is going to happen makes him feel more in control and less anxious. The caregiver can be part of the ritual and it doesn't have to be elaborate: when you come in, draw a picture together or read a story, then give him two hugs, a kiss, and say good-bye. Whatever the ritual is, it should be comforting to both you and your child and help you feel good when separating.

Think about how to come together again at the end of child care; it's equally important. Give him some undivided attention and understanding to help him with the switch from caregiver back to you. Consider taking a few minutes to talk about what he has done that day, read a story, or look at what he has made.

—Ideas found in "Making Child Care Even Better" by Sandi Kahn Shelton,
Working Mother, January 1997.

Help your child say good-bye when changing child care; switching child care providers can be a big event in his life. Don't underestimate the impact that saying good-bye to a significant person can have on your child. If your child is under the age of three, wait until a few weeks before the change to talk about it. Then, use simple, clear language to tell him about the change and what is coming next.

Consider ways that you can help your child learn to say good-bye. He can make or bring a thank-you gift, such as a homemade treat, a story he made up that you wrote down, a picture he drew, or a photo he's decorated of himself. In marking his good-bye in this way, he learns about showing gratitude to people, about good-byes, and last days. To help your child remember the caregiver, consider creating a book of his memories, including photos and short anecdotes about their time together.

—Ideas found in *Becoming the Parent You Want to Be* by Laura Davis and Janis Keyser,
Broadway Books, 1997.

Determine if another child or older sibling is ready to baby-sit a younger child:

- Age—is the child old enough to baby-sit? One set of guidelines from the Fairfax County (Virginia) Department of Human Development suggests that a child should be over the age of twelve to baby-sit, and that he or she should only be allowed to baby-sit for children over the age of four, for no more than four hours. Children over fourteen can be allowed to baby-sit infants and small children. Call your city or county department of human services or department of social services to find out what is recommended in your community. Age should not be the only or main factor in determining readiness to baby-sit.

- Physical capabilities—can the baby-sitter lift the child, handle feeding, take care of diapering?

- Maturity of thinking—will the baby-sitter recognize dangerous situations and make good decisions about how to handle them? He should be able to make emergency phone calls, if necessary, understand how to handle an emergency, recognize when he needs more help, and know who to call for help in the neighborhood.

- Emotional readiness—is the baby-sitter comfortable being alone at home and dealing with unexpected, possibly dangerous situations, if they arise?

Ask for good quality child care from your teenage baby-sitter. He should be able to play with your child and keep your child safe while you are away.

—Ideas found in "Guidelines for Baby-sitters," National Child Care Information Center.

Child Care

When using an in-home baby-sitter for the first time, train him; arrange for the new sitter to come early to orient him to your home, expectations, and rules:

- Give the new baby-sitter a tour of the home, showing him where the important things are: emergency phone numbers, first-aid kit, fire or burglar alarm system (if you have one), fire evacuation plan, and how to unlock doors and windows in case of an emergency.
- Make sure you leave important information: the address and phone number of where you will be, doctor's name and phone number, neighbor or relative to call in case of emergency, and the address and phone number of your home.
- If the baby-sitter is supposed to give your child any medicine, be clear about how much and when he should give it to the child.
- If your child is in diapers, show the baby-sitter how to change a diaper.
- If you expect a baby-sitter to use any appliances like the stove, show him how to use them.
- Make it clear what you expect the baby-sitter to do concerning bedtimes, meals, baths, play, and television.
- Clarify how you would like your baby-sitter to handle phone calls and expected/unexpected visitors.
- Be sure to tell the baby-sitter what the expectations are regarding snacks, watching television after your child is in bed, having guests over while baby-sitting, and making personal phone calls.

The more information you give the baby-sitter, the more confident he will be doing his job, and the more comfortable you will be leaving your child home with him.

> —Ideas found in *The New Complete Babysitter's Handbook*
> by Carol Barkin and Elizabeth James, Clarion Books, 1995.

Maintain a good relationship with your baby-sitter or child care provider. Make sure that everyone has the same understanding about fees, wages, hours, and expectations for care. Revisit your agreements and expectations from time to time. Be sure to communicate with your caregivers. Ask questions, provide information, and listen to them. If problems arise, deal with them right away. Perhaps most important, tell your caregivers how much you value and appreciate the work they do for you!

> —Ideas found in "A Nanny for Your Family...Answers to Questions Parents Often Ask About In-Home Child Care" prepared by the International Nanny Association, (www.nanny.org, 609-858-0808).

Help a child understand child care by reading more about it together:

 Adam's Daycare by Julie Ovenell-Carter

 Busy at Day Care Head to Toe by Patricia Demuth

 Shoes Like Miss Alice's by Angela Johnson

When to Get More Help

Children typically grow and learn new skills in their own time and at their own pace within the wide range of what is normal. Sometimes, children need a bit of extra help to keep their development on track, or to stay healthy and happy. Sometimes, parents need help providing for a child's needs or sorting out the best approaches to parenting.

Consider getting help for your child if he:

- Is distressed in child care after you leave him and is unable to become involved in activities for most of the day after a trial period.
- Has behavior problems in the child care setting that last for several weeks.
- Shows increased negative behavior at home that is hard to explain.
- Reports or shows signs of being abused or neglected in child care.
- Suddenly says he doesn't like his child care provider, or by words or actions begs not to be left at child care.
- Complains about feeling unsafe or about being teased or bullied by another child.

Consider getting help for yourself if you:

- Need help finding or paying for good quality child care.
- Find it difficult to communicate your needs and the needs of your child to the child care provider.
- Are not treated appropriately by your child care provider, or are not contacted for advice or instruction, or out of concern, when illness, accidents, or injuries occur.

You are the expert when it comes to your family and child. If you have a concern, trust your instinct and find someone trained to help you: health care providers, early intervention teams, mental health professionals, parent educators and consultants, or telephone help-line staff. Consider talking it over with friends and family, too. You don't need to worry alone! Turn to "Finding Help in Your Community" on page 4 to learn about finding help near you.

More Help and Information

Books for Parents

- *Child Care That Works: A Parent's Guide to Finding Quality Child Care* by Eva and Mon Cochran. Houghton Mifflin, 1997.
- *The Childcare Sourcebook: The Complete Guide to Finding and Managing Nannies, Au Pairs, Baby-sitters, Day Care, and After-School Programs* by Ellen O. Tauscher. Macmillan, 1996.
- *The Working Parents Handbook* by June S. Sale, Kit Kollenberg with Ellen Melinkoff. Simon & Schuster, 1996.
- *The Unofficial Guide to Childcare* by Ann Douglas. Macmillan, 1998.

Articles, Pamphlets, and Booklets

- *ABC's of Safe and Healthy Child Care* by Cynthia Hale. Centers for Disease Control & Prevention (CDC), U.S. Public Health Service, Dept. of Health & Human Services. Order through the Government Printing Office, Order Desk:

  202-512-1800, fax: 202-512-2250, www.access.gpo.gov

  Online at the CDC
  www.cdc.gov/ncidod/hip/abc/abc.htm
- "Baby-sitting Reminders," American Academy of Pediatrics, The Injury Prevention Program (TIPP). Call:

  The American Academy of Pediatrics
  800-433-9016, fax: 847-228-5097
  www.aap.org
- "The Super Sitter," U.S. Consumer Product Safety Commission. Call:

  U.S. Consumer Product Safety Commission
  800-638-2772, TTY: 800-638-8270
  Online at CPSC:
  www.cpsc.gov/cpscpub/pubs/4243.html
  Also available from the National Child Care Information Center.

Community Resources

- To find out if your state or county has an assistance program for child care, call your county social services department.

Government

- Contact the IRS for more information on the Dependent Care Tax Credit (DCTC) which is a federal tax credit for a portion of child care expenses. Call 800-829-3676 to order publications and forms, or download them from the IRS Web site: www.irs.us-treas.gov. Contact the department of revenue in your state for information on state tax credits for child care.

National Organizations

- Child Care Aware/National Association of Child Care Resource and Referral Agencies
  800-424-2246
  Web site: www.childcarerr.org
- National Association for the Education of Young Children (NAEYC)
  800-424-2460, fax: 202-328-1846
  Web site: www.naeyc.org

  Call or visit the Web site to get a list of NAEYC-accredited child care centers in your area.
- National Child Care Information Center
  800-616-2242, fax: 800-716-2242,
  TTY: 800-516-2242
  Web site: www.nccic.org
- National Resource Center for Health and Safety in Child Care
  800-598-KIDS (5437)
  Web site: http://nrc.uchsc.edu

  Call or visit the Web site for information about health and safety in child care and where to get help in your state for safety concerns.

Videos

- *Daycare Live!* Mother's Helper Inc.
- *Finding Quality Childcare.* Quartet Creative Series.

Childproofing and Safety

"Boy with a bandaide and tie"
by Will, age 4

Description

Childproofing is making a home, school, or day care safe for children. It means changing things, moving things, adding things, putting things out of reach, locking things away, supervising children, and using safe, healthy practices. Safety is the condition of freedom from danger, risk, or injury.

Realistic Expectations

- There are many reasons that young children are especially vulnerable to injury. They:
    - Need to touch, taste, feel, smell, and explore to learn.
    - Have limited understanding of consequences of their actions.
    - Like to imitate adults.
    - Get so involved in activities that they don't think past what they are doing.
    - Cannot judge what is safe.
- Young children experience and see the world in a very different way than adults. To them, everything is new, interesting, and intriguing. They do not yet know the difference between sharp or dull, warm or boiling, and poisonous or non-poisonous.
- Each year between 20 and 25 percent of all children in the United States suffer an injury that is bad enough to require a trip to the doctor, miss school, and /or require bed rest, according to the National Center for Injury Prevention and Control.
- Each year 40,000-50,000 children in the United States suffer permanent damage due to injuries, according to the American Academy of Pediatrics.
- Preventable deaths outnumber all other deaths in children over age one in the United States, according to the National Center for Injury Prevention and Control:
    - Car crashes are the leading cause of injury-related death for children between ages one and fourteen. Most were not wearing seat belts or were not in car seats, and 60 percent of children who died in crashes involving a drunk driver were in the drunk driver's car.
    - Drowning is the second leading cause of injury-related death for children ages zero to four. Drownings often occur when children wander out of the house and fall into a pool that is not fenced and locked.

Childproofing and Safety

- Most types of accidents involving children can be prevented by taking some simple precautions in situations that are known to be associated with injuries: hunger, fatigue, stress, illness or death in the family, pregnancy, births, changes in caregivers, moving, or visiting a new place with unfamiliar dangers.
- Injuries happen even to attentive parents' children during unexpected hectic everyday moments: the phone rings, the dinner burns, or another child cries.
- Slowly throughout childhood, children learn the difference between dangerous and safe things and require supervision, simple precautions to keep them from harm, and help in learning how to keep themselves safe.

Approaches

Childproof your home, and learn about ways to keep your child safe.

The following childproofing and safety precaution checklist is not meant to scare you! It is meant to inspire you to take action. Recognizing dangers in everyday objects and surroundings and taking steps to prevent injuries is something anyone can do. Your action might save a child's life or spare him discomfort or permanent damage to his body. It may give you some peace of mind as well.

How far and fast he can move, where he can reach, his understanding of the world, his ability to follow rules, and what attracts his attention change constantly. There are some general, sensible actions you can take that are based on typical ways that children think and act at different ages.

- 6-18 months. His curiosity has moved beyond himself to the world around him, and his ability to explore that world increases daily. His improved coordination and rapidly increasing ability to get around require constant watchfulness. Frequent room-by-room checking for possible hazards is extremely important at this age. When he grabs for an object that is unsafe, such as a purse or appliance, try offering something he can play with as a distraction.
- Toddlers. His mobility and curiosity, accompanied by the fact that a child at this stage will eat or drink even the worst-tasting substances, make poison prevention a critical priority. Use a firm "no" for really dangerous situations, such as a hot radiator, and explain why, "NO! the radiator is HOT!" At the same time, physically remove the dangerous object or move the child to reinforce the idea that "no" means "stop right now."
- Preschoolers. His ability to understand rules related to safety is improving, but he cannot be expected to be reliable about following them. While he is in the process of learning about dangers and safety, supervision and childproofing are still important, along with making safety rules, repeating them often, and applying them consistently. Explain why these rules must be obeyed.

Refer to this checklist frequently and rework your safety plan from time to time as the child grows older.

CHILDPROOFING YOUR HOME

☐ Keep a list of emergency phone numbers next to every phone.

☐ Assemble a first aid kit for both your home and your car. Keep each set out of the reach of children. Check the supplies from time to time, and replace used or dated items. The following should be in every first aid kit: roll of 3-inch wide gauze bandage, packet of individually wrapped 4-inch square sterile non-stick dressings, adhesive bandage strips, butterfly bandage tapes, thin adhesive strips, roll of absorbent cotton, children's acetaminophen chewable tablets or liquid, oral and rectal thermometers, petroleum jelly, ipecac syrup, tweezers, safety pins, 3 percent hydrogen peroxide, calamine lotion, antibiotic cream, bar of soap, flashlight, and antihistamine tablets or liquid.

☐ Try to see the world through your child's eyes. Get down on your hands and knees and search for small objects, dangling cords, electrical sockets, breakable objects, and dangerous corners.

☐ To prevent falls, install window guards that can be removed in case of a fire. Screens will not support a toddler's weight. Don't put furniture that can be climbed on underneath or near windows.

☐ Tie cords of blinds or curtains up out of reach or cut them off.

☐ Before putting your very young child down to play, get down on all fours yourself and search the floor for tiny objects, such as safety pins, buttons, needles, and paper clips. Vacuum rugs frequently.

☐ Search the undersides of tables and chairs for nails that stick out and rough surfaces that can cause splinters.

☐ Place gates at the top and bottom of staircases. Do not use accordion-style gates; they can trap a child's head and limbs. You may want to leave a few steps in front of the bottom gate so the child can practice climbing.

☐ Put safety guards in all unused electrical outlets.

☐ Do not let cords from appliances or lamps dangle within your child's reach.

☐ Put soft guards on the corners of sharp tables.

☐ Store glass and marble tables until the child is older.

☐ Remove breakable knickknacks from low tables.

☐ If the floor is slippery, do not put socks on your child once she can pull herself to her feet.

☐ Make sure that all rugs are taped down and carpets securely tacked.

☐ Test the stability of all furniture. Be sure it will not tip over when a child who is learning to walk leans on it.

☐ Latch all doors either open or closed. Swinging doors are especially dangerous. You may want to remove them until your child is older.

☐ Put decals or tape on glass doors at a toddler's eye level.

☐ Enclose radiators, floor registers, and other heat sources with wooden ornamental covers.

☐ Lock rooms that are not childproof.

☐ If you have a gun, keep the unloaded gun somewhere else, such as a hunting club, or turn it in at your local police station. If you must have a gun, keep it unloaded and locked away up high. Keep the ammunition locked in a separate place. Guns, especially handguns, do not belong around children.

Childproofing and Safety

CHILDPROOFING YOUR KITCHEN

❒ When cooking, use the back burners when possible, and turn pot handles inward so they do not stick out over the edge of the stove.

❒ If you can, remove the stove knobs when not in use.

❒ Remove dangerous items, including cleaning products, plastic bags, and sharp utensils from low cabinets and drawers, and put them somewhere that's not accessible to your child. Install "kiddy locks" (available at most hardware and department stores).

❒ Unplug and put away appliances when they are not in use. Be sure cords are tucked safely out of reach and out of sight.

❒ Be aware of your child's whereabouts when carrying hot liquids. Never carry your child in one arm and a hot liquid in the other—a trip could cause a nasty burn.

❒ Put all electronic equipment, such as the television and stereo, in closed cabinets or on shelves at adult height. Don't let appliance cords hang down.

❒ Use nonskid backing under throw rugs.

CHILDPROOFING YOUR BATHROOM

❒ Never leave a toddler unattended in the bathroom.

❒ Keep bathroom doors latched when not in use and if the door locks from inside, keep a key handy since it is easy for a child to lock herself in.

❒ Never leave an infant or young child unattended in the bath even for a second.

❒ Place skid-free mats inside and next to the bathtub.

❒ Keep medicines, razors, and other sharp objects and toiletries inside a locked medicine cabinet, including shampoo, toothpaste, mouthwash and hair conditioners.

❒ Cushion the tub faucet to prevent injury if a child falls against it.

❒ Keep toilet lids latched closed; locking devices are available. Teach older siblings to do this too, as soon as they learn to use the toilet.

❒ Make sure the trash can has a tightly fitting lid. Place razor blades and other dangerous objects into a trash can where there is no chance of the child getting into it.

❒ If you use electrical appliances in the bathroom, always unplug them and put them away (preferably in another room) when you are finished.

❒ Try not to use electric wall heaters. If you have one, tape over the controls.

❒ Set the water heater thermostat to 120 degrees Fahrenheit or lower.

CHILDPROOFING THE CHILD'S ROOM/S

❒ Check all furniture, especially second-hand furniture, to make sure it complies with current safety requirements and is age appropriate. New furniture should have the Juvenile Product Manufacturer's Association safety certification seal. Check furniture often for hazards caused by wear and tear.

❒ All fabrics in the child's room should be flame retardant: pajamas, sheets, and curtains.

❒ Cribs should have no more than 2⅜ inches between the bars, the mattress should fit snugly, mobiles should be removed (when the child can pull herself up to her hands and knees), bumpers should be removed (when the child can pull herself up to standing), and large toys or stuffed animals that can be used to climb out should not be in the crib.

❑ Once the child is about three feet tall, she should start sleeping in a bed.

❑ Be sure the changing table has a guard of at least two inches on all sides, and never leave the child unattended on the table or turn your back, even when she's strapped on.

❑ Keep diaper pails out of the reach of toddlers.

❑ Wait until children are good climbers—at least four or five years of age—before you buy bunk beds. If you buy them, make sure the beds are sturdy and well-constructed so they will not collapse; put the bed in a corner so two sides are walled in; place a guard that can't be rolled under on the other side; use a night-light by the ladder for middle of the night trips, be sure there are supports under the top mattress (the bed frame is not enough), and don't allow jumping or climbing on bunk beds.

CHILDPROOFING THE BASEMENT, LAUNDRY ROOM, AND UTILITY ROOM

❑ Store the iron unplugged with the cord wrapped around it. Never leave the iron unattended when in use and put it on a firm surface.

❑ Be sure all electrical appliances are well vented and properly grounded.

❑ Keep cleaning supplies and tools locked up and out of the reach of children.

❑ Never leave clothes to soak in pails or basins if there are young children nearby.

❑ Empty all buckets, fluid containers, and sinks immediately after finishing a task, and don't leave buckets unattended.

CHILDPROOFING YOUR GARAGE

❑ Be sure your child is away from an automatic garage door before you open or close it (there are new garage doors that automatically stop if a child or pet is in the way).

❑ Keep all chemicals and all tools up high in a locked closet or locker: hammer, screwdriver, paint, thinners, pesticides, fertilizer.

❑ If you have an old refrigerator or freezer, remove the door so children can't get trapped inside.

❑ Never allow the child to play in the garage or driveway.

CHILDPROOFING YOUR YARD

❑ Never let a small child play outside alone. Even a baby napping outdoors needs watching.

❑ Be on the lookout for things a child might put in his mouth: stones, twigs, animal droppings, or mushrooms.

❑ Keep children away from outdoor barbecues at all times, but especially when in use. If possible, cover propane tanks or lock them up.

❑ Check your yard for poisonous plants. Remove mushrooms, poison ivy, and other hazardous plants as soon as they appear. Teach your child never to eat things he finds in the garden unless you tell him it's safe. Common poisonous plants found in the garden and yard include buttercups, daffodil bulbs, English ivy, holly, mistletoe, tomato leaves, potato vines, rhododendrons, and rhubarb leaves. Brightly colored berries are especially attractive to young children, but many are poisonous. Be on the lookout.

❑ Teach your child to recognize and stay away from poison ivy, oak, and sumac.

❑ Avoid using pesticides or herbicides, especially in areas where children play. If you or your neighbors use these products, make sure children are indoors when the are applied, and do not allow children to play on the lawn for at least 48 hours after treatment.

Childproofing and Safety

❑ Don't mow the lawn when young children are around. Never let a child ride with you on a tractor or riding mower. Do not let children less than twelve years old use lawn mowers.

❑ Put lawn and garden equipment, such as hoses, rakes, shovels, and ropes away when not in use.

ANIMAL SAFETY

❑ Teach her that animals aren't toys. Most animal bites result from a child's rough play or teasing.

❑ Teach her not to bother a sleeping or eating animal.

❑ Don't leave small children alone with pets, especially when there is a new baby in the house. She may not recognize when the animal is getting upset or excited.

❑ Have your pets immunized for rabies and other diseases.

❑ Follow leash laws and keep your pet under control at all times.

❑ Teach her to not to approach an animal other than her own pet.

❑ Teach her not to run or make threatening gestures if a strange or barking dog approaches her.

❑ Teach her that wild animals are only for looking at from a distance and not for petting.

BICYCLE SAFETY

❑ If you decide to bike with a young child in a carrier, be sure the seat is securely attached over the rear wheel, and has the following features: a high back, shoulder harness, and lap belt, as well as spoke guards to prevent hands and feet from getting caught in the wheels. An infant bike helmet must always be worn and is even the law in some states.

❑ Never let your child ride on the handlebars of any bike.

❑ Wait to buy a tricycle until she has the necessary coordination to ride one and the maturity to follow your rules about when and where to ride (usually about age three).

❑ Don't buy your child a bicycle until she is physically able to ride one and to understand the rules of the road (usually about age six with training wheels).

❑ Insist that everyone in your family wear a properly fitting helmet that is approved by the American National Standards Institute (ANSI) or the Snell Memorial Foundation.

❑ Never let your child listen to headphones while biking; they're distracting and block out traffic sounds. Set a good example by not using them yourself.

❑ Make sure your child's bike is in good repair.

❑ Give her plenty of practice riding in safe places: paths, sidewalks, dirt lots, empty parking lots, or grassy yards.

❑ Begin to teach the child the rules of the road, but do not let her ride in the road or street until she is ten years of age.

CAR SAFETY

❑ Use a car safety seat EVERY TIME your child rides in the car.

❑ Always wear your seat belt yourself to set a good example.

❑ Refuse to move the car until everyone is buckled up and stays buckled up.

❏ Make sure the car seat meets safety standards, is right for the child's age and size, and is installed properly. If you have questions, lost the instructions, or need to find out about car seat recall, you can call the U.S. Department of Transportation's Auto Safety Hotline at 800-424-9393.

❏ Keep all children in the back seat.

❏ Never use rear-facing infant seats facing forward or in the front seat of a car equipped with airbags.

❏ Never let children younger than thirteen years ride in a front passenger seat that has airbags.

❏ Check metal parts and vinyl upholstery in the summertime to make sure they are not too hot for your child.

❏ Once your child has outgrown an auto booster seat (at about 50 pounds), be sure your car's seat belts fit your child properly. The shoulder strap should go across the shoulder, not the neck, and the lap belt should fit low across the hips, not the abdomen. If they do not, the child still needs a booster.

❏ Never, ever leave your infant or child alone in the car. A moment is all it takes for a child to lock herself in, shift gears, release emergency brakes, burn herself on a cigarette lighter, or become overheated. Also, a child alone in a car is a prime target for abduction.

❏ Don't drink and drive.

❏ Always walk behind your car to be sure the child is not there before you back out of your driveway.

❏ Never put children in the rear section of a station wagon or the back of a pickup truck.

CHOKING PREVENTION

❏ Cut or break food into child's bite-size pieces and chop foods with a tough texture into smaller than bite-size pieces: hot dogs or meat sticks.

❏ Encourage your child to chew their food well.

❏ Don't give your child hard, smooth foods such as nuts or hard candy that must be chewed with a grinding motion. Children can chew this way until about age four. Keep peanuts away from children under seven years.

❏ Don't let children eat or chew gum while playing or running. Teach them to chew and swallow before talking or laughing.

❏ Avoid foods that can slide into the windpipe, such as grapes, raw carrots or celery sticks, and hard candies.

❏ Choose toys and playthings carefully. According to government regulations, toys sold for children under three years cannot have parts smaller than 1¼ inches in diameter and 2½ inches long. If there are older children in the home, make sure that toys with small parts, such as construction kits, are well out of a toddler's reach.

❏ Keep rubber and latex balloons away from the young child; she may inhale them when she tries to blow them up or choke on a scrap of broken balloon. If you buy balloons, choose Mylar. Teach her never to put balloons in her mouth.

❏ Keep coins out of her reach.

FIRE INJURY PREVENTION

❏ Install at least one smoke detector on every floor. Test smoke detectors regularly (every month).

❏ Teach the child what to do in case of a fire: where to get out; stop, drop, and roll if her clothes are on fire. Practice every six months.

❏ Keep fire extinguishers in the kitchen, stairwells, and workrooms. Check them periodically to be sure they have not expired and practice using one before you need it.

❏ Put "child inside" decals on bedroom windows to alert firefighters to her whereabouts in a fire.

Childproofing and Safety

- ❑ Keep fire ladders in second-story bedrooms.
- ❑ Annually check electrical wiring for fraying, heating systems for safe pressure and venting, and fuses and circuit breakers for the right amperage.
- ❑ Keep space heaters away from curtains, drapes, and furniture. Only use them for short periods of time.
- ❑ Do not allow smoking in the house.
- ❑ Always put out candles and fireplace fires before going to bed.
- ❑ Never leave food on the stove unattended.
- ❑ Never smoke in bed.
- ❑ Have your chimney cleaned each year.
- ❑ Keep matches and lighters out of the reach of small children.

FOOD-BORNE ILLNESS PREVENTION

- ❑ Alert the manager of restaurants or supermarkets if you see unsafe handling of food: picking up meat with bare hands, failing to use gloves when handling baked goods; using a phone and then handling food without washing hands; touching hair, skin, and face while serving food.
- ❑ Wash your hands for at least twenty seconds with hot water and soap before you start preparing food, and wash them again as necessary while you're working. Always wash hands after going to the bathroom. Teach the child to do the same.
- ❑ If you have a break in the skin, use a waterproof bandage or wear rubber gloves.
- ❑ If you wear rubber gloves while preparing food, wash the gloves as often as you would wash your hands.
- ❑ Clean food preparation surfaces with hot, soapy water, then wipe with a weak solution of bleach (¼ cup diluted in 1 gallon of water). Plastic chopping boards can go right in the dishwasher for a thorough cleaning.
- ❑ When you wash dishes by hand, it's safest to let the dishes air dry.
- ❑ Boil dishcloths regularly and clean sponges with bleach. These materials can harbor germs unless kept clean.
- ❑ Keep your refrigerator at 41 degrees Fahrenheit or below.
- ❑ Return food to the refrigerator immediately after serving. Refrigerate freshly cooked food right away: don't cool it to room temperature first.
- ❑ Use leftovers promptly.
- ❑ Throw out food that smells "off" or looks discolored. Don't taste it to see whether it's bad.
- ❑ Buy food in good condition from traceable sources; be especially cautious about buying food from street vendors.
- ❑ Check that packaging is intact and cans are not dented or bulging. Don't look for bargains among bins of cans and packages that have lost their labels.
- ❑ Don't buy unpasteurized dairy products or fruit juices.
- ❑ Avoid fish and shellfish from non-commercial sources.
- ❑ Don't use raw windfall fruit (though it can safely be used when cooked for a long time such as in making fruit jellies and butters).
- ❑ Trim visible fat off meats before cooking to reduce levels of pollutants while at the same time cutting down on calories and fat content. Traces of pesticides and other environmental pollutants such as industrial wastes, when present, are likely to be found at higher concentrations in animal fats.
- ❑ Generally, choose mild cooking methods (boiling, steaming) to keep potentially toxic chemical by-products at the lowest possible levels. Many foods can be baked or parboiled, then finished off with just a minute or two on the grill to add flavor.

❑ If you have any doubt about your water supply, have it analyzed for bacteria count and chemical content. This is especially important if you have your own well water.

❑ At the supermarket, bag meats separately from fresh produce.

❑ Refrigerate or freeze raw meat as soon as you bring it home.

❑ Follow the safe handling labels on prepackaged raw meat and poultry.

❑ Remove giblets before you refrigerate or freeze poultry.

❑ Defrost frozen foods in the refrigerator, not on the countertop.

❑ Use separate cutting boards for raw meats and raw produce.

❑ When you use a cutting board to prepare raw meat, fish, or poultry, wash it with soap and hot water and rinse it with a mile bleach solution before using it again for any food.

❑ Knives and other utensils that have come in contact with raw meat should be washed and disinfected before being used again.

❑ Cook meat to the recommended temperature and use a meat thermometer if you find it difficult to judge whether or not meat is done.

❑ Beef and lamb can be eaten rare to medium, provided the internal temperature has reached 140 degrees Fahrenheit, the temperature that will kill most food-borne bacteria.

❑ Don't serve hamburgers rare. Ground meat is handled much more frequently than other meats during preparation and is therefore more likely to be contaminated. Hamburgers should be cooked until brownish-pink to brown in the center.

❑ Pork should be thoroughly cooked with no pink color, to prevent the spread of trichinosis parasites.

❑ Poultry is properly cooked when the thigh joints move easily and the juices run clear.

❑ If you stuff poultry, cook it immediately. Better yet, bake the stuffing in a separate dish.

HIGH CHAIR SAFETY

❑ Never leave the child unattended in the high chair.

❑ Always strap the child in securely, using both the waist and crotch straps, and position the chair far enough from walls and tables that she cannot reach them and push off.

LEAD POISONING PREVENTION

❑ Look for common sources of lead: paint in homes built before 1978; soil around homes that is contaminated with flaking paint or lead that was formerly added to gasoline; drinking water from plumbing with lead pipes or solder; antique or foreign-made furniture, toys, crystal, and pottery; some folk remedies such as Azarcon; and industries that release lead into the air.

❑ Clean up paint chips.

❑ Always wash the child's hands before eating and sleeping.

❑ Keep floors, windowsills, toys, pacifiers, stuffed animals, and all surfaces clean.

❑ Rinse sponges, mops, and dust rags thoroughly after cleaning.

❑ Remove shoes before entering the home to avoid tracking in lead from soil.

❑ Encourage the child to eat a healthy diet.

Childproofing and Safety

- ❐ In the morning, or when you haven't run the water for a while, flush out lead residue by leaving the faucet on until the water is as cold as it can get. Do this for every faucet used for drinking or cooking. Lead water pipes are common in old homes, and although lead water pipes are no longer allowed in construction, lead solder can still present a risk even in fairly new homes.

- ❐ Don't use hot tap water for cooking (hot water dissolves more lead from solder than cold water).

- ❐ If you must use a water softener, use it only for your hot water supply. Soft water leaches lead out of solder much more than hard water.

- ❐ If you have any reason to suspect lead, get more information on lead from The National Safety Council's National Lead Information Center at 800-424-LEAD. Talk to your child's doctor about whether she should have a blood test for lead.

OUTDOOR ELEMENTS SAFETY (COLD AND SUN)

- ❐ Make sure children are properly clothed for winter play: layering several pieces of clothing provides more protection against cold.

- ❐ Attach mittens or gloves with clips, not strings.

- ❐ Use hats and cover ears in cold weather.

- ❐ Limit time outside during periods of low temperature and high wind chill.

- ❐ Provide warming drinks at the end of outdoor play in winter.

- ❐ Take the child into a warm environment when she complains of feeling cold.

- ❐ Insist that the child use a sun block with a sun protection factor (SPF of 30 or higher on your child).

- ❐ Dress her in comfortable lightweight clothing, and include a hat that shades the face and ears.

- ❐ Have her wear sunglasses that provide ultraviolet protection.

PLAYGROUND SAFETY

- ❐ Keep the sandbox covered when it's not in use, especially if there are outdoor cats in the neighborhood.

- ❐ Change the sand frequently and try to prevent toddlers from putting it in their mouths.

- ❐ Be sure that swing sets, jungle gyms, and seesaws are well anchored. They should be set on either soil or rubber padding, not concrete.

- ❐ Check that swings are light but strong. The seat should be made of plastic or rubber. The set should be fenced in to keep small children from running close to the swings.

- ❐ Don't allow young children to play on trampolines, trapeze bars, or swinging rings, except in special children's gymnastics classes when an instructor is present. Do not buy home trampolines.

- ❐ Slides should be smooth with no protruding seams. They should not be made of metal, and the sides should be raised four inches. The platform should be protected with sides or guard rails. Be sure the landing surface is soft.

- ❐ Children less than three years old should not play on seesaws. Older children should use seesaws with others of approximately the same age and size.

POISONING PREVENTION

❐ Keep all medications and vitamins locked up high out of sight and reach. Put them away immediately after use, and don't leave them in purses or pockets—children have an uncanny way of finding them in unusual places.

❐ Buy products with child-resistant caps and use them.

❐ Never call medicine or vitamins candy when giving them to your child.

❐ Never leave cleaning fluids or the rags you clean with lying out.

❐ Keep cosmetics and personal-care products up high in childproof cabinets.

❐ Check on the plants in your home and yard to determine which ones are poisonous. Teach the child to never eat plants unless an adult says it is OK.

❐ Keep alcohol high in a locked cabinet, and empty and rinse glasses immediately after a party or gathering.

❐ Never smoke near a child because second-hand smoke is harmful to children, and tobacco products are poisonous to children if they eat them.

❐ Never store cleaning products or other toxic substances in old food containers or other harmless looking containers.

❐ Keep the Poison Control Center number posted by your phone. If your child has put something poisonous into his mouth, save it and call your Poison Center or doctor immediately.

❐ Keep syrup of ipecac on hand, and use it to make your child vomit up the poison only if told to do so by the Poison Center or your doctor.

POOL, LAKE, AND WATER SAFETY

❐ Supervise children in any water at all times: pails of water, toilets, wading pools, swimming pools, hot tubs, or bathtubs. Never take your eyes off the child while she is swimming: do not read, play cards, talk on the phone, mow the lawn, or do any other distracting activity.

❐ Empty or cover wading pools when not in use.

❐ When on any boat, be sure the child is wearing a safety-approved life jacket, even when sleeping.

❐ Don't allow running, rough play, or riding bikes near a pool. Do not allow glass or breakable dishware in a pool area.

❐ Do not take a baby in a pool until she is able to control her head, and never fully submerge a baby in water.

❐ Teach children to swim only with a buddy.

❐ Arrange for swimming lessons after the child is four years old, but don't rely on swimming lessons to save your children from drowning.

❐ Don't allow children in a hot tub.

❐ If you own a hot tub, keep it covered and locked.

❐ If you own a pool, fence it on all four sides and keep the gate locked at all times. Even in the winter, install a phone near the pool. Keep a safety ring with a rope and a pole beside the pool at all times. Lastly, use only battery-operated radios and other appliances by the pool—no electrical appliances—and learn CPR.

Childproofing and Safety

TRAVEL SAFETY

❏ Childproof your accommodations as soon as you arrive: a friend's or relative's house, hotel room, cabin, or campsite.

❏ Bring a small first-aid kit that includes: a children's pain killer/fever reducer, the medication you normally give the child for colds and coughs, motion sickness medicine, ipecac syrup, a children's electrolyte solution (for dehydration), sun block, bandages, antibiotic ointment, and baking soda (for marine stings).

❏ Before allowing your child to swim in the ocean, check water temperature and pollution levels. Make sure the water is free of jellyfish and other marine hazards.

❏ Encourage your child to wear beach shoes to avoid scratches from rocks, coral, and shells.

❏ Before traveling outside the country, check with your pediatrician that the child's immunizations are up to date and whether supplemental immunizations are needed.

❏ The safest way to fly is in a car seat. Set up car seats exactly as you would in your car, with infant seats facing backward. You will probably have to pay for the extra seat.

❏ Never let children under five fly alone; most airlines don't permit it.

WALKER INJURY PREVENTION

❏ The American Academy of Pediatrics strongly urges parents not to use mobile baby walkers.

> —Safety checklist from *Guide to Your Child's Symptoms* by Donald Schiff, M.D. and Stephen P. Shelov, M.D. © 1997 by American Academy of Pediatrics. Reprinted by permission of Villard Books, a division of Random House Inc.

Prevent carbon monoxide gas poisoning. Carbon monoxide gas cannot be seen, smelled, or tasted, making it vital that you take precautions to detect its presence.

• Purchase and install Underwriters Laboratories (UL) approved carbon monoxide detectors where they can be heard from all bedrooms with the doors closed. For added protection, install detectors near the furnace room, garage, fireplace, and any gas appliance such as a kitchen range or clothes dryer, or in rooms where people spend large amounts of time: living rooms, family rooms, and dining rooms.

• Clean, test, and maintain detectors frequently, according to the instructions you received at the time of your purchase.

• Maintain all of your combustion appliances: furnaces and ducts, fireplaces, wood stoves and chimneys, heaters, ranges, water heaters, and clothes dryers.

> —Ideas found in *The Healthy Home Handbook: All You Need to Know to Rid Your Home of Heath and Safety Hazards* by John Warde, Times Books, 1997.

Search for environmental hazards such as mercury, asbestos, pesticides, molds, lead, radon, solvents, PCBs, and air pollution. They can all negatively affect your child's health. Consider how many of these toxins are in your child's home or school and take appropriate steps to remedy any situations that are creating health hazards.

> —Ideas found in *Raising Children Toxic-Free: How to Keep Your Children Safe From Lead, Asbestos, Pesticides, and Other Environmental Hazards* by Herbert L. Needleman and Philip J. Landrigan, Farrar, Straus and Giroux, 1994.

Encourage your child to stay in her car seat without a fuss:

- Keep a police or fire fighter's hat for her to wear just for car time.
- Don't start your car until your child gets into the seat and is buckled in.
- Practice consistency. Don't deviate, not even once. Insist on using the car seat for all travel, not just in your car.
- Save special toys and books for your child to use only while she is in her car seat.
- Let your child check to see if you're using your seat belt, and then you check to see if she is buckled into her car seat.
- When you advance your child to a toddler seat, wrap it up and make it a special gift for her.
- As you buckle her up, play an imitation game where you do something like tapping your chin, and then she does the same.
- Recite favorite nursery rhymes and sing songs as you buckle up in your car.
- Place a sticker on her car seat that she can look at or peel off.
- Recite, "I love you too much to let you out of your car seat; I want you safe," as long as necessary when the going gets rough.
- Place the car seat where she can reach it easily and teach her to put the straps on herself. This involves her in the process.
- Start to leave earlier so there is time for her to do it herself.
- Talk about where you are going so the focus is on something other than the car seat and her cooperation.
- Have her pack a snack or a collection of toys in a lunch pail, and tell her that she can open the pail only after she is buckled in.

—*Help! For Parents of Children from Birth to Five*, a collection of ideas from parents, edited by Jean Illsley Clarke, HarperSanFrancisco, 1993.

Teach your child how to safely cross the street. Children under five years of age should always cross the street with an adult for several good reasons: her short height makes her difficult to see; she has poor judgment of speed and direction of sound; and her trusting nature may lead her to believe that drivers will always see her and be able to stop in time.

Still, she should be taught to respect the street as soon as she is old enough to walk around outside.

- Model and practice how to cross the street with her over and over again.
- Train her to always stop at the curb, even when there are no cars on the street. This habit will lower the chance of her dashing into the street when her mind is on something else.
- Teach her to look and listen for approaching cars by turning left, then right, then left again. You might say to the very young child while you demonstrate, "this way, that way, and this way again."
- Show her how to wait until the street is clear, and then walk, don't run, quickly across to the other side. Tell her not to dawdle, stop, or cross on the diagonal.

—Ideas found in *To Save a Child: Things You Can Do to Protect, Nurture & Teach Our Children* by Audrey E. Talkington and Barbara Albers Hill, Avery Publishing Group, 1993.

Childproofing and Safety

Follow basic safety rules to avoid becoming the victims of a crime. Often, the people who are looking for a victim to molest, steal a car from, abduct, or rob look for someone who looks vulnerable, or a home that appears easy to enter. Don't be that person. Secure your home and car:

- Lock the doors and windows of your home with high-quality locks.
- Make sure all of the entries to your home are well lit.
- Consider installing an alarm system in your home.
- Make it easy to get to a telephone from every room.
- Help organize a "block watch" program in your neighborhood; call your local police department for more information.
- Never leave your child alone in the car, even while you "keep your eye on her," for a minute.
- Keep your car doors locked at all times.

> —Ideas found in *Raising Safe Kids in an Unsafe World: 30 Simple Ways to Prevent Your Child From Becoming Lost, Abducted, or Abused* by Jan Wagner, Avon Books, 1996.

Teach your child to be careful with shopping carts. Each year over 20,000 children ages five and under are treated in hospital emergency rooms for injuries related to shopping carts, including falls and cuts. Falls from carts cause most injuries. Prevent shopping cart accidents:

- Use safety belts to restrain your child in shopping carts.
- Stay close to the cart.
- Do not let your child stand in the cart or push it.

> —Ideas found in "Shopping Cart Safety for Children," National Safe Kids Campaign.

Teach your child sled safety:

- Buy sledding equipment that is sturdy and well constructed.
- Choose gentle slopes that are free of ice and obstacles.
- Have her sit up straight, don't let her go down the hill headfirst or lying down.
- Don't let her sled across streets or driveways.
- Teach her how to stay out of the main path on the way up the hill.
- Always supervise her.

> —Ideas found in "Cold-Weather Smarts" by Rachelle Vander Schaaf, *Sesame Street Parents*, December 1997/January 1998.

! **WARNING!** Many products for children are found to be unsafe after they have been used in homes. Watch for notices of recalls regarding toys and equipment for children.

BE PREPARED FOR AN EMERGENCY.

- Keep information about yourself in a handy place at work. Keep information about you and your family in a handy place at home, such as on the refrigerator door or in your automobile glove compartment.

- Keep medical and insurance records up-to-date.

- Find out if your community is served by an emergency 9-1-1 telephone number. If it is not, look up the numbers for the police, fire department, EMS, and poison control center. Emergency numbers are usually listed in the front of the telephone book. Teach everyone in your home how and when to use these numbers.

- Keep emergency telephone numbers in a handy place, such as by the telephone or in the first aid kit. Include home and work numbers of family members and friends who can help. Be sure to keep both lists current.

- Keep a first aid kit handy in your home, automobile, workplace, and recreation area.

- Learn and practice first aid skills.

- Make sure your house or apartment number is easy to read. Numerals are easier to read than spelled-out numbers.

- Wear a medical alert tag if you have a potentially serious medical condition, such as epilepsy, diabetes, heart disease, or allergies.

—Courtesy of the American Red Cross. All Rights Reserved in all Countries.

WHEN TO CALL EMS

If the victim is unconscious, call 9-1-1 or your local emergency number immediately. Sometimes a conscious victim will tell you not to call an ambulance, and you may not be sure what to do. Call for an ambulance anyway if the victim:

- Is or becomes unconscious.
- Has trouble breathing or is breathing in a strange way.
- Has chest pain or pressure.
- Is bleeding severely.
- Has pressure or pain in the abdomen that does not go away.
- Is vomiting or passing blood.
- Has seizures, a severe headache, or slurred speech.
- Appears to have been poisoned.
- Has injuries to the head, neck, or back.
- Has possible broken bones.

ALSO CALL

Also call for any of these situations:

- Fire or explosion
- Downed electrical wires
- Swiftly moving or rapidly rising water
- Presence of poisonous gas
- Vehicle collisions
- Victims who cannot be moved easily

—Courtesy of the American Red Cross. All Rights Reserved in all Countries.

HOW TO CALL EMS

1 Call the emergency number. The number is 9-1-1 in many communities. Your work place may have its own emergency number to call. The person at the other end may be responsible for relaying information to emergency medical personnel in the surrounding community. Dial 0 (the Operator) if it is the assigned number in your facility or if you do not know the correct emergency number.

2 Give the dispatcher or operator the necessary information. Answer any questions he or she might ask. Most dispatchers or operators will ask:

- The exact location or address of the emergency. Include the name of the city or town, nearby intersections, landmarks, the building name, the floor, and the room number.

- The telephone number from which the call is being made.

- The caller's name.

- What happened—for example, a motor vehicle collision, fire, or fall.

- How many people are involved.

- The condition of the victim(s)—for example, unconsciousness or chest pains.

- What help (first aid) is being given.

3 Do not hang up until the dispatcher or operator states he or she has the necessary information. The dispatcher may be able to tell how to best care for the victim.

4 Return to the victim, and continue to care for the victim or offer assistance.

With a life-threatening emergency, the survival of a victim often depends on both professional medical help and the care you can provide. You will have to use your best judgment, based on knowledge of your surroundings and your training about when to call. Generally, *call FAST!*

—Courtesy of the American Red Cross. All Rights Reserved in all Countries.

Childproofing and Safety

Teach your child how to call for help if she's frightened, lost, hurt, or sick, or if someone else needs help. Children under five can not be expected to be reliable in reacting to emergencies, but children as young as three have called for help in emergencies. Begin to prepare your child by teaching her how to help in an emergency:

- Write the emergency number for your area near every phone in your home. Show it to your child. Program it into auto-dial or speed dial if you have one.
- As soon as she can learn, teach your child her home address.
- Have your child practice for an emergency. Teach her to:
    1. Dial the emergency number.
    2. Say, "I need help, my address is _____, and the problem is _____."
    3. Stay on the line until the operator says to hang up.

> —Ideas found in "Getting Help in a Crisis" by Terri Adams, Online, ParentTime,
> Available: www.parenttime.com.

Practice simple rituals to find the courage to let your child go out into a dangerous world. Parents of all cultures turn to some sort of rituals, or simple and repeated actions, to hold and keep the fears that they have for their children. Some rituals come from religion, some from folk practices, and others are created by parents as they go along, using whatever works for them. Most parents who use the rituals believe that doing so will help them manage their fears and protect their children:

- Prayers and blessings.
- Telling stories of sandmen, elves, fairies, and guardian angels.
- Imagining the child in safety.
- Singing lullabies and other bedtime rituals.
- Tucking the child in at night and checking on her after she is asleep.
- Keeping the child's picture at home, at the office, or in a wallet.
- Encouraging the child to bond with a stuffed animal or blanket.
- Calling out the same warnings, day after day: "Look both ways," "Buckle up," "Put on your hat."
- Phoning to the child when she is away or in child care.
- Naming the child's legal guardians or godparents.
- Working at making the world a better place for all children.

Rituals are not meant to replace things like teaching safety, being careful, and seeking medical attention when necessary. You still have to provide seat belts, helmets, and many, many lessons.

> —Ideas found in *Safe and Sound: Protecting Your Child in an Unpredictable World* by
> Vanessa L. Ochs, Penguin Books, 1995.

Help your child understand more about safety by reading about it together:

Dinosaurs, Beware! by Marc Brown and Stephen Krensky

Officer Buckle and Gloria by Peggy Rathmann

When to Get More Help

Children typically grow and learn new skills in their own time and at their own pace within the wide range of what is normal. Sometimes, children need a bit of extra help to keep their development on track, or to stay healthy and happy. Sometimes, parents need help in providing for a child's needs or sorting out the best approaches to parenting.

Consider getting help for your child if she:

- Frequently acts without regard to safety a lot more than other children her age.
- Reports being abused in any way.
- Reports conversations with or being approached by strangers in your yard, playground, friend's home, or child care setting.

Consider getting help for yourself if you:

- Need help paying for a car seat or any of the tools to childproof your home.
- Need help childproofing your home or inspecting it for hazards.

You are the expert when it comes to your family and child. If you have a concern, trust your instinct, and find someone trained to help you: health care providers, early intervention teams, mental health professionals, parent educators and consultants, or telephone help-line staff. Think about talking it over with friends and family, too. You don't need to worry alone! Turn to "Finding Help in Your Community" on page 4 to learn about finding help near you.

More Help and Information

Books for Parents

- *The Complete Guide to Making Your Home Safe* by Dave Heberle and Richard M. Scutella. Betterway Books, 1995.

- *Fifty Ways to Keep Your Child Safe: Physically, Emotionally, Medically, Environmentally* by Susan K. Golant. Contemporary Books, 1992.

- *Infant and Child CPR* by American National Red Cross. Mosby Lifeline, 1993.

- *Kidsafe: Everything You Need to Know to Make Your Child's Environment Safe* by Rae Tyson. Times Books, 1995.

- *Raising Children Toxic-Free: How to Keep Your Children Safe From Lead, Asbestos, Pesticides, and Other Environmental Hazards* by Herbert L. Needleman and Philip J. Landrigan. Farrar, Straus and Giroux, 1994.

- *Standard First Aid* by American National Red Cross. Mosby Lifeline, 1993.

- *To Save a Child: Things You Can Do To Protect, Nurture & Teach Our Children* by Audrey E. Talkington and Barbara Abers Hill. Avery Publishing Group, 1993.

Articles, Pamphlets, & Booklets

- "About Protecting Your Child," MetLife. Call: 800-METLIFE.

- "Air Bag Safety: Buckle Everyone! Children in Back!," Air Bag Safety Campaign, National Safety Council. (See National Organizations)

- "Protecting Children in Motor Vehicles: A Matter of Restraint," and "Precious Cargo: Protecting the Children Who Ride With You," American Medical Association and General Motors. Call 800-247-9168.

- "Safe Kids Buckle Up," National Safe Kids Campaign. Call 800-441-1888.

- The Injury Prevention Program (TIPP), American Academy of Pediatrics. Call or view online:
AAP Publications
800-433-9016, Fax: 847-228-1281
Web site: www.aap.org/family/tippmain.htm

- "Your Family Disaster Plan" and "The Emergency Preparedness Checklist" Family Emergency Preparedness, Family Protections Program, Federal Emergency Management Agency and the American Red Cross. Contact FEMA, your state or local emergency management agency or your local chapter of the American Red Cross.

Community Resources

- Poison Control: look in your local phone book to find a poison control center near you. Ask if they distribute "Mr. Yuk" stickers to put on dangerous products or poison prevention kits for parents.

Government

- Federal Emergency Management Agency (FEMA)
Web site: www.fema.gov

  FEMA for Kids: www.fema.gocv/kids/. Visit web site for safety and preparedness information, games and activities for children.

- U.S. Consumer Product Safety Commission
800-638-2772, 800-638-8270 (speech and hearing impaired)

  Call to report an unsafe consumer product or a product-related injury for publication listings.

- U.S. Dept. of Transportation, National Highway Traffic Safety Administration
800-424-9393
Web site: www. nhtsa.dot.gov

  Call for child passenger safety information, including "Safetyville: How to Make Your Child's World A Safer Place."

Mail Order Catalogs

- The Catalog for Safe Beginnings
  800-598-8911 Web site: www.safebeginnings.com

- The Right Start Catalog
  800-LITTLE-1 (800-548-8531)
  Web site: www.rightstart.com

National Organizations

- For a Safer America Coalition, Be Cool About Fire
  Safety Program
  Write for information and "Deputy Fire Marshal" kit:
  The Advertising Council
  1233 20th St. N.W., Washington, DC 20036

- National Safety Council
  800-621-7619
  Web site: www.nsc.org

- Children's Safety Network National Injury and Violence
  Prevention Resource Center
  617-969-7101 ext. 2207, Fax: 617-244-3436
  800-255-4276
  Web site: www.edc.orsg/HHD/csn

- National SAFE KIDS Campaign
  202-662-0600, Fax: 202-393-2072
  E-mail: info@safekids.org
  Web site: www.safekids.org

  Call or write for information on preventable childhood
  injuries.

- Window Covering Safety Council
  800-506-4636
  Call for a free looped window cords repair kit.

Recall Notices

Find information about consumer products that have been
recalled:

- *Consumer Reports* Magazine.

- Kidsource Online. Web site: www.kidsource.com

- ABC's of Parenting. Web site: www.abcparenting.com

- U.S. Consumer Gateway.
  Web site: www.consumer.gov/productsafety.htm

- U.S. Consumer Product Safety Commission

Videos

- *Child Safety Outdoors.* KidSafety of America.

- *Officer Buckle and Gloria.* Weston Woods.

Web Sites

- Child Passenger Safety Web.
  www.childsafety.org

- U.S. Consumer Gateway.
  www.consumer.gov/productsafety.htm

Communication

"What I like best about my body:
I like my ears because
I like to talk"

by Jakob, age 4

Description

Communication is the way people share information or messages with each other. It's what you say and how you say it through words, tone of voice, rhythm of the language, song, gestures, hand signals, body posture, clothing choices, facial expressions, listening, play, dance, art, and even silence. Communication is what gives people a chance to express hopes, dreams, problems, ideas, opinions, and feelings.

Realistic Expectations

- It's never too early to start talking to children. They need to hear language and words in order to learn the skills of communication.
- Young children learn to talk and communicate at individual times and at different rates. Typically:
  - Babies may not understand all the words but they do tune in to the feelings and moods of the message.
  - Children typically can understand more words than they can speak.
  - A language explosion happens at ages two and three when vocabulary increases rapidly.
  - By the time children are five years old, they can speak between 1,500 and 2,500 words.
- Many young children talk a lot because they enjoy practicing, and they have a limited ability to control the impulse to talk.
- Young children can think faster than they can talk and need more time than adults to get their message out.
- Communication is affected by: time of day, appearances, the place you are in, noise level, sights nearby, how you feel, being hungry, feeling tired, and how much time you have.
- Helping children learn to communicate and accept their feelings may lead to more positive behavior. Children who are frustrated by not being able to communicate will often whine, cry, throw tantrums, hit, or argue.
- Generally, communication in children is encouraged when:
  - They are allowed to say what they think and ask about anything.
  - Adults listen to children, and don't talk or lecture at them too much.
  - They are not forced to talk on demand; young children have a limited ability to immediately put thoughts into words.
  - The television and radio are turned off, and the telephone or doorbell is not allowed to interrupt.
  - Children are allowed to talk in their own time while they are doing something else, like playing or taking a walk.

- If children feel that they can talk to adults about anything, they may be more likely to report incidents of racism, prejudice, and abuse. If children feel that they will disappoint or anger parents by telling them something, they may decide to keep it to themselves.

- Physical violence typically starts with angry or frustrating communication. Expressing feelings with words leads to less fighting, hitting, shoving, and abuse. No matter how strong the emotions, people can communicate in non-violent, non-abusive ways.

- Being able to communicate in positive ways is something children will use and benefit from throughout their lives; it's never too early or too late to start learning communication skills.

Approaches

Open the doors to communication by talking respectfully *with* your child, not *to* or *at* him. Consider that there are many points of view and your child may have a different way of looking at things than you do. Explore solutions to a problem together with your child; this will give him an opportunity to be creative and helpful in the process, and you will be more likely to win his cooperation.

—Ideas found in *Children: The Challenge* by Rudolf Dreikurs, Plume, 1990 (© 1964).

Allow your child to talk and ask about anything. Encourage him to come to you with questions now so that when larger questions about things like drugs, sex, or violence come up later, he will know already that it is safe to talk to you. Begin early taking questions seriously and responding to them in a way that he will understand at his age. Give a child time to think, consider the possibilities, and make decisions. Adults who are open and provide answers create a setting where good communication can take place.

—Ideas found in *Questions Children Ask and How to Answer Them* by Miriam Stoppard, DK Publishing, 1997.

> *It's harder to get my son to talk now that he is in preschool. To encourage my son to tell what he did or how he feels, I create stories with silly characters, like Fritz, Frieda, Frazzle, and Frumble Fuzzy, who live with him and go to school with him. I ask him to help me fill in the details of the story like what they did or thought at school that day, and I find out much about how my son thinks and feels.*
>
> —Betsy, a Parenthood Web member

Create good communication in simple ways:

- To help your child learn to listen, softly touch him and say his name.
- Use a soft voice when you speak to him, and sometimes whisper so he can practice listening.
- Get down on your child's level and look into his eyes.
- Be kind, respectful, and polite when you talk to your child.
- Invite your child to tell you more by using language that encourages it: "Wow, can you tell me more?" or "I understand," or "I'm not sure if I understand, can you tell me again?"
- Turn off and tune out the distractions when your child wants to talk to you—offer him your full attention.

—Ideas found in "Communication Tips for Parents and Kids" from the California Consortium to Prevent Child Abuse, Online, KidSource, Available: www.kidsource.com.

Communication

Actively listen to and understand your child; it's an important part of communicating. Active listening, sometimes called reflective listening, is a way to communicate that shows you not only heard, but understood the person.

- When your child comes to you with a need of some kind, first think about what he is saying: what is the message he is trying to give you?

- Then, respond to your child by repeating back in your words what you think he is trying to say: "I hear you saying that you don't want to go to preschool."

- Your child will either say that you understand him or he will need to say more about the message: "No, I don't. I'm working on a puzzle now."

- As you continue to reflect back to the child, he may begin to think of ways to meet his need: "I see it's frustrating for you to stop in the middle. Are you almost done?" He might say: "Yes, I could go to school after I'm done."

Keep your thoughts and emotions out of the process and focus on the child. For active listening to work, you must be willing to: listen, help, accept a child's feelings and not be afraid of the intensity of them, trust that the child can handle his problems and feelings, and allow him to be responsible for them, and remain open to changing your mind.

> —Ideas found in *Discipline That Works: Promoting Self-Discipline in Children*
> by Thomas Gordon, Plume, 1991.

Identify and describe your child's feelings, one of the more difficult but important parts of communicating. Listen to your child, consider what emotion he is feeling, and think of one word that names it. Then tell him what you believe about how he is feeling. If your child says: "My sister grabbed my cookie and I want to punch her," then you might assume that he is angry. You could say, "That must have made you mad!" Listening and reflecting back what you hear will help your child help himself with the problem.

> —Ideas found in *How to Talk So Kids Will Listen and Listen So Kids Will Talk*
> by Adele Faber and Elaine Mazlish, Avon Books, 1980.

Be genuine with your child; he will feel heard and supported when he gets an honest reaction and response. If your child comes to you after being hurt, show him you understand his hurt by showing how bad you feel for him. Trying to mask your real feelings in a situation that makes you upset for the child may only make him feel worse.

> —Ideas found in *Parenting by Heart* by Ron Taffel, with Melinda Blau,
> Addison-Wesley Publishing, 1991.

Listen to your child with an open mind. Avoid listening only to wait until it is your turn to speak with your mind already set on the outcome. True listening means hearing the child without thinking of other things or letting your mind wander, considering what the child says before forming a response, and being open to the child's ideas as possible solutions.

> —Ideas found in *The Mother Dance: How Children Change Your Life* by Harriet Lerner,
> HarperCollins, 1998.

To encourage children to listen to you, communicate with I-messages instead of you-messages. Instead of framing your thoughts around what the child did wrong or what he should do, consider thinking about and telling him how the situation is affecting you:

- A description of the problem or what you see: "When this happens..."
- Your feeling about the situation: "I feel..."
- What the situation means for you or what you have to do about it; "because..."

If a child breaks a rule about throwing sand out of the sandbox, you could use an I-message: "When I see you throwing sand, I feel afraid because I might get sand in my eyes and that hurts." You are not blaming your child, and he learns that it's the consequences or potential consequences of his actions that are the problem and not he, himself. Next, trust the child to change his actions or find an answer to the problem.

> —Ideas found in *Raising a Responsible Child* by Don Dinkmeyer and Gary D. McKay,
> Simon & Schuster, 1996.

Consider the way you talk to your child; it is as important as what you talk about:

- Be trustworthy and talk about what you know; be honest about what you don't.
- Be brief and get to the heart of the matter. Avoid lecturing and arguing.
- Be clear; talk to your child with words and simple language that he can understand.
- Listen to what your child has to say and value his opinions. Ask him for his thoughts and ideas and avoid deciding for him what he should think.

> —Ideas found in *How to Talk to Your Kids About Really Important Things*
> by Charles E. Schaefer and Theresa foy Di Geronimo, Jossey-Bass Publishers, 1994.

With four children, just getting through our day doesn't leave us much time to talk. So, at bedtime, we all take turns talking about:

- *What happened today that made us happy.*
- *If anything made us sad.*
- *What might have made us angry.*
- *What we did that was kind today.*

We cover a lot this way and it's fun, too!

> —Jane from Sillwater, MN

Don't force your child to talk to you about a problem or crisis. Most people want to help a child who is hurting; it is important to patiently accept the information that your child is able to give you and read the nonverbal signs. Look at his body language, gestures, and mood for ideas about what he might be feeling. Gently encourage him to tell you more about what he is feeling. Then ask him: "What can I do for you? Can I help you?" The respect and patience that you show him will go a long way to help him with his problem.

> —Ideas found in *Different and Wonderful: Raising Black Children in a Race-Conscious Society*
> by Darlene P. and Derek S. Hopson, Simon & Schuster, 1992.

Communication

Calm down and cool off from a tense or angry situation before talking to your child about it. Find someone else to talk to if it helps, find a place to go, consider going for a walk. Everything you say to a child can harm or help him, so a calm frame of mind can make a big difference in helping your child.

—Ideas found in *Wonderful Ways to Love a Child* by Judy Ford, Conari Press, 1995.

When correcting your child, use words and descriptions that focus on the problem at hand and not words that label the child in a permanent way. When a child is told what he is or isn't, he may believe that the underlying cause for a specific situation is from something lacking in him as a person. Then he learns to be negative. When a child is told that something needs to be changed about a particular situation today, he sees that something can be done about it, and he learns to view the world more positively. When talking with your child about a problem:

- Be clear and honest about what the situation is: "If you can't put on your jacket when I ask you, then I may need to help you." Don't exaggerate: "You never do what I ask."
- Point out what might be causing the specific problem today: "If you talk louder, then Grandma will be able to hear you." Don't label the child: "You're a bad talker."

—Ideas found in *The Optimistic Child: A Proven Program to Safeguard Children Against Depression and Build Lifelong Resilience* by Martin E.P. Seligman et al, Houghton Mifflin, 1995.

Help your pre-verbal baby communicate by signals. Create signals with your baby that you use each time: you could put your hands to your cheek to signal nap time while telling him that it's time for a nap, or put your fingers to your lips to signal snack time as you ask him if he'd like a snack. Your baby will learn that he can communicate with words and actions, and you may encourage his use of both.

—Ideas found in *The Parents Answer Book*, (Parent's Magazine) Golden Books, 1998.

Put your words into actions sometimes. Instead of pushing a child with words, try leading him with your actions. If a child won't turn off the TV and come to dinner, try turning the TV off and gently leading him to the table, instead of coercing him with more and more words, threats, or yelling. Sometimes, you can communicate more by using less words.

—Ideas found in *Positive Discipline A-Z* (revised and expanded 2nd edition) by Jane Nelsen, Lynn Lott, and H. Stephen Glenn, Prima, 1999.

Communicate with your child through play. Your child cannot always express himself on demand, and often extends his real feelings, worries, and thoughts into play. First, watch how and what the child plays. Then join him on his level. If he is playing with dolls, figures, teddy bears, or puppets, become the voice of one of the toys and talk to the child as if you were that toy. Let the child be the leader in directing what to do. You may have the opportunity to play out a solution to a problem that the child is having in real life, play a new idea for him to consider in his real life, or just find out what's he's happy, sad, angry, or frustrated about.

—Ideas found in *Playwise: 365 Fun-Filled Activities for Building Character, Conscience, and Emotional Intelligence in Children* by Denise Chapman Weston and Mark S. Weston, G.P. Putnam's Sons, 1996.

Build family self-esteem with positive language; avoid miscommunication with negative words. Words send strong messages and lead to strong feelings. When you use negative words, like "dumb" and "I hate it when...," then people in the family will feel put down. When you use positive words, like "You are important" and "I like it when you...," the people in your family will feel valued and supported.

—Ideas found in *Making Peace in Your Stepfamily* by Harold Bloomfield and Robert B. Kory, Hyperion, 1993.

Avoid communicating unfairly to prevent talking from turning into fighting. Have a reasonable discussion where you exchange thoughts, understandings, and feelings, instead of a verbal fight where you try to hurt each other. Many tactics and words don't help solve a problem, but add to it. Some of the things to consider to prevent arguments:

- Avoid assuming that you know what the other person is thinking, and jumping to conclusions.
- Avoid changing the subject and bringing up other things that you are angry with the person about. Stick to the problem at hand.
- Avoid interrupting and avoid using silence to ignore. Let the person speak and then you respond.
- Don't yell, blame, intimidate, call names, compare the person to someone else, insult, or humiliate. Everyone, including you, makes mistakes—rubbing it in and making a person feel worse about it doesn't help.
- Feeling hurt and trying to make the other person feel guilty can be a way to manipulate someone to do what you want them to do. It's not a fair way to communicate.

> —Ideas found in *Family Communication* (revised edition) by Sven Wahlroos, Contemporary Books, 1995.

Use stories and books to start discussions at home. Talking about books together can bring a family closer and open up communication to reveal thoughts, opinions, ideas, differences, and agreements about topics that may not come up in everyday life. Some families have regular book discussion evenings.

> —Ideas found in "Sparking Conversation at Home" by Maeve Visser Knoth, *The Horn Book Magazine*, May-June 1997.

The Field Guide's Conversation Starters

- I hear a truck. What do you hear?
- What do you think about…?
- How do you think this works?
- I like green things. What do you like?
- You have such great ideas. What are your ideas about…?
- Why…?
- Can you smell anything?

- Remember what we did yesterday?
- How does it feel to be…?
- I remember when I was your age…
- I see the sun. What do you see?
- If you were an animal, what would you be? Why?
- Find a picture in this book of…
- I love you!

Help a child understand more about communication by reading about it together:

📖 *A is for Angry* by Sandra Boynton

📖 *Communication* by Aliki

📖 *If You Give a Moose a Muffin* by Laura Numeroff

📖 *Polar Bear, Polar Bear, What Do You Hear?* by Bill Martin, Jr.

📖 *Today I Feel Silly and Other Moods that Make My Day* by Jamie Lee Curtis

When to Get More Help

Children typically grow and learn new skills in their own time and at their own pace within the wide range of what is normal. Sometimes, children need a bit of extra help to keep their development on track, or to stay healthy and happy. Sometimes, parents need help in providing for a child's needs or sorting out the best approaches to parenting.

Consider getting help for your child if he:

- Does not do the following by his first birthday:
  - Turn to sounds.
  - Imitate sounds.
  - Say a single word.
- Does not do the following by two years:
  - Speak at least fifteen words by eighteen months.
  - Point to pictures of familiar things or something desired by eighteen months.
  - Pay attention to the ring of a telephone, doorbell, or someone entering the room.
  - Follow simple instructions.
  - Try to use words instead of gestures to express needs and use two-word sentences.
- Does not do the following by at least three years:
  - Have clear speech that is easy to understand by you.
  - Stop drooling unless it is related to teething.
- Does not do the following by at least four years:
  - Use sentences of more than three words.
  - State own name.
  - Ask questions and speak clearly.
- Does not do the following by at least five years:
  - Show an interest in listening to children's books and stories, cannot remember any part of the story, or doesn't understand it.
  - Speak clearly to be understood even by strangers.
  - Understand two-part commands using prepositions: "Put the cup on the table," or "Get the ball that is under the couch."
  - Use plurals or past tense properly most of the time.

Consider getting help for yourself if you:

- Often feel misunderstood or have a difficult time understanding others.
- Find yourself in power struggles that escalate into hitting or shouting.

You are the expert when it comes to your family and child. If you have a concern, trust your instinct and find someone trained to help you: health care providers, early intervention teams, mental health professionals, parent educators and consultants, or telephone help-line staff. Think about talking it over with friends and family, too. You don't need to worry alone! Turn to "Finding Help in Your Community" on page 4 to learn about finding help near you.

More Help and Information

Books for Parents

- *Baby Talk: The Art of Communicating with Infants and Toddlers* by Monica Devine. Plenum Press, 1991.

- *Family Communication* (revised edition) by Sven Wahlroos. Contemporary Books, 1995.

- *The Gentle Art of Communicating with Kids* by Suzette Haden Elgin. John Wiley & Sons, Inc., 1996.

- *How to Talk So Kids Will Listen and Listen So Kids Will Talk* by Adele Faber and Elaine Mazlish. Avon Books, 1980.

- *The Mom & Dad Conversation Piece: Creative Questions to Celebrate the Family* by Brett Nicholaus and Paul Lowrie. Ballantine, 1997.

- *Raising Peaceful Children in a Violent World* by Nancy Lee Cecil. Luramedia, 1995.

Articles, Pamphlets, & Booklets

- "Why Kids Ask Why...and the Answers They're Really Looking For" by Ava L. Siegler. *Child*, August 1998.

- "How Can Parents Model Good Listening Skills?" by Carl Smith, Online, ERIC Clearinghouse on Reading, English and Communication Skills, Available: www.accesseric.org/resources/parent/listenin.html

National Organizations

- ERIC Clearinghouse on Reading, English and Communication Skills
  800-759-4723, fax: 812-855-4220
  web site: www.indiana.edu/~eric _rec/

Cooperation and Power Struggles

by Tom

Description

Cooperation is the ability to work together toward a common goal and to solve problems together. It requires a willingness to work things out and comply with necessary plans, rules, and requests. Power struggles happen when parents and children don't agree on the solution, plan, or idea and neither is willing to give up control to cooperate.

Realistic Expectations

- Young children may not understand the meaning of the word "cooperate" or may have a different idea of what it means.
- If you ask young children to cooperate, be prepared—they may say "no."
- Children will be able to cooperate only with what they are developmentally able to do:
    - One-year-olds can follow one simple direction only.
    - Two-year-olds can follow two related directions.
    - Three-year-olds can follow three related instructions, or two to three unrelated instructions.
- Young children struggling to learn independence may have more difficulty cooperating.
- Preschoolers explore power: how things work, how things get done, and how they can make something happen. Power struggles happen between children who want something different than parents.
- Children may be more likely to cooperate when:
    - Their ideas and opinions are respected.
    - They are given choices.
    - They are allowed to help make decisions.
    - Their good behavior is noticed and appreciated.
    - They are valued as a member of the family.
- Children may be less likely to cooperate, and more likely to engage in a power struggle when:
    - Cooperation is demanded.
    - They are interrupted without warning from an activity they are enjoying.
    - Their routine is changed unexpectedly.
    - They hear "no" often from adults.
    - They get their way after arguing about it.

- A parent or caregiver punishes them harshly or hurts them.
- They don't know how to do a task or what they are being asked to do.
- They are asked to cooperate too often. Parents typically ask or command young children hundreds of times in a week.

- Dealing with problems before children lose control over them and teaching children how to release tension may prevent some power struggles and tantrums.

- Children learn cooperation from watching the adults around them who show them what cooperation looks like by doing it themselves.

- Young children have a limited ability to share, cooperate, and control their feelings. They may be able to cooperate one minute but not the next. Introducing children to cooperation early may lessen the number of power struggles.

Approaches

Win cooperation from your child instead of demanding it. If you try to demand cooperation, your child may resist, and a power struggle may take place. Yet even a very young child can learn cooperation if the adult helps. Act without frustration but with love and firmness, then your child is likely to react more positively and begin to learn cooperation.

—Ideas found in *Children: The Challenge* by Rudolf Driekurs, E.P. Dutton, 1964.

Expect cooperation from your child. Don't expect power struggles or you may be encouraging them. Instead, use language that tells a child that you know she will agree: "The clock shows it's time for a rest. I know you would like a story before a nap. Let's go."

—Ideas found in *Parenting Young Children: Systematic Training for Effective Parenting (STEP) of Children Under Six* by Don Dinkmeyer, Sr., et al., American Guidance Service, 1997.

Encourage your child to cooperate with you:

Solution 1: Make your request clear, short, and specific: "Please put your toys in the toy box."

Solution 2: Use the "When/Then" technique, also know as Grandma's Rule. Let the child know the sequence of her priorities: "When you have finished lunch, then you can play your new game."

Solution 3: Offer the child a choice: "Do you want milk or juice?" Another way to use this technique is to offer the time-focused choice: "Would you like to clean up now or in five minutes?" If she creates a third option, simply say, "That wasn't one of the choices," and restate the original question. If a child refuses to choose, you choose for her.

Solution 4: Use humor to gain cooperation. A bit of silliness can often diffuse the tension and get your child to cooperate willingly.

Avoid letting your emotions take control. Don't yell, threaten, criticize, or belittle. Instead, ask yourself a question, "What is the problem?" Then decide what approach you are going to use to solve the problem. Take a deep breath, and follow through on your plan.

—Elizabeth Pantley, author of *Perfect Parenting* and *Kid Cooperation*.

Cooperation and Power Struggles

Prevent power struggles: think about your child's request before responding and end arguments early. Think about what is the best decision for your child and don't give in to requests because it's easier. It's OK to change your mind after more careful thought, but don't allow your child to argue about it once you have made a thoughtful decision. Your child will test the limits or continue arguing to see if there are limits. Tell your child that you have made up your mind, will not change it, and to stop arguing about it. Then ignore it.

—Ideas found in *So This Is Normal Too?* by Deborah Hewitt, Redleaf Press, 1995.

To encourage cooperation and prevent power struggles with your child:

- Set and follow consistent routines: breakfast, getting dressed, washing face, brushing teeth and hair, then play time.
- Help her learn routines by offering her something she wants: "when your teeth are brushed, then you can play with the new puzzle."
- Show her that each person in the family is important and that sometimes someone else needs to be first or have attention; by waiting for her turn, she is being fair to everyone in the family.
- Expect the child to cooperate and offer a simple choice:

  "Time to go to the store. Do you want to pick out orange or apple juice this week?"
- Help your child understand when she is acting inappropriately and what she can do about it: "You're not allowed to throw your snack on the floor. Now we have to throw it away, but you can try again at snack time this afternoon."
- Decide which issues or problems are important to you. Perhaps stop struggling over the ones that aren't as important.

—Ideas found in *Living with the Active Alert* (revised and enlarged edition) by Linda S. Budd, Parenting Press, 1993.

Notice and comment on any attempt to cooperate, no matter how grudgingly it is given. Your child sincerely may not want to do what you want her to, so she may not cooperate cheerfully. But if she cooperates at all, even reluctantly, be sure to tell her that you appreciate it to encourage more cooperation.

—Ideas found in *Win the Whining War & Other Skirmishes* by Cynthia Whitham, Perspective Pub., 1991.

Help your child think for herself and solve her own problems. Influence her decisions with real information about why something should be done but avoid controlling her by telling her what to do, which leads to power struggles. When you nag, yell, or whine at your child to do something, you make it your problem to see that it gets done. If you allow your child to own the problem, then allow her to make the decisions about it, and be prepared to live with the consequences. Ask her to do something, then keep silent about it and it becomes her responsibility. For example, say: "I need you to put the truck back in your room before lunch. When Grandma comes over this afternoon, she could trip on it and get hurt." Then don't serve lunch until the truck is put away. Start small and increase responsibility as she gets older.

—Ideas found in *Winning at Parenting...Without Beating Your Kids* (Barbara Coloroso), Video, Kids Are Worth It!

Avoid power struggles by letting your child have the final say sometimes. Sometimes when your child just wants to argue, let her have the last word instead of battling with her.

> —Ideas found in *Positive Discipline A-Z* (revised and expanded 2nd edition) by
> Jane Nelsen, Lynn Lott, and H. Stephen Glenn, Prima, 1999.

Reduce the number of power struggles:

- Decide what is important to you and what isn't. Avoid a struggle over the things that don't really matter. Choose your struggles.
- Consider all the things that you ask your child to do. Reduce the number of things that you require of her by focusing on the most important things that you need her to do.
- Watch and notice all the times that your child does what you ask of her—you may be surprised at how often she cooperates!

> —Ideas found in "Power Struggles" by Beth Johnson, Online, ParentTime,
> Available: www.parenttime.com.

Encourage cooperation by respectfully making requests or directing your child. Think about the way in which you ask for or demand cooperation. Consider how it would feel to be blamed, ordered, called names, lectured at, warned, made to feel bad, or compared to other people: "How come you can't pick up the ball like your sister? I've told you a thousand times how stupid it is to leave it here so someone can trip and fall on it. Pick it up right now or you can forget ever seeing it again." This is not a situation in which your child is likely to feel good about herself and be inspired to cooperate.

Instead, try telling your child what the situation is and what is wrong with it: "The ball is at the bottom of the steps and in the way of someone trying to come down." Sometimes it only takes one word to communicate the problem or expectation. Perhaps the family has talked enough about the problem of leaving the ball by the stairs that all that may be needed is: "Ball." Invite cooperation without making your child feel bad and she will be much more likely to do it.

> —Ideas found in *How to Talk So Kids Will Listen and Listen So Kids Will Talk*
> by Adele Faber and Elaine Mazlish, Avon Books, 1980.

The Field Guide's Cooperation Starters

- I need your help.
- Please.
- Do you have a good idea?
- Let's choose together.

- How should we do this?
- I know you can do it!
- Your cooperation is great!
- Thank you.

Cooperation and Power Struggles

When you are in a power struggle, negotiate with your child when you can, be firm when you can't. Try to be flexible. Give in on things that aren't as important to you as they are to her. Allow her to offer ideas and choose options in situations where you can:

- Think about what is going on, where you are, how much time you have, and decide if you can negotiate with your child. Sometimes you can and sometimes you need to make a decision and stick to it. Tell your child which situation you are in: "We can negotiate about this together," or " No, we can't buy ice cream now; we don't have time to stop right now."

- Talk about what you see as the problem and what you would like to happen; listen to your child for her ideas and see if you can solve the problem together.

When you listen to a child and negotiate when you can, you give her the idea that she is important and that her ideas are valuable. Some circumstances do require setting a clear limit or making a firm decision. The wishes of all people in the family should be considered equally. It's hard, but your child can learn the important skills of talking, listening, negotiating, handling anger, and solving disagreements in a positive way.

—Ideas found in *Becoming The Parent You Want to Be* by Laura Davis and Janis Kayser, Broadway Books, 1997.

Help children understand more about cooperation and power struggles by reading about it together:

 Pelle's New Suit by Elsa Maartman Beskow

 *Stone Soup* by Marcia Brown

The Wizard, the Fairy, and the Magic Chicken by Helen Lester

When to Get More Help

Children typically grow and learn new skills in their own time and at their own pace within the wide range of what is normal. Sometimes, children need a bit of extra help to keep their development on track, or to stay healthy and happy. Sometimes, parents need help in providing for a child's needs or sorting out the best approaches to parenting.

Consider getting help for your child if she:

- Stands out as being a lot more uncooperative than other children her own age.
- Often overreacts to situations or events and does not respond to comfort.
- Does not show some ability to control behavior by four years.

You are the expert when it comes to your family and child. If you have a concern, trust your instinct, and find someone trained to help you: health care providers, early intervention teams, mental health professionals, parent educators and consultants, or telephone help-line staff. Think about talking it over with friends and family, too. You don't need to worry alone! Turn to "Finding Help in Your Community" on page 4 to learn about finding help near you.

More Help and Information

Books for Parents

- *Kid Cooperation: How to Stop Yelling, Nagging and Pleading and Get Kids to Cooperate* by Elizabeth Pantley. New Harbinger Publications, 1996.
- "Chapter 21 Negotiating Conflicts Between Parent and Child" in *Becoming The Parent You Want To Be* by Laura Davis and Janis Keyser. Broadway Books, 1997.
- *Positive Discipline for Preschoolers* (revised 2nd edition) by Jane Nelsen, Cheryl Erwin, and Roslyn Duffy. Prima Pub., 1998.

Videos

- *The Little Engine That Could.* MCA Universal Home Video.

Crying

Description

Crying is universal. Crying is a healthy way that children express emotion and/or communicate a need.

Realistic Expectations

- In infants, crying is their earliest language.
- You can't spoil babies in the first eight to ten months of their lives; ones who are responded to consistently when they cry, actually cry less by the time they are a year old, and they become more independent as toddlers and preschoolers.
- Some of the causes of crying in young children will seem trivial to adults, but are nonetheless very real to children. Children cry when they:
    - Feel emotionally overwhelmed
    - Are in pain or injured
    - Cannot find the words to express what they are trying to say
    - Fear losing a parent (separation anxiety)
    - Are overexcited
    - Are over-tired
    - Are fearful
    - Are bored
    - Want their own way and do not get it
    - Have bad dreams
    - Are nervous
- While it is important to always respond to children's needs with love and care when they cry, if adults over-react to children's crying, over time, children may learn to use crying instead of words to get what they want and to ask for attention.
- Sensitive children are more prone to both crying and laughing more quickly; their crying doesn't necessarily mean that they are generally unhappy.
- As children gain more language and can put their emotions and needs into words, and as they gain more skills in comforting themselves, the frequency of their crying usually decreases.
- When children's cries are handled well, they will learn to trust the world and believe in their own ability to get what they need. These things foster self-esteem and a sense of personal power.

Approaches

Attend to your young child who is crying, but also help him learn ways to comfort himself. Avoid being overly protective or rushing in to fix things every time he is frustrated; your overly anxious response to crying can sometimes make it worse. Respond to his cries, but at some point, gently push him to calm himself down. From about nine months on, it is especially important to teach your child ways to comfort himself. This doesn't mean leaving him to cry alone. Instead, your job is to decide how much attention each of his cries demands.

Figure out what his cries mean and help him to deal with the problem: if he doesn't want to stay in his bed, give him a hug, tell him you know he can do it, remind him that you are right outside his door, and keep encouraging him. Over time, his self-comforting tools lead to an inner sense of security and satisfaction at being able to do something for himself. Pacifiers, thumbs, teddy bears, blankets, or other comfort objects can be very helpful to the child who is learning to comfort himself. Often he will work them into a behavior pattern that can help him feel better.

—Ideas found in *Touchpoints* by T. Berry Brazelton, Addison-Wesley, 1992.

When being over-tired causes tears, give your child hugs, be patient, talk softly, and get him to bed quickly. When he is over-tired, even small discomforts can make him cry and make it difficult to comfort him. It is extra important for you to be calm and quiet. Sing a song, hold him, read a story, and keep speaking quietly.

—Ideas found in *Complete Baby and Child Care* by Miriam Stoppard,
Dorling Kindersley Publishing, 1995.

Comfort your child when he is hurting. When your child is physically or emotionally hurt, he is likely to want to be comforted, and you will likely want to comfort him. Go ahead and do so, but don't overdo your concern about the hurt, and move on as soon as possible. Expect that he will want to be more brave as he grows older. But for now, don't worry about comforting him too much.

—Ideas found in *Dr. Spock's Baby and Child Care* (7th edition)
by Benjamin Spock and Stephen Parker, Dutton, 1998.

Prevent crying in your child who cries easily and often. Crying is a healthy way to express emotion, but sometimes it can be a signal that the child needs something:

- Is he over-tired or hungry? If so, take steps to get him on a regular sleeping and eating schedule.
- Is he ill or becoming ill? Take him to the doctor to rule out physical causes.
- Is he frustrated because he cannot do something that could be taught? Teach him the skill: tying his shoe, pouring milk, putting on his shirt, etc.
- Is he frustrated because he cannot speak well enough to tell people what he wants? Teach him how to get what he wants without crying by using gestures or pointing.
- Does he seem to have the language, but not know how to ask for what he needs? Help him know what he wants and what he doesn't want and encourage him to speak up about it.
- Does he need encouragement? Praise him often when he is not crying: "I enjoyed our time together. I love being with you. Thanks for sharing your feelings with me."
- Does he spend too much time alone? Sometimes the child may just need more time with the people he loves.

Consider logging his crying in a journal for a few days, noting how often and when it happens. Look for patterns that might indicate trouble spots that you could change. Show him that you believe he can and will handle the situations that make him cry.

—Ideas found in *Positive Parenting From A to Z* by Karen Renshaw Joslin.
Fawcett Columbine: Ballantine Books, 1994.

Crying

! WARNING! Never shake a child and never harm a child with physical punishment.

Shaking a baby or child under the age of three can cause brain damage, blindness, paralysis, seizures, or death. Even a small amount of shaking or a less vigorous shaking can severely harm a young child.

The American Academy of Pediatrics (AAP) warns that children who are routinely disciplined with spanking and other physical forms of punishment are more likely to become aggressive and to learn that aggressive behavior is the way to solve problems. Spanking or hitting can also lead to injury and abuse, especially when it is done in anger.

Help your child know what to do when he cries so often that it seems to be getting in the way of his making friends or doing other things. Usually, a child who cries easily is more of a problem for the parents or older children than for the child himself. Children are usually forgiving of a young friend's crying. Be careful not to blow the situation out of proportion, but consider ways to help your child:

- When he is crying, don't discourage the crying; he may just become more upset.
- At the time of the crying, tell the child you understand that he is angry or sad or whatever emotion he may be feeling.
- When he calms down, talk about what things led up to his feeling that way, talk about other things he could have done besides crying; he may need you to provide him with most of the ideas. Consider rehearsing or role-playing the options with him.
- Check yourself to see if you are unknowingly rewarding his crying. If crying is the only way he can get your attention, he will cry often. Change your behavior and give him attention whenever he is acting in a positive way.

—Ideas found in *Toddlers and Preschoolers* by Lawrence Kutner, William Morrow, 1994.

Keep your own negative moods under control. Sensitive children may cry when they pick up on your own anxiety, tension, anger, depression, etc. You usually can't hide your strong emotions from children, and you don't need to. Explain your strong emotions to the child in simple terms, but don't over-burden him with your problems: "I am crying because I am sad that Grandma died." If you are in a stressful time, get support from and express your strong emotions to other adults so that these emotions don't have a negative impact on your child.

—Ideas found in *What to Expect the Toddler Years* by Arlene Eisenberg,
Heidi E. Murkoff, and Sandee E. Hathaway, Workman Pub., 1994.

Help your child understand more about crying by reading about it together:

 Cry Baby by Ruth Brown

 Sometimes I Feel Like A Mouse: A Book About Feelings by Jeanne Modesitt

 Today I Feel Silly & Other Moods That Make My Day by Jamie Lee Curtis

 What Makes Me Happy? by Catherine Anholt

When to Get More Help

Children typically grow and learn new skills in their own time and at their own pace within the wide range of what is normal. Sometimes, children need a bit of extra help to keep their development on track, or to stay healthy and happy. Sometimes, parents need help in providing for a child's needs or sorting out the best approaches to parenting.

Consider getting help for your child if he:

- Frequently cries, especially if there seems to be no reason.
- Generally cannot be comforted when crying or cannot be comforted when he is crying and ill.
- Never cries.

Consider getting help for yourself if you:

- Find yourself frustrated with the amount your child cries.

You are the expert when it comes to your family and child. If you have a concern, trust your instinct and find someone trained to help you: health care providers, early intervention teams, mental health professionals, parent educators and consultants, or telephone help-line staff. Think about talking it over with friends and family, too. You don't need to worry alone! Turn to "Finding Help in Your Community" on page 4 to learn about finding help near you.

More Help and Information

Books for Parents

- "Older Baby: Crying and Comforting," in *Dr. Miriam Stoppard's Complete Baby and Child Care* by Miriam Stoppard, Dorling Kindersley Publishing, 1995.

Dawdling

Description

Dawdling is consciously taking your time and being slow. When you ask your child to get her jacket on, and she agrees to do it, but decides to wait until she has added a few more blocks to her building, and then slowly goes to look for her jacket, that's dawdling.

Realistic Expectations

- What parents think of as dawdling, young children may think of as a normal or reasonable amount of time to complete their tasks. Young children require plenty of time to get dressed, get ready to go, eat their meals, play, and do whatever is asked of them.

- Young children have a limited ability to focus on a task, so sometimes what appears as dawdling is really distraction and a lack of focus. Sometimes young children become so involved in what they are doing and what they are thinking, that they don't hear adults.

- Children who by temperament, are slow to adapt to change or are easily distracted may dawdle more or have more difficulty focusing.

- Children who are nagged, scolded, threatened, and punished for dawdling or distraction may become more dependent on help and more absentminded. When children are not given responsibility but are pushed to do things, they may not learn to do them on their own.

- Young children have a limited sense of time and may not understand what adults mean by "in ten minutes" or "right now."

- Dawdling is a common concern of early childhood but typically passes with time in the school-age years.

Approaches

Help your child accomplish her tasks and routines until she is old enough to do them herself; avoid hurrying, pushing, and nagging. Take the time to show a child what the routines, tasks, and steps are to be done. Be patient and allow enough time to accomplish them in your child's own natural time.

—Ideas found in *Dr. Spock's Baby and Child Care* (7th edition)
by Benjamin Spock and Stephen J. Parker, Dutton, 1998.

Set schedules and routines to help reduce dawdling. Help your child understand what happens, when, and why so that she learns what she needs to do and what will happen when she does them. She may be less likely to dawdle after breakfast every day if she routinely looks forward to ten minutes of special play time with you.

—Ideas found in *The Parents Answer Book* (Parent's Magazine), Golden Books, 1998.

If your child is dawdling in accomplishing a task, look first at what you expect her to do and make sure that she can reasonably do it. If your child is having trouble getting her shoes on or pulling on her shirt and pants, sometimes making some simple changes can help stop the dawdling: find shoes that are easy to get on and see if she can do it by herself; make sure her clothes are not too small or too difficult to manage and see that she can manage them. Then when you are sure that she can do what you ask her to do, consider giving her a fun reason to get on with the job: "If you can get your pants and shirt on soon, then we'll have time to work on your puzzle for a few minutes before we go."

> —Ideas found in *Raising a Responsible Child* by Elizabeth Ellis, Carol Publishing Group, 1995.

Ignore the dawdling and praise your child when she finishes a task on time. Since pushing, prodding, and name-calling don't help your child stop dawdling and may make it worse, don't do it. It's a phase that will pass with time. Use patience and ignore the dawdling. Give positive comments to your child when she sticks with something and completes it: "Wow, you got ready for your bath so fast—that's so great!"

> —Ideas found in *Win the Whining War & Other Skirmishes* by Cynthia Whitham, Perspective Pub., 1991.

> At one point in my life (for about fifteen minutes), I was completely organized. We had more than enough time to get dressed, dawdle, brush teeth, and play games. I even got to work early.
>
> But this is not the norm! Normally, we are late. Having lived both extremes, I believe that kids will be kids and they are inherently slow. It's our responsibility as parents to head them off at the pass and pull them forward, rather than push them from behind.
>
> —Kim, St. Albert, Alberta, Canada

Help your child avoid dawdling:

- When you give her a task to do, make sure that there aren't other things around that will take her attention away from her task. Consider putting her shoes or jacket in the hall, away from toys or television, and asking her to put them on there.
- Let her know that you understand how she feels: "I know it's not always fun to have to get ready or eat breakfast when someone tells you to. I see that you feel mad at having to get ready in a hurry."
- Sometimes, let her dawdle and decide how fast to do a job. Consider letting her have one task a week that she can do on her own time.
- Make the task into a game or let her pretend to be something fun while doing a task.
- If there is a certain task that she tends to dawdle over, consider making it routine to complete that task at a similar time of day, such as before play or story time.
- Make sure that she has plenty of time to complete the task and then offer her a reward for doing the job well: "I'll set the timer for fifteen minutes. If you can get your pants and shirt on before the bell rings, then we can stop for ice cream before the library."

Keep in mind that most children need help and attention to finish a task. Praise your child well for trying, in addition to completing, a task.

> —Ideas found in *365 Wacky, Wonderful Ways to Get Your Children to Do What You Want* by Elizabeth Crary, Parenting Press, 1995.

Help a child understand more about dawdling by reading stories about it together:

I Just Forgot by Mercer Mayer

When the Fly Flew In... by Lisa Wetsberg Peters

> When my kids dawdle, we make getting out the door into a big game with lots of laughs. I command, "Ten Hut! Forward March! Hut two, three, four." Other times, I call out, "All aboard! Train leaving the station." Then we chug-chug-chug out the door holding each others waists or moving our arms like a train. It sure beats nagging at them to get a move on.
>
> —Sararose, member of the Parenthood Web

When to Get More Help

Children typically grow and learn new skills in their own time and at their own pace within the wide range of what is normal. Sometimes, children need a bit of extra help to keep their development on track, or to stay healthy and happy. Sometimes, parents need help in providing for a child's needs or sorting out the best approaches to parenting.

Consider getting help for your child if she:

- Appears to dawdle a lot more than other children her age.

Consider getting help for yourself, if you:

- Feel frustrated with your child frequently.

You are the expert when it comes to your family and child. If you have a concern, trust your instinct and find someone trained to help you: health care providers, early intervention teams, mental health professionals, parent educators and consultants, or telephone help-line staff. Think about talking it over with friends and family, too. You don't need to worry alone! Turn to "Finding Help in Your Community" on page 4 to learn about finding help near you.

More Help and Information

Books for Parents

- *The Parent's Answer Book* (Parent's Magazine). Golden Books, 1998.
- *Raising a Responsible Child: How Parents Can Avoid Overindulgent Behavior and Nurture Healthy Children* by Elizabeth Ellis, Carol Publishing Group, 1995.
- *Without Spanking or Spoiling: A Practical Approach to Toddler and Preschool Guidance* (2nd edition) by Elizabeth Crary. Parenting Press, 1993.

Death and Grief

"Great-grandpa when he was a baby"
by Kate, age 4

Description

Death is the end of life. It is when the heart stops beating, the brain stops thinking, and the body can no longer see, hear, smell, touch, taste, breathe, or feel. Death is an unchangeable, irreversible fact of life for every living thing.

Grief or mourning is the process of separating from someone or something important to you, and yet holding on to some connection. Grief can bring on deep, intense feelings. Children grieve not only for the death of parents, grandparents, siblings, loved ones, and pets, but also for losses due to abandonment, divorce, lack of contact with someone important, serious illness, and experiencing violence or war.

Realistic Expectations

- Children under the age of five don't have the ability to understand that death is final or that everyone dies. Even if they are told that death is forever, they may expect that someone who has died will come back.
- Children under the age of five are likely to ask the same questions about death many times.
- Young children grieve differently than adults. Children commonly react to a major loss in various ways while grieving:
  - Denial: behaving as if nothing has happened; the loss may be too much for them to deal with.
  - Anger: being mad at the adults who did not stop the death from happening or who can't make things the way they were before the loss. Or they might be angry at the person who died.
  - Guilt or shame: believing that they have caused the death, divorce, or event, or thinking something is wrong with them because of it.
  - Fear: wondering about their own death or deaths of others close to them, or having nightmares.
  - Intense sadness, anxiety, or depression, which may include: feeling tired, feeling sick, loss of appetite, difficulty concentrating, uninterested in daily activities, and choosing to spend time alone.
  - Panic: wondering what will happen to them and who will take care of them.
  - Regression: going back to earlier behaviors, such as thumb sucking, bedwetting, or having trouble separating.
  - Longing: wishing things could be the way they were before or that the person would come back.
  - Acceptance: feeling sadness over the loss but getting back to feeling good about themselves and life.

- It is common for young children to have no immediate reaction to a death. It may take them awhile to fully understand that the person is gone forever.
- Young children interpret language and words very literally. If you tell children that death is like going to sleep, they will likely be afraid to sleep. If you tell children that someone died because they were ill, they may become afraid that anyone who gets sick, including themselves, will die.
- Young children have a limited sense of time. To a young child, "very old" may mean ten instead of seventy. If you tell a child that someone died because they were very old, they may become afraid that parents, brothers, sisters, or anyone that seems old to them may die soon.
- Expect to help young children understand death that they see around them, in addition to the death of loved ones: deaths of people in the community, animals, Simba's father in *The Lion King*, an airplane crash and other deaths in the news, and dying in video games.
- When adults talk openly and with acceptance about death, children have positive role models to learn from. Children often imitate the reactions to death that they see from adults around them.
- Many experts agree that children should not be forced to attend a funeral, but that they should be allowed to say good-bye in some meaningful way.
- Grief over a significant loss takes a long time.

Approaches

Explain death to a child in simple language and relate it to all living things: "There is a beginning and an ending for everything that is alive. In between is living."

Point out that all living things—bugs, flowers, animals, and people—all have lives that start, grow, and end. Talk about specific plants or animals and show the child what a life cycle looks like. Explain that a lifetime can last for a few weeks, a few years, many years, or over one hundred years, but that each living thing has a lifetime that includes an ending.

> —Ideas found in *Lifetimes: A Beautiful Way to Explain Death to Children* by Bryan Mellonie and Robert Ingpen, Bantam Books, 1983.

Prepare your child for death by introducing the concept to him before someone close to him dies:

- First, consider your own feelings and experiences with death. Understand it yourself before talking to your child about it.
- Give your child accurate words and meanings. Avoid saying that death is "going to sleep" or that you have "lost" someone who has died in an effort to protect him; it may only confuse and frighten him.
- Take advantage of situations in everyday life in which you can explain death: a dead squirrel or a lifeless tree. Talk about how it doesn't move, grow, or feel anymore, and lacks life. Encourage your child to talk about feelings and let him know that it's natural to feel sad. When a pet dies, consider burying it and having a funeral ceremony.
- Read stories to him about death or dying that portray it in an accurate way, are not frightening, and that provide the information that you would like to give your child.

Allowing your child to learn about death as a part of life may help prepare him for the time when someone close to him dies.

> —Ideas found in *The Grieving Child: A Parent's Guide* by Helen Fitzgerald, Simon & Schuster, 1992.

Tell your child about a loss together as a family, and as soon as possible. Talk to your child in clear, definite terms that he can understand from his experience so that he will have less confusion, less reason to blame himself, and less opportunity to disbelieve it. Be sure to tell him:

- The loss is not his fault.
- He will be well cared for and by whom.
- It's natural for him to think and wonder about what happened.
- It's OK to feel the way he does for as long as he needs to, even if his feelings are not the same as others'.

As he asks questions, or you become more clear in your thinking, allow yourself to change, improve, or add to what you tell your child. Allow your child to ask you or tell you anything on his mind, and if he doesn't come to you, find ways to keep talking about it with him.

> —Ideas found in *Helping Children Cope with Separation and Loss*
> by Claudia Jewett Jarratt, Harvard Common Press, 1994.

Talk to your child about why people die. Consider telling your child that people die because it is possible, just like people fly into space because it's possible. Explore with your child the bigger picture of a person's life and death: "Aunt Fran lived a fun life and lived longer than most people, almost one hundred years, before she died," or "Grandpa was in a lot of pain before he died from cancer; now he doesn't hurt anymore."

> —Ideas found in *Gentle Closings: How to Say Goodbye to Someone You Love*
> by Ted Menten, Running Press, 1991.

Talk to your child about what happens to people when they die. Consider the age of the child and talk to him in terms that he can understand. The fact is that no one knows for sure what happens after death, but most people have beliefs about it. It's OK to let your child know that a parent or caregiver doesn't know everything, but you still need to give him an honest answer. Share your personal beliefs. Your child is likely to ask about where people go when they die, if they can visit someone after they die, and if they or you are going to die.

Explain death to your young child briefly in a way that is easy to understand and consoling: "We believe that people go to a safe place when they die," or "When someone dies, they live through us, our thoughts, the special times we shared, the things they taught us, and how they made us feel." Continue to give simple truthful answers like "It's not time for you to go there," and reassure your child that it won't be for a very long time.

> —Ideas found in *Big Lessons for Little People: Teaching Our Kids Right from Wrong While Keeping Them Healthy, Safe, and Happy* by Lois Nachamie, Dell Trade, 1997.

Allow your child to see you or other adults expressing grief. Cry or show your own sadness around your child, and he will learn that is OK for him to cry and be sad. Give him permission to show his feelings by showing your feelings and not denying your own grief. Be aware that if you show grief with extreme anger or out-of-control actions, you will teach the child to react to death in the same way.

> —Ideas found in *Helping Children Cope with the Loss of a Loved One:*
> *A Guide for Grownups* by William C. Kroen, Free Spirit Publishing, 1996.

Allow your child to attend a funeral if he doesn't appear afraid, if he is able to understand what it's for, if he appears able to stay in control, and if he wants to go. Funerals are a time to say good-bye and letting him be part of the good-bye ceremony may comfort him and help him work through his grief. If you take your child, be sure to tell him clearly and accurately what will happen. Consider having someone come to the funeral who can help with your child if he needs to leave and you need to stay. If you do not take your child to the funeral, consider giving him another opportunity to say good-bye, perhaps at the grave.

> —Ideas found in *Caring for Your Baby and Young Child* (American Academy of Pediatrics, revised edition) Bantam Books, 1998.

Death and Grief

Help your child deal with his feelings of loss:

- Help him talk about his feelings, then recognize and support them. Draw pictures together and ask him to draw his feelings, worries, family members, what's on his mind, or a picture of the person who has died. Play puppets together and bring out your child's feelings through play. Put on some music and ask your child what the music makes him think of. Let him know that is it OK for him to feel the way that he does. Ask him if he can pick out a color that looks like how he feels and then ask him to explain why he picked that color.
- Ask your child about any favorite times or memories he has about the person who has died.
- Read books together about death and ask him what he thinks or how he feels about the story.
- Ask your child what object, clothing, photograph, or memento helps him feel connected to the person who has died. Help him talk about why that object reminds him of the person.
- Help your child find a stone that can be his special worry stone. He can paint it, decorate it, carry it in his pocket, or hold it in his hand when he needs to release some tension by rubbing or holding it.
- Help your child say good-bye to the loved one. Plan a simple service, ritual, celebration, or event in which your child can say good-bye: planting something living, placing a note for the loved one in a balloon and letting it go, placing a picture or card at the grave, or any way your child can actively say good-bye.

> —Ideas found in "Special Needs of Bereaved Children: Effective Tools for Helping" by Maryanne Schreder in *Bereaved Children and Teens: A Support Guide for Parents and Professionals* edited by Earl A. Grollman, Beacon Press, 1995.

Find many ways to help a child say good-bye and remember the loved person who has died:

- Find pictures of the person or make drawings, and create a memory book.
- Write down memories, stories, poems, and thoughts about the person.
- Pick out something special that belonged to the loved one to help remember the person.
- Keep a photograph of the person where the child can look at it when he wants to.
- Visit the cemetery where the loved one is buried.
- Tell funny stories about the person.
- If the loved one taught the child something, encourage him to keep doing it.
- Plant a bush, tree, or flower in memory of the person.
- Give the loved one's name to a teddy bear or pet.
- Honor the person's birthday with a celebration.

Remember how good it feels to be alive and that enjoying life does not mean that you don't remember the loved one, but that you have room in your life for many things.

> —Ideas found in *When Dinosaurs Die: A Guide to Understanding Death* by Laurene Krasney Brown and Marc Brown, Little, Brown and Co., 1996.

Help a child understand more about death and loss by reading about it together:

- *The Dead Bird* by Margaret Wise Brown
- *Lifetimes: A Beautiful Way to Explain Death to Children* by Bryan Mellonie and Robert Ingpen
- *Nana Upstairs and Nana Downstairs* by Tomie De Paola
- *Pearl's Marigolds for Grandpa* by Jane Breskin Zalben
- *The Tenth Good Thing About Barney* by Judith Viorst (also available in video)
- *When A Pet Dies* by Fred Rogers
- *When I Die, Will I Get Better?* by Joeri Breebaart

When to Get More Help

C hildren typically grow and learn new skills in their own time and at their own pace within the wide range of what is normal. Sometimes, children need a bit of extra help to keep their development on track, or to stay healthy and happy. Sometimes, parents need help in providing for a child's needs or sorting out the best approaches to parenting.

Consider getting help for your child if he:

- Has experienced a profound loss: death of parent, sibling, friend, or grandparent that he was close to; or a divorce.
- Is unable to sleep, eat, or get back to doing daily activities as usual.
- Loses interest in activities, events, and people.
- Is afraid of being alone.
- Has prolonged periods of crying or temper tantrums.
- Frequently imitates a person who has recently died or talks about wanting to join them.
- Acts much younger than usual for a long time.

Consider getting help for yourself if you:

- Have experienced a loss and have a difficult time recovering from it.

You are the expert when it comes to your family and child. If you have a concern, trust your instinct, and find someone trained to help you: health care providers, early intervention teams, mental health professionals, parent educators and consultants, or telephone help-line staff. Think about talking it over with friends and family, too. You don't need to worry alone! Turn to "Finding Help in Your Community" on page 4 to learn about finding help near you.

More Help and Information

Books for Parents

- *Bereaved Children and Teens: A Support Guide for Parents and Professionals* edited by Earl A. Grollman, Beacon Press, 1995.
- *The Grieving Child: A Parent's Guide* by Helen Fitzgerald. Simon & Schuster, 1992.
- *Helping Children Cope with the Loss of a Loved One: A Guide for Grownups* by William C. Kroen. Free Spirit Publishing, 1996.
- *Helping Children Cope with Separation and Loss* by Claudia Jewett Jarratt. Harvard Common Press, 1994.

Articles, Pamphlets, & Booklets

- "Coping With Loss: Bereavement and Grief" from the National Mental Health Association, 800-969-6642, Web site: www.nmha.org

National Organizations

- The Dougy Center, The National Center for Grieving Children and Families
  Fax: 503-777-3097
  Web site: www.dougy.org

Web Sites

- GriefNet, an online death and grief resource.
  www.griefnet.org
- Growth House, a gateway to online resources on death and dying.
  www.growthhouse.org

Discipline Tools, Rules, and Limit Setting

Description

Discipline is the process of guiding and teaching children to have acceptable behavior within certain limits, to co-operate, to be responsible, and to think for themselves. Discipline is not the same as punishment. Punishment treats the *person* as wrong and deals with the past. Discipline treats the *act* as wrong and deals with the present and future. The goal for children is to gradually gain an inner discipline that will guide them in the world.

Realistic Expectations

- Children under age five are not motivated to follow rules in order to do what is right yet, but act more to gain approval from the important adults in their lives, or to avoid consequences. Knowing right from wrong is an abstract concept that takes time and experience to understand.
- Different ages and stages of development present different needs and discipline challenges:
  - At age one, children begin to learn that they cannot always behave as they please, but they cannot easily understand and follow rules, yet.
  - At age two, children only begin to follow simple rules and are not able to follow them consistently.
  - At age three, children can follow a few more rules, though still not consistently. Typically, they can come when asked, wait for a turn, avoid some dangers, and obey the adult in charge.
  - At age four, children still have limited self-control but can follow directions, obey an authority figure, return things to their place, and treat things with care.
- Many discipline problems can be prevented by childproofing your home and by following routines for eating, sleeping, resting, doing chores, and playing. Routines provide children with comforting structure that lets them know what to expect and when to expect it.
- Young children need adults to watch and guide them, and to protect them from harm because they do not yet consistently remember rules and limits. It is normal for young children to misbehave because they are just learning the rules.
- Physical punishment, such as spanking, hitting, slapping, and shaking is damaging to children. It may cause children to act out of fear, instead of a motivation to strive for responsible behavior. Children who are physically punished may develop low self-esteem and may increase their tendency toward aggression.
- It is estimated that 60-79% of child abuse cases began as a spanking.
- Learning *self*-discipline takes a childhood filled with patience, love, and limits provided by adults consistently and repeatedly.

Approaches

Treat your child with the same respect that you want for yourself. When you discipline your child, ask yourself if you are showing your child the kind of regard or consideration that you want them to give to you. If not, consider another approach.

> —Ideas found in *Kids Are Worth It!* by Barbara Coloroso, Avon Books, 1995.

Help your child put her energy to good use. Provide your child with many opportunities to run, jump, kick, sing, dance, throw, splash, pedal, and be active. Your young child has a lot of energy that needs a positive outlet or it may be expressed in misbehavior.

> —Ideas found in *What to Expect the Toddler Years* by Arlene Eisenberg,
> Heidi E. Murkoff, and Sandee E. Hathaway, Workman Pub., 1994.

When creating rules for your family, focus on simple positive messages that teach your child values. Establishing family ground rules is one of the best ways to set limits for your child. Rules should be simple, clear, and few in number. Avoid stating them as negatives such as no hitting, no eating in the living room, or no swearing. State the rules in positive language:

- We keep a clean house by picking up our own messes.
- We respect each other's privacy when others ask for space.
- We are considerate of others with the amount of noise we make.
- We are peaceful; we use our voices, not our hands to work out problems.

Use your family rules to guide your child toward the goals you have for her, to make things work smoothly, to keep her safe, and to help everyone to respect each other's needs.

> —Ideas found in *The Family Virtues Guide: Simple Ways to Bring Out the Best in
> Our Children and Ourselves* by Linda Kavelin Popov, Dan Popov, and John Kavelin,
> Plume, 1997.

Before you discipline your child, take the time to do some quick problem solving. Use the STAR method to help you think before you act.

- **S** Stop and focus. On yourself, your child, and the problem. Get an idea of where you are and where you want to go before you do something that may make life more difficult for you and your child.
- **T** Think of ideas. Lots of ideas. Different ideas.
- **A** Act effectively. The most wonderful plan will not work if you don't "do it." Pick your battles. Chose your timing. Get the support you need to carry out the plan.
- **R** Review, revise, reward. Few plans work completely the first time. Most successful parents need to tweak their plans several times before the situation is satisfactorily resolved. Reward yourself for effort or success.

> —From *Love & Limits: Guidance Tools for Creative Parenting* by Elizabeth Crary,
> Parenting Press, Inc., 1994. For more information, call 800-992-6657.

Consider your child's beliefs about herself and what the goals of her behavior and misbehavior may be; this will help you decide how to handle misbehavior and encourage positive behavior.

Goals of Misbehavior

Babies

- The concept of goals usually doesn't apply to infants.
- Assume that troubling behavior is baby's way of telling about a need.
- An older baby might seek attention or power. First assume that baby is using skills he/she has to get real needs met.
- Babies do not pursue revenge or display of inadequacy.

Toddlers

Belief	Goal	What do you usually feel/do?	How does child usually respond?	Age-level behavior	What can you do?
"I need to be noticed."	Attention	Annoyed. Nag, scold, remind.	Stops temporarily. Later, misbehaves again.	Whines	Give attention for positive behavior. Redirect child to other activity.
"You can't make me."	Power	Angry. Punish, fight back, or give in.	Continues to misbehave, defies you.	Answers your request with "NO!"	Give choices so child can make decision.
"You don't love me!"	Revenge	Hurt. Get back at child.	Misbehaves even more, keeps trying.	Hits or calls you name.	Avoid feeling hurt or punishing. Build trust, respect.

Preschoolers

Belief	Goal	What do you usually feel/do?	How does child usually respond?	Age-level behavior	What can you do?
"I want to be noticed or waited on."	Attention	Annoyed. Nag, scold, remind.	Stops temporarily. Later, misbehaves again.	"Watch me now!" Seeks constant attention from you.	Give attention for positive behavior when child does not seek it. Make time each day to give child full attention.
"I am in control. You can't make me!"	Power	Angry. Punish, fight back, or give in.	Continues to misbehave, defies you.	Has temper tantrums, resists minding you.	Don't fight or give in. Let consequence occur.
"You don't love me!"	Revenge	Hurt. Get back at child.	Misbehaves even more, keeps trying.	Screams, yells "I hate you!" "You don't love me!"	Avoid feeling hurt or punishing. Build trust, respect.
"I am helpless. I can't."	Display of inadequacy	Hopeless, like giving up. Give up, agree that child is helpless.	Does not respond or improve.	Whines, says "I can't do it."	Encourage any efforts. Don't pity.

—From Parenting Young Children: Systematic Training for Effective Parenting of Children Under Six (EC STEP) by Don Dinkmeyer Sr; Gary D. McKay et al © 1997, American Guidance Service, Inc., 4201 Woodland Road, Circle Pines, MN 55014-1796. Used with permission. All rights reserved.

Goals of Behavior

Babies

- Are beginning to form positive goals.
- Are learning to get some needs met through attention and power.
- Are learning to be involved, take part, by cooing, playing, cuddling.

Toddlers

Belief	Goal	What does child do?	How can you support child?
"I want to be like others."	Attention, involvement, to contribute	Copies parent sweeping, cooking, doing chores.	Notice, let child know you appreciate help.
"I can do it my way."	Power; independence	Wants to feed and undress self.	Let child do as much as possible for self.
"It's mine!"	Fairness, relationships with others	Learns to respect another child's toy.	Encourage child to share toy when done playing with it.
"I want to do it myself."	Competence	Attempts to do things on own.	Accept child's efforts.

Preschoolers

Belief	Goal	What does child do?	How can you support child?
"I belong when I contribute."	Attention, involvement, to contribute	Starts to clear dishes, put own laundry in hamper.	Notice, let child know you appreciate help.
"I can decide for myself. I can do it!"	Power; independence	Picks out clothes to wear.	Support, encourage child's efforts at doing things for self.
"I want to cooperate and get along with others."	Fairness, relationships with others	Shares toys rather than fight over them.	Notice, appreciate child's efforts to cooperate.
"I want to succeed."	Competence	Accepts own mistakes. If fails, tries again.	Accept child's mistakes and recognize progress.

—From *Parenting Young Children: Systematic Training for Effective Parenting of Children Under Six (EC STEP)* by Don Dinkmeyer Sr; Gary D. McKay et al © 1997, American Guidance Service, Inc., 4201 Woodland Road, Circle Pines, MN 55014-1796. Used with permission. All rights reserved.

Use four kinds of tools to discipline your child: nurturance, prevention, guidance, and consequence tools.

1. Nurturance tools give your child the time, love, care, attention, and affection she needs to develop into a capable and healthy adult. Your child is bound to misbehave, but when you give her affection and attention, she may be more likely to accept the limits you set because she will know that you are acting out of love and care for her.

2. Prevention tools help you think realistically about your child's behavior and may keep some problems from happening before they start. Use these tools often to avoid having to guide misbehavior.

3. Guidance tools. When nurturance and prevention tools don't stop your child from misbehaving, use guidance tools to show your child the behavior that you want her to learn. These tools teach the lessons, values, and skills that are important for self-worth, responsibility, problem solving, and self-control.

4. Consequence tools. When the other tools aren't enough to stop misbehavior, use consequences to teach a child what not to do. Consequences should occur close in time to the misbehavior, be consistent, make sense, be less severe than the misbehavior, and be used rarely. Always use consequences along with nurturance, prevention, and guidance tools.

There are many right ways to discipline your child. Be prepared with tools to guide your child toward good behavior. No one tool works every time, and there is no right tool for every situation. The more tools you have, the more effective you will be.

Nurturance Tools	
Provide real affection (all ages). Express unconditional positive feelings for your child.	**Trust and respect each other (all ages).** Encourage all family members to treat each other with respect. What your child becomes has a great deal to do with the example set by those who raise her. Be a parent who keeps promises and who is honest and sincere.
Really listen (all ages). When your child comes to you with a question or comment, stop what you are doing, look at your child, and really listen. Your listening ear is more important to your child than your advice. Watch your child; what you see can help tell you how she feels.	
	Spend time together (all ages). Someone once said, "Children spell love T-I-M-E." Words of love are important, but they don't take the place of time spent with your child. Find things to do together such as reading, playing games, doing chores, or anything enjoyable for both of you.
Love unconditionally (all ages). Your child needs to be accepted, trusted, even prized for who she is, not for what she does. Acceptance means that when your child doesn't behave, you still love her, while letting her know you don't approve of her behavior. This love and acceptance gives your child a sense of security, belonging, and support. Show love through hugs, kisses, or touch.	
	Show interest in what your child does (all ages). When you think your child is about to misbehave, ask her to talk about what she is doing. This may distract her from misbehaving.

Prevention Tools

Change your thinking about the misbehavior (all ages). Know what behavior is expected for your child's age, ability, and personality, and accept that behavior. Allow your child to make mistakes. Don't accept behavior that hurts others.

Example:
You no longer become angry when your toddler keeps climbing out of the stroller, because you understand that's how toddlers act.

Understand your child's point of view (all ages). You and your child may have different perspectives about what misbehavior is. Also, take time to think what may be going on in your child's life that may be a reason for the misbehavior.

Example:
Your child begins to tease the family dog after a new baby comes into your home.

Allow minor misbehavior (all ages). Don't respond to misbehavior if you have a more important goal you want to reach. Continue to watch the behavior in case it becomes troubling to others.

Example:
You see your three-year-old pour some of her juice in the bathtub to see the water turn purple. She is so intrigued by her experiment, you don't correct her.

Give specific instructions (all ages). Children don't always know the rule or know what you want them to do. Tell your child, but be careful not to be too controlling.

Example:
Say, "Hold my hand in the parking lot," or "Pick up your glass with both hands."

Model the desirable behavior yourself (all ages). Children strongly reflect the example set by those who raise them. Your behavior clearly tells your child what values and principles should guide her life. As a parent, you are always setting examples for your child to follow.

Example:
If you want your child to say "please" and "thank you" when asking for things, do the same yourself.

Prepare your child for a difficulty (4-18 years). When your child is faced with a problem that can't be changed or avoided, give her information to help her handle the situation.

Example:
Your four-year-old is going shopping to help pick out a toy for her cousin's birthday. Before leaving, you tell her that she can't get a toy for herself, making sure she understands the purpose of the trip before you leave.

Tell stories to make a point (all ages). Read or tell stories to your child to help her understand why something is important.

Example:
You read "The Little Engine That Could" to her when she is frustrated about not being able to do something.

Catch your child being good (all ages). Let your child know immediately when she's done something good. Give her affection and encouragement.

Example:
Give her a compliment: "It was nice of you to help your little sister get her jacket on."

Encourage humor and fun (all ages). Make things fun by doing the unexpected. Come up with a new twist to the usual routine.

Example:
If your child is grumbling about picking up her stuffed toys, make a game of it by shooting baskets with the toys into their storage box.

Distract or redirect your child (2-4 years). Physically steer your child away from a possible problem to a place where she can do a more acceptable activity.

Example:
If your two-year-old child is trying to climb on the cupboards, take her by the hand to an outdoor climber or playground.

Prevention Tools (continued)

Change the surroundings (all ages). Remove forbidden objects or change the environment to prevent the problem or misbehavior.

Example:
Your two-year-old is always climbing up the step stool in the kitchen. You fold the step stool and store it in a nearby closet.

Give your child a break to calm down (3-12 years). Gently remove your child from a difficult situation where she is losing self-control.

Example:
Your four-year-old is getting over-excited at her best friend's birthday party. You take her by the hand and say, "Let's go for a short walk up and down the apartment hall."

Change the activity (2-11 years). When your child is about to misbehave because she is tired or bored, find another interesting, acceptable activity.

Example:
When your child will not stay in her car seat because she is bored, give her a tape player and tape story for something to do.

Hold your child (all ages). When your child is distressed, a touch on the back or shoulder or being held close is comforting and reassuring. Often a child who is out of control also can be calmed by being held firmly but gently.

Example:
If your child is tired and seems ready to have a tantrum, pick her up and hug her for a few minutes in a quiet place.

Provide physical and emotional security (all ages). Children need to know that their basic needs for food, shelter, and clothing will be taken care of. Being gentle and dependable assures your child you are there for her.

Provide reassuring routines (2-16 years). Your child may sometimes misbehave because of stressful changes in her life. When routines are upset, be sure your child has familiar experiences.

Example:
Every morning you have your child get dressed after eating breakfast or every evening after your child is tucked into bed she listens to her tape recorder.

Move physically closer (all ages). Move near your child when she may lose self-control and misbehave. Your being nearby, in a warm and friendly way, may reduce her temptation to misbehave. It's equally important to move close to your child when making a request or command.

Example:
Your toddler bites when other children take toys from her. You notice a child has just taken a toy from your child so you move near her and watch.

Provide transitions (3-8 years). When young children have to change from a busy activity to a quiet activity, prepare them for the change.

Example:
After supper and a bath you read your child a story to quiet her down and get her ready for bed.

Discipline Tools, Rules, and Limit Setting

Guidance Tools

Explain limits (3-18 years). When your child doesn't understand what you expect of her, tell her the reasons for your limits.

Example:
Tell your three-year-old: "Play with the ball outside, not inside, because something might get broken."

Use humor (all ages). When a lighthearted approach might work, use humor to make a point or remind your child of what you expect of her. Avoid ridicule or sarcasm.

Example:
You asked your four-year-old to pick up her crayons from the kitchen table so you can set it for supper. She doesn't do it, and then asks what you will be having for dinner, to which you say, "Crayons I guess."

Provide a reminder of the rule (all ages). When your child forgets a rule, tell her the rule again as a positive reminder. Explain what will happen if the rule is not followed. Give the reminder once.

Example:
Say to a two-year-old: "The rule is to hold my hand in the store or you will need to ride in the stroller."

Make a polite request (all ages). Ask your child to change a minor misbehavior. Be specific and concise. If your child's behavior is totally unacceptable, don't use this tool.

Example:
If your four year old child is dumping blocks on the floor that you are vacuuming, say, "I need to get the house cleaned for company tomorrow. It would help me if you color at the table instead of taking out your train set and blocks."

Ask for the rule to be restated (3-18). If your child knows the rule, and is misbehaving anyway, ask her to stop what she is doing and tell you the rule she's breaking. Tell her when she's right.

Example:
Say, "What's the rule? No throwing balls in the house! That's right!"

Use "do" instead of "don't" (all ages). Your child will learn more effectively if you emphasize the positive. When children hear many negative words, the meaning of those words is weakened.

Example:
When your child runs in the house, say, "Outside is the place to run," instead of, "Don't run in the house!"

Ask for consequences (4-18 years). When your child doesn't seem concerned about the effect of her misbehavior, talk with her about how she and others have been affected by what she has done.

Example:
Say to your four-year-old, "You kept taking all the toys away when your friend came over to play. What happened because you did that?...That's right, she didn't want to play anymore and we had to take her home.... When your friends come to play you need to share your toys with them or they will want to leave."

Emphasize positive thinking (3-18 years). When your child feels discouraged, help her to look for the positives in what may seem like a negative situation.

Example:
Your four-year-old is grumbling about putting on her snowsuit. You encourage her to think about all of the things she loves to do in the cold, snowy weather: building snowmen, sliding, walking in freshly fallen snow.

Ask for solutions (4-18 years). After your child is calm enough to think, ask her how she might solve the problem. Have her think of as many solutions as possible and choose the best one. Be open to her ideas.

Example:
You say to your four-year-old, "You broke your sister's music box. What are some things you can do to solve this problem?" After some discussion, your child suggests that she will let her sister pick one of her music boxes to replace the one she broke.

Guidance Tools *(continued)*	
Help with frustrating tasks (all ages). When your child becomes frustrated to the point of losing control, help her just enough to solve the problem. Give some encouragement along with the help. *Example:* *Your three-year-old is becoming more and more frustrated as she tries to zip her jacket. You praise her efforts and help her by holding the bottom of the jacket zipper so she can zip it up.*	**Compromise (4-18 years).** Look for a chance to give your child a partial success when you have to say no to an overall request. *Example:* *Say, "We can't keep playing Checkers until you win. We'll play two games and then it's time for bed."*
	Ask for help to understand (4-18 years). Ask your child to tell you what she thinks is the problem. Talking about the problem may help your child think of solutions. *Example:* *Your four-year-old is coloring at the table and begins to cry. You don't know what is making her cry, so you say, "What are you crying for? Tell me, so I can try to help." Your child says, "I can't find my blue marker."*
Provide a hearing (all ages). When you are unsure about what happened and who was responsible for a problem, ask your child to describe it. Listen to her without criticizing or blaming. Then determine the extent of her responsibility for the problem. *Example:* *Say to your three-year-old who takes a toy away from a nine-month-old: "What is making the baby cry?"*	
	Show your child "how" (all ages). Sometimes your child doesn't understand what you want or know how to do what you expect. If necessary, demonstrate very specifically what you mean. *Example:* *If the child is whining, demonstrate what whining is, or if she is trying to learn to wipe up a spill, show her how to do it.*
Contract (all ages). Let your child do what she wants to do only after finishing what she has to do. The fun activity is the motivator for doing something more difficult. *Example:* *Your child has been whining for a drink. You say, "When you sit in your chair and ask me without whining then I'll get you something to drink."*	
	Redirect the child's thinking (3-18). When your child is arguing with you, avoid disagreement by mentally sidestepping the main argument and gently turning your child's thinking in a more positive direction. *Example:* *Your toddler resists being taken from her high chair. You say, "OK, tell me when you want to get down." After a few moments your child says, "I get down."*
Affirm feelings and thoughts (all ages). When your child is too emotional to think clearly, tell her the feelings and ideas that you believe she is having. Be sympathetic to your child's feelings and ideas. Don't tell her what she thinks and feels is wrong. *Example:* *Say to your four-year-old, "I know you want some-thing to drink RIGHT NOW, but we need to make some juice first."*	

Guidance Tools (continued)

Be consistent (all ages). Limits must be consistently applied and enforced. Your child is more likely to respect limits when she realizes that you mean what you say. Consistent limits provide security and direction for children.

Example:
You are tired and have had a bad day. Your child resists getting into her car seat. You consider letting her sit next to you since it is a one block ride, but you follow through with your routine of always insisting she wear a seat belt.

Offer substitutes (2-16 years). When your child is misbehaving with something, give her a similar, but more acceptable, replacement.

Example:
You see your toddler about to empty a drawer of pens and pencils. You pick her up and give her a bucket full of blocks she can empty instead to practice dumping.

Physically restrain your child (2-16 years). If your child is in an out-of-control rage, gently but firmly hold her to prevent her from harming herself or others. Speak in a reassuring, calm voice. Release your child as soon as the aggressive behavior stops. If you have to use this tool more than rarely with any age child, professional help is needed.

Example:
Your two-year-old lashes out, screaming and kicking in a violent outburst of temper. You approach her from behind, fold your arms across her chest, and hold her wrists in both of your hands until she is calm.

Remove your child from situations she cannot handle (2-16 years). Gently remove your child from a difficult situation where she is losing self-control.

Example:
Your school-age child and a friend are playing a board game. Your three-year-old is trying to play, but is unable to understand all the rules, and becomes frustrated. You say, "Let's go play a game of tag."

Have your child repeat the action (4-18 years). If your child is careless or not concerned about how she performs your reasonable request, have her repeat the action correctly.

Example:
When your four-year-old is told to pick up her crayons, she throws them in her closet on the floor. You say, "Pick your crayons up again, but this time put them in their box."

Ignore irrelevant behavior (all ages). Irrelevant behaviors are things your child does to keep you from enforcing a rule. The behavior is often irritating, but doesn't actually break the rule. Ignore this behavior (unless it bothers or is harmful to others) while enforcing the rule. Keep a neutral expression and look or move away. Paying attention to irrelevant behavior increases the chance of that behavior happening again.

Example:
Your three-year-old begins crying and complaining at the store when you will not buy her a toy. You keep shopping, don't say a word, and do not buy the toy.

Give permission (all ages). When you are not successful at stopping a minor form of misbehavior, ask yourself if you're expecting too much. You may decide to back off and admit defeat before you make the problem worse.

Example:
You insist that your four-year-old wear a dress to a party. She gets dressed and puts on her favorite sweater and pants. You argue about what she is wearing. Finally you realize it isn't that important that she wear a dress and you give her permission to let her decide what she will wear.

Say, "NO!" (all ages). When your child isn't sure how serious you are about a rule, get her attention and give a calm but firm sign of your disapproval.

Example:
You see your preschooler take several cookies right before dinner, you get her attention, and give her "the look." She puts the cookie back.

Guidance Tools (continued)	
Take a break yourself to calm down. Leave the situation to give yourself a break. Go to the bedroom for a few moments, or take a short walk. Ask a friend to watch your child, if needed.	**Put the situation in perspective.** It is important for you to understand why children misbehave. You can respond more effectively when you are aware of your child's motives and goals.
Relax. When you feel overwhelmed by stress, take a moment to release physical tension. Take a deep breath and sigh, smile to yourself, and release your muscle tension as you breathe out.	**Tap into your inner strength.** Imagine the problem situation and how you feel. Identify three feelings, thoughts, or experiences you want to have when the difficulty occurs. For example, you might want to be relaxed, patient, and courageous. When you experience the problem, re-experience the feelings and ideas you have associated with it.

Consequence Tools

Allow natural consequences (all ages). Let your child experience the natural results of her misbehavior. These results shouldn't be harmful to your child, but unpleasant enough to motivate your child to change.

Example:
You have warned your four-year-old about playing roughly with her butterfly net. You remain quiet one afternoon when you see her carrying her dolls in it. After a few moments, the net breaks and the child begins to cry.

Introduce logical consequences (all ages). Impose a penalty that is reasonable and logically connected to the misbehavior. The child is "disciplined" by this consequence of her action. Take away a privilege associated with your child's misbehavior. Explain what you're taking away in a firm but friendly manner.

Example:
Say, "You threw your trucks across the living room. Now it's time to put them away for the rest of the day."

Express disappointment (all ages). Describe your own honest feelings of discouragement or concern about your child's misbehavior. Your child wants to please you; your disappointment is a punishment.

Example:
Say, "I feel afraid and think you're lost when you hide underneath the clothing store racks when we're shopping and I can't see you."

Lose a privilege/earn back a privilege (ages 4-18). Loss of a privilege can be an effective tool. Explain what you're taking away and why in a firm but friendly manner. Make a bargain with your child. If there is something she wants to do, find a way she can earn that privilege by correcting misbehavior.

Example:
If your child rides her tricycle into the street, the tricycle could be taken away for a period of time.

Enforce a time-out (3-12 years). Time-out is a way of correcting behavior by placing your misbehaving child in a quiet place alone for a few minutes and then talking about the problem. Time-out is a short, boring time away from other people. The younger the child, the shorter the time-out. A good rule is to use one minute for every year of the child's age. You can use time-out with children when they are noisy, fighting, or doing something so annoying you can't ignore it.

It is best to approach time-out as a way to calm everyone involved, not as a way to punish your child. Never leave a child in a locked room, confined space, or other frightening location.

Example:
Tell your misbehaving four-year-old child, "You may get along with each other and continue to play, or not get along and take a four-minute time-out."

—Reprinted from *Positive Parenting: a Video-Based Parent Education Curriculum* (EP-6545), with the permission of the University of Minnesota Extension Service, 1997, 800-876-8636, www.extension.umn.edu

! **WARNING! Never shake a child and never harm a child with physical punishment.**

♦ Shaking a baby or child under the age of three can cause brain damage, blindness, paralysis, seizures, or death. Even a small amount of shaking or a less vigorous shaking can severely harm a young child.

The American Academy of Pediatrics (AAP) warns that children who are routinely disciplined with spanking and other physical forms of punishment are more likely to become aggressive and to learn that aggressive behavior is the way to solve problems. Spanking or hitting can also lead to injury and abuse, especially when it is done in anger.

Help your child learn to take time-out to "feel better" so she can then "do better." Time-out should never be used as a punishment, but instead should be used to teach children the value of taking time to help themselves to feel better. It should be used as a cooling-off period.

Do not use time-out with children younger than about 3½ years old. Until children reach the age of reason, which starts around three (and is an ongoing process that even some adults have not fully mastered), young children need constant supervision and removal, kindly and firmly, from what they can't do and guidance to an activity they can do. Say, "Let's take some time-out to read a book or listen to music until we feel better."

If your child is older then 3½ involve her in creating a nurturing (not a boring) place with stuffed animals, books, soft music, pillows, etc. Then let her choose time-out because it will "help her." Tell her that everyone needs time-out once in a while to have a place to sort out feelings, calm down, and then make a decision about what to do. When she has misbehaved or seems that she is ready to, encourage her to take a break for a short time and then to try again when she feels ready to change her behavior.

Remember, the point of time-out is to teach children that mistakes are opportunities to learn, to teach them life skills that will serve them when adults are not around, and to help them feel that they belong and are significant so they don't feel a need to engage in nonproductive behavior.

> —Jane Nelsen, author of *Time Out: Abuses and Effective Uses* and the
> Positive Discipline series.

For a spirited child, treat time-out with gentle care. When it seems that your child is losing control, help her to take a break and pull it together again to avoid unacceptable behavior.

- Teach your child how to take time-out to relax her body.
- Recognize when your child is about to lose control, and help her notice what is happening inside her body.
- Stay with her: talk softly to her, rub her back or find other ways to help her feel good physically.

> —Ideas found in *Raising Your Spirited Child* by Mary Sheedy Kurcinka, Harper Collins, 1991.

Many experts agree: Never use punishment that physically or emotionally hurts your child, including spanking, hitting, slapping, or shaking. Look at the facts:

- *Spanking leads to increased aggression in your child.*
- *Children who are spanked learn that hitting is an acceptable way to resolve conflict.*
- *Spanking leads to more spanking. It may immediately stop or reduce an undesirable behavior, but becomes less effective the more times you spank.*
- *Spanking can lead to injury or abuse of your child, especially when done in anger.*

Discipline methods, such as distraction, time-out, logical consequences, and teaching positive behavior are more effective than spanking in changing behavior in children.

Use humor in your discipline. Humor serves many purposes: it can defuse a power struggle or encourage you and your child not to take problems so seriously; it allows you to be genuine when you really want to laugh at a funny situation; it can reduce stress; it can reduce tension; and it can bring you closer to your child.

Be careful not to overuse humor. A little humor now and then will not destroy your discipline program, but it should not replace natural and logical consequences or be used to tell your child that she is charming when in fact she is doing something unacceptable or harmful. When it can reduce tension and anger to create a better situation for following through with a consequence, it can help the discipline process, heal wounds, lighten potentially heavy situations, and make life more pleasant.

> —Ideas found in *Am I in Trouble? Using Discipline to Teach Young Children Responsibility* by
> Richard L. Curwin and Allen N. Mendler, Network Publications, 1990.

Discipline Tools, Rules, and Limit Setting

Help your child understand more about rules and good behavior by reading about them together:

- *Mama, If You Had a Wish* by Jeanne Modesitt
- *Contrary Bear* by Phyllis Root
- *Contrary Mary* by Anita Jeram

When to Get Help

Children typically grow and learn new skills in their own time and at their own pace within the wide range of what is normal. Sometimes, children need a bit of extra help to keep their development on track, or to stay healthy and happy. Sometimes, parents need help providing for a child's needs or sorting out the best approaches to parenting.

Consider getting help for your child if she:

- Acts much younger than other children of the same age.
- Shows little or no improvement after you consistently try an approach to help her change a behavior for at least two months.
- Is frequently defiant and does not respond to your reasonable requests.
- Often overreacts to events and cannot be calmed down.
- Threatens others, is cruel to animals, or damages property often.
- Has had a significant change for the worse in her behavior for over a month.

Consider getting help for yourself if you:

- Run out of ideas for discipline or can't solve a problem on your own, and want ideas about other options or support.
- Were harshly or rarely disciplined as a child and are concerned you may follow the same pattern.
- Feel in danger of harming your child by disciplining her.

You are the expert when it comes to your family and child. If you have a concern, trust your instinct and find someone trained to help you: health care providers, early intervention teams, mental health professionals, parent educators and consultants, or telephone help-line staff. Think about talking it over with friends and family, too. You don't need to worry alone! Turn to "Finding Help in Your Community" on page 4 to learn about finding help near you.

More Help and Information

Books for Parents

- *A To Z Guide to Your Child's Behavior: A Parent's Easy and Authoritative Reference to Hundreds of Everyday Problems and Concerns From Birth to 12 Years* (Children's National Medical Center). Putnam Pub., 1993.

- *The Case Against Spanking: How to Discipline Your Child Without Hitting* by Irwin A. Hyman, Jossey-Bass, 1997

- *Discipline Without Shouting or Spanking: Practical Solutions to the Most Common Preschool Behavior Problems* by Jerry Wyckoff and Barbara C. Unell. Meadowbrook Press, 1984.

- *Love & Limits: Guidance Tools for Creative Parenting* by Elizabeth Crary. Parenting Press, 1994.

- From *Parenting Young Children: Systematic Training for Effective Parenting of Children Under Six (EC STEP)* by Don Dinkmeyer Sr.; Gary D. McKay et al © 1997, American Guidance Service, Inc.

- *Pick Up Your Socks: and Other Skills Growing Children Need* by Elizabeth Crary. Parenting Press 1990.

- *Playful Parenting: Turning the Dilemma of Discipline into Fun and Games* by Denise Chapman Weston and Mark S. Weston. Tarcher/Putnam 1993.

- *Positive Discipline A-Z: From Toddlers to Teens- 1001 Solutions to Everyday Parenting Problems; Positive Discipline: The First Three Years-Laying the Foundation for Raising a Capable, Confident Child; Positive Discipline for Preschoolers: For Their Early Years-Raising Children Who Are Responsible, Respectful, and Resourceful* (Revised Edition) by Jane Nelsen. Prima Publishing.

- *Positive Parenting From A to Z* by Karen Renshaw Joslin. Fawcett Columbine: Ballantine Books, 1994.

- *Time-In: When Time-Out Doesn't Work* by Jean Illsley Clarke. Parenting Press, 1998.

- *Win the Whining War & Other Skirmishes: A Family Peace Plan* by Cynthia Whitham. Perspective Pub., 1991.

- *Without Spanking or Spoiling: A Practical Approach to Toddler and Preschool Guidance* (2nd edition) by Elizabeth Crary. Parenting Press, 1993.

Hotlines

- Childhelp USA—National Child Abuse Hotline: 800-4-A-CHILD (800-422-4453)

National Organizations

- The Center for Effective Discipline, End Physical Punishment of Children (EPOCH-USA) 614-221-8829, Fax: 614-221-2110 Web site: www.stophitting.com

- Parents Anonymous 909-621-6184, Fax: 909-625-6304 Web site: www.parentsanonymous-natl.org

  Request or view online information about PA in your area.

Diversity and Acceptance

by Joe

Description

Diversity is variety. The people in the world present a variety of sizes, shapes, intellects, abilities, conditions of health, races, ethnic groups, religious beliefs, genders, sexual orientation, ages, family configurations, classes, and income levels. Acceptance of diversity means understanding the variety—how we are alike, how we are different—and treating all people with empathy and respect, regardless of differences.

Realistic Expectations

- Young children talk and ask questions about differences in people. They aren't color-blind, gender-blind, nor blind to diversity. Typical questions might be: "Why am I this color and my friend is a different one?," "Are people who live in houses better than people who live in apartments?" or "Why do I have two daddies and she only has one?"

- Babies as young as six months old have been observed noticing differences in people. Two-year-olds may not talk about differences but show their curiosity about them by touching and observing. Between three and five, children become aware of their physical characteristics and differences between themselves and others.

- Children under age five take language literally and are often confused when adults don't: African Americans are not literally black, as white Americans are not literally white.

- Young children tend to think that what is true for them is true for all: if children have only women caretakers, they may think that only women care for children.

- Children need to be told that behavior that appears different is not necessarily wrong and that people grow up with many differences in culture, beliefs, and attitudes which accounts for many differences in the way people act.

- Children who appear mean to others because they seem different from themselves may be behaving out of fear. They may see someone with a disability, a missing limb, or a serious disease, and be afraid that this could happen to them.

- Prejudice is a learned behavior. It is passed on to children in very subtle ways: looking fearfully at a stranger or group of people you see on the street, or using words suggestive of divisiveness such as "them" and "us." It is also passed on in more overt ways: not allowing a child to play with another child on the basis of gender, race, or other characteristic of diversity, and using language that slurs a group of people. Children also learn it from the media, books, music, and people outside the family. Anytime a person—adult or child—puts down, excludes, or overpowers another person on the basis of shape, size, gender, race, or any other factor of diversity, then that person is acting with prejudice.

- Acceptance is a learned behavior that becomes a common practice when children are taught about openness, patience, cooperation, many points of view, tolerance, flexibility, respect, and individuality. When children or adults view another person as an individual, not mainly as a member of a group, and treats him or her with empathy and respect, they are practicing acceptance.

Approaches

Most human beings agree on a basic set of principles that we can teach children. As difficult as they are to live by, they can be stated quite simply. We find these principles in proverbs, stories, poems, songs, prayers, legends, traditions, sayings, and literature. Among those principles are:

1. All people are valuable. No one is better than anyone else.
2. No one is perfect. We all make mistakes.
3. In some ways, we are just like everyone else on Earth. We all share the same feelings.
4. In some ways, we are different from everyone else on Earth. Each of us has a unique personality and appearance.
5. All people—no matter who they are, where they come from, what they believe, how they act, or what they look like—deserve respect and compassion.
6. Each of us is responsible for our own actions.
7. To be happy and secure, we need other people in our lives.
8. We should treat other people the way we want others to treat us.
   —From *Teaching Tolerance* by Sara Bullard, Doubleday, 1996.

To teach your child to understand diversity and practice appreciation of others, first help him take pride in who he is: his family's country of origin, and the cultures to which he belongs. When a child accepts and feels good about who he is, he can, in turn, appreciate others. Consider these gifts you can give to your child:

- Information about where he comes from: provide pictures, stories, jokes, sayings, toys, games, music, food, dance, language, books, art, costumes, or anything from your culture or country of origin.
- Relationships with grandparents, aunts, uncles, cousins, and close family friends.
- Stories and information about your family history: tell the child stories, show them pictures, and consider recording or transcribing family stories so they're not forgotten. If you're not aware of your family's background, do some research yourself.
- A positive attitude about a child's ethnicity, culture, gender, religion, family, abilities, health, height, weight, and neighborhood.
  —Ideas found in *Becoming The Parent You Want to Be* by Laura Davis, and Janis Keyser, Broadway Books, 1997.

To prevent prejudice, start early. Encourage your child to come to you with his observations, his questions, his concerns, and take them seriously. Think about your beliefs and feelings and talk to a child openly about his questions. This will be a good start in instilling positive attitudes and preventing prejudice.
  —Ideas found in *Raising the Rainbow Generation: Teaching Your Children to Be Successful in a Multicultural Society*, by Darlene Powell Hopson and Derek S. Hopson with Thomas Clavin, Simon & Schuster, 1993.

Diversity and Acceptance

> *I can only hope that we are raising our kids to embrace people who aren't exactly like them, and that their lives will be enriched by friends of different races and cultures.*
>
> —Cindy, a Parenthood Web member

To combat prejudice and foster acceptance:

- Help your child to feel secure and confident with himself. A child who feels good is not as likely to put another down. Notice things that are different and special about him and others around him.

- Give your child opportunities to meet and play with many kinds of people. Help him see that differences are to be appreciated and celebrated. Expose him to other cultures on television, in books, and in your community.

- Help your child to consider the feelings and opinions of others. A child who can put himself in another's shoes and show understanding of another is less likely to show prejudice.

- Make a clear expectation that prejudice will not be allowed. Your child should not make fun of another or leave another out on the basis of looks or background. Show him when it happens, what a stereotype is, how discrimination happens, and discuss why it's not fair. A child who can recognize prejudice will be less likely to practice it.

- Urge your child to stick up for another who is being treated unfairly. Consider giving her words to use, such as "Please stop! Don't call him/her any names. That's not right."

Be a model for your child in speaking out against prejudice. It can be difficult to say something to a friend, family member, or neighbor who is using offensive, biased language, but when you do, you show your child that it is wrong for everyone, even adults. A joke, a casual remark, or a prejudiced opinion should not be allowed. Just as you teach your child to stick up for others when they are being treated unjustly, so you should, too.

> —Ideas found in "What to Tell Your Child About Prejudice and Discrimination"
> by the National PTA and the Anti-Defamation League, 1994.
> Online: www.pta.org/programs/prejudic.htm

Be a positive role model and confront prejudice; children watch and learn from you. Be ready, willing, and able to respond to prejudicial remarks when you hear them, whether they are directed at you or another group of people.

The goal is to educate and create allies. Be non-judgmental and compassionate yet firm, when confronting people. If you assume the person is speaking out of ignorance, not maliciousness, then you can listen, ask questions, and provide more or new information rather than argue, humiliate, or shame him.

Some suggestions for what to say when someone makes a prejudicial comment:

"I am going to interrupt you because you have just offended me."

"I don't like that."

"What you just said could be heard as biased."

"Do you really believe that?"

"I'm sure you didn't mean to offend me, but you did. Let me tell you why..."

"What did you mean by that?" followed with "Why do you feel that way?"

"Perhaps you didn't mean it the way it sounded but this is how it felt when you said it..."

If you are visiting someone that you know is prejudiced in some way, consider preparing your child for the visit and then explain negative comments after the visit.

> —From *Lesbian Parenting: A Guide to Creating Families and Raising Children*
> by D. Merilee Clunis and G. Dorsey Green, Seal Press, 1995.

Begin to teach your child empathy—the ability to understand how someone else feels:

- Ask your child to consider how he would feel if he were in another person's place. Talk about how another person may feel as a result of his words or actions. Talk about why people may be feeling the way they are and think of a situation in your child's life that may help him realize what others are feeling. When your child hurts another person, it's a good time to ask him to think about how he would feel if he were the one being hurt.

- Expect your child to practice kindness and consideration; show him ways that he can do this and what kindness looks like. Show your approval of empathy, especially when he practices it. Help your child say no to people who make fun of him when he is being empathetic. Show that you don't like it when people aren't considerate.

- Talk to your child about his feelings and show him that his feelings are important, too. Allow him to have his way sometimes.

- Show your child that you are empathetic, too. Talk about how good it feels inside to be considerate of others' feelings, and to treat people how you would like to be treated.

Put yourself in another's place and if you can imagine what they are feeling, you are empathetic. When an adult or child feels empathy, they are more likely to want to help or protect others and less likely to want to hurt them. Don't expect your child to learn empathy and fairness by two or three, but if you start at this age, then when he is four or five, he may value treating people with fairness.

—Ideas found in *Bringing Up a Moral Child* by Michael Schulman and Eve Meckler,
Main Street Books, Doubleday, 1994.

> We have a very diverse group of friends—as a family, we get together on Saturday nights, sometimes ten or twelve people. It's important to have this extended family for our son—gay and straight, all different races, different religions. It's so wonderful to see him like everybody he meets and not be scared of those that are different from him. That's important to me—for him to not only tolerate diversity, but to embrace it. And he does.
>
> —Ray, San Diego

Start a discussion with your child about diversity by reading books together about many kinds of people, and from many parts of the world. A story like *Everybody Bakes Bread* by Norah Dooley teaches a child to respect differences and similarities. The child in the story goes door-to-door in her neighborhood in search of a rolling pin with which to make bread, only to discover that her multicultural neighbors make bread in a variety of wonderful ways. Everyone bakes bread but not everyone's bread looks the same. It's a joyous discovery.

Point out bias, prejudice, and stereotypes when you see it in books or the media. A stereotype shows itself when a group of people is generalized in a simple way. Talking about differences and similarities with respect, and showing your child what stereotypes and prejudice look like will help your child understand and accept diversity.

—Ideas found in "Young Children and Racism," by Debbie Reese,
National Parent Information Network's *Parent News*, March 1998.

Diversity and Acceptance

Make time to appreciate differences and teach tolerance through play:

More Than One Way to Slice It

Ask your child to help you prepare a sandwich. Before you cut it, ask him to consider all the possible ways to get the sandwich into pieces small enough to pick up and eat. Consider the many different tools to use and shapes you could make. Have him pick one idea to try on the first day and others on succeeding days. Help the child think about what he liked and why. If he chooses a favorite way or shape, occasionally encourage him to accept other ideas.

Help him practice difficult concepts like open-mindedness and cooperation by pointing out that there is more than one right way to do things: slice a sandwich, walk to the library, fold clothes, arrange toys. Showing him many ways to look at one thing helps him learn to accept many points of view, a concept that will serve him well later on.

> —Ideas found in *Ready, Set, Cooperate* by Marlene Barron with Karen Romano Young, John Wiley & Sons, Inc., 1996.

Celebrate the World

Learn about other cultures, their celebrations, their traditions, costumes, food, and instruments. Celebrate the holidays of other countries: Chinese New Year, the Nigerian Zolla Festival, or a Mexican fiesta.

> —Ideas found in *The Little Hands Big Fun Craft Book* by Judy Press, Williamson Publishing, 1996.

Who Am I?

To look at and appreciate differences, play "Who Am I?" with a child. Pretend you are someone the child knows well, like a friend or family member and describe the person. Don't say their name, but talk about personality and other things that make that person who they are.

> —Ideas found in *Teaching Tolerance* by Sara Bullard, Doubleday, 1996.

Help your child understand more about diversity by reading about it together:

- *All the Colors of the Earth* by Sheila Hamanaka
- *All the Colors We Are: The Story of How We Got Our Skin Color* by Katie Kissinger
- *Children Just Like Me* by Barnabas and Anabel Kindersley
- *Children Just Like Me: Our Favorite Stories* by Jamila Gavin
- *The Crayon Box That Talked* by Shame Derolf
- *In My Mother's House* by Ann Nolan Clark
- *This Is Our House* by Michael Rosen
- *We're Different, We're the Same* (a Sesame Street book) by Bobbi Jane Kates
- *Whoever You Are* by Mem Fox
- *Why Am I Different?* by Norma Simon
- *Wolf* by Sara Fanelli

When to Get More Help

Children typically grow and learn new skills in their own time and at their own pace within the wide range of what is normal. Sometimes, children need a bit of extra help to keep their development on track, or to stay healthy and happy. Sometimes, parents need help in providing for a child's needs or sorting out the best approaches to parenting.

Consider getting help for you or your child if:

- Either of you experience acts of prejudice due to differences: being avoided, being called names, being teased or joked about, or being the victim of violence.
- Witness or are exposed to a victim of violence or prejudice.
- Either of you avoid others due to differences.

You are the expert when it comes to your family and child. If you have a concern, trust your instinct and find someone trained to help you: health care providers, early intervention teams, mental health professionals, parent educators and consultants, or telephone help-line staff. Think about talking it over with friends and family, too. You don't need to worry alone! Turn to "Finding Help in Your Community" on page 4 to learn about finding help near you.

More Help and Information

Books for Parents

- *Child's Play Around the World: 170 Crafts, Games, and Projects for the Two-To-Six-Year-Olds* by Leslie Hamilton. Berkley Publishing Group. 1996.

- *I'm Chocolate, You're Vanilla: Raising Healthy Black and Biracial Children in a Race-Conscious World* by Marguerite A. Wright. Jossey-Bass, 1998.

- *The Little Hands Big Fun Craft Book* by Judy Press. Williamson Publishing, 1995.

- "Preparing Children to Live in a Richly Diverse World" from *Becoming the Parent You Want to Be* by Laura Davis and Janis Keyser. Broadway Books, 1997.

- *Raising the Rainbow Generation: Teaching Your Children to Be Successful in a Multicultural Society* by Darlene Powell Hopson and Derek S. Hopson with Thomas Clavin. Simon & Schuster, 1993.

- *Teaching Tolerance: Raising Open-Minded, Empathetic Children* by Sara Bullard. Doubleday, 1996.

- *Why Are All The Black Kids Sitting Together in the Cafeteria? and other Conversations About Race* by Beverly Daniel Tatum. Basic Books, 1997.

Articles, Pamphlets, & Booklets

- "Talking About Racism: An African-American Father Struggles With How to Explain Racism to His Children, by Leonard Pitts, Jr. Parenting Magazine, Online at ParentTime, available at www.parenttime.com.

- "What to Tell Your Child About Prejudice and Discrimination," National PTA and Anti-Defamation League, 1994. Call: (312) 670-6782. E-mail: info@pta.org. Or read at their Web site: www.pta.org., or the Anti-Defamation League Web site: www.adl.org.

Government

- Commission on Civil Rights.

  Complaints alleging denials of civil rights may be reported to:

  Complaints Referral, Commission on Civil Rights, 202-376-8513 or 800-552-6843

  A catalog of publications and Commission brochures are available from the Publications Office.

- Community Relations Service, Department of Justice.

  The mission of the Service is to prevent and resolve community conflicts and reduce community tensions arising from actions, policies, and practices perceived to be discriminatory on the basis of race, color, or national origin. For further information, contact any of the ten regional offices or:

  Director, Community Relations Service, Department of Justice, 202-305-2935, Fax: 202-305-3009 Web site: www.usdoj.gov/crs/crs.htm

Museums

- Museum of Tolerance, Los Angeles, CA Web site: www.wiesenthal.com/mot/index.html

National Organizations

- The Anti-Defamation League Materials Library 800-343-5540, Fax: 201-652-1973 Web address: www.adl.org.

- Parenting for Peace and Justice 314-533-4445, Fax: 314-533-1017 E-mail: ppjn@aol.com

Videos

- *Sesame Street Celebrates Around the World: A Monster New Year's Eve Party*, Children's Television Workshop, Random House, 1994. Sesame Street videos also include: *Big Bird in China*; *Big Bird in Japan*; and *Shalom Sesame*.

Divorce

Description

Divorce is the ending of a marriage, which inevitably changes a family. Ideally, new family structures are formed that nurture and support all of the adults and children.

Realistic Expectations

- Roughly one American child in three will see his or her parents divorce.
- Divorce creates a ripple effect of changes for the children involved: parents may have less money to spend; children may need to attend a new preschool or day care; children may need to live in a new home or in two homes; relationships with grandparents, aunts, and uncles may be strained; they may see less of their non-custodial parent; or they may see anger between parents.
- Because these changes happen at a time when it is important to feel a sense of stability, divorce creates a significant amount of stress in the lives of children.
- Children may show signs of tension for at least a couple of years after a divorce.
- Children may express their feelings and reactions about a divorce through behavior, not words: anger, temper tantrums, acting younger than they are, aggression, changes in patterns of eating and sleeping, nightmares, physical accidents, misbehavior, or extreme good behavior. When you see these behaviors, young children may:
  - Be frightened and confused by the threat to their security.
  - Fear that if parents stop loving each other, they could stop loving the child too.
  - Pretend the problem isn't real.
  - Feel a strong loss and have an urge to bring back the lost parent.
  - Feel responsible for a parent's fighting or leaving.
  - Have fantasies about reuniting parents.
  - Feel abandoned by the parent who leaves, and fear that the parent they live with will leave too.
  - Fear that no one will care for them.
  - Feel a deep sense of loneliness.
  - Blame one parent or the other.
  - Worry about where they will live and who will buy food.
- Some children may have strong feelings, fears, and reactions inside, without showing any behavior changes on the outside.
- Children who have difficulty adjusting to life in general will probably have more problems adjusting to the changes that a divorce brings.
- During and after a divorce, time with close friends and extended family can help children understand that even though many things are changing, there are many people who will remain constant in their lives: grandparents, uncles, aunts, cousins, teachers, day care providers, and neighbors.
- Children can be helped through a divorce in a positive way. Children who seem to show the least amount of trauma are those who: are able to remain in the same house, keep many of the same people around them, have at least one parent who is emotionally available enough to support them, remain near both parents during the divorce, and are not caught in the middle of fighting or violence before, during, or after the divorce.

Approaches

If you and your spouse are contemplating a separation or divorce, slow down and think carefully about the effects it will have on your child. Your child is bound to suffer in a divorce, but only you can decide which is better for her, the current situation or a divorce. It is well worth very careful thought.

—Ideas found in *Touchpoints* by T. Berry Brazelton, Addison-Wesley, 1992.

Reach out for support for yourself. Divorce and marital separation are considered to be life-crises, times when the demands of the situation will probably go beyond what you will have to give. Even if you are usually a person who is private or likes to stand on your own two feet, push yourself to ask for support and information from a variety of people: family members, friends, spiritual guides, mental health professionals, physicians, and attorneys.

—Ideas found in "Coping with Unexpected Marital Separation" by Barbara Mandell, *Family Information Services*, March 1998.

Consider getting professional help for your child during this time. Almost all parents have help getting through a divorce from friends and professionals. Your child deserves and needs the same to help her to understand what's happening and how she is feeling. Her pediatrician is a good place to start even though you may be offered the name of another person who specializes in handling young children in divorce situations.

—Ideas found in *Taking Care of Your Child* by Robert H. Pantell and James Fries, Perseus Books, 1999.

If your child is living with you and you're having a difficult time coping with your emotions and everyday life during the divorce, say so and get help to care for her. She will understandably be extra needy, clingy, and demanding during this time. Don't feel as if you have to keep your pain and anger from your child; tell her that you are sad or angry in simple terms. If you are acting strange and detached, your child will cope with it better in the comfort of her own home and routines than in a strange place. Invite a friend or family member to come and live with you in your home to help you for a time.

—Ideas found in *Your Baby and Child: From Birth to Age Five* (third edition) by Penelope Leach, Alfred A. Knopf, 1997.

Come to agreements about where your child will live, a visitation schedule, and child support with as little conflict as possible. Custody battles are expensive and draining for everyone involved, and very difficult for children. Don't use your child as a way of getting even with your former spouse. One of the best things you can do for your child who is experiencing a divorce is to come to an agreement without a long battle.

Get an education about custody, visitation, and child support to be able to reach a fair settlement that will best serve the needs of everyone in your family. Read about family law, and seek the help of a counselor, mediator, and/or a lawyer to help you make decisions.

—Ideas found in *Every Parent's Guide to the Law* by Deborah L. Forman, Harcourt Brace, 1998.

If you must divorce, strive for having as positive an experience as possible for everyone in your family. A good divorce has clear straightforward goals, and there are only three of them:

- Keep your family a family:
  - Accept that battles are destructive and can be avoided.
  - Recognize that compromise is absolutely necessary.
  - Construct a vision of your new family.
  - Make new rules for how the two households will be linked.
- Minimize the negative effects on your child:
  - Give your child time to adjust.
  - Accept that your child needs, and has a right to, both parents.
  - Cooperate with your ex-spouse if only for the sake of your child.
  - Establish a limited partnership agreement with clear rules.
  - Accept that your child's family will probably expand to include many others.
- Integrate your divorce in your life in a healthy way:
  - Remember the good, as well as the bad, parts of your marriage relationship.
  - Accept the inevitable mixture of feelings.
  - Face your losses without drowning in the pain.
  - Forgive yourself and your ex-spouse.
  - Let go of the anger.

> —Excerpts from *The Good Divorce: Keeping Your Family Together When Your Marriage Comes Apart* by Constance R. Ahrons. Copyright © 1994 by Constance R. Ahrons. Reprinted by permission of HarperCollins Publishers, Inc.

Help your child through a divorce by giving her messages that she needs to hear at this time:

1. I love you and I will not leave you.
2. You did not cause the divorce and you cannot change the situation. It's not your job.
3. It is OK to love your Father/Mother.
4. You can talk to me; I will listen.
5. It's OK to be sad, scared, happy, frustrated, or upset about the divorce.
6. You do not need to take care of me. I will take care of myself and get appropriate help when I need it.
7. Repeat: I love you and I will not leave you.

> —From "Parents Forever: Education for Families In Divorce Transition," (EP-6770)
> University of Minnesota Extension Service, 1997, 800-876-8636, www.extension.umn.edu

Divorce

Tell your child about the divorce at the right time, openly, honestly, and at her own level:

- Tell your young child one or two weeks before the split; it gives her enough time to prepare but not so much time that she will worry and wonder for too long.

- Tell her at home. Give her plenty of time to talk. She deserves time and privacy to cry, ask questions, and to be hugged.

- Wait until you have reached a state of emotional calm yourself. You can and should share some of your feelings of sadness and upset, but try not to dump a huge load on your child.

- Involve the other parent in telling your child a unified story. She is more likely to understand that it is true and final. If both of you can't be there, ask your spouse to call or write immediately after your talk with the child. If that is impossible, explain why to your child.

- Tell all of the children in your family at the same time. This will help cushion the blow and provide a sense of family support.

- Be honest and straightforward. This will give your child the clear message that the decision is final.

- Give many reassurances to your child that both of you will continue to love her even though you will not live together.

- Give many reassurances to your child that she did not cause this divorce, and she cannot fix it.

- Answer all of her questions, and expect many of them to be about what will happen next. Common questions will be: Why did this happen? What will happen to me? Where will I live? Where will the parent who is leaving live? Will I see the parent who is leaving again? When and where will I see the parent who is leaving?

> —Ideas found in *How to Talk to Your Kids About Really Important Things* by Charles E. Schaefer and Theresa Foy Di Geronimo, Jossey-Bass, 1994.

Change the language you use about divorce to change the way you and your child think and feel about it. Language can be powerful. Many of the typical words and phrases used to talk about divorce leave the impression of being broken or at a loss, or that parents are still connected to their old life together.

Instead of saying:	Try saying:
Visit.	Live with, be with, stay with.
I have children, but they live with their mother/father.	I have a family.
The children's mother/father left us.	I have a family.
The children are seeing/visiting their mother/father.	The children are with their mother/father at their other house, with their other family.
Motherless, fatherless, split or broken home, in-complete home.	The home, the family.
The children have one home and their mother/father visits.	The children have two homes, an expanded family.
The marriage broke up, failed.	The marriage ended.
Wife/husband ex-wife/husband.	Children's mother, children's father.

Using the right words can help you separate your old role as a mate from your continuing one as a parent.

> —Excerpted with the permission of Simon & Schuster from *Mom's House, Dad's House: A Complete Guide for Parents Who are Separated, Divorced, or Remarried* by Isolina Ricci, 1997. Copyright © 1980 by Isolina Ricci.

Help your child spend time with grandparents and other extended family members during and after a divorce. It may be difficult for you to deal with family members' emotions, but it is very important for your child to have as much time with her grandparents and other family members as she did before the divorce. By helping your child continue those relationships, she will have another avenue for support, and one more way of keeping as many things the same as possible when so many other things are changing. Grandparents, especially, also have an emotional tie to their grandchildren that needs to be respected during this time because the divorce is also difficult for them.

—Ideas found in *Dr. Spock's Baby and Child Care* (seventh edition)
by Benjamin Spock and Stephen J. Parker, Dutton, 1998.

If your child does not live with you, stay involved. Your child needs to know that even though you don't live with her anymore, she is still important to you and can count on you. Young children under three years need more frequent contact to maintain a strong relationship:

- Give her something to remind her of you when you aren't there: a book of photos, an old bathrobe, a favorite shirt, a pair of slippers, or a special toy.
- Consider visiting your child in her home if she is under two; she will be anxious when away from the parent she lives with full-time.
- Make a place for your child in your new home and make her feel like she belongs: give her a bed and storage space of her own, hang her artwork and family photographs on the walls, and if at all possible, give her a room of her own.
- Spend time alone with each child if you have more than one. Set aside time for you and your child to be together without interruption: it could be as simple as a fifteen-minute talking time before bed, reading a book together, or taking a walk.
- Invite your child's friends over to play; this makes even young children feel more at home.
- Be involved in the normal, everyday, mundane routines of your child's life. Talk to the other parent to learn about daily routines: food preferences, sleeping habits and routines, favorite activities, favorite books and toys, etc. Establish rules, routines, and responsibilities for her in your home that are as close to her other home as possible. Avoid being a "Disneyland Parent"—one who just gets together with your child for fun and games.
- Commit to actively participate in parenting your child every day: call her each day, find out how her day went, take her to dentist and doctor appointments, go to preschool conferences, check in with her day care provider, and know what she is doing, learning, and feeling in her life.

—Ideas found in *The Divorced Parent: Success Strategies for Raising Your Children After Separation* by Stephanie Marston, William Morrow, 1994.

Help your child deal with living in two homes by creating rituals and routines that help her make the changes from one to another more easily. Picking up her entire life and moving it from house to house twice a month, every weekend, or even every three days is likely to make your child out of sorts on the days she makes a change.

- Ask your child to help you create a ritual for when she arrives; it will help to ease the transition from one family and lifestyle to another. Some children will want to be alone, others may want a hearty welcome, and others may want a quick hello. A ritual might be singing a simple song, eating a meal, reading a certain book, going for a walk, or having a cup of tea or hot chocolate. Suggest that the other parent develop a transition ritual as well.
- Maintain as many routines and rituals as you can from before the divorce: the way you leave home in the mornings, how you say good-bye at day care or preschool, where you sit at the mealtime table.

• Think ahead about the family rituals that were a part of your family life that the divorce changed, and plan for how you will handle them: birthdays, holidays, gifts, shopping for clothes, medical appointments, Mother's Day, Fathers Day, etc. Which traditions do you want or need to change? What can you do to change the ritual, make it your own, or replace it? What do you need to do to make the new ritual happen?

—Ideas found in *The Single Parent's Almanac: Real-World Answers to Your Everyday Questions* by Linda Foust, Prima Publishing, 1996.

If you and your child are upset that your ex-spouse doesn't visit the child regularly, find ways to help both of you accept and acknowledge the situation, and to express your feelings about it:

• Let your child say the words she would like to write in a letter to the parent as you write them.

• Remind your child often that she is worthy of love, and that the parent's lack of visiting is not her problem to fix.

• Remind yourself often that you are not responsible for the actions of the other parent; focus on taking good care of yourself and your child.

• Join a support group that has other members who are dealing with the same problem.

• Say to yourself often, "This isn't how I wanted it to be, but I can build a new life."

• Let your child call the parent when she wants to see him or her.

• Acknowledge your child's feelings: say, "I see that you sometimes feel lonely for Daddy/ Mommy."

• Ask the other parent to join you in a session with a mediator or a counselor to help solve the problem.

• Find other loving adults, particularly the same sex as the missing parent, for your child to have relationships with: grandparents, aunt/uncles, teachers, neighbors, etc.

—From *Help! For Parents of Children from Birth to Five, a Collection of Ideas from Parents*, edited by Jean IllsleyClark, HarperSanFrancisco, 1993.

When the other parent has abandoned your child, try to face the reality, forgive, and to move on. The fact that there *is* another parent forces you to face him or her, either in person or within yourself. You can't control that other person. Perhaps you can't even really understand him or her. Forgiving certainly doesn't mean self-righteously pitying, or condoning harmful actions. Maybe in the end it means simply letting go, acknowledging that life brought two individuals together who in a magical moment created a child, and then moved on again into separate lives. As her parents, the welfare of your child rests appropriately with both of you. However, if the other parent doesn't take on the responsibility, spending time blaming him or her doesn't make you a more effective parent. Perhaps the most profound level of forgiveness is recognizing that whatever has happened between you and that other person is simply part of your own life story—a story that has left you with the gift of the child.

—Excerpt from *In Praise of Single Parents: Mothers and Fathers Embracing the Challenge*. Copyright © 1994 by Shoshana Alexander. Reprinted by permission of Houghton Mifflin Company. All rights reserved.

Use activities to help your child understand that she will be moving back and forth between homes.

- For your preschooler, draw pictures together of families. Encourage her to talk about her feelings as she does, and remind her that there are many different kinds of families.

- Mark the days off on a calendar until the next time she will see the other parent. Another way to help the young child measure time is by making a paper chain with the same number of links as the days until she will see the other parent. Remove a link each day.

- Play "house" or play with puppets, dolls, or small figures, acting out family members coming and going from home to home.

> —Ideas found in *Co-Parenting After Divorce: How to Raise Happy, Healthy Children in Two-Home Families* by Diana Shulman, Winnspeed Press, 1996.

Help your child understand more about divorce and separation by reading about it together:

Always My Dad by Sharon Dennis Wyeth

At Daddy's on Saturdays by Linda Walvoord Girard

Boundless Grace by Mary Hoffman

Good-Bye, Daddy! By Brigitte Weninger

It's Not Your Fault KoKo Bear by Vicki Lansky

Let's Talk About It: Divorce by Fred Rogers

When to Get More Help

Children typically grow and learn new skills in their own time and at their own pace within the wide range of what is normal. Sometimes, children need a bit of extra help to keep their development on track, or to stay healthy and happy. Sometimes, parents need help providing for a child's needs or sorting out the best approaches to parenting.

Consider getting help for your child if she:

- Shows signs of stress that last for a long time or unusual for her, such as acting younger than she is, seeming sad, withdrawn, or listless, fighting with friends for becoming aggressive, being very fearful, having lots of illness, or having lots of tantrums. It is often helpful for a child to have a relationship with a counselor or trusted adult to discuss issues, feelings, etc. as they arise. Issues may last a long time, or may surface again when other stressors occur, or when other life stages or changes occur.

- Regularly has a very difficult time going from parent to parent.

- Says she has been abused or neglected while with the other parent.

Consider getting help for yourself if you:

- Need support or ideas for handling the situation in a healthy manner.

- Need help finding or paying for legal advice or information.

- Need help finding new housing or other financial assistance.

- Are having trouble collecting support from your ex-partner.

- Feel sad, lonely, hopeless, exhausted, anxious, or fearful, and nothing you do seems to help you feel better.

- Need help explaining and dealing with your child's feelings about a parent who has abandoned her.

- Feel your child is being manipulated due to conflicts between you and her other parent.

You are the expert when it comes to your family and child. If you have a concern, trust your instinct and find someone trained to help you: health care providers, early intervention teams, mental health professionals, parent educators and consultants, or telephone help-line staff. Think about talking it over with friends and family, too. You don't need to worry alone! Turn to "Finding Help in Your Community" on page 4 to learn about finding help near you.

More Help and Information

Books for Parents

- *Vicki Lansky's Divorce Book For Parents: Helping Your Children Cope with Divorce and It's Aftermath* by Vicky Lansky. The Book Peddlers, 1996.
- *Divorce for Dummies* by John Ventura and Mary J. Reed. IDG Books, 1998.
- *Does Wednesday Mean Mom's House or Dad's?: Parenting While Living Apart* by Marc J. Ackerman. John Wiley & Sons, Inc., 1997.
- *Every Parent's Guide to the Law* by Deborah L. Forman. Harcourt Brace, 1998
- *The Good Divorce: Keeping Your Family Together When Your Marriage Comes Apart* by Constance Ahrons. HarperCollins, 1994.
- *Helping Your Kids Cope With Divorce the Sandcastles Way* by M. Gary Neuman and Patricia Romanowski. Times Books, 1998.
- *In Praise of Single Parents: Mothers and Fathers Embracing the Challenge* by Shoshana Alexander. Houghton Mifflin Co., 1994.
- "Separation/Divorce" in *What to Expect the Toddler Years* by Arlene Eisenberg, Heidi E. Murkoff, and Sandee E. Hathaway. Workman Pub., 1994.

Articles, Pamphlets, & Booklets

- "Divorce: Ten Things Your Mother Never Told You" by Vicki Lansky. Online. Divorce Online. Available: www.divorceonline.com.
- "Handbook on Child Support Enforcement" U.S. Department of Health and Human Services, Administration for Children and Families, Office of Child Support Enforcement. View online or request from:

  Consumer Information Center
  Pueblo, Colorado 81009
  888-8 PUEBLO (888-878-3256)
  Web site: www.pueblo.gsa.gov

Community Resources

- If you need help with child support issues or questions, call your state or county child-support enforcement agency. The Office of Child Support Enforcement Web site provides links to local agencies: www.acf.dhhs.gov/programs/cse.

National Organizations

- American Academy of Child and Adolescent Psychiatry
  800-333-7636
  Web site: www.aacap.org
  Request or view: Facts for Families.
- Children's Rights Council, Inc.
  202-547-6227
  Publishes quarterly "Speak Out for Children."
- Parents Without Partners International, Inc.
  312-644-6610
  Web site: www.parentswithoutpartners.org

Web Sites

- DivorceInfo. www.divorceinfo.com.
- Divorce Net. www.DivorceNet.com.
- Divorce Online. www.divorce-online.com.
- Divorce Source. www.divorcesource.com.
- Divorce Support. www.divorcesupport.com.
- Divorce Wizards. www.divorcewizards.com.
- CYFC Links:
  Divorce, Single Parenting and Step-Families.
  www.cyfc.umn.edu/Parenting/parentlink.html#divorce.
- Free Advice: www.freeadvice.com

Doctor, Dentist, and Hospital Visits

by Jakob

Description

Becoming partners with your child's pediatrician, dentist, and other health care providers and preparing your child for the visits will help you care for your child's health needs with ease, comfort, pleasure, and success.

Realistic Expectations

- Making and keeping routine doctor and dentist appointments at prescribed times is important in maintaining children's health.

- Routinely immunizing children will prevent many dangerous childhood diseases that have taken many children's lives or caused them much discomfort: chickenpox, diphtheria, rubella or German Measles, polio, pertussis or whooping cough, hepatitis B, mumps, tetanus, and measles.

- Healthy teeth help children chew well, learn to speak more quickly and clearly, and have attractive smiles.

- It is common and normal for children (especially between the ages of one and three) to be afraid of doctor and dentist visits, because they fear the unknown and want to resist being examined by a "stranger."

- Children will generally handle medical appointments or hospitalizations better and with less fear when they are:

  - Told shortly ahead of time what to expect.
  - Given the information over and over, accurately, honestly, and in simple ways.
  - Accompanied by a parent during the appointment or hospital stay.

  - Involved in their care as much as possible.
  - Given many opportunities to talk about the experience when they are home again.
  - Treated matter-of-factly about appointments.

- Children will have widely different reactions to hospitalization, depending on their age, temperament, past experience with the hospital setting, how well they have been prepared, parents' level of anxiety, and parents' attitude toward illness and health care. However, hospitalizations are always stressful to a degree for children. Common stresses include:

  - Feelings of helplessness and vulnerability.
  - Loss of control over own body.
  - Painful procedures.
  - Separation from family and friends.
  - Lack of understanding of the experience.
  - Being treated like a baby.
  - Fear of death or of being cut up.
  - Loss of privacy.
  - Being ill.

- Children *can* have *positive* experiences with hospitalization. They may even gain a sense of accomplishment from the experience if it is handled well.

- One of the best predictors of how children will cope with a hospitalization is the parents' level of anxiety: calm parents tend to have a calming effect on their children, while anxious parents may make children anxious.

- It is very common for young children to believe that they caused their illness and hospitalization because they were bad, even if they do not talk about it.

- Children have a need to ask the same questions over and over in order to process their fears and concerns.

- Children have very little understanding about how the body works: a common fear is that if there is a cut, everything inside will fall out.

- Children who get in the habit of routinely visiting the doctor and dentist at an early age are more likely to have good health care habits as adults.

Approaches

Find a health care provider that is a good fit for you and your child:

- If you are moving, ask your former health care provider, your real estate agent, or other parents for names of health care providers in the new community.

- Call a local hospital and ask if they have a referral service or can recommend health care providers in the area.

- Contact the American Academy of Pediatrics, Pediatrician Referral Source.

> —Ideas found in *How to Find the Perfect Pediatrician* by Margaret Redhead Cronin, in *Parenting*, March 1998.

Schedule and keep regular appointments for your child. The American Academy of Pediatrics (AAP) recommends routine checkups by one month, and then at two months, four months, six months, nine months, twelve months, fifteen months, eighteen months, twenty-four months, and each year after that. It is important that you feel you can trust your health care provider, that your questions will be answered, and that your concerns will be handled compassionately. It is also important for you to feel comfortable with the staff and the general atmosphere of the office.

> —Ideas found in *Caring for Your Baby and Young Child* (revised edition) from the American Academy of Pediatrics, Bantam Books, 1998.

Immunize your child on time to protect him from dangerous childhood diseases. The schedule changes slightly from time to time, but not a great deal. If you do not have a pediatrician or medical coverage, call the local health department or community health center for help. If you have concerns about immunizing your child, talk to your pediatrician or call the Immunization Hotline at 800-232-2522 (800-232-0233 for Spanish). The hotline can also give you information on where to get free immunizations in your area.

Here's the Schedule
*Recommended by the American Academy of Pediatrics

Vaccine	Birth	1	2	4	6	12	15	18	4–6	11–12	14–16
		Months							Years		
Hepatitis B Hepatitis B	■	■			■	■				(■)	
DTaP/DTP Diphtheria, Tetanus, Pertussis (Whooping Cough)			■	■	■		■		■		
Tetanus-Diphtheria Tetanus, Diphtheria											■
Haemophilus Haemophilus influenzae type b			■	■	■	■					
Polio Polio			■	■		■			■		
MMR Measles, Mumps, Rubella						■			■	■	
Varicella Chicken pox						■				(■)	

Shaded bars indicate range of acceptable ages for vaccination. These recommended ages should not be thought of as absolute. Vaccine schedules are changed as new vaccines, combinations of current vaccines, and indications are licensed.

(■) Previously unimmunized preadolescents/adolescents should be immunized.

(■) *Those who have not had a document case of chicken pox or have not been immunized should receive the vaccine.

** Two poliovirus vaccines are currently licensed in the U.S.: inactivated poliovirus vaccine (IPV) and Oral Polio Vaccine (OPV). Parents and providers may choose among these options: 1) 2 Doses of IPV followed by 2 doses of OPC; 2) 4 doses of IPV; 3) 4 doses of OPV. IPV is the only poliovirus vaccine recommended for immunocompromised persons and their household contacts. Consult your pediatrician.

If you don't have a pediatrician, or don't know where to go in your community for your child's vaccinations, the following toll-free Immunization Hotline can help you. Call **1-800-232-2522**.

—From "American Academy of Pediatrics Immunization Schedule,"
Online, Immunize for Healthy Lives/McDonald's,
Available: www.mcdonalds.com/community/health/index.html.

Evaluate the quality of medical care that your child is receiving. Ask questions and look for the following signs of good medical care:

- Does the practitioner listen to you and your child? You both must perceive the same problems.

- Does the practitioner encourage questions? Are your questions taken seriously?

- Do you receive satisfactory answers to your questions? The quick phrase, "She'll grow out of it" may not always be enough explanation.

- Does the practitioner take an appropriate medical history? Be wary of practitioners who most often listen for only a few seconds before deciding on a course of action; actions taken on a partial story are often in error. Injuries and simple problems may not require many questions by the provider, but a complicated illness requires more.

- Does the practitioner do a careful examination before ordering lab tests? A good medical history and physical examination will usually help a health care provider make an accurate diagnosis.

- Is your practitioner concerned about your child's development and about safety matters? About preventing illness or just treating it?

- Is there a backup person available when the practitioner is out of town on vacation or at meetings?

One of the most important factors in evaluating the provider is your confidence in the practitioner. Confidence will take time and experience to develop.

> —From *Taking Care of Your Child* (fifth edition) by Robert H. Pantell, and James Fries. Copyright 1999 by Robert Pantell, James Fries, and Donald Vickery. Reprinted by permission of Perseus Books Publishers, a member of Perseus Books, L.L.C.

Evaluate alternative therapies with the same consideration that you give to any medical care for your child. Look for:

- Safety and effectiveness of the therapy or treatment. Generally, safety means that the benefits outweigh the risks of a treatment or therapy. Ask your practitioner for information, and get scientific research from libraries, online computer services, or the National Institutes of Health.

- Expertise and qualifications of the health care practitioner.
  - Talk with the practitioner about his education, additional training, licenses, and certifications, both unconventional and conventional.
  - Talk to other people who have been seen by the practitioner.
  - Get information about a health care practitioner from local and state medical boards, other health regulatory boards or agencies, and consumer affairs departments. They can give you information about a particular practitioner's license, education, and accreditation, and whether there are any complaints registered against him.

- Quality of service. Visit the practitioner's office and look at the conditions there: how many patients are seen in a day, how much time does the practitioner spend with each patient, condition of the physical space, etc.

- Costs. Ask if costs are covered by your health care insurance. Many complementary and alternative treatments are not currently reimbursed by health insurance, and patients must pay directly for the service.

> —From "Considering Alternative Therapies?" Online, National Institutes of Health, Available: http://nccam.nih.gov/nccam/what-is-cam/consider.shtml.

Doctor, Dentist, and Hospital Visits

Think ahead about the extra challenges that emergency room visits with your child will present, so that you are prepared for them. In an emergency situation with your child:

- If there is time, take a few minutes to calm yourself down. Your child will become more anxious if you are.

- If there is time, call your child's doctor or clinic for directions on whether to go to the emergency room or to the clinic.

- Keep his health insurance card and immunization record in a handy spot to grab when you are leaving. If there is time, grab any medications he is taking and a few of his favorite toys.

- When you arrive in the Emergency Room, let a nurse know you are there immediately. He will decide how quickly your child needs to be seen.

- Ask for help if you need it to make phone calls to friends or family.

- You may have to wait, but if you feel you are not being seen soon enough, ask to see a nurse, social worker, or a patient advocate.

- Before you leave, be sure that you understand all of the instructions for care and medications. Most emergency rooms will write these instructions down for you. If they don't, ask them to.

> —Ideas found in "Emergency-room Visits" by Kate Jackson Kelly, *Parents*, April 1994.

Approach your child's medical appointments in a positive, upbeat, confident manner. Give your child patience and understanding about his fears and apprehensions, and then proceed firmly and with direction.

- Plan the appointment; give him a short warning (you are the best judge of how much time he needs) and then go without hesitating.

- If you have fears of your own, don't show them to him. Be matter-of-fact and reassuring. Tell him with confidence that the health care people are trustworthy and that he can handle the appointment.

- Avoid overprotection and pitying his fears about doctor and dentist visits; these responses are likely to lead to your child feeling sorry for himself or becoming more anxious. Likewise, threatening, scolding, name-calling, or punishing will not win cooperation or build self-confidence and self-esteem.

- Tell the office staff what you need: "William could use a little encouragement today." This models assertiveness for your child.

- During the appointment, praise your child for things he is doing well.

Remain kind and firm, but offer choices when you can: "You can sit in my lap to have your blood pressure taken or you can sit on the chair."

> —Ideas found in *Positive Parenting From A to Z* by Karen Renshaw Joslin,
> Fawcett Columbine: Ballantine Books, 1994.

Help your child reach adulthood without experiencing tooth decay and enjoy a lifetime of beautiful smiles:

- Schedule regular dental visits beginning by your child's first birthday.
- Put only water in a bottle that's used at naptime or bedtime.
- Ask your dentist about how to get the right amount of fluoride for your growing child.
- Provide your child with a balanced diet.
- Start brushing as soon as your child's first tooth appears.
- Brush and floss your child's teeth daily until he can be taught to do this alone.
- Ask your dentist about sealants.

THE DEVELOPING SMILE: TOOTH ERUPTION CHARTS

PRIMARY TEETH

Upper Teeth	Erupt	Shed
Central incisor	8-12 mos.	6-7 yrs.
Lateral incisor	9-13 mos.	7-8 yrs.
Canine (cuspid)	16-22 mos.	10-12 yrs.
First molar	13-19 mos.	9-11 yrs.
Second molar	25-33 mos.	10-12 yrs.

Lower Teeth	Erupt	Shed
Second molar	23-31 mos.	10-12 yrs.
First molar	14-18 mos.	9-11 yrs.
Canine (cuspid)	17-23 mos.	9-12 yrs.
Lateral incisor	10-16 mos.	7-8 yrs.
Central incisor	6-10 mos.	6-7 yrs.

PERMANENT TEETH

Upper Teeth	Erupt
Central incisor	7-8 yrs.
Lateral incisor	8-9 yrs.
Canine (cuspid)	11-12 yrs.
First premolar (first bicuspid)	10-11 yrs.
Second premolar (second bicuspid)	10-12 yrs.
First molar	6-7 yrs.
Second molar	12-13 yrs.
Third molar (wisdom tooth)	17-21 yrs.

Lower Teeth	Erupt
Third molar (wisdom tooth)	17-21 yrs.
Second molar	11-13 yrs.
First molar	6-7 yrs.
Second premolar (second bicuspid)	11-12 yrs.
First premolar (first bicuspid)	10-12 yrs.
Canine (cuspid)	9-10 yrs.
Lateral incisor	7-8 yrs.
Central incisor	6-7 yrs.

—From "Your Child's Teeth" by the American Dental Association, copyright 1997.

Doctor, Dentist, and Hospital Visits

Ask your child what he thinks will happen at the doctor or dentist visit. Take the opportunity to give him correct information if he has any mistaken ideas about what really will happen. He may have some concerns that you never would have imagined: "I will be left forever in the hospital," "the doctor can see my thoughts by looking at me," "there is no bathroom," or "the doctor will cut me with knives."

—Ideas found in *Toddlers and Preschoolers* by Lawrence Kutner, William Morrow, 1994.

Talk to your young child about what will happen at medical appointments. Always be honest, and give him an opportunity to talk about his fears. Here are some things you might say to your child about visiting a doctor:

- "The nurse may tell you to take off all your clothes except your underwear."

- "The doctor may ask you to step on a scale so he can weigh you and measure your height. This won't hurt at all."

- "The doctor may use an instrument called a stethoscope. This is simply a tube that lets the doctor hear the sounds of your heart and lungs. This does not hurt at all."

- "The doctor may take your blood pressure by pumping up a special cuff around your arm. This will give you a tight feeling around your arm for just a short time [demonstrate by lightly squeezing your child's arm], but it doesn't hurt."

- "The doctor or nurse may give you a shot. The shot will hurt for a minute or two, but it's very important to have this because the medicine you get from the needle will help protect your body against germs that could make you sick."

- "The doctor may take a blood sample by pricking your finger and taking out a little blood. The doctor will examine this blood to make sure that everything is okay. It will hurt when your finger is first pricked, but only for just a second."

Add any other details you know will be a part of your visit. If the doctor gives children some kind of treat at the end of the visit, be sure to emphasize this positive point.

Here are some things you might say to prepare your child for a trip to the dentist:

- "You're going to the dentist next Thursday. This is a doctor who takes care of teeth. The dentist wants to help you keep your teeth strong and healthy."

- "When we get to the dentist's office, you'll sit in a chair that's kind of like the recliner we have in the living room, but it's more fun because the dentist can make it go up and down."

- "The dentist or dental assistant will put a big bib on you. Everybody—even Mom and Dad—gets a bib at the dentist's. This keeps the patient's clothes dry while the dentist is cleaning their teeth."

- "There will be a bright light shining down on you. This helps the dentist see all your teeth."

- "The dentist puts his dental tools on a little tray by your chair. This tray holds things like little hand mirrors, metal toothpicks, and cotton balls."

- "The dentist will ask you to open your mouth real wide and then he'll put his little mirror into your mouth to look at all your teeth."

Then talk about other procedures that the dentist will use like x-ray, teeth cleaning, suctioning with the tube, etc.

—Reprinted with permission from *How to Talk to Your Kids About Really Important Things: For Children Four to Twelve*, by Charles E. Schaefer, Jossey-Bass.
Copyright © 1994 Charles E. Shaefer and Theresa Foy Digeronimo.
All rights reserved.

Help your child get over his fears of doctor and dentist visits:

• Hold your child in your lap while the doctor examines him.

• Bring favorite toys and games to focus his attention away from the procedures and to comfort him.

• Do pretend checkups at home through play. A toy doctor kit is a very worthwhile, inexpensive investment. Let him be the patient sometimes and the doctor sometimes. Play out many procedures that he might encounter: getting a throat culture, getting a cast, giving a urine sample, getting called out of the waiting room, getting weighed, having a temperature taken, and having his blood pressure measured.

• Take him to the doctor or dentist office one or two times when he does not have an appointment just to have fun and become familiar with the place: read a book in the waiting room, look at the fish, and talk to the receptionist.

• Don't over-prepare. Too much buildup can increase his anxiety: tell a two or three year old on the day of the visit, and a four or five year old the day before.

• Don't use words that have unpleasant meanings like needle, hurt, or drill.

• Don't lie. If he asks if he will get a throat culture, don't lie, but try to focus on the positive: "Yes you will, it will be uncomfortable for just a few seconds, and then it will be over. It will help the doctor know how to help you get well."

• Read stories to him about animals and children visiting the dentist and doctor.

• Keep your own anxieties to yourself, both verbally and nonverbally.

> —Ideas found in "When Kids Hate the Doctor: The Best Way to Help Them Cope"
> by Susan King, *Redbook*, July 1995.

Prepare your child for hospital visits before he has a problem or an illness that requires him to go there. Make teaching your child about the hospital as common as talking about other places like the laundromat, museum, or library. Point to your local hospital as you drive by. Take advantage of opportunities to visit a hospital when someone you know is admitted there. Look at the many books and videos about hospitals. These things will help him to cope with a hospitalization later if one should be necessary.

> —Ideas found in *Child Care A to Z: the First Five Years* by Richard C. Woolfson,
> Meadowbrook Press, 1997.

If your child is hospitalized ask your doctor or hospital for *A Patient's Bill Of Rights*. It was produced by the American Hospital Association to inform patients and their families of what they can expect from the hospital and staff during a hospital visit. As your child's guardian, it is your responsibility to understand what will happen, what kind of service you should expect, and to discuss any concerns that you have with hospital staff. If you have more concerns, keep asking questions until you get the help you need.

> —Ideas found in *Take This Book to the Hospital With You*, by Charles B. Inlander,
> and Ed Weiner, People's Medical Society, 1997.

Stay with your child during hospitalizations. He needs personal care from people who know him well to be able to cope with the strange things, people, and events in the hospital. If he is separated from everyone he trusts and loves, it can be an avoidable, terrible emotional experience for him.

> —Ideas found in *Your Baby & Child: From Birth to Age Five* by Penelope Leach,
> Alfred A. Knopf, 1997.

Doctor, Dentist, and Hospital Visits

Support your child during a hospital visit in ways that will help him learn and grow from it. It is possible for children to grow in self-esteem and maturity by conquering their fears and anxieties. The following tips will help you both:

- Prepare yourself, and keep your anxieties from your child. Your own anxiety will effect how your child handles a hospital stay. Ask all of the questions you need to get the information you want.

- Spend at least the first night in the hospital with your child, even if the hospital puts up a fight about it. The presence of a parent is vital to your child's comfort through painful procedures and when separated from home and all that he knows.

- When you must leave your child, prepare him and never slip out. Before you leave, help him to trust a special nurse or staff member. Promise that you will return at a certain time, and follow through with your promise.

- When it's possible, have other friends and family members visit.

- Prepare him in advance if it is a planned visit. Be honest, complete, and simple in your descriptions of what will happen.

- Take a tour of the hospital in advance if they offer one.

- Never say, "Don't cry," or "Don't be afraid."

- If he will be having surgery, tell him that he will be asleep and not feel anything during the surgery. Tell him about what to expect when he awakens.

- Reassure him that you will be in the hospital to help him get through it.

- Reassure him that he is not responsible for making his illness happen; or in other words, he did not do anything wrong to wind up in a hospital bed. Encourage him to talk about his feelings over and over.

- Explain all procedures in very simple terms, and tell him why they are happening and how they will help him in the long run.

- Congratulate him after each procedure that he completes. Remind him that he did it!

- Solicit the help of a child life or child activity specialist to learn about the best ways for your child to work out his feelings and concerns and to meet other children.

- Let your child do whatever he can for himself to help combat feelings of helplessness.

- After the hospitalization is over, let him feel a sense of conquering the situation. Celebrate it. Remind him that he has managed it with success.

- Expect a reaction when he goes home; reactions are normal and healthy. He may regress to an earlier stage of development: a child who has been toilet trained for months may start wetting his pants again. Let him talk about and play out his feelings about the hospitalization once he is home.

—Ideas found in *Touchpoints* by T. Berry Brazelton, Addison-Wesley, 1992.

Help your child understand more about doctor, dentist, and hospital visits by reading about them together:

Barney Goes to the Dentist by Linda Cress Dowdy

Curious George Goes to the Hospital by Hans Augusto Rey

Dentists by Dee Ready

Going to the Doctor by T. Berry Brazelton, M.D.

Just Going to the Dentist by Mercer Mayer

Let's Talk about Going to the Doctor by Marianne Johnston

Let's Talk About Going to the Hospital by Marianne Johnston

The Berenstain Bears Go to the Doctor by Stan and Jan Berenstain

The Berenstain Bears Visit the Dentist by Stan and Jan Berenstain

The Crocodile and the Dentist by Taro Gomi

Tubes in My Ears: My Trip to the Hospital by Virginia Dooley

When to Get More Help

Children typically grow and learn new skills in their own time and at their own pace within the wide range of what is normal. Sometimes, children need a bit of extra help to keep their development on track, or to stay healthy and happy. Sometimes, parents need help providing for a child's needs or sorting out the best approaches to parenting.

Consider getting help for your child if he:

- Expresses a great deal of anxiety prior to medical visits.
- Develops new fears of separation, other fears, sleep disturbances, or acts much younger than his age after being in the hospital.

Consider getting help for yourself if you:

- Need help finding or paying for medical care for your child.
- Have leftover fears from your childhood medical experiences that you seem to be passing on to your child.

You are the expert when it comes to your family and child. If you have a concern, trust your instinct and find someone trained to help you: health care providers, early intervention teams, mental health professionals, parent educators and consultants, or telephone help-line staff. Think about talking it over with friends and family, too. You don't need to worry alone! Turn to "Finding Help in Your Community" on page 4 to learn about finding help near you.

More Help and Information

Books for Parents

- *Going to the Doctor* by T. Berry Brazelton. Addison-Wesley, 1996. A children's book with a chapter for adults with tips on how to ease your child through the stress of the visit

- *Take This Book to the Hospital with You: A Consumer Guide to Surviving Your Hospital Stay* by Charles B. Inlander and Ed Weiner. People's Medical Society, 1997. This is a nice, simple overview of the inner workings of a hospital, and advice and information on how to advocate for the patient and know and protect their rights.

- "Your Child's Doctor," Chapter 47 in *Touchpoints* by T. Berry Brazelton. Addison-Wesley, 1992.

- *Your Child's Medical Journal: Keeping Track of Your Child's Personal Health History from Conception through Adulthood* by Sharon Larsen. Harmony Books, 1999.

Articles, Pamphlets, & Booklets

- "Considering Alternative Therapies," National Institute of Health, National Center for Complimentary and Alternative Medicine. Write or call the Clearinghouse. Available online: http://nccam.nih.gov/nccam/what-is-cam/conisder.shtml.

- "Your Child's Teeth," American Dental Association. Ask your dentist, call or write the ADA.

Community Resources

- To find a pediatrician in your area, send a stamped self-addressed envelope with your request for a pediatrician referral in your area to:

  American Academy of Pediatrics
  P.O. Box 927, Elk Grove, IL 60009
  (see National Organizations)

Government

- National Institutes of Health, National Center for Complimentary and Alternative Medicine Clearinghouse (NCCAM)
  888-644-6226, TTY/TDY: same
  Web site:http://nccam.nih.gov/nccam/

Hotlines

- The Center for Disease Control Immunization Hotline: 800-232-2522, Spanish: 800-232-0233

National Organizations

- American Academy of Pediatric Dentistry
  312-337-2169, Fax: 312-337-6329
  Web site: www.aapd.org

- American Academy of Pediatrics
  800-433-9016, Fax: 847-228-1281
  Web site: www.aap.org

- American Dental Association
  ADA, Division of Communications
  312-440-2500, fax: 312-440-2800
  Web Site: www.ada.org

- American Medical Association
  800-AMA-3211
  Web site: www.ama-assn.org

Videos

- *Sesame Street Home Video Visits the Hospital.* Sony Wonder.

Web Sites

- Dr. Rabbit's No Cavities Clubhouse.
  Web site: www.colgate.com/Kids-world/index.html.

- Immunofacts. Web site: www.immunofacts.com.

- The Virtual Children's Hospital®.
  Web site: http://vch.vh.org.

Drug, Alcohol, and Smoking Abuse Prevention

—by Tennae

Description

The use of alcohol, tobacco products, and legal and illegal drugs is common in the United States, yet each one carries the risk of misuse, abuse, and addiction. Addiction is a physical dependence, or when a person's behavior is taken over by a substance to the point that it interferes with health or well-being.

Realistic Expectations

- In the United States, it is estimated that addiction to drugs, cigarettes, and alcohol directly or indirectly accounts for one-third of all hospital admissions, one-quarter of all deaths, and a majority of serious crimes.
- American children are smoking, drinking, and using drugs at young ages:
  - More than half of all eighth graders have tried alcohol at least once, and that they have their first drink, on average, at age eleven.
  - Three thousand children start smoking every day.
- Children of smokers are more likely to start smoking themselves, and the younger children are when they start using tobacco products, the more likely they are to become addicted to them.
- Children of alcohol or drug abusers are three to five times more likely than other children to develop addictions and a variety of other problem behaviors later in life.
- School age children and teens say that they turn to alcohol and other drugs for a variety of reasons: to fit in by doing what their friends are doing, to escape from painful parts of their lives, to fight off boredom, to have fun, to take risks, and/or to satisfy their curiosity.
- Young children are not ready to learn complicated facts about alcohol and drugs, but they can learn simple lessons about decision making, following rules, and problem solving. They are greatly influenced by observing their parents making responsible decisions about using drugs, alcohol, and tobacco.

Drug, Alcohol, and Smoking Abuse Prevention

Approaches

Take steps while your child is very young to prevent alcohol and other drug use later; don't wait until you think she has a problem. The attitudes and habits that your child learns in early childhood will be the foundation for decisions she makes later in her life. Show her that you love her, that she can trust you, and that she can talk to you about any problem.

- Teach positive values or standards about right and wrong. School age children, teens, and adults often are able to say no to alcohol or other drugs because they have strong beliefs against using them based on the values they have been taught at home.

- Make and enforce rules. Be specific, be consistent, and be reasonable. With a young child, set rules about playing fair, telling the truth, sharing toys, etc.

- Learn about alcohol, tobacco, and other drugs. Know their effects on the mind and body, and the symptoms of their use, misuse, and addiction; this will help you to honestly monitor your own habits, and to be able to give accurate information to your child when she asks for it.

- Talk to your child and really listen to her. Make sure she learns that she can bring any of her problems and questions to you.

- Give your child opportunities to be competent and successful. Praise her for the many things she does right. This will teach her to feel good about herself and develop her self-confidence.

- Model good behavior. Your child watches you very closely, and copies your actions. She learns by example: if she sees you having a drink every day to unwind after work, she will come to believe it is the way to relax.

- Create opportunities for your child to safely make choices in everyday life. Show her that you believe in her ability to make good decisions by giving her the opportunities to make choices: "Would you like to wear white or red socks today?" or "Why don't you choose the fruit for snack today?"

- Teach her how to get along with other people. When she is a school age child or teen, she may be less likely to try drugs if she is not shy or does not feel clumsy socially.

- Set aside regular times to give your child your attention and have fun with you: play a game, read a book, go for a walk, or look at the stars.

Work to build trust and respect between you and your child, and to keep the lines of communication open. Talk to her throughout her childhood at a level she can understand, about the prevalence and dangers of alcohol and drug misuse. Communicate your love for her and your desire for her to be drug and alcohol free.

> —Ideas found in "Growing Up Drug Free: A Parent's Guide To Prevention,"
> U.S. Department of Education.

Talk to your child about drugs, alcohol, and smoking using words and ideas that she can understand at her age. Change the information you give her as she grows in understanding, adding more complex ideas as you go. Most two to four year-olds will not ask questions about these matters. If they do, you can adapt the following answers to fit their questions.

If your four to six-year-old asks if smoking is bad for you, you might say, "It always is bad for you. It hurts the smoker's lungs and heart, and also the lungs and heart of the people around the smoker. It is very hard to stop smoking, so it is better never to start at all."

If a four to six-year-old asks what alcohol is, you might say, "Alcohol is a chemical that is in some drinks like wine and beer. Drinking a little alcohol makes people feel relaxed, but drinking too much makes people get out of control and feel sick. So, a little bit of alcohol isn't bad for most grown-ups, but too much can act like a poison. Children should never drink alcohol."

> —Ideas found in *Questions Children Ask & How to Answer Them* by Miriam Stoppard,
> DK Publishing, 1997.

Take steps to prevent your child from starting smoking:

- Don't smoke, or if you do smoke, don't smoke in front of her. Don't let her handle your cigarettes, pipe, cigar, or matches.
- Don't allow smoking in your home, including older siblings and visitors; ask everyone to smoke outside if they have to smoke at all.
- Make it clear to your child that you don't approve of smoking.
- Warn her about the dangers of smoking.

> —Ideas found in "Children and Smoking: A Message to Parents,"
> American Heart Association, 1996.

If you smoke, quit for you and for your child. The impact that smoking has on you and your child is great:

- Children who live in secondhand smoke, or the cigarette, pipe, or cigar smoke from another person's habit, have more ear infections, pneumonia, bronchitis, and lung diseases, and are more likely to develop asthma.
- Women who smoke while pregnant risk miscarriage and having a baby with a low birth weight. Low weight babies often have health problems and are more likely to need special care in the hospital and need to stay longer.
- Men who smoke around pregnant women also raise the risk of the woman delivering a baby with a low birth weight.
- Smoking is the greatest source of preventable death in our society. Smoking accounts for one out of every six or seven deaths each year in the United States.
- Every year, more Americans die from smoking-related diseases than from AIDS, drug abuse, car accidents, and murder - combined.
- Eighty-seven percent of all lung cancer cases are caused by smoking.
- One out of every two long-term smokers die because of smoking.
- Smokers die on average six to eight years younger than non-smokers do.

Talk to your doctor about a program to help you quit smoking. There are over forty-six million ex-smokers, and you can become one of them!

> —From *The American Lung Association 7 Steps to a Smoke-Free Life* by Edwin B. Fisher,
> Copyright © 1998, Lifetime Media, Inc. Reprinted by permission of John Wiley & Sons, Inc.

If you are concerned that you or someone in your family is abusing drugs or alcohol, consider how the abuse might be impacting your child and reach out for help. A parent's alcohol or drug dependence has a negative impact on a child in many ways; it typically:

- Causes a variety of difficult feelings, including shame, guilt, pain, loneliness, resentment, general frustration, and/or loack of confidence in a child.
- Models inappropriate use of alcohol and drugs that the child is likely to copy as a young adult and adult.
- Causes the child to focus attention on developing survival skills to help her cope with the stress of her environment, instead of developing the positive, typical life skills needed to become a healthy adult.
- Causes the child to miss out on having the security of a home where parents are fully available to help her thrive and grow.

Additionally, the child may suffer from a wide range of developmental problems if the mother used drugs or alcohol during pregnancy.

Drug, Alcohol, and Smoking Abuse Prevention

The most important things you can do for your child are to openly acknowledge the problem and to get help for both of you from someone outside of the family. Consider getting help from:

- A therapist/counselor; look for one with a good background in chemical dependency, family systems, and the developmental needs of children.

- A self-help group for yourself, and a support group for your child. 12-step programs, like Alcoholics Anonymous, are organizations that support and encourage adults as they recover from alcohol or drug dependency. Al-anon, Alateen, Alatot, and Children Are People are examples of programs designed to help either adults or children solve the problems that are typical when living with an alcoholic or other drug-dependent person. These support groups are free and designed to help you and your family within the safety of a group of people who all have the same concerns as you do. You will not be asked to give your name unless you choose to, and there are rules about keeping all of the information shared in a group confidential.

> —Ideas found in *Parenting for Prevention: How to Raise a Child to Say No to Alcohol and Other Drugs* by David J. Wilmes, Hazelden, 1995.

If your family is working to overcome an alcohol problem, help your child understand more about alcohol abuse and addiction by reading about families who have been in the same situation:

 I Wish Daddy Didn't Drink So Much by Judith Vigna

When Someone in the Family Drinks Too Much by Richard C. Langsen

Daddy Doesn't Have to Be a Giant Anymore by Jane Resh Thomas

When to Get Help

Children typically grow and learn new skills in their own time and at their own pace within the wide range of what is normal. Sometimes, children need a bit of extra help to keep their development on track, or to stay healthy and happy. Sometimes, parents need help in providing for a child's needs or sorting out the best approaches to parenting.

Consider getting help for you and your child if she:

- Has mental health or behavior problems. If someone in your home is struggling with a drug or alcohol problem, your child may be telling you with his behavior that the person needs to get help for the well being of everyone in the family.

Consider getting help for yourself if you or a family member:

- Smoke or chew tobacco and would like to quit.
- Might have a drug or alcohol problem. One yes answer to the following suggests the possibility of a drinking or drug problem, and more than one suggests a high probability:
  - Have you ever felt you should cut down on your drinking or drug use?
  - Have people annoyed you by criticizing your drinking or drug use?
  - Have you ever felt bad or guilty about your drinking or drug use?
  - Have you ever had a drink or taken drugs first thing in the morning to steady your nerves or to get rid of a hangover?

You are the expert when it comes to your family and child. If you have a concern, trust your instinct and find someone trained to help you: health care providers, early intervention teams, mental health professionals, parent educators and consultants, or telephone help-line staff. Think about talking it over with friends and family, too. You don't need to worry alone! Turn to "Finding Help in Your Community" on page 4 to learn about finding help near you.

More Help and Information

Books for Parents

- *All Kids are Our Kids: What Communities Must Do to Raise Caring and Responsible Children and Adolescents* by Peter L. Benson. Jossey-Bass, 1997.
- *The American Lung Association 7 Steps to a Smoke-Free Life* by Edwin B. Fisher, Jr. with Toni L. Goldfarb. J. Wiley & Sons, 1998.
- *HELP! For Kids and Parents About Drugs* by Jean Illsley Clarke, Carole Gesme, Marion London, and Donald Brundage. HarperSanFrancisco, 1993.
- *Parenting for Prevention: How to Raise a Child to Say No to Alcohol and Other Drugs* by David J. Wilmes. Hazelden, 1995.

Articles, Pamphlets, & Booklets

- "Children and Smoking: A Message to Parents." American Heart Association. Request from AHA: 800-242-8721. Available online: www.amhrt.org.
- "Drunk Driving: An Unacknowledged Form of Child Endangerment." Mothers Against Drunk Driving. (see National Organizations)
- "Facts About Nicotine Addiction and Cigarettes." American Lung Association. (see National Organizations)
- "Growing Up Drug-Free." and "Schools Without Drugs"(for information on individual drugs and their effect on the body) U.S. Department of Education. Request from:
  888-8 PUEBLO (888-878-3256)
  Web site: www.pueblo.gsa.gov
- "Raising a Drug-Free Child: by Nancy W. Hall, *Parents* January 1998.
- "Quitting Spitting: More Than Enough Reasons to Stop Using Spit Tobacco NOW!" American Cancer Society. (see National Organizations)

Government

- Children and Tobacco Consumer Information, U.S. Food & Drug Administration
  1-888-FDA-4KIDS
  Web site:
  www.fda.gov/opacom/campaigns/tobacco.html
- CDC's Tips, Tobacco Information and Prevention Source, Centers for Disease Control
  800-CDC-1311
  Web site: http://www.cdc.gov/nccdphp/osh/index.htm
- National Institutes of Health:
  National Cancer Institute, Cancer Information Service:
  800-4-CANCER,
  Web site: www.nci.nih.gov
  National Institute on Alcohol Abuse and Alcoholism
  P.O. Box 10686, Rockville, MD 20849-0686
  Web site: www.niaaa.nih.gov
  National Institute on Drug Abuse
  888-644-6432, TTY: 888-889-6432
  www.nida.nih.gov

Hotlines

- National Institute on Drug Abuse Hotline:
  800-662-HELP

National Organizations

- Al-Anon Family Group Headquarters Inc.
  888-4AL-ANON
  E-mail: wso@al-anon.org
  Web site: www.Al-Anon-Alateen.org

- Alcoholics Anonymous, World Services
  212-870-3400
  Web site: www.alcoholics-anonymous.org
  Look in your local phone book to find and AA chapter
  near you.

- American Cancer Society
  800-ACS-2345
  Web site: www.cancer.org

- American Lung Association
  212-315-8700
  800-LUNG-USA - for local American Lung Association
  Web site: www.lungusa.org

- Hazelden, alcoholism and chemical dependency
  recovery help.
  800-257-7810
  Web site: www.hazelden.org

- Mothers Against Drunk Driving (MADD)
  800-GET-MADD
  E-mail: victims@madd.org
  Web site: www.madd.org

- National Clearinghouse for Alcohol and Drug
  Information
  800-729-6686, TDD: 800-487-4889
  Web site: www.health.org

- National Center for Tobacco-Free Kids
  800-284-KIDS
  E-mail: info@tobaccofreekids.org
  Web site: www.tobaccofreekids.org

Web Sites

- QuitNet, information on quitting smoking.
  www.quitnet.org

- Web of Addictions. www.well.com

Eating Habits and Mealtimes

Description

Young children with healthy eating habits like to eat, are interested in food, can eat until they are full and then stop, and can enjoy eating in other places besides home. Over time, children with healthy eating habits add to those skills: learning to try new foods and like them, having good table manners, and making do with less-favorite foods.

Realistic Expectations

- Children will typically eat and grow physically at the pace that is right for their own body.
- Children know when they are hungry, when they are full, and how much they need to eat.
- Children need a fairly consistent eating and snack schedule, and a variety of healthy foods; this helps children to regulate their appetites and expand their tastes. The predictability of mealtimes and snacktimes is emotionally reassuring for young eaters.
- Children need not eat a large variety of foods at one sitting, but they should be offered a good variety each day. Children can get just as much nutrition out of well-planned snacks as they do out of meals.
- Since children's nutritional needs are different from adults, and their stomachs are smaller, they need one-quarter to one-third of an adult-sized food portion, and snacks between meals.
- Children need more fat in their diets until they are two years of age.
- Children are more sensitive to the smell, taste, and texture of food than adults. They typically react negatively to new foods, but they are more likely to try them if they are allowed to spit out the food if they don't like it. It may take up to twenty tries during twenty different meals before they will swallow and accept the new food.
- Temperament can impact the way that children approach and enjoy food; some children have regular eating habits and take to most new foods easily, some have irregular eating habits and are slow to accept new foods, some fall somewhere in between regular and irregular, and the remaining children show a mix of regularity and irregularity in their reactions to food.
- Unpredictable and picky eating are common and normal in most young children at some time: they may have clear food preferences, want only one food over and over, decide they hate certain foods that they once loved, and have appetites that change often.
- Typically, steady growth is the best proof that children are getting the right amount of food for their unique needs.
- Expect to see any or all of these mealtime behaviors in toddlers:
    - Have increasing interest in feeding themselves.
    - Use their hands and fingers to pick up foods.
    - Learn to stab food with a dull fork.
    - Hold a cup to drink, but spill liquids frequently.
    - Show a preference for unusual food combinations.
    - Play with food, create a mess, and sometimes throw food when finished eating.
    - Have a low tolerance for sitting at the table for more than five to ten minutes.

- Leave the table and return again and again to eat if permitted.
- Enjoy imitating mealtime behavior of adults.
- Expect to see any or all of these mealtime behaviors in preschoolers:
  - Begin to eat neatly with no help.
  - Begin to use small spoons and forks well.
  - Use a dull knife awkwardly, but still need assistance cutting food.
  - Drink from a cup without a lid.
  - Serve themselves from a platter, dish, or pitcher.
  - Dislike foods mixed together.
  - Use simple table manners but interrupt conversation to gain attention.
  - Prefer play to eating, but can remain at the table for five to fifteen minutes.
  - Enjoy helping to set or clear the table.
- Children learn eating habits by watching adults and older children and imitating them.
- A positive feeding relationship between parent and child throughout childhood is important; it promotes healthy eating habits and helps to prevent eating disorders in adulthood.
- As children grow, develop, and reach adulthood, some of their most vivid and fond memories may be of time spent together as a family at mealtimes.

Approaches

Provide your child with a variety of healthy foods based on the Food Guide Pyramid.

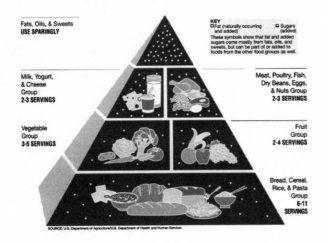

—From the U.S. Department of Agriculture

Eating Habits and Mealtimes

Provide your child with foods in child-sized portions. Suggested serving sizes based on the Dietary Guidelines for Americans for healthy children 1 - 3 and 4 - 5 years of age are:

FOOD PYRAMID GROUPS AND RECOMMENDED PORTION SIZES

Food Group	Recommended Daily Servings	Portion Size Guidelines 1-3 years	4-5 years
Grain Group	≥ 6 servings		
	Bread	¼-½ slice	1 slice
	Buns, bagels, muffins	¼-½	½
	Crackers	2-3	4-6
	Dry cereal	¼-⅓ cup	⅓ cup
	Cooked cereal	¼-⅓ cup	½ cup
	Rice, pasta	¼-⅓ cup	½ cup
Fruit/Vegetable Groups			
Vitamin C sources	≥ 1 serving		
	Whole	½ small	½-1 small
	Cooked, canned, or chopped raw	⅓ cup	½ cup
	Juice	⅓ cup	½ cup
Vitamin A sources	≥ 1 serving		
	Cooked, canned, or chopped raw	¼ cup	¼-½ cup
	Juice	¼-⅓ cup	½ cup
Other fruits/vegetables (including potato)	≥ 3 servings		
	Cooked, canned, or chopped raw	¼ cup	½ cup
	Whole	¼-½ piece	½-1 piece
	Juice	¼ cup	½ cup
Milk Group	3 servings		
	Milk, yogurt	½ cup	¾ cup
	Cheese	½ oz.	¾ oz.
Meat Group	2 servings		
	Lean meat, chicken, fish	1-3 tbsp.	4-5 tbsp.
	Dry beans and peas	1-3 tbsp.	2-4 tbsp.
	Egg	1	1
Fat Group	3-4 servings (depends on calorie needs)		
	Margarine, butter, oils	1 tsp.	1 tsp.

—Copyright 1998, The American Dietetic Association. *Pediatric Manual of Clinical Dietetics.* Used by permission.

! WARNING! Children under three years are more likely to choke on small, round, or sticky foods: hot dogs, nuts, popcorn, peanuts, whole grapes, raw vegetables, gum, and hard candy. Supervise them when they are eating, remind them to chew well, and insist that they sit down to eat.

Create pleasant mealtimes to help your child develop healthy eating habits and create memories that will last a lifetime:

- Serve meals and snacks on a predictable but flexible schedule.
- Prepare simple meals.
- Use your child's favorite plate, bowl, cup, and utensils.
- Give your child small portions on a small plate, or let him serve himself when he is able to do so.
- Give your child a small amount to drink at one time (spills will be smaller!)
- Allow your child to ask for more food and drink.
- Tolerate mealtime messiness as your child learns to eat independently and neatly.
- Focus attention and conversation on the child to increase your child's interest in staying at the table.
- Give your child one to two minutes of uninterrupted time to share the events of the day.
- Allow your child to leave the table when he has finished eating.
- Do not insist that your child finish the meal before having dessert. Consider serving dessert with the meal to downplay its importance.
- Use mealtimes as opportunities to compliment your child for any good behaviors, good deeds, or nice work performed that day.

> —From *The Yale Guide to Children's Nutrition*, William V. Tamborlane, Editor, Yale University Press. Copyright 1997.

Make a clear division of responsibility in feeding the child and live by it: you are responsible for what, when, and where food is offered to the child; the child is responsible for how much he eats. Let him go by what he feels inside to determine how much he needs to eat at meals and snack time. As long as you are doing your part by putting the right foods out at the right time, trust your child to eat what's right for him and to grow into the body that's right for him.

- Parents have a responsibility to:
  - Choose and buy healthy food.
  - Make meals.
  - Coordinate the timing of meals and snacks.
  - Provide food in a form he can handle.
  - Allow him to be as independent with eating as he is capable of.
  - Make family mealtimes pleasant.
  - Help him to share in family meals.
  - Help him to pay attention to his eating.
- The child is responsible for:
  - How much he eats.
  - Whether he eats.
  - How his body turns out.

The way to get him to eat is *not to try*. You have to let it be his idea. Parents can either help or disturb children's ability to try new foods and to know when they are full. You shouldn't force your child to eat, or restrict the amount of food he eats. Either one can make his eating worse, make him grow poorly, and make him feel bad about him-

Eating Habits and Mealtimes

self, his body, and his eating. Either can also make meals and feeding change from a fun and satisfying process into a battle in which nobody wins.

The way eating is managed with children can have an enormous impact on the way a child feels about himself and about the world.

—Excerpted with permission from *How to Get Your Kid to Eat…But Not Too Much* by Ellyn Satter, Bull Publishing, 1987.

Encourage your child to recognize when he is hungry and when he is full. Regularly ask him the following three questions:

• Does your body feel hungry? Help him to tune into body signals, like a growling stomach, to decide if he is really hungry or just bored and looking for something to do.

• What do you want to eat? Ask him if he wants something sweet, salty, or spicy; something hot, cold, or at room temperature; something soft, chewy, or crunchy.

• Are you full? Only he knows when he's full. Tell him to start with small amounts of food, assure him that he can always have more, and tell him to eat just until he is full.

Over time, he will learn to be in touch with his body's cues about when to eat and when to stop. These are some of the keys to healthy eating and lifelong weight control.

—Ideas found in "Was Your Daughter Born to Diet?" by Debra Waterhouse, *Parents*, January 1997.

Allow your child to make some choices about food. Food is a safe area for the child to experiment with choice. Be somewhat flexible about what he chooses to eat. Don't worry about the quality of each and every meal. Instead, watch his food intake over the course of several days or a week; when given a balanced, wide variety of choices of food for snacks and meals, most children more than meet their nutritional requirements and stay right along their growth curve.

—Ideas found in *Let Them Eat Cake! The Case Against Overcontrolling What Children Want To Eat: The Pediatrician's Guide to Safe and Healthy Food and Growth* by Ronald E. Kleinman, Michael S. Jellinek, and Julie Houston, Villard, 1994.

Keep encouraging your child to try new foods. While picky eating is very common in young children, it is still important to encourage him to remain open to new foods.

• Offer just one new food at a time, and let him know ahead of time what it tastes like: sweet, salty, or sour.

• Let him decide the amount to try, even if it is as small as a half teaspoon.

• Show him how to carefully spit the food into a napkin if he decides he doesn't want to swallow it, and tell him that is OK.

• Keep offering a new food over and over. Don't give up, someday he will give it a try.

• Be a good role model: he is more likely to drink milk and eat vegetables if you do.

• Occasionally have him eat with friends or siblings that are good eaters when you introduce him to new foods.

• Serve an unfamiliar food with familiar ones: if he likes pudding, use it as a dip for trying pineapple spears or kiwi.

• Serve foods with bright colors and interesting textures; he may be intrigued enough to try them.

• Involve him in preparing the new food. Even young children can help stir, mash, pour and measure.

- Never force him to try a food. Offer it. If he does not want it, simply take it away and present it again at a different time.
- Talk about the food pyramid with preschoolers as you prepare a meal or snack.
- Read stories about food. He may want to try food mentioned in stories.

—From "A Dozen Ways to Get Kids To Try New Foods."
Courtesy of NATIONAL DAIRY COUNCIL ®.

The Field Guide Fun Food Tips

- Freeze a whole banana and then serve with a spoon! It tastes like banana ice cream!
- Serve frozen peas or other vegetables right out of the freezer as finger food—they're sweet.
- Puzzle sandwiches: Cut a sandwich into odd shapes that fit together like a puzzle.
- Serve crepes with many different fillings.
- Make and use sprinkles: Chop, grind, or mix together ⅓ cup granola, ⅓ cup nuts, and ⅓ cup wheat germ. Sprinkle on yogurt, fruit, ice cream, cottage cheese.
- Serve shape pancakes: When frying pancakes, pour the batter into numbers, letters, or shapes. Let your child choose some shapes to have you prepare.
- Try having breakfast foods for dinner, and left-overs from dinner for breakfast.
- Mix plain sparkling water with fruit juice and add chunks of fruit for decoration.
- Have a winter picnic on a blanket in the house!
- Cut sandwiches, bologna, or cheese into shapes with cookie cutters.

- Prepare soft shell tortillas with melted cheese, chopped vegetables, meat, or refried beans—roll like a jellyroll or sprinkled flat like a pizza.
- Dip less desired foods in appealing dips: cheese dip, bean dip, sweet mustard, ketchup, cream dips, salsa, yogurt, honey, etc.
- Create international meals: plan a meal with a theme from another culture.
- Make a variety of healthy shakes loaded with fruit, yogurt, and honey.
- Bake a simple muffin or quick bread recipe with your child. Have a tea party, using the baked goods for the treat.
- Make kabobs or "hors d'oeuvres" using pretzels for skewers, with meatballs, fruit chunks, cheese cubes, salami, etc.
- Make cinnamon apples: Cut apples into slices and place a small amount of cinnamon sugar on the plate. Let your child dip the apples into the cinnamon
- Same food, more fun: Prepare foods that you can eat with your fingers and then serve in muffin tins, pie plates, or allow your child to occasionally use a fancy plate or serving dish.

Teach your child about the joy of food and nutrition through experience:

- Let him help plan, prepare, and serve simple snacks and meals.
- Use children's cookbooks with your preschooler.
- Plant an herb garden in a window or a vegetable garden outside.
- Visit a farm or farmer's market.
- Cook foods from different cultures.
- Bake breads in shapes of animals.
- Put real food in the child's kitchen play space for playing "house."

—Ideas found in *Healthy Eating From the Start: Nutrition Education for Young Children*,
Online, National Association for the Education of Young Children, 1996,
Available: www.NAEYC.org.

Eating Habits and Mealtimes

Help your child understand more about eating habits, mealtimes, and food by reading about it together:

- *Bread and Jam for Frances* by Russell Hoban
- *Bread is for Eating* by David Gershator
- *D.W. the Picky Eater* by Marc Tolon Brown
- *Eat Up, Gemma* by Sarah Hayes
- *Eating the Alphabet: Fruits and Vegetables from A to Z* by Lois Ehlert
- *Gregory the Terrible Eater* by Mitchell Sharmat
- *Let's Eat!* by Ana Zamorano
- *Lunch!* by Denise Fleming
- *Never Take a Pig to Lunch: And Other Poems About the Fun of Eating* by Nadine B. Westcott
- *Pretend Soup and Other Real Recipes: A Cookbook for Preschoolers and Up* by Mollie Katzen
- *The Book of Children's Foods* (cookbook) by Lorna Rhodes
- *The Please Touch Cookbook* from the Please Touch Museum

When to Get More Help

Children typically grow and learn new skills in their own time and at their own pace within the wide range of what is normal. Sometimes, children need a bit of extra help to keep their development on track, or to stay healthy and happy. Sometimes, parents need help providing for a child's needs or sorting out the best approaches to parenting.

Consider getting help for your child if he:

- Causes you concern over his eating habits, appetite, or patterns of weight gain or loss. If so, see his health care provider or a registered dietitian.

Consider getting help for you and your child if you:

- Are unable to pay for food for your family.
- Are frequently worried about your child's eating and growth.
- Find yourself in frequent battles over food with your child, or mealtimes are consistently unpleasant.
- Frequently use food as a reward or a bribe.
- Have unresolved eating issues of your own, or worry that you might have an eating disorder.

You are the expert when it comes to your family and child. If you have a concern, trust your instinct and find someone trained to help you: registered dietitians, lactation specialists, health care providers, early intervention teams, parent educators and consultants, mental health professionals, or telephone help-line staff. Think about talking it over with friends and family, too. You don't need to worry alone! Turn to "Finding Help in Your Community" on page 4 to learn about finding help near you.

More Help and Information

Books for Parents

- *American Academy of Pediatrics Guide to Your Child's Nutrition: Feeding Children of All Ages.* Villard Books, 1999.
- *Child of Mine: Feeding With Love and Good Sense* by Ellyn Satter. Bull Publishing, 1991.
- *Fat-Proof Your Child* by Joesph C. Piscatella and Bernie Piscatella. Workman Publishing, 1997.
- *First Meals: Fast, Healthy, and fun Foods to Tempt Infants and Toddlers from Baby's First Foods to Favorite Family Feasts* by Annabel Karmel. DK Publishing, 1999.
- *How to Get Your Kid to Eat... But Not Too Much* by Ellyn Satter. Bull Publishing, 1987.
- *Taming of the C.A.N.D.Y. Monster: Continuously Advertised Nutritionally Deficient Yummies: A Cookbook to Get Kids to Eat Less Junkfood* by Vicki Lansky. The Book Peddlers, 1999.
- *The Yale Guide to Children's Nutrition* by William V. Tamborlane, M.D., Editor. Yale University Press, 1997.

Articles, Pamphlets, & Brochures

- "Exploring Healthy Eating: Activities for Parents," Prepared by Center on Hunger, Poverty and Nutrition Policy, Tufts University. Request from:
  National Maternal and Child Health Clearinghouse
  703-356-1964, Fax: 703-821-2098
  E-mail: nmchc@circsol.com
  Web site: www.nmchc.org

Community Resources

Call your city or county social services department for information on:

- The Food Stamp Program, which helps low-income families buy food.
- The Special Supplemental Nutrition Program for Women, Infants, and Children (WIC) provides health referrals and food assistance to women, infants, and children who are in need.

Government

- Check the Consumer Information Catalog (CIC) to order publications on children, food, and food safety. Write, call, or view online:
  CIC
  Pueblo, Colorado 81009
  888-8 PUEBLO (888-878-3256)
  Web site: www.pueblo.gsa.gov

Hotlines

- Food Information & Seafood Hotline, Center for Food Safety and Applied Nutrition, U.S. Food & Drug Administration: 800-FDA-4010 (800-332-4010)
- For customized answers to your food and nutrition questions by a registered dietitian, call 900-CALL-AN-RD (900-225-5267). The cost of the call will be $1.95 for the first minute and $.95 for each additional minute.

National Organizations

- International Food Information Council (IFIC)
  202-296-6540, Fax: 202-296-6547
  E-mail: foodinfo@ific.health.org
  Web site: http://ificinfo.health.org

Videos

- *Breadtime Tales.* Kelvin 5400, Inc.
- *Magic School Bus for Lunch.* Kid Vision.

Web Sites

- American Dietetic Association: www.eatright.org
- KidsHealth: www. kidshealth.org.

Family

"My Family" by Jakob, age 4

Description

A family is two or more people who have made a commitment to belong to each other. A family shares love, experiences, traditions, rituals, time, responsibilities, connection, and pride in being a family. The many kinds of typical families include those with adopted children, single parents, grandparents as parents, teenage parents, working parents, stay-at-home parents, gay and lesbian parents, parents from many cultures, races, and ethnic backgrounds, and families in step-relationships.

Realistic Expectations

- Children learn about who they are, how they are alike, and how they are different from other people. A sense of being part of something larger and a sense of individuality start in a healthy family.

- Children have a strong need to feel a sense of belonging. The family is the first group that children typically belong to and feel a sense of connection with. The connections that children make here can lead the way to a life full of connections, love, and interdependence.

- Connections within a family are key to children's well-being: children from homes with strong connections tend to have more confidence, happiness and success as adults; children from homes without a strong sense of family connection tend to be more fearful, anxious and depressed as adults.

- Family problems and stress happen. Families that expect problems and find ways to deal with them tend to be healthier.

- Real families rarely resemble TV families. In real life, it usually takes longer than 30 or 60 minutes to solve a problem.

- Creating a strong and connected family is something we all can do.

Approaches

Decide what "family" means to you. No matter what kind of family you grew up in or find yourself in now, you can follow your own dream of what family should be. Circumstances may change your family situation, but even so, many of the main ingredients of family can remain intact, including love, commitment, and the sharing of home, experience, history, and rituals.

—Ideas found in *Mom's House, Dad's House* by Isolina Ricci, Ph.D. Fireside, 1997.

These traits are commonly found in healthy families:

- The healthy family communicates and listens. It fosters table time and conversation.
- The healthy family affirms and supports one another.
- The healthy family teaches respect for one another.
- The healthy family develops a sense of trust.
- The healthy family has a sense of play and humor.
- The healthy family has a balance of interaction among members.
- The healthy family shares leisure time.
- The healthy family exhibits a sense of shared responsibility.
- The healthy family teaches a sense of right and wrong.
- The healthy family has a strong sense of family in which rituals and tradition abound.
- The healthy family has a shared religious core.
- The healthy family respects the privacy of one another.
- The healthy family values service to others.

There is no such thing as a "perfect family" and no one family exhibits all of these traits. Families are families, after all, with warts and beauty marks unique to themselves. Instead of setting up an impossible, perfect family model to imitate, focus on your own family's health by becoming aware of the traits commonly found in healthy families, study the hallmarks of them, and look at family strengths.

—From *Traits of a Healthy Family* by Dolores Curran, Ballantine, 1983.

Give your child the gift of extended family and community: mothers, fathers, grandparents, cousins, uncles, and aunts. Provide your child with love, security, a sense of the strengths of the past, and the tools for success in the future through family and you will prepare her well. Extended family will help her grow and bloom.

—Ideas found in *Raising Black Children* by James P. Comer and Alvin F. Poussaint, Plume, 1992.

Family

Provide your child with the essential building blocks of family and community life that she needs to grow and develop.

DEVELOPMENTAL ASSETS FOR INFANTS AND TODDLERS *(Birth to Age 2)*

EXTERNAL ASSETS

ASSET TYPE	ASSET NAME AND DEFINITION

Support

1. Family support—Family life provides high levels of love and support.
2. Positive family communication—Parent(s) communicate with the child in positive ways. Parent(s) respond immediately to the child and respect the child.
3. Other adult resources—Parent(s) receive support from three of more nonparent adults and ask for help when needed. The child receives love and comfort from at least one nonparent adult.
4. Caring neighborhood—Child experiences caring neighbors.
5. Caring out-of-home climate—Child is in caring, encouraging environments outside the home.
6. Parent involvement in out-of-home situations—Parent(s) are actively involved in helping the child succeed in situations outside the home.

Empowerment

7. Children valued—The family places the child at the center of family life.
8. Child has role in family life—The family involves the child in family life.
9. Service to others—Parent(s) serve others in the community.
10. Safety—Child has a safe environment at home, in out-of-home settings, and in the neighborhood.

Boundaries and Expectations

11. Family boundaries—Parent(s) are aware of the child's preferences and adapt the environment to best suit the child's needs. Parent(s) begin setting limits as the child becomes mobile.
12. Out-of-home boundaries—Child care and other out-of-home environments have clear rules and consequences while consistently providing the child with appropriate stimulation and enough rest.
13. Neighborhood boundaries—Neighbors take responsibility for monitoring child's behavior as the child begins to play and interact outside the home.
14. Adult role models—Parent(s) and other adults model positive, responsible behavior.
15. Positive peer observation—Child observes positive peer interactions of siblings and other children and has opportunities for beginning interactions with children of various ages.
16. Expectations for growth—Parent(s) are realistic in their expectations of development at this age. Parent(s) encourage development but do not push the child beyond his or her own pace.

Constructive Use of Time

17. Creative activities—Parent(s) daily expose the child to music, art, or other creative activities.
18. Out-of-home activities—Parent(s) expose the child to limited but stimulating situations outside of the home. Family attends events with the child's needs in mind.
19. Religious community—Family attends religious programs or services on a regular basis while keeping the child's needs in mind.
20. Positive, supervised time at home—Parent(s) supervise the child at all times and provide predictable and enjoyable routines at home.

INTERNAL ASSETS

ASSET TYPE	ASSET NAME AND DEFINITION
21.	Achievement expectation—Family members are motivated to do well at work, school, and in the community, and model this to the child.
22.	Engagement expectation—The family models responsive and attentive attitudes at work, school, in the community, and at home.
23.	Stimulating activity—Parent(s) encourage the child to explore and provide stimulating toys that match the child's emerging skills. Parent(s) are sensitive to the child's level of development and tolerance for movement, sounds, and duration of activity.
24.	Enjoyment of learning—Parent(s) enjoy learning, and demonstrate this through their own learning activities.
25.	Reading for pleasure—Parent(s) read to the child daily in enjoyable ways.

Positive Values

26.	Family values caring—Parent(s) convey their beliefs about helping others by modeling their helping behaviors.
27.	Family values equality and social justice—Parent(s) place a high value on promoting equality and reducing hunger and poverty, and model these beliefs.
28.	Family values integrity—Parent(s) act on convictions and stand up for their beliefs, and communicate and model this in the family.
29.	Family values honesty—Parent(s) tell the truth and convey their belief in honesty through their actions.
30.	Family values responsibility—Parent(s) accept and take personal responsibility.
31.	Family values healthy lifestyle and sexual attitudes—Parent(s) love the child, setting the foundation for the child to develop healthy sexual attitudes and beliefs. Parent(s) model, monitor, and teach the importance of good health habits, such as providing good nutritional choices and adequate rest and play time.

Social Competencies

32.	Planning and decision-making observation—Parent(s) make all safety and care decisions for the child and then model these behaviors. Parent(s) allow the child to make simple choices as the child becomes more independently mobile.
33.	Interpersonal observation—Parent(s) model positive and constructive interactions with other people. Parent(s) accept and are responsive to the child's expression of feelings, interpreting those expressions as cues to the child's needs.
34.	Cultural observation—Parent(s) have knowledge of and are comfortable with people of different cultural/racial/ethnic backgrounds, and model this to the child.
35.	Resistance observation—Parent(s) model resistance skills by their own behaviors. Parent(s) are not overwhelmed by the child's needs and thereby demonstrate appropriate resistance skills.
36.	Peaceful conflict resolution observation—Parent(s) behave in acceptable, nonviolent ways and assist the child to develop these skills when faced with challenging or frustrating circumstances by helping the child solve problems.

Positive Identity

37.	Family has personal power—Parent(s) feel they have control over things that happen to them and model coping skills, demonstrating healthy ways to deal with frustrations and challenges.
38.	Family models high self-esteem—Parent(s) model high self-esteem and create an environment where the child can develop positive self-esteem, giving the child positive feedback and reinforcement about skills and competencies.
39.	Family has a sense of purpose—Parent(s) report that their lives have purpose and model these beliefs through their behaviors.
40.	Family has a positive view of the future—Parent(s) are optimistic about their personal future and work to provide a positive future for the child.

DEVELOPMENTAL ASSETS FOR PRESCHOOLERS *(Ages 3 to 5)*

EXTERNAL ASSETS

ASSET TYPE	ASSET NAME AND DEFINITION

Support

1. Family support—Family life provides high levels of love and support.

2. Positive family communication—Parent(s) and child communicate positively. Child seeks out parent(s) for assistance with difficult tasks or situations.

3. Other adult resources—Child receives support from at least one nonparent adult. Parent(s) have support from individuals outside the home.

4. Caring neighborhood—Child experiences caring neighbor.

5. Caring out-of-home climate—Child is in caring, encouraging environments outside the home.

6. Parent involvement in out-of-home situations—Parent(s) are actively involved in helping child succeed in situations outside the home.

Empowerment

7. Children valued—Parent(s) and other adults value and appreciate children.

8. Children given useful roles—Parent(s) and other adults take child into account when making decisions and gradually include the child in decisions.

9. Service to others—The family serves others in the community together.

10. Safety—Child has a safe environment at home, in out-of-home settings, and in the neighborhood.

Boundaries and Expectations

11. Family boundaries—Family has clear rules and consequences. Family monitors the child and consistently demonstrates appropriate behavior through modeling and limit setting.

12. Out-of-home boundaries—Neighbors, child care, preschool, and community provide clear rules and consequences.

13. Neighborhood boundaries—Neighbors take responsibility for monitoring child's behavior.

14. Adult role models—Parent(s) and other adults model positive, responsible behavior.

15. Positive peer interactions—Child's interactions with other children are encouraged and promoted. Child is given opportunities to play with other children in a safe, well-supervised setting.

16. Expectations for growth—Adults have realistic expectations of development at this age. Parent(s), caregivers, and other adults encourage child to achieve and develop his or her unique talents.

Constructive Use of Time

17. Creative activities—Child participates in music, art, or dramatic play on a daily basis.

18. Out-of-home activities—Child interacts with children outside the family. Family attends events with the child's needs in mind.

19. Religious community—Family attends religious programs or services on a regular basis while keeping the child's needs in mind.

20. Positive, supervised time at home—Child is supervised by an adult at all times. Child spends most evenings and weekends at home with parent(s) in predictable, fun, enjoyable routines.

INTERNAL ASSETS

ASSET TYPE   **ASSET NAME AND DEFINITION**

Commitment to Learning

21. Achievement expectation—Parent(s) and other adults convey and reinforce expectations to do well at work, school, in the community, and within the family.

22. Engagement expectation—The family models responsive and attentive attitudes at work, school, in the community, and at home.

23. Stimulating activity—Parent(s) and other adults encourage the child to explore and provide stimulating toys that match the child's emerging skills. Parent(s) and other adults are sensitive to the child's level of development.

24. Enjoyment of learning—Parent(s) and other adults enjoy learning and engage the child in learning activities.

25. Reading for pleasure—Caring adult(s) read to the child for at least 30 minutes a day.

Positive Values

26. Family values caring—Child is encouraged to express sympathy for someone who is distressed and to share his or her possessions with others.

27. Family values equality and social justice—Parent(s) place a high value on promoting equality and reducing hunger and poverty, and model these beliefs.

28. Family values integrity—Parent(s) act on convictions and stand up for their beliefs, and communicate and model this in the family

29. Family values honesty—Child learns the difference between truth and lying.

30. Family values responsibility—Child learns that actions have an effect on other people.

31. Family values healthy lifestyle and sexual attitudes—Parent(s) and other adults model, monitor, and teach the importance of good health habits. Child learns healthy sexual attitudes and beliefs and to respect others.

Social Competencies

32. Planning and decision-making practice—Child begins to make simple choices, solve simple problems, and develop simple plans at an age-appropriate level.

33. Interpersonal interactions—Child plays and interacts with other children and adults. Child freely expresses feelings and is taught to articulate feelings verbally. Parent(s) and other adults model and teach empathy.

34. Cultural interactions—Child is positively exposed to information and people of different cultural/racial/ethnic backgrounds.

35. Resistance practice—Child is taught to resist participating in behavior that is inappropriate or dangerous.

36. Peaceful conflict resolution practice—Parent(s) and other adults model peaceful conflict resolution. Child is taught and begins to practice nonviolent, acceptable ways to deal with challenging and frustrating situations.

Positive Identity

37. Family has personal power—Parent(s) feel they have control over things that happen to them and model coping skills, demonstrating healthy ways to deal with frustrations and challenges.

38. Family models high self-esteem—Parent(s) model high self-esteem and create an environment where the child can develop positive self-esteem, giving the child positive feedback and reinforcement about skills and competencies.

39. Family has a sense of purpose—Parent(s) report that their lives have purpose and model these beliefs through their behaviors.

40. Family has a positive view of the future—Parent(s) are optimistic about their personal future and work to provide a positive future for the child.

—Reprinted with permission from Nancy Leffert, Peter L. Benson, and Jolene L. Roehlkepartain, *Starting Out Right: Developmental Assets for Children,* © 1997 by Search Institute, 700 S. Third Street, Suite 210, Minneapolis, MN 55415; 800-888-7828.

Develop a sense of purpose and direction in your family. Families often have problems and feel lost, but the secret to becoming a good family is knowing where you are headed and why. Lead with initiative and follow your purpose, instead of being guided by events and circumstances. Don't just survive, lead your family to purpose and direction. Know what you want for your family, make it a priority, and then work to get there together.

> —Ideas found in *The 7 Habits of Highly Effective Families* by Stephen Covey, Golden Books, 1997.

Explore the richness of family history. It may explain the origin of some of the long-held attitudes and beliefs of a family and help you discover the impact that previous generations had on the family, positive or negative. It may uncover stories of strength and determination, of believing in self-worth, and of standing up for rights that can contribute to pride, trust, and identity in the family today. Take strength from the relatives who came before you and valued themselves, even when society didn't. Involve your child in the exploration. It will directly contribute to her feelings of self-worth.

> —Ideas found in *Different and Wonderful: Raising Black Children in a Race-Conscious Society* by Darlene Powell Hopson and Derek S. Hopson, Fireside, 1992.

Make an effort to be a part of your community. Belonging to community starts with each new relationship with a child or adult that develops. Seek help and support from the people in your area; offer help and support when you can give it. Look for and participate in events and groups in your community. The many benefits of making connections in the community include:

- Understanding how families are different and how they are the same.
- Gaining the knowledge that there is more to life than fulfilling one's own needs.
- A sense of security in connecting to a larger group.
- Greater self-esteem and happiness due to identifying with a community—something strong and important.
- The opportunity to learn about and be a part of the bigger picture: we all have a part to play in the success of the community.

Building connections in the family and community takes effort and time, but the rewards are great.

> —Ideas found in *Playwise: 365 Fun-Filled Activities for Building Character, Conscience, and Emotional Intelligence in Children* by Denise Chapman Weston and Mark S. Weston, G.P. Putnam's Sons, 1996.

Teach your child the values of the family through everyday interactions and events. Set a positive example for your child in the way you handle everyday situations, in the things that you resolve to do, in the way you handle mistakes, in the commitments that you make, in the explanations you give, in interactions with family and friends, and in the importance that you place on family. For example, if a family value is to spend time together, and the evening dinner or story time is constantly interrupted with work-related phone calls, then your child may learn that family time is not as important as work. When your child sees you setting aside special time just for family, she learns that family is a priority.

> —Ideas found in *Becoming the Parent You Want to Be* by Laura Davis and Janis Keyser, Broadway Books, 1997.

Keep a sense of humor; it is essential. Over time, problems sometimes become funny family stories. It may take time to see the humor in it all, but look for opportunities to create a classic family story. Every family has them. Consider writing them down.

—Ideas found in *I Didn't Plan to Be a Witch: And Other Surprises of a Joyful Mother* by Linda Eyre, Simon & Schuster, 1996.

Strengthen family connections through rituals. A routine is something a person does regularly, like brushing his teeth. A family ritual is regular, deliberate, planned time together; it signifies something more important and has purpose.

Telling stories is often a routine activity in waiting rooms, or happens when spare time presents itself at home. But if every Sunday evening becomes "family storytelling time," it takes on new meaning, as something family members can look forward to. When life intrudes on time together, preserve and honor the family rituals so connections can grow stronger.

Give your family these gifts through rituals:

- Expectations of what will happen and when. If a child knows that her father will not leave the house in the morning without giving her a hug, a kiss, and a "have a fun day," then your child can expect this special moment each day and look forward to it.

- A sense of "family," its personality and what makes it unique. The storytelling family may think of themselves as "the Sunday Night Storytelling Family." A family that bikes together regularly may think of themselves and be seen by others as the family of bike riders in the neighborhood.

- An understanding of who is included and important in the family: "Grandma's friend, Roy, has come to Sunday dinner for as long as I can remember," "Mr. Jordan, who lives alone next door, always comes to my family birthday party," or "The relatives from Tennessee always come to Grandma's reunion."

- Reinforcement of values: if a family value is to care for each other when someone needs help, then the weekly Saturday trip to take homebound Grandma grocery shopping and out for ice cream demonstrates support of that value.

- Time to connect with each other.

Although, rituals can and should be changed or adopted as families change and grow, using them consistently in family life builds strength in your family.

—Ideas found in *The Intentional Family* by William J. Doherty, Addison-Wesley, 1997.

Allow your child to create her own rituals that help her understand the world. For example, a child who asks for her pillow to be turned and fluffed before a hug each night at bedtime is creating a ritual. It may not be obvious to the parent why these things give her comfort or security, but it is important to recognize that they do and to support the ritual.

Rituals allow families to build relationships, to ease transitions, to help in grieving, to express values, and to honor and celebrate many facets of life.

—Ideas found in *Rituals for Our Times* by Evan Imber-Black and Janine Roberts, Jason-Aronson, 1998.

Family

Help your family connect in small ways, as well; your child will appreciate and remember these special moments. An unplanned stop for ice cream or pizza to talk, throwing the ball around together in the yard, or an unexpected kiss can create lasting memories of feeling connected to family. Your child will likely remember and appreciate the things you do together more than the toys or things she's been given.

> —Ideas found in *Familyhood: Nurturing the Values That Matter* by Lee Salk, Simon & Schuster, 1992.

Share things, places, stories, and songs to create connections within the family. Enjoy the togetherness in "our special neighbors," "our yard," "our biking path," or "our pizza shop." Create your own "our _____." These small things help a sense of family grow.

> —Ideas found in *Fun Time, Family Time* by Susan K. Perry, Avon Books, 1996.

Create family history with your child by making a family story tape. Ask grandparents to share a favorite family story or to tell a story or two about when they were young or when their children were young. Audio tape or videotape their storytelling. This gift of themselves will be enjoyed now and will bring alive the past for many generations.

> —Ideas found in *I Heard It Through the Playground* by Joel Fram, Carol Boswell, and Margaret Mass, HarperPerennial, 1993.

Create family history with your child by making a family book. Ask relatives to note a special memory about your family, the children in the family, or to write a favorite family story. Have each person write their contribution in a book and pass it on to another family member. Or collect individual stories and bind them into a special family book.

> —Ideas from *Teaching Tolerance* by Sara Bullard, Doubleday, 1997.

Help your child understand more about family by reading about it together:

 *Celebrating Families* by Rosmarie Hausherr.

 *Daddy Calls Me Man* by Angela Johnson

 Family Time (A Super Chubby book) by Margaret Miller

Fathers, Mothers, Sisters, Brothers: A Collection of Family Poems by Mary Ann Hoberman

Hooray for Me! by Remy Charlip

"More More More" Said the Baby: 3 Love Stories by Vera B. Williams

My Mom and Dad Make Me Laugh by Nick Sharratt

So Much by Trish Cooke

Take Time to Relax by Nancy Carlson

When to Get More Help

C hildren typically grow and learn new skills in their own time and at their own pace within the wide range of what is normal. Sometimes, children need a bit of extra help to keep their development on track, or to stay healthy and happy. Sometimes, parents need help providing for a child's needs or sorting out the best approaches to parenting.

Consider getting help for yourself if you:

- Need help providing food, shelter, clothing or medical care for your child.

- Have difficulty providing love, attention, emotional care, and guidance to your child.

- Have difficulty enjoying your child.

- Have difficulty understanding your child.

- Have difficulty communicating with your child.

- Have very few family members or friends nearby to help and support your family.

- Have a serious or ongoing stress or conflicts in your family.

You are the expert when it comes to your family and child. If you have a concern, trust your instinct and find someone trained to help you: health care providers, early intervention teams, mental health professionals, parent educators and consultants, or telephone help-line staff. Consider talking it over with friends and family, too. You don't need to worry alone! Turn to "Finding Help in Your Community" on page 4 to learn about finding help near you.

More Help and Information for ALL FAMILIES

Books for Parents

- *The 7 Habits of Highly Effective Families* by Stephen Covey. Golden Books, 1997.
- *Ancestors: A Beginner's Guide to Family History and Genealogy* by Jim and Terry Willard with Jane Wilson. Houghton Mifflin, 1997.
- *The Family Virtues Guide: Simple Ways to Bring Out the Best in Our Children and Ourselves* by Linda Kavelin Popov. Plume, 1997.
- *Fun Time, Family Time* by Susan K. Perry. Avon Books, 1996.
- *The Heart of a Family: Searching America for New Traditions That Fulfill Us* by Meg Cox. Random House, 1998.
- *The Intentional Family: How to Build Family Ties in Our Modern World* by William J. Doherty. Addison-Wesley, 1997.
- *Once Upon A Family: Read-Aloud Stories and Activities That Nurture Healthy Kids* by Jean Grasso Fitzpatrick. Viking Press, 1998.
- *Raising a Family: Living on Planet Parenthood* by Jeanne and Don Elium. Celestial Arts Publishing, 1997.
- *The Shelter of Each Other: Rebuilding Our Families* by Mary Pipher. Ballantine, 1997.
- *To Our Children's Children: Preserving Family Histories for Generations to Come* by Bob Greene and D. G. Fulford. Doubleday, 1993.
- *Traits of a Healthy Family* by Dolores Curran. Ballantine, 1983.

National Organizations

- National Genealogical Society
  800-473-0060
  Web site: www.ngsgenealogy.org

Videos

- *A Family Concert: Featuring the Roches and the Music Workshop for Kids.* Baby Music Boom.
- *Family Tales* (Maurice Sendak's Little Bear). Paramount.
- *The Patchwork Quilt* (Reading Rainbow). Lancit Media Productions.

Web Sites

- Children's Defensefund's Parent Resource Network: www.childrensdefense.org/prn.html
- Family.com (Disney's family web site): www.family.com
- Family Resource Online: www.familyresource.com

More Help and Information for Families with ADOPTED OR FOSTER CHILDREN

Books for Children

- *An Mei's Strange and Wondrous Journey* by Stephan Molnar-Fenton. DK Publishing Inc., 1998.
- *Beginnings: How Families Come to Be* by Virginia Kroll. Concept Books, 1994.
- *How I Was Adopted: Samantha's Story* by Joanna Cole. William Morrow & Co., Inc., 1995.
- *A Mother for Choco* by Keiko Kasza. G. P. Putnam's Sons, 1992.
- *Over the Moon: An Adoption Tale* by Karen Katz. Henry Holt, 1997.
- *Seeds of Love: For Brothers and Sisters of International Adoption* by Mary E. Petertyl. Folio One Pub., 1997.
- *Tell Me Again About the Night I Was Born* by Jamie Lee Curtis. HarperCollins Juvenile Books, 1996.
- *Through Moon and Stars and Night Skies* by Ann Turner. HarperCollins, 1990.

Books for Parents

- *Birthmothers: Women Who Have Relinquished Babies for Adoption Tell Their Stories* by Merry B. Jones. Chicago Review Press, 1993
- *Raising Adopted Children: A Manual for Adoptive Parents* by Lois Ruskai Melina. HarperCollins, 1986.
- *Real Parents, Real Children: Parenting the Adopted Child* by Holly Van Gulden and Lisa M. Bartels-Rabb. Crossroad Publishing Co., 1995.
- *Talking with Young Children About Adoption* by Mary Watkins and Susan Fisher. Yale University Press, 1995.

Magazines and Newsletters

- *Adoptive Familes*, Adoptive Families of America.
- *Roots & Wings*, P.O. Box 577, Hackettstown, NJ 07840, (908) 637-8828.

Mail Order Books

- Adoption Book Catalog—Tapestry Books
  800-765-2367
  Web site: www.tapestrybooks.com

National Organizations

- Adoptive Families of America
  800-372-3300
  Web site: www.adoptivefam.org
- National Foster Parent Association
  800-557-5238
  Web address: www.kidsource.com/NFPA/index.html

Web Sites

- AdoptINFO, Children, Youth and Family Consortium: www.cyfc.umn.edu/Adoptinfo/
- Foster Parent Community: www.fosterparents.com
- Foster Parent Home Page: www.fostercare.org/FPHP

More Help And Information for BLENDED FAMILIES

Books for Children

- *Boundless Grace: Sequel to Amazing Grace* by Mary Hoffman. Dial Books for Young Readers, 1995.

- *Getting Used to Harry* by Cari Best. Orchard Books, 1996.

- *Room for a Stepdaddy* by Jean Thor Cook. Albert Whitman & Co., 1995.

- *Stepfamilies* by Fred Rogers (Let's Talk About It series). G. P. Putnam's Sons, 1997.

Books for Parents

- *The Combined Family: A Guide to Creating Successful Step-Relationships* by Taube S. Kaufman. Plenum Publishing Corp., 1993.

- *Making Peace in Your Stepfamily: Surviving and Thriving as Parents and Stepparents* by Harold H. Bloomfield with Robert B. Kory. Hyperion, 1993.

- *Mom's House, Dad's House: A Complete Guide for Parents Who Are Separated, Divorced, or Remarried (second edition)* by Isolina Ricci. Fireside, 1997.

- *Positive Discipline for Blended Families: Nurturing Harmony, Respect, and Unity in Your New Stepfamily* by Jane Nelsen, Cheryl Erwin, and H. Stephen Glenn. Prima Publishing, 1997.

National Organizations

- The Stepfamily Association of America
  800-735-7837
  Publishes "Stepfamilies" quarterly newsletter.
  Web site: www.stepfam.org

- Stepfamily Foundation, Inc.
  212-877-3244, fax: 212-362-7030
  24 hour information line: 212-799-STEP
  Web site: www.stepfamily.org

More Help and Information for Families of COLOR AND CULTURAL DIVERSITY

Books for Children

- *Abuela's Weave* by Omar Castaneda. Lee & Low Books, 1995.
- *Dia's Story Cloth* by Dia Cha. Lee & Low Books, Inc., 1996.
- *Families: Poems Celebrating the African American Experience*, selected by Dorothy S. Strickland and Michael R. Strickland. Boyds Mills, 1994.
- *Family Pictures = Cuadros de Familia* by Carmen Lomas Garza. Childrens Book Press, 1990.
- *Giving Thanks: A Native American Good Morning Message* by Chief Jake Swamp. Lee & Low Books, 1995.
- *Journey Between Two Worlds Series*, Lerner Publications Company. Although these books are written for older children, they look at families from all over the world and their journey to come to the United States. Adults will need to explain the text, but children will enjoy the photographs and art. Titles include: *An Armenian Family*; *A Bosnian Family*; *An Eritrean Family*; *A Guatemalan Family*; *A Hmong Family*; *A Kurdish Family*; *A Haitian Family*; *A Nicaraguan Family*; *A Sudanese Family*; and more.
- *Nappy Hair* by Carolivia Herron. Knopf, 1997.

Books for Parents

- *American Family Album Series* by Dorothy and Thomas Hoobler, Oxford University Press. Titles include: *The African-American Family*; *The Chinese American Family*; *The Cuban American Family*; *The Japanese American Family*; *The Jewish American Family*; *The Mexican American Family*; and more.
- *Black Parenting Book: Caring for Our Children in the First Five Years* by Anne C. Beal, Linda Villarosa, and Allison Abnero. Broadway Books, 1998.
- *Raising Black Children: Two Leading Psychiatrists Confront the Educational, Social, and Emotional Problems Facing Black Children* by James P. Comer and Alvin F. Poussaint. Plume, 1992.
- *Raising Nuestros Ninos: Bring Up Latino Children in a Bicultural World* by Gloria Rodriguez. Fireside, 1999.
- *Raising the Rainbow Generation: Teaching Your Children to Be Successful in a Multicultural Society* by Darlene Powell Hopson. Simon & Schuster, 1993.
- *Raising Your Jewish/Christian Child: How Interfaith Parents Can Give Children the Best of Both Their Heritages* by Lee F. Gruzen. Newmarket Press, 1990.
- *Of Many Colors: Portraits of Multiracial Families* photos by Gigi Kaeser; interviews by Peggy Gillespie. University of Massachusetts Press, 1997.

National Organizations

- National Black Child Development Institute 800-556-2234, fax: 202-234-1738 E-Mail: moreinfo@nbcdi.org Web site: www.nbcdi.org

Web Sites

- The Bilingual Family Web Page: www.net.no/cindy/biling-fam.html
- "Mutli-racial Families in Children's Books," an annotated bibliography by Wendy Betts: www.armory.com/~web/fambooks.html
- "Children's Books about Jewish Religion and Culture," an annotated bibliography by Wendy Betts: www.armory.com/~web/jbooks.html
- Jewish Family and Life: www.jewishfamily.com
- "Multiracial Families in Children's Books," an annotated bibliography by Wendy Betts: www.armory.com/~web/fambooks.html
- Native American Books, books by and about Native Americans: http://indy4.fdl.cc.mn.us/~isk/books/bookmenu.html
- Watoto World, the web site for African American children, parents and educators: www.melanet.com/watoto

NOTE: The authors made every attempt to locate parenting resources for families of a wide range of cultural diversity with young children, to include as much as we could, and exclude no one. Please ask your local librarians or booksellers for more help and information regarding your information need.

More Help and Information for FATHERS

Books for Children

- *The Daddy Book* by Ann Morris (World's Family series). Silver Press, 1995.
- *Daddy Makes the Best Spaghetti* by Anna Grossnickle Hines. Clarion Books, 1988.
- *Lots of Dads* by Sheely Rotner and Sheila Kelly. Dial Books for Young Readers, 1997.
- *Daddy and I* (a Black Butterfly Board Book) by Eloise Greenfield. Black Butterfly Children, 1991.
- *Papa, Please Get the Moon for Me* by Eric Carle. Simon & Schuster, 1986.

Books for Parents

- *The New Father: A Dad's Guide to the Toddler Years* by Armin Brott. Abbeville Press, 1998.
- *The Father's Almanac*, Revised (2nd edition) by S. Adams Sullivan. Doubleday, 1992.
- *The Prodigal Father: Reuniting Fathers and Their Children* by Mark Bryan. Clarkson N. Potter, Inc., 1997.

National Organizations

- National Center for Fathering
  800-593-DADS, fax: 913-384-4665
  www.fathers.com

Web Sites

- Father Net: www.cyfc.umn.edu/Fathernet
- Fathering Magazine: www.fathermag.com

More Help and Information for
GAY AND LESBIAN PARENTS

Books for Children

- *Asha's Mums* by Rosamund Elwin and Michele Paulse. Women's Press, 1990.
- *Daddy's Roommate* by Michael Willhoite. Alyson Publications, 1990.
- *Heather Has 2 Mommies* by Leslea Newman. Alyson Publications, 1991.
- *One Dad, Two Dads, Brown Dad, Blue Dads* by Johnny Valentine. Alyson Publications, 1994.

Books for Parents

- *The Lesbian and Gay Parenting Handbook: Creating and Raising Our Families* by April Martin. HarperPerennial, 1993.
- *The Lesbian Parenting Book: A Guide to Creating Families and Raising Children* by D. Merilee Clunis and G. Dorsey Green. Seal Press, 1995.
- *Reinventing the Family: The Emerging Story of Lesbian and Gay Parents* by Laura Benkov. Crown Publishers, Inc., 1994.

Hotlines

- Gay & Lesbian National Hotline
  888-THE-GLNH (843-4564).
  Web site: www.glnh.org

National Organizations

- Family Pride Coalition
  619-296-0199, fax: 619-296-0699
  E-mail: pride@familypride.org
  Publishes "The Parent's Network" electronic newsletter.
  Web site: www.familypride.org
- National Center for Lesbian Rights
  415-392-NCLR(6257), fax: 415-392-8442
  E-mail: info@nclrights.org.
  Web site: www.nclrights.org

Web Sites

- Children, Youth and Family Consortium, University of Minnesota, "Resources for Children and Families on the Web: Gay, Lesbian, Transgender, Bisexual": http://www.cyfc.umn.edu/cyfclinks.html
- Family Q—the Internet Resource for Lesbian Moms and Gay Dads: www.studio8prod.com/familyq

More Help and Information for GRANDPARENTS

Books for Children

- *Fireflies for Nathan* by Shulamith Levey Oppenheim. William Morrow, 1994.
- *Our Granny* by Margaret Wild. Ticknor & Fields Books for Young Readers, 1994.
- *A Window of Time* by Audrey O. Leighton with Jeffrey R. LaCure. NADJA Publishing, 1995.

Books for Parents

- *The Essential Grandparent: A Guide for Making a Difference* by Lillian Carson. Health Communications, Inc., 1996.
- *Grandparenting in a Changing World* by Eda LeShan. Newmarket Press, 1993.
- *Grandparenting Today: Making the Most of Your Grandparenting Skills With Grandchildren of All Ages* by Eleanor Berman, Editor. Putnam Publishing Group, 1997.
- *Raising Our Children's Children* by Deborah Doucette-Dudman. Fairview Press, 1996.

Articles And Booklets

- *A Grandparents' Guide for Family Nurturing and Safety* (606E), CPSC, 1997. Order a free copy from the Consumer Information Catalog, P.O. Box 100, Pueblo, CO 81002, 888-878-3256. Web site: www.pueblo.gsa.gov
- Grandparents Minisection: "The Grandparent Bond," "We Are Family," "Birth of a Grandma," "The Grand(parent) Tour." *Parents Magazine*, March 1997.

National Organizations

- American Association of Retired Persons (AARP) Grandparent Information Center 202-343-2296.

  Parenting Grandchildren: A Voice for Grandparents newsletter & tip sheets for grandparents.

  Website: www.aarp.org
- Foundation for Grandparenting
  E-Mail: gpfound@trail.com
  Web site: www.grandparenting.org

More Help and Information for MOTHERS

Books for Children

- *Hazel's Amazing Mother* by Rosemary Wells. Dial Books for Young Readers, 1985.
- *If You Were My Bunny* by Kate McMullan. Scholastic, Inc., 1996.
- *Indigo and Moonlight Gold* by Jan Spivey Gilchrist. Black Butterfly Children's Books, 1993.
- *Lots of Moms* by Shelley Rotner and Sheila M. Kelly. Dial Books for Young Readers, 1996.
- *Mama, Do You Love Me?* by Barbara Joosse. Chronicle Books, 1991.
- *The Mommy Book* by Ann Morris (World's Family Series). Silver Press, 1996.
- *Tell Me a Story, Mama* by Angela Johnson. Orchard Books, 1989.
- *The Way Mothers Are* by Miriam Schlein. Albert Whitman & Co., 1993.

Books for Parents

- *Are We Having Fun Yet? The 16 Secrets of Happy Parenting* by Kay Willis and Maryann Bucknum Brinley. Warner Books, 1997.
- *I Didn't Plan to Be a Witch: And Other Surprises of a Joyful Mother* by Linda Eyre. Simon & Schuster, 1996.

Magazines And Newsletters

- *Mothering Magazine*
  505-986-8335
  E-Mail: mother@ni.net

Web Sites

- The Mommy Times: www.mommytimes.com
- HipMama: www.hipmama.com
- Moms Online: www.momsonline.com

More Help and Information for Families with ONLY CHILDREN

Books for Parents

- *Keys to Parenting the Only Child* by Carl E. Pickhardt. Barron's Educational Series, 1997.
- *Parenting an Only Child: the Joys and Challenges of Raising Your One and Only* by Susan Newman. Doubleday, 1990.
- *You and Your Only Child: the Joys, Myths and Challenges of Raising an Only Child* by Patricia Ann Nachman with Andrea Thompson. HarperCollins, 1997.

Books for Children

- *Louanne Pig in the Perfect Family* by Nany L. Carlson. Puffin Books, 1986.

Magazines and Newsletters

- *Only Child News.* Only Child Enterprises, Inc.
  323-937-6815
  Web site: www.onlychild.com

Web Sites

- Only Child: www.onlychild.com/

More Help and Information for SINGLE PARENTS

Books for Children

- *Casey's New Hat* by Tricia Gardello. Houghton Mifflin, 1997.
- *A Chair for My Mother* by Vera B. Williams. Greenwillow, 1983.
- *Oma and Bobo* by Amy Schwartz. Bradbury Press, 1987.
- *The Paper Crane* by Molly Bang. Greenwillow Books, 1985.
- *Walking with Mama* by Barbara White Stynes and Glenn J. Hovemann. Dawn Publications, 1997.

Books for Parents

- *The Complete Single Mother* by Andrea Engber and Leah Klungness. Adams, 1995.
- *In Praise of Single Parents: Mothers and Fathers Embracing the Challenge* by Shoshana Alexander. Houghton Mifflin Co., 1994.
- *Mom's House, Dad's House: A Complete Guide for Parents Who Are Separated, Divorced, or Remarried* by Isolina Ricci. Fireside, 1997.
- *On Our Own: Unmarried Motherhood in America* by Melissa Ludtke. Random House, 1997.
- *Single Mothers by Choice: A Guidebook for Single Women Who Are Considering or Have Chosen Motherhood* by Jane Mattes. Times Books, 1994.

National Organizations

- Children's Rights Council, Inc.
  202-547-6227
  Publishes quarterly "Speak Out for Children."
  www.vix.com/crc/
- National Organization of Single Mothers
  704-888-MOMS
- Parents Without Partners International, Inc.
  312-644-6610
  E-mail: pwp@jti.net
  Web site: www.parentswithoutpartners.org
- Single Mothers By Choice
  212-988-0993
- Single Parents Association
  800-704-2102
  Web site: www.singleparents.org/

More Help and Information for
PARENTS WITH SPECIAL NEEDS

Books for Children

- *Lucy's Picture* by Nicola Moon. Dial Books for Young Readers, 1995.
- *Mama Zooms* by Jane Cowen-Fletcher. Scholastic Inc., 1993.
- *My First Book of Sign Language* by Joan Holub. Troll, 1996.
- *When Mommy Is Sick* by Ferne Sherkin-Langer. Albert Whitman & Co., 1995.

Books for Parents

- *Disabled Parents: Dispelling the Myths* by Michele Wates. Radcliffe Medical Press, 1997.
- *How to Help Children Through a Parent's Serious Illness* by Kathleen McCue with Ron Bonn. St. Martin's Press, 1996.
- *When a Parent Has Cancer: A Guide to Caring for Your Children* by Wendy Schlessel Harpham. HarperCollins, 1997.

Magazines & Books on Audio Tape or in Braille

- Magazines on Tape, Personal Audio, Inc. 13 Branch Street, Methuen, MA 01844, 888-GET-A-TAPE (888-438-2827). You can buy a subscription or single tape in the Parenting series or the single issue Child Development tape. Web site: www.personalaudio.com

- National Library Service for the Blind & Physically Handicapped administers a free program to circulate reading materials to people who are unable to read or use standard print due to visual or physical limitations. Ask about free subscriptions to magazines on audio tape. Call your local library for more information or contact: National Library Service for the Blind and Physically Handicapped, Books for Blind and Physically Handicapped Individuals, Library of Congress, Washington, D.C. 20542.

  Web site: www.loc.gov/nls

- Recording for the Blind and Dyslexic, 20 Roszel Road, Princeton, NJ, 08540. A national non-profit organization that loans recorded books to people who cannot read standard print.

  800-803-7201

  Web site: www.rfbd.org

National Organizations

- National Information Center for Children and Youth with Disabilities (NICHCY) 800-695-0285 (Voice/TTY) E-mail: nichcy@aed.org Web site: www.nichcy.org

- Through the Looking Glass 800-644-2666, fax: 510-848-4445. Publishes "Parents with Disabilities" newsletter. Web site: www.lookingglass.org

Web Sites

- The Family Village: www.familyvillage.wisc.edu

- Steven Sell's Disability Management Page—linking people with disabilities and chronic health conditions to resources, products and services that promote active, healthy independent living: www.disability.com

- Trish & John's Resources for Parents with Disabilities, includes information on books, toys, accessible & adaptive parenting products, internet resources & parent chat. Web address: http://ourworld.compuserv.com/homepages/Trish_and_John/resource.htm

More Help and Information for STAY-AT-HOME PARENTS

Books for Children
- *I Know What You Do When I Go to School* by Ann E. Cannon. Gibbs Smith Publisher, 1996.

Books for Parents
- *From Briefcase to Diaper Bag; How I Quit My Job, Stayed Home with My Kids and Lived to Tell...* by Katie Kelley Dorn. Times Books, 1995.
- *Myth of the Welfare Queen: A Pulitzer Prize-Winning Journalist's Portrait of Women on the Line* by David Zucchino. Scribner, 1997.
- *Staying Home: From Full-Time Professional to Full-Time Parent* by Darcie Sanders and Martha Bullen. Little Brown & Co., 1992.
- *What's A Smart Woman Like You Doing at Home?* by Linda Burton, Janet Dittmer, and Cheri Loveless. Mothers At Home, 1992.

National Organizations
- At-Home Dad Network & Newsletter
  E-mail: athomedad@aol.com
- FEMALE—Formerly Employed Mothers at Loose Ends
  630-941-3553
  Web site: www.FEMALEhome.org
- National Association of At-Home Mothers
  888-650-3953
  E-mail: ahmrc@lisco.com
  Publish *At-Home Mother*.

Newletters
- *Welcome Home*, published by Mothers at Home, 800-783-4666. Web site: www.mah.org

Web Sites
- Slowlane.com: the Online Resource for Stay-At-Home Dads

  www.slowlane.com

More Help and Information for TEENAGE PARENTS

Books for Children
- *Do I Have A Daddy? A Story About A Single-Parent Child with a Special Section for Single Mothers and Fathers* by Jeanne Warren Lindsay. Morning Glory Press, 1991.

Books for Parents
- *Teen Dads: Rights, Responsibilities and Joys* by Jeanne Warren Lindsay. Morning Glory Press, 1993.
- *Discipline From Birth to Three: How Teen Parents Can Prevent and Deal with Discipline Problems with Babies and Toddlers* by Jeanne Warren Lindsay and Sally McCullough. Morning Glory Press, Inc., 1998.

More Help And Information for Families with TWINS AND MULTIPLES

Books for Children

- *Dragon Scales and Willow Leaves* by Terryl Givens. G.P. Putnam Sons, 1997.
- *Just Not the Same* by Addie Lacoe. Houghton Mifflin, 1992.
- *Twin Pickle* by Ann Doro. Bill Martin Books, 1996.
- *The Twins Two By Two* by Catherine and Laurence Anholt. Candlewick Press, 1992.
- *Twinnies* by Eve Bunting. Harcourt Brace, 1997.

Books for Parents

- *Double Duty: The Parents' Guide to Raising Twins from Pregnancy Through the School Years* by Christina Baglivi Tinglof. Contemporary Books, 1998.
- *Mothering Twins: From Hearing the News to Beyond the Terrible Twos* by Linda Albi, et al. Fireside, 1993.
- *Multiple Blessings: From Pregnancy Through Childhood, a Guide for Parents of Twins, Triplets, or More* by Betty Rothbart. Hearst Books, 1994.
- *The Parents' Guide to Raising Twins* by Elizabeth Friedrich and Cherry Rowland, St. Martin's Press, 1990.
- *Twins, Triplets and More: Their Nature, Development and Care* by Elizabeth M. Bryan. St. Martin's Press, 1992.

Magazines and Newsletters

- *TWINS Magazine*, "The Magazine for Parents of Multiples"
  888-55-TWINS, fax: 303-290-9025

National Organizations

- Mothers of Supertwins (MOST)
  516-859-1110, fax: 516-859-3580
  E-mail: Maureen@MOSTonline.org
  Web site: www.mostonline.org
- National Organization of Mothers of Twins Clubs, Inc.
  800-243-2276
  Web site: www.nomotc.org

More Help and Information for WORKING PARENTS

Books for Children

- *Daddies at Work* by Eve Merriam. Simon & Schuster Books for Young Readers, 1989.
- *Lyle at the Office* by Bernard Waber. Houghton Mifflin, 1994.
- *Mommy's Office* by Barbara Shook Hazen. Atheneum, 1992.
- *My Working Mom* by Peter Glassman. William Morrow & Co., 1994.
- *Worksong* by Gary Paulsen. Harcourt Brace & Co., 1997.
- *You're My Nikki* by Phyllis Rose Eisenberg. Dial Books for Young Readers, 1992.

Books for Parents

- *A Mother's Place: Taking the Debate About Working Mothers Beyond Guilt and Shame* by Susan Chira. HarperCollins, 1998.
- *The Time Bind: When Work Becomes Home and Home Becomes Work* by Arlie Russell Hochschild. Metropolitan Books, 1997.
- *Working and Caring* by T. Berry Brazelton. Addison-Wesley Publishing Co., 1987.
- *Working Fathers: New Strategies for Balancing Work and Family* by James A. Levine and Todd L. Pittinsky. Addison-Wesley Publishing Co., Inc., 1997.
- *The Working Parents Handbook* by June S. Sale, Kit Kollenberg, with Ellen Melinloff. Fireside Books, 1996.
- *The Working Parents Help Book: Practical Advice for Dealing With the Day-to-Day Challenges of Kids and Careers* by Susan Crites Price and Tom Prince. Petersons Guides, 1996.

Government

- For information on the Family and Medical Leave Act (FMLA), contact:

  Office of the Administrator. Wage and Hour Division, Dept. of Labor
  Room S-3502, 200 Constitution Ave NW
  Washington, DC 20210
  202-219-8305

  Or look in your local telephone directory under U.S. Government, Dept. of Labor, Employment Standards Adm., Wage and Hour Div., for the regional office nearest you.

Magazines

- *Working Mother*, 135 West 50th St., 16th Floor, New York, NY 10020, 1-800-627-0690.

Web Sites

- WAHM: The Online Magazine for Work at Home Moms: www.wahm.com

Fears

Description

Fear is intense worry, concern, panic, or distress that comes from being near real or imagined danger. People usually experience fear if they perceive danger, and before or just after an actual dangerous event. Fear is a normal, natural part of life.

Realistic Expectations

- Children are born with two natural fears: the fear of falling and the fear of loud, sudden noises.
- Common early childhood fears include:
    - Strangers—begins around eight months.
    - Separation—begins around or before age one.
    - The bath and being sucked down the drain—begins around age one.
    - The potty and being flushed down the toilet—begins around age two.
    - Bugs and animals—begins around age two.
    - Thunder, storms, and loud noises—begins around age two.
    - The dark, shadows, and dark closets—begins around age three.
    - Being hurt—begins between age one and two.
- Children under five have a limited ability to tell fantasy from reality, and dreams from reality; an imagined or dream "monster" may be just as scary to them as if it were real.
- Children may be afraid of unusual things, due to their limited understanding of words and limited sense of size: an airplane getting smaller in the sky may make a child afraid that the people on it are disappearing, a child may be afraid of a first haircut because "cuts" usually hurt, or a child may be afraid that he could get flushed down the toilet because he sees other things disappearing there.
- Physical reactions to fear are common: shaking, breathing fast, shortness of breath, heart beating faster, lump in the throat, crying, or dry mouth.
- Some children develop more fears than others: shy children, children with great imaginations, and sensitive children are among those that may be likely to develop more fears.
- Some children are more fearless than others: extroverts, children who don't notice when they are interrupting or disrupting, and children who learn less from what they see are among those that may have fewer fears than others.
- Children's fears are affected by what they are exposed to during the day. Scary movies or television shows, and frightening or traumatic events, can make fears more intense.
- Babies and young toddlers (under age two) who can't understand or follow directions with more than one part, respond better to comfort that is non-verbal: a touch, a whisper, humming, swinging, rocking.
- Children ages two to four can help you to comfort them by looking, listening, and talking about stories, but they continue to appreciate some of the earlier comforts like touching and singing.

- Beginning around age four, children can learn relaxation techniques to calm their fears: breathing, counting, focusing attention on something else.
- Some fears help prevent people from acting recklessly or unsafely: being afraid of getting hit by a car or other fears of personal injury.
- Learning to use and manage fear is a skill that children will use for the rest of their lives.

Approaches

Help your child get ready for changes that might frighten him to lessen fear. Talk to your child about the change or new experience before it happens. Tell him what is going to happen, when, who will be involved, and how it might make him feel. Allow him to talk, ask questions about it, and make choices when he can. Visit the new place or practice the new experience before he must do it in everyday life, if you can. Be understanding and supportive of your child's fear, give him plenty of time, and avoid filling his day with more than he can handle.

> —Ideas found in *Living with the Active Alert Child* (revised and enlarged edition) by Linda S. Budd, Parenting Press, 1993.

Listen to and reassure your child, then point out the reasons for your child's fear; let him know that all children his age have fears. Tell him that he is growing up and learning so many new things, such as how to get along without you at times, and how to speak for himself. Let him know you understand that learning and growing can be scary. Tell him about a time when you were scared as a child, and what you did to get over it. Show him that you know how he feels and that it's OK to be scared sometimes.

> —Ideas found in *Touchpoints* by T. Berry Brazelton, Addison-Wesley, 1992.

> *Many experts agree:* Take your child's fears seriously and avoid shaming, embarrassing, or making fun of your child for having fears.

Help your child with a fear:

- Regard his fears as real to him.
- Learn about what fears young children typically have so you won't take too seriously the common fears that usually pass with time.
- Let him avoid what he is afraid of for a while before trying to help him get over a fear.
- Prevent him from taking part in situations that you know are fearful to him: if you know he's afraid of loud sounds, don't visit a fire station right now.
- Try to help him get used to what he is afraid of gradually. Little by little, expose him to whatever he fears: if he is afraid of loud noises, play soft sounds and gradually increase the volume.
- Look for the cause of a big or general fear to see if there is a particular part of it that is really the problem: if he seems afraid of preschool, find out what in particular is bothering him. Perhaps, the teacher signals that it's time to go in from the playground with a loud noise of some kind. If you cannot assess the reason for your child's fear, or it seems unusually strong, ask a professional for help.

> —Ideas found in *Child Behavior* by Frances L. Ilg, Louise Bates Ames, and Sidney M. Baker, Harper and Row, 1981.

Give your child information about the fear to help lessen it. Tell your child in simple terms what is happening: "The loud sound comes from a big, red fire engine, like the one that you got to climb on at the fire station. It makes a loud sound so people will hear it coming and get out of the way. It needs to go fast and not stop so it can get to the fire as fast as it can to put it out." Help the child understand what is going on and why, and he may feel more in control and less afraid.

> —Ideas found in *Marguerite Kelly's Family Almanac* by Marguerite Kelly, Simon & Schuster, 1994.

Reassure your child that you or his caregiver will keep him safe and always watch out for him. Remind your child that you will know where he is at all times and that he can know where you are anytime, so that you are caring for him even when you are not together. Tell him how you keep yourself safe and well by eating well, wearing a seat belt, and protecting yourself in other ways. Showing the child that you will care for him and yourself provides a feeling of safety for him.

> —Ideas found in "Helping Children Handle Their Fears," *UCLA Working Parents Newsletter*, Online Sample Issue, 1994. Website: www.childcare.ucla.edu/nsample.htm

Allow your child to cope with fear, and comfort him. Help him face fears and ask for help if he needs it, and express your belief in his ability to handle his fears. Then offer comfort that is appropriate to your child's age. If a baby shows fear by crying, hold him and comfort him. If a young child is afraid to go to a new place for the first time, comfort him by helping him through the experience.

Teach him to cope with the fear instead of removing the fear or protecting him from it. Ask your toddler to become involved with what he is afraid of. The bath may be less frightening if your child can turn the water on and off. Show him that he can have some control over the thing that frightens him. Help preschoolers gain some control over the imaginary creatures that scare him: use quiet music to ward off evil creatures, use magic powers to shoo monsters away, or allow you child to sleep with a light on.

> —Ideas found in *Once Upon a Family: Read-Aloud Stories And Activities That Nurture Healthy Kids* by Jean Grasso Fitzpatrick, Viking, 1998.

Help your child overcome a fear that's real to him, yet poses no real danger:

1. Listen to your child when he tells you that he has a fear, even if it sounds silly to you: "I'm afraid that the spider on the ceiling will crawl on me."

2. Come up with a plan for facing up to the fear: "We could bring the spider down and find a new home for him outside. Where do you think the spider would like to live?"

3. Follow through with the plan together. Let your child take the step that confronts the fear, but stay with him if he needs you: "I put the spider in this clear container. Would you like to carry it outside to the tree and let the spider out? I'll go with you."

Your child can learn courage if you help him practice standing up to fears that pose no harm. When you take seriously what is a real concern to your child, he learns to trust you and feel safe telling you his thoughts and feelings.

> —Ideas found in "Helping Your Child Learn Responsible Behavior: With Activities for Children" by Edwin J. and Alice B. Delattre, U.S. Department of Education, Office of Educational Research and Improvement.

Comfort your child and help him learn how to relax when he is afraid. Comfort your baby with touch, holding, rocking, singing, blowing bubbles, or toys to distract him from his fear. In addition, for your toddler, try to get him to participate: ask him questions about pictures in a book, or let him open the doors in a lift-the-flap book. In addition to all of the above, try letting a three- or four-year-old child do something active, and as he does it, he will become less scared or worried or anxious, and more joyful. Learn more about using distraction and imagination to help your child manage fear.

> —Ideas found in *No More Monsters in the Closet: Teaching Your Children to Overcome Everyday Fears and Phobias* by Jeffrey L. Brown, with Julie Davis, Prince Paperbacks, 1995.

Help your child cope with monsters under the bed, nightmares, scary vacuum cleaners, and the fear of being flushed down the drain:

Reassure your child that you have never seen a monster in your home. Look together under the bed, in the closet, or in the corner. Perhaps sweep out the closet or under the bed to convince him it's not there. The monster is probably very real to him, and don't try to convince him it's not. Simply tell him that you don't believe in monsters, but that you understand how real it is to him.

> —Ideas found in *How to Read Your Child Like a Book* by Lynn Weiss, Meadowbrook Press, 1997.

Recognize that a nightmare is real to the child and tell him you understand how scary it is. Avoid telling him that it was only a dream or what you think the dream means. Instead, explain how dreams come from inside him and that he can control them. If the dream still bothers him in the morning, consider asking him to draw a picture of his dream to help him manage his fear of it and express his feelings about it.

> —Ideas found in "I'm Scared!" by Sue Wallace, *Parents*, August 1998.

Play pretend with your child's doll or stuffed animal, and let the doll face the fear of the vacuum. Pretend that the doll is examining the vacuum cleaner in great detail. Then allow the doll to take a ride on the vacuum while it is running. Perhaps if your child sees that his doll is not afraid and not being hurt, he will conquer his fear.

> —Ideas found in *I Heard It Through the Playground*, by Joel Fram, Carol Boswell, and Margaret Maas, Harper Perennial, 1993.

Let your child take a sponge-bath or shower if he's afraid of being washed down the drain, and let him use a container or potty for toileting if he's afraid of being flushed down the toilet. Let your child avoid the things that scare him. Give him time to get over it and gain confidence. Helping him learn more about size and what can fit where may help reduce these fears.

> —Ideas found in *Guide To Your Child's Symptoms* (American Academy of Pediatrics), Villard, 1997.

Help your child learn more about facing fears by reading about it together:

 Brave Georgie Goat by Denis Roche

 Can't Sleep by Chris Raschka

 Dog Donovan by Diana Hendry

 Go Away, Big Green Monster! by Ed Emberley

 The Story of a Blue Bird by Tomek Bogacki

 There's a Nightmare in My Closet by Mercer Mayer

When to Get More Help

C hildren typically grow and learn new skills in their own time and at their own pace within the wide range of what is normal. Sometimes, children need a bit of extra help to keep their development on track, or to stay healthy and happy. Sometimes, parents need help providing for a child's needs or sorting out the best approaches to parenting.

Consider getting help for your child if he:

- Does not respond to comfort when fearful.
- Has strong fears that develop earlier and last longer than other children his age.
- Has fears that are interfering with everyday activities.
- Has fears that are causing problems with making friends.
- Has fears that are disrupting normal sleep patterns.
- Has fears that are leading to compulsive behavior.
- Does not know the difference between fantasy and reality most of the time by age five.
- Does not move beyond being extremely fearful by age five.

You are the expert when it comes to your family and child. If you have a concern, trust your instinct, and find someone trained to help you: health care providers, early intervention teams, mental health professionals, parent educators and consultants, or telephone help-line staff. Consider talking it over with friends and family, too. You don't need to worry alone! Turn to "Finding Help in Your Community" on page 4 to learn about finding help near you.

More Help and Information

Books for Parents

- "Chapter 22: Fears" in *Touchpoints* by T. Berry Brazelton. Addison-Wesley, 1992.
- *Mommy, I'm Scared: How TV and Movies Frighten Children and What We Can Do to Protect Them* by Joanne Cantor, Harcourt, Brace, & Co., 1998.
- *Monsters Under the Bed and Other Childhood Fears: Helping Your Child Overcome Anxieties, Fears, and Phobias* by Stephen W. Garber, Marianne Garber and Robyn Freedman Spizman, Villard Books, 1993.
- *No More Monsters in the Closet: Teaching Children to Overcome Everyday Fears and Phobias* by Jeffrey L. Brown, with Julie Davis, Prince Paperbacks, 1995.

Fighting, Hitting, Biting, and Aggression

by Jakob

Description

Children typically hit, bite, slap, yell, tease, grab, break or throw things in the course of growing up. Aggression is the act of attacking people or property. What may seem like aggression in children under age five, may really be children struggling to understand limits, to learn new skills, to communicate, and to gain control of their emotions. With help as they grow, children learn to solve problems in non-aggressive ways.

Realistic Expectations

- Almost all children between the ages of one and four experiment with aggression.
- Children act aggressively for many reasons:
  - Limited ability to see things from another person's point of view
  - Low tolerance for frustration
  - Limited ability to control strong urges
  - Limited ability to plan ahead and think through possible consequences
  - Limited ability to use language to get a point across
  - To seek attention
  - Pain or illness
  - Imitation
  - Experimentation (if I do this what reaction will I get?)
  - Tension release
  - Jealousy
  - Trying to communicate affection
  - An accident
  - Desire to have needs met immediately
  - Difficulty sharing
  - Anger

- Children who are routinely disciplined with spanking and other physical forms of punishment are more likely to act aggressively and learn that aggressive behavior is the way to solve problems.
- Children are typically capable of learning the rule "don't hurt people or animals" after two and one-half years.
- Children who learn to control their aggression will gain more self-discipline, empathy, and relationship skills that will benefit them throughout their lives.

Fighting, Hitting, Biting, and Aggression

Approaches

Look for possible causes of aggressive behavior. Hitting, pushing, shoving, kicking, teasing, and other types of aggression can be normal from time to time. However, if a pattern develops, try to find a possible cause. If you uncover a cause for the aggression, take action to help your child fix the problem. Don't just accept your child's aggressive behavior if it becomes a pattern.

> —Ideas found in *Raising Preschoolers: Parenting For Today* by Sylvia Rimm, Three Rivers Press, 1997.

! **WARNING! Never shake a child and never harm a child with physical punishment.**

Shaking a baby or child under the age of three can cause brain damage, blindness, paralysis, seizures, or death. Even a small amount of shaking or a less vigorous shaking can severely harm a young child.

The American Academy of Pediatrics (AAP) warns that children who are routinely disciplined with spanking and other physical forms of punishment are more likely to become aggressive and to learn that aggressive behavior is the way to solve problems. Spanking or hitting can also lead to injury and abuse, especially when it is done in anger.

Help your child to learn to control her aggression:

- Try tempting your child with an activity when it looks like she may be becoming aggressive.
- Do not reward her by giving her the thing she was fighting over.
- Compliment her peaceful behavior when you see it.
- Consider the possibility that she needs more positive attention and find ways to give it to her.
- Consider whether there has been a change in her routine that has been unsettling and make adjustments if necessary or comfort her through inevitable changes.
- Teach her that it is never OK to hurt someone.
- Never try to teach her a lesson by hitting, biting, or kicking her back..
- Talk in a matter-of-fact way about how it would feel if someone hurt her, but don't scold, threaten, or talk continually about it.
- When your child is aggressive toward you, tell her that you don't like that kind of treatment and that you won't let her hurt you. Move away, and only start playing with her again when she is able to stop being aggressive.
- Move your toddler away from the person she hit and say, "No. We don't hit."
- Give your preschooler who has been aggressive a short time-out, and tell her why she needs to cool off.

> —Ideas found in *A To Z Guide to Your Child's Behavior*, (Children's National Medical Center), Putnam Pub., 1993.

Fighting, Hitting, Biting, and Aggression

Teach your preschool child to be assertive when she feels like she might hurt someone, or when someone might hurt her:

- Teach your child to stick up for herself. Tell her to say, "No, I don't like that."
- Remind her to tell an adult if a situation is getting too hard for her to handle alone.
- Teach her to try to notice when she is bothered by something and then change activities: go for a walk around the room, draw a picture, or sing.

> —Ideas found in *How to Read Your Child Like a Book* by Lynn Weiss, Meadowbrook Press, 1997.

Deal with conflict in a healthy way to show your child how to do the same. Conflict is a natural part of all relationships. It is the absence of healthy conflict that can lead people to fight in destructive ways. The rules for healthy conflict can help family members maintain a safe structure in which change can happen constructively, not destructively:

- Say what you think the problem is.
- Assert your ideas with respect, and without aggression.
- Listen with an open mind, an open ear, and an open heart.
- Attack the problem, not the person.
- Show respect for the other person's feelings.
- Be responsible for your thoughts, feelings, and actions.

> —From Jeffry Jeanetta-Wark, M.A., LICSW.

Help your child prevent a buildup of anger and aggression through daily exercise. Be sure your child gets the opportunity to exercise every day as a way to work off anger, and as an outlet for aggressive feelings. Exercise is simply good for the body and brain!

> —Ideas found in *When You Worry About the Child You Love* by Edward Hallowell, M.D., Simon & Schuster, 1996.

Teach your child how to get along with other children:

- Show her how to invite another child to play without being aggressive. Some children don't know how to interact with other children yet; she may push another over with the intention of saying hello or inviting the child to play. Teach your child to say, "Hello, can we play?" and to shake hands or gently pat the other child's back.
- Help her learn to find enough space for her activity and to give anyone around her enough space. Sometimes accidents happen when there is not enough space in which to play; it may appear to her that another child hit her, when in fact that other child was bumped by a passing child and was pushed. Try to give your child enough space to play in, and help her to define her space.
- Set limits that help her learn when to stop. Sometimes children love to roughhouse play, but don't know when to stop or how to stay in bounds. Set limits. Each person needs to be ready and willing to play and know to stop when someone says, "Stop—enough!" It is also difficult for children to just walk away from roughhousing once they get going. Try giving her something to do with her hands to help with the transition: finger-painting, modeling dough, or playing catch.

> —Ideas found in *So This Is Normal Too?* by Deborah Hewitt, Redleaf Press, 1995.

Fighting, Hitting, Biting, and Aggression

Let your child work out conflicts on her own whenever she can, but listen nearby and be ready to step in to help when she needs it. Resolving conflict is new for your child, and she still needs lots of help. If frustrations are rising quickly, step in and offer ideas: "Sophia, you could play with the other truck until Elise is ready to give you a turn."

If your child has been hurt or has hurt someone, you need to step in and stop the fight. Comfort the victim, and offer her another activity. Then discipline the aggressive child: calmly explain that biting, hitting, etc., is not accepted. Remind her of the consequences: "If you bite again, you will have to sit in the chair for a few minutes." If she bites again, put her in the chair.

> —Ideas found in *What to Expect the Toddler Years* by Arlene Eisenberg, Heidi E. Murkoff, and Sandee E. Hathaway, Workman Pub., 1994.

Show and teach your child peaceful options to use in a conflict:
- I can talk the problem over and listen to what the other person has to say.
- I can walk away.
- I can say, "I'm sorry."
- I can do something else.
- I can take turns.
- I can share.
- I can ignore the behavior.
- I can compromise or find a middle ground.
- I can give the other person a hug.
- I can ask for help.

Practice these with your child if she is over age three, and hang a copy of the list in a noticeable spot in your home to remind you to use it. Learning these ten responses will go a long way toward helping your child be prepared to handle conflict.

> —Excerpted from *Raising Peaceful Children In A Violent World* by Nancy Lee Cecil, with Patricia L. Roberts, copyright 1995. Reprinted by permission of Innisfree Press, Inc., Philadelphia, PA.

Help the child stop biting; while it may be common, it should be stopped.
- Supervise your child closely around other children.
- Give her attention for her positive behavior.
- When she is becoming angry or frustrated, redirect her to another activity.
- Give your child the words for what she is feeling: "You feel angry and frustrated because you want the doll."
- Think about skills that your child may be behind in that might cause her frustration. If you are concerned, talk to your child's healthcare provider.
- Be consistent about setting limits with your child, especially about aggressive acts.
- Avoid physical punishment or exposure to violence.
- When your child bites, put her in a time-out with a short explanation: "I know you are mad, but people are not for biting."

- Offer a teething ring, small pillow, or cloth to bite, and tell her that she can bite things but not people; this should be done in a positive, not punitive, way.
- Clearly express your negative emotions but stay calm and in control.
- Make sure that anyone caring for your child is responding in the same way to the biting, and not using physical punishment.
- Do not bite back!

> —Ideas found in "Biting" by Barbara Howard, *Behavioral and Developmental Pediatrics*, (edited by Steven Parker and Barry Zuckerman,) Little, Brown and Company, 1995.

One of the ways I've grown as a parent is in learning to react a little less. We developed a mantra that our son heard before and after each incident or time-out: "We don't bite/hit/kick/pinch. It hurts people. We won't let you do anything that will hurt you or someone else." As soon as he was calm enough, it helped to talk about what was behind it, "We use words, not biting. Is there something wrong? Are you feeling _____?" This eventually worked and we see the benefit of it now.

—Betsy, Parenthoodweb member.

When my 18-month-old started biting, whenever I was quick enough, I would say, "Zerberts!" as he put his mouth on me to bite. Instead of biting, he would give me a zerbert (raspberries or blowing on the skin). Then I would giggle, and he would get sidetracked and go from being angry to being happy instead.

—Maria, Caledonia, MN

Consider the reasons for your child's biting, and make a plan to help her stop. Children may bite for different reasons, and not all will respond to the same reaction.

- The experimental biter. Your infant or young child may take an experimental bite out of a mother's breast or a caregiver's shoulder. When this occurs, give prompt, clear signals to communicate that children must not bite people. Say, "No!" Give her a wide variety of other things to chew, smell, touch, and taste. This type of biter may also be motivated by teething pain. Offer her appropriate things to chew on for relief: teething biscuits, a teething ring, or frozen bagels.
- The frustrated biter. Some biters lack the skills to cope with situations such as the desire for an adult's attention or for another child's toy. Even though your child may not have intended to harm another person, react with disapproval. First, tend to the victim. Then explain to the biter that biting hurts others and is not allowed. Later teach her the language to show her feelings or get what she needs. Praise her when she communicates peacefully. Watch for signs or rising frustration, and intervene.
- The threatened biter. Some children, feeling they are in danger, bite in self-defense. They may be overwhelmed by their surroundings, and bite as a means of regaining control. In this case, do the same as above, but also assure your child that her rights and possessions are safe. Stressful situations in your child's life can contribute to feeling threatened: the death of a grandparent, a mother returning to work, or the separation of parents.

Fighting, Hitting, Biting, and Aggression

- The power biter. Some children experience a strong need for control. As soon as they see the response they get from biting, they want to see the reaction again, and know that biting will probably get the reaction. Give the biter choices throughout the day and praise her for positive behavior. If the biter gets attention when she is not biting, she will not have to resort to aggressive behavior to feel a sense of power.

You can guide your child toward self-control and away from biting. The key is understanding.

—From "Biters: Why They Do It and What to Do About It," National Association for the Education of Young Children, 1997.

Help your child understand more about strong feelings and aggression by reading about them together:

 *A Weekend With Wendell* by Kevin Henkes

Bootsie Barker Bites by Barbara Bottner

Dark Day, Light Night by Jan Carr

Lilly's Purple Plastic Purse by Kevin Henkes

Make Someone Smile: And 40 More Ways to Be a Peaceful Person by Judy Lalli

Mean Soup by Betsy Everitt

Snail Started It! By Katja Reider

The Grouchy Ladybug by Eric Carle

When to Get More Help

Children typically grow and learn new skills in their own time and at their own pace within the wide range of what is normal. Sometimes, children need a bit of extra help to keep their development on track, or to stay healthy and happy. Sometimes, parents need help providing for a child's needs or sorting out the best approaches to parenting.

Consider getting help for your child if she:

- Does not stop extremely aggressive behavior toward other people or things by age three.
- Becomes easily frustrated and angry with requests from family members or when doing simple tasks.
- Does not show some self-control of aggressive behavior when angry by age four.
- Frequently bites others.
- Is frequently picked on by other children.
- When behavior often hurts or causes injury to persons, things, or animals.

You are the expert when it comes to your family and child. If you have a concern, trust your instinct and find someone trained to help you: health care providers, early intervention teams, mental health professionals, parent educators and consultants, or telephone help-line staff. Consider talking it over with friends and family, too. You don't need to worry alone! Turn to "Finding Help in Your Community" on page 4 to learn about finding help near you.

More Help and Information

Books for Parents

- *HELP! The Kids Are at It Again: Using Kid's Quarrels to Teach People Skills* by Elizabeth Crary. Parenting Press Inc., 1997

- *Child Magazine's Guide to Quarreling: Help Your Children Fight Less and Get Along More* by Gail E. Hudson. Pocket Books, 1997.

- *Make Someone Smile: and 40 More Ways to Be a Peaceful Person* by Judy Lalli. Free Spirit Publishing, 1996.

Articles, Pamphlets, and Booklets

- "Teaching Children Not to Be—or Be Victims of—Bullies." Call or write:

  National Association for the Education of Young Children (NAEYC)

  1509 16th St. NW, Washington, DC 20036-1426

  800-424-2460, Fax: 202-328-1846

  Web site: www.naeyc.org

  Available online:
  www.naeyc.org/resources/eyly/1996/14.htm

Friends

Description

Friends are people that children enjoy being with, doing things with, developing relationships with, and learning things from. When children feel affection for and develop a relationship with a companion, they have a friend.

Realistic Expectations

- Becoming a good friend involves mastering a combination of skills that typically are not mastered until the school-age years. Young children are only beginning to learn the skills needed to be a good friend:

    – Expressing feelings, needs, wishes, and requests.

    – Listening and understanding others.

    – Following simple social rules.

    – Taking turns.

    – Working things out together and compromising.

    – Empathizing, or understanding how another person feels.

- Around age one or two, young children enjoy playing similar things *near* each other in parallel play. Around three or four, children start to play cooperatively *with* each other.

- Until approximately age three, young children believe that toys, objects, and sometimes other children are part of themselves and not separate, so they may touch, poke, or grab another child in play.

- Until around age four, children have difficulty sharing. It is common for them to share or be kind one minute and appear selfish the next.

- Three- and four-year-olds may feel that if they don't win at a game, then they are not a good person.

- Generally, young children will get along better when they are not hungry, sick, or tired, and they are not expected to play together for long periods of time (one to two hours is usually enough).

- Children who are more intense may have a more difficult time taking turns with toys or switching activities with friends.

- Children who have more difficulty making friends may have more success playing with children that are slightly older.

- Imaginary friends are normal and start to show up around age two and a half. By age five or six, most children are done with imaginary friends. Over half of all children will have an imaginary friend at some point.

- Children who appear shy, bossy, or selfish may be struggling to learn new social skills, an experience which can be stressful. Children can change rapidly as they grow and develop. Labeling them in a certain way, such as quiet or loud, may cause them to behave in that way.

- Rules and values vary from home to home. When friends visit a new home, talking with the adult who will be in charge of the children about expectations for care and supervision can avoid problems later on.

- Children learn by watching the adults that they are with. If the adults have enjoyable, respectful relationships with friends, children are more likely to enjoy good friendships, too.

Approaches

Introduce your child to friends his own age at age two. Although two-year-olds are both demanding and re-spectful of others, they learn so much from being together: how to do things they hadn't thought of before, as well as new behaviors and social skills. Try not to get in the way of their play or their developing relationship; the more children are allowed to interact with each other, the greater the opportunity they have to learn about them-selves and each other.

—Ideas found in *Touchpoints* by T. Berry Brazelton, Addison-Wesley, 1992.

Talk to your child about what friendship means. Tell him:

- Friends are people who like each other and want to do things together.
- People can have friends in many places and friends of many different ages.
- Friends don't always see things or do things in the same way, but you can learn new ways of doing things from friends.
- It can be hard to have friends and share, take turns, or not get your way.
- You can still be friends even if a friend makes you mad or sad, or if you don't play together all the time. Friends can also make you feel better and share great, fun times.

—Ideas found in *Making Friends* by Fred Rogers, Punt & Grosset, 1987.

Allow your child to choose some of his own friends, but use your judgment on when to help with a relation-ship. Your child may ask to play with a child that you would not have chosen for a playmate. Consider that if the relationship is not hurtful, that your child can learn positive things from people who are quite different from him: a quiet child who may be attracted to a bossy or assertive child may learn to stand up for himself more, or an active child may learn some of the pleasures of playing at activities that a quieter child prefers. Step in and help when there is name-calling, or other behavior that hurts your child, but try to help your child learn how to deal with challenging relationships instead of protecting him from them—he will have the opportunity to gain more confidence in social situations.

—Ideas found in *Child-Wise* by Cathy Rindner Tempelsman, Hearst Books, 1994.

Before friends come over, set up your home for a successful play time. Put out a few simple things that most young children have fun with so that they can play as independently as possible. Then let them direct their play. Consider providing things that you know the children will enjoy, like:

- A large box that can be decorated and made into a variety of things: store, bus, fishing boat, tunnel
- A safe place to work freely, and art supplies: crayons, markers, play dough, stickers
- Puzzles
- Dress-up or make-believe clothes and props
- Music

A safe place with some simple suggestions of things to do can provide young children with enough that they need to explore play and friendship without being overwhelmed about new situations or too many toys.

—Ideas found in *Parenting Your Toddler: The Expert's Guide to the Tough and Tender Years* by Patricia H. Shimm and Kate Ballen, Addison-Wesley, 1995.

Help your child include others in his play and deal with exclusionary play—it will strengthen his concept of friendship. When children try to exclude others from their play, talk to them about their play and what they're doing. Acknowledge and describe the play you see. Children may be more likely to include another child if it's clear that they will still be able to continue their play theme. Ask the children who are doing the excluding for their ideas. Offer them suggestions as to how a friend might be able to help or be included: "What do you need done with this bag of blocks? Could your friend help you build the town?" Be sure to ask the child who is being left out is he would like to play. Ask him if he has ideas about how he might participate. Children will be more receptive if they are encouraged, not forced, to play together.

> —Ideas found in *Becoming the Parent You Want to Be* by Laura Davis and Janis Keyser, Broadway Books, 1997.

Teach your child about personal space. Explain to him that everyone needs some space around them that makes them feel comfortable. Show him that by getting too close, his friend may want to move away from him, or his friend may feel afraid or angry until he can get a comfortable space again. Helping your child learn this important skill may improve his friendships.

> —Ideas found in *Living With the Active Alert Child: Groundbreaking Strategies for Parents* (revised and enlarged edition) by Linda S. Budd, Parenting Press, 1993.

Expect your child to follow the same rules and good behavior when a friend is visiting or when visiting a friend. Even though rules vary from family to family, you can set limits on what is acceptable or not acceptable in your home. If your child expects to behave differently because a friend does, explain that rules are different in different families, but that you expect him to follow your rules. If he won't, offer him the choice of following your family's rules or not playing with the friend.

> —Ideas found in *Positive Parenting from A to Z* by Karen Renshaw Joslin, Fawcett Columbine: Ballantine Books, 1994.

When your child makes a new friend and is invited to play in their home without you, consider safety first. Don't leave a child in a home or environment that you have not checked for safety. Don't leave a child with people that you have not met or talked to first. Consider going to the home the first time and making sure that it is childproofed, that guns are stored and locked, that a pool is enclosed, and that the children will be supervised to your satisfaction by a responsible adult or babysitter. If you have any suspicions that the child will not be safe, excuse yourself and the child from the play date.

> —Ideas found in "Play Nice!" by Colleen Davis Gardephe and Theresa Kump, *Parents*, October 1997.

Allow your child the experience of having an imaginary friend if they bring one home. Be positive and follow your child's direction with the friend. If the child asks if his friend can have a blanket, allow him to give him a blanket, but avoid suggesting what the imaginary friend needs or wants. Don't suggest to your child that his friend wants him to do or not do something, like picking up toys. Also, don't allow the child to use his friend to get out of doing something by blaming it on the imaginary friend. Encourage your child to express himself in a wide variety of ways and use his imagination often.

> —Ideas found in *What to Expect the Toddler Years* by Arlene Eisenberg, Heidi E. Murkoff, and Sandee E. Hathaway, Workman Pub., 1994.

Help your child learn more about friendship by reading about it together:

Arnie and the New Kid by Nancy Carlson

Friends by Rachel Isadora

Friends by Kim Lewis

Harry and Willy and Carrothead by Judith Caseley

How to Be a Friend: A Guide to Making Friends and Keeping Them by Laurene Krasny Brown

Jessica by Kevin Henkes

Making Friends by Fred Rogers

Yo! Yes? by Chris Rashka

When to Get More Help

Children typically grow and learn new skills in their own time and at their own pace within the wide range of what is normal. Sometimes, children need a bit of extra help to keep their development on track, or to stay healthy and happy. Sometimes, parents need help providing for a child's needs or sorting out the best approaches to parenting.

Consider getting help for your child if he:

- Seems to be replacing real relationships with imaginary friendships or spending most of his days with imaginary friends instead of connecting with real people.
- Does not show some interest in other children by age three.
- Does not stop extremely aggressive behavior toward other people by age four.
- Does not play with other children by age five.
- Does not know the difference between fantasy and reality most of the time by age five.

You are the expert when it comes to your family and child. If you have a concern, trust your instinct and find someone trained to help you: health care providers, early intervention teams, mental health professionals, parent educators and consultants, or telephone help-line staff. Consider talking it over with friends and family, too. You don't need to worry alone! Turn to "Finding Help in Your Community" on page 4 to learn about finding help near you.

More Help and Information

Books for Parents

- "Children's Friendships: Cooperation and Conflict, Chapter 23" in *Becoming the Parent You Want to Be* by Laura Davis and Janis Keyser. Broadway Books, 1997.

- "Friends, Chapter 45" in *Touchpoints* by T. Berry Brazelton. Addison-Wesley, 1992.

- "Socialization, Chapter 1" in *Parenting Your Toddler: The Expert's Guide to the Tough and Tender Years* by Patricia H. Shimm and Kate Ballen. Addison-Wesley, 1995.

Articles

- "Play Nice! An Age-By-Age Guide to Keeping Tempers and Friendships Intact" by Colleen Davis Gardephe and Theresa Kump, *Parents*, October 1997.

Videos

- *The Ezra Jack Keats Library*, includes "Peter's Chair." Children's Circle.

- *That's What Friends Are For.* New Leaf Media.

"Once upon a time there was a girl named Kim. She had a friend named Matti."

by Jennifer, age 4

Holidays

Description

A holiday is a day or group of days set aside to remember or celebrate an event. Holidays are meant to divert people from daily routines and refresh them. They can be national events, community celebrations, religious occasions, ceremonies, rituals, fairs, festivals, sport tournaments, anniversaries, and school releases. Holidays often involve time off from work, school, or day care, and decorations, symbols, food, and family time.

Realistic Expectations

- Through holidays, children can learn the importance of celebration, relaxation, ritual, and other important values that enhance life and build strong connections within the family and community.
- Stress is common at holiday time: trying to do too much, expecting too much, too much family togetherness, and spending time with extended family can lead to tension.
- Children also experience stress at holiday time for various reasons: appealing presents and decorations around their home that they aren't allowed to touch, new music, new stories, new food, new rituals to learn, and the tension and stress of the adults around them.
- Someone who is grieving a loss, such as the death of a parent or a divorce, may be sadder during holidays.
- It is not an adult's job to fulfill every dream, desire, or wish of a child. Children need help understanding what they should expect when giving and receiving gifts and that their desires are being influenced by the advertisements they see.
- If the emphasis surrounding a holiday is placed on gifts, food, clothes, decorations, candy, and toys, expect a child to associate holidays with things.
- If the emphasis is on family celebration, friends, giving, and thinking of others, expect children to experience and associate holidays with people and sharing.
- Toddlers may be overwhelmed by too many gifts. Don't expect them to appear grateful. They may be just as happy with the box and ribbon as with the gift inside.
- Children notice differences and similarities in holiday celebrations. Expect them to ask questions about why not all families celebrate the same holidays and about why families celebrate in different ways.
- Holidays rarely are perfect and people often expect too much. When families expect that some of the food won't turn out, some of the toys may not work, and sometimes people won't get along, and focus on the positive experiences surrounding a holiday instead, then it's likely that childhood memories of holidays will be warm and positive.

Approaches

Help your child understand what a holiday celebrates: change of year or seasons, struggle for independence, remembrance of heroes, friendship, appreciation, religious occasions, and historical events. Teach her the history and tradition behind a holiday: "The Fourth of July is not just a day for fireworks, but a day that celebrates the independence of our whole country."

—Ideas found in *Roots & Wings: Affirming Culture in Early Childhood Settings* by Stacey York, Toys 'n Things Press, 1991.

Provide your child with opportunities to celebrate! Even if you do not believe in observing certain holidays, give your child the experience of celebrating special occasions. Find a day or occasion that has meaning for you and teach your child the value in stopping to notice and appreciate important moments in life. This will give her lasting memories of family time and add value to her life.

—Ideas found in *Raising Black Children* by James P. Comer and Alvin F. Poussaint, Plume, 1992.

Introduce a toddler to a holiday without forcing her to participate; let her experience the holiday in her own way. Holidays can be confusing for children ages three and under. A toddler may not understand what all the fuss is about and so may not appreciate all the work and tradition surrounding the holiday. Introduce him to holiday traditions but don't force him to engage in things like sitting on Santa's lap, or saying "trick or treat" at each house. He may not enjoy the same activities, food, and traditions as adults; think of activities that will appeal to him at his stage in life.

Keep on schedule during holidays and try to follow regular routines for eating and sleeping to help her enjoy the holidays as much as she can. The first few days after a holiday may be difficult, as a young child unwinds from the excitement. Don't plan more exciting activities for this time, but try to relax.

—Ideas found in *What to Expect the Toddler Years* by Arlene Eisenberg, Heidi E. Murkoff, and Sandee E. Hathaway, Workman Publishing, 1994.

Decide for yourself what kind of holiday will hold the most meaning for your family. Form your own traditions and hang on to the traditions from the past that still work for your family. Let go of unrealistic expectations and everyone else's idea of what a holiday should be. Design your holiday so that the emphasis is on being together as a family, and schedule your activities to meet your family's needs. In the end, the holiday will be more satisfying for all of you.

—Ideas found in "Careful Planning Can Keep Holidays Happy" by Ron Pitzer, Online, Children, Youth and Family Consortium's Electronic Clearinghouse, Available: www.cyfc.umn.edu

Prepare your child for problems that may come up:
- What to do if she gets a gift she doesn't like.
- How to handle having visitors that disrupt the household.
- What to do with plans that mean being away from home for a long time.
- How much candy and treats are allowed when so much is available.
- Anything that may have been a problem in the past.

—Ideas found in *Positive Parenting from A to Z* by Karen Renshaw Joslin, Fawcett Columbine: Ballantine Books, 1994.

Help your child understand that holidays aren't just about spending money. Show her that generosity, tradition, and family togetherness are the greater rewards. Consider working as a family to shop for and create gifts for others. When making gifts of food, don't expect perfection. Concentrate instead on the joy of being and working together. Let even the youngest child contribute. It will be more rewarding to give a gift that everyone contributed to than to give a perfectly crafted gift.

> —Ideas found in *Positive Discipline A-Z (revised and expanded 2nd edition)* by Jane Nelsen,
> Lynn Lott, and H. Stephen Glenn, Prima, 1999.

Help your child learn the joys of giving and generosity. She may get so excited about her own wants and wish lists at holiday times, that she may need reminding about the spirit of giving. Have each family member pick one person outside the family to do something for. It could be buying a gift for a child who might not receive one or helping an elderly person prepare for a holiday. Your child can get excited about giving, too.

> —Ideas found in "Take It Easy" by Karen Miles, *Woman's Day*, December 16, 1997.

To bring new life into a holiday, create a new ritual. Plan an activity for the family that you've never done before. It could be something as simple as making a holiday-related snow or sand sculpture, or it could be starting a new tradition of attending a holiday play, service, or celebration. Consider visiting someone who is homebound or checking out the stars on a holiday night. Create a new food to add to the traditional holiday menu. Look for the true meaning of your holiday.

> —Ideas found in "Keep the Best, Create the Rest" by Helen Zelon,
> *Family Circle*, December 17, 1997.

Consider having a celebration for no particular reason. Create some family time for just having fun together. Invite friends, play games, have a cake, dress up or dress casually, and make it a special party. This helps your child appreciate the present instead of constantly looking forward to the next holiday or birthday.

> —Ideas found in *New Traditions* by Susan Abel Lieberman, Noonday Press, 1990.

What do you tell children about Leprechauns, the Easter Bunny, Santa Claus, the Tooth Fairy, or other characters often associated with holidays or celebrations—do you tell your child that they are real or do you tell them the truth? Ideas from the Parenthood Web Member Board:

"I don't consider it lying. I am not hurting the kids by fostering a sense of enchantment and excitement in them. It is the magic of the make-believe that makes these entities real to a child. So, I am never going to tell them Santa/Easter Bunny/Tooth Fairy are not real, because they live in one's heart."

"Our child has as much fun knowing it is Mom and Dad. We do different things sometimes. The last tooth got a teddy bear. I think make-believe is great and our children's imagination is able to grow knowing we are all playing a game."

"As parents we walk the fine line between fact and fiction. When your child is scared, don't you tell them that you will always protect them, even though you know in your heart, you can't always? If the only thing your child ever holds against you is that you allowed him to believe in Santa Claus, you have done a fine job indeed."

Help a child understand and appreciate holidays by reading stories about them and doing activities together:

Children Just Like Me: Celebrations by Anabel Kindersley

The Family Read-Aloud Holiday Treasury, selected by Alice Low

The Make-Something Club Is Back!: More Fun with Crafts, Foods, and Gifts by Frances Zweifel

When to Get More Help

When deciding whether children need some extra help, usually it is best to look for patterns in behavior and skills that stay constant over a period of time. Holidays are typically isolated events that are often stressful in the life of your child. Therefore, you should not make general judgments about how he is developing, or decisions about getting more help at this time.

More Help and Information

Books for Parents

- *The Early Childhood Almanac: Activities for Every Month of the Year* by Dana Newmann. Center for Applied Research in Education (a Simon & Schuster Co.), 1998.

- *The Heart of a Family: Searching America for New Traditions That Fulfill Us* by Meg Cox. Random House, 1998.

- *New Traditions: Redefining Celebrations for Today's Family* by Susan Abel Lieberman. Noonday Press, 1990.

Videos

- *Sesame Street Celebrates Around the World*, Sony Wonder.

Independence

Description

The ability to make choices, confidently master new skills, and understand limits are the foundations of independence. Independent children want to decide for themselves, do it themselves, take care of themselves, finish it themselves, tell it themselves, and feed themselves—or at least try. Independence in children leads to becoming responsible, self-reliant adults.

Realistic Expectations

- When parents or caregivers do things for children and don't allow them to do things for themselves, they may be indirectly telling children that they don't think they are capable, independent people.

- Between ages one and two children practice separateness. Creating a sense of self as separate from others is the first step toward independence. This budding independence often sounds like: "No, no, no!" or "Mine!" Children need to practice their separateness from parents or caregivers in this way to develop their sense of self.

- Children who are allowed to say "No!" without getting into trouble learn confidence in being themselves. Children who are not allowed to say "No!" learn that being separate is not a good thing; they may think that they have to say "Yes" in order to be loved.

- Children have a limited ability to focus, concentrate, and play independently. This ability varies widely in children. At ages three and four, children typically are able to focus for between five and twenty minutes.

- Brief periods of safe time to play by themselves (while parents supervise from a distance) are of great benefit to children: they practice new skills, think, explore, and learn to enjoy themselves independently.

- Independence in young children is encouraged when:
  - Children are taught skills that they can safely master.
  - Children are allowed to do what they are able to do for themselves—safely.
  - Books, toys, and activities are provided that are interesting and age-appropriate.
  - The atmosphere is positive, and correction or criticism is not excessive.

- Fear of trying, low assertiveness, and low self-esteem can occur if young children are not allowed to achieve some independence. Frustration and the feeling of failure can result when too much independence is expected. Children may learn to feel capable and good about themselves when allowed to master the skills of independence that are right for their age.

- Children who expect an adult to do everything for them may not feel capable of doing things for themselves and may need more encouragement to work or play independently.

- Children may not want to try something independently because they don't know how to do it.

- Pushing children to become independent in tasks before they are ready may actually cause learning to occur later.

- The process of becoming independent begins at birth, when babies first turn their heads by themselves to find food, and continues on throughout childhood. It takes time and patient, caring adults to help children become independent!

Approaches

Help your child safely learn to be independent:

- Arrange your home so that your child can do things independently: place books, art supplies, music tapes, and toys in low areas so he can easily take them out and put them away, place and choose clothing so that your child can dress himself, leave some unbreakable dishes out or in a low cupboard where he can help himself, put some juice or milk in a child-sized pitcher so he can pour for himself sometimes, place some healthy snacks or cereal in a location where he can help himself at the appropriate time.

- Allow your child to have his own ideas, opinions, thoughts, and to make age-appropriate decisions. Ask him to choose which cup, plate, socks, shirt, fruit he would like that day. Allow him to disagree with you and say "No" sometimes.

Be realistic in terms of what your child can do. Try to set him up for success by giving him tasks, choices, and situations that he can work towards and confidently master. Support your child's struggles by offering encouragement, rather than rescuing.

—Ideas found in *Becoming the Parent You Want to Be* by Laura Davis and Janis Keyser, Broadway Books, 1997.

Foster your toddler's ability to play independently! When your toddler is involved in something, avoid interrupting or interacting with him for a short time. Begin your own work. If he starts to complain, wait a little while before going to him as long as nothing is wrong with him. Encourage his independent play by leaving him alone for a few more minutes each day over a period of many days. Tell him how proud you are of him when he plays contentedly by himself!

—Ideas found in "Raising an Independent Child" by Debra Kent, *Parenting*, June/July 1998.

Encourage your child to play by himself sometimes:

- Recognize that he may not be able to play alone yet.
- Tell him that you need to do something for ten minutes, but then you will play with him.
- Set a timer—for only a few minutes, to start—and tell your child that he can come for you when the bell goes off.
- Put together a box of toys that he can play with when you need him to play alone.

—Ideas found in *Help! For Parents of Children from Birth to Five*, a collection of ideas from parents edited by Jean Illsley Clarke, HarperSanFrancisco, 1993.

Find opportunities for your child to practice independence:

- Ask him to do small things for you: put a paper in the trash, unload a shopping bag, or get a book from the next room.
- Encourage him to make decisions and provide opportunities for him: "Which shirt would you like to wear today, the red one or the black one?"
- Help him learn about himself by asking him questions about his likes and dislikes and his opinions on matters: "Do you think that dog is cute?" "Do you like carrots?""
- Take care of him when he's hurt, return to him when you say that you will, and comfort him when he needs it. If he knows that you will help him when he needs it, he's more likely to share his feelings.

- Encourage the idea of doing things together, and tell him that together you can do anything. It will give him the self-confidence to try.

When he feels good about himself, in part because you show him that you feel good about him, he will have the confidence to explore life independently as he grows.

> —Ideas found in *The New Parent* by Miriam Stoppard, DK Publishing, 1998.

Give your child opportunities to try, stumble, and make mistakes. When you are afraid to let a child try, consider the consequences of his efforts. If he can safely do something on his own, let him try. If he doesn't know how to do something safely, show him. From successes, he will learn the feeling of accomplishment. From stumbling, he will learn skills to overcome obstacles. Teach him that he can learn as much from mistakes as he can from accomplishments. Independence is achieved through each trial and error, if you give your child the chance.

> —Ideas found in *Positive Discipline A-Z* by Jane Nelsen, Lynn Lott and H. Stephen Glenn, Prima Pub., 1993.

Encourage independence in your timid or fearful young child:

- Ask your child to join in activities. If he doesn't want to do something himself, ask him to help: "If I get the play dough out, will you help me make a snake?"
- Get his ideas about things: "Do you think we should color the tree red today?" "What toy car should go next to this building in the town?" "Should we have apples or oranges for lunch?"
- Show your child how to do new things. He will feel more confidence to tackle a task or activity if he has the know-how to do it.

> —Ideas found in *What to Expect the Toddler Years* by Arlene Eisenberg, Heidi Murkoff, and Sandee Hathaway, Workman Pub., 1994.

Notice when a child tries to accomplish something independently and help him feel good about his growing independence. The desire to do something and the capability to do it foster independence. Watch for accomplishments but also acknowledge effort. Your recognition of both steps toward independence is important to a child's self-confidence.

> —Ideas found in *The Parent's Journal Guide to Raising Great Kids* by Bobbi Conner, Bantam Books, 1997.

Help your child understand more about independence by reading about it together:

 All by Myself by Mercer Mayer

 Cat's Kittens by Paul Rogers

 I Can (Baby Beginner Board Books) by Helen Oxenbury

 I Can Do It! Featuring Jim Henson's Sesame Street Muppets by Sarah Albee

I Like Me! by Nancy Calson; *Me Gusto Como Soy!* translated by Dolores Koch

When to Get More Help

Children typically grow and learn new skills in their own time and at their own pace within the wide range of what is normal. Sometimes, children need a bit of extra help to keep their development on track, or to stay healthy and happy. Sometimes, parents need help providing for a child's needs or sorting out the best approaches to parenting.

Consider getting help for your child if he:

- Does not show a balance of being connected to you and becoming increasingly less dependent on you, little by little, after one year of age.
- Demonstrates anxious behavior (stomachaches, fearfulness, etc.) prior to periods of separation.
- Does not separate from you without extreme difficulty by age three.

Consider getting help for yourself if you:

- Have trouble allowing independence in your child.
- Wonder about your expectations for your child's independent behavior.

You are the expert when it comes to your family and child. If you have a concern, trust your instinct and find someone trained to help you: health care providers, early intervention teams, mental health professionals, parent educators and consultants, or telephone help-line staff. Consider talking it over with friends and family, too. You don't need to worry alone! Turn to "Finding Help in Your Community" on page 4 to learn about finding help near you.

More Help and Information

Books for Parents

- "Independence" in *The Parent's Journal Guide to Raising Great Kids* by Bobbi Conner, Bantam Books, 1997.
- *Toddlers and Parents: A Declaration of Independence* by T. Berry Brazelton. Delta/S. Lawrence, 1989.

Videos

- *I Can Do It! (Kidsongs)*. Sony Wonder.

Interrupting

by Tennae

Description

Interrupting is breaking in on or stopping a conversation or activity by talking or making noise.

Realistic Expectations

- Interrupting is a normal, common behavior of young children. They see themselves as the center of the world and assume that everyone else does too.
- Children under five have a limited ability to delay gratification or wait. It is typical for them to want what they want, when they want it, and interrupt you to get it.
- Children thrive on attention and may interrupt to get it; young children need a lot of attention.
- Children may feel threatened when their parents give attention to someone else, even by talking on the phone. They need help learning how to take care of themselves while a parent or caregiver attends to someone else.
- Children may become impatient and interrupt because they don't have the words to express themselves.
- Children who are included in conversations with adults may learn to interrupt less.
- If children receive attention for interrupting, they may continue interrupting. If they get attention for patience, waiting, and occupying themselves for a few minutes, they may practice these positive skills.

Approaches

Take the time to show your child how to wait:

- Consider creating a hand signal or cue that means please wait a minute. Practice the signal and waiting. Don't make your child wait more than a few minutes.
- Show your child what interrupting looks and feels like by making a game out of it.
- Talk about what will happen. If you need to make a phone call or have some uninterrupted minutes, let your child know ahead of time. If there is something she needs, consider providing it before your uninterrupted time.
- When your child has practiced and understands the signal for *wait*, then begin to use it in everyday life. Remain unemotional if she continues to interrupt after the signal is given and ignore the interruption, leaving the room if possible.
- Notice and praise your child when she is not interrupting.

> —Ideas found in *Positive Parenting from A to Z* by Karen Renshaw Joslin, Fawcett Columbine: Ballantine Books, 1994.

Interrupting

Prevent interrupting by helping your child become occupied. Ask your child if she would like to be near you while you make a phone call or finish your activity. Ask her to get something to read or play with, and to bring it near you. Consider creating and labeling a special place—like a bag, shelf or crate—for toys to be used only when you are on the phone or need uninterrupted time. Before you make your phone call or begin your uninterrupted activity, tell your child about it and ask her to have fun with the special toys reserved for this occasion. She will learn an important new skill: the ability to occupy herself while you give attention elsewhere.

> —Ideas found in *Positive Discipline A-Z* (revised and expanded 2nd edition) by Jane Nelsen, Lynn Lott, and H. Stephen Glenn, Prima, 1999.

Show your child how to interrupt appropriately by saying, "Please, excuse me." Pay attention to interruptions only when the child does so politely.

> —Ideas found in *Win the Whining War & Other Skirmishes* by Cynthia Whitham, Perspective Publishing, Inc., 1991.

With my four-year-old, we use the basic technique of ignoring him. If he does not interrupt politely—"Mom, can I tell you something, please?"—then I simply pretend that I have not heard him. Occasionally, he forgets this, so I remind him that he must wait. We don't tell him to wait because we are the grown-ups, we tell him that he must wait because interrupting anyone is rude. We are not allowed to interrupt him either.

Sometimes, the value of the message your child is bringing overrides the value of the lesson you are trying to teach. If my kids want to interrupt because they want me to put in a video or get a cup of water or something like that, the rule definitely applies! But suppose your child has just seen the first butterfly of spring or is bringing you a gift of his crayon art? Certainly, joy overrules propriety!

> —Debbie, Louisville, Kentucky

Set limits on interrupting. Remain calm and don't give your child whatever it is that she wants. Ask her to move away from you for a little while, and then come back to try again. Giving attention to your child when she interrupts by getting upset and yelling may actually cause her to interrupt more often.

> —Ideas found in *A to Z Guide to Your Child's Behavior* (Children's National Medical Center), Putnam Pub., 1993.

Show your child how to listen and wait for a turn to talk. Avoid interrupting your child, especially when another adult calls or comes in. Be respectful of your child's need for your attention to teach her how to be respectful of you.

> —Ideas found in *The Parents Answer Book (Parents Magazine)*, Golden Books, 1998.

Help your child understand more about waiting and time by reading about it together:

 My First Book of Time by Claire Llewellyn

 Phone Book (Pop-Up) by Jan Pienkowski

 Wait Skates! by Mildred D. Johnson

When to Get More Help

C hildren typically grow and learn new skills in their own time and at their own pace within the wide range of what is normal. Sometimes, children need a bit of extra help to keep their development on track, or to stay healthy and happy. Sometimes, parents need help providing for a child's needs or sorting out the best approaches to parenting.

Consider getting help for your child if she:

- Shows little or no improvement after you try an approach to help her change the interrupting for at least two months.

You are the expert when it comes to your child. If you have a concern, trust your instinct and find someone trained to help you: health care providers, early intervention teams, mental health professionals, parent educators and consultants, or telephone help-line staff. Consider talking it over with friends and family, too. You don't need to worry alone! Turn to "Finding Help in Your Community" on page 4 to learn about finding help near you.

More Help and Information

Books for Parents

- "Attention-Seeking;" " Interrupting" in *A to Z Guide to Your Child's Behavior* (Children's National Medical Center). Putnam Pub., 1993.

- "Patience" in *20 Teachable Virtues: Practical Ways to Pass on Lessons of Virtue and Character to Your Children* by Barbara C. Unell and Jerry L. Wycoff., Berkley Pub. Group, 1995.

Kindergarten

"School bus"
by Maura, age 5

Description

Kindergarten is an introduction to elementary school, in which young children begin to learn the routines and demands of learning in a group. Kindergarten, whether public or private, may be half day or whole day.

Realistic Expectations

- Children develop at different rates, so there is always a wide range of skills in any kindergarten class: some children may already be able to read, and others may not know the letters of the alphabet; some children can cooperate with other children, and others need help.

- Usually, schools require children to be five years of age by a certain date to be eligible to enter public-school kindergarten. Cut-off dates differ from state to state.

- Age should not be the only consideration in deciding whether a child is ready for school, because readiness for kindergarten depends on various factors. Still, most children typically do best in school with children their own age as long as schools do their job of individualizing their curriculum and services for each student.

- Individual schools or districts may have varying guidelines on what they expect of children upon entering kindergarten. Generally, experts agree that ideally, to be ready for kindergarten children should demonstrate the following: physical well being, positive self-esteem, ability to speak and listen, curiosity, ability to work and play with adults and other children, comfort being away from parents, and an ability to solve problems and think creatively.

- Five-year-olds can change and mature quickly; a child who may not seem ready for school in the spring may be ready in the fall when school begins.

- The transition to kindergarten may be easier for children who have some experience with other children and adults.

- Kindergarten can be an exciting turning point for children and their parents: the beginning of a lifetime of learning opportunities in a school setting.

Approaches

Help your child get ready for kindergarten by providing many opportunities to develop his body and mind. To provide for good health and physical well-being, see to it that your child:

- Eats a balanced diet.
- Receives regular medical and dental care and has had all the necessary immunizations.
- Gets plenty of rest.
- Runs, jumps, plays outdoors, and does other activities that help develop large muscles and provide exercise.
- Works puzzles, scribbles, colors, paints, and does other activities that help develop small muscles.

To help your child prepare for the social and emotional challenges, see to it that he:

- Is learning to be confident enough to explore and try new things.
- Is learning to work well alone and to do many tasks for himself.
- Has many opportunities to be with other children and is learning to cooperate with them.
- Is curious and is motivated to learn.
- Is learning to finish tasks (for example, picks up own toys).
- Is learning to use self-control.
- Can follow simple instructions.
- Helps with family chores.

To help your child learn language and gain knowledge about the world, see to it that he:

- Has many opportunities to play.
- Is read to every day.
- Has access to books and other reading materials.
- Has his television viewing monitored by an adult.
- Is encouraged to ask questions.
- Is encouraged to solve problems.
- Has opportunities to notice similarities and differences.
- Is encouraged to sort and classify things (for example, looking for red cars on the highway).
- Is learning to write his name and address
- Is learning to count and plays counting games.
- Is learning to identify shapes and colors.
- Has opportunities to draw, listen to and make music, and to dance.
- Has opportunities to get firsthand experiences to do things in the world - to see and touch objects, hear new sounds, smell and taste foods, and watch things move.

All children are unique. They grow and develop at different rates, and no one accomplishment guarantees that a child is ready for school.

—From "Helping Your Child Get Ready for School," U.S. Department of Education, 1992.

Kindergarten

Resist the temptation to *push* **your child toward doing letter and number work on paper or to read before kindergarten;** *expose* **your child to letters and numbers without** *pushing* **him to learn to read or do math.** Children who are rushed into reading or writing before they are ready miss important steps that give them a foundation for later learning, and they may lose their joy in learning. What your child needs before kindergarten is to:

- Play with objects enough to know what words mean so that he can later understand them when he reads them: a tennis ball is small, a golf ball is smaller, a marble is smallest.

- Use his fingers to develop the muscles he will need for writing: string beads, play with play dough, button his clothes, cut and paste, pour, and draw.

- Have hands-on opportunities to count objects, sort them into piles, take some away from the pile, and add some, in order to understand what is going on behind written number problems: putting three pennies in a pile, adding three more to the pile, and then counting all of them gives him the experience he needs to be able to understand what is happening in a number problem like $3 + 3 = 6$ when he sees it later in elementary school.

Give him plenty of time to play and explore so that he will learn to ask questions, make predictions, check for accuracy, and ask more questions. When he learns through play, he will see himself as a discoverer and an inventor!

> —Ideas found in *A Parent's Guide to Early Childhood Education* by Diane Trister Dodge and Joanna Phinney, Teaching Strategies, Inc., 1990.

Teach your child a few basic skills before kindergarten. Children develop at different rates, and different schools have different expectations for children when they begin kindergarten. Some skills signal that a child is probably ready to begin kindergarten. The child should:

- Know his first and last name.
- Be able to tell you his address or phone number.
- Know his parents' or guardians' names.
- Catch a large ball most of the time.
- Be able to run and stop on a signal.
- Be able to hop on one foot and skip—usually.
- Be able to hold a pencil or crayon.
- Be able to use scissors.
- Like to write and draw, and can usually write his first name.
- Be able to count (usually to ten).
- Be able to copy shapes (circles, squares, triangles, and rectangles).
- Be able to sort things in categories by color, shape, and kind.
- Be able to fill in the missing part in pictures of people, animals, or a house.

Call your school district for information on specific expectations.

> —From *Parent Involvement Begins at Birth: Collaboration Between Parents and Teachers of Children in the Early Years* by Sally Goldberg. Copyright © 1997 by Allyn and Bacon. Adapted by permission.

Learn about "good" kindergarten classrooms, and make sure that these qualities and conditions are present in your kindergarten. Kindergarten is a time for children to expand their love of learning, their general knowledge, their ability to get along with others, and their interest in reaching out to the world. It is important that children still get to be children. Here are ten signs of a good kindergarten classroom:

1. Children are playing and working with materials or other children. They are not aimlessly wandering or forced to sit quietly for long periods of time.

2. Children have access to various activities throughout the day, such as block building, pretend play, picture books, paints, and other art materials, and table toys such as building blocks, pegboards, and puzzles. Children are not all doing the same things at the same time.

3. Teachers work with individual children, small groups, and the whole group at different times during the day. They do not spend time *only* with the entire group.

4. The classroom is decorated with children's original artwork, their own writing with invented spelling, and dictated stories.

5. Children learn numbers and the alphabet in the context of their everyday experiences. Exploring the natural world of plants and animals, cooking, taking attendance, and serving snacks are all meaningful activities to children.

6. Children work on projects and have long periods of time (at least one hour) to play and explore. Filling out worksheets should not be their primary activity.

7. Children have an opportunity to play outside every day that weather permits. This play is never sacrificed for more instructional time.

8. Teachers read books to children throughout the day, not just at group story time.

9. Curriculum is adapted for those who are ahead as well as those who need additional help. Because children differ in experiences and background, they do not learn the same things at the same time in the same way.

10. Children and their parents look forward to school. Parents feel safe sending their child to kindergarten. Children are happy; they are not crying or regularly sick.

Individual kindergarten classrooms will vary, and the things each teacher teaches will vary according to the interests and backgrounds of the children. But all developmentally appropriate kindergarten classrooms will have one thing in common: the focus will be on the development of the child as a whole.

> —From the "Top 10 Signs of a Good Kindergarten Classroom," 1996. Reprinted with permission from the National Association for the Education of Young Children.

Schedule a routine physical examination with your child's pediatrician prior to starting kindergarten; many states require it. The pediatrician should check the child's vision, hearing, overall physical development, and be sure that his immunizations are up to date. If you have any concerns about whether or not your child is ready to begin kindergarten, talk to your pediatrician about it. He or she will be able to help you decide or make arrangements to talk to another professional who can help.

> —Ideas found in *Caring for Your Baby and Young Child* (revised edition) from the American Academy of Pediatrics, Bantam Books, 1998.

Kindergarten

If you are concerned that your child may not be ready for kindergarten when he is of age to attend, give it careful thought and consult with others who can help you make a decision. Most children are ready for kindergarten at the age schools recommend, but sometimes, they seem "too young," especially those whose birthdays fall right before the age cut-off date. Some children may receive needed help in the kindergarten program that will allow them to "catch up," while some may benefit from one more year of maturation while attending a preschool or receiving home schooling. Whether to send your child to kindergarten or hold him back is not an easy decision to make because many variables impact the decision.

Talk to your child's preschool teacher (if he is enrolled in one), pediatrician, caregivers, and/or kindergarten teachers or administrators from the school in which you plan to enroll him. Discuss your child's unique personality, needs, and strengths, and the schools expectations, goals, approaches and services; while making a decision, consider how your child and the school will work together.

—Ideas found in *Kindergarten Ready or Not?* By Sean A. Walmsley and
Bonnie Brown Walmsley, Heinemann, 1996.

Visit your child's new school to make connections with the place and people there; it will help him feel more comfortable on his first day of school and throughout the year. One of the most important ways you can influence your child's success in school is to stay involved in his education. Build a respectful and friendly relationship with your child's teacher, and help him to do the same; it acts as the connection between your child's home and school experience, making it easier to pass between the two worlds. To begin building these strong connections and help your child feel good about his first day:

- Attend the kindergarten visiting day that most schools have before school begins. Introduce yourself to your child's teacher and spend a few minutes talking to him or her with the child. Meet other children and their parents. If you miss this meeting, arrange for another.
- Take the time to share important information you know about your child with his teacher: any medical information, the way he learns best, special needs, fears, etc.
- Tour the school and play on the playground.
- Obtain and hang a list of school phone numbers in a convenient place at home so that you can stay in touch with the teacher with notes and phone calls.
- Plan to volunteer in or visit your child's classroom often.

—Ideas found in *The Kindergarten Survival Handbook: The Before School Checklist and
A Guide for Parents* by Allana Cummings Elovson, Parent Education Resources, 1993.

Help the child who has fears of going to kindergarten. Some children are excited and make the transition to kindergarten with amazing ease. Some have fears: "Will I find friends there? Will I like the teacher? Will I be able to find the bathroom? Will I miss my bus? Will I get lost?" Talk to him about his fears. Listen to him, then state back to him what you believe he is feeling: "I know that starting kindergarten is scary for you. You are worried about finding your way to the bus, aren't you?" This will let him know that you understand, and that he can trust you with his feelings. Don't tell him that he shouldn't feel the way he does by saying things like, "Be a big boy" or "Don't be silly—it will be fun."

Once you have acknowledged his feelings, give him reassurances and any information he needs: "I know you can find the drinking fountain at your new school just like you did at preschool. Your teacher will probably show you right away, but if not, you can ask him to show you." Try to help him feel excited by remaining positive yourself, but let him have his own feelings about school. Continue to talk about his fears as they arise.

Read books about going to kindergarten, and make a visit to the classroom before the first day to help him become more familiar with what the experience will be.

—Ideas found in *Kindergarten—It Isn't What It Used to Be* (updated edition) by Susan K. Golant, and Mitch Golant, Lowell House, 1997

Help your child understand more about kindergarten by reading about it together:

Kindergarten Kids by Ellen B. Senisi

Learning Is Fun with Mrs. Perez by Alice K. Flanagan

Miss Bindergarten Gets Ready for Kindergarten by Joseph Slate

Sparky and Eddie: The First Day of School by Tony Johnston

When You Go to Kindergarten by James Howe

When to Get More Help

Children typically grow and learn new skills in their own time and at their own pace within the wide range of what is normal. Sometimes, children need a bit of extra help to keep their development on track, or to stay healthy and happy. Sometimes, parents need help providing for a child's needs or sorting out the best approaches to parenting.

Consider getting help for your child if he:

- Acts much younger than other children his age and does not seem ready for kindergarten the year before he should start.
- Seems like he is ready for kindergarten but just misses the age cut-off in your school district.
- Has not been immunized and you would like him to be.
- Is three or four years old and you would like him to be in a preschool program and need help finding or paying for one.

You are the expert when it comes to your family and child. If you have a concern, trust your instinct and find someone trained to help you: health care providers, early intervention teams, mental health professionals, parent educators and consultants, or telephone help-line staff. Consider talking it over with friends and family, too. You don't need to worry alone! Turn to "Finding Help in Your Community" on page 4 to learn about finding help near you.

More Help and Information

Books for Parents

- *Kindergarten—It Isn't What It Used to Be* (updated edition) by Susan K. Golant, and Mitch Golant, Lowell House, 1997

- *Kindergarten Ready or Not?* by Sean A. Walmsley and Bonnie Brown Walmsley, Heinemann, 1996.

- *The Kindergarten Survival Handbook: The Before School Checklist and Guide for Parents* by Allana Cummings Elovson, Parent Education Resources, 1993.

- *MegaSkills®: Building Children's Achievement for the Information Age* (new and expanded edition) by Dorothy Rich. Houghton Mifflin, 1998.

- "Evaluation and Testing, Chapter 3," and "Samples from Tests and Assessments, Appendix D" in *Helping Children Grow Up in the 90's: Resources Book for Parents and Teachers*, National Association of School Psychologists, 1992.

Articles, Pamphlets, and Booklets

- "Your Child's First Day at School" from Metropolitan Life Insurance Company. Request: 800-METLIFE. Web site: www.metlife.com.

- "A Good Kindergarten for Your Child" and " Ready or Not...Preparing Young Children for the Classroom" from National Association for the Education of Young Children (NAEYC). (See National Organizations)

- "Helping Your Child Get Ready for School: With Activities for Children From Birth Through Age 5" by Nancy Paulu. Online. U.S. Department of Education, Office of Educational Research and Improvement. Available to order through the consumer Information Center, Pueblo, Colorado 81009, 888-8-PUEBLO (1-888-878-3256) or read online: www.pueblo.gsa.gov/cic_text/children/getready/getready.txt

Community and Government Resources

- Head Start Bureau

  Web site: www.acf.dhhs.gov/programs/hsb/

  Head Start is a national program which provides educational, medical, dental, nutritional, and social services for low-income, pre-school children, ages three to five, and their families. Look in your local phone book, on the web site, or call your local school district to find the Head Start program nearest you.

National Organizations

- National Association for the Education of Young Children (NAEYC)

  800-424-2460, Fax: 202-328-1846

  Web site: www.naeyc.org

Web Sites

- Family Education Network (FEN): http://familyeducation.com.

- Kidsource: Education—Early Learning.

  www.kidsource.com/kidsource/pages/ed.early.html

- ReadyWeb: an electronic collection of resources on school readiness for parents and educators: http://readyweb.crc.uiuc.edu/

- School Express: www.schoolexpress.com

Lying

Description

Lying is *deliberately* telling someone something untrue. A falsehood, a fib, a "white lie," and not telling the whole truth are all ways to purposefully deceive someone. Fantasy is not considered a lie.

Realistic Expectations

- It is normal for children to exaggerate the truth and to fib. Some children start as young as three, and by age six, most, if not all, children will lie. Most experts agree that children don't deliberately lie until age three or four because they don't have the skills needed to lie.

- Children ages four and five typically tell tall tales, brag, and exaggerate the truth: "My mom is the fastest runner in the whole world." "Bye, Dad, I'm going to England now." "I can jump higher than Michael Jordan!" Telling stories is different from lying; it is a child's way of stretching his imagination, experimenting with language, and making himself look good.

- Children have huge imaginations, often live in a fantasy world, and may not be able to tell the difference between what's real and what isn't. Telling about their fantasy is not the same as intentionally lying.

- Children under five are just beginning to develop a sense of right and wrong. They may not know lying is wrong.

- Children with low self-esteem may be more likely to exaggerate about themselves in order to help feel good.

- Sometimes what appears to be a lie is really a difference of opinion. If two children tell different versions of the same event, they are not intentionally lying but telling the truth as they see it.

- Children may lie to test the limits or to see if they can trick you. Children experiment with power and language as they learn the ways of the world.

- Toddlers and preschoolers may tell you something that is not true to cover up a mistake or bad behavior. They may think that by telling something that they wish was true, it becomes true.

- Some children lie because they don't feel safe telling the truth and fear harsh punishments or criticism. Children who lie often to cover up mistakes need reassurance that everyone misbehaves at times and that this doesn't make them a bad person.

- Sometimes children lie to deal with a stressful situation: a child who is having a problem at day care may invent a story to avoid going there.

- Children under age five typically do not have the knowledge or words to lie about being physically or sexually abused. Take their stories of abuse seriously and don't assume that they are lying.

- Parents tell stories, myths, and tall tales to children. The existence of the tooth fairy is one example.

- Children will be more honest if their parents or caretakers are honest.

Approaches

Show understanding of your child's wishful thinking. Sometimes your child may tell what she wishes were true as if it is true: "Mom said I could have only ice cream for breakfast every day." Don't call her on lying. Instead, tell her that you see how much she would like to have ice cream for breakfast every day, but that she will have to be happy with regular breakfast food.

> —Ideas found in *Raising Black Children* by James P. Comer, and Alvin F. Poussaint, Plume, 1992.

Encourage truthfulness by allowing your child to come to you with mistakes without fear of anger and punishment. Let her know that she can come to you for help and you will accept her mistakes calmly and without anger. If she is punished for telling the truth, she will soon learn not to tell the truth.

> —Ideas found in *Your Baby & Child* (3rd edition) by Penelope Leach, Alfred A. Knopf, 1997.

Avoid inviting lying by asking a question that will get your child into trouble if she answers truthfully. For example, if your child has ice cream on her face and there is ice cream on the floor, don't ask your child if she spilled ice cream. You already know what happened. Look to what you can do to solve a problem instead of being concerned about blaming your child. Consider telling her: "I see you spilled ice cream. I'll get a sponge and you can help me clean it up." This will prevent her from lying to cover up mistakes or out of fear of punishment.

> —Ideas found in *Positive Discipline A-Z* (revised and expanded 2nd edition) by Jane Nelsen, Lynn Lott, and H. Stephen Glenn Prima, 1999.

Make it easier for your child to tell the truth. When your child lies, stay calm and look for the reason. Your child may need more affection and praise to build self-esteem if she lies about her abilities. She may lie out of fear of punishment. Physical punishment actually causes a child to lie more to avoid the punishment. Instead, assure your child that you love her no matter what she does and even when you are angry with her. Explain to your child why lying is wrong and tell a story that she can understand about why lying is wrong, like "The Boy Who Cried Wolf." Making it easier for your child to tell the truth will prevent lying.

> —Ideas found in *Complete Baby and Child Care* by Miriam Stoppard, Dorling Kindersley, 1995.

Encourage honesty in preschoolers by teaching the concepts of truth and lying. Ask, "Do you know the difference between something that's true and something that's not true? Let's see if you do. I'll say something and you say 'True' or 'Not true.'" Start with simple facts and move toward things relating to behavior, for example:

- The sky is green. (Kids say, "Not true.")
- We see with our eyes. (Kids say, "True")
- Ants are bigger than elephants.
- Take a cookie out of a jar and eat it. Then say, "I didn't eat the cookie."
- Drop a toy on the couch. Then say, "Yes, I left my toy on the couch."

Then say, "You really can tell the difference between what's true and not true, can't you? Do you know what it's called when someone says something that's not true? It's called a *lie*."

> —Reprinted with the permission of Simon & Schuster from *Teaching Your Children Values* by Linda and Richard Eyre, Copyright © 1993 by R.M. Eyre & Associates, Inc.

Respect privacy and honesty in your home to prevent lying. Allow yourself to have privacy without lying to your child or keeping secrets. Between four and six, she can understand that not everything is for or about her. Explain that adults have things that they do without children and that some of them are done in private. Allow your child to have privacy, and practice independence. If she is not ready to tell you something, respect her wishes. Don't put her in a position that tempts her to lie to protect her own privacy.

> —Ideas found in *Why Kids Lie* by Paul Ekman, with Mary Ann Mason Ekman and Tom Ekman, Penguin Books, 1991.

Help your child learn the difference between fantasy and reality. Play make-believe with your child and make up stories that aren't real. When something realistic is on television or in a movie, talk about what is real and what is not. Talk about exaggeration of the truth and point it out in his story.

> —Ideas found in *Positive Parenting from A to Z* by Karen Renshaw Joslin, Fawcett Columbine: Ballantine Books, 1994.

Teach your child the difference between partial truths and the entire truth. A toddler may only remember or report a portion of what really took place: if she comes to tell you that her friend broke her truck, she may leave out the part about how she, herself, threw it at a tree, and the friend only picked up the broken pieces. Kindly explain how the entire truth is important to understanding what happened before accusing someone of doing something.

> —Ideas found in *What to Expect the Toddler Years* by Arlene Eisenberg, Workman Pub., 1994.

Help your child understand more about lying by reading about it together:

 The Berenstain Bears and the Truth by Stan and Jan Berenstain

 Heat Wave (a tall tale) by Helen Ketteman

"The Shepherd Boy and the Wolf" in *The Children's Aesop* by Stephanie Calmenson
(Or any version of "The Boy Who Cried Wolf")

When to Get More Help

Children typically grow and learn new skills in their own time and at their own pace within the wide range of what is normal. Sometimes, children need a bit of extra help to keep their development on track, or to stay healthy and happy. Sometimes, parents need help providing for a child's needs or sorting out the best approaches to parenting.

Consider getting help for your child if he:

- Lies and is also in a very stressful situation: a child who is having a problem at day care, with a divorce at home, or with moving to a new home.

- Does not know the difference between fantasy and reality by five years of age.

- Tells you he has been physically or sexually abused and you wonder if he is lying. Don't assume that he is lying; young children typically do not have the knowledge or words to lie about being abused.

You are the expert when it comes to your family and child. If you have a concern, trust your instinct and find someone trained to help you: health care providers, early intervention teams, mental health professionals, parent educators and consultants, or telephone help-line staff. Consider talking it over with friends and family, too. You don't need to worry alone! Turn to "Finding Help in Your Community" on page 4 to learn about finding help near you.

More Help and Information

Books for Parents

- "Fabricating" and "Lying" in *Positive Discipline A-Z* (revised and expanded 2nd edition), by Jane Nelsen, Lynn Lott, and H. Stephen Glenn. Prima, 1999.

- "Lying" in *Complete Baby and Child Care* by Miriam Stoppard. Dorling Kindersley, 1995.

- *Why Kids Lie: How Parents Can Encourage Truthfulness* by Paul Ekman, with Mary Ann Mason Ekman and Tom Ekman, Penguin Books, 1991.

Videos

- *Responsibility/Truth*, The New Captain Kangaroo Series. Twentieth Century Fox Home Entertainment.

- *Telling the Truth*, Sesame Street Guide to Life Series. Sony.

Manners

Description

Manners are the conventions, considerations, and tact that people use with each other. These customs reflect values in a family, community, or culture. Using good manners shows that you have respect and consideration for others, value courtesy in society, and know how to be polite.

Realistic Expectations

- There are hundreds of rules and conventions that are known as manners: No interrupting, say "Please" when asking for something, say "Thank you " when receiving something, say "Excuse me," when interrupting or bumping someone, no elbows on the table, be quiet when someone else is speaking, take turns in line, give up your seat for an elderly person, ask before borrowing, say "Hello" when you meet someone and "Good-bye" when you leave, sit down during a meal, no talking with your mouth full, wipe your face with your napkin and not your shirt, and many, many more.

- Though children under age five are aware of some manners, they have a limited ability to use them consistently. Young children typically don't yet have the self-control that is necessary to consistently: politely ask when they want something, wait a turn, be quiet, hold off saying what they think, or express feelings in adult ways. They may know that they need to stand in line to buy juice, but they may not have the self-control to wait and they may try to run to the front of the line.

- Preschoolers begin to understand that there are different ways to treat people and that they have a choice in how they treat people, including using manners. Babies and toddlers don't have that understanding yet, so they can't make choices about whether or not to use manners.

- Many children under age five are not comfortable greeting and talking to people they don't know. They may not be willing to say hello to someone that you introduce them to.

- Children often learn more by watching what you do than by being told what to do. Children who live with good manners at home are more likely to use good manners in time. Children who see adults and older children out of control, acting ill-mannered, or who are used to being ordered or commanded to do things, are likely to learn that good manners are not very important.

- Children gain self-confidence and self-esteem from knowing the right way to act and being allowed to act appropriately for their age.

- Learning manners takes time. Teaching simple manners in the early years is a positive start and will make it easier for children to learn and adopt a wider set of manners when they are older.

Approaches

Help your child with the first steps in learning manners: to enjoy other people and feel good about himself. To help your child enjoy other people, don't force him to speak to someone new at age two, three, or four. Avoid drawing attention to your child and embarrassing him. If your child learns that people don't make him uncomfortable, and he's allowed to speak to them when and if he wants to, learning adult manners will follow.

> —Ideas found in *Dr. Spock's Baby and Child Care* (7th edition) by Benjamin Spock and
> Stephen J. Parker, Dutton, 1998.

Help your child understand why manners are important, not just what they are. Explain to him the value of being considerate of someone else in addition to the rule: " We wait in line without complaining because the people ahead of us got here first and it's fair that they get to have a turn first," or "We hold the door open for Grandma because she can't get through the door with her walker very easily by herself. Holding the door for her shows her that we care for her." If you teach your child to be considerate and thoughtful, manners will likely come more easily to him in time.

> —Ideas found in *What to Expect the Toddler Years* by Arlene Eisenberg, Heidi E. Murkoff and
> Sandee E. Hathaway, Workman Pub., 1994.

Strike a balance between meeting your child where he is at developmentally and expecting him to follow through consistently with manners. Learn about what your child is developmentally capable of and not capable of. Young children are just learning skills that they need to be able to use table manners. Still, even one-year olds sometimes say "Tanks," "Pease," and "Scuse me!" Look for and compliment good manners when you see your child using them. As skills emerge, teach and help your child practice new manners.

> —Deb Kratz, co-author of *The Field Guide to Parenting*.

Teach your preschool child to say "Please" and "Thank you" and to use other simple manners, without requiring that he use them every time. Tell him specifically what is expected in terms of good behavior: say "please" when asking for something, say "thank you" when it is given, say "excuse me" when you bump into someone or accidentally interrupt, and be quiet or use a quiet voice at times. Be understanding of your child because these skills are new and take time to learn. Forcing him to use them may only cause a power struggle. Remind him to use manners without blaming him or making him feel bad when he forgets. Be sure to tell your child what manners are for: to show respect and thoughtfulness to others.

> —Ideas found in *The Parents Answer Book*, (Parents Magazine), Golden Books, 1998.

Show your child how to be polite and give him a chance to practice. Practice manners and consideration yourself: listen, don't interrupt, speak politely, share, be kind—not hurtful, and use good language. Tell him what to say to be polite: "Hello" for when you are meeting someone; "Good-bye" for when you end a conversation or leave; "Excuse me" for when you burp, bump into someone, or interrupt; and "I'm sorry" for when you make a mistake or say something that hurts someone. Teach him that he can show good manners by actions, too: taking turns, waiting patiently, picking up his toys.

Consider ways that your child can practice: have a tea party with stuffed animals, play pretend grocery store, take him to the library or post office and allow him to ask politely for something. Remind him politely when he forgets manners and be sure to watch and praise his good manners when he uses them.

> —Ideas found in *Parenting Works! Facilitator's Guide* (MELD), Blue Penguin, 1996.

Help your child understand that using manners is more than saying "Please" and "Thank you," it's also about respecting the feelings of others. Tell your child that making fun of someone, or name calling is not using good manners. Helping a friend when they need it, sharing, giving each friend some attention when you invite them over, and using words instead of hitting, grabbing, or fighting is using good manners. Explain to your child that paying attention when someone talks to you, and waiting for your turn to speak, are also ways to use good manners. It shows that you care about and respect how other people feel

—Ideas found in *Perfect Pigs: An Introduction to Manners* by Marc Brown and Stephen Krensky, Little Brown & Co., 1983.

Around age four, after your child understands the manners of home, begin to teach him manners to use out in the world. Before going out to someone else's home, or to a social gathering, talk to the child about how he could act, and consider practicing: "Often when I meet someone new or see someone I haven't seen for awhile, I shake their hand. People at the wedding we are going to might ask to shake your hand too. Do you want to try with me first? Now that you know how, maybe you can shake hands at the wedding just like me."

—Ideas found in *Touchpoints* by T. Berry Brazelton, Addison-Wesley, 1992.

Teach your child to whisper and tell him when it is appropriate. There are many public places where it's not appropriate to talk out loud—like during a movie, a religious service, or a meeting. Before expecting your child to behave at these places, show him how to whisper. Talk about when it's OK to use your regular voice, a loud or outside voice, and a quiet or inside voice.

—Ideas found in *Practical Parenting Tips* (revised and updated edition) by Vicki Lansky, Meadowbrook Press, 1992.

Invite your child's initiative in coming up with ways to show consideration for others. There are many ways to thank someone for a gift, a favor, or for doing something nice, just like there are many ways to ask someone for something. Your child may be more likely to participate if he is allowed to express himself in his own way or come up with his own ideas of expressing appreciation. "How should we celebrate your grandma's birthday?" is more likely to get an enthusiastic response, such as, "I want to make her a sculpture out of wood and paint it with sparkly paint!" than a command to go make Grandma a birthday card.

—Ideas found in *Becoming the Parent You Want to Be* by Laura Davis and Janis Keyser, Broadway Books, 1997.

Help your child learn more about manners by reading about them together:

 *Eat Your Peas, Louise!* by Pegeen Snow

Hello! Good-bye; and Manners by Aliki

Me First by Helen Lester

My Dog Never Says Please by Suzanne Williams

No Bad Bears: Ophelia's Book of Manners by Michele Durkson Clise

No One Told the Aardvark by Deborah Eaton and Susan Halter

Oops! Excuse Me Please! And Other Mannerly Tales by Bob McGrath

Pass the Fritters, Critters by Cheryl Chapman

Perfect Pigs by Marc Brown and Stephen Krensky

When to Get More Help

Children typically grow and learn new skills in their own time and at their own pace within the wide range of what is normal. Sometimes, children need a bit of extra help to keep their development on track, or to stay healthy and happy. Sometimes, parents need help providing for a child's needs or sorting out the best approaches to parenting.

Consider getting help for your child if he:

- Cannot follow simple instructions by two years of age.
- Cannot show some ability to control his behavior by at least five years of age.

Consider getting help for yourself if you:

- Aren't sure what is expected behavior at any age.

You are the expert when it comes to your family and child. If you have a concern, trust your instinct and find someone trained to help you: health care providers, early intervention teams, mental health professionals, parent educators and consultants, or telephone help-line staff. Consider talking it over with friends and family, too. You don't need to worry alone! Turn to "Finding Help in Your Community" on page 4 to learn about finding help near you.

More Help and Information

Books for Parents

- *Elbows Off the Table, Napkin in the Lap, No Video Games During Dinner: The Modern Guide to Teaching Children Good Manners* by Carol Wallace. St. Martin's Press, 1996.
- *Teaching Your Children Values* by Linda and Richard Eyre. Simon & Schuster, 1993.

Articles, Pamphlets and Booklets

- "Special Section: Manners," *Parents*, December 1996.

Moving

by Tennae

Description

Moving is transferring a family's belongings, furnishings, and emotions from one home to another. Families move for a wide variety of reasons, including a parent's job relocation, need for a larger or smaller home, need for a different neighborhood, economic realities, eviction, divorce, separation, or simply a desire for a change. Home can be anywhere the family lives together and creates a home: your own house, a friend or relative's home, an apartment or condominium, a townhouse, a hotel room, etc.

Realistic Expectations

- Children may not understand what moving means:
  - They may think that moving away from a house means moving away from all the belongings inside the house, too.
  - They may think that it is their fault that the family is moving.
  - They may need reassurance that they will move with the family, and not be left behind.
  - They may not realize that moving is permanent and may expect to go to the previous home again after moving.
- Children under five do not fully understand the concept of time and will need help understanding when the move will take place.
- It is common for children's behavior to regress around moving time:
  - Toddlers may react to the stress of moving by having more tantrums.
  - Preschoolers may become clingy and fear separation.
  - Children who are potty trained may begin to have accidents.
  - Children who usually sleep well may not be able to sleep through the night or may need a night light.
- Changes in routine or habits, such as potty training or weaning, will be more difficult and stressful if started shortly before or after a move.
- Some children do not talk about their worry related to a move. A preschool child who does not appear interested or is not asking questions may need help talking about it and may need reassurance about the move.
- Almost all children adjust to a move if they are prepared for it, but it may take several months to adjust to a new home.
- Children get their cues from adults. If the adults are positive about the move, the children are likely to be positive, too.

Approaches

To have a successful move:

- Pay attention to the ending of things as well as the beginning of something new.
- Keep your family together and comfort each other.
- Allow your child to help and feel like they are an important part of the moving process.
- Show your child a positive attitude about the move and change.
- Plan well and enjoy your move!

—Ideas found in "Moving with Kids" by Katharine Canfield, Online, MoversNet: www.usps.gov/moversnet.

Prepare for a move by separating the task into three stages:

1. The Preparation Stage involves the decision-making, house-hunting, buying and selling, and planning. It also includes the emotional steps of anticipation, excitement, waiting, and worrying.

2. The Work Stage or the "cardboard box" stage of the move consists of the actual physical labor that includes cleaning, sorting, storing, wrapping, packing, junking, hauling, and loading at one end and unpacking at the other. Involve everyone so they feel like an integral part of the moving process.

3. The Settling-In Stage is the equally important process of getting acquainted with your new neighborhood and community. It includes meeting neighbors, becoming familiar with new jobs and schools, dealing with the sadness of saying good-bye, overcoming anxieties and fears about your new setting, finding new "favorite" places, and establishing new friendships.

Moving is a family endeavor. Every person is essential to its success. Each stage in the process offers an opportunity to learn new ways of being with one another that honor each person's valuable contribution to the family. Only when all three stages are completed can you call your new house a home. Only then is your move really over.

—From *Moving with Children* by Thomas T. Olkowski and Lynn Parker, Gylantic Pub.Co., 1993.

Prepare your child for a move and help her in the process of moving:

- Tell her the news before you start packing boxes—but not too far in advance of the move.
- Talk honestly with her about your feelings and what you will feel sad about leaving behind.
- Speak to her in simple terms about why you are moving.
- Look for fun things that your child will enjoy in the new neighborhood and new home and then tell her about them.
- Visit the new home, neighborhood, and day care or school together.
- Play make-believe moving so she can begin to understand what it is about and let out some of her feelings about it.
- Include your child in the move by letting her help pack.
- Pack her things last and unpack them first. Let her help unpack.
- Involve her in leaving the old house and arriving at the new house.
- Be calm and understanding with your child.
- Get to know your new community.

—Ideas found in *What to Expect the Toddler Years* by Arlene Eisenberg, Heidi E. Murkoff, and Sandee Hathaway, Workman Pub., 1994.

Follow normal routines and schedules as much as possible during moving time. Let your child know what to expect when things won't follow the regular schedule. Find time to play with her, and talk about your feelings and hers. Be positive about the move. Let her help you pack and give her choices about where to put her things in the new home. Remember to laugh, and to use humor and silliness to help get over any stress or sadness that may occur.

> —Ideas found in *Positive Parenting from A to Z* by Karen Renshaw Joslin, Fawcett Columbine: Ballantine Books, 1994.

Tell your child that her feelings about moving are OK; don't try to change her mind about them or rescue her from sadness. She can learn to cope with change if she's allowed to. Tell her that you understand and tell her about a time when you had to make a big change. Avoid trying to make things easier for her with new things, bribes, or rewards.

> —Ideas found in *Positive Discipline A-Z* by Jane Nelsen, Lynn Lott, and H Stephen Glenn, Prima, 1999.

> *The hardest part about moving for me has been my wanting to make things perfect for the kids—make sure they have new friends fast, are happy fast, feel at home fast—and understanding that feeling a part of a new community takes time for everyone, and different amounts of time for everyone. Give yourself and your children a break and try enjoying each other's company while you make inroads into becoming part of a new community.*
>
> —Jodie, on moving from Minneapolis to Mahtomedi

Avoid making promises that you can't keep. Let your child feel sad if she needs to about what she is leaving behind. Don't build expectations or make promises about things that you have no control over: whether there will be new friends, whether she will enjoy the new neighborhood, school, or day care. Most children do make great new friends and enjoy their new home, but some don't.

> —Ideas found in *A to Z Guide to Your Child's Behavior* (Children's National Medical Center), Putnam Pub., 1993.

After a move, take care to keep in touch with old friends while encouraging new friendships for your child. Bring her back to see friends from the old neighborhood and have them visit the new home. Talk about these friends, look at pictures, call them, and write or send pictures to them.

Start with one or two new friends and take the children out together to give them a chance to become good friends. If the new neighborhood, school, or day care has what seems like a close or closed group of kids, you can help her find a way into the group through a friendship with at least one of the children in the group.

> —Ideas found in *Touchpoints* by T. Berry Brazelton, Addison-Wesley, 1992.

Help a child understand more about moving by reading about it together:

- *Alexander, Who's Not (Do You Hear Me? I Mean It!) Going to Move* by Judith Viorst
- *Annie Bananie* by Leah Komaiko
- *The Berenstain Bears' Moving Day* by Stan and Jan Berenstain
- *Goodbye House* by Frank Asch
- *I'm Not Moving, Mama* by Nancy White Carlstrom
- *Ira Says Goodbye* by Bernard Waber
- *The Leaving Morning* by Angela Johnson
- *The Lost and Found House* by Michael Cadnum

When to Get More Help

Children typically grow and learn new skills in their own time and at their own pace within the wide range of what is normal. Sometimes, children need a bit of extra help to keep their development on track, or to stay healthy and happy. Sometimes, parents need help providing for a child's needs or sorting out the best approaches to parenting.

Consider getting help for your child if she:

- Cries frequently or seems extremely sad.
- Appears withdrawn.
- Shows signs of stress, disappointment, or depression.
- Has disturbed sleeping and eating patterns and acts much younger than his age for a period of time after the move.
- Is reluctant to separate from family members.
- Seems excessively worried or fearful about the new situation.
- Seems in denial about the move.
- Has increased or unusual and lasting anger and tantrums.

*Note: Any of the above behaviors are common in young children during a move, and usually pass quickly; if they do not, and instead last for a period of time that seems extreme to you, seek advice.

You are the expert when it comes to your family and child. If you have a concern, trust your instinct and find someone trained to help you: health care providers, early intervention teams, mental health professionals, parent educators and consultants, or telephone help-line staff. Consider talking it over with friends and family, too. You don't need to worry alone! Turn to "Finding Help in Your Community" on page 4 to learn about finding help near you.

More Help and Information

Books for Parents

- *Moving with Children: A Parent's Guide to Moving with Children* by Thomas T. Olkowski and Lynn Parker. Gylantic Pub. Co., 1993.
- *Steiners' Complete How-To-Move Handbook* by Clyde Steiner and Shari Steiner. Dell Publishing, 1996.

Articles, Brochures, and Activity Guides

- "Children and Family Moves," AACAP Facts for Families, Fact No. 14.

  Write to:

  American Academy of Child & Adolescent Psychiatry
  P.O. Box 96106, Washington DC, 20090-6109
  www.aacap.org
- "Mover's Guide" published by TMSI and the U.S. Postal Service. Available at U.S. Post Offices and an expanded version is available online through MoversNet. See websites below.
- "Moving and Children" from the American Moving & Storage Association

  1611 Duke St., Alexandria, VA 22314-3482.
  Send a request for the brochure with a SASE.
  www.amconf.org

Community Resources

- Real Estate Agent: Ask your real estate agent if the realty company offers any moving kits or books for children.
- Moving Company: Several moving companies have moving kits or books for children and have information for parents on how to move with children. Ask your moving company or check the phone book for a company in your area.

Videos

- *Ira Says Goodbye* (based on the story by Bernard Waber). Loma Linda University.
- *Let's Get A Move On: A Kid's Video Guide to a Family Move.* Kidvidz.

Web Sites

- Atlas Van Lines provides information on how to move and online games for kids: www.atlasvanlines.com
- MoversNet: www.usps.gov/moversnet
- Relocation Central: The Online Guide for People on the Move: www.relocationcentral.com
- Relocation Online: www.relocationonline.com

Parents: Taking Care of Ourselves

Description

Taking care of ourselves as parents includes attending to our physical, emotional, mental, social, and spiritual needs. It allows us to be the best that we can be for our children.

Realistic Expectations

- Studies repeatedly show that warmth, caring, and responsiveness from adults are what's most important for the well being of children. Parents can best meet the challenge of providing those things when they attend to their own basic needs.

- Everyone has an equal amount of time to spend in work, play, leisure, and rest: 1440 minutes in a day, 168 hours in a week.

- Time for yourself is not a luxury but a necessity. Everyone benefits from taking time to refresh and care for themselves.

- All families benefit from support from others in raising children.

- Balancing the care of children and self requires choices, priorities, sacrifices, compromises, delegating, eliminating, simplifying, learning to say no, and sharing tasks.

Approaches

Commit to caring for yourself. Instead of endless self-sacrifice and denial of your needs, focus on making yourself the best person you are capable of becoming. When you grow and develop, your child does too. Just as the earth revolves around the sun for life-sustaining energy, your child thrives on the nurturing, caring, and warmth that you provide.

This commitment to self does not mean, however, that your child is left alone while you pursue meditation or skiing in some distant location. This commitment to self also does not mean giving yourself permission to accept a job in which one-hundred-hour workweeks are common. Simply stated, commitment to self does not give you permission to abandon, minimize, ignore, or in any other way compromise your responsibilities and duties as a parent.

What this commitment to self does mean is that you take responsibility to develop your own unique talents, skills, mind, and spiritual center to their fullest, and do not use your children as an excuse for not moving ahead with your own life. Developing your talents, skills, and mind can include anything from taking classes for fun, to going back to school, to developing a hobby or work that you love, to reading a book, to having a discussion with a friend. Finding a spiritual center does not need to be a traditional belief; god can be anything, look like anything, and be called by any name or not named at all. Just know that you are not alone and find peace by focusing on something bigger than yourself.

Make your own development a priority and consider both yourself and your child, in everything that you do, every day.

—From *The Complete Single Mother* by Andrea Engber and Leah Klungness,
Adams Media Corporation, 1995.

Actively maintain your health so you can enjoy your child far into the future. Heart disease, cancer, emphysema, and liver cirrhosis are chronic, long-term illnesses that can be prevented or postponed by following a plan for good health:

- Exercise.
- Eat a healthy diet. Especially cut down on fat.
- If you smoke, stop.
- If you use alcohol, do so in moderation, or no more than two drinks a day.
- Control your weight.
- Avoid injury: use seatbelts; don't drink or use drugs and drive a vehicle or boat; reducing fire hazards in your home—use smoke alarms and keep clutter to a minimum; prevent gun accidents by keeping them out of your home or locking the ammunition away from the gun.
- Maintain preventive care with a doctor. Have periodic checkups as recommended by your health care provider and seek advice if you have concerns about your health.

> —From *Take Care of Yourself: The Complete Illustrated Guide to Medical Self-Care* (6th edition) by Donald M. Vickery MD and James Fries MD, Copyright © 1996 by Donald M. Vickery and James F. Fries. Reprinted by permission of Perseus Books Publishers, a member of Perseus Books, L.L.C.

Stop expecting to find time, instead create time. Think about all that you do in a day. Consider writing everything down and how long it takes to do it. If this day is unusual in some way, consider tracking what you do for two or three days. Once you can clearly see how you spend your time, then you can look at what's important, make changes, and create time for things that are missing.

> —Ideas found in *The Joy of Twins and Other Multiple Births* by Pamela Patrick Novotny, Crown Publishers, 1998.

Take control of your time! If it's the little things that eat up your day, try to:

- Set priorities; consider making a list and marking the tasks of greatest importance.
- Put a task, chore, or problem away if it doesn't seem manageable at present. Take an hour or several days off and return to it when you have a fresh perspective.
- Take the time to do a job the right way the first time; it can take more time to fix mistakes than it does to do it correctly in the first place.
- Do your work and don't take on the work of others; ask for help if you need it.
- Use time spent waiting to finish other small chores.
- Take care of yourself! You will be able to get more done if you are feeling well, refreshed, relaxed, and calm.

> —Ideas found in "You Can Get Control of Your Time" from the Working Parent Resource Center, *Family Information Services*, January 1997.

Keep your smile and keep laughing. Look for humor in everyday situations. Humor can help you look at a situation in a different way and possibly learn something new from it. Laughter and humor can lighten your attitude, give you a sense of joy, and prevent stress. Besides, laughing feels good.

> —Ideas found in *Restoring Balance to A Mother's Busy Life* by Beth Wilson, Contemporary Books, 1996.

Simplify your life by saying no. If someone asks you to do something you don't want to do, just say, "No thank you." If you have a hard time saying no, buy some time, "I need to check my calendar and think about it," or "Maybe another time."

—Ideas found in *Simplify Your Life: 100 Ways to Slow Down and Enjoy the Things That Really Matter* by Elaine St. James, Hyperion, 1994.

Think about what you do with your time and look for a good reason why you do what you do. If you don't have a good reason, consider giving it up. If you do something out of habit, because you fear saying "No," or simply because other people expect you to, reconsider. If you find that you are spending or making time for something that is really not that important to you, set it aside and spend your time on things that really do matter to you.

—Ideas found in *The Single Parent's Almanac* by Linda Foust, Prima Pub., 1996.

Make time for play, dreams, and enjoyment! The first step in making dreams come true is to be aware of them. Make a list of the things you've always wanted to do no matter how far from coming true they may seem. Make time in your life for fun and recreation in the same way that you do for work and the other things that need to get done. Don't end up regretting not having time—plan to work and play. Play, dreams, and fun are important to both body and soul.

—Ideas found in *Shelter for the Spirit* by Victoria Moran, HarperCollins, 1997.

Find your own special place that nurtures you and inspires you to dream, even if it is a place only in your imagination or heart; go there often. For author Frances Hodgson Burnett, the special place was her garden, which she referred to as her private study. Her garden was an outdoor space surrounded by brick walls which she transformed into a rose garden by planting hundreds of rosebushes. It was there that she rebuilt her life after a difficult time, and wrote *The Secret Garden*, a story of two unhappy children who brought back to life an abandoned and overgrown garden hidden behind stone walls. For both the author and the characters in her book, reviving the garden was a metaphor for restoring dreams and spirit.

Create an outdoor sanctuary for your own secret garden. If you have a backyard place, arrange a comfortable chair and a small table in a shady nook, or hang a hammock. If you are in an apartment, arrange some potted flowers and a comfortable chair on a deck or in a common area, or claim a spot as "your spot" at a local park.

As Louise Driscoll said, "Within your heart, keep one still, secret spot where dreams may go."

—Ideas found in *Simple Abundance: A Daybook of Comfort and Joy* by Sarah Ban Breathnach, Warner Books, 1995.

Face each day with a positive outlook, believing that what you do not understand today, you may understand tomorrow. Parenting is a journey. Sometimes it can feel like you don't know where you are going, even though you have a sense you will know you have arrived when you get there. Soren Kierkegaard said, "Life must be understood backward. But, it must be lived forward."

Get away from your work, it is not a gift, but a right. You do not have to get everything done today, it will all be there waiting tomorrow. Marian Dollive said, "There's nothing quite so valuable as work. That's why it's a good idea to leave some for tomorrow."

—Ideas found in *Meditations for Parents Who Do Too Much* by Jonathon Lazear and Wendy Lazear, Simon & Schuster, 1993.

The Field Guide Collection of Ideas
for Nurturing Mind, Body, and Soul

Buy or pick a bouquet of flowers.

Watch the sky.

Knead and bake bread.

Have a good cry.

Go fishing.

Go out: to a museum, library, bookstore, or restaurant.

Go for a walk or a hike.

Meditate or chant.

Ask for a foot, neck, or full body massage.

Go somewhere you have never been before and wander around.

Cook a pot of soup.

Have a good meal delivered to your home.

Put together a collection of things that you love: photos from a trip, letters from friends, shells, or treasured rocks.

Surround yourself with scents: eucalyptus, oils, sachets, perfumes, candles, or incense.

Watch a fire: make one outside or in a fireplace, or light a candle.

Make a list of the abundance or blessings in your life.

Make or listen to music: sing, whistle, or play an instrument!

Go to an estate or garage sale and take advantage of a good deal.

Dance.

Make a list of movies you want to see, go rent or see one of them.

Doodle, draw, or paint.

Call your parents and tell them you love them!

Plant a flower in an indoor pot or window box.

Make a tape of your favorite songs and play it.

Have a cup of tea.

Eat chocolate.

Take a class and learn something new.

Take a nap under a comforter.

Start or write in a journal.

Do something very physical: tennis, biking, jogging, or skiing.

Read a book.

Call a friend who makes you laugh.

Talk to your child. Tell him a story about something great that happened when you were his age—ask him what great thing happened to him today.

Listen when your child tells you he loves you: it may come in the way of a gift of the first weed of the spring, a scribble drawing, a touch on the cheek, or a quick smile.

Be a child again and play make-believe with your child, or do something you loved as a child.

Surprise someone with some home made cookies or a flower from your garden.

Explore your back yard or a park with your child from your child's point of view & enjoy the wonder of it.

Ask a shut-in neighbor if you can pick up something for them next time you are at the store.

Hug your child.

Sleep in late on the weekend.

Parents: Taking Care of Ourselves

Use affirmations, or words of encouragement, to nurture yourself. Self-affirmations are all the things you say, do, think, and feel that show that you are lovable and capable. Say the following words to yourself from time to time, or ask someone to say them to you:

- My needs are important.
- I can be uniquely myself, and honor the uniqueness of others.
- I can be independent and interdependent.
- Through the years, I can expand my commitments to my own growth, to my family, my friends, my community, and to all humankind.
- I can build and examine my commitments to my values and causes, my roles, and my tasks.
- I can be responsible for my contributions to each of my commitments.
- I can be creative, competent, productive, and joyful.
- I can trust my inner wisdom.
- I can say my hellos and good-byes to people, roles, dreams, and decisions.
- I can finish each part of my journey and look forward to the next.
- My love matures and expands.
- I am lovable at every age!

You can start using the affirmations by saying the messages to yourself as "you" messages, speaking from your own nurturing parent to the child within you — "I'm glad *you're* alive." Later, you can affirm yourself with an "I" message, when the child within is willing to make that statement as a celebration or to claim that statement as a conviction that the inner child does believe or wants to believe — "I'm glad *I'm* alive."

> —From *Growing Up Again: Parenting Ourselves, Parenting Our Children*, by Jean Illsley Clarke and Connie Dawson, copyright 1989, 1998 by Jean Illsley Clarke and Connie Dawson. Reprinted by permission of Hazelden Foundation, Center City, MN.

When you're having a bad day, consider strategies to help you get your day back on track:

- Stop mentally attacking yourself for what happened earlier in the day. Everyone has bad days. Step back and find humor in your situation.
- Take a short mental vacation. Remember one of your "peak parent" moments: digging at the beach, dancing in the living room, or cuddling at bedtime. Or close your eyes and imagine you are relaxing next to a mountain stream or at your favorite vacation spot.
- Evaluate the remainder of your day. Simplify as much as possible. Eliminate bothersome tasks and focus, if possible, on completing a task that will give you a sense of accomplishment and control.
- Reduce the noise, smells, and the confusion around you. Excess stimuli intensify the stress.
- Turn to written phrases and passages that provide you with meaning and inspiration.
- Stand up and stretch your arms above your head. Stretch left and hold 1-2-3-4. Stretch right and hold. Repeat several times. After your stretch, wiggle your fingers and toes.
- Go for a ten to fifteen minute walk. Focus on the sights and sounds around you.
- Eat a healthy lunch. Skipping lunch because you're behind will only worsen your mood and your problem solving ability.
- Find a way to make someone else happy. Doing for others has an amazing impact on your own sense of personal satisfaction.

- Have a good laugh. Pull out the latest comic page from the newspaper, look at a joke book or visit a friend or co-worker who is known for a fine sense of humor.

- Avoid as much as possible negative people who will bring you down. Instead seek out people with a positive outlook.

—From "Bad Hair Days for Parents" by Jerri Wolfe, *Family Information Services*, 1995.

Be good to yourself by taking time to spend with your child. It is true what everyone is saying around you, "Childhood passes so quickly." Even though now, the days may at times seem long, later, the years will seem short. One of the greatest gifts that you can give to yourself is to spend time with your child, before it slips away. Take some moments for yourself today and each day, to laugh, cry, play, explore, worry, wonder, and dream with your child.

—Deb Kratz, co-author of *The Field Guide to Parenting*

Honor and value yourself as a parent. Washing clothes and preparing food for children are necessary accomplishments that can be seen and crossed off a list, but many things that you do that are vital to your child's development and well-being aren't always noticed or valued—notice and value them for yourself. Some of these things that can't be precisely measured or recorded may be among the most important things you do with your child: listening to him, showing him how to fit a peg in a pegboard, telling a story, laughing together, singing a song, looking at a tree, having an imaginary tea party, comforting hurt feelings, and more.

—Shelley Butler, co-author of *The Field Guide to Parenting*

Discover the gifts your child gives to you; they can change your life. As a parent, you probably spend a lot of time thinking about being a good parent and what you can do for your child. Take time to appreciate the gifts your child gives to you:

- Remarkable, intense, unconditional love and admiration just for being you.
- Trust that you are the strongest, wisest person in the world.
- The chance to find new or special emotions, strengths and skills in yourself.
- The opportunity to be a child again by sharing the joy and wonder of her world through play.

Your child is the best present you will ever be given, accept her gifts and enjoy!

—Ideas found in *Caring for Your Baby and Young Child* (American Academy of Pediatrics, revised edition), Bantam Books, 1998.

Help a child understand more about parents taking care of themselves by reading about it together:

 Bunnies and Their Hobbies by Nancy Carlson

 *Getting Used to Harry* by Cari Best

 *Love You Forever* by Robert Munsch

The Perfectly Orderly House by Ellen Kindt McKenzie

Take Time to Relax by Nancy Carlson

When to Get More Help

Sometimes, parents need a bit of extra help to stay healthy and happy.

Consider getting help for yourself if you:

- Feel isolated or alone frequently.

- Feel sad, tired, or depressed, especially if you are a woman who has recently given birth to a child.

- Feel unusually fearful, nervous, or upset when there is not an obvious reason or problem.

- Feel that you are sleeping too much, having trouble sleeping through the night, or cannot easily fall asleep.

- Feel out of control with your anger or other emotions.

- Feel that you have a problem with weight control, drugs, alcohol, or tobacco use.

- Are unable to find or pay for food, clothing, shelter, and medical care for you and your child.

If you have a concern, trust your instinct and find someone trained to help you: health care providers, early intervention teams, mental health professionals, parent educators and consultants, or telephone help-line staff. Consider talking it over with friends and family, too. You don't need to worry alone! Turn to "Finding Help in Your Community" on page 4 to learn about finding help near you.

More Help and Information

Books for Parents

- *Celebrate Your self: Enhancing Your Self-Esteem* by Dorothy Corkille Briggs. Doubleday, 1986.

- "Taking a Closer Look at You—Chapter 9" in *The Complete Single Mother: Reassuring Answers to Your Most Challenging Concerns* by Andrea Engber and Leah Klungness. Adams Media Corporation, 1995.

- *Chore Wars: How Households Can Share the Work and Keep the Peace* by James Thornton. Conari Press, 1997.

- *Halving It All: How Equally Shared Parenting Works* by Francine M. Deutsch. Harvard Univ. Press, 1999.

- *Restoring Balance to a Mother's Busy Life* by Beth Wilson. Contemporary Books, 1996.

- *Simple Abundance: A Daybook of Comfort and Joy* by Sarah Ban Breathnach. Warner Books, 1995.

- *Working Fathers: New Strategies for Balancing Work and Family* by James A. Levine and Todd L. Pittinsky. Addison-Wesley, 1997.

- *You Might As Well Laugh: Surviving the Joys of Parenthood* by Sandi Kahn Shelton. Bancroft Press, 1997.

Web Sites

- The Reflecting Pool at the WonderWise Parent www.ksu.edu/wwparent/reflect/reflect.htm

Play, Learning, and Intelligence

by Joe

Description

Play, a natural part of early childhood, means engaging in amusement, creativity, sport, or other recreation. Children learn, gain knowledge and master skills through play and simple, everyday experiences. Intelligence is the ability to understand, learn, use knowledge, and master skills.

Realistic Expectations

- All children are naturally curious and eager to experience, play, and learn.
- Children do not separate play, learning, and work. For them, living is playing and playing is living.
- Through play, children learn about their world, gathering information with all of their senses by interacting with the things and people around them.
- The way children play changes as they grow and change.
- Young children do not think like adults. They think concretely, in the here and now; their ability to reason unfolds throughout childhood.
- Repetition helps children learn. That's why they enjoy doing the same activity, singing the same song, or reading the same book over and over.
- There is no one way to learn. Each person has a blend of strengths, talents, and weaknesses that come together to comprise their unique style of learning.
- There are many ways to be intelligent, and many of those are not measured by standard IQ tests. Dr. Howard Gardner identifies eight types of intelligence: linguistic, logical-mathematical, spatial, musical, bodily kinesthetic, interpersonal, intrapersonal, and naturalist.
- It is play and simple everyday experiences that feed the child's growing mind: talking, singing, touching, tasting, smelling new scents, playing rhyming word games, making a dam or river in the sand, counting apples at the grocery store, seeing new sights, listening to sounds, dancing, playing, listening to stories, etc. Children need to share time and experiences with a warm, caring, and attentive parent or caregiver.

- During the early childhood years, attitudes toward learning are formed that will guide the child for the rest of his or her life:
  - Children who are often told, "No!" or "Be careful!" may become fearful of the world and learning; children who are pushed and pressured to learn may become stressed and find learning unpleasant.
  - Children who are encouraged to explore and have fun doing so learn to love learning!

Approaches

Learn about brain development in the early years. Humans have instinctively shared experiences with their young children throughout time, but now we have scientific research that explains the importance of these behaviors.

Babies are born with brains that are still growing. During the first three years of life—especially during the first year—the amount of brain development is enormous! The human brain contains billions of nerve cells, or *neurons*, that look like miniature trees, with networks of branches that reach toward each other. The "branches" are actually *dendrites*, that form the connections, or pathways, upon which information travels through the brain: the stove is hot, the flower smells nice, the milk is sweet, the loud noise is frightening, or the light is bright. These connections are formed on the "use it or lose it principle." Each experience the child has actually causes the dendrites to grow.

On the other hand, without experiences to stimulate them, dendrites wither and die, and the pathways are lost. There are special times during childhood when the brain is particularly efficient at learning certain skills. With some of these skills, if the right experience doesn't happen at the critical time, the child's ability to learn that particular skill is lost, or the skill will be much more difficult to learn later.

The experiences that a child has in early childhood, or the lack of them, will have a profound impact on brain development that lasts a lifetime. A rich assortment of early experiences allows the child to reach his full intellectual potential. A lack of experiences can endanger a young child's brain function and development.

> —Ideas from *Magic Trees of the Mind* by Marian Diamond and Janet Hopson, Dutton, 1998.

Help your child reach his full potential. Medical research shows us that to thrive, children need simple basics. Your child needs physical health, sound nutrition, a safe environment, and nurturing caregivers who give him lots of consistent love and stimulation. Give your child the basics:

- *Get physical:* Expose your child to as many physical activities as possible.
- *Talk:* Expose him to a variety of vocabulary words—repetition counts; use a slow, friendly tone of voice, respond to jabber, and ask questions.
- *Make music:* Play any kind of music, dance together, sing to him and with him, and play with rhythm instruments.
- *Allow quiet times:* Limit television, slow your pace, and give him time to figure things out.
- *Read:* There is something particularly wonderful about reading with your child!

> —From Hilary Pert Stecklein, M.D., founder of Reading Rx—a reading program dedicated to promoting literacy.

Encourage your child to explore! Curiosity is the foundation for the love of learning; be careful not to label it as negative or bad behavior. Your child learns to understand his world by connecting with objects and people. A child will naturally reach out to the shiny object or obvious feature on a person, a crystal vase, shiny jewelry on grandma, colorful gardens, furry gerbils, lights and ornaments on a Christmas tree, or the ears and nose of grandpa. His body and its senses lead the way; his mind follows. To firmly plant the seeds of learning, encourage him to be curious, to reach out, to touch, and to explore.

> —From Joan Henderson, Parent Educator, Canada.

Play, Learning, and Intelligence

Make the world your child's classroom. Pay attention to what he does, answer his questions, and help him explore the things he is interested in. He will learn from anything and everything he sees, wherever he is, because children are fascinated by the objects and tools that they see being used around them in everyday life—usually more so than toys and learning games that are manufactured for them.

—Ideas found in *Learning All the Time* by John Holt, Addison-Wesley, 1989.

Let your child get dirty, sometimes. Many things that are good for him and his spirit will make a mess and get him dirty: jumping in mud puddles, digging in dirt, splashing in water—to name just a few. If he is always told not to get dirty or make a mess, he will become cautious and timid instead of free, warm, and life-loving.

—Ideas found in *Dr. Spock's Baby and Child Care* (7th edition) by Benjamin Spock and Stephen J. Parker, Dutton, 1998.

Learn about and value your child's play. Through play, your child will:

- Problem solve and experiment with how the world works. When playing with sand, he explores, predicts, tests, and shapes his ideas about weight, measurement, cause and effect, and much more.
- Feel control over his world. When your child plays at being the dad, giving orders, or being the scary monster, he becomes large and powerful in the safety of a make-believe world.
- Build self-esteem. Making a sandcastle or a tower with blocks in his own way creates confidence and feelings of success.
- Practice language. Words and ideas are used throughout play, such as: mine, yours, blocks, car, under, over, into, scary, happy, baby, etc.
- Strengthen creativity, imagination, and an appreciation for beauty. Making a dog out of play dough, studying the patterns of frost or raindrops on a window, or taking a trip to another city through make-believe, tickles fantasy and joy.
- Practice and build social skills. Playing games and having tea parties with teddy bears or young friends allows lots of practice in taking turns, having conversations, helping, sharing, and getting along with others.
- Express and process feelings. A child who is nervous about changing to a new child care center might act out the scene with his doll, making the doll sad, mad, excited, and nervous while playing. Similarly, a child who has witnessed violence may play-act the scene and the many emotions that he observed.
- Take risks without worrying about failing, following rules, or succeeding. In his own play, your child can choose his own activities, is usually not interfered with by adults, and can change rules.
- Reduce stress. Tension is released by squishing modeling dough, laughing, or finding shapes in clouds.
- Have fun!

—Ideas found in *The Preschool Years* by Ellen Galinsky and Judy Davis, Times Books, 1988.

Be a good teacher by following your child's lead and being positive and patient:

- If your child shows no interest in an activity, let him quit and move on to something else. It could mean he's not ready for it. When he is ready, he is likely to learn more quickly and easily. Pushing a child will do more harm than good.
- Before you won't allow your child to have an activity, ask yourself if it's really going to hurt anything if he gets dirty, makes noise, makes a mess, or uses something in an unusual way. If it's safe, let him try things, investigate, question, and make messes. That's how he learns about his world.

- Provide him with many firsthand experiences: the zoo, museums, parks, art shows, live concerts, etc. Actively experiencing something is more valuable learning than passively reading about it or watching it on television.

- Be patient when your child asks you to show him something over and over again. Learning takes time, and children learn through repetition.

- Work with young children for short periods of time (fifteen minutes or less.)

- Give your child time to solve his own problems. If he expresses some frustration, recognize his dilemma and show your confidence in his ability to get out of the situation: "I see you are having trouble getting your shorts on. Do you think turning it right-side-out would help?" If he still has trouble after trying, of course help him.

- Let him do things for himself whenever he can. Even if it is faster for you to do it, let him try, and offer help only if he asks for it.

- Have an enthusiastic attitude toward discovering and practicing new skills and ideas. Your positive attitude about learning will rub off on him.

- Let him invent his own variations of games and activities sometimes. He may be exercising creativity or trying to better suit his own abilities and interests.

- Strike a balance between spending time playing and talking with him and making time for unscheduled, free time to play with friends or be by himself.

- Let him make mistakes, and talk to him about how making mistakes is a part of learning.

> —Ideas found in *Parents Are Teachers Too* by Claudia Jones, Williamson Pub. Co., 1988.

Model behaviors and skills for him. He learns a great deal through watching and imitating adults and other children. When you show him something new, try to do things very slowly and carefully so that he can easily copy you and learn the skill by doing it himself. Help him to learn things step-by-step by teaching one thing at a time, making sure he accomplishes the first thing before moving on to the next.

> —Ideas found in *Montessori Play and Learn: A Parents' Guide to Purposeful Play From Two to Six* by Lesley Britton, Crown Publishers, 1992.

Get to know your child's learning style; each person has ways that he learns best. There are tools to help you identify your own learning styles, and to begin to uncover your child's. One popular tool is the Walter Barbe-Raymond Swassing model that is based on three modes of taking in and processing information:

- Auditory learners learn best when they hear information or say it to themselves.

- Visual learners learn best when they can see something.

- Kinesthetic learners learn best when they are in motion.

Each of us uses all three, but we benefit most when using our strongest method of learning.

> —Ideas found in *Every Child Can Succeed: Making the Most of Your Child's Learning Style* by Cynthia Ulrich Tobias, Focus on the Family, 1996.

Learn about the seven types of intelligence. According to Howard Gardner's multiple intelligence theory, each of us has seven intelligences, or ways to be smart. Each type of intelligence gives us something to offer to the world. What makes us unique is how much or how little we have of each type of intelligence. Do not be quick to label your child as one type. Give him opportunities to learn in all areas, and recognize different strengths as they emerge.

- Linguistic or word smart — best at using the written or spoken word to communicate: an adult with strong linguistic intelligence might be a journalist, lawyer, or storyteller.

- Logical-Mathematical or logic smart — good with numbers, patterns and logical reasoning: an adult with strong logical-mathematical intelligence might be a scientist, accountant, or computer programmer.

- Spatial or picture smart — best at thinking in pictures or images following directions, visualizing and drawing accurately: an adult with strong spatial intelligence might be an artist, chess player, sailor, or map-maker.

- Musical or music smart — good at keeping time with music, singing in tune, and perceiving and appreciating melodies: an adult with strong music intelligence might be a musician, either professional or amateur.

- Bodily kinesthetic or body smart — good at controlling their own body movements skillfully: an adult with strong bodily kinesthetic intelligence might be an actress, athlete, surgeon, or carpenter.

- Interpersonal or person smart — good at understanding and working with other people, and seeing things from their perspective: an adult with strong interpersonal intelligence might be a pastor, teacher, counselor, or good friend.

- Intrapersonal or self smart — good at being contemplative or introspective: an adult with strong intrapersonal intelligence will be someone who is deeply in touch with their own thoughts, feelings, and beliefs.

By exploring all of their intelligences, children can become well-rounded individuals who are successful in many aspects of life.

> —From "Seven Ways for Young Children to be Smart 1997." Reprinted with permission from the National Association for the Education of Young Children.

Note: Howard Gardner's reframed theory of intelligence describes an eighth intelligence—naturalistic intelligence—which allows people to distinguish among, classify, and use features of the environment. An adult with strong naturalistic intelligence might be a farmer, gardener, botanist, geologist, florist, or archaeologist. All eight intelligences, and the possibility of even more yet to be identified, are discussed in the article "Project Summit—The Theory of Multiple Intelligences" available on website http://pzweb.harvard.edu/SUMIT/MISUMIT.HTM and in the book *Intelligence Reframed*, by Howard Gardner, Perseus Books, Fall 1999.

Develop MegaSkills®, or the inner engines of learning, in your child. A MegaSkill is like the gas that makes the car go, the yeast that makes the bread rise, or a megaphone that sends the voice farther than it can ordinarily reach. That's what MegaSkills do for the bits and pieces of learning that children receive. It is generally agreed that children need certain basic skills (usually called the three Rs) in order to succeed. But for children to be able to learn the basic skills at school, they need to learn another important set of basics at home.

- Confidence: feeling able to do it.
- Motivation: wanting to do it.
- Effort: willing to work hard.
- Responsibility: doing what's right.
- Initiative: moving into action.
- Perseverance: completing what you start.
- Caring: showing concern for others.
- Teamwork: working with others.
- Common sense: using good judgment.
- Problem solving: putting what you know and what you can do into action.
- Focus: concentrating with a goal in mind.

MegaSkills keep children enjoying reading long after they learn to decode the alphabet, and help them later in life to deal with challenges like sex, drugs, and AIDS. They can be taught these skills at home by parents through simple activities. The happiest and most successful adults are those who possess MegaSkills qualities and, of course, a sense of humor.

—From MegaSkills® by Dorothy Rich, Houghton Mifflin Company, 1998.
For more information, go to web site: www.MegaSkillsHSI.org.

Consider how you want to handle play that imitates violent or sexist themes. Children naturally act out in play the things they experience and see in their surroundings. Violence and inequities between the sexes are still very prevalent, so it is difficult to fully protect your child from them. These themes are bound to show up in children's play.

Research shows that while aggressive play and violent play-themes are universal, giving children toy guns designed to look like real ones, playing violent games with them, or modeling violence, increases the amount and intensity of their violent play. A middle ground approach makes the most sense. Consider banning weapons and super-heroes from your home, but calmly accept the games that come from his imagination, such as when he makes a gun from tinker toys, points it at his friend and says, "Got you!" Just don't further encourage violent play by asking questions or playing along.

Girls are likely to play with dolls that are fashioned after adult figures, or pretend themselves to be beautiful women, acting out scenes of victims being rescued by powerful males. It is important for your girl to know that she *could* play and do things that she sees portrayed as "for boys", even if she decides not to do them.

The greatest influence you will have on children is your own behavior. Tell them that you disagree with violence, and then show them with your everyday actions. Show them through your own example that the only experiences that a person cannot have because of gender are those related to reproductive functions. Expose them to people who share these values, and talk about it when you see examples of those who don't.

Don't expect to achieve gender-free play or a gender-blind child. Your best hope is to offer both sexes a full range of toys, whether they are traditionally thought of as "boy toys" or "girl toys." Doing so keeps a world of possibilities open to them through play.

—Ideas found in *Your Baby & Child: From Birth to Age Five* (3rd edition) by Penelope Leach. Alfred A. Knopf, 1997.

When a girl wants to play with a doll that represents an unrealistic image of women, consider playing with her and challenging her to play beyond the doll's role as beauty queen. Too often, a girl will play that the doll is a mother or is preoccupied about her appearance. Help her think up new ways to play with the doll that represent the many roles women play in real life: pretend that the doll is a mayor in charge of organizing the rescue effort following a tornado, make believe that the doll plays professional basketball, travels to fun and exotic places, and does many kinds of work. By playing with her, you can help a girl see many possibilities for herself as she becomes a woman.

—Ideas found in *How to Mother a Successful Daughter: A Practical Guide to Empowering Girls from Birth to Eighteen* by Nicky Marone, Random House, 1998.

When your child wants to play guns, war, and other pretend violence, teach him how to play safely and challenge him to look beyond the shooting:

- Make sure he knows that play that is hurtful or scary to another is not allowed.
- Whatever you decide about playing with guns, set rules and explain them: "No shooting people, only trees" or "We don't allow shooting in the house near people, only in the yard."

- Consider challenging your child to find another purpose for his pretend gun: the yardstick that he shoots with could be a walking stick to hike with.
- Consider talking to your child about the concept of "bad guys" and what that means: people aren't bad or good, but they can do hurtful things. A person who does a bad thing may be a "regular" guy who makes a mistake. Or a person who does bad things may need help realizing he is hurting people and should stop. Talking to a preschooler about this sets the stage for real understanding later on.
- Provide opportunities for other types of play which allow your child to feel capable and powerful.

> —Ideas found in *Becoming the Parent You Want to Be* by Laura Davis and Janis Keyser, Broadway Books, 1997.

Help your child understand more about learning by reading about it together:

📖 *Child's Book of Play in Art: Great Picture, Great Fun* by Lucy Micklethwait

📖 *Finger Rhymes* by Marc Tolon Brown

📖 *Is That Josie?* by Keiko Narahashi

📖 *Let's Play: Traditional Games of Childhood* by Camilla Gryski

📖 *Piggies* by Audrey Wood

📖 *Please Touch Cookbook* by Please Touch Museum

📖 *The Lap-Time Song and Play Book* by Jane Yolen

📖 *The Line Up Book* by Marisabina Russo

📖 *You and Me, Little Bear* by Martin Waddell

When to Get More Help

Children typically grow and learn new skills in their own time and at their own pace within the wide range of what is normal. Sometimes, children need a bit of extra help to keep their development on track, or to stay healthy and happy. Sometimes, parents need help providing for a child's needs or sorting out the best approaches to parenting.

Consider getting help for your child if he:

- Was making progress but is losing skills such as talking, walking, self-control, etc.
- Is significantly late in developing a skill or is behind in developing many skills listed for his age in Your Growing Child.

You are the expert when it comes to your family and child. If you have a concern, trust your instinct and find someone trained to help you: health care providers, early intervention teams, mental health professionals, parent educators and consultants, or telephone help-line staff. Consider talking it over with friends and family, too. You don't need to worry alone! Turn to "Finding Help in Your Community" on page 4 to learn about finding help near you.

More Help and Information

Books for Parents

- *300 Three-Minute Games: Quick and Easy Activities of 2-5 Year Olds* by Jackie Silberg. Gryphon House, 1997.
- *Awakening Your Child's Natural Genius: Enhancing Curiosity, Creativity, and Learning Ability* by Thomas Armstrong. J. P. Tarcher, 1991.
- *Disney's Family Fun Crafts: 500 Creative Activities for You and Your Kids.* Hyperion, 1997.
- *Every Child Can Succeed: Making the Most of Your Child's Learning Style* by Cynthia Ulrich Tobias. Focus on the Family, 1996.
- *Frames of Mind: The Theory of Multiple Intelligences* by Howard E. Gardner. Basic Books, 1983.
- *How Children Learn* by John Holt. Addison Wesley, 1989.
- *Know Your Child: An Authoritative Guide For Today's Parents* by Stella Chess and Alexander Thomas. Basic Books, 1987.
- *Magic Trees of the Mind: How to Nurture Your Child's Intelligence, Creativity, and Healthy Emotions from Birth Through Adolescence* by Marian Diamond and Janet Hopson. Dutton, 1998.
- *MegaSkills®: Building Children's Achievement for the Information Age* (new and expanded edition) by Dorothy Rich. Houghton Mifflin Company, 1998.
- *Montessori Play and Learn: A Parents' Guide to Purposeful Play From Two to Six* by Lesley Britton. Crown Publishers, 1992.
- Ready, Set, Learn Series by Marlene Barron. John Wiley & Sons.
- *The Second Cooperative Sports & Games Book* by Terry Orlick. Pantheon Books, 1982.
- *Turn Off the TV and—* by Anne Rogovin. Abingdon Press, 1995.
- *Who's Calling the Shots? How to Respond Effectively to Children's Fascination with War Play and War Toys* by Nancy Carlsson-Paige and Diane E. Levin. New Society Publishers, 1990.
- *Your Child at Play: One to Two Years; Your Child at Play: Two to Three Years; Your Child at Play: Three to Five Years* (2nd edition) by Marilyn Segal. Newmarket Press, 1998.

Articles, Pamphlets, and Booklets

- "Special Report: How A Child's Brain Develops." *Time,* February 3, 1997.
- "Your Child From Birth to Three." *Newsweek,* Spring/Summer 1997.

Videos

- *Doing Things: Eating, Washing, In Motion.* Bo-Peep Productions.
- *The First Years Last Forever,* a Johnson & Johnson presentation. Reiner Foundation. Available to borrow free of charge from public libraries and Blockbuster Video, or call 1-888-447-3400 for information about ordering an inexpensive copy.
- *Food For Thought,* Health Partners. An inexpensive copy is available through Reading Rx, PO Box 26085, Shoreview, MN 55126-0085, or call 1-651-490-7694, or e-mail: ReadingRx@aol.com.
- *Squiggles, Dots and Lines.* Kidvidz.
- *Toddler Takes: Toddlers at Play.* Tow Truck Productions.

National Organizations

- I am Your Child Foundation
  P.O. Box 15605, Beverly Hills, CA 90209
  Website: www.iamyourchild.org

Web Sites

- Kidsource: www.kidsource.com
- Parenting Me: www.parentingme.com
- ParenthoodWeb: www.parenthoodweb.com

Preschool

Description

Preschool, also called nursery school, is an educational program for children not old enough to attend kindergarten. Intended for the early childhood years, preschools typically do not stress formal lessons, but emphasize learning through play and social interaction.

Realistic Expectations

- Children who feel confident about learning have a greater chance of doing well in school. Young children who are encouraged to enjoy exploring and experimenting gain confidence about learning.
- Preschool is not a necessity for all children. Children who have a lot of social experiences with other children and adults, and many opportunities to grow and learn, may get what they need to grow, develop, and get ready for kindergarten at home or day care.
- Preschool may be particularly helpful for children who don't have many chances to visit parks, playgrounds, or places to run and jump, and for those who don't have many other opportunities to play with other children.
- A quality program can have a positive impact on children's growth and development, yet a recent report by the Carnegie Corporation showed that less than 25 percent of preschools in the U.S. were satisfactory.
- Starting a new school is typically an anxious time for most young children, but those age two or three may have more trouble separating from parents at preschool. It may take a month or more for young children to separate easily from you at school.
- Children who are pushed to learn or perform in the preschool years tend to experience low motivation in the school years.
- Children in the preschool years learn best through play.
- With a positive start in preschool, children may look forward to elementary school with confidence and excitement.

Approaches

When choosing a preschool, look for the basic requirements of a good program:

- Positive objectives for your child and a philosophy that you agree with: helping her feel confident and good about herself, helping her with independence skills, and a chance for her to learn about being with other children and adults. Watch out for programs that promise to make a child smart and those that push a child to learn.
- Small class size: ages two to three, ten children or less; age four and up, no more than twenty children.
- An adequate number of adults per number of children; generally, a lower ratio is necessary for younger children.
- Trained teachers who have education in child development or early childhood education. Beware of schools that have a high turn-over rate among the staff and teachers.
- Rules and consequences: consistent, clear rules that still allow your child freedom to explore and learn.

- Safe environment: all areas that the child has access to should be child-proofed, a staff member should be trained in first aid, CPR, and choking in children.
- Clean and healthy environment: diaper-changing area should be separate from other areas, child-sized sinks should be available, children should be encouraged to wash hands, and a policy about illness should include isolating a child with fever and sending home a child with an infectious disease.

> —Ideas found in *Caring for Your Baby and Young Child* (American Academy of Pediatrics), Bantam Books, 1998.

Choose a preschool that emphasizes social and emotional skills; it will help your child feel good about herself as she learns to play with other children. When choosing a preschool, look at the staff and whether they encourage the children to play or push the children to perform. Watch for too much directed learning time which can take away from time to learn social tasks. The important experiences your child should have at preschool are: being with other children, learning how to interact with other adults, and learning about himself in relation to other children his age.

> —Ideas found in *Touchpoints* by T. Berry Brazelton, Addison-Wesley, 1992.

Decide what kind of preschool program is best for your child. You should make your decision after thinking about your own educational philosophy, considering your family's lifestyle, and trying to match your child's personality and needs to the programs that you have seen. Consider the many decisions to make in picking a preschool:

- What kind of school and approach to learning would be best for the child? Choose between:
  - Traditional nursery schools, based on the theories of Jean Piaget, which approach learning through play and have organized areas of activity that usually include art, music, science, reading, make-believe play, and blocks.
  - Montessori schools, where multi-age groups use specific materials to learn concepts and ideas in a specific sequence, where daily chores and tasks foster self-competence, and where the older children teach the younger children.
  - Waldorf or Rudolf Steiner schools emphasize creativity and free-thinking, and learning through artistic mediums.

  All of these share a developmental approach to preschool which means that the curriculum is based on age-appropriate play, activities, and materials.
- Do you prefer a public or private program?
- Are you looking for a preschool affiliated with a church or synagogue or do you prefer a non-religious school?
- How many hours a day do you want or need your child to be at preschool: full-day, half-day, or a program with extended day-care hours?
- Would your child do better in a morning class or afternoon class?
- How many days per week do you want your child to attend preschool: every day or a few days per week?
- Would your child fit better in a single-age group or multi-age group?

Choosing a preschool is a personal decision—one that has to be a good match for your child, and for you.

> —From *Smart Start* by Marian Edelman Borden. Copyright © 1997 by Marian Edelman Borden. Reprinted by permission of Facts on File, Inc.

Help your child prepare physically, socially, emotionally, and intellectually for preschool success:

- Make sure your child gets good food, enough sleep, plenty of safe play time, medical and dental care, and the opportunity to run, jump, and be physical.
- Provide opportunities for your child to learn kindness, respect, and patience, and to practice sharing and helping others. She learns best from your example.
- Allow your child to learn through exploration and play.
- Talk to her about everything, listen to her, answer her questions, encourage her to talk and express her ideas, and read to her.

—Ideas found in "Ready or Not... Preparing Young Children for the Classroom,"
National Association for the Education of Young Children, 1997.

Help a child prepare for the start of school:

- Give your child some notice of when the program will start; how much notice you give her should depend on whether your child has smoother transitions with more or less time to prepare.
- Be realistic about school and not overly excited; provide information about what will happen there and who will be there.
- Give your child some frame of reference about when she will go to school and how long she will stay there, keeping in mind that preschoolers have a vague sense of time. Consider telling her that school will begin after breakfast (or lunch) and you will come get her before lunch (or dinner).
- Allow your child to have her own feelings about school without being told what she should or will feel. Don't make promises that you can't keep about how much your child will enjoy school.
- Set up a visit to the new school before it begins.
- Begin any new routines or schedules before school starts.

—Ideas found in *The Preschool Years* by Ellen Galinsky and Judy Davis, Times Books, 1988.

> I think no matter what age you begin those little degrees of separation, it's hard on us and on our kids. I also know that to a certain extent, your child's ability to handle change will be a reflection of how you feel about it. Your child is facing the challenge of being separated from you, but also a world of growth opportunities that belong to him as an individual. No matter how gently it happens, it's hard to cope with going from the intimacy of pregnancy to the independence of preschool!
>
> —Debbie, Louisville, Kentucky

Share what you know about your child with her preschool teachers! To help your child have the best year at preschool that she possible can, let her teachers know all about her: abilities, fears, the things she's curious about, the things she likes to do, temperment, how she gets along with other children and adults.

As the school year continues, let her teachers know about special things that happen in your child's life, things that change, or anything that may change how she acts at school. The more teachers know about your child and what to expect, the better they will be able to help her.

—Ideas found in *Everything You Always Wanted to Know About Preschool—But Didn't Know Whom to Ask* by Ellen Booth Church with Deb Matthews, Scholastic, Inc., 1996.

Avoid pressuring your child to talk about preschool; instead ask her about particular things that may have happened there. She may find telling you about preschool difficult since young children have limited abilities to talk about feelings and happenings. Avoid asking non-specific questions like, "What happened today?" Instead, help her to put her feelings and experiences into words by asking questions about particular parts of her preschool day:

- "I remember visiting the monkey room that had a climbing gym in it. Did you get to play in the monkey room today?"
- "I know you love to paint and that your teacher said you could paint today if you wanted to. Tell me about the colors you painted with!"

—Ideas found in "Avoiding the Long Goodbye" by Patricia Henderson Shimm with Kate Ballen, *Parenting*, September 1998.

Help your child learn more about preschool by reading about it together:

 *Three-Star Billy* by Pat Hutchins.

When Daddy Came to School by Julie Brillhart.

When to Get More Help

Children typically grow and learn new skills in their own time and at their own pace within the wide range of what is normal. Sometimes, children need a bit of extra help to keep their development on track, or to stay healthy and happy. Sometimes, parents need help providing for a child's needs or sorting out the best approaches to parenting.

Consider getting help for your child if she:

- Is distressed in preschool after you leave her and is unable to get involved in activities for most of the day, or to adjust to the new place, people, and routines.
- Has behavior problems in preschool that last for several weeks.
- Reports or shows signs of being abused or neglected in preschool.
- Suddenly says she doesn't like her preschool staff or teachers, or by words or actions begs not to be left at preschool.
- Complains about feeling unsafe or being teased or bullied by another child.

Consider getting help for yourself if you:

- Would like your three- or four-year-old to be in a preschool program and need help finding or paying for one.

You are the expert when it comes to your family and child. If you have a concern, trust your instinct and find someone trained to help you: health care providers, early intervention teams, mental health professionals, parent educators and consultants, or telephone help-line staff. Consider talking it over with friends and family, too. You don't need to worry alone! Turn to "Finding Help in Your Community" on page 4 to learn about finding help near you.

More Help and Information

Books for Parents

- *Everything You Always Wanted to Know About Preschool—But Didn't Know Whom to Ask* by Ellen Booth Church with Deb Matthews. Scholastic, Inc., 1996.
- *Smart Start: The Parents' Guide to Preschool Education* by Marian Edelman Borden. Facts on File, Inc., 1997.
- "When Others Care for Your Child" in *What to Expect the Toddler Years* by Arlene Eisenberg, Heidi E. Murkoff and Sandee E. Hathaway. Workman Pub., 1994.

Articles, Pamphlets, and Booklets

- From the National Association for the Education of Young Children (NAEYC): See *National Organizations*

  "A Good Preschool for Your Child"
  (NAEYC order # 517)

  "How to Choose a Good Early Childhood Program"
  (# 525)

  "What Are the Benefits of High Quality Early Childhood Programs?" (# 540)

Community and Government Resources

- Head Start Bureau

  Web site: www.acf.dhhs.gov/programs/hsb/

  Head Start is a national program which provides educational, medical, dental, nutritional, and social services for low-income, pre-school children, ages three to five, and their families. Look in your local phone book, on the web site, or call your local school district to find the Head Start program nearest you.

National Organizations

- National Association for the Education of Young Children (NAEYC)

  800-424-2460, Fax: 202-328-1846

  E-Mail: naeyc@naecy.org

  Web site: www.naeyc.org

Videos

- *Preschool Power 8* from the Preschool Power series. Concept Associates.

Reading
and Books

Description

Reading is the activity of figuring out that the characters on the page are letters, that letters put together form words, and that those words communicate meaning. Through reading and telling stories together, young children and adults are able to share words that express feelings, ideas, and information that young children can interpret, understand, and apply in their own lives. Reading materials are books, brochures, magazines, maps, mail, newspapers, signs, shopping lists, posters, pamphlets, comics, coupons, cereal boxes, or anything that you can read to yourself or to your child.

Realistic Expectations

- If adults show children what reading looks like by reading near them, they will want to read and look at books, too.
- Babies explore books in their own ways: bending, biting, dropping, looking at the pictures, and listening to the words.
- Older babies or toddlers with an active temperament may not sit still for a whole book. They may listen to a few pages at a time, and may enjoy reading more when the stories or poems have action, invite participation, or encourage movement.
- Many children by the age of three can recognize a few dozen words that they see often in their everyday life, such as "McDonald's" or "STOP." Parents are not always aware when their child begins to read words.
- Attention span lengthens with age. An older baby can listen to simple stories with a few words on each page. Young children can listen to longer and more complex stories as they grow. Don't expect most five-year-olds to sit through chapter books.
- The average age that children learn to read is six and a half. Many experts agree that there is no advantage in pushing them to read earlier.
- Children listen and understand on a higher reading level than they can read. Children benefit from being read to from birth throughout the school years.
- Reading is for everyone, girls and boys, mothers and fathers. Children need to see and hear both women and men reading. Boys tend to be better readers when fathers read to them and when they see fathers reading to themselves.
- Children and adults don't always agree on choices of books. Reading together will be most successful when both parent and child enjoy the story.
- Books on tape, book software, videos made from books, and television that promotes reading are good, but they are not a substitute for reading to children, talking about books with them, and having fun with stories.
- If adults read to young children often in a relaxed atmosphere of fun and enjoyment, children are likely to develop a love of books and reading, which is the best preparation for learning to read.

Approaches

Feed your child's mind for it to grow and develop. Just as a child's body needs nourishment and exercise to grow, a child's mind needs to be fed in order for it to grow and develop. New sensations and experiences cause new pathways in the brain to connect. The brain responds to voice, color, touch, taste, smell, shape, etc., and creates new pathways that build intelligence. That's why reading to babies and young children is so important. Without these early rich experiences, the brain doesn't grow as much and children tend to have a more difficult time learning later on. Spend time reading, playing, singing, and talking to a child every day and ask that whoever is with your child do the same.

> —Ideas found in *Food for Thought* (video), Health Partners.

Give your child positive experiences with books early so that he will associate reading with fun. Read to your child early. Children love to imitate and will pretend to read if they see the people around them reading. Match reading to your child's interest level and attention span. Read a book and talk about it. Ask your child questions about it, even if they can't answer you yet. Let your child interrupt for questions. Encourage the enjoyment of books, not the ability to read.

> —Ideas found in *The Read-Aloud Handbook* (4th edition) by Jim Trelease, Penguin Books, 1995.

Teach your child some of the basics about reading. Most of the things that adults take for granted about reading need to be taught to a child. Show the child how to hold a book right side up, where the beginning of the book is, how to turn the pages at the right point in the story, where the words are on the page, and where to find his favorite books at home.

> —Ideas found in *Read to Me: Raising Kids Who Love to Read* by Bernice E. Cullinan, Scholastic, Inc., 1992.

Allow your child to look at, chew, hold, bite, drop, and practice turning the pages of books. Exploring books through touch is an important part of learning to love books. Give your child the opportunity to be physical with books. Make sure that books are within his reach and available to him in the same way that toys are. Caring for books is a skill that your child will learn by watching the way people around him take care of books. Save library books and other special books for times when you can read together. Choose books for young children carefully, as the images and ideas presented help your child shape his vision of the world.

> —Ideas found in *Becoming the Parent You Want to Be: A Sourcebook of Strategies for the First Five Years* by Laura Davis and Janis Keyser, Broadway Books, 1997.

Encourage reading by making it an enjoyable experience:

- Make sure that you and your child want to read.
- Find an enjoyable place to sit together and be comfortable.
- Make sure the television, radio, or other distractions are turned off.
- Let your child choose which books to read. Be ready to read favorites over and over.
- Be sure that your child can see the pages. Point to words or pictures and repeated phrases.
- Read with feeling and enthusiasm. Change the speed of the story, sometimes reading slower or faster.
- If your child wiggles and appears uninterested, consider finishing the story later.

Reading and Books

- Create a special reading time each day, but don't limit yourself to reading at that time only. Waiting rooms and car, bus, or plane rides all provide opportunities to look at books.

Reading together in a relaxed and enjoyable way creates closeness between children and adults at the same time that it prepares kids for reading later on.

—Ideas found in "How to Raise a Reader: Sharing Books with Infants and Toddlers,"
American Library Association, 1992.

Help your child learn to love reading:

- Read out loud to your child and be prepared to do it every day.
- Show your child that you read.
- Have reading materials of all kinds around the house.
- Take your child to the library and bookstore often and let him choose.
- Encourage him to find out more about anything that appeals to him.
- Ask an older child to read to a younger one.
- Place a limit on how much time your child spends watching TV, playing video games, and using the computer.
- Make time for reading, but don't require any particular book or topic.
- Ask book professionals for help finding books.
- Talk about reading with your child—your reading and theirs.
- Watch for author appearances and book signings in your area and take your child to meet authors.

Take time, make time, and read!

—Ideas found in "Readerly Advice," by Michael Dirda, *The Writer*, January 1998.

> *Read to your friend. Pick out a story that you know well. Even if you can't read the words yet, tell him the story as you turn the pages. Show him the funny parts. Ask him to "read" one of his favorite stories to you.*
>
> —Leah, age 5

Tell your child stories anytime, and make up your own! Stories are great at bedtime, but they are great to tell at many other times, too: in the car, on a bus, on your way somewhere, after your child has had a bad or sad experience, when your child is sick, on holidays, and at many other times. Try telling your child a story of your own making and ask him to help. Use your imagination and have fun!

—Ideas found in *I'll Tell You a Story, I'll Sing You a Song* by Christine Allison, Delacorte, 1987.

Tell your child stories from books instead of reading them, sometimes. Your child will love to hear stories over and over, and telling stories can allow you to be more open and creative in making the story come alive. You can take stories from books that may be too long or involved to read to your child at his age, and make them come alive in a way that is right for him. Storytelling gives your child the opportunity to create his own pictures in his mind instead of just looking at those provided for him.

—Ideas found in *Picture Book Storytelling: Literature Activities for Young Children* by Janice J. Beaty, Harcourt Brace, 1994.

Invite your child to participate when reading or telling rhyme, rhythm, and repeating phrases. Give your child either real or homemade instruments such as rattles, maracas, tambourines, a box with cereal or pasta in it, or a pot and a spoon to shake or tap out the rhythm in the story as you read it. Practice by saying the words and having children shake or tap out the syllables with you on their instruments: "Don-key, don-key, old and gray, o-pen your mouth, and gent-ly bray."

—Ideas found in *The R.I.F. Guide to Encouraging Young Readers* by Reading Is Fundamental, Inc., Doubleday, 1987.

When choosing books for your child, consider:

- Books for babies and toddlers under age two should be durable. Consider board, or vinyl books. Books with one image on a page and books that show something within the experience of a child, like an orange or a car, are good for youngest readers.
- Two-year-olds can enjoy short stories and like stories about things they know about: colors, shapes, animals, trucks, and kids. Rhyme and repetition are popular at this age.
- Preschoolers still enjoy stories about things they know and rhymes, but they can listen to longer stories. Also, they may like non-scary folk or fantasy tales. They are ready to hear about real things such as stars, planets, food, trucks, and the earth. They will enjoy lively and colorful concept books that show letters, numbers, and words.

—Ideas found in *The Best Toys, Books, Videos, and Software for Kids 1998* by Joanne Oppenheim, Prima Publishing, 1997.

Choose good quality stories; they can help prepare a child for life. Look for books that:

- Tell a story about good qualities of people, like honesty and persistence.
- Tell a story filled with lifelike characters.
- Tell an engaging story that holds your child's attention.
- Don't try to manipulate your child into better behavior, but tell a good story.
- Allow the main character to stumble and learn something new about himself.
- Introduce a child to new things, ideas, and imagery.

Your child can learn from the trials and tribulations and the joys and successes of characters in a story without having to go through the experience himself. If he does encounter a similar challenge in life, he will have some understanding of it.

—Ideas found in *Books That Build Character: A Guide to Teaching Your Child Moral Values Through Stories* by William Kilpatrick, and Gregory and Suzanne M. Wolfe, Simon & Schuster, 1994.

Find books and reading experiences for your child in many places:

- Make use of your local public library. Explore all the areas of the library: the non-fiction area, picture book area, easy reader shelf, and the book tape, CD, magazines, and video racks. Most libraries offer free preschool story times and other programs that invite fun at the library. Librarians are trained to answer questions and suggest books. Encourage your child to ask questions and take advantage of their help yourself.
- Watch the newspaper for book readings, story times, author or book character appearances, and book activity events at local bookstores, toy stores, and museums. Many are free!

Reading and Books

- Borrow books from your friends, neighbors, and family. Suggest putting in a children's lending library at your preschool or church. Consider trading books with another family. Pass on books to younger siblings, cousins, or friends, and make it known that you would appreciate having books passed to you.

- Find new children's books to buy at bookstores (some specialize in children's books), most discount department stores (not always the best selection), through book clubs, mail order booksellers, booksellers on the web, or at book fairs. Suggest to friends and relatives that books make excellent gifts for children.

- Find used children's books to buy or trade at used bookstores, garage sales, library sales and bookstores, and children's' consignment shops.

Expose your child to many kinds of books, authors, and book experiences. Through the fun and excitement that your child shares with you in reading at an early age, a lifelong love of reading is likely to follow.

—Shelley Butler, co-author of *The Field Guide to Parenting*

The Field Guide Children's Book Shelf

Award-Winning Books

Drummer Hoff by Barbara Emberley: 1968 Caldecott Medal

In Daddy's Arms I Am Tall: African Americans Celebrating Fathers by Javaka Steptoe: 1998 Coretta Scott King Award

Madeline's Rescue by L. Bemelmans: 1954 Caldecott Medal

Make Way for Ducklings by Robert McCloskey: 1942 Caldecott Medal

Many Moons by James Thurber and illustrated by Louis Slobodkin: 1944 Caledcott Medal

Snapshots from the Wedding, by Gary Soto and illustrated by Stephanie Garcia: 1998 Pura Belpre Illustrator Award

Snowflake Bentley by Jaqueline Briggs Martin and illustrated by Mary Azarian: 1999 Caldecott Medal

The Adventures of Sparrowboy, written and illustrated by Brian Pinkney: 1997 Boston Globe-Horn Book Award for Picture Book

Board Books

Fire Engine (Snap Shot series)

I Spy Little Book by Jean Marzollo.

Jesse Bear, What Will You Wear? by Nancy White Carlstrom

What Is It? by Tana Hoban

Poetry and Rhyme

The Arnold Lobel Book of Mother Goose by Arnold Lobel

Finger Rhymes by Marc Brown

Life Doesn't Frighten Me by Maya Angelou

Read-Aloud Rhymes for the Very Young, selected by Jack Prelutsky

You Be Good & I'll Be Night by Eve Merriam

Preschool-Kindergarten Beginning Readers

B is for Books (a Sesame Street Book) by Annie Cobb

Bob Books for Beginning Readers (series) by Bobby Lynn Maslen

Itchy, Itchy Chicken Pox by Grace MacCarone

Series Books

Arthur books by Marc Brown

Clifford books by Norman Bridwell

Curious George books by Margaret and H.A. Rey

Frances books by Russell Hoban

Harold (and the Purple Crayon) books by Crockett Johnson

Little Critter books by Mercer Mayer

Magic School Bus books by Joanna Cole

Pippo books by Helen Oxenbury

Spot books by Eric Hill

Wordless Books

Good Dog Carl by Alexandra Day

Pancakes for Breakfast by Tomie dePaola

The Field Guide Children's Book Shelf (continued)

Books About Real Life and Real Things

Bye-Bye Diapers (a Sesame Street book) by Ellen Weiss

Moving (a First Experience book) by Fred Rogers.

The Universe (First Discovery Books series)

What's Inside? Trucks (What's Inside series).

What's It Like to Be a Fish? (a Let's-Read-and-Find-Out-Science Stage 1 book) by Wendy Pfeffer.

Zoo Animals (Eye Openers series)

Chapter Books for Young Children

Adventures of Laura and Jack by Laura Ingalls Wilder

Pirates Past Noon (Magic Tree House Series) by Mary Pope Osborne

Concept Books

123 by William Wegman

Alphabet City by Stephen T. Johnson

Alphabatics by Suse MacDonald

The Best Word Book Ever by Richard Scarry

Chicka Chicka Sticka Sticka by Bill Martin Jr. and John Archambault

Counting Crocodiles by Judy Sierra

My First Word Book by Angela Wilkes

More Great Authors Who Have Written Many Books For Children

Janet and Allen Ahlberg: Each Peach Pear Plum; The Jolly Postman

Aliki: My Visit to the Aquarium; Hands

Byron Barton: Dinosaurs, Dinosaurs; Machines at Work

Jan Brett: The Hat; The Mitten

Margaret Wise Brown: Goodnight Moon; The Runaway Bunny

Ashley Bryan: All Day, All Night: A Child's First Book of African-American Spirituals; Turtle Knows Your Name

Virginia Lee Burton: Mike Mulligan and His Steam Shovel; Katy and the Big Snow

Eric Carle: The Grouchy Ladybug; The Mixed-Up Chameleon

Nancy Carlson: I Like Me; A Visit to Grandma's

Donald Crews: Freight Train; Rain; School Bus

Tomie dePaola: Strega Nona; Legend of the Bluebonnet

Lois Ehlert: Eating the Alphabet; Planting a Rainbow

Mem Fox: Whoever You Are; Koala Lou

Don Freeman: Corduroy; A Pocket for Corduroy

Kevin Henkes: Julius, The Baby of the World; Owen

Shirley Hughes: All About Alfie

Angela Johnson: Shoes Like Miss Alice's; Daddy Calls Me Man

Ezra Jack Keats: The Snowy Day; Regards to the Man in the Moon

Jack Kent: There's No Such Things as a Dragon; Joey

Helen Lester: Me First; Princess Penelope's Parrot

Leo Lionni: Alexander and the Wind-Up Mouse; Frederick

Pat Mora: Uno, Dos, Tres: 1,2,3; A Birthday Basket for Tia

Robert Munsch: Mud Puddle; The Fire Station

Jan Ormerod: The Saucepan Game

Marcus Pfister: The Rainbow Fish; Dazzle the Dinosaur

Beatrix Potter: The Tale of Peter Rabbit; Tale of Mr. Jeremy Fisher

Chris Raschka: Yo! Yes?; Simple Gifts: A Shaker Hymn

Anne Rockwell: Fire Engines; Planes

Maurice Sendak: Where the Wild Things Are; In the Night Kitchen; others.

Dr. Seuss: Green Eggs and Ham; If I Ran the Circus

Shel Silverstein: The Giving Tree; The Missing Piece

Judith Viorst: Alexander and the Terrible, Horrible, No Good, Very Bad Day

Bernard Waber: Lyle, Lyle, Crocodile; Ira Sleeps Over

Rosemary Wells: Bunny Cakes; Max's First Word

The Field Guide Children's Book Shelf (continued)

Folk Tales & Tales From Other Countries

Anansi the Spider, and others by Gerald McDermott

The Bootmaker and the Elves by Susan Lowell

Brother Rabbit: a Cambodian Tale by Minfong Ho and Saphan Ros

Lift-the-Flap, Pop-Up, Hide and Seek Books, Touch and Feel Books

Alpha Bugs by David Carter

Dear Zoo by Rod Campbell

Dinnertime (a Minipops book) by Jan Pienkowski

Fuzzy Yellow Ducklings: Fold-Out Fun With Textures, Colors, Shapes, Animals by Matthew Van Fleet

Pat the Bunny by Dorothy Kunhardt

Popposites: A Lift, Pull, and Pop Book of Opposites by Roger Culbertson

Magazines for Children

Babybug

Click

Highlights for Children

Humpty Dumpty's Magazine

Ladybug

Sesame Street Magazine

Turtle Magazine for Preschool Kids

Your Big Backyard

Picture Books with Patterns or Repeated Phrases

Brown Bear, Brown Bear, What Do You See; Polar Bear, Polar Bear, What Do You Hear? by Bill Martin Jr.

Hey! Get Off Our Train by John Burningham

If You Give a Moose a Muffin by Laura Jappe Numeroff

Is That Josie? by Keiko Narahashi

Sheep in a Jeep by Nancy Shaw

Help your child learn more about books by reading about them together:

 The Babies Are Coming! by Amy Hest

 A Book Takes Root: The Making of a Picture Book by Michael Kehoe

 Tomas and the Library Lady by Pat Mora

"There is a fossil and it was 200 million years ago. And someone rode on a big dinosaur, Tyrannosaurus, and then he hopped off and then he died."

by Joey, age 4

When to Get More Help

Children typically grow and learn new skills in their own time and at their own pace within the wide range of what is normal. Sometimes, children need a bit of extra help to keep their development on track, or to stay healthy and happy. Sometimes, parents need help providing for a child's needs or sorting out the best approaches to parenting.

Consider getting help for your child if he:

- Does not show an interest in listening to children's books and stories by at least four years of age.
- Does not remember any part of the story or doesn't understand it by at least four years of age.

Consider getting help for yourself if you:

- Would like to learn to read better. Also consider helping any adults you know who never learned to read or to read well get help.

You are the expert when it comes to your family and child. If you have a concern, trust your instinct and find someone trained to help you: health care providers, early intervention teams, mental health professionals, parent educators and consultants, or telephone help-line staff. Consider talking it over with friends and family, too. You don't need to worry alone! Turn to "Finding Help in Your Community" on page 4 to learn about finding help near you.

More Help and Information

Books for Parents

- *99 Ways to Get Kids to Love Reading and 100 Books They'll Love* by Mary Leonhardt. Three Rivers Press, 1997.
- *Great Books for Boys: More than 600 Books for Boys 2 to 14* by Kathleen Odean. Ballantine Books, 1998.
- *Great Books for Girls: More than 600 Books to Inspire Today's Girls and Tomorrow's Women* by Kathleen Odean. Ballantine Books, 1997.
- *Raising a Reader: Make Your Child a Reader for Life* by Paul Kropp. Main Street Books, 1996.
- *The Read-Aloud Handbook*, Fourth Edition by Jim Trelease. Penguin Books, 1995.

Booksellers by Mail

- Amazon.com, an online bookseller: www.amazon.com
- Chinaberry Book Service
  800-776-2242

Government

- *America Reads Challenge: Read*Write*Now!*; *Helping Your Child Learn to Read: With Activities for Children from Infancy Through Age 10* by Bernice Cullinan & Brod Bagert. U.S. Dept. of Education, Office of Educational Research & Improvement, 1993. Available through the Consumer Information Center, Pueblo, CO 81099 or online through the U.S. Dept. of Education Web site: www.ed.gov/pubs (look under publications for parents, and then in the "Help Your Child" series).

Hotlines

- National Literacy Hotline: 800-228-8813

Magazines

- *Bulletin of the Center for Children's Books*, University of Illinois Press
  217-333-8935
  E-Mail: puboff@ alexia.lis.uiuc.edu
  Web site: http://edfu.lis.uiuc.edu/puboff/bccb/
- *Horn Book Magazine: About Books for Children and Young Adults*
  800-325-1170
  E-mail: infor@hbook.com
  Web site: www.hbook.com

National Organizations

- Children's Book Council (CBC), Inc.
  E-mail: staff@cbcbooks.org
  Web site: www.cbcbooks.org.
- International Reading Association
  800-336-7323
  Website:www.reading.org
- National Storytelling Association
  800-525-4514, Fax: 423-753-9331
  Web site: www.storynet.org
- Reading Is Fundamental, Inc.
  877-RIF-READ
  Web site: www.si.edu/rif/

Videos for children

- *Arthur's Eyes*. Random House Home Video.
- *Children's Circle Video Series* videos include: *Ezra Jack Keats Library* and *More Stories for the Very Young*. Children's Circle.
- *Little Bear Family Tales*. Paramount.
- *On the Day You Were Born* (Notes Alive series, Minnesota Orchestra Visual Entertainment).

Web Sites

- "100 Picture Books Everyone Should Know," prepared by the Office of Children's Services at the New York Public Library: www.nypl.org/branch/kids/gloria.html
- American Library Association, "For Parents & Kids" resources: www.ala.org
- The Children's Literature Web Guide: www.acs.ucalgary.ca/~dkbrown
- Internet Public Library, select Youth Division for online stories, poems, picture books, activities and links to children's sites: www.ipl.org

Responsibility

by Rachel, age 5

Description

Responsibility means acting wisely without being guided, told, pressured, or threatened into action. It is the ability to make decisions and be accountable for them. Children learn to be responsible by feeding themselves, sleeping independently, dressing themselves, playing independently, helping with simple chores, and behaving within limits.

Realistic Expectations

- Children who are given responsibility for tasks that they are capable of are likely to have a greater sense of belonging in the family, and develop a belief that they can contribute to life in a meaningful way.
- For children to succeed in their responsibilities:
  - Chores, tasks, and expectations must fit their age and developmental level. Children can't do what they aren't capable of doing yet.
  - They will need help and reminders to accomplish tasks. Most children won't be able to be fully responsible for chores and everyday tasks like dressing, without reminders or supervision, until age ten or older.
  - Tasks must be manageable, large tasks must be broken down into steps, and children must be clearly taught how to do them.
- Children will be *less* likely to learn responsibility when:
  - Chores or tasks are done out of fear of punishment or getting hurt.
  - They are not allowed to experience the consequences of their actions.
  - They are rescued often from unpleasant situations when they do not necessarily need help..
- Children may not understand what responsibility means and why responsibilities like going to work and keeping a home clean are important to adults.
- Children spend a lot of time learning many personal responsibilities: potty learning, dressing, eating, washing hands, and sleeping. Don't expect them to have a lot of time for chores.
- Children who are distracted easily may need more help learning to fulfill responsibilities.
- Children may be eager to help out with a chore when it is new, but they may lose interest in it after they've done it a few times.
- Giving children tasks that are real and help the family may encourage children to want to do them more and give them a greater sense of accomplishment.
- Learning responsibility is a lifelong process that parents introduce to young children. They have a limited capacity for responsibility and are only just beginning to learn the skills necessary to become a responsible person.

Approaches

Talk to your child about the meaning of responsibility. Learning to be responsible means learning to:

- Think about the feelings of others and treat people fairly.
- Tell the truth, even if it means admitting mistakes.
- Do the right thing, even if it means not getting your way or losing something that you want.
- Develop self-control.
- Feel good about yourself and your accomplishments, and be satisfied with appropriate behavior, what you can do, and achieving new things.

A child will learn best from experience, so look for ways in everyday life to show her what responsibility looks like and for opportunities for her to practice it.

> —Ideas found in "Helping Your Child Learn Responsible Behavior" by Edwin J. and Alice B. Delattre, U.S. Department of Education, Office of Educational Research and Improvement, 1993.

Encourage your child to begin to learn responsibility through language:

- Ask directly for what you want or need.
- Think and feel for yourself, not for others.
- Be responsible for your own feelings and be responsive to the feelings of others.
- Say "yes" and "no."
- Respond to questions with straight answers.

When all family members make a habit of speaking responsibly, it helps the family attain healthy levels of caring, independence, and interdependence.

> —From *Growing Up Again: Parenting Ourselves, Parenting Our Children* by Jean Illsley Clark and Connie Dawson, copyright 1989, 1998 by Jean Illsley Clarke and Connie Dawson. Reprinted by permission of Hazelden Foundation, Center City, MN.

Increase the level of responsibility and decision-making for your child as she grows and gets older. Starting at age two, give your child small chores that she can accomplish, and add responsibility each year as she gains new skills. Help her develop her own reasons for wanting to help; don't tie chores to money. If you pay her for doing chores, you teach her that a task or responsibility is only worth doing if you get paid, and that good work is always rewarded. Instead, tell her that she is an important person to the family, and that you are counting on her to be responsible and to help. If you start when she is young, then by the time she understands that there is a difference between work and play, she will already be part of the family system for getting things done.

> —Ideas found in *Winning at Parenting...Without Beating Your Kids*, Video, Kids Are Worth It!

Introduce your child to the skills she needs to become a responsible person. The process takes many years. Start early; show your child what responsible adults look like by practicing responsibility yourself and providing your child with opportunities to practice the skills she is developing. To become responsible, your child needs to learn these skills:

- Decision-making. Start by offering your child simple choices: "Do you want to play in the sandbox or on the playground?" Then, as she gets older, talk about her options and the results of the choices she makes.

- Self-motivation. Young children respond to praise, and feeling good makes them want to fulfill their responsibilities.
- Ability to remember responsibilities (limited in young children).
- Ability to speak responsibly about a situation.

> —Ideas found in *Pick Up Your Socks—And Other Skills Growing Children Need!* by Elizabeth Crary, Parenting Press, 1990

Teach your child to accept responsibility for her actions, good and bad. Discuss with your child what you feel you do well and what you feel you may need to improve on. When you make a mistake, admit it and tell her how you could have handled it better. Encourage her to take credit for the things that she does well but also to take responsibility for her mistakes. Show your child that you believe in her ability to act responsibly.

> —Ideas found in *Teaching Your Children Values* by Linda and Richard Eyre. Simon & Schuster, 1993.

Help your child learn from her mistakes. Part of learning responsibility is learning to accept making mistakes and then trying again next time. Help your child learn this by providing an environment of respect and learning, rather than one of criticism and blame.

> —Ideas found in *Parenting Works! Facilitator's Guide* (MELD), Blue Penguin, 1996.

Assign tasks that your child can reasonably accomplish at her age and developmental level. Avoid assigning tasks to your baby or child under age two and a half. She is very busy with developmental tasks such as learning how to use her body, how to talk, and how to make things work. Start giving your preschooler small jobs—like hanging her jacket on a hook, picking up toys, putting crayons back in the box or napkins on the table, or other simple but helpful tasks.

> —Ideas found in *The Parent's Journal Guide to Raising Great Kids* by Bobbi Conner, Bantam Books, 1997.

Consider the many ways to help your child get a job done:
- Praise your child for her help and work for her effort, not whether the job is done perfectly or not. Praise goes a long way toward teaching responsibility—further than bribes or rewards for jobs well done.
- Help your child get the job done. She'll be more likely to do it if you're there with her.
- Make it easy for her to put things away by designating a place to put them that she can easily find and understand.
- Add some fun to the process. Put on some music or tell silly stories about the toys.
- Divide the task into smaller parts. It will be less overwhelming to your child to pick something specific to start with: "Let's pick up all the blocks first."
- Set a routine for the job: "All toys in the box before dinner."
- Try teamwork when you need to get things done in a hurry. Ask everybody in the family to pitch in and see how much they can get picked up in five minutes or less.
- Ask your child to help get something specific done instead of blaming her for making a mess.
- Sometimes only a word is needed: "Jacket!" If she already knows that her jacket is supposed to be on the hook instead of the floor, she'll get it.

> —Ideas found in *Chore Wars* by James Thornton, Conari Press, 1997.

Responsibility

When your child is overwhelmed by the task of picking up her toys, consider making fewer toys available:

- Give your child fewer toys at birthdays or holidays.
- Put away some of the toys for a time so that when you take them out again they will be something "new" to play with. At the same time, take some of the toys that are already out and put them away.
- Keep some toys available—but out of reach—for special times and times when you want to monitor the number of toys your child already has out.
- Consider making a rule: "If you can't pick it up, then you can't play with it." Then when your child refuses or is too overwhelmed to pick it up, put it away for awhile.

—Ideas found in *Raising a Responsible Child* by Elizabeth Ellis, Carol Publishing, 1995.

Help your child understand money. Talk about the different responsibilities that go along with money: working for it, saving, sharing with people less fortunate, and spending wisely. When you think your child understands that money is exchanged for goods and that people work for money, and when you think she is ready to take on the responsibility of chores and money, then it may be time to start an allowance. Introducing her to responsible uses of money now will benefit her later on.

—Ideas found in *Money Doesn't Grow on Trees* by Neale S. Godfrey and Carolina Edwards, Simon & Schuster, 1994.

Ask your child to be a delivery person as a way to help out. Your child will enjoy delivering things that you need. Allow her to deliver a message to someone in the next room, or ask her to pick up some dirty clothes and deliver them to the laundry room. When you appreciate it, she will feel good about being able to help and important.

—Ideas found in *Raising Preschoolers* by Sylvia Rimm and Katie Couric, Three Rivers Press, 1997.

Avoid bribing your child to get her to act responsibly. If your child will only do what she needs or should do because there is a reward waiting for her if she does, then she may not be learning responsible behavior. She needs to learn to act correctly because it makes her feel good, not because there is a payoff. Try to change behavior without rewards. Use rewards for good behavior sparingly, but not if your child demands it.

—Ideas found in "What's In It for Me?" by Margery D. Rosen, *Child*, November 1998.

Help a child understand more about responsibility by reading about it together:

 *Clean Your Room, Harvey Moon!* by Pat Cummings

 The Day That Henry Cleaned His Room by Sarah Wilson

It Wasn't My Fault by Helen Lester

Jelly Beans for Sale by Bruce McMillan

Jobs People Do by Christopher Maynard

Katy and the Big Snow by Virginia Lee Burton

 Pigsty by Mark Teague

When to Get More Help

C hildren typically grow and learn new skills in their own time and at their own pace within the wide range of what is normal. Sometimes, children need a bit of extra help to keep their development on track, or to stay healthy and happy. Sometimes, parents need help providing for a child's needs or sorting out the best approaches to parenting.

You are the expert when it comes to your family and child. If you have a concern, trust your instinct and find someone trained to help you: health care providers, early intervention teams, mental health professionals, parent educators and consultants, or telephone help-line staff. Consider talking it over with friends and family, too. You don't need to worry alone! Turn to "Finding Help in Your Community" on page 4 to learn about finding help near you.

More Help and Information

Books for Parents

- *Money Doesn't Grow on Trees: A Parent's Guide to Raising Financially Responsible Children* by Neale S. Godfrey and Carolina Edwards. Simon & Schuster, 1994.

- *Pick Up Your Socks—And Other Skills Growing Children Need!* by Elizabeth Crary. Parenting Press, 1990.

- *Raising a Responsible Child: How Parents Can Avoid Overindulgent Behavior and Nurture Healthy Children* by Elizabeth Ellis. Carol Publishing, 1995.

- *Raising a Responsible Child: How to Prepare Your Child for Today's Complex World* (revised and updated edition) by Don Dinkmeyer, and Gary D. McKay. Simon & Schuster, 1996.

Government

- "Helping Your Child Learn Responsible Behavior: With Activities for Children" by Edwin J. and Alice B. Delattre, U.S. Department of Education, Office of Educational Research and Improvement. Available through the Consumer Information Center, Pueblo, CO 81099 or online through the U.S. Dept. of Education Web site: www.ed.gov/pubs/parents/behavior/index.html

Self-Esteem

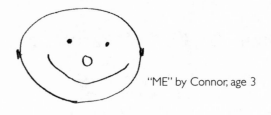

"ME" by Connor, age 3

Description

Self-esteem is the ability to appreciate your own value and importance. Feeling loved, lovable, capable, self-confident, responsible, accepted, valued, and close to the ideal you create for yourself are all characteristics of self-esteem. All children and adults have self-esteem, but some people achieve high self-esteem while others struggle with low self-esteem.

Realistic Expectations

- The process of developing self-esteem begins at birth and continues throughout life. Parents start the process by simply loving their child, but as the child grows, the ways to encourage healthy self-esteem changes.

- Children develop high self-esteem through:
    - Mastering skills and tasks.
    - Experiencing love and acceptance.
    - Encouragement of effort and achievement.
    - Being and feeling valued.
    - Learning to value their own qualities, such as persistence, caring, curiosity, or others.

- Having high self-esteem does not mean that you are conceited, selfish, or think you are better than anyone else.

- Failing at something does not cause low self-esteem; the way children learn to deal with failure affects self-esteem. If children know that it's acceptable to make mistakes and learn from them, they will be more likely to have high self-esteem than children who believe it's wrong to fail.

- Children who have spirited, challenging, or active temperaments may be more at risk for low self-esteem.

- Too much praise or praise that is not associated with an activity or achievement may actually lower self-esteem. Children who are praised too much may come to depend on praise for satisfaction or motivation.

- Divorce, death, traumas, and stress typically affect self-esteem. People who are involved in stressful situations are at risk for low self-esteem. However, when stressful situations are handled well, people may feel a boost in self-esteem.

- Being loved and feeling loved or lovable may be two separate things; people may be loved but if they don't feel loved and don't feel that they are lovable people, their self-esteem suffers.

- Low self-esteem in school-age children and teenagers has been linked to poor school performance and greater risks of drug or alcohol abuse, involvement in crime, violence, and suicide.

- Parents who feel good about themselves and have high self-esteem will be better able to help children learn the skills needed to achieve high self-esteem. Children may be more likely to have low self-esteem when parents have low self-esteem.

- Gaining a healthy, positive self-image and high self-esteem will positively affect every other area of a person's life.

Approaches

To help your child achieve high self-esteem, meet his basic needs:

- Connection. People need to feel connected to other people in order to feel special, safe, and secure. Help your child develop his first connections within the family by making him feel loved and safe.

- Individuality. Everyone is different, so everyone has their own gifts to offer. Appreciate what's different about your child and yourself, and what makes each person a one-of-a-kind.

- Authority and independence. Help your child learn to make decisions, have an effect on situations, master skills, and solve problems. Support his efforts to be independent, develop his capabilities, and act with authority and power in some areas of his life.

- Open communication. Allow your child to be open about his feelings, to say what he thinks, to request help when he needs it, and to speak up about what he wants.

If your child experiences connections and belonging, is appreciated for being who he is, is allowed to act with independence and power, and has the freedom to speak and ask, then he will have a good environment in which to develop high self-esteem.

—Ideas found in *The Magic of Encouragement* by Stephanie Marston, W. Morrow, 1990.

Take care of yourself and build your own self-esteem; before you can help your child, you need to have the skills to accept and love yourself:

- Make and keep promises to yourself, and take control of the things you want to change. You may be very responsible to your job, friends, family and community, but when you decide to make a change or do something for yourself, do you follow through? If you can, you will feel better, stronger, and more in control.

- When mistakes occur, be kind to yourself and others. Learn to let go of bad feelings and forgive others and yourself. The sooner you can do that, the greater the chance of feeling good about yourself again.

- Take chances. If you can learn to face things that may have an unknown outcome, your self-esteem will grow. Set manageable, specific, realistic goals: instead of choosing not to make new friends, call the new neighbor and ask him to go for a walk today.

- Be honest with yourself about your achievements and abilities. If you do a good job, admit it. If you deserve recognition for something, accept it.

Self-esteem is an ongoing process, not something you either have or don't have. Expect that some days you may have more than others, but you can learn the abilities needed to gain and keep a high self-esteem.

—Ideas found in "Increase Your Self-Esteem" by Ron Pitzer, Online, Children, Youth and Family Consortium's Electronic Clearinghouse, www.cyfc.umn.edu.

Self-Esteem

Help your child grow up with self-esteem by asserting that you believe your child is lovable and capable. By giving your child messages that he is loved and capable, you help his efforts to master developmental skills. Be sincere in giving these messages of affirmation:

- From six to eighteen months, support the child for working at the developmental tasks of the "doing" stage. Offer him these messages:

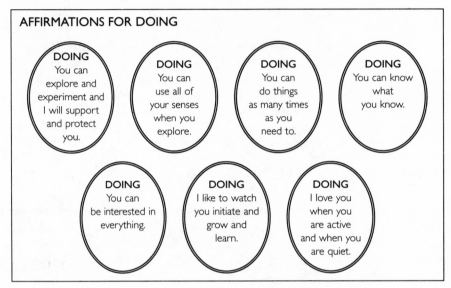

AFFIRMATIONS FOR DOING

DOING You can explore and experiment and I will support and protect you.

DOING You can use all of your senses when you explore.

DOING You can do things as many times as you need to.

DOING You can know what you know.

DOING You can be interested in everything.

DOING I like to watch you initiate and grow and learn.

DOING I love you when you are active and when you are quiet.

- From eighteen months to three years, support the child for working at the developmental tasks of the "thinking" stage. Offer him these messages:

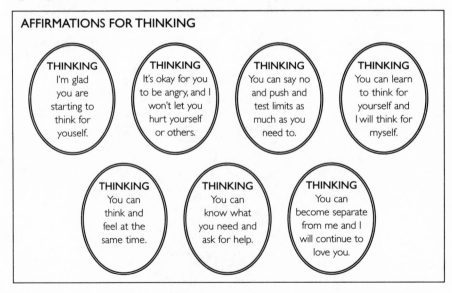

AFFIRMATIONS FOR THINKING

THINKING I'm glad you are starting to think for youself.

THINKING It's okay for you to be angry, and I won't let you hurt yourself or others.

THINKING You can say no and push and test limits as much as you need to.

THINKING You can learn to think for yourself and I will think for myself.

THINKING You can think and feel at the same time.

THINKING You can know what you need and ask for help.

THINKING You can become separate from me and I will continue to love you.

- From three years to six years, support the child for working at the developmental tasks of the "identity and power" stage. Offer him these messages:

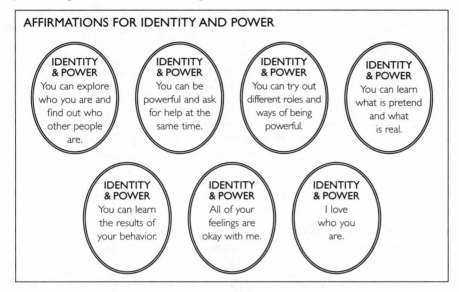

AFFIRMATIONS FOR IDENTITY AND POWER

IDENTITY & POWER
You can explore who you are and find out who other people are.

IDENTITY & POWER
You can be powerful and ask for help at the same time.

IDENTITY & POWER
You can try out different roles and ways of being powerful.

IDENTITY & POWER
You can learn what is pretend and what is real.

IDENTITY & POWER
You can learn the results of your behavior.

IDENTITY & POWER
All of your feelings are okay with me.

IDENTITY & POWER
I love who you are.

Support your child's efforts to work and master tasks that are appropriate for his age. Allow him to grow up at his own pace. Messages of love and belief in your child given with honest admiration will encourage his self-esteem.

> —From *Growing Up Again: Parenting Ourselves, Parenting Our Children* by Jean Illsley Clark and Connie Dawson, copyright 1989, 1998 by Jean Illsley Clarke and Connie Dawson. Reprinted by permission of Hazelden Foundation, Center City, MN.

Help your child gain a positive self-image. Notice, comment, and point out the good things about your child. Reinforce the idea that many different people are great and wonderful, too. Consider the language you use to describe people. If your child repeatedly hears comments like, "Your dark skin reminds me of Grandpa and he was the most handsome man in our family," and "Our friend's light skin is beautiful, and our dark skin is beautiful," your child will come to recognize that he and many other kinds of people are terrific the way they are. Help your child feel good about his self-image while introducing the idea that although other people are different, your child is great the way he is.

> —Ideas found in *Different and Wonderful: Raising Black Children in a Race-Conscious Society* by Darlene Powell Hopson and Derek S. Hopson, Simon & Schuster, 1992.

Raise your child to be confident by following five principles of self-esteem; it's critical for the lifelong welfare of your child that you invest time and effort in building his self-esteem:

1. Listen to and acknowledge the thoughts and feelings of your child. When you give him your full attention, listen, and empathize, you communicate that you accept him and that he counts.

2. Structure situations to help your child experience feelings of success. Set clear and appropriate expectations, provide a reasonable amount of help and adequate incentives, and remove some of the obstacles to success.

3. Give your child a feeling of reasonable control over his life.

4. Communicate to your child that he is lovable and capable. Reinforce the idea that he is worthy to be loved, not just that he is loved.

5. Model a positive view of yourself to your child. Be aware of how you talk about yourself and react to circumstances of life. Show your child what healthy self-esteem looks like; this modeling is vital to developing healthy self-esteem in your child.

> —From *Self-Esteem for Tots to Teens: How You Can Help Your Children Feel More Confident and Lovable* by Eugene Anderson, George Redman, Charlotte Rogers, Parenting & Teaching Publications, 1991. 800-8-ESTEEM.

Accept your child as he is and appreciate the many qualities that make him a special, unique individual; this is one of the most important things you can do for a child to help him develop high self-esteem. Focus on the positive skills, traits, and abilities and be willing to accept mistakes, challenges, and difficulties. Try to be realistic about your child: he was born with a certain temperament, he may or may not behave, learn, or fit in with other children his age, and he is not perfect. Understand that there are many ways of growing up, of doing, and of being that parents did not cause or cannot change. Look for, point out, and celebrate the special and great things about your child.

> —*Living with the Active Alert Child: Groundbreaking Strategies for Parents* (revised and enlarged edition) by Linda S. Budd, Parenting Press, 1993.

Show your child honest love and help him feel lovable by giving him your full attention at times. A child needs to feel that he is loved and lovable to develop high self-esteem. Adults who protect, but overprotect; who give to their child, but give too much; who spend time with a child, but their thoughts are elsewhere; who talk to a child, but find fault or compare, are not giving a child honest, genuine love and attention. Open yourself to the special things about the child and find time to be with him—giving your whole self, an open mind, a full heart, and your physical presence. This kind of focus on a child will communicate love and caring, and fosters a child's self-esteem.

> —Ideas found in *Your Child's Self-Esteem* by Dorothy Corkille Briggs, Doubleday, 1970.

Help your child acquire optimism: a positive, active attitude about when, how, and why things occur in his own life. Encourage your child to do well: to master skills, persist in trying, tolerate frustration, and cope with failure in a positive way. Self-esteem follows from doing well.

Help a child think realistically and optimistically:

- Avoid using words that describe an absolute—always, never, best, worst, most, least: "You are the worst at picking up, but the best at making a mess." Say instead: "Let's work on getting these toys picked up."

- Help him focus on what happened in that instance rather than talking about what always or never happens: "I see you are mad at your sister *right now*." Avoid saying: "You *always* yell at your sister *every time* you play together."

- Help your child understand what specifically is going on: "I see you didn't like it when Amy grabbed your block." Help your child steer away from pessimistic thinking like, "She *never* plays fair with me; she must hate me."

- Help your child think about mistakes or failures and interpret events in a specific way, rather than in a universal way, and to prevent him from blaming them on a general imperfection in himself:

  - "I broke the cup because I picked it up when I wasn't supposed to," instead of "I broke the cup because I'm so dumb and bad."

     – "Steven doesn't want to play with me today, because I slipped and stepped on his foot," instead of "Steven won't play with me because I always hurt him."

Self-esteem follows as a result of having a positive attitude and doing well in life, mastering age-appropriate tasks, and acquiring more confidence to learn new ones.

> —Ideas found in *The Optimistic Child* by Martin E. P. Seligman, et al., Houghton Mifflin, 1995.

Avoid linking love to behavior; love that is tied to a child being or doing something does not feel like love. Don't use love as a way to get the child to do or stop doing anything. If you say, "I love you when you go to bed without a fuss," or "I love you because you are so happy all the time," a child learns that he has to meet these conditions to be loved. A genuine "I love you," or "Thank you for going to bed without a fuss tonight," in other words, unconditional love, contributes more to your child feeling loved.

> —Ideas found in *The Winning Family: Increasing Self-Esteem in Your Children and Yourself* by Louise Hart, Celestial Arts, 1993.

Show your child respect and consideration to boost his self-esteem. Say "please" and "thank you," ask before you borrow things, knock before you enter, and observe other manners and courtesies with your child as you do with adults. When correcting or disciplining your child, give him information about his actions, words, or behavior without attacking his whole being: say, "You may not hit the dog," instead of "You are a bad boy to hit the dog." Avoid putting him down, calling him names, or making him feel like he is a bad person. Using respect and consideration with a child will add to his self-esteem.

> —Ideas found in *Practical Parenting Tips* (Revised and updated edition) by Vicki Lansky, Meadowbrook Press, 1992.

Help a child learn more about self-esteem by reading about it together:

The Biggest Boy by Kevin Henkes

Dark Day, Light Night by Jan Carr

Guess How Much I Love You by Sam McBratney

I Like Me by Nancy Carlson; *Me Gusto Como Soy* translated by Dolores Koch

Koala Lou by Mem Fox

Little Mo by Martin Waddell

The Mixed-Up Chameleon by Eric Carle

Quick as a Cricket by Audrey Wood

Something Special by David McPhail

The Talking Cloth by Rhonda Mitchell

We Can Do It! by Laura Dwight

When to Get More Help

Children typically grow and learn new skills in their own time and at their own pace within the wide range of what is normal. Sometimes, children need a bit of extra help to keep their development on track, or to stay healthy and happy. Sometimes, parents need help providing for a child's needs or sorting out the best approaches to parenting.

Consider getting help for you or your child if either of you:

- Frequently thinks or makes unkind or unflattering remarks about yourself.
- Is often overly aggressive or hostile toward others.
- Is overly passive.
- Is a perfectionist or unable to recognize your own accomplishments.

You are the expert when it comes to your family and child. If you have a concern, trust your instinct and find someone trained to help you: health care providers, early intervention teams, mental health professionals, parent educators and consultants, or telephone help-line staff. Consider talking it over with friends and family, too. You don't need to worry alone! Turn to "Finding Help in Your Community" on page 4 to learn about finding help near you.

More Help and Information

Books for Parents

- *Growing Up Again: Parenting Ourselves, Parenting Our Children* by Jean Illsley Clark and Connie Dawson. Hazelden, 1998.
- *How to Develop Self-Esteem in Your Child: 6 Vital Ingredients* by Betty B. Youngs. Fawcett Columbine, 1993.
- *The Magic of Encouragement* by Stephanie Marston. W. Morrow, 1990.
- *The Optimistic Child* by Martin E. P. Seligman, et al. Houghton Mifflin, 1995.
- *Self-Esteem: A Family Affair* by Jean Illsley Clarke. Hazelden, 1998.
- *Self-Esteem for Tots to Teens: How You Can Help Your Children Feel More Confident and Lovable* by Eugene Anderson, George Redman, Charlotte Rogers. Parenting & Teaching Publications, 1991. 800-8-ESTEEM (800-837-8336).
- *The Winning Family: Increasing Self-Esteem in Your Children and Yourself* by Louise Hart. Celestial Arts, 1993.
- *Your Child's Self-Esteem* by Dorothy Corkille Briggs. Doubleday, 1970.

Articles, Pamphlets and Booklets

- "Self-Esteem and Your Children: You are the Key" National Association for the Education of Your Children

  800-424-2460, Fax: 202-328-1846

  Web site: www.naeyc.org.

Separation Anxiety and Attachment

Description

Separation anxiety is the conflicting feelings that children have when they part from the person or people to whom they are most attached. While children are experimenting with their independence, they may leave you for a moment at a time, but keep you in sight. If you try to do the same thing, and leave for a moment, they may react by crying and trying to find you because they fear losing you. This reaction is separation anxiety; it is a normal process in children's development.

Attachment is a close and secure relationship that develops gradually over time; it builds over days, weeks, months, and years of childhood. Both the child and the parent participate in this relationship.

Realistic Expectations

- Secure attachments occur when parents are sensitive and responsive to children's needs: when the child cries after a bad dream, a parent responds promptly; when the child smiles at the feel of a breeze on the cheek, a parent smiles; when the child says, "Look at the soft kitty!" a parent replies, "Yes, I see!" These children come to see the world as safe, trustworthy, predictable, and kind.

- Feeling secure in a relationship typically leads to a secure feeling inside children that leads them to become independent, to explore freely, to dive into learning, and to desire making friends.

- Children whose parents do not consistently respond to their signals and emotional needs may learn to mistrust that others will be there for them; as a result of this mistrust, some children may isolate themselves while others may become extremely dependent, clingy, and easily upset.

- As children become more independent, they become torn between their desire to move away from you and their fears of losing you.

- Separation anxiety usually peaks between ten and eighteen months. Strong separation reactions typically can appear as early as six months and last throughout the preschool years.

- Not all children show extreme separation anxiety: some cry loudly, some whimper, some cling, some seem depressed, some dive right into activity, some observe, and some just say "bye-bye."

- Young children have a limited sense of time and memory, so they do not know when or if you will come back. Little by little, as children's memories and sense of time develop, their ability to hold you in their thoughts comforts them, and they learn that you will come back.

- Separation anxiety is likely to be more intense in new environments, or in children who have other stresses in their lives such as moving or a new baby in the family.

- Parents also have feelings of anxiety when they separate from their children; they may feel a loss when they leave their small child in someone else's care.

- The positive benefits that come from a secure attachment in early childhood will positively impact children throughout their lives.

Approaches

To develop a secure attachment with your child, become the best parent you can be. Building a secure attachment with your child is one of the most important things you can do for her. Taking care of yourself, and understanding how children and parents grow will help you build upon a strong foundation:

- Meet your own needs for emotional support, housing, food, clothing, transportation, and health care.

- Understand the development of your child, how she grows, what she is able to do at certain ages, and what she is not yet capable of doing in order to have more realistic expectations for how she will behave.

- Consider your own childhood and the care you received as a child. Recognize that the way you were parented is a strong influence on the parenting that you give your child. Make conscious choices about the kind of parent you want to be, the things from your childhood that you want to repeat, and the things that you want to be different for your child. If you have experiences from your childhood that have not been resolved or are still causing you pain, consider getting help to resolve them.

> —Ideas found in "Understanding Attachment and Bonding Between Parent and Child" by Martha Farrell Erickson, *Family Information Services*, 1997.

Give your child love and attention. In addition to building a secure relationship, this feeds your child's mind and stimulates brain growth. There are many ways to show love and give attention:

- Don't worry about spoiling your child with too much love. Comfort her whenever she is hurt, frightened, or insecure. Rather then making a "baby" out of your child, this will create a sense of security and help her learn to soothe herself.

- Tell her with touch that you love her: pick her up, hug, cuddle, pat, rub, or gently tickle her.

- Respect her and praise her for her accomplishments.

- Tell her with words that you love her.

- Avoid criticism, punishment, or teasing.

- Keep her as free from stress as you can.

> —Ideas found in *Magic Trees of the Mind* by Marian Diamond, Dutton, 1998.

I have many warm memories of me as a small boy with my father. I still remember that every night at bedtime, I'd jump into my P.J.s, brush my teeth, crawl into bed, and yell downstairs to my dad that I was ready for him to come and say good-night. I would "hide" by being small and flat under the sheets and calm myself into absolute silence. I first heard my own heart beat, then I heard dad's old leather moccasins on the worn wooden steps, which uttered the creaks that I knew well.

Most nights, dad would play along with this game, and at just the right time, I'd jump out from under the sheets and laugh my head off. Dad would act surprised, then casually snuggle next to me while we'd talk awhile about things like birthday parties and what silly things the dog did that evening. Then we would kiss and hug good night before he returned downstairs. Looking back on those moments of magical thinking, boyish glee, and paternal affection, I realize they were important rituals of attachment. The opportunities to invent rituals are with us throughout our lifetime and their influence can endure for generations.

—Jeffry, Wisconsin

Let your child practice separating through play. Help your child cope with her feelings of separation anxiety by using stuffed animals, dolls, or a dollhouse to play that a child is separating from an adult. Talk about the situation as you play, and ask her how the animals feel.

> —Ideas found in *A To Z Guide to Your Child's Behavior* (Children's National Medical Center), Putnam Pub., 1993.

Understand and encourage your child's attachment to a comfort object; it can help her manage separations. Children often get attached to, or can be helped to attach to, a blanket, stuffed animal, scrap of fabric, a piece of your clothing, a towel, etc. These objects can soothe and provide a sense of security that can help ease your child through separations. Often, the objects have silky, nubby, or fuzzy textures that are pleasing to stroke or rub. Children use the object when they need to and grow out of it when they learn other ways to cope with change.

> —Ideas found in "The Portable Pal" by Amy Engeler, *Parents Magazine*, January 1998.

Create routines and rituals for leaving your child and reuniting with her. Make your child's schedule as regular as possible, if it is going to include separations. A predictable routine allows your child to set an internal clock that begins to tell her when to expect your comings and goings. If you work sporadic hours it may take longer for your child to adjust to separations. Here are some suggestions:

- Create rituals (such as reading together, taking a walk, cuddling on the couch) that work in your family for re-connecting after you have been separated from each other.
- Clear your own mind before you arrive home: take a walk, go for a run, meditate, sing in the car (for a few minutes), or find another activity that helps you switch gears and prepare to meet your family.
- Take ten or fifteen minutes to be available to her when you are first reunited: talk, sing, share a book, play, or do any other activity that you enjoy together.
- Do something physical or affectionate together: hug, cuddle, give a back rub, wrestle, play ball, or share any other loving gesture.
- Talk about your days. Sometimes, it is easier for your child to share if you start first or if you mention a specific thing that you know happened in her day.
- Have your child help with some daily routines: getting the mail, watering the garden or plants, feeding the cat, or bringing in the newspaper.

Over time you and your child will develop your own strategies for coming back together again.

> —Ideas found in *Becoming the Parent You Want to Be* by Laura Davis and Janet Keyser, Broadway Books, 1997.

Teach your child that she can be separated from you for a time and still be safe, secure, and happy. Help her deal with strong feelings about separation:

- Encourage her exploration: tell her, "I like it when you look at things. You are safe here."
- Reassure her that you will be there when she comes back after exploring: "Go and see that baby in the other room and I will be right here waiting for you."
- Put some limits on her clinging to you. If she clutches your leg frequently and is reluctant to leave your side, offer her a choice: "I need to vacuum now. Do you want to sit in the chair where you can watch, or do you want to draw at the kitchen table? I will be right here."
- When you are out of her sight in another room, talk to her. Tell her what you are doing.

Separation Anxiety and Attachment

• Plan some short separations from each other. Find a capable person to care for her, and then leave for a short time. Short times away from you followed by your return will teach her that you do come back.

The child's urge to leave you and become more independent increases her need to be sure that you won't leave her for good. This natural process is often frightening for her, and she needs your support and encouragement.

> —Ideas found in *How to Read Your Child Like a Book* by Lynn Weiss, Meadowbrook Press, 1997.

Ease your child's separation anxiety when you must leave her:

• Always tell your child that you are leaving and that you will be back. It's best not to sneak away. Children don't understand the concept of time at this age, so saying you'll be back in an hour won't mean much. As you tell her when you will return, state it in relation to an activity: "I will see you after you have music time and snack."

• Similarly, don't try to prepare your child much in advance; phrases like, "in a little while" or "this evening" will mean nothing to her. Ten or fifteen minutes before you leave, simply and honestly state that you are leaving and that you will return.

• Expect your child to react, but try not to cry or be visibly upset in front of her. If you remain calm and confident in her ability to handle the separation, it will help her.

• Try telling your child what to do while you're gone. Setting her up with specific projects gives a comforting sense that everything is still under control and gives her something else to think about.

• Help your child by naming and reflecting back her feelings of fear, sadness, or anger. It may help to predict a happy outcome: "I know you are really sad now, but remember what fun you had last time? I know you will have fun when you are finished feeling sad."

• Consider showing your child where you will be if you will be in the same building.

• Bring a comfort or transitional object from home, or give her something of yours.

> —From Robbinsdale Early Childhood and Family Education Curriculum.

Be aware of and express your own feelings of loss when you turn the child over to another for care. Know that it is common and normal for parents who are attached to their child to feel lonely, sad, guilty, and helpless when they leave their child. Recognize the feelings in yourself if they exist, and allow them to surface. Expressing these normal, universal feelings can lead to defusing and mastering them, without lessening the deep relationship you have with your child.

> —Ideas found in *Touchpoints* by T. Berry Brazelton, Addison-Wesley, 1992.

Help your child understand more about separation by reading about it together:

 Even If I Spill My Milk? By Anna Grossnickle Hines

 I'll See You When the Moon Is Full by Susi Gregg Fowler

 Owl Babies by Martin Waddell

 The Good-Bye Book by Judith Viorst

When to Get More Help

C hildren typically grow and learn new skills in their own time and at their own pace within the wide range of what is normal. Sometimes, children need a bit of extra help to keep their development on track, or to stay healthy and happy. Sometimes, parents need help providing for a child's needs or sorting out the best approaches to parenting.

Consider getting help for your child if she:

- Does not become connected to you or another caregiver.
- Does not become increasingly more independent after one year.
- Is frequently so distressed when you leave her in the care of another that she is unable to get involved in activities for of the time she is away from you.

Consider getting help for yourself if you:

- Feel disconnected from your child.
- Have extreme difficulties separating from your child.

You are the expert when it comes to your family and child. If you have a concern, trust your instinct and find someone trained to help you: health care providers, early intervention teams, mental health professionals, parent educators and consultants, or telephone help-line staff. Think about talking it over with friends and family, too. You don't need to worry alone! Turn to "Finding Help in Your Community" on page 4 to learn about finding help near you.

More Help and Information

Books for Parents

- "The Dance of Separation, Chapter 13," in *Becoming the Parent You Want to Be: A Source Book of Strategies for the First Five Years* by Laura Davis and Janet Keyser. Broadway Books, 1997.
- *First Feelings: Milestones in the Emotional Development of Your Baby and Child* by Stanley I. Greenspan and Nancy Thorndike Greenspan. Penguin, 1994.

Sexuality

"Mamma with a
baby inside her."
by Hannah, age 4½

Description

Developing one's sexuality is a lifelong process. Children begin to learn about themselves as sexual people from the time they are born. Infants and young children enjoy the pleasures of touch and being touched by another human being, as well as discovering, touching, and exploring their bodies. Preschool children learn which gender they are, consider what it means to be a boy or a girl, begin to understand privacy and boundaries about their bodies, and begin to wonder about where babies come from.

Realistic Expectations

- Infants and children develop positive attitudes about their bodies when adults give them plenty of loving physical non-sexual touch: holding, massaging, kissing, hugging, or gentle tickling.
- Parents, extended family, friends, religion, and the media all influence the messages people receive about sexuality from birth and throughout life.
- Children naturally take pleasure from exploring or touching their body, including their genitals. Many children will masturbate, or excite their own genitals; it is a normal behavior that provides information about one's own body, what the genitals feel like, and how they work.
- Between eighteen months and three years, children are learning whether they are a boy or girl. Around three to four years of age, children become sure of their own gender. At that time, they also become curious about body differences between boys and girls, and often will play house or doctor to explore the bodies of their friends.
- Around age three, many children form a strong attachment to the parent of the opposite sex, or to another adult of the opposite sex, if one does not live in the home of the child.
- Three- to four-year-olds can begin to accept and learn about the need for privacy—their own and others'.
- Around age three, children may begin to ask simple questions about bodies, birth, and reproduction: "Where do babies come from? How do babies get out of a mommy's tummy? What is a vagina? Why do women have breasts?"
- Most children under age five only want very simple information about bodies. They don't typically think about, understand, or ask about more complicated things like how the baby gets into the mother's body or about sexual acts.
- Children are interested in learning the names for all body parts and functions, including the genitals: penis, breasts, vulva, vagina, scrotum, testicles, urinating, having a bowel movement, etc.
- If parents create a home where children are free to talk or ask about anything, then children will learn that sexuality is a safe and open topic for discussion.
- Children who feel positive about their bodies have gained a major component of self-esteem, and have a significant contribution toward feeling positive about their sexuality.

Approaches

Communicate positively, matter-of-factly, and at your child's age level about bodies and sexuality. This will foster open communication that will be increasingly important as your child becomes a teen. In early childhood, your child's needs are simple:

Infants and toddlers (birth to two years)

- Teach your child the names of body parts, including the genitals. Give accurate names for all body parts to give a simple message that his or her entire body is natural, healthy, and wonderful (not dirty, secretive, or bad).
- React calmly when your child touches his or her genitals; this will give the message that sexual feelings are normal and healthy. Avoid shaming since this may lead him or her to believe that parts of the body are bad.
- Answer questions, hold, hug, talk with, and respond to your child's needs; this lets him or her know that he or she is lovable and helps to build trust for open discussions and relationships over time.

Preschoolers (three to four years)

- Continue all of the above.
- Answer your child's questions about where babies come from, giving simple answers: "Babies come from a mama's body." Typically children at this age do not need or want to know the facts about sex or how the baby got into the body.
- Teach your child to take good care of his or her body: wash, brush teeth, eat good foods, rest, sleep, and exercise.
- Teach your child about privacy: you want privacy if the bathroom door or your bedroom door is closed, and he or she should masturbate in a private place.
- Teach your child about healthy touches, unhealthy touches, and body boundaries: no one has a right to touch his or her body unless he or she wants them to. Teach your child to tell you if anyone touches him or her in an uncomfortable way.

—Ideas found in "Communication Tips for Parents," Online, Sexuality Information and Education Council of the United States (SIECUS), 1998: www.siecus.org.

When talking to your child about sexuality, consider what you want to tell your child. Before you can talk to your child about sex or sexuality, you need to know the answers and know how you feel about the topic. Think about what your parents told you as a child and what was helpful or hurtful. Improve what they did—add or subtract as you see useful. Also, consider your beliefs, values, and comfort level about sexuality and your own sex life, body, and all of its processes: menstruation, masturbation, foreplay, intercourse, ejaculation, etc. Many adults have conflicts or questions about all of these things. Examine your feelings and talk them through with another adult; your discomfort or joy will probably show to your child.

—Ideas found in *What Should I Tell the Kids: A Parent's Guide to Real Problems in the Real World* by Ava L. Siegler, Dutton, 1993.

Answer your child's questions with direct, natural, simple answers. Tell your child the truth in language he or she can understand. Relax for now, most children can't handle the details about sexual intercourse before at least six to eight years of age. Think ahead about answers to typical sexuality questions:

- "Babies grow in a place near their mommy's stomach called the uterus."
- "Sex is a sort of hugging for two adults to be very close to each other so they can cuddle and kiss."

- "All girls have a vagina. It is an opening into a girl's body that is between her legs. Boys don't have a vagina, they have a penis."

- "Breasts make milk for babies. Women who have had a baby can feed the baby that way if they decide to."

- "A penis is something that all boys have. A boy gets rid of urine through it. All penises grow hard sometimes, especially if you touch them. Daddy has a penis, but his is bigger than yours. Girls don't have a penis, they have a vagina that is inside of their body."

    —Ideas found in *Questions Children Ask and How to Answer Them* by Miriam Stoppard, DK Publishing 1997.

Treat masturbation as normal, and then discuss it in terms of manners rather than right and wrong behavior. Self-stimulation of genitals is common and normal. Consider it his or her own business but ask that it be done in a private room. If he or she is masturbating in front of others, calmly give a reminder about privacy. Tell your child that it is fine to masturbate, but it is not polite to do it in front of others.

    —Ideas found in *A to Z Guide to Your Child's Behavior* (Children's National Medical Center), Putnam Pub., 1993.

Treat nakedness with respect. Nudity can be very natural between parents and children. It can provide an opportunity for your child to ask questions, and for you to teach him or her about appropriate and inappropriate touching. Set limits with him or her about touching and poking your genitals and breasts. If he or she is showing any discomfort over either of you being naked, cover up. Both of these things will teach him or her that everyone has the right to put limits on having their body seen and/or touched by others.

If your family does feel comfortable with nudity at home, tell your child that other people may not be comfortable with it. Teach him or her to respect differences by letting him or her know when nudity is appropriate and when it is not: "There are manners about going without our clothes. When we have company, when we are outside, or when we are at other people's houses, we keep our clothes on."

    —Ideas found in *Positive Parenting from A to Z* by Karen Renshaw Joslin, Fawcett Columbine: Ballantine Books, 1994.

Pay attention to the music, or the positive, reassuring attitude that you convey when you talk to your child about sexuality; it is not just what you say, but how you say it that is important. When you listen to a piece of music and really like it, you often end up humming the melody. People rarely sing the lyrics, because they can't remember them. The same can be true in talking about sex with your child: he or she may not remember many of your actual words, but they will remember the tone of the conversation and the feelings he or she had during it. If the attitudes are positive, children will likely remember that:

- Their questions were always accepted and answered.

- Their emotions and concerns were treated as normal.

- They received positive messages about the human body.

- There was acceptance of the need for caring touch among all human beings.

Over time, your child may adopt, with increasing comfort, the language you use when you discuss sexuality issues with him or her in an open and unembarrassed manner. Hopefully, more and more clearly, your child will hear and appreciate the music.

    —Adapted with permission from *When Sex Is the Subject* by Pamela M. Wilson, ETR Associates, Santa Cruz, CA., 1991.

Begin talking to your child about caring for and treating his or her body with respect in the preschool years. Waiting until your child is an adolescent who comes home and surprises you with clothing, a new pierced something, or a tattoo that you may not approve of, is not the time to start talking about how you feel about honoring and respecting bodies. Start now. There are no guarantees about what your child will learn and apply later, but the early talks you have with your child will hopefully act as an anchor as he or she goes out into the world later to make his or her own decisions about standards.

> —Ideas found in *How to Talk to Your Child About Sex* by Linda and Richard Eyre, Golden Books, 1998.

Respond to children who are exploring their bodies together. We sometimes find ourselves surprised to discover our young children exploring each other's bodies. It is common for children to be interested in and to explore their friend's bodies. Ideally, we want children to feel comfortable about their natural curiosity, yet still be safe. We want them to learn how their bodies work, to enjoy their bodies, to set appropriate boundaries, and also what is socially acceptable.

- Share your observation with them and ask them for information about what they're doing. "I see you have your clothes off. Tell me about the game."

- Buy yourself some time to regroup if you don't trust your first instinct or don't know what to do. You can ask your children to put their clothes on and find another game. Explain that you can talk a little later about questions they might have. Tell them you want them to have safe ways to learn about their bodies.

- Acknowledge children's curiosity, encourage their questions and let them know the family and safety rules. "I know you are curious about your body. I want to tell you what our family's rules are and I wonder if you have any questions for me."

- Make sure you are within hearing or visual range of children who are at the stage of being fascinated with their bodies. Doors should stay open.

- Teach them to say "no." Tell them that it is never OK for anyone to touch any part of them without permission, and that they always have the right to say no. Let them know that they can get help from an adult if their request is not being respected.

- Talk to the other child's family about what happened and make a plan about guidelines for future play times.

- Give children other options of things to play.

- Watch for power imbalances in the relationship. Do both children feel fee to say "no?" Help the children involved if an imbalance exists.

- If there is information that your child is looking for, provide it with books, pictures, dolls, or talking together.

> —Ideas found in *Becoming the Parent You Want to Be* by Laura Davis and Janis Keyser, Broadway Books, 1997.

Raise children to be aware of and to assert themselves about their personal boundaries. By four years of age, teach your child:

- That no one has a right to touch his or her private parts without permission from him or her, that no one has a right to make him or her touch their private parts, and that no one has a right to ask him or her to keep it a secret if either of the above happen.

- To tell if something uncomfortable has happened. Reassure him or her that they will never be in trouble with you for telling, even if they broke a rule like leaving the yard without telling you.

- That he or she can always say no to unwanted touches, even if they seem well intentioned—like hugs or tickles that don't feel good.

- To say, "NO!" in a loud, clear voice. Practice it with him or her.

Listen carefully and with an open mind if your child says that an adult or older child touched him or her in a way that was uncomfortable, then get help for you and your child to explore what happened.

> —Ideas found in *Beyond the Birds and the Bees* by Beverly Engel, Pocket Books, 1997.

Show your love for another adult in your child's presence: touch, squeeze, kiss, make time for fun, show concern for each other's feelings, laugh, respect each other, work together in a positive way on projects, or share jobs around the home. Your child is watching your relationship closely. Show your child that affection and respect are important ingredients in a loving relationship.

> —Ideas found in *Raising a Son: Parents and the Making of a Healthy Man* by Don Elium and Jeanne Elium, Celestial Arts, 1996.

Help your child understand more about sexuality and his or her body by reading about it together:

 Did the Sun Shine Before You Were Born? By Sol and Judith Gordon (note: this book has one page that talks about intercourse, but no picture of it - the text could be skipped for a younger child)

 If You Were Born a Kitten by Marion Dane Bauer

The Bare Naked Book by Kathy Stinson

What's Inside? Baby by Dorling Kindersley Limited

 *What's the Big Secret?: Talking About Sex with Girls and Boys* by Laurie Krasny Brown and Mark Tolon Brown. (note: this book has one page that talks about intercourse, but no picture of it - the text could be skipped for a younger child)

When to Get More Help

Children typically grow and learn new skills in their own time and at their own pace within the wide range of what is normal. Sometimes, children need a bit of extra help to keep their development on track, or to stay healthy and happy. Sometimes, parents need help providing for a child's needs or sorting out the best approaches to parenting.

Consider getting help for your child if she:

- Masturbates compulsively every day, or to the extent that it interferes with other activities.
- Keeps masturbating in public after you have worked with her for a period of time to encourage doing so only in private.
- Behaves in a sexual manner or says sexual things that seem too advanced for her age.
- Reports or shows any signs of being sexually abused.

Consider getting help for yourself if you:

- Were sexually abused or think you may have been, and have never talked to a counselor or doctor about it.
- Feel at risk of having sexual contact with your child.

You are the expert when it comes to your family and child. If you have a concern, trust your instinct and find someone trained to help you: health care providers, early intervention teams, mental health professionals, parent educators and consultants, or telephone help-line staff. Think about talking it over with friends and family, too. You don't need to worry alone! Turn to "Finding Help in Your Community" on page 4 to learn about finding help near you.

More Help and Information

Books for Parents

- *Beyond the Birds and the Bees: Fostering Your Child's Healthy Sexual Development* by Beverly Engel. Pocket Books, 1997.
- *How to Talk to Your Child About Sex: It's Best to Start Early, But It's Never Too Late — A Step-By-Step Guide for Every Age* by Linda Eyre and Richard M. Eyre. Golden Books, 1998.
- *Questions Children Ask and How to Answer Them* by Miriam Stoppard. DK Publishing, 1997.
- *When Sex Is the Subject* by Pamela M. Wilson. Network Publications, 1991.

National Organizations

- Sexuality Information and Education Council of the United States (SIECUS)
  212-819-9770, Fax: 212-819-9776
  E-mail: siecus@siecus.org
  Web site: www.siecus.org.

Sharing

Description

Sharing is dividing things between people, taking turns, lending possessions, or borrowing from someone else. When children divide a group of toys so that each have some to play with or they play together with something like a truck or doll, they are sharing.

Realistic Expectations

- Sharing is a set of skills that takes many years to learn, and involves:
    - Understanding that things are separate from you.
    - A sense of future time, in order to understand that you will get your possessions back at a later date.
    - Trust that the person really will give it back.
    - Understanding what another person feels, or empathy.
    - Ability to express wishes, feelings, desires, needs.
- The rate that children develop sharing skills varies, but typically, between the ages of eighteen months and two years, they begin to see things as separate from themselves. Even then, children may believe they are giving away a part of themselves if they have to give up one of their things.
- Understanding ownership is one of the first steps in learning to share. Children need to experience possessing things before they can understand the concept of sharing. When children say "Mine!" they are just beginning to understand ownership—at around age two.
- It is normal for children to be protective of their things. Deciding who can and can't use their things is a way for children to feel in control of a small part of their world.
- Children sometimes grab things from one another because they don't have the language skills to express themselves yet.
- Children may have a harder time sharing when:
    - Self-esteem is low and they may use ownership of things to feel good about themselves.
    - Moving, divorce, or other stresses are taking place.
    - Jealous of a sibling.
    - Intense by nature.
    - Forced to share (many experts agree: forcing a child may actually delay learning to share).
- Children often have a harder time sharing with siblings than with friends, because they are also competing with siblings for parental attention.
- Children who live in a home where cooperation and sharing is practiced by the adults will be more likely to learn to share.

Approaches

Help your child understand what ownership means, and help him sort out which things belong to him. At eighteen months or two years, your child is just beginning to understand that he possesses things of his own, but it may not be clear to him yet which things are his and which belong to someone else. Help him understand ownership by talking with him about what belongs to whom in your home: "I noticed that you are playing with your sister's toothbrush that has a duck on it. Here is your toothbrush with the big yellow bird on it."

—Ideas found in "One for You, One for Me" by Marie Faust Evitt, *Child*, March 1998.

Talk about what sharing means, show your child what sharing looks like, and praise any effort by your child to share. Point out to your child when you share with him: "I'm going to have a peach, but I'll give you some. That's sharing. I like sharing my peach with you." Then when a child offers to share with you or a friend, be sure to notice it: "It made your friend happy when you gave him half of the blocks. That's great that you are sharing!"

—Ideas found in *1,2,3—The Toddler Years* by Irene Van der Zande with Santa Cruz Toddler CareCenter Staff, The Center, 1986.

Avoid coercing or forcing him to share; he won't be able to do much sharing at early ages. Don't worry about it! To teach your child to share:

- Practice sharing through play: try picking out a toy, doll, or animal, and give it to your child. Ask your child if you can have the toy again. After he masters this, ask him to give you one of his toys. Keep it in his view while you play with it very briefly, then give it back.
- Allow your child to pick out a few special toys that he never has to share. Avoid having him bring these toys to preschool or day care, where he may be expected to share them.

—Ideas found in *Toddlers and Preschoolers* by Lawrence Kutner, William Morrow, 1994.

Encourage a child to ask for something that he wants instead of grabbing it. Part of sharing is learning to negotiate for things that you want. Ask your child to use words: "May I use that crayon please?" Let a child know that you have confidence that he can use words and work things out.

—Ideas found in "Learning to Share" by Nancy Seid, *Parents*, July 1998.

Help your child learn to share:

- Ask children to take turns with toys that they both want to use. Set a timer and explain that when the timer goes off it is time for the next turn.
- Put away some toys that have proven too difficult to share.
- Make sure that your child gets to go first sometimes, but also second sometimes, in turn taking. Also, make sure that sometimes your child has the first choice of something you share, and sometimes he doesn't.

Learning to share means showing what sharing looks like, how it works, and what is fair for everyone.

—Ideas found in *Parenting Works! Facilitator's Guide* (MELD), Blue Penguin, 1996.

Always ask your child first, before lending one of his toys or possessions to another. If you give a child this courtesy about his things, he may be more likely to share in the future and less likely to be possessive about his things—because he will know that his ownership is respected.

—Ideas found in *What to Expect the Toddler Years* by Arlene Eisenberg, Heidi E. Murkoff, and Sandee E. Hathaway Workman Pub., 1994.

Express your wishes about sharing, without blaming your child for being selfish. Try encouraging a child to share by telling him how it makes you feel when he doesn't—and what you would like to see instead: "You don't seem to be using the green paint right now. I feel bad when you won't let Juwan have it. I'd really like it if you would let him have it for a few minutes and then you can trade colors with him." Helping your child to share can show him the benefits of sharing; but calling him selfish, or getting mad at him when he doesn't share, will only make him feel that there is something wrong with him.

> —Ideas found in *Positive Discipline A-Z* (revised and expanded 2nd edition) by Jane Nelsen, Lynn Lott, and H. Stephen Glenn, Prima, 1999.

Avoid fights and conflicts over sharing toys, by planning ahead. When your child plays with a friend or sibling, consider providing:

- Enough toys so that children don't need to compete to get one.
- A good variety of toys.
- More than one of some inexpensive toys: dolls, cars, and stuffed animals.

> —Ideas found in *Pathways To Play* by Sandra Heidemann, and Deborah Hewitt, Redleaf Press, 1992.

When sharing becomes too difficult, offer your child a choice about sharing. After you have allowed your child to put away special things, and talked about what things are to be shared, he still may have trouble taking turns or sharing things. Offer your child a choice between taking turns and sharing or not playing with the toy or friend for awhile.

> —Ideas found in *Positive Parenting From A to Z* by Karen Renshaw Joslin, Fawcett Columbine: Ballantine Books, 1994.

Teach your child the concept of half, to help him understand sharing. Show how one thing can be made into enough for two by giving half to each:

- Show how splitting one whole pizza in half makes two pieces that can be shared between two people.
- Show how pouring half a can of a drink into one glass and the other half into another glass makes two glasses of something to drink.
- Ask your child for his ideas on how to make one thing into enough for two, or how to share one whole thing.
- Draw pictures together of whole things that people can eat and share. Then, outline or cut the whole into pieces to see how the whole can be divided and shared.
- Bake or cook something together, and show how to measure halves: half a cup, half a teaspoon, half of a lemon, half of an onion.
- Take a look at things around you and talk about how they can be shared or split in half: chairs, juice, apples, a group of toy animals.

> —Ideas found in *Give Me Half!* (MathStart series) by Stuart J. Murphy, HarperCollins, 1996.

Help your child understand sharing by reading more about it:

The Doorbell Rang by Pat Hutchins

Give Me Half! by Stuart J. Murphy

Me First by Helen Lester

Oh, Bother! Someone Won't Share by Betty Birney

One of Each by Mary Ann Hoberman

Rabbit and Hare Divide an Apple by Harriet Ziefert

When to Get More Help

Children typically grow and learn new skills in their own time and at their own pace within the wide range of what is normal. Sometimes, children need a bit of extra help to keep their development on track, or to stay healthy and happy. Sometimes, parents need help providing for a child's needs or sorting out the best approaches to parenting.

Consider getting help for your child if he:

- Does not show some ability to share by four years of age.

You are the expert when it comes to your family and child. If you have a concern, trust your instinct and find someone trained to help you: health care providers, early intervention teams, mental health professionals, parent educators and consultants, or telephone help-line staff. Consider talking it over with friends and family, too. You don't need to worry alone! Turn to "Finding Help in Your Community" on page 4 to learn about finding help near you.

More Help and Information

Books for Parents

- "Sharing" in *Positive Parenting From A to Z* by Karen Renshaw Joslin. Fawcett Columbine: Ballantine Books, 1994.
- "What Enables Children to Share" in *Becoming The Parent You Want To Be* by Laura Davis and Janis Keyser, Broadway Books, 1997.

Videos

- *Five Lionni Classics: The Animal Fables of Leo Lionni.* Random House Home Video.
- *Learning to Share.* Children's Television Workshop.

Web Sites

- "Social Studies" by Debra Kent. Online. ParentTime. Available: www.parenttime.com

Siblings

"Me & My Brother"
by Jakob, age 5

Description

Siblings are brothers and sisters. Siblings may live together or apart, may come from the same parents or not, may be the same or different genders, may be twins, multiples, or separated in age by many years. All siblings are individual people with unique, distinct personalities who share love and rivalry.

Realistic Expectations

- Siblings grow and develop at their own rate, each different from the other. Siblings, even twins or multiples can look, act, and behave in different or similar ways, and develop at different rates.
- Siblings tend to get along better when:
    - They each feel they are loved equally.
    - Their parents have a good relationship.
    - They experience a sense of belonging in the family.
    - They each get attention from parent(s).
- Jealousy of a new baby, which is normal, tends to be strongest for siblings who are between eighteen months and three years. Children feel that their family has been invaded and feel a loss of time and attention from parents.
- Just before or after the birth of a new baby is not the best time to make any big changes in children's routines. Switching from a crib to a bed, toilet training, moving, or starting a new school may be overwhelming and difficult for young children while they are adjusting to the major change of a new sibling entering the family.
- Children may not realize that the new baby is going to live with them forever or that their parents are the baby's parents, too.
- Ambivalence toward siblings is typical. It is common for siblings to be fighting one minute and be comforting the next.
- It is common for parents to prefer one sibling over another depending on ages, interests, abilities, and temperament. It is also common for these preferences to change over time as the children grow and change.
- Parents tend to have high expectations, show more affection, and be more strict in their discipline with first-born children.
- Comparing and labeling siblings, favorably or unfavorably, usually causes resentment. Children can sense when they are being compared to a sibling, whether it is openly expressed or not.
- Siblings argue and fight for many reasons:
    - Jealousy (some children feel that their sibling is liked or loved more).
    - Too much togetherness (some children have a lower tolerance for spending lots of time with a sibling).

- Independence (some younger children argue to prove their independence from older siblings).
- Possessiveness of things (children want control over their own things and argue or fight when that control is threatened).
- Temperament (children with differing temperaments may have more trouble getting along together— certain combinations of temperaments may not be a good match).
- Lacking the skills needed to share, compromise, control impulses, and negotiate.

- Siblings who are punished for actions related to the other sibling may come to resent their sibling and blame the sibling for the punishment.
- The sibling relationship is often the one constant connection that people have in their lives, from the beginning to the end of life. Helping young children foster good, positive sibling relationships can bring about many years of love, support, and belonging.

Approaches

Love each child unconditionally for who they are. Help siblings see that, although they are different, they are loved and appreciated for the unique things that make each of them special.

> —Ideas found in *Positive Discipline A-Z* (revised and expanded 2nd edition) by Jane Nelsen, Lynn Lott, and H. Stephen Glenn, Prima, 1999.

Prepare your child for the arrival of a new baby:
- Tell a child about a new baby on the way three or four months before the birth, which is a more manageable amount of time for a toddler or preschooler to anticipate an event than seven or nine months. Don't wait until you run the risk of the child hearing about the baby from someone else, but try not to tell a young child too early.
- Encourage questions and answer them in an age-appropriate way. Tell him the correct words for body parts: "uterus," not "tummy."
- Avoid telling the child how he will feel: "You're going to love having a baby sister!"
- Talk about what it will be like when the baby comes, stressing the positives of being an older child, but don't paint too rosy of a picture of what a new baby is like. Help him realize that it will be a long time before a baby can become a playmate.
- Take the child along on prenatal doctor's visits.
- Let him feel the baby kicking.
- Sign your child up for an age-appropriate sibling preparation class; classes are often available at the hospital for free. Show him the hospital where the baby will be born and take a tour if one is offered.
- Ask the child to pick out a name for the baby.
- Let him help pick out a new toy for the baby and prepare the baby's room and equipment.
- Show him pictures of when he was a baby and tell him your happy memories. Remind him how much he has learned to do and how competent he is.

Although there is no fool-proof method for preparing your child for the arrival of a new sibling, you can help him understand what will happen.

> —Ideas found in *Loving Each One Best* by Nancy Samalin, Bantam Books, 1996.

If your child is about to become a sibling, avoid pressuring him to grow up faster, act older than his age, or act younger than his age. Reassure him that you love him just the way he is. By understanding what is typical for children at that age and parenting him accordingly, you can avoid some of the bad feelings he may have about the new baby if he is expected to act either older or younger than he is.

—Ideas found in *Parenting Works! Facilitator's Guide* (MELD), Blue Penguin, 1996.

Accept that each child needs attention, and tell your children that is alright to ask for it. Siblings may squabble less if each child feels a sense of belonging. Help each child see that attention comes in many forms: help in making her bed, reading a book together, taking a walk together, a pat on the back, or a kiss. Tell her that you enjoy her company or having her in your family. Giving each child time, and talking about how much each of them means to you, helps them feel a sense of belonging.

Show your children how they also get attention from other people: caregivers, neighbors, relatives, friends, and even people you know who work in stores, libraries, or parks that you visit often. Teach your children about appropriate ways to ask for attention, and talk about when you can or can't give it to them. Grabbing a toy away from a sibling is not OK, but asking you to help color a picture is. Be sure to respond to their requests for attention when they ask in appropriate ways.

—Ideas found in *Help! The Kids Are at It Again* by Elizabeth Crary, Parenting Press, 1997.

Teach each child how to get along with and be responsible for their sibling; it's one of the most important things that you can help them learn. Instead of trying to avoid, prevent, or cure sibling rivalry, teach children to share and to help each other. From this they will learn to feel responsible for a sibling, the family and for others.

—Ideas found in *Touchpoints* by T. Berry Brazelton, Addison-Wesley, 1992.

Help each child express their jealous feelings instead of trying to make the feelings disappear. Your children can learn an important life lesson in acknowledging and dealing with jealousy. If they are taught to deal with feelings now, they may be better at dealing with competition and jealousy as an adult. Give your children words and actions to help them take control of their feelings: "I can see that you are mad at your brother. Instead of hitting, see if you can touch him gently to stop him from taking your toy."

—Ideas found in *Dr. Spock's Baby and Child Care* (7th edition) by Benjamin Spock and Stephen J. Parker, Dutton, 1998.

Nurture the sibling relationship by showing both children the many roles that they can play with their sibling:

- Give an older child some responsibility (an amount that is appropriate for her age) for a younger child, and encourage her to be a caregiver.
- Encourage your child to teach her sibling about something that she is good at.
- Encourage both siblings to comfort and care for the other when the body or feelings are hurt.
- Consider giving the siblings a job that requires teamwork to complete, so they both learn the value of working together.

—Ideas found in "Peaceable Siblings" by William and Martha Sears, Online at ParentTime: www.parenttime.com.

Foster a good sibling relationship with positive measures:

- Notice and comment when siblings are getting along well or working together to complete a task. Emphasize that families work together and care for each other.

- Look at your significant relationship and make sure that you are showing siblings a positive example in your life.

- Avoid showing favoritism or comparing siblings. Instead, talk about how you could do things better to get along.

- Find time for both children and help them understand what makes them special.

Children who feel good about themselves, see a positive example, and learn the skills to deal with things they don't like, will have the start of a positive relationship with a sibling.

> —Ideas found in "He Started It!" by Lisa Connors McDonough, *Child*, December/January 1998.

Instead of punishing a sibling for hurting her younger brother or sister, consider helping her solve the problem that made her angry in the first place. Listen to what your child is telling you about why she hurt her sibling. Show her you understand: "I see that you got very angry when your sister knocked down the tower that you built. It can be very frustrating to work on something and have someone else knock it down."

Next, tell your child how you feel about it: "It makes me feel bad to see either of you get hurt or pushed." Enlist your child's help in finding a solution, and consider making a list of options to try instead of pushing, hitting, or fighting. Listen to all the ideas without criticizing, even the ideas that involve taking the sibling back to the hospital where she came from. Come to an agreement on some final solutions.

Give your child words and actions that she can use to avoid conflict with her sibling: "If you see your sister about to knock something down, you can gently stop her hand and say, 'I'm not done with this yet. You can have some of these other blocks to stack and knock down if you want.'" Be sure to tell your child that if none of the solutions work, she can always ask you for help.

> —Ideas found in *Siblings Without Rivalry* (10th edition) by Adele Faber and Elaine Mazlish, Avon Books, 1998.

Help your child see that it's OK for an older or younger sibling to play differently. Differences in ages can mean differences in abilities, attention span, and physical strength. Emphasize the playing instead of the outcome. It can be a challenge to find a game or activity for children of different ages, but help siblings learn patience with those who are more advanced in their skills and those who are less skillful. Emphasize the importance of doing your best instead of winning.

> —Ideas found in *101 Activities for Siblings Who Squabble* by Linda Williams Aber, St. Martin's Griffin, 1995.

Give each sibling a turn to be king or queen for a day. To avoid fights over whose turn it is to decide or go first, consider letting each child have a whole day in the week in which she gets to make the decisions, have the first turn, and help choose what to eat.

> —Ideas found in *Practical Parenting Tips* (revised and updated edition) by Vicki Lansky, Meadowbrook Press, 1992.

Help your child understand more about siblings by reading about them together:

Big Help by Anna Grossnickle Hines

Do Like Kyla by Angela Johnson

I Love You the Purplest by Barbara Joosse

Julius, the Baby of the World by Kevin Henkes

The Lapsnatcher by Bruce Coville

My Rotten Redheaded Older Brother by Patricia Polacco

The New Baby at Your House by Joanna Cole

Tell Me Again About the Night I Was Born by Jamie Lee Curtis

Twin Pickle by Ann Doro

We're Very Good Friends, My Brother and I by P.K. Hallinan

When to Get More Help

Children typically grow and learn new skills in their own time and at their own pace within the wide range of what is normal. Sometimes, children need a bit of extra help to keep their development on track, or to stay healthy and happy. Sometimes, parents need help providing for a child's needs or sorting out the best approaches to parenting.

Consider getting help for your child if she:

- Frequently injures, threatens or tries to hurt a sibling.

Consider getting help for yourself if you:

- Frequently label one child as good or bad.
- Frequently compare siblings' behaviors, talents, skills and personalities in front of the children.
- Have an awareness of a strong or intense attraction to one child.

You are the expert when it comes to your family and child. If you have a concern, trust your instinct and find someone trained to help you: health care providers, early intervention teams, mental health professionals, parent educators and consultants, or telephone help-line staff. Consider talking it over with friends and family, too. You don't need to worry alone! Turn to "Finding Help in Your Community" on page 4 to learn about finding help near you.

More Help and Information

Books for Parents

- *101 Activities for Siblings Who Squabble: Projects and Games to Entertain and Keep the Peace* by Linda Williams Aber. St. Martin's Griffin, 1995.

- *And Baby Makes Four: Welcoming a Second Child Into the Family* by Hilory Wagner. Avon Books, 1998.

- *Beyond Sibling Rivalry: How to Help Your Children Become Cooperative, Caring, and Compassionate* by Peter Goldenthal. H. Holt, 1999.

- *From One Child to Two* by Judy Dunn. Ballantine Books, 1995.

- *Help! The Kids Are at It Again* by Elizabeth Crary. Parenting Press, 1997.

- *Loving Each One Best: A Caring and Practical Approach to Raising Siblings* by Nancy Samalin with Catherine Whitney. Bantam Books, 1996.

- *Siblings Without Rivalry: How to Help Your Children Live Together So You Can Live Too* (10th edition) by Adele Faber and Elaine Mazlish. Avon Books, 1998.

- *Welcoming Your Second Baby* by Vicki Lansky. Bantam, 1995.

Videos

- *Arthur's Baby.* Random House/Sony.

- *Hey, What About Me?* Kidvidz.

Sleep

Description

Sleep is a time for the body and mind to get rest. The sleep cycle has two basic states of sleep: active or REM (rapid eye movement) sleep and quiet or NREM (non-rapid eye movement) sleep. Dreaming takes place in active sleep, deep sleep takes place during the quiet state. These two states alternate within sleep cycles that occur throughout a night of sleep. A good night's sleep, or an adequate amount of uninterrupted sleep, is vital to good health. "Sleeping through the night" usually means that children sleep in their beds without calling to a parent during the night; they may actually wake up for brief waking periods between sleep cycles, but can get themselves back to sleep independently.

Realistic Expectations

- Most growth occurs during sleep. Children learn best, feel best, and are the least accident-prone when they are well rested.
- Children have shorter cycles of active and deep sleep than adults, so they have more brief waking periods.
- Typically children and adults wake briefly several times a night as they move between active sleep and deep sleep. Children wake more than adults. Usually, they fall back to sleep without remembering waking up if conditions (pillows, sound, security objects, light, etc.) are the same as when they fell asleep. These conditions are called sleep associations.
- Developing sleep associations is a task that all children need to do at some point to develop healthy sleep patterns for life.
- A fairly regular schedule of waking time, mealtimes, nap time, and bedtime helps to set children's internal body rhythms, one of which is sleep. If the daily schedule varies too much from day to day, sleep patterns will suffer.
- Daytime events may interfere with sound sleep: vacations, changing the clock seasonally, a new baby in the house, or moving.
- Physical conditions and illness may interfere with sleep: colds, allergies, fever, ear infections, intestinal pains, teething, enlarged adenoids and more.
- Half of all children under six will experience some kind of sleep difficulty.
- Children who do not get enough sleep may be difficult to awaken in the morning, frequently irritable, easily frustrated, or may fall asleep during playtime or dinner.

• The physical need for amounts of nighttime sleep and daytime naps changes for children as they grow. Individual needs for sleep will vary, but there are common patterns:

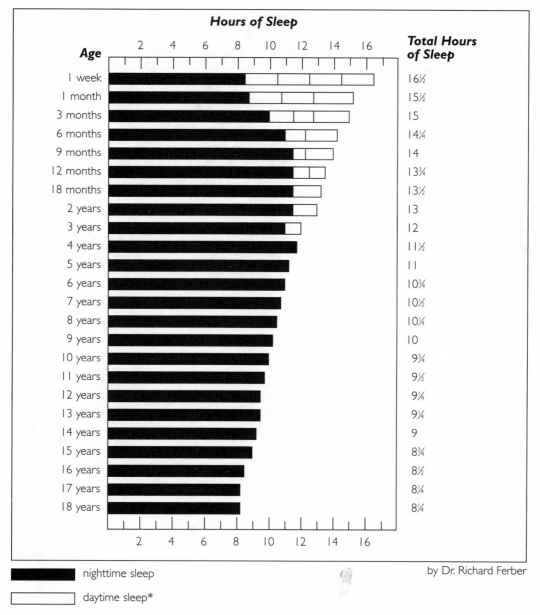

Hours of Sleep

Age	Total Hours of Sleep
1 week	16½
1 month	15½
3 months	15
6 months	14¼
9 months	14
12 months	13¾
18 months	13½
2 years	13
3 years	12
4 years	11½
5 years	11
6 years	10¾
7 years	10½
8 years	10¼
9 years	10
10 years	9¾
11 years	9½
12 years	9¼
13 years	9¼
14 years	9
15 years	8¾
16 years	8½
17 years	8¼
18 years	8¼

■ nighttime sleep

□ daytime sleep*

by Dr. Richard Ferber

*Divided into typical number of naps per day. Length of naps may be quite variable.

—Reprinted with the permission of Simon & Schuster from *How to Solve Your Child's Sleep Problems* by Richard Ferber. Copyright © 1985 by Richard Ferber, M.D.

Sleep

- Children may give up naps as early as two years of age. Still, they will need a rest period in the afternoon for approximately one hour to read or play quietly.
- Normal developmental tasks will affect sleep:
  - Separation issues peak typically at twelve months, and reoccur periodically after that. Children may not want parents to leave the room at bedtime or naptime.
  - Power struggles are common from eighteen months on, as children express their independence. Children may resist going to sleep or bed.
  - Nightmares and fears of the dark, imaginary monsters, and other real things are especially strong for children between the ages of two and six. Children may need extra reassurance at bedtime or during the night.
  - Children may show an occasional preference for comfort from one parent over another. Bedtime routines may be more difficult for the other parent during those times.
  - Children are going through so many developmental changes from one to five years of age that they actually may practice new challenges in their sleep. Children may wake more frequently in the night during times of developmental leaps.
  - Children are excited about life, so they may have a hard time making the transition from fun-filled days to quiet naps or bedtime.
- Healthy sleep habits are learned skills. When parents value healthy sleep and teach good habits, children are likely to continue those habits into their adult life.

Approaches

Many experts agree:

There are a wide variety of beliefs, styles and approaches to helping your child learn to sleep. They range from having your whole family sleep together in the same bed to letting your child cry herself to sleep in another room. Still, there are many things that many experts do agree on about sleep:

- *Follow a fairly regular schedule of waking time, nap times, and bedtime.*

- *Consider the amount of food and drink you offer. Too much or too little food and drink throughout the day and before bedtime can disturb sleep. If your child drinks too much liquid before bedtime, she will awaken from the urge to urinate or from a wet diaper. If she is hungry she will awaken early. Provide your child with balanced meals and snacks on a fairly regular schedule during the day, then trust that she does not need any feeding in the night. Keep a bedtime drink of water at your child's bedside each night if it comforts her.*

- *Encourage exercise. A child without enough exercise during the day will have a difficult time winding down at night.*

- *Provide a calming, consistent and reassuring bedtime ritual or routine; it is important from birth on. It should be long enough to ease a transition from a busy day to a quiet night, but should also be time limited. One to five year olds thrive on routines, taking great comfort from them. An example of a ritual would be taking a bath, having a snack, brushing teeth, reading two books, singing a song and then turning the lights out. Another example would be simply to read one book, talk about the day, and say goodnight.*

- *Help your child attach to a security object such as a special blanket, stuffed animal, or a piece of your clothing. These things may ease her transition to bed and sleep, by giving her something to hold for comfort.*

- *Avoid television before bedtime. It can create fears or excite your child.*

- *Do not let your child fall asleep with a bottle. It can cause severe decaying of the teeth.*

- *If you are trying to change sleep habits, give a new sleep approach a fair trial of a week or two. Don't change your approach in the middle of the night.*

- *Check for simple things first if your child has trouble falling asleep or is wakeful during the night:*

  - *Room temperature. Rooms that are too hot or too cold can wake children. Adjust room temperatures and bedtime clothing accordingly.*

  - *Noise. Noises inside and outside the home or apartment can wake your child. White noise such as a fan or radio static may be helpful for some children to block out noise. Some children are soothed by the sound of soft radio music or household noise outside their door, others are disturbed by it.*

  - *Light. The amount of light that children want in their rooms, or that they can tolerate is individual. Some prefer darkness, others prefer night-lights. Experiment to learn what works for your child. If you have a consistently early riser, or are having difficulty getting your child to sleep before dark or at naptime, consider room-darkening shades to block window light.*

- *When children awaken during the night due to illness, a nightmare, or other fears, they need and deserve your love, attention, and reassurance.*

Encourage your child to learn to comfort herself to sleep, but give her the support and encouragement she needs to do so. Decide clearly on a program before you begin. Review your child's daytime schedule and sleep needs, to be sure you have appropriate expectations. After a bedtime ritual and settling your child in for the night with a blanket or special toy, pat her soothingly, say goodnight, and reassure her that she can go to sleep on her own. Leave the room.

If she cries, go to her, give her a pat of encouragement, and leave the room again. Be as unexciting as you can, and do not pick her up. Soothe her with your hand briefly, but leave her in her crib or bed.

After a period of going to her each time, begin to stay out of her room. Just call to her with reassurance from down the hall. Finally, let her give it her best try alone by waiting at least fifteen minutes before going in for the first time or for subsequent times. Eventually, she will learn her own methods of self-comfort.

—Ideas found in *Touchpoints* by T. Berry Brazelton, Addison-Wesley, 1992.

Let your child achieve independent sleep associations, but comfort her on a specific planned schedule. After five or six months of age, your goal should be to help your child learn to fall asleep alone, without being held, rocked, nursed, or using a bottle or pacifier. To help her, you must be out of your child's room when she falls asleep.

After a bedtime ritual, say goodnight and leave the room. If she cries wait for five minutes, then go to her. Take one or two minutes to calm her with a word or two, or a pat of reassurance, then leave the room. If she continues to cry, wait 10 minutes and return for the same brief reassurance and leave the room. Then go to her every 15 minutes briefly, as above, until she falls asleep. Each night, add five minutes onto the intervals:

Days	Minutes between reassuring visits
1	5, 10, 15, 15, 15, until asleep.
2	10, 15, 20, 20, 20, until asleep.
3	15, 20, 25, 25, 25, until asleep.
If needed, keep adding five minutes per day to the above schedule until the child masters falling asleep on her own.	

By the seventh day your child will most likely be sleeping very well.

—Ideas found in *Solve Your Child's Sleep Problems* by Richard Ferber, M.D., Simon and Schuster, 1985.

Sleep together as a family, or in a "family bed." Children are less able than adults to handle nighttime upsets, so they need their parents to be available during the night. Sleep sharing, or sharing your bed with your child, is one way of developing trust and a connection to her. It also helps her to develop a healthy sleep attitude and an understanding that sleep is a pleasant state to enter.

The benefits of sharing a bed with your child can be a harmonious relationship and sound sleep for all. However, family bed is not for everyone. Be prepared that the age most children will seek independence and ask to have their own bed is two to three years. If either parent is uncomfortable with this arrangement, it should be discussed and resolved, or discontinued.

—Ideas found in *The Discipline Book* by William Sears, M.D., Little, Brown and Company, 1995.

Sleeping together in a bed as a family does not have to be an all-or-none-proposition. Try a variation with your young child:

- Let your child sleep on a mattress, futon, or sleeping bag in your room.
- Let your child start out in her bed, but tell her she is welcome to come into your bed during the night.
- Let your child fall asleep in your bed, but tell her you will carry her into her own bed when she falls asleep.
- Let her sleep in bed with a sibling.
- Get into bed with your child in her bed until she falls asleep.
- Set times when your child may come into your bed: morning cuddling everyday, when she is sick, or weekend family times.

> —Ideas found in *Getting Your Child To Sleep... and Back to Sleep* by Vicki Lansky, The Book Peddlers, 1991.

Make a clear decision to live with a sleep problem for a certain period of time. There are many good reasons why you might decide to temporarily live with your child's current sleep situation even if it is a problem. If your life is or will soon be in upheaval, if any family member is ill, if you feel your child is in a fragile state or a developmental leap, or if you simply don't feel ready to take on the challenge, you can decide to put off a change until you and your child are ready.

> —Ideas found in *The Sleep Book for Tired Parents* by Rebecca Huntley, Parenting Press, 1991.

If your child learns how to climb out of her crib, make sure she is safe, and then try some things to encourage her to stay in her crib if it is not yet time for her to move to a bed. When your child figures out how to get out of her crib, you can try other things before moving her to a bed right away. Some children try to climb out of their cribs as early as eighteen months of age, others won't even try until they are at least two and a half. Some never do. First remove any dangers that exist if she climbs out again: put pillows on the floor and move nearby pieces of furniture and cords. Then try different things until one works to help her to stay put:

- Move her crib mattress to the lowest setting.
- Take out all of the bumpers and large toys in the crib.
- Don't give her a reward for climbing out of her crib by giving her attention for it.
- Be firm and tell her, "No climbing!" This may be more effective if you can catch her before she is successful at climbing out.
- If all else fails, lower her side bar and put a stool nearby so she can easily climb in and out without a fall. If your child is likely to start wandering around the house, consider putting up a gate at her bedroom door, or putting a bell on it to alert you.

> —Ideas found in *Sleeping Through the Night* by Jodi A. Mindell, HarperPerennial, 1997.

If your child won't stay in her bedroom at night, encourage her to stay put:

- Show her how to use a special doll or stuffed animal (the bigger the better) for comfort instead of looking for you.
- Leave a night-light on in her room.
- Leave a radio on at low volume in her room.
- Offer her books or quiet toys to play with in her bed at bedtime.
- Explain that grown-up time begins after her bedtime so she needs to stay in bed.

- Play a story or lullabies on a cassette tape in her room.
- Leave her door open and her light on in the hall.
- Ask her what she needs to help her to stay in bed.
- As long as she stays in her room, don't insist that she stay in bed. You can move her into bed later.
- Get her a new sleeping bag to sleep in on her bed, or some new sheets.

> —From *Help! For Parents of Children from Birth to Five*, a collection of ideas from parents, edited by Jean Illsley Clarke, HarperSanFrancisco, 1993.

Help her to feel comfortable at bedtime and to look forward to it:

- Put her pajamas in the clothes dryer for a few minutes to warm them and make them cozy (make sure they are not too hot before she jumps into them).
- Set up an aquarium with a light to use as a night light and for her to watch as she drifts off to sleep.
- Tell her to think very hard about something she would like to dream about.
- Use a baby monitor in reverse: let her listen to *you* after she is in bed.
- Sit just outside her door doing something quiet as she drifts off to sleep: read a book, balance your checkbook, or match socks.
- Leave a sport or bicycle water bottle filled with water by her bedside for her to use during the night.
- Let her listen to a story tape with an accompanying book, or a tape of you or another favorite person reading or telling a story.

> —Ideas found in *I Heard It Through The Playground*, by Joel Fram, Carol Boswell, and Margaret Mass, HarperPerennial, 1993.

Learn to tell the difference between night terrors and nightmares, and how to help your child during each one:

Nightmares are bad dreams. Your child may cry and seem frightened, but is easily awakened. She may be afraid to go back to sleep, fearing that the dream will come back. Handle nightmares by comforting your child: hug her, tell her she had a bad dream, tell her she is safe, and stay with her until she is calm. Follow your child's lead about whether she wants to talk about the dream; some children do and some don't, and many under five can't.

Night terrors are incomplete awakenings between sleep cycles. She may seem frightened or upset: crying, moaning, talking, kicking, thrashing, or sitting up. She may appear both asleep and awake at the same time, or appear completely awake, look right at you, but not seem to recognize you. Typically she settles back to sleep, and she will not remember a thing the next morning. Handle a night terror by staying nearby, but simply let it run its course. Do not try to wake her up or ask her questions the next day about it; doing either may just make her feel uncomfortable or confused.

> —Ideas found in *Keys To Children's Sleep Problems* by Susan E. Gottlieb, Barrons Educational Series Inc., 1993.

If your child who is younger than five years still wets the bed, understand that it probably is not a cause for concern. In children under five years, bedwetting is typically not a cause for concern, and will eventually resolve itself. However, if your child has been dry at night for several months and then begins wetting, talk to her health care provider.

> —Ideas found in *American Academy of Pediatrics Guide To Your Child's Symptoms*, Villard, 1997.

Use bedtime as an opportunity to create closeness with your child by taking time to talk.

- Talk about the past: "Remember when…." (we went camping, we brought your baby brother home, we rode on the train).
- Ask her questions about her day: "What was the best thing that happened to you? What was the worst thing? What was the funniest thing?"
- Tell each other things that you love about each other.

—Ideas from "Bedtime Without Struggling" by Kathryn Kvols and Helen Hall, Online, Positive Parenting On-line!, Available: www.positiveparenting.com/bedtime.html.

Use bedtime as an opportunity to listen to quiet music:

♫ *A Child's Celebration of Lullaby*. Music For Little People.

♫ *The Planet Sleeps*. Sony Wonder.

♫ *The Sun is Low Upon the Lake*. Lyric Partners.

Help your child understand more about sleep by reading about it together:

A Bedtime Story by Mem Fox

The Boy Who Wouldn't Go To Bed by Helen Cooper

A Good Night's Sleep by Allan Fowler

Can't You Sleep, Little Bear? By Martin Waddell

Can't Sleep by Chris Raschka

Good Night Moon by Margaret Wise Brown

Hush!: A Thai Lullaby by Minfong Ho

Some Sleep Standing Up by Susan Stockdale

Sleep, Sleep, Sleep: A Lullaby for Little Ones Around the World by Nancy Van Laan

Sweet Dreams by Sue Porter

Tell Me Something Happy Before I Go To Sleep by Joyce Dunbar

Ten, Nine, Eight by Molly Bang

Time for Bed by Mem Fox

Time To Sleep by Denise Fleming

When to Get More Help

Children typically grow and learn new skills in their own time and at their own pace within the wide range of what is normal. Sometimes, children need a bit of extra help to keep their development on track, or to stay healthy and happy. Sometimes, parents need help providing for a child's needs or sorting out the best approaches to parenting.

Consider getting help for your child if she:

- Has nightmares or night terrors for more than one month, that increase in frequency or intensity, that are accompanied by daytime fears, or that frequently disrupt her sleep patterns.
- Still has sleep problems after you have tried an approach faithfully for one month or longer.
- Is very sensitive and becomes upset over whatever you do to try to help her get to sleep.
- Shows any signs of a medical problem or physical condition that you think might be interfering with her sleep.
- Continues to wet the bed beyond age five or starts wetting the bed after months of dryness.

Consider getting help for yourself if you:

- Have difficulty following through with a sleep plan once you create one.
- Are being affected negatively by her sleep habits: exhaustion, anger, disagreements with a spouse, etc.

You are the expert when it comes to your family and child. If you have a concern, trust your instinct and find someone trained to help you: health care providers, early intervention teams, mental health professionals, parent educators and consultants, or telephone help-line staff. Think about talking it over with friends and family, too. You don't need to worry alone! Turn to "Finding Help in Your Community" on page 4 to learn about finding help near you.

More Help and Information

Books for Parents

- *Getting Your Child To Sleep—And Back To Sleep: Tips for Parents of Infants, Toddlers and Preschoolers* by Vicki Lansky. The Book Peddlers, 1991
- *Keys To Children's Sleep Problems* by Susan E. Gottlieb. Barrons Educational Series, 1993.
- *Sleep: How To Teach Your Child to Sleep Like a Baby* by Tamara Eberlein. Pocket Books, 1996.
- *Sleeping Through the Night: How Infants, Toddlers, and Their Parents Can Get a Good Night's Sleep* by Jodi A. Mindell. HarperPerennial, 1997.
- *Solve Your Child's Sleep Problems* by Richard Ferber. Simon and Schuster, 1985.
- *The Family Bed* by Tine Thevenin. Avery Publishing Group, 1987
- *The Sleep Book for Tired Parents* by Rebecca Huntley. Parenting Press, 1991.

Articles, Pamphlets, and Booklets

- "Sleep Problems in Children: Guidelines for Parents." Call or write: American Academy of Pediatrics, Div of Publications, 800-433-9016, Fax: 847-228-1281 Web site: www.aap.org
- "Solved! The Mysteries of Toddler Naps" by Nancy Kalish. *Parenting*, August 1998. Also available online at ParentTime: www.parenttime.com (on the home page, type "naps" in the "what are you looking for" box, then scroll down to title).

Video

- *Good Night Baby, Baby Good Night*. Company Company Partners.
- *Sweet Dreams, Spot*. Disney.

Web Sites

- Sleep Net (with links to more than 130 sleep information sites): www.sleepnet.com

Special Needs—
Finding Help and Support

Description

Children with special needs include those with: hearing, speech, language, vision, orthopedic, or other health impairments, developmental disabilities, serious emotional disturbances, autism, traumatic brain injuries, and learning disabilities. Children with special needs are more like typically developing children than they are different from them, but sometimes benefit from extra help and support. There are a wide variety of services available to help you and your family.

Realistic Expectations

- Each year approximately 750,000 newborns may have or be at risk for having disabilities that will significantly affect their physical or mental development, according to the American Academy of Pediatrics.

- Infants, toddlers, and preschoolers who have a disability or who have delayed development may be eligible for a variety of services that support families as they help their children grow, such as home visits, preschool classes, occupational therapy, physical therapy, speech therapy, respite services, mental health services, medical coverage, or social security benefits.

- A "free, appropriate, and public education" is a federally mandated right of children of all ages with disabilities. The Education for All Handicapped Children Act, known as EHA, and the Individuals with Disabilities Education Act (IDEA) and Public Law 99-457 mandate that states must make an effort to find, evaluate, support and educate children with disabilities from birth throughout childhood.

Approaches

If you are concerned that your child may have a disability, your child has a right to a *free evaluation* to determine if he is eligible for early intervention or special education and related special services; this is available to *any* child. Usually the evaluation is done by a team of professionals which may include a psychologist, social worker, teacher, nurse, occupational therapist, speech therapist, and/or physical therapist. A typical evaluation includes some developmental testing, and then reviewing those results and many different pieces of information:

- Your child's medical history.
- Observations and feedback from all members of the evaluation team, including parents.
- Any other important observations, records, and/or reports about your child.

To request an evaluation for children birth to five years, talk to your pediatrician, public health department, school district, or contact the National Information Center for Children and Youth with Disabilities (NICHCY) to find out about services for your child in your area.

> —From "A Parent's Guide: Accessing Programs for Infants, Toddlers, and Preschoolers With Disabilities," National Information Center for Children and Youth with Disabilities, 1994.

Special Needs—Finding Help and Support

If you have asked for an assessment of your child, become part of the team. A developmental assessment is a way of learning about your child's capabilities, and to determine if there is a need to give him extra help to reach his potential. If you have requested an assessment:

- Share your wisdom about your child; your expertise is being the parent and knowing your child better than anyone else. Your gut feelings and personal observations count.

- Make use of other team members' expertise; their job is to help you and your family.

- Don't worry about learning all the technical terms; these can be defined for you. Explaining in your terms what is going on with your child is fine and will be understood by everyone.

- Don't be afraid to disagree; if professionals see your child differently than you, ask for more discussion. Tell the team what parts seem inaccurate about your child.

- Designate a partner to bring to meetings: a spouse, friend or family member. The support person can help take notes, keep track of information, and review the discussion with you later.

- Make sure your own needs are met. Spending time on a process that misses what you are concerned about delays your ability to help your child. Make your needs clear.

> —From "Tips for Surviving Your Child's Developmental Assessment," Online, Zero to Three: National Center for Infants, Toddlers, and Families: www.zerotothree.org.

If your child is identified as qualifying for special services, know your rights and responsibilities in his special education process. You have very specific rights to participate in the educational decision-making process about your child. Many organizations have information to help guide you through the special education process. Since specific criteria and procedures used by school districts vary, it is important to familiarize yourself with the information provided by state and local agencies. Your local school district's director of special education and his or her staff may be helpful in finding such information and guiding you through the process.

Additional resources are available from national disability organizations. Some of them may have state and local chapters near you. All states now have federally supported parent information and training centers, which provide information and advocacy services.

As your child progresses through educational systems, knowing and following through on your rights and responsibilities ensures that you are a partner with the professionals who will influence your child's future.

> —From "Rights and Responsibilities of Parents of Children With Disabilities," Online, National Parent Information Network, Available: www.npin.org.

Actively participate in your child's special education process. To the extent appropriate, your child should be educated with children who do not have disabilities. A written educational or service plan is a written statement of the program designed to meet your child's unique needs. The plan is called an Individual Education Plan (IEP) for children over three years of age, and Individual Family Service Plan (IFSP) for children birth to 3 years.

Be a good team member:

- Attend all the meetings about your child.

- Learn more about your child's disability.

- Be a good listener. Ask questions.

- Listen to what other people say about your child.

- Share what you know about your child. You are the expert about your child! Tell the team what he likes or does not like, the ways he learns best, and what he does well.

- When you don't agree, talk about it. Look for compromise in ways that are all right for your child and family.

- Know your rights.
- Keep good records of all meetings and conversations. Date them.
- Put requests in writing if you can, and keep copies.

If you have a concern, or if you disagree with the plans for your child, call your service coordinator to request a conference or meeting to resolve your concerns informally. If you can't work out problems this way, call an advocate at your state's parent training and information center. An advocate there will help you decide what you can do and help you learn your rights.

—From "Families are Important: An Early Childhood Guidebook for Families of Young Children with Disabilities" by Maria Anderson, Pacer Center © 1997. www.pacer.org 4826 Chicago Ave. So., Minneapolis, MN 55417; 612-827-2966.

Take some advice from experienced parents:
- Remember that your child is more like other children than unlike them.
- Take time for yourself.
- Help is available: don't be afraid to ask.
- Talk to other parents: join a parents group.
- Trust your gut! You are your child's expert; you know what he needs.

—Excerpt from *After the Tears: Parents Talk About Raising a Child With a Disability* by Robin Simons, copyright © 1987 by The Children's Museum of Denver, Inc., reprinted by permission of Harcourt Brace & Company.

As a pediatric nurse practitioner who works with children, I know that children with special needs move through the same developmental phases and stages as do all children, and that all children have strengths and weaknesses.

As a parent of a child with special needs, I expect a similar journey as all parents, but there is always a tension present. At each intersection along the way, tuning into my awareness of the differences, adjusting my dreams, and allowing time to grieve has been important to me. This adjustment has been like meandering with an unclear destination, rather than following a known paved road.

—Barb, Pediatric Nurse Practitioner and parent, Eden Prairie, MN

Allow yourself to grieve the loss of dreams you had for yourself and your child. Most parents have an image of a child without a disability, and thoughts about their life with that child, long before the child is born. The news of a disability or birth anomaly can be the loss of dreams for you and your family, a loss that needs to be grieved. Here are some suggestions when facing such losses:

- Grieve the loss of dreams. This may be the hardest task, but it is crucial. Stay with your grief, honor the feelings and thoughts you have, don't push them away. Listen to what your grief is telling you. Allow yourself to cry, scream, write, wail, or be quiet.
- Know that you are giving up or altering significant dreams. Be honest about it. Be realistic about your losses. Put things in perspective. Don't let your anger or sadness get in the way of important memories of what was, or tarnish the possibilities for what can yet be.
- Keep dreaming! Do not let the loss of dreams prevent new dreams and possibilities.

- Know that you are not alone. Even though you may think and feel that no one knows what you have experienced, there are ways you can connect and find kindred spirits.

- Build on your support system. Educate your friends, neighbors, and support system about your loss. An act of self-care or self-nurturance on your own behalf, is to say to your friends, "No, I'm not talking about the Down syndrome, the heart problem, or the cancer. I'm talking about *my loss of dreams*. Let me tell you more about it. Are you willing to listen?" You may also want to find a support group, a counselor, or a therapist.

Give yourself permission to grieve, alone or with others. Then, continue dreaming. Dream new dreams that fit with your life now and for the days ahead.

> —Adapted with permission from *Loss of Dreams: A Special Kind of Grief* by Ted Bowman. Copies of this booklet are available for $5.00 from Ted Bowman, 2111 Knapp Street, St. Paul, MN 55108-1814.

Involve friends and relatives with your child with special needs:

- Set the tone. They will take their cues from you: if you talk comfortably about your child, with a sense of humor and a positive attitude, they will be more likely to do the same.

- Give information and take the initiative. Friends may not want to intrude, and you may interpret this as disinterest. Explain what the problem is, what it's like for you, and what you will be doing about it. Tell them what you need, and what helps: special toys, an evening out, a weekend away. Consider having a family meeting, or sending a letter; include brochures about the disability.

- Get them involved: take them to visit your child's programs and to meet other children with disabilities, and to meet and talk with the professionals who are working with him.

- Whenever anyone offers help, accept it.

- Let them know you appreciate them for thinking of you.

- Put yourself in their place. If this had happened to someone else in the family instead of you, what would have helped you to understand and to reach out to them?

- If your friends and relatives are not all that you hoped for them to be, be forgiving and patient with them. They may be clumsy, shy, or uncomfortable; they may hurt your feelings with insensitive remarks. Give them the benefit of the doubt. Just like you, they're new at learning about how to deal with your child's special needs.

> —From *Nobody's Perfect: Living and Growing With Children Who Have Special Needs* by Nancy B. Miller, P. H. Brookes, 1994.

Keep your child's medical records in good order. It is useful to keep copies of medical records about the child in one organized place. The information legally belongs to parents. Usually, you can call the medical records department or ask the child's doctor to give you or mail you the copies.

Consider buying a three-ring binder and dividing the information into sections by dates or types of tests and information, whichever works best for you. Some parents like to keep all of the child's records, others keep only the records that they feel may be useful in the future. You should keep:

- A summary of your child's medical history: any diagnoses, complications, medications, or other important information.

- A record of significant telephone conversations: use blank pages to record the date of the call, the person you spoke to, their telephone number and title, the main points of your conversation, any plans or decisions made.

- Business cards from doctors, agencies, or companies (buy a plastic pocket sheet designed for business cards and put it in the three ring binder, or just tape the cards to an 8½" x11" sheet of paper in the binder).

- Copies of hospital discharge plans and orders.
- Dates of immunizations.
- Dates of surgical procedures and tests.
- Allergies to drugs and other substances.
- Medications the child has used, the reason for using the medication, the dosage, the results and why the medication was stopped.
- Records of unusual reactions to medical experiences.
- Reports from specialists and therapists.
- Birth certificate.
- A list of communicable diseases the child has had.
- Laboratory reports.
- X-ray, MRI, CT scans, or other diagnostic testing reports.
- Treatment plans.
- Dates of follow-up appointments.

Consider saving financial records about the child's health care, too:

- Dates of services, where provided, and by whom.
- Names, addresses, telephone numbers, and policies of your insurance company or state financial program.
- Notes on how the insurance company or state program responded to your claims.
- Social security number.
- Letters of medical necessity.
- Copies of any appeals you have made with the insurance company or state program.
- Letters from your insurance company or state financial programs.
- Receipts for co-payments, deductibles or other fees you pay.

> —From "Speaking Up For Your Child," Pathfinder Resources, Inc.
> For information about ordering materials and educational opportunities for families and professionals, call 651-647-6905 or go to web site: www.Pathfinder-resources.com. 2324 University Ave. W, Suite 105, St. Paul, MN 55114.

Help your child understand more about children with special needs through reading:

- *Arnie and the New Kid* by Nancy Carlson
- *Big Brother Dustin* by Alden R. Carter
- *Dad and Me in the Morning* by Patricia Lakin
- *Harry and Willy and Carrothead* by Judith Caseley
- *Kathy's Hats: A Story of Hope* by Trudy Krisher
- *Mandy Sue Day* by Roberta Karim
- *Moses Goes to a Concert* by Isaac Millman
- *My Buddy* by Audrey Osofsky
- *Seal Surfer* by Michael Foreman
- *We Can Do It!* by Laura Dwight

When to Get More Help

Children typically grow and learn new skills in their own time and at their own pace within the wide range of what is normal. Sometimes, children need a bit of extra help to keep their development on track, or to stay healthy and happy. Sometimes, parents need help providing for a child's needs or sorting out the best approaches to parenting.

Consider getting help for your child if he:

- Is missing any of the skills in Part I: When to Get More Help in *The Field Guide*.
- Needs special services or equipment that would cost more than you can afford to pay.

Consider getting help for yourself if you:

- Feel isolated or alone.
- Have felt tired or depressed for more than one month, especially if you are a woman who has recently birthed a child.

You are the expert when it comes to your family and child. If you have a concern, trust your instinct and find someone trained to help you: health care providers, teachers, social workers, parent educators, mental health workers, or telephone help-line staff. Consider talking it over with friends and family, too. You don't need to worry alone! Turn to "Finding Help in Your Community" on page 4 to learn about finding help near you.

More Help and Information

Books for Parents

- *After the Tears: Parents Talk About Raising a Child with a Disability* by Robin Simons. Harcourt Brace Jovanovich, 1987.

- *The Child With Special Needs: Encouraging Intellectual and Emotional Growth* by Stanley I. Greenspan, Serena Wieder, and Robin Simons. Addison-Wesley, 1998

- *Every Parent's Guide to the Law* by Deborah L. Forman. Harcourt Brace, 1998.

- *Keys to Parenting the Gifted Child* by Sylvia Rimm. Barrons, 1994.

- *Nobody's Perfect: Living and Growing with Children Who Have Special Needs* by Nancy B. Miller. P.H. Brookes, 1994.

- *Since Owen: A Parent-to-Parent Guide for Care of the Disabled Child* by Charles R. Callanan. Johns Hopkins University Press, 1990.

- *Steps to Independence: Teaching Everyday Skills to Children With Special Needs* by Bruce L. Baker, Alan J. Brightman, and Jan B. Blacher. P. H. Brookes, 1997.

- "Using Ordinary Toys for Kids with Special Needs" in *Oppenheim Toy Portfolio, 1999: The Best Toys, Books, Videos & Software for Kids* (6th edition) by Joanne F. Oppenheim, Stephanie Oppenheim, and James Oppenheim. Oppenheim Toy Portfolio, 1998.

Articles, Pamphlets, and Booklets

- "Accessing Programs for Infants, Toddlers, and Preschoolers with Disabilities,"
  "Assessing Children for the Presence of a Disability,"
  "Parenting a Child with Special Needs: A Guide to Reading and Resources."
  "Disability Fact Sheets" from the National Information Center for Children and Youth with Disabilities (see National Organizations).

- "All About Me," (a comprehensive record-keeping system for families with children with special needs) by C. Allshouse, Pathfinder Resources, 1997.

- "Guide to Toys for Children Who Are Blind or Visually Impaired" from The American Foundation for the Blind at 800-232-5463.

- "Learning Disabilities." National Institutes of Health, National Institute of Mental Health.

- "Resources for Families and People Who Work With Families." Beach Center on Families and Disability (See National Organizations).

- "Speaking Up for Your Child: Advocating in the Health Care System for Your Child with Special Needs" (a booklet designed to help families to develop skills to foster partnerships with professionals that work with their children) by C. Allshouse, Pathfinder Resources, 1997. 651-647-6905, www.Pathfinder-resources.com

- "Toys 'R' Us Toy Guide for Differently Abled Kids" Request from Toys "R" Us: 461 From Rd. Paramus, NJ 07652, 201-262-7800.

Community Resources

- Early Intervention Services Program for Infants and Toddlers, Special Education: The Individuals with Disabilities Education Act (IDEA) ensures that all children who have special health care needs will have access to the services that they need. Call your state department of education, your state department of health and human services, your local school district, or the National Information Center for Children and Youth with Disabilities (800-695-0285) to find the early intervention or special education program in your area (see National Organizations).

- Parent Training and Information Centers: to find a parent training and information center in your area, call your school district, county social services agency, or your local public library. To find a list of parent training and information centers and community groups in the United States online, go to the PACER web site: www.pacer.org/natl/tnatl.htm. Contact PACER at 612-827-2966.

Government

- National Institutes of Health (for access to all the institutes, go to the Web site: www.nih.gov/icd/):

  National Institute of Child Health and Human Development: 800-370-2943

  National Institute of Deafness and Other Communicative Disorders: 800-241-1044, TTY: 800-241-1055

  National Institute of Mental Health: 301-443-4513

Magazines and Newsletters

- *The Exceptional Parent.* To order: P.O. Box 2078, Marion, OH 43305; 877-372-7368; web site:

  www.pedianet.com/eparent/

National Organizations

- Beach Center on Families and Disability, The University of Kansas
  785-864-7600, fax: 785-864-7605
  E-mail: Beach@dole.lsi.ukans.edu
  Web site: www.lsi.ukans.edu/beach/beachhp.htm

- ERIC Clearinghouse on Disabilities and Gifted Education
  The Council for Exceptional Children (CEC)
  800-328-0272
  E-mail: ericec@cec.sped.org
  Web site: www.cec.sped.org/ericec.htm

- Learning Disabilities Association
  412-341-1515, Fax: 412-344-0224
  E-mail: ldanatl@usaor.net
  Web site: www.ldanatl.org

- National Association for Gifted Children
  202-785-4268
  Web site: www.nagc.org

- National Information Center for Children and Youth with Disabilities (NICHCY)
  800-695-0285, Fax: 202-884-8441
  E-mail: nichcy@aed.org
  Web site: www.nichcy.org

- National Lekotek Center
  800-366-7529

  Call for information about suitable toys for disabled children, or to find the Lekotek Center nearest to you.

- Through the Looking Glass
  800-644-2666
  Fax: 510-848-4445
  www.lookingglass.org

Web Sites

- National Parent Information Network (NPIN). Resources for Parents: Full Texts of Parenting Related Materials: Children With Special Needs.

  http://ericps.crc.uiuc.edu/npin/respar/texts/special.html

- PACER: National Resources and WWW Links.

  www.pacer.org/natl/tnrwwwl.htm

Spirituality

"Rainbow" by Tom

Description

Spirituality is how people think about and include religious, sacred, or inner spirit in their lives; it is a way of looking at and approaching life. Spirituality can create a sense of connection and belonging to the larger world, to all people, and to a larger purpose in life. For many, it involves a belief in something greater than themselves, and the faith that people are not alone. Spirituality can add to life: peace, comfort, purpose, hope, and a moral or ethical standard for behaving. Some say that learning to be spiritual is learning to be human.

Realistic Expectations

- Preschoolers are especially interested in where things come from, who made them, and why: "Where does the sky come from and who made it?" Asking these types of questions is their way of beginning to understand larger issues such as creation, or where the world came from.

- Children under five have limited ability to understand the abstract concepts of spirituality, prayer, church or god. Young children tend to understand a spirit or a god in human terms only.

- By age six, children have an understanding or concept of god, whether it has come from organized religion, the family, media, or from hearing people say "Oh, my god!"

- Children do notice differences in what families believe and how they practice or act on their beliefs, in the same way children notice differences in gender, age, race, and abilities, and they will have questions about it.

- Children learn values, morals, and spirituality both through organized, conscious efforts to teach them and in lessons learned through everyday experiences.

- Children have limited ability to consistently practice values such as honesty or unselfishness. However, the introduction to these things as young children will lay the foundation for learning and practicing them for the rest of their lives.

Approaches

Give your child a sense of what you believe in and stand for as a family; show her your family values. Pass on to your child: a sense of right and wrong, fairness, justice, honesty, compassion, tolerance, God, working hard, duty, honor, charity, ethics, morals, or whatever it is you believe in and hold true. People need to feel connected, to feel like they belong, and to have a moral code, role models, and a foundation of good conduct, all of which can start in the family.

Teach and show your child your moral or spiritual values and beliefs by taking a stand, and helping your child understand that she is not alone in the world, that she has connections to people, how people came into being, and the meaning of being human. Pass on your beliefs through rituals practiced in the family, by giving and doing for others, by teaching sacrifice and responsibility, and by connecting to people outside the family.

—Ideas found in *Parenting by Heart* by Ron Taffel with Melinda Blau, Addison-Wesley, 1991.

Spirituality

Define success for your child, not in terms of money or things, but in terms of compassion, kindness, love, joy, connection—those things that contribute to who a person is inside, not what a person has or does. Teach your child that she is here for a reason and that she has purpose, so she will learn to approach her future in a conscious effort to satisfy herself on the inside, within her spirit. This may be the best thing you can do to make certain she has success in life.

> —Ideas found in *The Seven Spiritual Laws for Parents* by Deepak Chopra, Harmony Books, 1997.

Pass on values to your child so she can begin to learn to live by them. Help your child see the rewards in practicing behavior that is good for both herself and others. Start simply with young children. When your child practices a value, be sure to give her a lot of praise. If a value in your house is self-reliance, then encourage your child to choose and do things for herself. Tell her what a good job she did in putting on her own pants, or choosing her own spoon. She will come to learn that her actions in doing things for herself are valued at home, and she will continue to practice self-reliance as she grows.

> —Ideas found in *Teaching Your Children Values* by Linda and Richard Eyre, Simon & Schuster, 1993.

Help your child learn virtues to help her spirit grow. Accept your child as a person with a spirit that needs to master and understand her world. Virtues, values, or a code of conduct help her do this. Teach her the many virtues you value: assertiveness, caring, compassion, confidence, creativity, determination, flexibility, helpfulness, joyfulness, kindness, love, patience, respect, self-discipline, tolerance, trust, and more.

Allow her to face challenges that create a chance to learn, and name the virtue for her. Allow your child to try something new, even though she may be afraid of it, and she can learn courage; tell her that this is courage. Allow your child to speak and ask about anything, and she can learn assertiveness; tell her how proud you are when she is assertive in asking for what she needs. Allow your child to wait sometimes, and she can learn patience; tell her when she is being patient. A growing spirit full of virtue will give your child real joy and happiness.

> —Ideas found in *The Family Virtues Guide: Simple Ways to Bring Out The Best in Our Children and Ourselves* by Linda Kavelin Popov with Dan Popov and John Kavelin, Plume, 1997.

Allow your child to ask questions, to wonder, and to imagine; this will nurture her spirit. Each time your child asks a question, she is putting together the pieces of her world and strengthening her connection to it. Avoid giving her too many details, adult explanations, or long lectures about life. Give your child simple, clear answers that she can understand from her experience and from things, people, and places she knows. Help her spirit grow—and strengthen your relationship with her by helping your child see that life has meaning, what that meaning is to you, and by helping her explore and trust her own meanings.

> —Ideas found in *Small Wonder* by Jean Grasso Fitzpatrick, Viking, 1994.

Introduce your child to nature and the natural world to teach the idea that life is purposeful and connected. Take your child outside and explore: let her hold a ladybug, encourage her to listen to the rustle of leaves, to notice what she can smell, and ask her what the puddle of rainwater feels like. Listen to and answer her questions. Talk about how everything in nature has a purpose, and how nature can give strength and comfort. Consider celebrating the start and end of seasons. The wonder that she experiences in nature is one of many ways that will help her spirit grow.

> —Ideas found in *10 Principles for Spiritual Parenting: Nurturing Your Child's Soul* by Mimi Doe Walsh with Marsha Fayfield Walch, HarperCollins, 1998.

Explain differences in beliefs to your child when she asks about them. Tell your child that people believe in different things, come from many different places and that everyone should be allowed to believe in whatever god or spirit they choose. It's OK for people to have differences in what they believe in. Avoid telling your child that one way is better than another. Acknowledge differences, and encourage children of different faiths, beliefs, and nationalities to play together.

> —Ideas found in *Question Children Ask & How to Answer Them* by Miriam Stoppard, DK Publishing, 1997.

Prepare to talk to your child about God. Your child will likely ask you about God because the belief in God is so great in our culture and communities that your child won't be able to help noticing and wondering. Whether you believe in God, a divine being, or that there is no greater being, take time to think about and understand your own spirituality. Think about what your ideas, beliefs, and feelings are about God or a greater spirit. Then, be honest with your child about it.

> —Ideas found in *Raising Spiritual Children In a Material World* by Phil Catalfo, Berkley Books, 1997.

Help a child understand spirituality by reading about it together:

- *Did You Hear the Wind Sing Your Name?* by Sandra De Coteau
- *Draw Me a Star* by Eric Carle
- *Giving Thanks* by Chief Jake Swamp
- *Guess How Much I Love You* by Sam McBratney
- *Life is Fun!* by Nancy Carlson
- *Old Turtle* by Douglas Wood
- *One Earth, One Spirit,* compiled by Tessa Strickland
- *The Other Way to Listen* by Byrd Baylor and Peter Parnall
- *The Talking Cloth* by Rhonda Mitchell

When to Get More Help

You are the expert when it comes to your family and child. If you have a concern, trust your instinct, and seek spiritual counsel. If you find you are unable to answer questions your child poses, help is available from a pastor, priest, or other spiritual advisor.

More Help and Information

Books for Parents

- *10 Principles for Spiritual Parenting: Nurturing Your Child's Soul* by Mimi Doe Walsh, with Marsha Fayfield Walch. HarperCollins, 1998.

- *Bringing Up a Moral Child: A New Approach for Teaching Your Child to Be Kind, Just, and Responsible* by Michael Shulman and Eve Mekler. Main Street Books/Doubleday, 1994.

- *The Family Virtues Guide: Simple Ways to Bring Out The Best in Our Children and Ourselves* by Linda Kavelin Popov with Dan Popov and John Kavelin. Plume, 1997.

- *Raising Spiritual Children In a Material World* by Phil Catalfo. Berkley Books, 1997.

- *Small Wonder: How to Answer Your Child's Impossible Questions About Life* by Jean Grasso Fitzpatrick. Viking, 1994.

- *The Spiritual Life of Children* by Robert Coles. Houghton Mifflin, 1990.

- *Teaching Your Children Values* by Linda and Richard Eyre. Simon & Schuster, 1993.

- *The Values Book: Teaching 16 Basic Values to Young Children* by Pam Schiller and Tamera Bryant. Gryphon House, 1998.

Web Sites

- ConsciousKids, ConsciousParents—an online bookstore for parents and children.

  www.eastwest.com/consciouskids/index.htm

- Parenting Q&A—from the select-a-topic menu, choose "Religion & Spirituality."

  www.parentingqa.com

Stress

by Tom

Description

Stress is a physical reaction in the body that happens when a person is challenged physically or mentally. Some stress in life is normal; it can happen in both positive and negative situations. Ideally, once a stress reaction has given the person a burst of energy to help them get through the challenge, the body returns to a calm state. However, if the person remains in stress a great deal of the time, their health and well-being are threatened.

Realistic Expectations

- When children or adults experience stress, they experience changes in their body that make them more alert and give them increased energy: breathing, heart-rate, and blood pressure increase, sugar is sent to the bloodstream, and blood is sent to the brain and muscles. People need to release the energy caused by stress or over time it can cause damage to the body.

- In adults, too much stress can lead to overeating, drug and alcohol overuse, muscle tension, elevated blood pressure, anxiety disorders, depression, anger, a weakened immune system, increased distractibility, headaches, memory problems, sleep disorders, decreased enjoyment in life, decreased productivity, and a decrease in ability to relate to others.

- In children, too much stress can lead to: excessive or continued bedwetting or wetting pants after being trained, being afraid or upset with no apparent cause, weight gain or weight loss, upset stomach, ear, hair, or eyebrow tugging, defiance, irritability, explosive crying, night terrors or nightmares, begging for attention, being withdrawn, an increase in fears, sleeping poorly, nervous tics, thumb-sucking, hiding, increased fighting or arguing with friends or siblings, temper tantrums, seeming blue or lonely, or excessive masturbation.

- The very nature of childhood can be stressful because it involves constant growth and change that usually involves giving things up, meeting new situations, overcoming obstacles, and learning new things. Each age holds unique stresses for both of you; children under the age of five can be stressed and stressful to live with because they typically:

  - Get into everything because they are physically active and curious.

  - Have strong feelings and fears and are just learning to control them.

  - Seek lots of attention.

  - Make many mistakes as they learn.

  - Begin to try to make their own choices and assert themselves.

- Typical causes of "stress overload" in both children and adults include a hectic schedule, major life changes (moving, birth of a sibling, divorce, new day care arrangements), mastering new skills, being in new situations, and high stress levels of other family members.

- Each person handles stress differently: one person may be slightly uncomfortable in a given situation, while another may get a stomachache from it.

- A number of factors help children and adults cope well with stress: high self-esteem, a sense of being in control of one's life, family and friends for support, a flexible and hopeful personality, the ability to express feelings honestly and directly, a sense of humor, satisfying work, being a good listener, good nutrition, routine exercise, and time to relax.

- While stress cannot be eliminated, there are many things that adults can do to help themselves and their children to manage it. Children who learn to manage their stress during childhood are likely to carry those skills with them into adulthood.

Approaches

Consider ways that parenting is stressful and take steps to lower your stress. Take care of yourself apart from your child. Being a good role model is one of the most important things you can do as a parent to inspire your child to keep his stress level low as he grows.

- Schedule time for physical activity, emotional release, friendships, and to be alone.

- Read and learn about children. Try to stay one step ahead in what you know about children and their development.

- Join or create a parenting support group. Talking with other parents about parenting challenges can be a great support system.

- Value the relationship with your child's other parent. Model respect, courtesy, and kindness.

- Get help if you need it. If you are stuck in your parenting, consider taking a class or talking to a health care provider. No one needs to worry alone about a child!

- Lighten up about parenting and have some fun. Decide to enjoy parenting, and don't focus only on the work and obligations of it.

- Read, take a class, or see your health care provider about a stress management plan.

> —Ideas found in *Stress and Your Child: Helping Kids Cope with the Strains and Pressures of Life* (revised edition) by Bettie B. Youngs, Fawcett Books, 1995.

Raise your awareness about the amount of stress you have in your life, and find ways to manage it. Each person handles stress differently. Some people actually seek out situations which may appear stressful to others. The key is determining your personal tolerance levels for stressful situations:

- Do minor problems and disappointments upset you excessively?
- Do the small pleasures of life fail to satisfy you?
- Are you unable to stop thinking of your worries?
- Do you feel inadequate or suffer from self-doubt?
- Are you constantly tired?
- Do you experience flashes of anger over situations which used to not bother you?
- Have you noticed a change in sleeping or eating patterns?

- Do you suffer from chronic pain, headaches, or backaches?

If you answered yes to most of these questions, consider the following suggestions:

- Be realistic. If you feel overwhelmed by some activities (yours and/or your family's) learn to say NO! Eliminate an activity that is not absolutely necessary or ask someone else to help. You may be taking on more responsibility than you can or should handle. If you meet resistance, give reasons why you're making the changes. Be willing to listen to others' suggestions and be ready to compromise.

- Shed the "superman/woman" urge. No one is perfect, so don't expect perfection from yourself or others. Ask yourself: What really needs to be done? How much can I do? Is the deadline realistic? What adjustments can I make? Don't hesitate to ask for help if you need it.

- Meditate. Just ten to twenty minutes of quiet reflection may bring relief from chronic stress as well as increase your tolerance to it. Use the time to listen to music, relax, and try to think of pleasant things or nothing at all.

- Visualize. Use your imagination and picture how you can manage a stressful situation more successfully.

- Take one thing at a time. The best way to cope with feeling overwhelmed is to take one task at a time. Pick one urgent task and work on it. Once you accomplish that task, choose the next one. The positive feeling of "checking off" work is very satisfying.

- Exercise. Regular exercise relieves stress. Twenty to thirty minutes of physical activity benefits both the body and the mind.

- Allow yourself a hobby. Take a break from your worries by doing something you enjoy. Whether it's gardening or painting, schedule time to indulge your interest.

- Adopt a healthy lifestyle. Good nutrition, rest, exercise, balancing work and play, and limiting your intake of caffeine and alcohol all help to keep stress levels in check.

- Share your feelings. Stay in touch with friends and family, even if it's only by telephone. Let them provide love, support, and guidance. Don't try to cope alone.

- Give in occasionally. Be flexible! If you find that you're in conflicts constantly, rethink your position. Arguing only intensifies stressful feelings. If you know you are right, stand your ground, but do so calmly and rationally. Make allowances for other's opinions and be prepared to compromise. If you are willing to give in, others may meet you halfway. Not only will you reduce your stress, you may find better solutions to your problems.

- Go easy with criticism. You may expect too much of yourself and others. Try not to feel frustrated, let down, disappointed, even trapped when another person does not measure up. The "other person" may be a wife, a husband, or a child whom you are trying to change to suit yourself. Remember that everyone is unique, and has his or her own virtues, shortcomings, and right to develop as an individual.

> —From "Stress: Coping With Everyday Problems," National Mental Health Association. www.NMHA.org.

Live as if you had only a few minutes left. Use the these ten "TA-DAHs" that can take you outside of yourself and heal your negative thoughts:

1. Trade frowns for smiles.
2. Talk to yourself in fun ways.
3. Touch someone else's life.
4. Take time to listen to yourself.
5. Treat yourself to pleasure and passion.
6. Turn on your imagination.
7. Tidy up your life.
8. Tap into the universe of humor.
9. Try to be different.
10. Tolerate more, and give thanks often.

> —From *Relax - You May Only Have a Few Minutes Left: Using the Power of Humor to Overcome Stress in Your Life and Work* by Loretta LaRoche, Villard Books, 1998.

Practice proven stress relievers!

- Get up fifteen minutes earlier in the morning.

- Don't rely on your memory; write down appointment times, when to pick up the laundry, when the library books are due, etc.

- Don't put up with something that doesn't work right: fix your alarm clock, wallet, shoe laces—whatever is an aggravation.

- Relax your standards; the world won't end if the grass doesn't get mowed this weekend.

- Turn needs into wants; our only true needs are food, water, and keeping warm.

- Every day do something you really enjoy.

- Allow yourself time, every day, for privacy, quiet, and looking inside.

- Eliminate (or minimize) the amount of caffeine in your diet, get enough sleep, and don't forget to take a lunch break, even if it is just for fifteen to twenty minutes.

- Forget about counting to ten, count to one thousand before doing something or saying anything that could make matters worse.

- Have an optimistic view of the world. Believe that most people are doing the best they can.

> —From "52 Proven Stress Reducers," National Headache Foundation.
> 1-888-NHF-5552, www.headaches.org.

Learn to live in the present to ward off stress. Children have an amazing ability to give all of their attention to the thing, person, or activity that they are with at the time; adults on the other hand are often in a hurry, and trying to get to the next thing. Doing so leaves them unable to really appreciate and enjoy the present. Amidst this preoccupation, you will miss out on fully being with the child, and the child will miss out on being with you. You also may spoil the child's natural ability to become absorbed in the tiny wonders of life or in the here and now. You don't need to carve out more time for doing things with the child. On the contrary, just appreciate each moment or brief bit of time with your child, really focusing on and connecting with the wonder and timelessness of his world: sing, watch the ant build its hole, smell the flowers as you pass them, or feel the grass between your toes.

> —Ideas found in "Break the Hurry Habit" by Janis Graham, *Working Mother*, April 1996.

Set aside uninterrupted time for play and family. With all the available technology, your home may be as chaotic as Grand Central Station. It might be necessary to turn off the telephone, beeper, or cell phone to get some quiet family time. Make play your goal, and see how leisurely a weekend can be. Set aside an uninterrupted half-hour a day to play, and let your child be your guide. Follow him. You don't have to change your whole lifestyle to relieve stress; just try a few simple things.

> —Ideas found in "Build a Stress-Proof Nest" by Ron Taffel, *Parents*, September 1997.

Set a child-friendly pace and rhythm to life. Young children are not mini-adults. Children live in a certain timelessness all of their own, that is filled with continuous moments in which to play, and days that spill into each other. Adults live in a world that requires and rewards productivity and efficiency. If you try to force your child to keep your pace, he will likely become hurried and stressed. Try instead to learn to operate in both worlds, shifting from one pace to the other. Share his childhood for a part of each day by putting your other demands aside. Some of his pace may rub off on you while you are there.

> —Ideas found in *The Parent's Journal Guide to Raising Great Kids* by Bobbi Conner,
> Bantam Books, 1997.

Give your child the space to enjoy his childhood. Be aware that many of the spaces for children's play have been shrinking: extra rooms that were once playrooms are being replaced by studies, studios, offices, or bedrooms for nannies or aging grandparents. Many playgrounds are no longer considered safe due to rising crime. The end result for children is that they have less space in which to roam and play. Find space for your child to run, jump, and play; without it he runs a greater risk of becoming stressed.

> —Ideas found in *Ties That Stress: The New Family Imbalance* by David Elkind, Harvard University Press, 1994.

Give thought to the areas of your child's life that may be stressful and to the sum total of stress in his life.

A STRESS TEST FOR CHILDREN

Children, then, are stressed by a wide variety of incidents — some positive, others benign, many negative. Like the many adult stress tests given today, we can chart a child's stress level by assessing the stressors he or she has undergone recently. The following scale gives an estimate of the impact of various changes in a child's life that hurry and stress them. Add up the total points for all of the items your child has experienced in the last year. If your child scored below 150, he or she is about average with respect to stress load. If your child's score was between 150 and 300, he or she has a better than average chance of showing some symptoms of stress. If your child's score was above 300, there is a strong likelihood he or she will experience a serious change in health and/or behavior.

Stress	Child's Points	Score	Child's Stress	Points	Score
Parent dies	100		Change in responsibilities at home	29	
Parents divorce	73		Older brother or sister leaves home	29	
Parents separate	65		Trouble with grandparents	29	
Parent travels as part of job	63		Outstanding personal achievement	28	
Close family member dies	63		Move to another city	26	
Personal illness or injury	53		Move to another part of town	26	
Parent remarries	50		Receiving or losing a pet	25	
Parent fired from job	47		Change in personal habits	24	
Parents reconcile	45		Trouble with teacher	24	
Mother goes to work	45		Change in hours with baby sitter or at day-care center	20	
Change in health of a family member	44		Move to a new house	20	
Mother becomes pregnant	40		Change to a new school	20	
School difficulties	39		Change in play habits	19	
Birth of a sibling	39		Vacations with family	19	
School readjustment (new teacher or class)	39		Change in friends	18	
Change in family's financial condition	38		Attend a summer camp	17	
Injury or illness of a close friend	37		Change in sleeping habits	16	
Starts a new (or changes) an extracurricular activity (music lessons, Brownies, and so forth)	36		Change in number of family get-togethers	15	
			Change in eating habits	15	
Change in number of fights with siblings	35		Change in amount of TV viewing	13	
Threat of violence at school	31		Birthday party	12	
Theft of personal possessions	30		Punished for not "telling the truth"	11	

If your child received a high score, don't look back, look ahead. Take action to reduce the overall amount of stress in his life.

> —From *The Hurried Child: Growing Up Too Fast, Too Soon* by David Elkind. Copyright © 1988, 1981 by David Elkind. Reprinted by permission of Perseus Books Publishers, a member of Perseus Books, L.L.C.

Help your child unwind in times of stress. Encourage activities that are likely to relieve stress in young children:

- Hugging and cuddling
- Gentle tickling
- Back or foot rubs
- Story-telling
- A warm bath
- Painting or drawing
- Playing with clay
- Water or sand play
- Watching fish in an aquarium
- Blowing bubbles
- Petting animals: real or stuffed
- Talking
- Thinking about quiet places

> —Ideas found in *What to Expect the Toddler Years* by Arlene Eisenberg, Heidi E. Murkoff, and Sandee E. Hathaway, Workman Pub., 1994.

Use movement and music to release stress in your child:

- Sing to the tune "If you're happy and you know it," making up words that add feelings as you go: "If you're happy and you know it clap and smile…." or "If you're angry and you know it stomp your feet…" or "If you're frightened and you know it hug yourself." If you don't know this song, just make one up to a tune you know.
- Turn on music to fit the mood that you think your child is in, and have him move with it.
- Do "body mirror" movement with your child, taking turns being the leader: face each other and have one of you "mirror" the hand, arm, and body movements of the other.
- Walk very, very slowly in a circle, and encourage your child to feel each muscle as he moves.
- Be rag dolls together by bending at the waist and letting heads, arms and hands hang loose and dangle to release tension in tight muscles.

> —Ideas found in "The Teaching Parent: Teaching Children to Deal With Stress" by Martha Bullock Lamberts, *Family Information Services*, 1995.

Help your preschooler learn to recognize and release tension in his body. These exercises are especially helpful to a child who may have a hard time talking about his feelings.

1. Breath in and out a few times, looking in a mirror. Smile at yourself. Wrinkle your whole face, moving from your eyebrows, to your eyes, to your nose, to your cheeks, to your mouth. If a place feels tight, tell it to get soft.

2. When you are angry, sad, happy, scared, worried, or any other feeling, think of different things you could do with the feeling and do one of them: if you feel angry you could hit a pillow, jump up and down, stomp your feet, or draw a picture with red; if you're worried you could dump the worry in a box, imagine yourself bigger than the worry, or have someone hug it away.

> —Ideas found in *Stress-Proofing Your Child: Mind-Body Exercises to Enhance Your Child's Health* by Sheldon Lewis and Sheila Kay Lewis, Bantam, 1996.

Help your child understand more about stress by reading about it together:

📖 *The Berenstain Bears and Too Much Pressure* by Jan and Stan Berenstain

📖 *Dinosaurs Alive and Well: A Guide to Good Health* by Laurie Krasny Brown

When to Get More Help

Children typically grow and learn new skills in their own time and at their own pace within the wide range of what is normal. Sometimes, children need a bit of extra help to keep their development on track, or to stay healthy and happy. Sometimes, parents need help providing for a child's needs or sorting out the best approaches to parenting.

Consider getting help for your child if he:

- Is under long-term stress.

Consider getting help for yourself if you:

- Meet the criteria on the preceding checklist from the National Mental Health Association.
- Are under long-term stress.

You are the expert when it comes to your family and child. If you have a concern, trust your instinct and find someone trained to help you: health care providers, early intervention teams, mental health professionals, parent educators and consultants, or telephone help-line staff. Consider talking it over with friends and family, too. You don't need to worry alone! Turn to "Finding Help in Your Community" on page 4 to learn about finding help near you.

More Help and Information

Books for Parents

- *Don't Sweat the Small Stuff ... And It's All Small Stuff: Simple Ways to Keep the Little Things From Taking Over Your Life* by Richard Carlson. Hyperion, 1997.

- *Kidstress: What It Is, How It Feels, How to Help* by Georgia Witkin. Viking, 1999.

- *Loving Each One Best: A Caring and Practical Approach To Raising Siblings*, by Nancy Samalin and Catherine Whitney. Bantam, 1996.

- *Meditations for Parents Who Do Too Much* by Jonathon Lazear and Wendy Lazear. Simon and Schuster, 1993.

- *Relax - You May Only Have a Few Minutes Left: Using the Power of Humor to Overcome Stress in Your Life and Work* by Loretta Laroche. Villard, 1998.

- *Simplify Your Life: 100 Ways To Slow Down And Enjoy The Things That Really Matter* by Elaine St. James. Hyperion, 1994

- *Stress and Your Child: Helping Kids Cope with the Strains and Pressures of Life* by Bettie B. Youngs. Fawcett Columbine, 1995

- *Stress-Proofing Your Child: Mind-Body Exercises to Enhance Your Child's Health* by Sheldon Lewis and Sheila Kay Lewis. Bantam, 1996.

- *Ties That Stress: The New Family Imbalance* by David Elkind. Harvard University Press, 1994.

- *What Do You Really Want for Your Children? Chapter 5*, by Wayne Dyer. Avon, 1997.

Articles, Pamphlets, and Booklets

- "Replacing Stress with Peace," from Principles of Parenting series, Auburn University. Available online through web site: www.humsci.auburn.edu/parent/stress/index.html

- "52 Proven Stress Reducers," National Headache Foundation. Call:

  National Headache Foundation
  888-NHF-5552
  Web site: www.headaches.org

National Organizations

- National Mental Health Association
  800-433-5959

  Web site: www.nmha.org

Swearing

Description

Swearing is cursing, using profane, abusive, offensive, dirty, or foul language, or making obscene gestures. Young children usually swear to experiment with language while adults often swear out of anger.

Realistic Expectations

- Children sometimes use unacceptable language without knowing the meaning of the words. If they hear swearing from other children, adults, television, movies, music, or from parents, they are likely to repeat it.
- Sometimes children use unacceptable words without knowing that they aren't supposed to. If it's acceptable for adults in the house to swear, children may assume that it is acceptable for them, too.
- Children under five often swear to get a reaction. Although they may not know what the words mean, they do have an understanding that certain off-limit words are used with more strength and feeling, and carry a power that most other words don't have. If a word gets a strong reaction, they will be likely to use it again.
- Typically, children will experiment with swearing and testing the language limits at ages four and five.
- Children need help learning appropriate words and actions to use when they are angry or frustrated.

Approaches

Respond calmly, without anger, to your child's swearing. Consider designating a place in your home where your child may go to swear and then join you when she is finished. The following are other possibilities: let your child know in a matter-of-fact way how it makes you feel: "I feel uncomfortable when you swear, and I would appreciate it if you would use another word to describe how you feel." Be kind, firm, and tell your child: "We do not use those words in our home." Decide what you will do, not what you will try to get your child to do. If your child will not stop swearing or go to another place to swear, then consider letting her know that you will leave the room every time she talks that way. Then do it.

> —Ideas found in *Positive Discipline A-Z* (revised and expanded 2nd edition) by Jane Nelsen, Lynn Lott, and H. Stephen Glenn, Prima, 1999.

Make clear to your child that inappropriate language is not allowed. If your child swears, tell her calmly and clearly without anger, that those words are not OK to use. Then be sure that no one in your family is using the words, or your child will be likely to say them again.

> —Ideas found in *The Parents Answer Books* (Parents Magazine), Golden Books, 1998.

Don't give your child attention for swearing, at home or in public. Let her experiment at home but tell her that you don't like the words. Reacting strongly will only give her the attention she seeks, and entice her to use the words again. If she uses bad language in public, consider setting up a consequence with her. Before you go out again, discuss together what will happen if she uses inappropriate words. Try to help her remember when she slips and praise her when she remembers on her own.

> —Ideas found in *Touchpoints* by T. Berry Brazelton, Addison-Wesley, 1992.

Ignore swearing, but notice acceptable language, and create your own fun words to replace unacceptable words. If your child is using bad words to get your reaction, then ignore it and don't give her the attention. Do give her attention when she is using acceptable language. Consider making up your own "bad language." Have fun with it and think up silly words to use as swear words: "poodleknuckles" or "dribbledress." The silliness will help ease the tension while allowing a child to express frustration or anger with more acceptable words.

> —Ideas found in *Win the Whining War & Other Skirmishes* by Cynthia Whitham,
> Perspective Pub., 1991.

If your child is imitating someone else, encourage her to use her own words. If you observe a child hearing and then repeating bad words, consider telling her gently to think and talk for herself. "You have such good words of your own. Why not use those?"

> —Ideas found in *So This Is Normal Too?* by Deborah Hewitt, Redleaf Press, 1995.

If your child is swearing out of anger, help her find better ways to show her feelings. Let her know that it's all right to be mad and to talk about it: "It's all right that you are really mad. Do you want to tell me what makes you mad?" Give her actions or words to show her feelings: punch her bed pillow, or say, "I'm really, really mad," or "That's not fair!" If she is frustrated and needs help, teach her how to let you know.

> —Ideas found in *What to Expect the Toddler Years* by Arlene Eisenberg, Heidi E. Murkoff, and
> Sandee E. Hathaway, Workman Pub., 1994.

! **WARNING!** Washing a child's mouth out with soap and making a child taste or eat soap may be hazardous to your child's health. Some children are allergic to soap and become ill or have a serious reaction. Soap is not intended for ingestion—don't put it in a child's mouth!

Show your child what kindness looks like. Help your child be aware of the feelings of others and the impact that good words and bad words have on people, but don't punish her for mistakes. She learns most from what she sees. Make sure that you and the people around your child are kind to each other, in order for her to have a good example to follow.

> —Ideas found in *20 Teachable Virtues: Practical Ways to Pass on Lessons of Virtue and Character
> to Your Children* by Barbara C. Unell and Jerry L. Wyckoff, Berkeley Pub. Group, 1995.

Help your child understand more about swearing and feelings by reading about it together:

 Andrew's Angry Words by Dorothea Lachner

 C Is For Curious: An A B C Of Feelings by Woodleigh Hubbard

 Elbert's Bad Word by Audrey Wood

 Sometimes I Feel Like a Mouse: A Book About Feelings by Jeanne Modesitt

When to Get More Help

Children typically grow and learn new skills in their own time and at their own pace within the wide range of what is normal. Sometimes, children need a bit of extra help to keep their development on track, or to stay healthy and happy. Sometimes, parents need help providing for a child's needs or sorting out the best approaches to parenting.

Consider getting help for your child if she:

- Shows little or no improvement after you try an approach to help her change the swearing for at least two months.

You are the expert when it comes to your child. If you have a concern, trust your instinct and find someone trained to help you: health care providers, early intervention teams, mental health professionals, parent educators and consultants, or telephone help-line staff. Consider talking it over with friends and family, too. You don't need to worry alone! Turn to "Finding Help in Your Community" on page 4 to learn about finding help near you.

More Help and Information

Books for Parents

- "Dirty Words" in *Positive Parenting From A to Z* by Karen Renshaw Joslin. Fawcett Columbine: Ballantine Books, 1994.
- "Manners" (Includes swearing) in *Touchpoints* by T. Berry Brazelton. Addison-Wesley, 1992.
- "Respect" in *Teaching Your Children Values* by Linda and Richard Eyre. Simon & Schuster, 1993.

Articles

- "Should you pitch a fit when your kid says ... !#*@%!#@!?" by Tamara Eberlein. *Parenting*, February 1997.

Talking Back

Description

Talking back is when children boldly, rudely, or disrespectfully reply to an adult. Talking back can be blunt, as in "No, I don't want it. Grandma's spaghetti is yucky," or it can be simply "Bad daddy!" A refusal to cooperate, such as "you do it" or "no, you're mean," is also talking back.

Realistic Expectations

- Children may not realize that they are being disrespectful with back talk. They may believe that they are expressing a point of view about the situation. They may be trying to offer an appropriate reason for behavior without knowing an appropriate way to express it.

- Talking back is a normal way for children to practice being assertive. They need to experiment with language and limits in order to learn them.

- Children who hear a lot of disrespectful talk will learn to talk disrespectfully.

- Talking back may be a sign of stress, discouragement or unhappiness.

- Children test a parent or caregiver with behaviors like talking back only if they feel safe with that adult. If children are talking back to adults, it may be a sign that they feel confident that they will be loved no matter what.

- Children need help learning how to be respectful. Children who hear polite, respectful language will eventually adopt it.

Approaches

Discuss back talk calmly and present an alternative to talking back. If your child sounds angry or frustrated, tell him what you are hearing and show that you understand: "You seem frustrated about being asked to pick up your toys." Talk about his feelings and yours, and be honest about how back talk feels to you. Tell him what else he could say: "Instead of 'Blech, no salami,' try 'May I please have peanut butter?'" Notice and comment when he makes respectful and polite requests and holds back rude behavior.

> —Ideas found in *Positive Parenting From A to Z* by Karen Renshaw Joslin.
> Fawcett Columbine: Ballantine Books, 1994.

Give your child a choice when he is being disrespectful: either talk respectfully or don't talk to you at all. Tell your child that you will leave the room if he is going to talk back or talk rudely, and that you want to listen to him when he can talk politely. After allowing him some time to calm down, ask your child if he is ready to talk in a respectful way. Always show and express love and affection for your child.

> —Ideas found in *Positive Discipline A-Z* by Jane Nelsen, Lynn Lott, and H. Stephen Glenn.
> Prima Pub., 1993.

When your child talks back to get attention, ignore it. If you take away the reward of talking back, which is your attention (even if it is angry attention), then he'll eventually stop it. When your child does what you ask without rudeness or complaint, notice and praise the good behavior.

> —Ideas found in *Win the Whining War & Other Skirmishes* by Cynthia Whitham,
> Perspective Pub., 1991.

Ask your child to please stop talking back, and try again in a nicer way. Don't be afraid to say "no" to your child and stick to it when something is not negotiable. Allowing your child to talk back to you does not do him any favors. He learns to be rude and that can be hard to change later on. Teaching him now to handle his frustration in an appropriate way when you say "no" is better in the long run than giving in to rude behavior to avoid his frustration.

> —Ideas found in "Taming Back Talk" by Jan Faull, available online at www.family.com.

Teach respect through play. Use the Definitions Game to get *respect* into the vocabulary of small children, so that both you and they can *use* the word. Tell them that *respect* means "acting nice and talking nice and minding." Then tell them about Mikey. Ask them whether Mikey was showing respect after each sentence:

- Mikey's mom asked him to clean up his room and he yelled, "I don't want to!" (*No.*)
- He said, "Please, may I be excused?" (*Yes.*)
- He looked his grandpa in the eye and said, "Fine sir," when Grandpa said "How are you?" (*Yes.*)
- When he couldn't put the puzzle together, he said, "I'm just stupid." (*No.*)

> —Reprinted with the permission of Simon & Schuster from *Teaching Your Children Values* by Linda and Richard Eyre. Copyright © 1993 by R.M. Eyre & Associates, Inc.

Help your child understand more about talking back by reading about it together:

 The Berenstain Bears and the Trouble With Grownups by Stan and Jan Berenstain

 Jason's Bus Ride by Harriet Ziefert

When to Get More Help

C hildren typically grow and learn new skills in their own time and at their own pace within the wide range of what is normal. Sometimes, children need a bit of extra help to keep their development on track, or to stay healthy and happy. Sometimes, parents need help providing for a child's needs or sorting out the best approaches to parenting.

Consider getting help for your child if he:

- Shows little or no improvement after you try an approach—for at least two months—to help him change the talking back.

- Does not show some self-control of aggressive behavior (when angry or upset) by four years of age.

You are the expert when it comes to your family and child. If you have a concern, trust your instinct and find someone trained to help you: health care providers, early intervention teams, mental health professionals, parent educators and consultants, or telephone help-line staff. Consider talking it over with friends and family, too. You don't need to worry alone! Turn to "Finding Help in Your Community" on page 4 to learn about finding help near you.

More Help and Information

Books for Parents

- *Backtalk: Four Steps to Ending Rude Behavior in Your Kids* by Audrey Ricker and Carolyn Crowder. Simon and Schuster, 1998.

- "Respect" in *Teaching Your Children Values* by Linda and Richard Eyre, Simon & Schuster, 1993.

- "Talking Back" in *Positive Parenting from A to Z* by Karen Renshaw Joslin Fawcett. Columbine: Ballantine Books, 1994.

Web Sites

- "Taming Back Talk" by Jan Faull and "What Back Talkers Should Say Instead" on www.family.com

Tantrums

by Jennifer, age 2

Description

A tantrum is a fit of frustration or anger. Behavior during tantrums can include whining, crying, making the body stiff, kicking, screaming, thrashing around on the ground, head banging, throwing things, breath holding, breaking things, biting, and yelling. A tantrum can serve as a safety valve that lets off steam when pressure is high.

Realistic Expectations

- Tantrums may begin as early as nine months, but most often begin around eighteen months.
- Almost all children between one and three have tantrums. Many children continue to have tantrums after age three, but typically do not have as many. By age four, tantrums are typically rare.
- Tantrums can be triggered by almost anything, anytime, especially in two-year-old children.
- Children begin having tantrums as a tension release, but when adults give the tantrums too much attention or give in to their demands, children may learn to use tantrums to get attention or to get their own way.
- Children may be terrified by their own rage during tantrums.
- Children can have tantrums that are a spillover of emotion from things like too much stimulation, too many transitions, or too much stress.
- Children who are helped to deal with tantrums in a positive way may learn to soothe themselves, and learn to control their behavior while they express strong emotions. These are valuable skills that will benefit them for a lifetime.

Approaches

Prevent some tantrums by understanding and reducing common frustrations. You can't avoid all tantrums, but giving some thought to your child's days and your expectations of her can help you make adjustments that might prevent some tantrums. There are many common frustrations that can lead to tantrums. Your child may be:

- Unable to put feelings, needs, or desires into words.
- Unable to coordinate her body and mind to do the new things she is trying to do.
- Trying to play with toys that are too difficult for her.
- Unable to get what she wants from people, or unable to get them to do what she is asking them to do.
- Expected to sit still for a long time: in a car, during church, shopping, etc.
- Expected not to touch things in a new and interesting place.
- Stopped from doing something all by herself.

- Feeling rushed when she wants to explore or play.
- Expected to keep a schedule with too many planned events in a day.
- Unable to understand instructions or requests.
- Stopped from playing, to do something undesirable like eating or going to bed.
- Overstimulated by attending events like holidays, birthday parties, and family reunions.

It is easy to push your child too far without realizing it, until it is too late and a tantrum erupts. Everything is new and stimulating to her—*everything*. Sensory overload can happen quickly! Plan ahead for calm, well-paced days, with a balance of planned activities and free time. If she is also hungry, tired, stressed or ill, plan even more carefully, because this will lower her frustration level even further.

> —Ideas found in *Tantrums: Secrets to Calming the Storm* by Ann E. LaForge,
> Pocket Books, 1996.

Help your child weather the storm of a tantrum by staying calm yourself and by showing respect for her feelings. What she needs most is for you to stay in control and to remain calm. Don't give attention to her tantrum, and absolutely *do not* have a tantrum of your own. This doesn't mean that you should put up with bad behavior. Instead, you should stay near her and attend to her feelings and behavior. Let her know that it is OK for her to have strong feelings, but that you expect her to express them with words and actions that do not harm anyone or anything.

> —Ideas found in "Understanding Tantrums" by Linda Johnston, *Family Information Services*,
> 1998.

! **WARNING! Never shake a child and never harm a child with physical punishment.**

- Shaking a baby or child under the age of three can cause brain damage, blindness, paralysis, seizures, or death. Even a small amount of shaking or a less vigorous shaking can severely harm a young child.

  The American Academy of Pediatrics (AAP) warns that children who are routinely disciplined with spanking and other physical forms of punishment are more likely to become aggressive and to learn that aggressive behavior is the way to solve problems. Spanking or hitting can also lead to injury and abuse, especially when it is done in anger.

Respond to tantrums in a positive way. Some tantrums will happen; there are a variety of ways to handle them. Usually it is best to just ignore tantrums. Keep doing whatever you were doing before the tantrum began, or do something that makes you look busy: sweep the floor while you sing or whistle, pick up around the house, or anything that keeps you moving. This teaches her that she cannot get what she wants by "making a fuss." If ignoring doesn't work quickly (and often it doesn't), try one of the following ideas:

- Describe her feelings to her: "You seem very angry." This teaches her to name her emotions.
- Describe your feelings to her: "I feel upset when you act like this." This helps her to think of how her behavior is affecting the people around her.
- Remove her from the scene. Be calm, and lead her to her room or a chair in the same room. Tell her she should stay there until she feels ready to come back and be with you and anyone else who was there, at which time she will be welcome. This teaches her that she can express her anger and frustration any way she wants in privacy, but not in public, and teaches her to find ways to work through her emotions on her own.

- Distract her with something else. Sometimes seeing something fun or someone else having fun without her draws her away from a tantrum: a book, singing, a puzzle, or a game. This teaches her that she can refocus energy and move on to something else if she so chooses.

- Walk away if you believe the tantrum is meant to manipulate. Let your child know you will not participate at all, to teach her that she will not gain anything with this behavior.

- Decide to give in occasionally, if it makes sense. Usually it is best to stick with your expectation of her once you have taken a stand and made a clear statement about it. However, if you feel you have made an unreasonable or excessively controlling request, trust your instinct and give in to your common sense. Tell your child and explain your reason for changing your mind as soon as you can so she doesn't learn that persistence pays.

Your child is trying to express her independence; tantrums will pass as she finds other ways to do so.

> —Ideas found in *No More Tantrums: A Parent's Guide to Taming Your Toddler and Keeping Your Cool* by Diane Mason, Gayle Jensen, and Carolyn Ryzewicz, Contemporary Books, 1997.

Keep your child safe during the tantrum and stay calm yourself, but otherwise, let it pass in its own time. Be sure your child will not hurt herself while she is in the tantrum. Hold her if she will let you and if it is calming for her; if she can't bear being held, move her away from things she might break, run into, or be harmed by in any way. There are several things you should not do during a tantrum:

- Don't try to argue with your child; she is beyond reason in the midst of a tantrum.

- Don't scream back; her anger may be contagious, but joining in can fuel hers.

- Don't let her feel either rewarded or punished for having a tantrum; the fact that she had a tantrum shouldn't change anything. If you had just said that she couldn't eat ice cream, don't give it to her after the tantrum, but if you had planned on going out for ice-cream before the tantrum, go out once she is calm.

- Don't let tantrums embarrass you in public or around other people such that you more easily give in to her demands; if she learns you will be easier to push over in public, she will quickly use it against you.

Have faith that she will grow to be reasonable over time.

> —Ideas found in *Your Baby & Child: From Birth to Age Five* (3rd edition) by Penelope Leach. Alfred A. Knopf, 1997.

If your child is having tantrums frequently, step back and see if you can remove some of the causes of her frustration. Sometimes parents are not tactful enough at interacting with a young child, and unknowingly contribute to frustration that can lead to tantrums. You may be contributing unknowingly to your child's frustration. Your child will be less frustrated if she is:

- Allowed to play freely outdoors (with supervision in safe environment) without having you follow her around too closely.

- Provided with enough things to play with and do indoors.

- Free to explore and touch things (as long as they are safe) without always being told "NO!"

- Given fair warnings when her play will be interrupted.

Some temper tantrums don't mean anything, but if they are frequent, consider what role you may have in fueling them.

> —Ideas found in *Dr. Spock's Baby and Child Care* (7th edition) by Benjamin Spock and Stephen J. Parker, Dutton, 1998.

Tantrums

Plan ahead to prevent a tantrum, if your child typically doesn't want to leave a friend's house. These tantrums are common. Try one of these ideas:

- Create a departure routine to follow each time she says goodbye to the friend: she puts on her coat, she hugs the friend, and she pats the dog good-bye.
- Say: "I'm so glad you had a good time. Let's figure out when we can do it again." Make a date before leaving.
- Call ten minutes before you arrive to pick her up to give her a ten-minute warning.
- At another time, ask her to help decide what she needs in order to leave easily.
- Acknowledge her feelings about not wanting to leave: "I know it is hard to say good-bye to a friend when you have had such a good time. We will come again."

> —From *Help! For Parents of Children from Birth to Five*, a collection of ideas from parents, edited by Jean Illsley Clarke, HarperSanFrancisco, 1993.

Plan ahead for handling your child's public tantrums. Don't worry about the people around you; most of them have been there too. Have the courage to follow through with a consistent response to her tantrums:

- When she begins to have a tantrum, announce to her firmly that you will ignore the tantrum.
- Proceed to ignore the tantrum, but keep your child in sight; make small talk with the adults around you or carry on with whatever you are doing.
- The moment she makes an attempt to calm herself, praise her.
- If she doesn't calm down, give a warning: "You must stop screaming or we will have to leave."
- If she still does not calm down, try one more warning, but then quickly follow through and take her outside, into another room, or into the car. If she does not follow you, pick her up and carry her, even if she is kicking and screaming.
- Give her a chance to regain control. If she cannot quickly stop the tantrum, go home.

If tantrums in public have become a common problem with your child, consider doing a "practice run" to the place they typically happen. The truth is, if you have plans to get your weekly grocery shopping done, and your child has a tantrum, leaving becomes a consequence for *you*, and you will be less likely to follow through with your plan to discipline her. Set up a situation where your child will have the consequence, not you: make a grocery store run when you are not really needing to shop, at a time that you are feeling up to the challenge of disciplining a tantrum in public. If she does have a tantrum, follow the above discipline plan and go home swiftly if need be. If she manages not to have a tantrum, all the better. Praise her and enjoy the time together.

> —Ideas found in *Win the Whining War & Other Skirmishes* by Cynthia Whitham, Perspective Pub., 1991.

If you have a spirited child, handle tantrums gently. Your child needs you to help her find the root of the problem, and to stop it. Stay with her. Some children like to be touched with a back scratch or hug, others need space and will respond better if you don't touch them but stand near them. Respect your child's unique needs. Look for possible causes and remedies: if you know she is tired, get her to a place she can rest; if you know she is hungry, get her some food.

If your child is still having a tantrum after ten to fifteen minutes, gently tell her to stop. Softly but firmly talk to her while she is crying about what is triggering the tantrum. Give her the words for what is happening: "It is time to stop screaming now. You were sitting for so long in the car, that your body got frustrated because it wanted to play."

Have rules and consequences in place that you have talked about before your child is in the throws of a tantrum. Help her learn that she has strong emotions, and that she needs to control herself within limits. Define the limits clearly: it is okay to stomp, hit a pillow, ask to be held, or scream when you are mad, but it is not okay to hurt someone, call names, swear, trash a room, or break things. Be very clear about what the consequences are for breaking the rule: if you mess your room up during a tantrum, you help put things back in place.

—Ideas found in *Raising Your Spirited Child: A Guide for Parents Whose Child Is More Intense, Sensitive, Perceptive, Persistent, Energetic* by Mary Sheedy Kurcinka, HarperCollins, 1991.

Help your child understand more about tantrums and strong emotions by reading about it together:

The Chocolate-Covered-Cookie-Tantrum by Deborah Blumenthal

Three-Star Billy by Pat Hutchins

The Good-Bye Book by Judith Viorst

When to Get Help

Children typically grow and learn new skills in their own time and at their own pace within the wide range of what is normal. Sometimes, children need a bit of extra help to keep their development on track, or to stay healthy and happy. Sometimes, parents need help providing for a child's needs or sorting out the best approaches to parenting.

Consider getting help for your child if she:

- Holds her breath or faints during a tantrum.
- Has more and more tantrums that are more severe each day as time goes on.
- Has intense tantrums after age four.
- Frequently causes injury to herself or others, or damage to property.
- Has additional behaviors that concern you, such as frequent nightmares, fears, listlessness, or very extreme mood swings.
- Has a great deal of difficulty or frustration with communicating.
- Does not show a range of emotions: joy, anger, sorrow, grief, enthusiasm, excitement, frustration, love and affection.

Consider getting help for yourself if you:

- Find it difficult to stay in control of yourself and your emotions during her tantrums.
- Have questions about handling tantrums.

You are the expert when it comes to your family and child. If you have a concern, trust your instinct and find someone trained to help you: health care providers, early intervention teams, mental health professionals, parent educators and consultants, or telephone help-line staff. Consider talking it over with friends and family, too. You don't need to worry alone! Turn to "Finding Help in Your Community" on page 4 to learn about finding help near you.

More Help and Information

Books for Parents

- "Responding to Crying and Tantrums, Chapter 11" in *Becoming The Parent You Want To Be: A Source Book of Strategies for the First Five Years* by Laura Davis and Janis Keyser, Broadway Books, 1997.

- *Tantrums: Secrets to Calming the Storm* by Ann E. LaForge, Pocket Books, 1996.

- "What's Important to Know: Taming Tantrums," in *What to Expect the Toddler Years* by Arlene Eisenberg, Heidi Murkoff, and Sandee E. Hathaway, Workman Pub., 1994.

- *I'm Two Years Old!* and *I'm Three Years Old!* by Jerri Wolfe, Pocket Books, 1998. These books are written in a style that really gives you the perspective of a two and three year old.

Tattling

Description

Tattling is telling or complaining about the actions or plans of another. Gossiping is a form of tattling. Usually, tattling involves breaking a rule, doing something wrong, or planning something against the rules.

Realistic Expectations

- Telling on someone is appropriate and should be encouraged when children are scared, being bothered, touched in an uncomfortable way, hurt, threatened, in danger, or concerned about something.

- Tattling is normal in young children. Toddlers and preschoolers tattle while learning social skills. Five-through seven-year-olds tattle as they focus on learning rules, and right from wrong.

- Children tattle on other children for many reasons:
    - To get another child in trouble.
    - To get something they want, when someone else is an obstacle.
    - To get attention or make themselves look good.
    - To prove they know the rules.
    - To exercise power over another child.
    - To stop someone from getting hurt.
    - Because they don't know how to solve a problem on their own.

Approaches

Teach your child the difference between *telling* when someone needs help and *tattling* to get someone in trouble or to get attention. Make it clear that telling an adult when someone is hurt is not the same as tattling. Your child should know that he should always come to an adult when he sees someone hurting someone else, when he is scared, when he is in danger, when he is uncomfortable about a situation or about being touched, and when toys, pets, or things need protecting.

Practice with your child telling the difference between telling and tattling by showing your child an example of children telling, and another of children tattling. For example, Mark and Jan are in the sandbox where the rule is to keep the sand in the box. When Jan throws sand out of the box, Mark asks her to stop, and she does. Mark runs over to the daycare teacher and tells that Jan was throwing sand.

Ask your child whether Mark was telling or tattling. Help him see that Mark was tattling to get Jan in trouble. Jan stopped throwing the sand, no one was getting hurt, so Mark really didn't need help. Ask your child to consider what Mark could have done instead and what your child would do if he were Mark.

—Ideas found in *Telling Isn't Tattling* by Kathryn M. Hammerseng, Parenting Press, 1995.
For more information, call 1-800-992-6657.

Tattling

Teach your child alternatives to tattling. Practice approaches to various problems that your child can solve himself, before they come up. Ask him for his ideas about handling various problems on his own, and then share yours. Some of the things a child could do instead of tattling are: go away and calm down, take turns, share, ask the other person to quit doing whatever is bothersome, and try again to work it out.

> —Ideas found in "Reforming a Tattletale" by Deborah Beroset, *Parents*, January 1998.

When two children are tattling on each other, give them the choice: either work it out or play separately. When children realize you aren't going to settle things for them, they will most likely choose to work it out and continue playing together.

> —Ideas found in *Win the Whining War & Other Skirmishes* by Cynthia Whitham,
> Perspective Pub., 1991.

Help your child learn when a problem is not his and belongs to someone else. If your child tattles on another child for doing something to someone else, help him see that it's really none of his business, as long as everyone is safe. If Jimmy takes a toy from Amy and your child tattles on Jimmy, tell him: "This is Amy's problem, not yours, and since she is not hurt or in danger, let's let Amy take care of it."

> —Ideas found in *Positive Parenting From A to Z* by Karen Renshaw Joslin.
> Fawcett Columbine: Ballantine Books, 1994.

> My three-year old is really starting to get into tattling. When it is a disagreement over a toy or who is going to ride the bike, first I try to let them work it out themselves. If one of my kids hit, pinch, etc., I encourage them to come and tell me instead of striking back. Because they are still pretty young I do find myself getting involved quite a bit, but I am trying to teach them how to work things out between themselves (easier said than done).
>
> —Tara, Alaska

When your child tattles to get someone else in trouble, tell your child that you don't approve of tattling, then explain how he could help instead: "Brothers, sisters, and friends help each other out; they don't try to get each other in trouble. Instead of telling me that Alex is breaking the rule about watching more than one TV show, try asking him to turn the TV off and play."

> —Ideas found in *Bringing Up A Moral Child* by Michael Schulman and Eve Mekler,
> Doubleday, 1994.

Help your child understand more about tattling and loyalty by reading about it:

 Amos and Boris by William Steig

 Let's Talk About Tattling by Joy Wilt Berry

 Telling Isn't Tattling by Kathryn M. Hammerseng

When to Get More Help

Children typically grow and learn new skills in their own time and at their own pace within the wide range of what is normal. Sometimes, children need a bit of extra help to keep their development on track, or to stay healthy and happy. Sometimes, parents need help providing for a child's needs or sorting out the best approaches to parenting.

Consider getting help for your child if he:

- Shows little or no improvement after you try an approach—for at least two months—to help him change the tattling.
- Cannot communicate effectively with peers to resolve conflicts.
- Reports being abused in any way.

You are the expert when it comes to your family and child. If you have a concern, trust your instinct and find someone trained to help you: health care providers, early intervention teams, mental health professionals, parent educators and consultants, or telephone help-line staff. Consider talking it over with friends and family, too. You don't need to worry alone! Turn to "Finding Help in Your Community" on page 4 to learn about finding help near you.

More Help and Information

Books for Parents

- "Tattling" in *Positive Parenting From A to Z* by Karen Renshaw Joslin. Fawcett Columbine: Ballantine Books, 1994.
- *Telling Isn't Tattling* by Kathryn M. Hammerseng. Parenting Press, 1995. For more information, call 1-800-992-6657.
- "Unselfishness and Sensitivity" in *Teaching Your Children Values* by Linda and Richard Eyre. Simon & Schuster, 1993.

Teasing and Name-Calling

Description

Teasing is pestering, annoying, name-calling, or making fun of someone else. It can be done good-naturedly, in fun, or it can be deliberately hurtful. Name-calling is referring to someone by something other than his given name or accepted nickname.

Realistic Expectations

- Teasing often begins in children as young as two years old. As they offer you a book and then slyly take it back before you can reach it, they are teasing in fun, practicing new social skills, and testing out newly discovered power.
- Children under three have only a vague understanding of hurting the feelings of others.
- Most children experiment with teasing and name-calling by the time they are three or four.
- Toddlers take words literally and may not understand even the loving teasing of adults. For example, a toddler who hears, "You're so silly, you will turn into a goose," may believe he will turn into a goose.
- Preschoolers usually enjoy teasing that is done in fun. Now that they understand some basic concepts, they find the humor in teasing: "I see you have new shoes on—have you ever seen three more beautiful feet?"
- Sensitive children may not appreciate teasing at all, even if it is done in fun.
- Children may be more likely to tease and call names if the children or adults around them do.
- Most children do not start teasing and name-calling out of anger or to hurt someone until after age five.

Approaches

Help your child who is teasing see when teasing is hurtful, and show your teased child how to handle it. Talk about when teasing is fun and when it isn't. Allow your child to have fun playing with words, but don't let her hurt people's feelings. Show her the difference between a nickname and calling people names: Elizabeth enjoys being called "Lizzie" as her nickname. She does not like to be made fun of by being called "Lizard."

Help your child to deal with being teased. Give your child words to use to ask the other child to stop. If the teasing doesn't stop, encourage your child to walk away, and ask for help if she needs it. Explain that by staying calm, the teasing child will not get what she wants—a reaction from your child of being upset.

—Ideas found in *Positive Parenting from A to Z* by Karen Renshaw Joslin.
Fawcett Columbine: Ballantine Books, 1994.

If your child is teasing others hurtfully, ask her how she would feel if she were being teased. If the teasing persists after talking to her about why she is teasing, how she would feel being teased, and asking her to stop, then consider giving a warning and a consequence, like a time-out.

—Ideas found in *A to Z Guide to Your Child's Behavior*, Putnam Pub., 1993.

Do not allow teasing or name-calling that points out differences in physical characteristics, disabilities, race, or gender. Tell your child that name-calling hurts people's feelings. Be honest with your child about the person involved and offer explanations about the person. Consider whether your child is being introduced to many kinds of people so that she doesn't find differences out of the ordinary. Also, consider whether your child was repeating something she heard and where she may have heard it. Explain that this kind of teasing is wrong.

> —Ideas found in *Becoming the Parent You Want to Be* by Laura Davis and Janis Keyser, Broadway Books, 1997.

Let your child know that you don't like name-calling, but that she can try it out in private if she wants to. Explain that certain names and words can hurt people just like kicking or biting them can. Don't expect her to have self-control yet. Do show her how she can tell someone that she is upset with them in a better way. Then, if she wants to experiment with language, allow her to try things out when she is alone.

> —Ideas found in *What to Expect the Toddler Years* by Arlene Eisenberg, Heidi E. Murkoff, and Sandee E. Hathaway, Workman Pub., 1994.

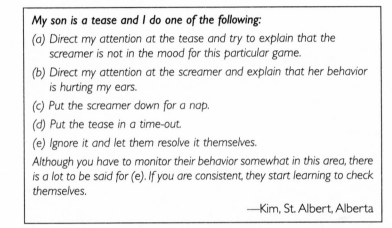

My son is a tease and I do one of the following:

(a) *Direct my attention at the tease and try to explain that the screamer is not in the mood for this particular game.*

(b) *Direct my attention at the screamer and explain that her behavior is hurting my ears.*

(c) *Put the screamer down for a nap.*

(d) *Put the tease in a time-out.*

(e) *Ignore it and let them resolve it themselves.*

Although you have to monitor their behavior somewhat in this area, there is a lot to be said for (e). If you are consistent, they start learning to check themselves.

> —Kim, St. Albert, Alberta

Teach your child kindness. Help her to notice when something—like teasing—is bothering someone, and then to stop. Point out when people are in need of help or need care. Practice kindness to all people. People who practice kindness are more likely to refrain from hurtful teasing or name-calling.

> —Ideas found in *The Family Virtues Guide: Simple Ways to Bring Out the Best in Our Children and Ourselves* by Linda Kavelin Popov, Plume, 1997.

Help your child learn more about teasing and name calling by reading about it together:

 Anansi and the Talking Melon by Eric A. Kimmel

 The Berenstain Bears and Too Much Teasing by Stan and Jan Berenstain

 Chrysanthemum by Kevin Henkes

Princess Penelope's Parrot by Helen Lester

Snail Started It by Katja Reider and Angela von Roehl

When to Get More Help

Children typically grow and learn new skills in their own time and at their own pace within the wide range of what is normal. Sometimes, children need a bit of extra help to keep their development on track, or to stay healthy and happy. Sometimes, parents need help providing for a child's needs or sorting out the best approaches to parenting.

Consider getting help for your child if she:

- Shows little or no improvement after you try an approach to help change the teasing for at least two months.
- Frequently threatens others, or is cruel toward other children or animals.

You are the expert when it comes to your child. If you have a concern, trust your instinct and find someone trained to help you: health care providers, early intervention teams, mental health professionals, parent educators and consultants, or telephone help-line staff. Consider talking it over with friends and family, too. You don't need to worry alone! Turn to "Finding Help in Your Community" on page 4 to learn about finding help near you.

More Help and Information

Books for Parents

- "Name-Calling" in *Discipline Without Shouting or Spanking* by Jerry Wyckoff and Barbara C. Unell. Meadowbrook Press, 1984.
- "Name-Calling" in *What to Expect the Toddler Years* by Arlene Eisenberg, Heidi E. Murkoff, and Sandee E. Hathaway. Workman Pub., 1994.
- "Tolerance" in *20 Teachable Virtues* by Barbara C. Unell and Jerry L. Wyckoff. Berkley Pub. Group, 1995.
- "Unselfishness & Sensitivity" in *Teaching Your Children Values* by Linda and Richard Eyre. Simon & Schuster, 1993.

Television, Videos, Computers, and Media

by Tom

Description

Television, movies, videos, video games, computers, software, and other media are an important part of our culture and should be used wisely. Use media reasonably and by choice, not out of habit, and determine which are appropriate for your child.

Realistic Expectations

- Wisely chosen television programming, videos, movies, and computer software can provide learning experiences, fun, and a positive influence for children when used in moderation.

- Children under five typically cannot distinguish between what's real and what's unreal, and so they are particularly vulnerable to the effects of media.

- Engaging in passive activities like watching television or playing video or computer games for long periods of time may interfere with children's growth and development. The more time children spend looking at screens, the less time they spend actively exploring their world, learning, running, jumping, climbing, and growing.

- Children imitate what they see and hear. If they see adults using media wisely, they may learn to use media wisely. If they see adults watching television several times a day, or for an excessive amount of time, they may learn to do that also.

- Don't assume that because a program, movie, video, video game or software product is labeled and marketed for children that it is not violent or scary. Studies show that Saturday morning cartoons contain twenty to twenty-five acts of violence per hour, while a prime time show for adults contains two to five acts of violence per hour.

- Many studies conducted over the last forty years show that heavy exposure to violence on television is harmful to children, can reinforce negative values, and poses several risks. Children may:

  - Learn to be less sensitive to the pain of others or may become immune to images of violence.

  - Slowly learn to accept violence as a way to solve problems.

  - Imitate violence.

  - Become more fearful of the world.

Television, Videos, Computers, and Media

- Even though a child does not have nightmares or may not appear scared or anxious about what they are viewing, this does not mean that a child is not affected by it.
- Don't assume that caregivers, neighbors, or other parents share your media values. Talking to other adults about your expectations before children spend time with them may protect children from media that parents do not want their children exposed to.
- V-chip technology allows people to block programming from their TV sets and computers with TV capabilities. The v-chip can block all shows with a TV rating that you choose from the TV ratings system now being used, but cannot block an individual show.
- Children learn and grow best from time spent with caring people, not from electronic media.

Approaches

Top TV Tips: Building a Balanced TV Diet

You are your children's first and most influential teacher. The values and coping behaviors your children learn now will last a lifetime. Use TV to promote your children's health by building a balanced TV diet.

1. Watch What They Eat and Watch What They Watch

   How much your kids eat has a big impact on their health; so does the amount of TV they watch.

   THINGS TO DO:

   - Start by charting your family's current TV intake; list all TV shows watched in a week.
   - Discuss how much time your family spends with TV, which programs are worthwhile, and which can be dropped in favor of other activities.

   The American Academy of Pediatrics recommends:

   - Parents should limit their children's TV viewing to one or two hours of quality programming a day.
   - Parents should take advantage of high-quality programs offered on videocassettes or from other sources.

2. Know What's Inside the Box

   You carefully read the labels on foods your children eat. Do the same with TV. Lots of sweets are not good for kids. Neither are programs with violence, lewd language and sexual overtones.

   WHAT TO DO?

   - Read the TV listings and reviews.
   - Preview programs before your kids see them. Talk to teachers and pediatricians to see what they recommend.
   - Select TV programs that build interest in other activities, such as reading, hobbies, or the outdoors.

3. Add Plenty of Nutritious Content

   Look for TV "main dishes" with educational content and positive characters and values.

   RESEARCH SHOWS

   - Both school readiness and verbal and math abilities were greater in children who watched "Sesame Street" and other educational programs.

      University of Kansas, Center for Research on the Influence of Television on Children, May 1995.

4. Sit Down With a Good "TV Meal"—Don't Just Snack Away

Don't let your children just "watch TV." The next time your children ask, "Can I watch TV?" ask them what *specific program* they want to watch. Help your children get in the habit of watching one TV program, then turning the TV off and doing something else. Involve your children in setting TV rules.

SOME IDEAS

- Don't let your children watch TV until after their homework or chores are done.
- Make that extra effort to watch some shows together. By watching together, you're telling your children you care. "Co-viewing" can lead to lasting educational benefits.
- Tape quality shows and view them at a later time.

5. Put Down the Clicker and Get Some Family Exercise

TV should not replace active play. Your TV diet will be most successful when it includes lots of "family exercises," such as family discussions and activities.

TV programs should be springboards that spur curiosity, discussion, and learning.

PARENT ACTION

- Talk with your children. Ask them, "What did you learn from that program?" or "Why do you like to watch that character?"
- When you see a portrayal that offends you, let your children know. Teach your children that programs that glorify violence or promiscuity and present gender, racial, cultural, or other stereotypes are against your values.
- Weave a "web of learning" for your children. Good TV programs can spark interest in related books, conversations and activities.

> —Reprinted from "The Smart Parent's Guide to Kids' TV," a publication of PBS and the American Academy of Pediatrics.
>
> **NOTE:** *In 1999, the AAP amended their position on children and television viewing. The AAP does not recommend television viewing for children ages two or younger until more is known about the effects of viewing on young children.*

Many experts agree that combined screen time (television, video, video game, computer use) for children should be limited to one hour per day or less, even if the program, video, software, or game is considered educational. Too much screen time can take away from the time that children spend in play and other activities that help children develop language, social, thinking, and motor skills.

Choose media wisely. Our children deserve the best entertainment we can offer. The following lists summarize the qualities to look for in TV programs, movies, and video games. Choose ones that:

- ❏ Portray suffering and the human condition sensitively
- ❏ Evoke thoughtful family discussion
- ❏ Reflect your priorities and values
- ❏ Enhance your child's learning about herself and others

Television, Videos, Computers, and Media

Choose video and computer games that:

❏ Demand mental ability, not only the use of the trigger finger

❏ Require thought and problem-solving skills

❏ Develop skills that will be carried into adult life and work

❏ Link the child to the culture of the real world

❏ Spur the child's curiosity and creativity

—Excerpt from *Screen Smarts* copyright © 1996 by Gloria DeGaetano and Kathleen Bander. Reprinted by permission of Houghton Mifflin Company. All rights reserved.

QUESTIONS TO HELP PARENTS AND CHILDREN TALK ABOUT TV AND OTHER MEDIA

- Talk about your reactions—both positive and negative—to what you each see.

  "What did you think about that show/game?"

  "I liked it when _____ happened. What did you think about that?"

  "I didn't like it when _____ . I wish they didn't have to hurt each other. What do you think?"

- Help sort out fantasy from reality.

  "What was pretend and what was real? How could you tell?" (Help sort out points of confusion by saying things such as "In real life things don't work that way.")

  "I wonder how they made _____ happen on that show. What do you think?"

- Help children compare what they saw to their own experience.

  "Could anything like _____ happen in our lives? When? How would it be the same? different?"

  "What would you do if you were in that situation?"

- Talk directly about the violence and other mean-spirited behavior children see on the screen.

  "What do you think about how _____ solved her/his problem? If you had a problem like that, what could you do? or say?"

  "Can you think of a way to solve that problem so that no one gets hurt or everyone stays safe?"

- Ask questions that focus on stereotyped images and behaviors.

  "I wonder why it's always men with big muscles who go to fight. Did you notice that? What do you think about it?"

  "It seems like the women always need to get rescued by the men. Have you noticed that? I wonder why."

  "I wonder why the 'bad guys' have foreign accents. Or why they always wear dark colors."

—From *Remote Control Childhood: Combating the Hazards of Media Culture* by Diane E. Levin. Reprinted with permission from the National Association for the Education of Young Children, 1998.

Judge the effectiveness of screen violence. An extensive body of research suggests that several important variables determine how effective media messages are at teaching aggression to children:

- Do we identify with the character? The more we identify and empathize with a character, the more likely we are to imitate that character.

- Is the violence reinforced? Does crime pay? Violence that is rewarded or seems justified is far more likely to be imitated than violence that seems unjustified.

- Is the violence seen as real or make-believe? Violence that is realistic is more likely to have an effect on people than violence that is unrealistic. It is important to note that Big Bird is "real" for the three-year-old and the Incredible Hulk is "real" for the five-year-old. It is not until a child is almost nine years old that "real" means about the same thing that it does for adults.

Keep in mind: *Parental involvement greatly enhances the prosocial effects, while reducing the antisocial effects, of media on children.*

—From *Viewing Violence* by Madeline Levine, Doubleday, 1996.

Use parental guidelines and ratings, but don't rely on them. Guidelines and ratings are helpful but won't tell you if your particular child will find something scary. Even G-rated movies can be frightening to young children. You know your child best. When in doubt, view the program first.

—Ideas found in *Mommy, I'm Scared: How TV and Movies Frighten Children and What We Can Do to Protect Them* by Joanne Cantor, Harcourt, Brace, & Co., 1998.

TV PARENTAL GUIDELINES

The following categories apply to programs designed solely for children:

TV-Y   All Children. *This program is designed to be appropriate for all children.* Whether animated or live-action, the themes and elements in this program are specifically designed for a very young audience, including children from ages 2-6. This program is not expected to frighten younger children.

TV-Y7   Directed to Older Children. *This program is designed for children age 7 and above.* It may be more appropriate for children who have acquired the developmental skills needed to distinguish between make-believe and reality. Themes and elements in this program may include mild fantasy violence or comedic violence, or may frighten children under the age of 7. Therefore, parents may wish to consider the suitability of this program for their very young children. Note: For those programs where fantasy violence may be more intense or more combative than other programs in this category, such programs will be designed TV-Y7-FV.

The following categories apply to programs designed for the entire audience:

TV-G   General Audience. *Most parents would find this program suitable for all ages.* Although this rating does not signify a program designed specifically for children, most parents may let younger children watch this program unattended. it contains little or no violence, no strong language and little or no sexual dialogue or situations.

TV-PG   Parental Guidance Suggested. *This program contains material that parents may find unsuitable for younger children.* Many parents may want to watch it with their younger children. The theme itself may call for parental guidance and/or the program contains one or more of the following: moderate violence (V), some sexual situations (S), infrequent coarse language (L), or some suggestive dialogue (D).

TV-14   Parents Strongly Cautioned. *This program contains some material that many parents would find unsuitable for children under 14 years of age.* Parents are strongly urged to exercise greater care in monitoring this program and are cautioned against letting children under the age of 14 watch unattended. This program contains one or more of the following: intense violence (V), intense sexual situations (S), strong coarse language (L), or intensely suggestive dialogue (D).

TV-MA   Mature Audience Only. *This program is specifically designed to be viewed by adults and therefore may be unsuitable for children under 17.* This program contains one or more of the following: graphic violence (V), explicit sexual activity (S), or crude indecent language (L).

—TV Parental Guidelines reprinted with permission from the TV Parental Guidelines Council, P.O. Box 14097, Washington, DC 20004.

Movie Ratings

G: "General Audiences. All Ages Admitted"

This is a film which contains nothing in theme, language, nudity and sex, violence, etc. which would, in the view of the Rating Board, be offensive to parents whose younger children view the film. The G rating is not a "certificate of approval," nor does it signify a children's film.

Some snippets of language may go beyond polite conversation but they are common everyday expressions. No strong words are present in G-rated films. The violence is at a minimum. Nudity and sex scenes are not present nor is there drug use content.

PG: "Parental Guidance Suggested. Some Material May Not Be Suitable for Children."

This is a film which clearly needs to be examined or inquired into by parents before they let their children attend. The label PG plainly states that parents may consider some material unsuitable for their children, but the parent must make the decision.

Parents are warned against sending their children, unseen or without inquiry, to PG-rated movies.

The theme of a PG-rated film may itself call for parental guidance. There may be some profanity in these films. There may be violence or brief nudity. But these elements are not deemed so intense as to require that parents be strongly cautioned beyond the suggestion of parental guidance. There is no drug use content in a PG-rated film.

PG-13: "Parents Strongly Cautioned. Some Material May Be Inappropriate for Children Under 13."

PG-13 is a sterner warning to parents to determine for themselves the attendance in particular of their younger children as they might consider some of the material not suited for them. Parents, by the rating, are alerted to be careful about the attendance of their under-teenage children.

A PG-13 film is one which, in the view of the Rating Board, leaps beyond the boundaries of the PG rating in theme, violence, nudity, sensuality, language, or other elements, but does not quite fit within the restricted R category. Any drug use content will initially require at least a PG-13 rating.

If nudity is sexually oriented, the film will generally not be found in the PG-13 category. If violence is too rough or persistent, the film goes into the R (restricted) rating. A film's single use of one of the harsher sexually-driven words, though only as an expletive, shall initially require the Rating Board to issue that film at least a PG-13 rating. More than one such expletive must lead the Rating Board to insure a film an R rating, as must even one of these words used in a sexual context.

R: "Restricted. Under 17 Requires Accompanying Parent or Adult Guardian."

In the opinion of the Rating Board, this film definitely contains adult material. Parents are strongly urged to find out more about this film before they allow their children to accompany them.

An R-rated film may include hard language, or tough violence, or nudity within sensual scenes, or drug abuse or other elements, or a combination of some of the above, so that parents are counseled, in advance, to take this advisory rating very seriously.

NC-17: "No One 17 And Under Admitted."

This rating declares that the Rating Board believes that this is a film that most parents will consider patently too adult for their children 17 and under. No children will be admitted. NC-17 does not necessarily mean "obscene or pornographic" in the oft-accepted or legal meaning of those words. The reason for the application of an NC-17 rating can be violence or sex or aberrational behavior or drug abuse or any other elements which, when present, most parents would consider too strong and therefore off-limits for viewing by their children.

> —Excerpts from "The Voluntary Movie Rating System" by Jack Valenti, the Motion Picture of America Association, 1996.

ESRB Rating Symbols & Content Descriptors for Video Games & PC Software

Look for these ratings on the front of the package and, for more information, look for content descriptors on the back of the package.

Early Childhood

Titles rated "Early Childhood (EC)" have content suitable for children ages three and older and do not contain any material that parents would find inappropriate.

Kids to Adults

Titles rated "Kids to Adult (K-A)" have content suitable for persons ages six and older. These titles will appeal to people of many ages and tastes. They may contain minimal violence, some comic mischief (for example, slapstick comedy), or some crude language.

Everyone

As of January 1, 1998, the new "Everyone" designation will replace the "Kids to Adults" rating. Titles rated "Everyone (E)" have content suitable for persons ages six and older. These titles will appeal to people of many ages and tastes. They may contain minimal violence, some comic mischief (for example, slapstick comedy), or some crude language.

Teen

Titles rated "Teen (T)" have content suitable for persons ages 13 and older. Titles in this category may contain violent content, mild or strong language, and/or suggestive themes.

Mature

Titles rated "Mature (M)" have content suitable for persons ages 17 and older. These products may include more intense violence or language than products in the Teen category. In addition, these titles may also include mature sexual themes.

Adults Only

Titles rated "Adults Only (AO)" have content suitable only for adults. These products may include graphic depictions of sex and/or violence. Adults Only products are not intended to be sold or rented to persons under the age of 18.

Rating Pending

Product has been submitted to the ESRB and is awaiting final rating.

Content Descriptors

When consumers look on the back of a package, they may see any of the following phrases that further describe the product's content.

VIOLENCE

MILD ANIMATED VIOLENCE
Contains scenes involving characters/animated/pixelated characters in the depiction of unsafe or hazardous acts or violent situations.

MILD REALISTIC VIOLENCE
Contains scenes involving characters in the depiction of unsafe or hazardous acts or violent situations in realistic or photographic detail.

COMIC MISCHIEF
Scenes depicting activities that have been characterized as slapstick or gross vulgar humor.

ANIMATED VIOLENCE
Contains depictions of aggressive conflict involving cartoon/animated/pixilated characters.

REALISTIC VIOLENCE
Contains realistic or photographic-like depictions of body parts.

ANIMATED BLOOD AND GORE
Animated/pixilated or cartoon-like depictions of mutilation or dismemberment of body parts.

REALISTIC BLOOD AND GORE
Representations of blood and/or gore in realistic or photographic-like detail.

ANIMATED BLOOD
Animated/pixilated or cartoon-like depictions of blood.

REALISTIC BLOOD
Representations of blood in a realistic or photographic-like detail.

LANGUAGE

MILD LANGUAGE
Product contains the use of the word like "damn".

STRONG LANGUAGE
Commonly referenced four-letter words to include anatomical references.

SEXUAL CONTENT

SUGGESTIVE THEMES
Mild provocative references or material.

MATURE SEXUAL THEMES
Contains provocative material: including depiction of the human body either animated or photographic-like formats.

STRONG SEXUAL CONTENT
Graphic depiction of sexual behavior and/or the human form (i.e. frontal nudity) in either animated or photographic-like detail.

EARLY CHILDHOOD

SOME ADULT ASSISTANCE MAY BE NEEDED

READING SKILLS

FINE MOTOR SKILLS

HIGHER LEVEL THINKING SKILLS

OTHER DESCRIPTORS

GAMING
The depiction of betting-like behavior.

USE OF TOBACCO AND ALCOHOL
Product contains images of the use of tobacco and/or alcohol in a manner which condones or glorifies their use.

USE OF DRUGS
Product contains images of the use of drugs in a manner which condones or glorifies their use.

INFORMATIONAL
Overall content provides data, facts, resource information, reference materials or instructional text.

EDUTAINMENT
Content provides user with specific skills development or reinforcement learning within an entertainment setting. Skill development is an integral part of product.

—Please be advised that the ESRB rating icons "EC," "K-A," "E," "T," "M," and "AO" are copyrighted works and certification marks owned by the Interactive Digital Software Association and the Entertainment Software Rating Board and may only be used with their permission and authority. Under no circumstances may the rating icons by self-applied to any product that has not been rated by the ESRB. For information about whether a product has been rated by the ESRB, please call the ESRB at (212) 759-0700 or 1-800-771-3772.

Evaluate any video game before you buy it. Consider trying a demo and if that is not available, read the box thoroughly. Sometimes you can tell from the label if a game is particularly violent or has sexual content. Ask for the option of a full refund or exchange if the game turns out to be violent or has sexual content. Try out the game yourself before giving it to your child.

> —Ideas found in "Video Games—A Note of Caution" by Dr. William Cockburn,
> Online, ParenthoodWeb: www.parenthoodweb.com.

When you and your child use the Internet, consider safety issues. Violent, sexual, and inappropriate material, and messages that demean people, are easy to find or stumble across. Monitor your child's use of the Internet and discuss guidelines such as never giving out your name, address, or phone number without permission.

> —Ideas found in "Child Safety on the Information Superhighway," National Center for
> Missing and Exploited Children, 1994.

Help your child learn more about television and other media by reading about it together:

Arthur's Computer Disaster; Arthur's TV Trouble by Marc Brown

Berenstain Bears and Too Much TV by Stan and Jan Berenstain

Mouse TV by Matt Novak

Take a Look, It's In a Book: How Television is Made at Reading Rainbow by Ronnie Krauss

When to Get More Help

Children typically grow and learn new skills in their own time and at their own pace within the wide range of what is normal. Sometimes, children need a bit of extra help to keep their development on track, or to stay healthy and happy. Sometimes, parents need help providing for a child's needs or sorting out the best approaches to parenting.

Consider getting help for your child if she:

- Frequently watches television up close after being asked not to (it is common for children to want to get close to the screen, but it may be a sign of a vision problem; usually there would be other symptoms, if that is the case).
- Spends excessive amounts of time watching television or playing computer or video games, preferring them to more engaging activities, or cannot be encouraged into other interests.
- Repeats scenes from television or cartoon shows that result in frequent cruelty toward other children or animals, threatening others, playing with fire, harming property, or engaging in play that has violent themes.

Consider getting help for the sake of all children if:

- You become aware of child pornography while online, or in any other form. Immediately report it to the National Center for Missing and Exploited Children by calling 800-843-5678.

You are the expert when it comes to your child. If you have a concern, trust your instinct and find someone trained to help you: health care providers, early intervention teams, mental health professionals, parent educators and consultants, or telephone help-line staff. Consider talking it over with friends and family, too. You don't need to worry alone! Turn to "Finding Help in Your Community" on page 4 to learn about finding help near you.

More Help and Information

Books for Parents

- *The Computer Museum Guide to the Best Software for Kids* by Cathy Minraker and Alison Elliot. HarperPerennial, 1995.

- *Facets Non-Violent, Non-Sexist Children's Video Guide.* Facets Multimedia, Inc., 1996. 800-331-6197.

- *The Internet Kids & Family Yellow Pages, 1999 Edition* by Jean Armour Polly. Osborne McGraw-Hill, 1998.

- *Mommy, I'm Scared: How TV and Movies Frighten Children and What We Can Do to Protect Them* by Joanne Cantor, Harcourt, Brace, & Co., 1998.

- *Screen Smarts: A Family Guide to Media Literacy* by Gloria DeGaetano and Kathleen Barder. Houghton Mifflin Co., 1996.

- *Stay Tuned: Raising Media-Savvy Kids in the Age of the Channel-Surfing Couch Potato* by Jane Murphy and Karen Tucker. Doubleday, 1996.

- *Viewing Violence: How Media Violence Affects Your Child's and Adolescent's Development* by Madeline Levine. Doubleday, 1996.

Articles, Pamphlets and Booklets

- "Child Safety on the Information Superhighway" National Center for Missing and Exploited Children 1-800-843-5678.
  Available online through Eugene School District 4J: www.4jlane.edu/safety/childtoc.html

- "How to Make the Right Choices for You and Your Family," Entertainment Software Rating Board (ESRB). Call, write or view online (see National Organizations)

- "Media Violence and Young Children" National Association for the Education of Young Children
  800-424-2460
  fax: 202-328-1846
  Web site: www.naeyc.org

- "Parent's Guide to the Internet" U.S. Department of Education, Office of Educational Research and Improvement, Office of Educational Technology, 1997.
  800-USA-LEARN
  Available online at the web site: www.ed.gov/pubs/parents/internet

- "Television and the Family," American Academy of Pediatrics
  800-228-5005
  Available online at: www.aap.org/family/mnbroc.cfm

Government

- Federal Communications Commission (FCC) 888CALL-FCC (888-225-5322), TTY: 202-418-2555

  Web site: www.fcc.gov.

  To find out how to submit informal or formal comments on proceedings and rules that are currently being considered before the commission, call or write the FCC, visit the web site and the Children's Educational Television Web site.

More Help and Information (continued)

Magazines and Newsletters

- *Children's Software Review*
  800-993-9499
  Search the online database of software reviews at their Web site: www2.childrenssoftware.com/childrenssoftware/

- *Parenting*; *Parents*; *Child*; *Family PC*; and other parenting or media magazines regularly review children's media.

National Organizations

- Center for Media Literacy
  800-226-9494
  E-Mail: cml@medialit.org
  Web site: www. medialit.org

- Coalition for Quality Children's Media
  505-989-8076.
  Evaluates children's media and publishes KIDS FIRST™ Directory.
  Search online database of endorsed children's media at their web site: www.cqcm.org/kidsfirst

- Entertainment Software Rating Board (ESRB), for information of video game and computer software game ratings.
  800-771-3772
  E-Mail: info@esrb.org
  Web site: www.esrb.org
  ESRB rates software, video games, and web sites.

- National Institute on Media and the Family
  888-672-5437
  Search the online database of media at their web site: www.mediaandthefamily.org

- Motion Picture Association of America (MPAA), for information on movie ratings
  202-293-1966
  Web site: www.mpaa.org
  Search the online movie rating database

- TV Parental Guidelines Council
  202-879-9364
  Web site: www.tvguidelines.org

Videos

- *Taking Charge of Your TV*, hosted by Rosie O'Donnell, produced by HBO for The Family Community and Critical Viewing Project. For a free copy call 800-452-6351. Or call the National Cable Television Association (NCTA) for this video and other information on critical viewing: 202-775-3550.

Web Sites

- Media Literacy Online Project: find links to articles, guides, and research. Web address: http://interact.uoregon.edu/MediaLit/HomePage

- Netparents.org: Resources for Internet Parents has information on internet ratings, blocking software, and a good list of links, "Starting Points for Kid-Friendly Net Access."
  www.netparents.org

- "Surfin the Net for Kids and Families," by Ann Treacy and Lori Beck.
  www.cyfc.umm.edu/surfin.html

- Yahooligans.com is a good starting place for surfing the web with children: www.yahooligans.com.

Temperament and Personality

Description

Temperament is a person's normal, natural style of behaving and responding to the world. The wide range of temperaments helps explain the wide range of behavior and disposition. Temperament does not dictate what children will do but helps understand how they do it.

Personality is the traits and characteristics that people are born with (nature) combined with the effect of people and environment (nurture). Personality is affected by many factors including temperament, birth order, family size, life events, serious illnesses, deaths, family moves, economic status, gender, intelligence, age, health, and parenting.

Realistic Expectations

- The temperament that children exhibit in childhood is likely to be similar to their temperament as an adult. Although there is some consistency in temperament, it is not an accurate predictor of personality, success, or failure as an adult.

- Typical behavior for children of a certain age and at a certain stage of development is often mistakenly identified as temperament. Children may be behaving in a developmentally appropriate way, rather than having a challenging temperament.

- Behavior is affected by how children feel. Children experience physical sensations differently. Children who feel overwhelmed, irritated, or uncomfortable with the sensations (taste, touch, sound, sight, smell) around them may behave in more challenging ways.

- Labels such as shy, easy, difficult, loud, or impulsive can damage self-esteem. They create expectations for children to act a certain way, and prevent them from branching out beyond the label, and they can last into adulthood.

- Temperament has a large impact on family relationships and children's health and behavior, and it influences the way adults treat children. Due to temperament differences, two children can experience the same family very differently: An outgoing, easy-to-adapt child may ask and receive more affection than a sibling who is sensitive or slow-to-warm up.

- Temperament traits that seem difficult to handle in children, like persistence, are often valuable characteristics to have as an adult.

- Bad parenting is not necessarily the cause when children develop behavior problems or exhibit difficult behavior. Some challenging behaviors are due to a child's environment being out of sync with her temperament and personality.

- Children's temperament can have an effect on how parents judge themselves and their parenting skills. Parents with children who have "easy" temperaments tend to feel successful while parents of challenging, spirited, or "difficult" children tend to feel more helpless and less successful.

- Understanding temperament and personality can improve parent-child relationships. Parents who understand temperament and personality may enjoy their child's unique strengths more and experience greater family harmony. How parents communicate with children has a lasting effect on their personality.

Approaches

"Personality Type" is a system for understanding four different components or "dimensions" that make up a person's personality and give information about the different operating styles that people have. Think of each dimension as a scale—a continuum between opposite extremes—like this:

Extroversion ——————————|—————————— Introversion

> Relates to where people get their energy: from being with people, or from being alone.

Sensing ——————————|—————————— Intuition

> Explains the way people take in information and learn about the world: from the five senses gathered through experience, or from meanings, connections, and possibilities related to information from the *sixth sense*.

Thinking ——————————|—————————— Feeling

> Interprets the ways people make decisions: by using objective information and considering logical consequences, or based on feelings, values, and consideration of how the decision will affect people.

Judging ——————————|—————————— Perceiving

> Help to understand how people organize the world around them: by preferring the process of making decisions and settling things, or by preferring the process of gathering information.

Personality type provides many useful insights about a person's behavior, motivations, and tendencies. Personality type is only one layer of a person. Two deeper layers are temperament and the level of intensity of each trait.

> —From *Nurture by Nature: Understanding Your Child's Personality Type and Become a Better Parent* by Paul D. Tieger and Barbara Barron-Tieger, Little, Brown and Company, 1997.

Many experts agree that people have tendencies to behave and react in consistent ways that are referred to as *temperament.* Based on the work of Stella Chess and Alexander Thomas, nine temperament traits or styles of behavior have been identified:

- *Activity Level*—the amount of movement and activity in daily circumstances on a scale from low to high.
- *Rhythmicity or Regularity*—the amount of regularity in daily activities like eating and sleeping on a scale from irregular to regular.
- *Mood*—the tendency to have happy or unhappy behavior and reactions on a scale from negative to positive.
- *Threshold or Sensitivity*—the amount of noise, pain, activity, or other stimulation that causes a response on a scale from low to high sensitivity.
- *Intensity or intensity of reaction*—the amount of energy put into reactions on a scale from low to high, or mild to strong.
- *Approach/Withdrawal*—the tendency shown when first reacting to new people or situations on a scale from ease of approach to withdrawal from new situation.
- *Adaptability*—the tendency toward changes in daily life on a scale from low to high adaptability.
- *Attention Span and Persistence*—the length of time spent on an activity, regardless of distractions; how long and how important it is to stick with an activity on a scale from low to high attention span and persistence.
- *Distractibility*—the tendency toward continuing activity when faced with noise, other activity or interruption on a scale of low to high distractibility.

Temperament and Personality

Work with your child's temperament, not against it. Seek professional help in profiling your child's temperament. The following table summarizes the main points regarding management of the high and low ends of the nine temperament characteristics:

SUMMARY OF MANAGEMENT APPROACHES	
HIGH ACTIVITY Help the child find ample opportunity for physical activity. Avoid unnecessary restrictions of activity. Demand restraint of motion appropriate for age when necessary.	**LOW ACTIVITY** Allow extra time to complete tasks. Set realistic limits, such as meeting the school bus on time. Do not criticize slow speed.
HIGH REGULARITY In an infant, plan feedings and other activities on a schedule. In an older child, advise of expected disruptions of the schedule.	**LOW REGULARITY** In an infant, first try to accommodate the preference for irregularity, then gradually steer her toward a more regular schedule. An older child can be expected increasingly to regularize his eating and sleeping times, even if he does not feel hungry or sleepy on schedule.
APPROACHING OR BOLD INITIAL REACTION Reinforce with praise if positive. Remember that the initial positive reaction may not last. Be aware of the child's boldness in dangerous situations.	**WITHDRAWING OR INHIBITED INITIAL REACTION** Avoid overload of new experiences. Prepare the child for new situations and introduce her to them slowly. Do not push too hard. Praise her for overcoming her fears of novelty. Encourage self-management as the child grows older.
HIGH ADAPTABILITY Look out for possible susceptibility to unfavorable influences in school and elsewhere.	**LOW ADAPTABILITY** Avoid unnecessary requirements to adapt. Reduce or spread out necessary adaptations, arranging for gradual changes in stages. Do not push too hard or too quickly. Give advance warnings about what to expect. Teach social skills to expedite adaptation. Maintain reasonable expectations for change. Support and praise effort.

SUMMARY OF MANAGEMENT APPROACHES (CONTINUED)

HIGH INTENSITY	LOW INTENSITY
Intensity may exaggerate the apparent importance of response.	Try to read the child's real need, and do not mistake it as trivial just because it is mildly expressed.
Avoid reacting to the child with the same intensity; try to read the child's real need and respond calmly to that need.	Take complaints seriously.
Do not give in just to make peace.	
Enjoy intense positive responses.	

POSITIVE MOOD	NEGATIVE MOOD
Encourage positive and friendly responses.	Remember that it is just your child's style, unless there is an underlying behavioral or emotional problem.
Look out only for those situations in which your child's outward positive behavior may mask true distress, such as with pain, and situations in which being too friendly may be troublesome, such as with strangers.	Do not let the child's mood make you feel guilty or angry; his mood is not your fault.
	Ignore as many of the glum, unfriendly responses as possible; however, try to spot and deal with the real distress.
	Advise an older child to try harder to be pleasant with people.

HIGH PERSISTENCE AND ATTENTION SPAN	LOW PERSISTENCE AND ATTENTION SPAN
Redirect a persistent toddler whose persistence is annoying.	The child may need help organizing tasks into shorter segments with periodic breaks; however, the responsibility for completion of the task belongs with the child.
In an older child, warn about the need to end or interrupt activity when continued for too long.	Reward the adequate completion of the task and not the speed with which it is done.
Reassure the child that leaving some tasks unfinished is acceptable.	

HIGH DISTRACTIBILITY	LOW DISTRACTIBILITY
If the problem involves an older child, try to eliminate or reduce competing stimuli.	If the child ignores necessary interruptions, do not assume it is deliberate disobedience.
Gently redirect the child to the task at hand when necessary; however, encourage the child to assume his own responsibility for doing this.	
Praise adequately for completing the task.	

HIGH SENSITIVITY	LOW SENSITIVITY
Avoid excessive stimulation.	Look out for underreporting of pain and other distress.
Eliminate overestimating extreme responses to stimuli.	Help the child develop an awareness of important internal and external stimuli.
Help the child understand this trait in himself.	
Support and encourage the child's sensitivity to the feelings of others.	

Temperament and Personality

"Goodness of fit" between your child's temperament and your child's environment impacts whether your child is growing and developing with ease. When expectations for your child match your child's traits, tendencies, and abilities, then the fit between the child and her parents or caregivers is good. This is a healthy environment for your child to grow in. When the environment for a child is not a good fit with her temperament, she may experience stress and may not develop in a healthy way.

Sometimes, opposite temperaments complement each other; sometimes, they don't. Parent and child with different temperaments can have healthy relationships by working towards "goodness of fit." "Goodness of fit" can be achieved by:

- Setting reasonable demands and expectations for your child molded to his temperament traits and yours.
- Changing expectations as your child grows and changes.
- Adapting parenting strategies to plan for temperament tendencies.
- Helping your child adapt his tendencies to grow, develop, and be comfortable in the real world.

> —Ideas found in *Know Your Child* by Stella Chess and Alexander Thomas, Basic Books, 1987.

Adjust your home to fit the needs of your child's temperament. If your home doesn't seem to work for your child, consider her temperament and what changes around the home you could make that might create an easier environment for her to live in. For example, if your child is easily distracted, you may want to consider keeping fewer toys available at any one time. If your child is extremely regular, you may want to provide a consistent time for sleeping, eating, and other activities.

> —Ideas found in *Understanding Temperament: Strategies for Creating Family Harmony* by Lyndall Shick, Parenting Press, 1998.

What distinguishes a truly challenging child is that she is simply more of everything—more intense, more excitable, more stubborn, more talkative, more defiant, and more rambunctious. A challenging child makes extraordinary demands on families and takes extra time, patience, and work. Focusing on the positives instead of the negatives may help you appreciate your child more. Here are eight great traits of challenging children:

- They are leaders. They're not content to sit back and let others tell them what to do.
- They march to a different drummer. They're unique and have an original take on life.
- They are creative and have intense feelings. They find colors, sounds, and movement fascinating and stimulating.
- They are memorable. People notice them; they don't just fade into the woodwork.
- They are independent thinkers. They demand answers and search for reasons and meaning.
- They have high energy. They won't sit in a stupor, vegging out in front of the TV.
- They usually know what they want. They're not wishy-washy.
- They are often sensitive and demonstrative. Their expressions of love are spontaneous and sincere.

> —Ideas found in "The Challenging Child" by Nancy Samalin, *Parents*, November 1997.

Be aware of your child's many attributes. Avoid labels for many reasons:

- Labels may not accurately reflect your child: Labeling your child as one temperament trait may not take into account her age, developmental stage, health, or personality. A child may be labeled as crabby when she may be just tired. A child may be labeled as selfish when she is just exhibiting the normal wariness of sharing of her age.
- Labeling your child may cause her to think she's supposed to act that way: Even a seemingly positive label like "Smiley" can give a child the impression that she is supposed to act happy and not show sadness or anger.

- Labels may keep you from seeing the many other sides of your child. Your child is never just one trait, and labeling her in one way does not take into account the whole child. A slow to warm child may also be adaptable, persistent, regular, and energetic. Even the most hard to live with temperament traits can be seen as assets if looked at in the right way. A child who is given a negative label like "Slowpoke" may really be persistent and thorough. A child who appears shy and is slow to warm up to new situations may really be the belle of the ball once she gets over her initial reaction.

- Your child is changing and a label that seems true today may not fit tomorrow. Labels may keep you from noticing all the growing and maturing your child is doing by focusing your view of her in one way.

Look at your child's many qualities and attributes. You may not be able to change a child's temperament, but you can alter your outlook of it and think positively.

—Ideas found in "Rebels, & Jokers: How Labeling Hurts Kids" by Tamara Eberlein, *Parents*, February 1997.

Help a child understand more about temperament and personality by reading about it together:

Can't Sit Still by Karen E. Lotz

Curious George books by H.A. & Margret Rey

Red Is Best by Kathy Stinson

Piggy's Birthday Dream by Anke de Vries

The Snow Fairy and the Spaceman by Catherine Anholt

Spinky Sulks by William Steig

Stop That Garbage Truck! by Linda Glaser

Where's Julius? by John Burningham

When To Get More Help

Children typically grow and learn new skills in their own time and at their own pace within the wide range of what is normal. Sometimes, children need a bit of extra help to keep their development on track, or to stay healthy and happy. Sometimes, parents need help providing for a child's needs or sorting out the best approaches to parenting.

Consider getting help for your child if she:

- Has a strong temperament type that leaves you wondering if she has a problem that needs attention. Sometimes it is difficult to tell the difference between normal behavior that springs from a strong temperament or personality type, and signs of possible problems: a child who rarely speaks in preschool may just be very introverted, or she may be overly stressed by the situation; a child who runs much of the time in preschool may just be very active or she may be showing signs of attention deficit disorder. Usually, children are just fine, or you will get more information as she grows that will clarify a problem if one exists. If you have questions about drawing the line between what is normal temperament or personality, and what is behavior that deserves special attention, ask for help to sort it out.

Consider getting help for yourself if you:

- Have a temperament or personality that clashes with your child's, and you find yourself in frequent conflicts with her.

You are the expert when it comes to your family and child. If you have a concern, trust your instinct and find someone trained to help you: health care providers, early intervention teams, mental health professionals, parent educators and consultants, or telephone help-line staff. Consider talking it over with friends and family, too. You don't need to worry alone! Turn to "Finding Help in Your Community" on page 4 to learn about finding help near you.

More Help And Information

Books for Parents

- *The Challenging Child: Understanding, Raising and Enjoying the Five "Difficult" Types of Children* by Stanley I. Greenspan with Jacqueline Salmon. Addison-Wesley Pub. Co., 1995.

- *The Edison Trait: Saving the Spirit of Your Non-Conforming Child* by Lucy Jo Palladino. Times Books, 1997.

- *Know Your Child* by Stella Chess and Alexander Thomas. Basic Books, 1987.

- *Living with the Active Alert Child: Groundbreaking Strategies for Parents* by Linda S. Budd. Parenting Press, 1993.

- *Nurture by Nature: Understanding Your Child's Personality Type and Become a Better Parent* by Paul D. Tieger and Barbara Barron-Tieger. Little, Brown and Company, 1997.

- *Raising Your Spirited Child: A Guide for Parents Whose Child Is More Intense, Sensitive, Perceptive, Persistent, Energetic* by Mary Sheedy Kurcinka. HarperCollins, 1991.

- *Raising Your Spirited Child Workbook* by Mary Sheedy Kurcinka. HarperCollins, 1998.

- *Temperament Tools: Working With Your Child's Inborn Tools* by Helen Neville and Dianne Clark Johnson. Parenting Press, 1998.

- *Understanding Temperament: Strategies for Creating Family Harmony* by Lyndall Shick. Parenting Press, 1998.

- *Understanding Your Child's Temperament* by William B. Carey. Macmillan, 1997.

National Organizations

- Association for Psychological Type
  816-444-3500, Fax: 816-444-0330
  Web site: www.aptcentral.org

Videos

- *Flexible, Fearful, or Feisty: the Different Temperaments of Infants and Toddlers.* California State Department of Education, 1990.

Web Sites

- Personalitytype.com, the web site of Paul Tieger and Barbara Barron Tieger: www.personalitytype.com.

Thumbs, Fingers, and Pacifiers

Description

Children begin sucking thumbs, fingers, and pacifiers during infancy when the need for sucking is strong. Babies learn that sucking can be comforting and that they have the power to calm themselves. Sucking for comfort is a normal, natural part of infancy that typically continues into toddlerhood and later.

Realistic Expectations

- It is typical for children to become attached to comforting security objects, like pacifiers and thumbs, by the time they are one year old. It is a sign of growing independence when they can comfort themselves in this way.

- By age two, children become less dependent on pacifiers and thumbs, but the desire for sucking can continue until age six or eight.

- Most children give up thumbsucking between two and four and pacifiers by age four.

- When sucking occurs for much of the day, this habit can interfere with learning other coping skills, with speech and language development, and with play—when a thumb in the mouth prevents a child from using both hands.

- Children tend to suck more when they are tired, sick, anxious, or bored.

- The American Dental Association says: "Children should have ceased sucking by the time the permanent front teeth are about to erupt." Permanent teeth typically erupt at age six and later.

- Punishment, nagging, humiliation, teasing, and harsh words are not effective methods to help a child stop a sucking habit and may make the habit worse by upsetting children and increasing their need for their security object.

- A sucking habit provides comfort and security. Children need help, extra support, and comfort when giving up the habit.

Approaches

The first approach to dealing with your child's thumb, finger or pacifier habit is to ignore it. Give it time, it will usually go away on it's own.

>—Ideas found in *Caring for Your Baby and Young Child* (revised edition, American Academy of Pediatrics), Bantam Books, 1998.

Allow your young child to keep his comfort habit of thumb or pacifier sucking. It's not necessary to try to break him of his habit before age four; most children quit on their own by then anyway. If he seems to be sucking much of the time, try to identify what may be causing his need for extra comfort. Then give him more of your time and attention to comfort him.

>—Ideas found in *Your Child: What Every Parent Needs to Know About Childhood Development from Birth to Preadolescence*, HarperCollins, 1998.

Thumbs, Fingers, and Pacifiers

Prevent the need for sucking by giving your child attention and time:

- Spend time with your child to help him feel loved.

- Allow extra time to show your child a new task or activity to reduce stress and the need for sucking.

- Allow extra time for your child to do what he needs to do to prevent frustration and reduce the need for sucking as a comfort.

- Help your child understand and name his feelings; listen to him.

- If you remain patient and avoid being negative about his sucking, but give him attention to reduce his need to suck, your child will stop sucking in his own time.

—Ideas found in *Positive Parenting from A to Z* by Karen Renshaw Joslin,
Fawcett Columbine: Ballantine Books, 1994.

> **!** **WARNING!** The American Academy of Pediatrics advises: Never tie a pacifier to a crib, bed, or around a child's neck! It is dangerous and can lead to serious injury or death.

> *I helped my three-year-old give up her pacifier by telling her that when she was ready to throw it away, that we could go to the store and buy any doll she wanted. Then, I dropped it; I did not say another word about it.*
>
> *One week later, we were out running errands when she told me she was ready to throw away the binky, she wanted a doll. I called daddy and told him the house should be binky-free when we got home. While he took care of that, Andrea picked out a bunny baby. She cried the first night, but the second night was a breeze. Now when she sees babies with pacifiers, she proudly announces that she threw away her binky, and that she has a new doll!*
>
> —Allison, Crawfordville, FL

You can't make your child quit sucking but you can help him want to quit:

- Talk to him about it—when and how to quit.

- Get help from the pediatrician, dentist, friends, relatives, siblings, or anyone who might be able to help the child feel as though he wants to quit.

- Be positive and point out that older children don't suck on fingers, thumbs, or pacifiers. Point out other babyish things that he used to do but doesn't do any longer: feeding himself, getting himself dressed, putting on his own shoes.

- Consider offering an older toddler an incentive to quit, like a new toy, treat, or special outing.

- Keep his hands and mouth busy with talking, making music, singing, or a snack at a needy time of day

—Ideas found in *What to Expect the Toddler Years* by Arlene Eisenberg, Heidi E. Murkoff,
and Sandee E. Hathaway, Workman Pub., 1994.

Help your child understand more about sucking habits by reading about them together:

📖 *David Decides About Thumbsucking* by Susan Heitler

📖 *Harold's Hideaway Thumb* by Harriet Sonnenschein

When to Get More Help

C hildren typically grow and learn new skills in their own time and at their own pace within the wide range of what is normal. Sometimes, children need a bit of extra help to keep their development on track, or to stay healthy and happy. Sometimes, parents need help providing for a child's needs or sorting out the best approaches to parenting.

Consider getting help for your child if he:

- Sucks his thumb or pacifier so much that it interferes with his learning to talk or eat.
- Sucks his thumb so much that it interferes with using his hands for playing.
- Seems to be affecting the shape of his mouth or teeth with his thumb or pacifier sucking.

You are the expert when it comes to your family and child. If you have a concern, trust your instinct and find someone trained to help you: health care providers, early intervention teams, mental health professionals, parent educators and consultants, or telephone help-line staff. Consider talking it over with friends and family, too. You don't need to worry alone! Turn to "Finding Help in Your Community" on page 4 to learn about finding help near you.

More Help and Information

Books for Parents

- "Handling Sucking Habits Now" in *What to Expect the Toddler Years* by Arlene Eisenberg, Heidi E. Murkoff, and Sandee E. Hathaway. Workman Pub., 1994
- "Thumb and Finger Sucking" in *Caring for Your Baby and Your Child* (American Academy of Pediatrics, revised edition) Bantam Books, 1998.

Articles, Pamphlets, and Booklets

- "Your Child's Teeth." Request from your dentists or call: American Dental Association, Div. of Communications 312-440-2500; Fax: 312-440-2800

Toilet Learning

Description

Toilet learning is the process by which children are taught how to go to the toilet on their own signal, needing little outside help. Toilet training is the help and guidance that adults give children to help them learn.

Realistic Expectations

- There is no exact timetable that can tell you when a child is ready to learn to use the toilet. Waiting for signs of readiness before beginning toilet training will lead to greater success; training too early is more difficult and less effective.

- Two years is the *minimum* age usually recommended to start toilet training for children.

- The time at which children are physically and emotionally ready varies from child to child. No two children are alike.

- Children younger than eighteen months do not have the bladder and bowel control to be toilet trained. Between eighteen and thirty months, children begin to show signs of being physically ready.

- Most children learn to use the toilet with some assistance between two and three years of age, and then regularly without being asked between three and a half and four.

- The majority of toilet training takes about six months, but the whole process can take years if you include wiping well and nighttime dryness.

- The typical order for achieving bowel and bladder control is: 1) nighttime bowel control, 2) daytime bowel control, 3) daytime bladder control, and 4) nighttime bladder control.

- Most children stay dry all night regularly about six months after they have mastered toilet training. But many, up to 15%, continue to wet the bed regularly until age five or later.

- Boys tend to train later than girls: only about half of boys are toilet trained by age three, while two-thirds of girls are trained by age three.

- Expect that people of previous generations may have ideas and beliefs about toilet learning that differ from recent expert thought on the subject.

- Independence in toilet training may take place at a later age in children with special needs.

- Learning to use the toilet will be more difficult during times of stress: birth of a sibling, moving, or divorcing.

- At the time most children become physically ready to learn to use the toilet, they are at the stage of wanting to do things for themselves, but at the same time are having difficulty doing so; this can both motivate children to learn to use the toilet and make it more frustrating.

- A parent's frustration over toilet training has led to child abuse in many cases.

- Children who learn about body parts and body functions in a positive way learn positive feelings about their sexuality.

- Learning to use the toilet independently is an important event, one that can result in a tremendous sense of accomplishment for children.

Approaches

Prepare your child for toilet learning first through diapering experiences. Instead of distracting your child from the diaper change and rushing through it, make eye contact and talk to him about everything that you are doing: "I'm going to change your diaper now. Here's the wet cloth on your bottom to clean you. Here's the clean dry diaper."

As soon as your child is able, have him help with diaper changes: ask him to bring the clean diaper, choose where to get dressed, unfasten the old diaper, help wipe himself, help pull up his own pants, and wash his hands. Once your child has done some of the tasks of diaper changing, he will be more prepared for learning to use the toilet independently.

—Ideas found in *Becoming the Parent You Want to Be* by Laura Davis and Janet Keyser, Broadway Books, 1997.

Let your child decide when it is time for him to learn to use the toilet or potty-chair. Know the right time to start the process by watching for readiness signs that he gives you. In the end, the timing and the achievement have to be your child's. If you believe your child is not ready to learn to use the toilet, then avoid following the advice of others that tells you to start anyway.

—Ideas found in *Touchpoints* by T. Berry Brazelton, Addison-Wesley, 1992.

Have a response ready when friends, neighbors, relatives, and other adults try to pressure you to toilet train your child earlier than your child is ready to learn:

- Explain that most children younger than eighteen months don't have enough awareness of how their bodies work to learn to use the toilet.
- Say, "It goes faster and easier when you train a child who is two and a half or so because the sphincter muscles are ready then."
- Explain that you don't feel he is ready. Then don't let yourself be pressured.
- Say, "I'm sorry, but we don't agree on this issue. Let's talk about something else."
- Find a way to remind the person that it will be your decision.

—From *Help! For Parents of Children from Birth to Five*, a collection of ideas from parents, edited by Jean Illsley Clarke, HarperSanFrancisco, 1993.

To prepare yourself for toilet training your child, sort out your own feelings. Many parents are anxious about toilet training: they may be uncomfortable with bowel and bladder functions, they may feel pressure to have the child succeed the right way at the right time, or they may feel in a hurry to get the job done so the child can get into preschool. One of the first steps in toilet training your child should be to resolve some of these concerns for yourself.

—Ideas found in *Dr. Spock's Baby and Child Care* (7th edition) by Benjamin Spock and Stephen J. Parker, Dutton, 1998.

Watch for all of the physical signs of readiness before beginning toilet training:

- Diaper is not always wet: he is dry for about two hours at a time during the day or is dry after naps.
- Bowel movements come at regular times.
- He shows awareness that he is about to urinate or have a bowel movement: goes off into a corner, grimaces, grunts, holds his crotch, or says he needs to go.

—Ideas found in *Caring for Your Baby and Young Child: Birth to Age 5* (American Academy of Pediatrics), Bantam Books, 1998.

Toilet Learning

Watch for developmental signs of readiness before beginning to toilet train your child. Your child should:

- Be able to follow simple two-step directions: "Take your pants off and sit on the toilet."
- Be able to communicate his need to go.
- Imitate actions of others.
- Generally be willing to cooperate and please you.
- Want to be independent about self-care activities—dressing, brushing teeth, or eating.
- Be able to get to the toilet.
- Be aware of a wet or soiled diaper.
- Be able to pull pants up and down.
- Be able to sit still for five minutes without help.
- Be interested in using the toilet.

> —Ideas found in "Toilet Training" by Steven Parker, *Behavioral and Developmental Pediatrics* (edited by Steven Parker and Barry Zuckerman), Little, Brown and Company, 1995.

Be patient about beginning and completing toilet training. Don't push your child, or expect too much too soon; you can do more harm than good. Children are born wanting to be clean and dry. Try not to interfere with his desire and timeline. Allow your child to achieve the task of learning to use the toilet happily.

> —Ideas found in *Complete Baby and Child Care* by Miriam Stoppard. Dorling Kindersley, 1995.

Don't push your child to be trained by a certain date just to get into preschool or a child care setting; that arbitrary timeline may not be right for him. Talk to the person in charge of the preschool or child care setting and see if they can be more flexible than the policy states. Wearing pull-up pants during preschool for the child who rarely urinates or has a bowel movement during that time may be acceptable. If there doesn't seem to be a solution, try to find a preschool or child-care center that will accommodate your child's needs on his own timeline.

> —Ideas found in "Will She Ever Learn to Use the Potty?" by Kathryn E. Livingston, *Parenting Magazine*, April 1998.

Many experts agree:

Wait until you see clear signs of readiness before trying to toilet train your child.

Use accurate names for body parts whenever talking to children: penis, vagina, buttocks, etc.

Use words that you will be comfortable hearing for body functions: poo-poo, tinkle, poop, etc.; whatever words you choose are fine, as long as you do not use negative words like yucky or stinky, and that you do teach the child the correct terms sometime.

When you see signs of readiness in your child, begin toilet training. One simple way to be sure you are not rushing your child is to wait until at least the second summer of his life, and then watch and wait for signs of readiness. Then, three weeks or so before beginning training:

- Read to your child about using the toilet.
- Make opportunities for him to see older children and family members using the toilet.
- Buy or borrow a potty-chair for him. Let him get used to sitting on it with his clothes on.
- Describe what goes on in the bathroom. In general, teach your child to use the toilet function words that you are comfortable with: pee-pee or number two. Avoid teaching words that treat natural functions as disgusting or shameful like: dirty or yucky.
- Point out the negative aspects of wearing soiled diapers: "Oh that must feel awful—all cold and wet! Here, I'll put on a dry one. Doesn't that feel good?"
- Let him teach his doll or stuffed animal to use the toilet. Drink and wet dolls are especially good.
- Encourage him to notice when he is going to the bathroom: he will probably grunt, squat, turn red in the face, or stop playing for a moment.
- Talk about toilet training as an important step in growing up: feeling clean and dry, wearing underwear, and not having to stop playing for diaper changes. Make it something to look forward to.

Begin actual training, expecting it to last for at least three days. Expect the whole process of becoming independent and accident free will take much longer—the training period is a time that you give him focused attention and training to help him learn the basics:

- Set a time to begin when you can spend at least three days with your child; it's important to follow through once a start is made. Choose a stress and hassle-free time.
- That morning put inexpensive cloth training pants on your child, NOT DISPOSABLE TRAINING PANTS! Cloth underwear creates awareness of the discomfort of wetness. Get them two or three sizes larger than your child's regular size so they'll be easy to pull off and on. You may even want to let him go without underwear when you are present and in the privacy of your own home.
- Tell your child to let you know if he feels the need to go. For the next three days, put your child on the potty-chair or toilet ten minutes after each meal. Also, give him extra fruit juice and water several times during the day between meals, and put him on the potty-chair or toilet ten minutes or so after those drinks. Make this sitting time "happy time." Stay there with your child. Sing songs, tell stories, make faces and play finger games. NEVER TIE OR BELT A CHILD ON A TOILET OR POTTY-CHAIR!
- After ten minutes, no more, take your child off. Praise success with clapping, hugs, or maybe even calling grandma. Consider putting a star on the back of the toilet or potty-chair for each time he successfully potties in the toilet or potty-chair. If he doesn't produce anything, ignore it.
- If your child has an accident, sympathize and calmly help him change his underwear.
- If he has trouble beginning to urinate, try turning the faucet on and letting it run.
- Let him use a little potty-chair or the family toilet, whichever he wants. Some children like to straddle the toilet and face backward.
- Teach a boy to push his penis downward so the stream of urine goes into the bowl.
- Some children will be afraid to flush or are protective of flushing their stool away. Let your child go to another room before you flush for him, or try to explain: "This is extra that you don't need."
- Teach girls to wipe from front to back to help prevent infections. Teach both boys and girls to wipe more than once when they have a bowel movement, each time with clean tissue until the tissue remains clean.
- Teach your child to wash his hands with soap every time he uses the toilet. Be sure he can reach a sink.

- Don't expect your child to go "cold turkey" and never wear a diaper again, even to bed, once he's started toilet training. Don't worry about nighttime dryness while he is learning to use the toilet during the day. It will come later.

Expect that the process will take some time! Once he has mastered the basics, it will still take time for him to be accident free. Ignore failure, reward success, expect accidents, and be patient!

—From "Toilet Training" by Martha Bullock, *Family Information Services*, March 1995.

Inspire the child to use the toilet by making it fun:

- Put a drop or red or blue food coloring in the toilet water and tell your child that if he urinates in the toilet, the color will change to orange or green.
- Put a piece of O-shaped cereal in the toilet and have a boy aim for the center.
- Use incentives: treats, pieces of candy, real kisses and hugs, coins, or stickers.
- Buy underpants that look like mom's or dad's.

—Ideas found in *I Heard It Through the Playground*, by Joel Fram, Carol Boswell, and Margaret Maas, HarperPerennial, 1993.

Help your child deal with bedwetting. Recognize that in children under five years, bladder control is largely involuntary, and bedwetting is not done on purpose.

- Never punish, scold, or embarrass your child for wetting the bed—these are NOT helpful. Don't let others tease him either.
- Talk about bedwetting as an "accident." Assure your child that you know he is not doing it on purpose. Explain that he will outgrow this.
- Ask your child to go to the bathroom before bedtime.
- Make sure he has a light to get to the toilet at night and that his pajama bottoms are easy to pull up and down.
- If your child has been dry at night for a few months and then begins to wet the bed, mention the wetting to his doctor to rule out a physical cause.
- Make cleaning up as hassle free as you can. Consider these tips:
  - Use a good, fitted, plastic cover for the mattress and pillow.
  - Consider using disposable pants that are made to pull up and down.
  - Make the bed up with two sets of mattress covers and sheets, so that you can strip one easily.
  - Lay a large towel over the spot your child is likely to wet, if he wakes up quickly enough after wetting, he may be able to learn to pull the towel off before the bed gets wet, and to drop it in a bucket near the bed.
  - Keep a sleeping bag in the child's room for him to move to after wetting the bed instead of changing the sheets at night.

—Ideas found in *Toilet Training: A Practical Guide to Daytime and Nighttime Training* by Vicki Lansky, Bantam Books, 1993.

Be patient. No matter what you read in books, or what anyone tells you, toilet training cannot be learned in a day. It is a process that will take time and lots of practice. Face it with a good sense of humor.

—Ideas found in *Kids Are Worth It!* by Barbara Coloroso, William Morrow, 1994.

Read with the child to learn more about using the toilet. Books are very useful in the process of toilet training:

- *Everyone Poops* by Taro Gomi
- *Going to the Potty* by Fred Rogers
- *I Have to Go!* By Robert Munsch
- *I Want My Potty* by Tony Ross
- *Koko Bear's New Potty* by Vicki Lansky
- *On Your Potty* by Virginia Miller
- *Once Upon a Potty: Hers* by Alona Frankel
- *Once Upon a Potty: His* by Alona Frankel
- *P. J. & Puppy* by Cathryn Falwell
- *Sam's Potty* by Barbro Lindgren
- *The Princess and the Potty* by Wendy Cheyette Lewison
- *Uh Oh! Gotta Go!: Potty Tales from Toddlers* by Bob McGrath
- *What Do You Do With A Potty?: An Important Pop-up Book* by Marianne Borgardt
- *Your New Potty* by Joanna Cole

When to Get More Help

Children typically grow and learn new skills in their own time and at their own pace within the wide range of what is normal. Sometimes, children need a bit of extra help to keep their development on track, or to stay healthy and happy. Sometimes, parents need help providing for a child's needs or sorting out the best approaches to parenting.

Consider getting help for your child if he:

- Continues to wet the bed beyond age five or if he starts wetting the bed after months of dryness.
- Is wetting during the day after having achieved dryness.
- Is bothered by not being able to achieve bowel or bladder control.
- Does not show some interest in using the toilet or potty-chair by age four years.

You are the expert when it comes to your family and child. If you have a concern, trust your instinct and find someone trained to help you: health care providers, early intervention teams, mental health professionals, parent educators and consultants, or telephone help-line staff. Consider talking it over with friends and family, too. You don't need to worry alone! Turn to "Finding Help in Your Community" on page 4 to learn about finding help near you.

More Help and Information

Books for Parents

- "All About Toilet Learning, Chapter Nineteen" in *What to Expect the Toddler Years* by Arlene Eisenberg, Heidi E. Murkoff, and Sandee E. Hathaway. Workman Pub., 1994.
- "Toilet Mastery" in *Your Baby & Child: From Birth to Age Five* (3rd edition) by Penelope Leach. Alfred A. Knopf, 1997.
- "Toilet Training" in *Touchpoints* by T. Berry Brazelton. Addison-Wesley, 1992.
- *Toilet Training: A Practical Guide to Daytime and Nighttime Training* by Vicki Lansky, Bantam, 1993.

Videos

- *It's Potty Time*. A Vision.
- *It's Time To Potty with Martha Lambert*. Power To Create.
- *Now I Can Potty*. K.I.D.S.
- *Once Upon A Potty For Her, Once Upon A Potty For Him*. Frappe Productions.
- *Toilet Training Your Child*, created with T. Berry Brazelton, M.D. Consumer Vision Inc.

Web Sites

- Your Mining Co. Guide to Parenting Babies & Toddlers. Choose "Potty Training" from the Net Links menu: http://babyparenting.miningco.com

Toys

by Tennae

Description

Toys are objects to play with. They can be simple, complicated, manufactured, handmade, realistic, natural, found, or purchased: a cardboard box, an elaborately formed plastic castle, a doll made from sticks and string, a walking and talking doll, a glass tea set, or tea cups made from acorn tops. Some toys provide likenesses of real things, some are likenesses of imagined things, and some provide the opportunity for children to create real or imagined things. Good toys encourage children to imagine, think, and do.

Realistic Expectations

- Children learn about their world, themselves, and others through the *experience* of playing with toys. Children retain only 10 percent of what they hear and 50 percent of what they see, but they retain 90 percent of what they *experience*.

- Toys provide children with opportunities to explore how things work, strengthen and coordinate their large and small muscles, expand their imaginations, solve problems, and learn to cooperate.

- Children's skill levels and interests are constantly changing. As they grow, their interest in toys changes and grows.

- Good quality, simple, basic toys:
  - Encourage many kinds of imaginary play in children because they can be used several ways.
  - Provide a variety of experiences—children may build a wall with blocks and then jump over it.
  - May be used for many years—a one-year-old will typically pile blocks in a heap, a two-year-old will stack them, a three-year-old will build a house, and a four-year-old will build a whole city.

- In eager attempts to explore and learn, children may find unusual ways to use toys: jumping on them, pounding on them, or taking them apart.

- If children have outgrown a toy, they can become bored with it. If they are not yet ready to understand it, they can become frustrated. Either reaction can lead to carelessness and misuse of the toy and make it unsafe.

- Toys are generally safe, but accidents can happen:
  - Injuries include cuts, burns, small parts becoming lodged in noses or ears, eye injuries from guns that shoot objects, and hearing damage from loud noises.
  - Toy-related deaths occur from choking, strangulation by long cords, or electrocution.
  - Younger children are attracted to older children's toys, many of which are hazardous to them.

- Children have difficulty sharing toys until at least age three or four. It is typical for one-year-olds and two-year-olds to grab toys from each other.

- Having too many toys in one place at one time can overwhelm children and actually inhibit their creativity.

- Children under age five lack the reasoning abilities and life experiences needed to understand complicated adult issues raised by certain toys: dolls that engage in war or dress provocatively. Toys like these can be confusing to children.

- Children won't care if toys are bought, borrowed, found, handed down, store-bought, or homemade, as long as they are fun and interesting. However, as they become exposed to advertisements for toys and other children's toys, their interest in and desire for specific toys is likely to increase.

- Toys are children's first belongings and provide some of their first learning experiences. If toys are fun and interesting, playing with them can help children begin a lifelong love of learning.

Approaches

Expose both boys and girls to a wide variety of toys that encourage involved play:

- Hands-on toys such as squeeze toys, balls, puzzles, beads, and board or card games build hand-eye coordination, encourage ideas about how things work, and foster cooperation and problem solving.

- Books and recordings are sources of joy for children and adults. Children who are read to in their early years usually become better readers.

- Art materials foster creativity and build skills that lead to reading, writing, and seeing beauty in life.

- Construction items such as blocks, building sets, and woodworking supplies are excellent ways to help children learn about science and number ideas. They also contribute to muscle strength and coordination.

- Experimental materials such as sand, water, clay, and musical instruments are ideal learning tools because children have so much control over them; they relish their feel and sound.

- Active play equipment builds strong muscles and confidence to meet physical challenges. Old tires and climbing frames are great to balance, jump, climb, and play on with other children. Swings, slides, and rocking toys challenge children's balance and viewpoint.

- Pretend objects such as dolls, stuffed animals, dramatic figures, and dress-up clothes give children a chance to try new behaviors and use their imaginations. This type of play also helps children understand the world and how we can work together. It gives children opportunities to imitate adults at work or at play.

Choose toys carefully because in so doing you will be setting the stage for how and what your child will learn with the toys and materials you select.

> —From "Toys: Tools for Learning." Reprinted with permission from the National Association for the Education of Young Children.

Be safe about toys:

- Childproof your home because everything looks like a toy to a child.

- Read and heed age guideline labels on toys as a place to begin. Toy manufacturers add labels with age and safety recommendations to *most, but not all* toys. The suggestions are based on guidelines from the Consumer Product Safety Commission. It is important to note that toy safety standards are voluntary, so you can never really be certain that safety standards are being followed; use your own judgment.

- Age guidelines are meant to reflect the safety of a toy based on the child's physical and mental ability to play with the toy, the child's play needs and interests, and the specific safety aspects of a particular toy: "Not recommended for children under three."

- Match toys with your child's skill level and interests. Sometimes toy companies are wrong about their age recommendations; use the guideline as a place to start, then use your own judgment based on what you know about your child.

- Avoid the following in toys for young children:
    - Parts that could pull off and/or fit into a child's mouth, nose, or ear
    - Exposed wires
    - Balloons
    - Parts that get hot
    - Lead paint
    - Poisonous materials
    - Breakable parts
    - Sharp points or edges
    - Things that shoot parts
    - Electric toys
    - Long cords or strings
    - Springs, gears, or hinged parts that could pinch or entrap tiny fingers

- Immediately throw away all wrappings from new toys. They may contain harmful things like plastic bags, staples, or Styrofoam.

- Supervise your child with all toys. Supervision is important even with toys that are carefully selected with his age and interest in mind: even a ball can become dangerous if an unsupervised child follows one into the street or lake.

- Watch your child extra carefully when there are older children's toys nearby. Toys that may be appropriate for older children can be harmful in the hands of children that are too young to use them safely.

- Put toys in their place and teach your child to do the same to avoid tripping accidents.

- If you use a toy chest, choose it carefully. Look for smooth, finished edges and a strong lid with safe hinges that will not pinch skin, as well as locking supports that keep it open and prevent it from falling on the child. It should have ventilation holes (or no cover at all) to prevent suffocation if the child becomes trapped inside.

- Maintain toys by examining them routinely for damage, wear, or broken parts: splinters, rust, chipping paint, loose eyes, exposed wires, etc. Repair, replace, or throw away damaged or worn toys.

- Call the Consumer Product Safety Commission (CPSC) at 800-638-2772 or TDD 800-638-8270 for information on recall warnings about toys, to report accidents, or to suggest toys that you believe should be recalled. The CPSC is the federal government agency that investigates concerns, complaints, and accident reports about toys from consumers.

> —From "For Kid's Sake: Think Toy Safety," CPSC Document #4281, U.S. Consumer Product Safety Commission, 1996.

Toys

Select toys wisely. In addition to the safety guidelines, think about the following:

- Choose toys your child is developmentally ready for. Think more about the kinds of toys that she does spend time playing with than the types of toys she is begging for because she saw them on television or at a friend's home.

- Non-toys can be just as appealing and have just as much value as store-bought ones—boxes, paper bags, sand, mixing bowls, blankets over chairs for tents, unopened or empty boxes of food.

- Strike a balance—while variety is important, avoid having too many toys at once. If your child does have a lot of toys, rotate them by leaving some out and putting the rest away in a closet or on a shelf that is out of sight. In a week or two, trade some of the ones that are out for some that are in storage.

- Look for toys that can be played with in many different ways and that encourage your child to be active instead of just watching—she will learn more from a set of blocks that can become many things and that requires her imagination, concentration and skill than she will from an electric train set that she can only watch move when she turns a switch.

- If there are toys that go against your values, think ahead about what your values are about allowing your child to own them. You may decide to ban certain toys or work out a compromise. Either way, explain to her why you decided what you did in a way that she can understand: to the four-year-old who is shooting at her little brother with a gun she made from a stick, you might say, "I don't want to have toy guns in the house because real guns kill and hurt people. If you are going to shoot that 'gun,' you may not shoot people, only targets like the tree or couch."

- Anticipate that she will play with toys in her own way, whatever that is. Let her do so unless it goes against your values or is dangerous: it is acceptable and creative when she turns a chair over and uses it for a feed trough for her horse, but it is dangerous and unacceptable if she decides to jump on your bass drum for a trampoline.

> —Ideas found in *What to Expect the Toddler Years* by Arlene Eisenberg, Heidi E. Murkoff, and Sandee E. Hathaway, Workman Pub., 1994.

- **Provide "non-toy" things and make your own toys.** Your child's curiosity drives her need to do, to find out, and to know. All you really need to do is surround her with things to explore, to wonder about, and to discover. Fancy learning materials are nice, but by no means necessary. Trinkets and simple materials can become active learning toys that your child can't keep her hands off.

> —Ideas found in *Do Touch: Instant, Easy Hands-on Learning Experiences for Young Children* by Labritta Gilbert, Gryphon House Press, 1989.

Begin to teach your preschool child to be a good consumer through toys. Even though she is young to understand these concepts, you can begin to talk to her about the techniques advertisers use to sell products that make toys and other products look great—even better than they might be in real life. There are five important things to teach children about commercials:

- Toys are often depicted as being incredible and indestructible.

- Commercials often create emotions that make you feel good.

- The children in commercials are often a little older than those that would be using the toy in real life: in a commercial, an eight- or nine-year-old child actor may play with a toy that is really designed for a five-year-old.

- Commercials show the actor's and toy's best performance: to sell a ball, brilliant catches and perfect throws are shown instead of the many fumbles that really happen.

- Sports heroes and movie stars tell children what to eat, wear, and play with, but they are paid generously for the endorsement and may not even like or use the product in real life.

> —From "Taking Charge of Your TELEVISION," The Family and Community Critical Viewing Project, 1995.

The Field Guide Toy Chest

Classic Toys for Ages One to Four.

- Activity boards with things to push, pull, open, close, etc.
- Balls.
- Blocks.
- Books.
- Boxes of all sizes.
- Bubbles.
- Climbing/sliding toy.
- Construction sets.
- Crayons, markers, and paper.
- Dolls and accessories: bed, blanket, bottle, etc.
- Dress-up box: hats, purses, scarves, shoes, etc.
- Finger-paints.
- Housekeeping toys: dishes, telephone, broom, food, sink, stove, etc.
- Natural materials: sticks, stones, seeds, water, dirt, sand, shells, leaves, etc.
- Nesting or fitting toys.
- Pail and shovel.
- Play dough.
- Play houses.
- Play vehicles: trucks, cars, trains, bulldozers, etc.
- Pounding toys.
- Puppets—hand and finger.
- Push and pull toys: wheelbarrow, wagon, doll buggy, etc.
- Puzzles.
- Sand and water toys.
- Shape sorters.
- Simple musical instruments: bells, maracas, keyboard, tambourine, xylophone, drum, cymbals, or sticks.
- Stuffed animals.
- Wind-up music box.

NOTE: Many toys come in a range of skill levels. When selecting a toy, match it to your child's skill level—look for the manufacturer's age recommendation on the package to start, but then use your own judgement as to whether the toy is appropriate for your child.

Great Toys for Age One.

- All toys in "Classic Toys for Ages One to Four."
- Jack-in-the-box type toys that give a response to a simple action.
- Pots and pans with covers.
- Riding toys.
- Small toys or objects (large enough not to be choking hazards) and a large container for putting inside and dumping out again.
- Stacking toys.

Great Toys for Age Two.

- All toys in "Classic Toys for Ages One to Four."
- Baskets, boxes, bags, etc. to fill with collections.
- Lacing toys and beads and string.
- Paints and brushes.
- Pegs and pegboard.
- Printing and stamping equipment.
- Riding toy or tricycle.
- Scissors—child's blunt end safety.
- Science tools: magnets, magnifying glass, stethoscope, kaleidoscope, and binoculars.
- Simple matching games.
- Toy people or animal sets.

Great Toys for Age Three.

- All toys in "Classic Toys for Ages One to Four" and in "Great Toys for Age Two."
- Balancing boards—low.
- Board games with rules and turn taking.
- Doll clothing with large fasteners.
- Parquetry or colorful design blocks.
- Toys and games that teach colors, sizes, shapes.

Great Toys for Age Four.

- All toys in "Classic Toys for Ages One to Four," "Great Toys for Age Two," and "Great Toys for Age Three."
- Jump rope.
- Ring toss.
- Scrapbook.
- Real tools such as camera, hammer, or flashlight (with training and supervision).

! **WARNING!** Always supervise your child with toys, making sure they are safe and appropriate for his skill level, and that they are not choking hazards.

Help your child understand more about toys by reading about them together:

📖 *Alexander and the Wind-Up Mouse* by Leo Lionni

📖 *Bunnies and Their Hobbies* by Nancy Carlson

📖 *Guns: What You Should Know* by Rachel Ellenberg Schulson

📖 *The Make-Something Club Is Back!: More Fun with Crafts, Food, and Gifts* by Frances W. Zweifel

📖 *Max's Toys: A Counting Book* by Rosemary Wells

📖 *Spot's Toy Box* by Eric Hill

📖 *What's Inside? Toys* by Dorling Kindersley

When to Get More Help

C hildren typically grow and learn new skills in their own time and at their own pace within the wide range of what is normal. Sometimes, children need a bit of extra help to keep their development on track, or to stay healthy and happy. Sometimes, parents need help providing for a child's needs or sorting out the best approaches to parenting.

Consider getting help for your child if she:

- Shows little interest in toys.
- Is a child with special needs and needs some of her toys adapted.
- Frequently breaks toys.

Consider getting help for yourself if you:

- Would like more toys for your child but can't afford them.

You are the expert when it comes to your family and child. If you have a concern, trust your instinct and find someone trained to help you: health care providers, early intervention teams, mental health professionals, parent educators and consultants, or telephone help-line staff. Consider talking it over with friends and family, too. You don't need to worry alone! Turn to "Finding Help in Your Community" on page 4 to learn about finding help near you.

More Help and Information

Books for Parents

- *The Little Hands Big Fun Craft Book: Creative Fun For 2-To-6-Year-Olds* by Judy Press. Williamson Pub, 1996.
- *Oppenheim Toy Portfolio, 1999: The Best Toys, Books, Videos, and Software for Kids* (6th edition) by Joanne F. Oppenheim, Stephanie Oppenheim, and James Oppenheim. Oppenheim Toy Portfolio, 1998.
- *The Toys R Us Guide to Choosing the Right Toys for Your Child* by Sandy MacDonald. Pocket Books, 1996.
- *Who's Calling the Shots?: How to Respond Effectively to Children's Fascination with War Play and War Toys* by Nancy Carlsson-Paige and Diane E. Levin. New Society Publishers, 1990.

Articles, Pamphlets, and Booklets

- "Toys 'R' Us Toy Guide for Differently Abled Kids." Request from:
  Toys "R" Us
  201-262-7800
- "Toys: Tools for Learning." Request from:
  National Association for the Education of Young Children (NAEYC)
  800-424-2460, Fax: 202-328-1846
  Web site: www.naeyc.org

Community Resources

To locate a toy lending library in your community, call:
- USA Toy Library Association
  847-864-3330, fax:847-864-3331
  www.sjdccd.cc.ca.us/toylibrary/
- National Lekotek Center: 800-366-PLAY

Government

U.S. Consumer Product Safety Commission (CPSC)
800-638-2772 (English/Spanish), 800-638-8270 (speech and hearing impaired)
www.cpsc.gov
Contact CPSC to report an unsafe consumer product or a product-related injury, for publication listings, or to ask for information.

Magazines and Newsletters

- *Oppenheim Toy Portfolio*. Order from:
  Oppenheim Toy Portfolio, Inc.
  212-598-0502
  Web site: www.toyportfolio.com

Mail Order

- Animal Town: 800-445-8642
- Back to Basics Toys: 800-356-5360, Web site: www.backtobasicstoys.com
- Constructive Playthings: 800-832-0572, Web site: www.constplay.com
- Dick Blick Art Materials: 800-447-8192, Web site: www.dickblick.com
- Hand in Hand: 800-872-9745
- Hearth Song: 800-325-2502, Web site: www.hearth-song.com
- Music for Little People: 800-346-4445

Recall Notices

Find information about toys and child equipment that have been recalled:
- ABC's of Parenting. Web site: www.abcparenting.com.
- *Consumer Reports* Magazine.
- Kidsource Online. Web site: www.kidsource.com.
- U.S. Consumer Gateway. Web site: www.consumer.gov/productsafety.htm.
- U.S. Consumer Product Safety Commission.

Web Sites

- Crayola: www.crayola.com
- Dr. Toy: www.drtoy.com
- eToys: www.etoys.com
- Holt Educational Outlet: www.holtoutlet.com
- KidSource Online. Choose "Toys & Games.": www.kidsource.com
- Toys R Us: www.toysrus.com
- Toysmart: www.toysmart.com

Transitions and Security Blankets

"Baby bear in a crib"
by Will

Description

Transitions are the changes, moves, switches, or passages from one activity to another, or from one place to another. The beginning or ending of something is a transition, as is a change in expectations. Getting dressed, going places, a change in routine or plan, losing something, switching from playtime to mealtime, a change in the weather, and bed time are everyday transitions.

A security blanket, teddy bear, transitional object, or security object are things children can hold, cuddle, and take comfort from by themselves. Children commonly choose teddy bears, baby blankets, clean diapers, stuffed animals, dolls, or a piece of their mother's or primary caregiver's clothing, but a transitional object can be anything that helps a child move from one activity or feeling to another. Some children don't attach to a security object. They adopt comfort habits such as thumb or pacifier sucking, rhythmic sounds, pulling on their ear or hair, and rocking. Security objects help children learn the important ability to comfort themselves and are often used during transitions from one thing to another. These objects help children feel secure because children can control them during times in their lives when they have little control.

Realistic Expectations

- Children vary greatly in their ability to handle transitions and their need for security blankets. Most children have difficulty with transitions at some point in early childhood.

- Though babies typically attach to a security blanket or transitional object between six and twelve months, attachment to security blankets usually peaks between eighteen and thirty months.

- By ages three and four, children have achieved some independence and are assertive about what they do and don't want to do. Transitions may be more difficult at this age.

- It is common for children to be fiercely attached to the security object, to refuse to allow it to be washed, and to grieve if it is lost.

- Security objects can help children learn to sleep independently. If they have a comfort object that reminds them that you are nearby when they are going to sleep or when they wake in the night, it lessens the need for you to be there in person.

- Children typically outgrow their need for security objects by the time they are four or five years old, but expect them to keep their security objects through the elementary school-age years, and perhaps even take them to college with them. Many experts agree it's not necessary to wean them from these things unless the attachment interferes with typical play and activity.

- Children who do not adapt easily, due to their temperament, will have more trouble making changes and transitions.

- Transitional objects or security blankets help children separate from parent or primary caregiver. In the transition from needing and being very dependent on adults to being independent and separating easily from them, children use an object that reminds them of their primary caregiver to bridge the gap between needing and not needing the person.

- Children under five have few of the skills needed to make smooth transitions. They have limited ability to understand time, to wait to get what they want, to compromise, and to use language to communicate frustration.

- Transitions are difficult for young children who tend to focus on the present and may not understand that they can return to a place or activity. It may feel to them that if they can't do it now, they won't ever be able to do it again.

- Routines generally help young children make smoother transitions. If children know what to expect, it may be easier to switch gears.

- Learning to comfort yourself and take comfort from what is around you is one of the major steps toward becoming a responsible and independent adult.

Approaches

Ease your child's transitions by helping him understand them. Recognize how hard it can be for your child to make changes, and acknowledge his feelings: "I understand that it's hard for you to leave Grandma's house; it's OK to feel sad about it. Can I help you find Grandma to give her a hug good-bye?" If your child knows that there's nothing wrong with how he feels, and that you are there to help him, it may make the transition easier for him.

> —Ideas found in "I'm Not Going" by Margery D. Rosen, *Child*, September 1998.

Learn to identify transitions in your child's life. Consider a regular day and how many times you ask your child to move from one thing to another. Think about your child and the comfort level he has with transitions. Instead of expecting him to handle many transitions during the day, structure your day to make the number of transitions manageable for your child. If cutting back on some transitions makes for a more successful day, then respect your child's need for fewer transitions.

> —Ideas found in *Raising Your Spirited Child* by Mary Sheedy Kurcinka, HarperCollins, 1991.

Plan ahead to help your child through transitions that tend to be difficult for him. If you know that leaving to go home from somewhere, or moving from play time to the car for day care are difficult times for your child, think of things to make those times easier for him: bring a snack to eat in the car or stroller, suggest a game to play on the way, or bring a favorite toy to play with when he gets into the car seat or stroller.

> —Ideas found in "It's Time to Go" by Cindy Schweich Handler, *Parents*, November 1997.

To smooth a transition for your child, let him know what, when, and where it will happen:

- Tell him before it is going to happen that it will happen soon: "Three more pushes on the swing and then it's time to go home."

- Give him some information about what is happening and suggest a transition activity: "We're going home now so that I can start dinner. On the way you can show me all the cars you can find."

- Tell him what will happen next: "When we get home, you can color or play with play dough on the table while I make dinner."

Transitions and Security Blankets

- Make a ritual of leaving: have him go pat his favorite swing and say "So long, see ya next time!"
- Ask him to help in the transition: "Can you help me push your sister in the stroller to the car?"
- Find an object to help him make the transition: "Let's go see pooh bear —he's waiting for you in the car" or "Would you like to bring this leaf home?"

> —Ideas found in *Becoming the Parent You Want to Be* by Laura Davis and Janis Keyser, Broadway Books, 1997.

Break down a task or activity into smaller steps to help your child make a transition. Instead of telling your child that it's time to stop playing and put away all the toys, consider asking the child to do one thing at a time: "It's time to hunt for the blocks and put them in their bucket." Then, when that is done, ask the child to put away the next set of things: "Now, it's time to put all the cars and trucks back into the box." Some tasks are overwhelming for young children. Breaking down a task can help your child see that the next step is not so overwhelming.

> —Ideas found in "Coping with Stressful Transitions" by W. Thomas Boyce, in *Behavioral and Developmental Pediatrics: A Handbook for Primary Care*, Little, Brown and Co., 1995.

> *My father used to swing me up on his back and start singing "here we go to the living room, into the bedroom, out through the hall, into the dining room" to a tune that he undoubtedly made up as we went. When we'd get to the dining room, he'd plop me down in my chair for dinner. Instead of the usual grumbling about it, I remember enjoying coming to dinner on those occasions when he made it fun. I knew that he wanted me to come to dinner, but what I didn't realize was that he was smoothing the transition from one activity to another for me.*
>
> —Shelley, Shoreview, MN

Allow your child to have a security object and help him choose one if he doesn't. Try drawing attention to a security blanket, teddy, or lovey during your bedtime routine. Place a soft toy or blanket in his crib or bed. He may learn to substitute it for you when he needs some comfort. When he does become attached to an object, consider keeping a spare on hand to avoid the risk of losing it.

> —Ideas found in *Caring for Your Baby and Young Child* (American Academy of Pediatrics), Bantam Books, 1998.

If your child decides on a blanket or old piece of clothing as a security object, cut it up into pieces as soon as you see that he is attached to it. You will be able to exchange the dirty pieces for the clean ones when he's not looking, and wash them.

> —Ideas found in *Practical Parenting Tips* by Vicki Lansky, Meadowbrook Press, 1992.

Allow your child to give up a security object in his own time; don't take it away suddenly. If you notice that your child no longer uses his security object regularly for comfort, don't praise his independence or remove it from his possessions. It is important for your child to have his beloved object around and to say farewell to it when he wants to. Having it around may show a child how much he has grown, when he remembers how important it used to be to him.

> —Ideas found in *Your Child's Emotional Health* (Philadelphia Child Guidance Center), Macmillan, 1993.

Help your child deal with a lost security object by showing him that you understand his loss. Tell him you feel bad about it, too, and that it's a sad thing to lose something so important. Show that you understand how he feels. Consider the right time to introduce a new security object. For a pre-talking child, help him find something new. For a talking child, gently ask him if he has any ideas of what he might like to have in place of his lost object. For the older child who no longer needs a security object, consider giving it up altogether.

—Ideas found in "The Power of Loveys" by Carol Lynn Mithers, *Child*, April 1998.

Help your child learn more about transitions and security blankets by reading about them together:

Alfie Gives a Hand by Shirley Hughes

D.W.'s Lost Blankie by Marc Brown

Franklin's Blanket by Paulette Bourgeois

Owen by Kevin Henkes

Prince Peter and the Teddy Bear by David McKee

The Surprise Family by Lynn Reiser

Teddy Bear Tears by Jim Aylesworth

When to Get More Help

Children typically grow and learn new skills in their own time and at their own pace within the wide range of what is normal. Sometimes, children need a bit of extra help to keep their development on track, or to stay healthy and happy. Sometimes, parents need help providing for a child's needs or sorting out the best approaches to parenting.

Consider getting help for your child if he:

- Prefers his comfort habit or object to the comfort of you or others when he is fearful, irritable, or anxious.
- Does not seem connected to you.
- Uses a comfort object so much that it frequently gets in the way of activities or playing with other children.
- Does not separate from parents without excessive clinging and crying by age three.
- Does not move beyond being extremely fearful, timid, or anxious by age five.

You are the expert when it comes to your family and child. If you have a concern, trust your instinct and find someone trained to help you: health care providers, early intervention teams, mental health professionals, parent educators and consultants, or telephone help-line staff. Consider talking it over with friends and family, too. You don't need to worry alone! Turn to "Finding Help in Your Community" on page 4 to learn about finding help near you.

More Help and Information

Books for Parents

- "Continued Use of a Comfort Object" in *What to Expect the Toddler Years* by Arlene Eisenberg, Heidi E. Murkoff, and Sandee E. Hathaway. Workman Pub., 1994.

- "Transition Games" and "Waiting Games" in *300 Three Minute Games: Quick and Easy Activities for 2 - 5 Year Olds* by Jackie Silberg. Gryphon House, Inc., 1997.

- "Transitional Objects" in *Caring for Your Baby and Young Child* (American Academy of Pediatrics), Bantam Books, 1998.

Articles, Pamphlets, and Booklets

- "I'm Not Going" by Margery D. Rosen. *Child*, September 1998.

- "What They Do for Comfort" by Penelope Leach. *Child*, October 1998.

Travel–In Town and Out of Town

by Joe

Description

Travel is making a journey from one place to another. Traveling in town may mean a trip to the corner grocery store or a thirty-minute ride to Grandma's house across the city. Traveling out of town may involve air, bus, or train travel, a lengthy car ride, hotels or resorts, camping, adventuring, or visiting friends and relatives.

Realistic Expectations

- Children will travel around town or out of town better when they are not hungry, sick, tired, or bored.
- Children who are light sleepers will generally travel better just after waking in the morning or after a nap.
- Aboard airplanes, children who weigh under forty pounds travel most safely in a child-restraint system or a car seat that is approved for use in airplanes.
- Taking off and landing in an airplane can be more painful or uncomfortable for children whose ears are not fully developed yet.
- Hotels, motels, inns, cabins, or other people's homes may not be childproofed—expect to make a room safe for your child wherever you stay.
- Parents often feel pressure to enjoy their vacation and expect it to be perfect.
- Traveling can be stressful for children and they may whine, cry, or complain more than they do at home. They will get excited, tired, hungry, bored, and over stimulated at times, and they won't have as many familiar things or surroundings to comfort them. They may feel homesick and may ask to go home.
- Children may not know what traveling means, or what is expected of them when traveling.
- Traveling with children can be a time to bring the family closer together and to create lasting memories for a lifetime.

Approaches

Before traveling around town with your child, plan the outing and prepare for success:

- Schedule trips when your child is usually the most agreeable and easy to get along with, and when she is well-rested and not hungry.

- Tell your child what the rules are and what you expect from her before you leave: no yelling, no running, and no whining or begging for treats.

- Play pretend shopping or errands with your child before you take her on an actual trip around town.

- Start with a short trip, then increase the duration on later trips.

- Pay attention to your child. Talk to her about what you are doing—point out colors, shapes, sizes, numbers, and uses for items. Let your child be your assistant and help. Play games: "How many red things can you count?" or "Where are your toes?" or "Who can find the apples first?"

- Tell her "No" when she is not following the rules, then ignore the behavior until she stops it. This will only work to change unwanted behavior if you are consistent and don't give in to whining, crying, yelling, or begging.

- Praise good behavior. Let her know that you believe she can behave and appreciate it when she does. Tell yourself you are doing a good job, too.

- Give your child a reward, treat, or special privilege for helpful behavior: a chance to watch a special video, time to have a friend over, an opportunity to play a game with you, a sticker on a good behavior chart, the change from a purchase, or the privilege of picking out something at the store.

- Be aware of your feelings on outings. If there is one behavior that especially bothers you in your child, concentrate on changing that. If you are worried about money while shopping, be aware, don't take it out on your child, and let her know what is bothering you. If you are embarrassed by your child's behavior, keep in mind that most parents experience embarrassing moments with their children in public.

- Learn to recognize when you are losing control. Some signs might be that your neck gets tight or your stomach aches. Take some deep breaths and try to relax.

You are not alone. Find someone to talk to about your feelings and experiences in taking the child on outings. Look for a parent support group or more information on parenting in your community.

> —From "Shopping With Your Children" by the Family Support Network.

Let the child know what, where, when, who, and how long the trip around town will last before taking her on an outing. Then be sure that you do what you say and don't expect your child to enjoy staying somewhere longer than planned. When she does a good job, tell her. The more good feelings she has about going out with you, the more she is likely to enjoy it and not misbehave next time.

> —Ideas found in *Simplify Your Life With Kids: 100 Ways to Make Family Life Easier and More Fun* by Elaine St. James with Vera Cole, Andrews McMeel Publishing, 1997.

Before taking your child out in public, talk about what kind of behavior you expect, and choose a sign, code word, or signal to use with each other. Tell your child that you expect her to stay close to you, and to use her regular or soft voice. Think of a word or signal that either of you can use when you want to get the other's attention: tugging your ear might mean to listen, or holding up your hand could mean to stop. Be sure to tell your child that you expect good behavior. Consider telling her that perhaps, if she follows the rules and signals, she may get a reward. Keep in mind that praise and a hug for good behavior will lead to more good behavior next time.

> —Ideas found in "Sing a Song of Spinach" by the National Committee to Prevent Child Abuse.

When your child asks "Are we there yet?" have fun with her by playing games. Use trips around town or longer trips to enjoy each other, and build a stronger relationship. Consider what she's interested in right now, what she's learning, what she's trying to master, and choose things to play and talk about that relate. Pick one or two games per week to try out in the car. Play games with letters, numbers, colors, letters, shapes, names, sounds, rhymes, or animals. Talk and sing with her. On a long or short trip, playing together helps a child learn, is fun, builds memories, and provides time to enjoy being together.

> —Ideas found in *Kids on Board: Fun Things to Do While Commuting or Road Tripping with Children* by Robyn Freedman Spizman, Fairview Press, 1997.

Help your child learn how to behave safely and respectfully in a restaurant:

- Ask your child to stay with you at your table, unless you leave the table together. Hold your child's hand or carry her around the restaurant. Wandering or running around where people are carrying food and glassware could cause an accident.

- Bring some things to keep your child busy while you wait: books, toys, supplies to draw or color. Play games of your own.

- If your child is really hungry, ask for something for her to eat right away.

- Help your child become aware of the people around her. Tell her that if she is banging, screaming, yelling, or bumping the seat next to her, she is probably disturbing the people around her and she should stop. Tell her that she'll have to move if she can't.

- Tell your child how to show appreciation to the people who waited on you: say thank you when the wait person helps you or brings you what you asked for, and together, leave a tip to show gratitude for their work and kindness.

> —Ideas found in *Big Lessons for Little People* by Lois Nachamie, Dell Trade, 1997.

When traveling with your child out of town, keep plans simple, and don't forget to pack your sense of humor. It may be easier to travel to one place and stay there with your young child. Limit the trip to traveling there and back. Expect to operate at your child's speed and enjoy time looking at the world through her eyes.

> —Ideas found in *Gutsy Mamas: Travel Tips and Wisdom for Mothers on the Road* by Marybeth Bond, Travelers' Tales, 1997.

Plan a family trip with your child's age, abilities, and interests in mind. Consider that if your child enjoys the trip, then all of you are more likely to enjoy it, too. Plan a realistic schedule for things that each person wants to do in a way that accommodates your child's need for eating, resting, and playing, but be prepared to be flexible if one activity turns into something that takes more or less time than you planned. Schedule activities but leave some time open for play. Plan to keep your child on schedule with eating, napping, and bedtime as much as possible. Good planning for a trip that keeps your child's needs in mind will be a great start to a memorable family vacation.

> —Ideas found in *The Penny Whistle Traveling with Kids Book: Whether by Boat, Train, Car, or Plane—How to Make the Best Ever Trip with Kids of All Ages* by Meredith Brokaw and Annie Gilbar, Simon & Schuster, 1995.

When reserving a hotel room, arrange for accommodations that are safe for your child. Ask the reservation clerk for a room without a balcony that is large enough to accommodate a crib and to reserve and guarantee a crib, if your child needs one.

> —Ideas found in *The Working Parents Handbook* by June S. Sale and Kit Kollenberg with Ellen Melinkoff, Simon & Schuster, 1996.

Travel—In Town and Out of Town

When planning a tour or guided vacation, make sure it accommodates your child. Ask if there will be other children, make sure any necessary gear is the right size for your child, and find out if child-friendly food is provided, the activities are appropriate for your child's age, the staff has worked with children of your child's age before, and if there are any special activities for your child.

—Ideas found in *Fodor's Family Adventures*, Fodor's Travel Publications, 1998.

Start getting ready for a family trip out of town one week before you leave. Make a list of things to do each day that includes packing and arranging for care of the home, mail, pets, and newspaper. It takes time to get ready for a vacation—give yourself some to prepare.

—Ideas found in *Family Travel: Terrific New Vacations for Today's Families* by Evelyn Kaye,
Blue Penguin Publications, 1993.

The Field Guide Travel Bag

- Your child's security blanket, teddy, lovey, or special toy
- Books and book tapes
- Cassette player and music tapes
- Small toys, puppets, and games
- Art supplies: crayons, markers, paper, scissors, glue stick (all non-toxic)
- A surprise or two: small toys, books or tapes from the library that are new to the child; new crayons or markers; a roll of masking tape
- A child's flashlight
- Snacks, drinks, sip cups:

  crackers, dry cereal, bagels, cereal bars, fruit, juice or juice boxes, water, and other healthy, non-salty, non-sticky finger foods
- Wet wipes for diaper changes and quick hand, face, or spill clean-up

- Prescription medicines
- For illness and cuts, scrapes, bumps:

  first aid kit, children's analgesic, phone number of the child's pediatrician, child's medical record number, and list of current medications. When traveling overseas, bring photocopied medical records, passport or visa and certified birth certificates
- Sunglasses
- Sunscreen
- Diapers or pull-ups
- Extra change of clothing
- Bibs
- Sealable plastic bags for dirty clothes, diapers, and bibs
- Tissues

Consider boarding an airplane with your child last instead of first. Allow your child to run, jump, and climb as long as she can before getting on the plane where she will not have much space to be active. The plane trip may seem shorter if she doesn't have to be on the plane any longer than necessary.

—Ideas found in "Trains, Planes & Automobiles" by Kathryn E. Livingston,
Parenting, June/July 1998.

Prepare for a long car trip with a young child:

- In addition to clothes, toys, and snacks, pack a pillow and blanket for your child.

- Plan to stop and get out of the car every two hours or so. Stretch, run, play, have a picnic, and use the restroom. In rain, snow, cold, or heat, stop at a shopping mall to get some exercise.

- Pack the car for fun. Bring a portable lap desk, tray, or anything to write or draw on, and art supplies. Put some toys in the backseat and some in the trunk, so when you stop you can switch or bring out a "new" toy for your child if she's bored.

- Plan to enjoy the trip while traveling in the car. Play games, listen to music, or read stories.

> —Ideas found in *Trouble-Free Travel with Children* by Vicki Lansky, Book Peddlers, 1996.

Be prepared for challenging behavior while on vacation. It's common for families to have high expectations for their trip and to experience some crabbiness and fatigue. Children need to eat more frequently, go to the bathroom more frequently, and tend to need more physical outlets for their energy. Prevent some crabbiness by tending to these physical needs often and dressing her in comfortable clothes. Also, guide your child's behavior in the car before problems occur:

- Give each child his own snacks, books, toys, drawing materials, and books. Bring music or recorded stories to listen to.

- Lay out the rules and limits. Some might be:

    - All passengers must be belted into car seats or wearing seatbelts.

    - Everyone must talk in a regular tone of voice that is not too loud; no shouting.

- Watch for the times when your child is following the rules and behaving well. Tell her how happy you are about it.

- Help your child understand time by dividing into sections. Set a timer and tell your child that when the bell rings, it will be time for a rest stop, snack, or surprise.

> —Ideas found in "Time for Summer Vacation" by Martha Farrell Erickson, Ph.D., *Family Information Services*, March 1997.

Prepare for travel with children by reading stories about it together and choosing books to bring with you:

 *Berenstain Bears and Too Much Vacation* by Stan and Jan Berenstain

 *Bigmama's* by Donald Crews

 *The Brass Ring* by Nancy Tafuri

 *On Our Vacation* by Anne Rockwell

 *The Relatives Came* by Cynthia Rylant

 *Sheep in a Jeep* by Nancy Shaw

 *Shopping Trip* by Helen Oxenbury

 *Up North at The Cabin* by Marsha Wilson Chall

When to Get More Help

Children typically grow and learn new skills in their own time and at their own pace within the wide range of what is normal. Sometimes, children need a bit of extra help to keep their development on track, or to stay healthy and happy. Sometimes, parents need help providing for a child's needs or sorting out the best approaches to parenting.

Consider getting help for yourself if you:

- Need help finding or purchasing a car seat for your child.
- Frequently feel embarrassed or as though you are about to lose control when you are out around town with your child.

You are the expert when it comes to your family and child. If you have a concern, trust your instinct and find someone trained to help you: health care providers, teachers, social workers, parent educators, mental health workers, or telephone help-line staff. Consider talking it over with friends and family, too. You don't need to worry alone! Turn to "Finding Help in Your Community" on page 4 to learn about finding help near you.

More Help and Information

Books for Parents

- *Fodor's Family Adventures* (2nd edition). Fodor's Travel Publications, 1998.
- *Family Travel: Terrific New Vacations for Today's Families* by Evelyn Kaye. Blue Penguin Publications, 1993.
- *Gutsy Mamas: Travel Tips and Wisdom for Mothers on the Road* by Marybeth Bond. Travelers' Tales, 1997.
- *Kids on Board: Fun Things to Do While Commuting or Road Tripping with Children* by Robyn Freedman Spizman. Fairview Press, 1997.
- *The Penny Whistle Traveling with Kids Book: Whether by Boat, Train, Car, or Plane—How to Make the Best Ever Trip with Kids of All Ages* by Meredith Brokaw and Annie Gilbar, Simon & Schuster, 1995.
- *Simplify Family Travel* by Christine Loomis. Reader's Digest, 1998.
- *Trouble-Free Travel with Children: Helpful Hints for Parents on the Go* by Vicki Lansky. Book Peddlers, 1996.

Community

- To find a discount program for child safety seats, call your state or local SAFE KIDS Coalition, or contact the National SAFE KIDS Campaign office: 202-662-0600, Web site: www.safekids.org.
- Check with you health care provider to see if they lend car seats or if they have a program for reduced prices on new car seats.

Government

- For foreign travel warnings and public announcements: U.S. Department of State, Bureau of Consular Affairs
  Call 24 hours: 202-647-5225
  Fax: 202-647-3000
  Read on web site: http://209.67.208.64/index.html
- To obtain an international driver's license:
  First check with the embassy or consulate of the country that you would like to drive in to find out if you need an international license or road permit and what the insurance requirements are.

  Obtain license from American Automobile Club (AAA) or other auto club:
  Apply through the AAA web site: www.aaa.com or look in your local phone book to find a AAA near you.

Magazines and Newsletters

- *Family Fun*, Disney Magazine Publishing Inc., monthly.

Web Sites

- ABC's of Parenting: under "Family" choose "Travel" for links to travel-related web sites: www.abcparenting.com/

Violence in a Child's World

Description

Violence is the act of using force or power to hurt people. Violence takes many forms: using fear, pain, or hurt to make another do something against their wishes; using words to scare, bully, embarrass, or demean; hurting someone physically, damaging the things someone cares about; or touching someone against their wishes. Hitting, slapping, rape, robbery, murder, unwanted sexual touching, verbal threats, drive-by shootings, vandalizing property, and hate crimes are examples of violence that can be present in a child's world.

Realistic Expectations

- Violence touches all children on some level: some see violence on television or in newspapers, some witness real life violence, some are victims of violence, and some behave violently.
- A basic need of children is to feel safe. When children are exposed to violence or violent images, it can be traumatic and make them feel insecure.
- Age impacts how children react to violence:
  - Infants and toddlers are likely to feel insecure and express it by showing more separation anxiety when their parents leave them in the care of others.
  - Preschool children are likely to copy violence, act tough, or to be aggressive.
- The impact on young children exposed to violence may go unnoticed by parents; because children are just beginning to learn about emotions and to use language, most will have a hard time understanding and expressing their fears and pain.
- Children are more likely to have stronger reactions to violence if they have experienced a traumatic incident in the past, are grieving a loss, or are ill.
- Children are more likely to cope positively with being exposed to violence if they have a stable emotional relationship with at least one parent or other significant adult, have an easygoing temperament, have parents and other adults who model behavior that encourages peaceful solutions for coping with problems, are older at the time of the exposure, or have support from persons outside the family.
- Children who live with violence at home often feel that they are to blame for the abuse; this is particularly frustrating for them because while they are feeling responsible for it, they are powerless to stop it.
- Many children who have witnessed or have been victims of violence develop psychological disorders that result in a variety of problems including sleep disturbances, inability to concentrate, flashbacks, images of terror, and nightmares.
- When children see or experience violence being used as a way to solve problems, they are more likely to use violence themselves when they feel angry, frustrated, or overwhelmed.
- Violence is often passed from generation to generation. Children who directly witness or experience violence in their families are more likely to abuse or be abused by a partner as an adult.
- Adults can have a great impact on reducing violence in the child's world and the world at large; most of the factors that feed violence are situations adults can prevent.
- Violence is a learned behavior. Violence can be unlearned.

Approaches

Pay attention to what your child is seeing, hearing, and feeling about the world. In early childhood, life experiences draw an inner "map" that will be your child's guide for the rest of his life. He is like a sponge; he soaks up what is around him and then releases it when squeezed. Some children will have maps in which they are central figures, powerful, and surrounded by friends. Others will have maps in which they are surrounded by enemies, or are insignificant specks stuck off in the corner.

Be cautious and conservative about exposing your child to the nastiness of the world. Let him play freely. Let him take childhood at a child's pace. Keep the dark side of adult life within the adult circle as much as possible. Be the guardian of his childhood and shield him from premature exposure to violence.

—From *Raising Children in a Socially Toxic Environment* by James Garbarino, Jossey-Bass, 1995.

> *I believe that one day, for one moment, there will be peace among everybody. People and animals all over the world will stop fighting and hating and they will think to themselves, "What is the reason for weapons? What are their purposes? Killing? Hurting? What for?" That little voice inside people will take over and people will start to think, "What a wonderful Earth this is."*
>
> —From Ben, nine years, as told to Misti Snow in
> *Take Time to Play Checkers*, Viking Press, 1992.

Decrease the amount of violence around your child to prevent violent behavior in him. Violence teaches violence! Violent behavior in your child can be decreased or prevented if you protect him from the following things:

- Being the victim of physical abuse and/or sexual abuse.
- Witnessing violence in his home and/or community.
- Seeing violence in the media (television, movies, or computer games).
- Guns in his home.

Some of these things may be impossible for you to control, but most of them are within your reach; take action now to protect him.

—Ideas found in "Facts for Families: Understanding Violent Behavior in Children & Adolescents," American Academy of Child & Adolescent Psychiatry, 1997.

Approach conflicts as a process of family problem solving. Remaining calm, being respectful, and involving preschool children will be constructive in the long run. Consider these steps in the process:

- Calm down, figure out what the problem is, and address what is fueling your emotions.
- Find a good time to discuss the problem. Don't wait too long with preschool children and make sure you won't be interrupted or intruded upon.
- Set some simple basic rules of respectful communication that include not blaming a person about past mistakes and focusing on the problem at hand.
- Show your child you understand and accept his feelings; he will need help naming his feelings and reassurance that feelings like anger are acceptable. Share your feelings.
- Talk about what the problem is.

- Consider everyone's thoughts, solutions, or ideas pertaining to the problem and support the child in contributing to the process.
- Talk about the solutions you like and don't like and see if you can agree on some. Pick one.
- Watch for the results and open the discussion again if the problem isn't being solved.

> —Ideas found in *The Lesbian Parenting Book: A Guide to Creating Families and Raising Children* by D. Merilee Clunis and G. Dorsey Green, Seal Press, 1995.

When it is possible, share child rearing with your partner. Accept that both men and women have the capacity to love and nurture children. If nurturing becomes accepted behavior for all, it may have an impact on decreasing violence in our culture.

> —Ideas found in *Boys Will Be Boys: Breaking the Link Between Masculinity and Violence* by Myriam Miedzian, Doubleday, 1991.

Help your child understand when he is exposed to actual violence or accounts of violence against someone close to him:

- Be honest about the violent situation. Give him information at the level he can understand.
- Explain that even though bad things happen to children every once in awhile, most children go through each day with no harm.
- Provide extra emotional support for him: hugs, time together, and words of comfort.
- Avoid passing on your own anxiety to him. If you are feeling anxious about the situation, deal with your feelings before your child is affected.
- Be reassuring by telling him what you and the others who care for him are doing to ensure *his* safety.
- Tell him what he can do to be safe on his own—like yelling, "No!" asking for help, and not talking to strangers.
- Keep an eye open for any signs of anxiety, and get help if you are concerned.

He may react strongly to violent events; be prepared.

> —Ideas found in "Talking To Your Children About Violence Against Kids" by Sharon Hills-Bonczyk, *Family Information Services*, 1998.

Protect your child from viewing violence on television and at the movies. Children younger than seven are especially influenced by what they see on the screen. After viewing violence, they are more likely to behave in aggressive or harmful ways toward others, they may become less sensitive to the pain and suffering of others, and they may become more fearful of the world around them.

> —From "Media Violence and Children: A Guide for Parents" by Joan Horton and Jenni Zimmer, 1994. Reprinted with permission from the National Association for the Education of Young Children, 1994.

Take action to protect your family from violence in your community. Don't feel helpless against crime—prevent it or fight back against violence:

- Set up a Neighborhood Watch or a community patrol; your local police will help you.
- Make sure your streets and homes are well-lighted.
- Help make sure that all the youth in the neighborhood have positive ways to spend their spare time through organized recreation, tutoring programs, part-time work, and volunteer opportunities. You don't need to take this one on alone! Encourage local agencies, schools, officials, or community groups to create programs that will fill these needs in your community.

- Build a partnership with police that is focused on solving problems rather than reacting to crises. Make it possible for neighbors to report suspicious activity or crimes without fear of retaliation.
- Take advantage of safety in numbers and hold group activities to show you're determined to drive out crime and drugs.
- Clean up the neighborhood! Involve everyone-teens, children, and senior citizens. Graffiti, litter, abandoned cars, and run-down buildings tell criminals that you don't care about where you live or about each other. Call your local public works department and ask for help cleaning up.
- Ask local officials to use new ways to get criminals out of your building or neighborhood. These include enforcing anti-noise laws, housing codes, health and fire codes, anti-nuisance laws, and drug-free clauses in rental leases.
- Work with schools to establish drug-free zones.
- Work with recreation officials to do the same for parks.
- Develop and share a phone list of local organizations that can provide counseling, job training, guidance, and other services that can help neighbors.

> —Ideas from "Ten Things Adults Can Do To Stop Violence,"
> Online, National Crime Prevention Council: www.ncpc.org.

Teach your child what to do if he finds a gun. Tell your child first to STOP! Be sure to tell him: "NEVER touch a gun." Then, teach him to walk away from the gun and tell an adult. These simple instructions could save a life.

> —Ideas found in "Find a Gun? Here's What to Do," National Crime Prevention Council.

If you learn or suspect that an adult you know is being abused by a partner, offer support:

- Listen and believe the person.
- Acknowledge that violence is wrong. Nobody deserves to be hit.
- Don't pass judgment on either of the people involved, and assure the person that help is available for both of them.
- Tell the person that they can take steps to stop the abuse:
  - Join a support group
  - Stay at an emergency shelter
  - Seek legal remedies or advice
  - Seek counseling
- Ask, "Are you safe right now? Where will you go after you leave me?" Help the person find the phone number of a shelter, doctor, or social worker if they are willing to get help now.
- Resist expecting a quick fix. Victims often need time before they are willing to accept help. Leave the door open to talking again.
- Set up a time to meet again.
- If children or adults who cannot make decisions for themselves are being abused, report it to the proper authorities: the numbers are in your local telephone book under "child abuse/protection and adult protection" in your county office.

> —From "Domestic Violence: Treating the Abused and the Abuser," *Minnesota Medicine*,
> October 1997.

Help your child understand more about violence by reading about it together:

 A Safe Place by Maxine Trottier, for children over the age of four who have experienced living in a shelter for battered women.

 King of the Playground by Phyllis Reynolds Naylor

 Life Doesn't Frighten Me by Maya Angelou

 Smoky Night by Eve Bunting, for children over the age of four who have experienced rioting.

 The Butter Battle Book by Dr. Seuss

 Why Did It Happen?: Helping Young Children Cope In a Violent World by Janice Cohn, for children over the age of four who have experienced a violent crime.

When to Get More Help

Children typically grow and learn new skills in their own time and at their own pace within the wide range of what is normal. Sometimes, children need a bit of extra help to keep their development on track, or to stay healthy and happy. Sometimes, parents need help providing for a child's needs or sorting out the best approaches to parenting.

Consider getting help for your child if he:

- Has witnessed or experienced acts of violence.
- Has many temper tantrums in a single day, several of which last for more than fifteen minutes, or often cannot be calmed by you.
- Has many aggressive outbursts, often for no reason.
- Is extremely active, impulsive, and fearless.
- Does not seem attached to you; for example, he does not touch, look for, or return to you in strange places.
- Frequently is cruel toward other children or animals, threatens others, plays with fire, harms property, or engages in play that has excessively violent themes.

Consider getting help for yourself if you:

- Are in a relationship where someone hits, shoves, or slaps you; uses looks or actions to intimidate you; attempts to control who you see, where you go, or what you do; calls you names; or humiliates you in front of others.
- Inflict power, force, or harm on another.
- Believe or worry that you could be violent or hurt your child.

You are the expert when it comes to your family and child. If you have a concern, trust your instinct and find someone trained to help you: health care providers, early intervention teams, mental health professionals, parent educators and consultants, or telephone help-line staff. Consider talking it over with friends and family, too. You don't need to worry alone! Turn to "Finding Help in Your Community" on page 4 to learn about finding help near you.

More Help and Information

Books for Parents

- *Raising Children in a Socially Toxic Environment* by James Garbarino. Jossey-Bass, 1995.
- *Teaching Peace: How to Raise Children to Live in Harmony—Without Fear, Without Prejudice, Without Violence* by Jan Arnow. Berkley Publishing, 1995.
- *Raising Peaceful Children in a Violent World* by Nancy Lee Cecil and Patricia L. Roberts. Innisfree Press, 1995.
- *When Nothing Makes Sense: Disaster, Crisis, and Their Effects on Children* by Gerald Deskin and Greg Steckler, Fairview Press, 1996

Articles, Pamphlets, and Booklets

- "Families Creating a Circle of Peace" by Jim McGinnes, et al. Institute for Peace and Justice, 1996. (see National Organizations for address)
- "Guns and Other Weapons," "Making Children, Families, and Communities Safer from Violence" and other valuable resources from National Crime Prevention Council. Call, write or view online. (see National Organizations for address)
- "NAEYC position Statement on: Violence in the Lives of Children." Request from:

  National Association for the Education of Young Children (NAEYC)
  800-424-2460, Fax: 202-328-1846
  Web site: www.naeyc.org

Hotlines

- National Domestic Violence Hotline: 800-799-SAFE (800-799-7233)
- National Victim Center: 800-FYI-CALL (800-394-2255)

Magazines and Newsletters

- Seeds of Promise, quarterly reports. Children, Youth, and Family Consortium, University of Minnesota: www.cyfc.umn.edu. or call 612-625-7248.

National Organizations

- Children's Defense Fund
  202-628-8787
  E-mail: cdinfo@childrensdefense.org
  Web site: www.childrensdefense.org
- National Crime Prevention Council
  202-466-6272, Fax: 202-296-1356
  Web site: www.ncpc.org
- Parenting for Peace and Justice Network, The Institute for Peace and Justice
  314-533-4445, Fax: 533-1017
  E-mail: ppjn@aol.com

Web Sites

- Pavnet Online, Partnerships Against Violence Network: www.pavnet.org

Whining and Complaining

Description

Whining is a dissatisfied, nasal, complaining, unacceptable tone of voice that makes even a request for a hug sound like fingernails on a blackboard. Complaining is a form of whining that expresses dissatisfaction, unhappiness, resentment, or pain.

Realistic Expectations

- Whining usually begins around age two when children start to understand how they feel and what they want, but haven't developed enough language to express themselves.

- Whining sometimes decreases around age three and a half, but it is common for it to continue to age five or later.

- Whining and complaining are common in children when they are hungry, tired, sick, bored, frustrated, stressed, confused, or not getting enough attention.

- Children that eat well, sleep well, get help in tasks that they are struggling to master, understand what is expected of them, understand what the rules are, and get plenty of love and attention may be less likely to whine and complain.

- Some types of temperaments are more prone to whining: children who do not adapt to new situations easily, children who have trouble with transitions, and children who are persistent.

- Children who have a sensitive and intense temperament may complain often because they may react more strongly to situations, changes, and to temperatures, tastes, and smells.

- Children often whine because they hear whining parents, caregivers, teachers, or siblings. Decreasing the amount of whining around children may decrease their whining.

- Giving in to whining, punishing whining, or getting angry about it will reward children. Either positive attention or negative attention reinforces whining.

- Learning to express yourself appropriately is a learned skill that takes time, but is a valuable skill to have as an adult.

Approaches

Find the reason for whining. Keep notes for a few days to recall when your child whines unacceptably. Look for a pattern: before mealtime, while playing a particular game, or due to boredom at a certain time each day. If you find the trigger for whining, you may be able to prevent it by changing it's cause.

> —Ideas found in *Your Child's Emotional Health* (Philadelphia Child Guidance Center), Macmillan, 1994.

Respond to your child's requests. Answer appropriate requests as soon as you can. If necessary, interrupt what you are doing to tell your child that you will give her your attention soon. Ignoring your child's requests may cause her to start whining, while giving attention to her requests may help prevent it.

—Ideas found in "Please Stop Whining!" by Ronald L. Pitzer, *Young Families*, Fall 1993.

Show your child what whining is and practice what it isn't. Believe it or not, your child may not know what whining is or how irritating it can be. Try tape recording your child both whining and using her pleasant voice. Find a time when she is not whining to play the tape in order to show her exactly what whining is and what it isn't. Show her how to use words by telling her what you see: "I can see that you are very sad." Then, help her to say why and practice using her non-whining voice. Catch the child using a non-whining voice often and praise it.

—Ideas found in *What to Expect the Toddler Years* by Arlene Eisenberg, Heidi E. Murkoff, and Sandee E. Hathaway, Workman Pub., 1996.

Draw a child's attention away from the cause of whining. If the child is whining for something she can't have or do, try distracting her with something she can have or can do: "You may not climb on the kitchen table. Let me help you put some cushions on the floor and we'll climb there." If she is whining due to frustration about something that she's not able to do yet, point out a skill that she has mastered: "I can see that you are frustrated because you want to ride a big bike like your brother. I'm so proud of the way you peddle your trike—will you show me?"

—Ideas found in *Toddlers and Preschoolers* by Lawrence Kutner, William Morrow, Inc., 1994.

Deal with whining by ignoring it:

- Give your child a warning. Tell her that you will not respond to her if she whines. Then, after a reminder, ignore the whining. Notice her efforts to stop whining, no matter how small, and praise her when she uses a better voice.

- Give the child a cue. Each time whining occurs, repeat the same phrase or gesture, then ignore the whining: say "I can't hear you properly" or touch your ear to indicate whining.

- Completely ignore whining. After you have made clear what whining is and that it is not acceptable, simply don't respond to it when it occurs.

—Ideas found in *Win the Whining War and Other Skirmishes* by Cynthia Whitman, Perspective Publishing, Inc., 1991.

Create a whining spot. If you have demonstrated what whining sounds like and shown what you expect, and the child continues to whine, she may need to vent some frustration. Explain to her, without anger, that if she must whine, she will have to do it away from you. Ask her to go to the whining spot, a place you have decided upon earlier. This is not a punishment, but a way to let a child express frustration in an acceptable way. Tell the child that when she's ready, she can come back.

—Ideas found in *Discipline Without Shouting or Spanking* by Jerry Wyckoff and Barbara C. Unell, Meadowbrook Press, 1984.

> I don't recognize whining—I tell my child: "I can't understand you when you talk like that—when you talk in a regular, pleasant voice, I can help you." Then be consistent.
>
> —Mary Lou, Spring Grove, MN

When your child complains, notice and tell her what you see her feeling, then ask her for her ideas on how to make the situation better for herself: "I can see that you like your favorite cup. Instead of complaining about the one I picked out, what else could you do?" Use positive language yourself and notice the good things that the child does.

> —Ideas found in *Positive Parenting from A to Z* by Karen Renshaw Joslin.
> Fawcett Columbine: Ballantine Books, 1994.

Help a child learn to stop whining by reading about it together:

Berenstain Bears Get the Gimmies by Stan and Jan Berenstain

Me First by Helen Lester

When to Get More Help

Children typically grow and learn new skills in their own time and at their own pace within the wide range of what is normal. Sometimes, children need a bit of extra help to keep their development on track, or to stay healthy and happy. Sometimes, parents need help providing for a child's needs or sorting out the best approaches to parenting.

Consider getting help for your child if she:

- Whines enough to get your attention for several months and is misunderstood frequently (could be a signal of a speech and language delay).
- Whines excessively for a period of one or two weeks (may signal a physical problem).

You are the expert when it comes to your family and child. If you have a concern, trust your instinct and find someone trained to help you: health care providers, early intervention teams, mental health professionals, parent educators and consultants, or telephone help-line staff. Consider talking it over with friends and family, too. You don't need to worry alone! Turn to "Finding Help in Your Community" on page 4 to learn about finding help near you.

More Help and Information

Books for Parents

- *Child Magazine's Guide to Whining: Tactics for Taming Demanding Behavior* by Tamara Eberlein. Pocket Books, 1997.
- *Win the Whining War and Other Skirmishes* by Cynthia Whitman. Perspective Pub., 1991.

Articles

- "No More Whining," by Paula Spencer. *Parenting*, April 1997. Available online at ParentTime: www.parenttime.com. Enter "whining" in the "Search Our Site" box and hit "Go."

Index

teaching about personal space,
368
two-year olds, 367
videos, 370
visiting friends' homes, 368
when to get help, 369
functions, naming and describing, 52

G

gay parents, resources for, 347
gender identity
books for parents, 202
books to read with your child,
201
definition of, 196
helping boys with, 200
helping girls with, 199
instilling values and expectations,
198
realistic expectations for, 196–97
removing gender-based
limitations, 199
responding to questions about
anatomy, 197
treating children equally, 198
when to get help, 201
gluing
activities, 135–36
checking materials for toxicity,
135
preventing choking, 136
glurch, 160
goop, 160
grandparents, resources for, 348
grief. See death and grief
gross motor development. See hand
and body movement

H

habits, bad
accepting normal behaviors, 186
books for parents, 188
books to read with your child,
187
definition of, 186
realistic expectations for, 186
stopping, 187
when to get help, 188
hand and body movement
four-year-olds, 84–87

one-year-olds, 18–21
three-year-olds, 62–65
two-year-olds, 40–43
hand-eye coordination. See
coordination, hand-eye
handicapped children. See children
with special needs
health care
books and articles for parents,
316
books to read with your child,
315
choosing providers, 4–5, 307
considering alternative therapies,
309
dental checkups, 69, 311
emergency room visits, 310
evaluating quality of care, 309
government resources, 316
hospitalizations, 313–14
hotlines, 316
immunizations, 308
medical checkups, 307
national organization resources,
316
preparing for appointments, 310,
312–13
realistic expectations for, 306–7
tooth eruption charts, 311
videos, 316
Web sites, 316
when to get help, 315
high chair safety, 235
hitting. See aggression
holidays
books for parents, 374
books to read with your child,
374
definition of, 371
encouraging celebrations, 372,
373
establishing family
traditions/rituals, 372, 373
fact vs. fantasy, 373
and money, 373
preparing for likely problems, 372
realistic expectations for, 371
teaching the joy of giving, 373
teaching your child the meaning
of, 372
videos, 374
when to get help, 374
homes security, 240
hopping. See jumping and hopping

hospital visits. See health care
household jobs
four-year-olds, 88, 90
one-year-olds, 22, 24
three-year-olds, 66, 68
two-year-olds, 44, 46

I

imaginary friends
allowing your child to have, 368
four-year-olds, 81, 83
three-year-olds, 59, 61
two-year-olds, 37, 39
imitating
four-year-olds, 96, 98
one-year-olds, 30, 32
three-year-olds, 74, 76
two-year-olds, 52, 54
immunizations, 308
independence
allowing for mistakes, 377
books for parents, 378
books to read with your child,
377
definition of, 375
encouraging solitary play, 376
four-year-olds, 80, 82
helping your child learn, 376–77
one-year-olds, 14, 16
realistic expectations for, 375
three-year-olds, 58, 60
for timid/fearful children, 377
two-year-olds, 36, 38
videos, 378
when to get help, 378
instructions, understanding and
following
four-year-olds, 93, 94
one-year-olds, 27, 29
three-year-olds, 71, 73
two-year-olds, 49, 51
intelligence. See play and learning
interrupting
books for parents, 381
books to read with your child,
380
definition of, 379
polite, 380
preventing, 380
realistic expectations for, 379
setting limits on, 380
when to get help, 381

J

jobs. *See* household jobs
jumping and hopping
    activities, 137–38
    books to read with your child, 139
    four-year-olds, 84, 86
    three-year-olds, 62, 64
    two-year-olds, 40, 42

K

kicking
    activities, 119
    four-year-olds, 84, 86
    three-year-olds, 62, 64
    two-year-olds, 40, 42
kindergarten
    books and articles for parents, 388
    books to read with your child, 387
    definition of, 382
    government resources, 388
    helping your child prepare for, 383–84
    important skills for, 384
    making the decision, 386
    national organization resources, 388
    overcoming fears of, 386–87
    physical exams prior to, 385
    realistic expectations for, 382
    signs of a good classroom, 385
    visiting the school, 386
    Web sites, 388
    when to get help, 387

L

lacing, 167
ladders, climbing
    four-year-olds, 84, 86
    three-year-olds, 62, 64
    two-year-olds, 40, 42
language development. *See* communication; conversation; language rules, understanding; sentences, speaking in; talking; words, understanding and using
language rules, understanding
    four-year-olds, 92, 94

three-year-olds, 70, 72
    two-year-olds, 49, 50
    See also communication; conversation; phrases, speaking in; sentences, speaking in; talking; words, understanding and using
lead poisoning, preventing, 235–36
learning and play. *See* play and learning
lesbian parents, resources for, 347
letters, recognizing
    activities, 140–42
    books to read with your child, 143
    four-year-olds, 96
limits, setting. *See* discipline and disciplining
lying
    books for parents, 392
    books to read with your child, 391
    definition of, 389
    distinguishing between fantasy and reality, 391
    distinguishing between full and partial truth, 391
    encouraging truthfulness, 390
    realistic expectations for, 389
    respecting privacy, 391
    teaching truth *vs.* lying, 390
    videos, 392
    when to get help, 392
    wishful thinking and, 390

M

make-believe, playing
    activities for, 144–45
    assembling a make-believe play box, 145
    books to read with your child, 146
    four-year-olds, 96, 98
    preventing choking, 145
    three-year-olds, 74, 76
    two-year-olds, 52, 54
manners
    age-appropriate, 394
    books and articles for parents, 396
    books to read with your child, 395

definition of, 393
    encouraging initiative in, 395
    helping your child with the first steps, 394
    modeling polite behavior, 394
    realistic expectations for, 393
    teaching new behaviors, 394, 395
    teaching reasons for, 394, 395
    when to get help, 396
    whispering and, 395
    See also eating; interrupting; talking back
manners, mealtime. *See* eating
masturbation, 37, 59, 81, 450
matching
    activities, 147–48
    books to read with your child, 148
    one-year-olds, 31, 33
    preventing choking, 148
    two-year-olds, 53, 55
mealtimes. *See* eating
measuring, 149
media
    books and articles for parents, 520
    books to read with your child, 519
    building a balanced television diet, 512–13
    definition of, 511
    evaluating before you buy, 519
    government resources, 520
    Internet issues, 519
    judging screen violence, 515
    limiting screen time, 513
    magazines, 521
    movie ratings, 516
    national organization resources, 521
    qualities to look for, 513–14
    realistic expectations for, 511–12
    software ratings and content descriptors, 517–18
    talking with your child about, 514
    television ratings, 515
    video games ratings and content descriptors, 517–18
    video resources, 521
    Web sites, 521
    when to get help, 519
medical care. *See* health care
mental health professionals, finding, 5

bicycle safety, 232
four-year-olds, 84, 86
one-year-olds, 19, 21
safety considerations for, 173
three-year-olds, 62, 64
two-year-olds, 40, 42
routines. See rules and routines,
    understanding and following
rules and routines, understanding
    and following
four-year-olds, 88, 90
one-year-olds, 22, 24
three-year-olds, 66, 68
two-year-olds, 44, 46
    See also discipline and disciplining
running
activities, 161–62
four-year-olds, 84, 86
one-year-olds, 18, 20
three-year-olds, 62, 64
two-year-olds, 40, 42

S

safety
animal safety, 232
bicycle safety, 232
books and articles for parents,
    246
books to read with your child,
    244
calling emergency medical
    services, 242–44
carbon monoxide poisoning
    prevention, 238
car safety, 232–33, 239
catalogs, 247
childproofing
    basements, 231
    bathrooms, 230
    childrens' rooms, 230–31
    garages, 231
    homes, 228–29
    kitchens, 230
    laundry rooms, 231
    utility rooms, 231
    yards, 231–32
choking prevention
    coins as hazards, 150
    during craft activities, 136,
        148, 160, 167
    when eating, 47, 69, 233, 326

while playing make-believe,
    145
cold weather safety, 236
crossing streets, 239
definition of, 227
emergency preparedness, 241
finding the courage to let
    children go, 244
fire injury prevention, 233–34
food-borne illness prevention,
    234–35
government resources, 246
high chair safety, 235
home security, 240
identifying environmental
    hazards, 238
lead poisoning prevention,
    235–36
national organization resources,
    247
playground safety, 236
poisoning prevention, 237
pool safety, 237
realistic expectations for, 227–28
recall notice information, 247
shopping cart safety, 240
sled safety, 240
sun safety, 236
teaching children to call for help,
    244
travel safety, 238
videos, 247
walker injury prevention, 238
water safety, 237
Web sites, 247
when to get help, 245
scooping, 174
scribbling
one-year-olds, 19, 21
two-year-olds, 41, 43
security objects. See transitions and
    security objects
self-esteem
accepting your child, 440
books and articles for parents,
    442
books to read with your child,
    441
child's vs. parent's, 437
definition of, 436
developing a positive self-image,
    439
developing optimism, 440–41

four-year-olds, 80, 82
giving messages of affirmation,
    438–39
giving unconditional love, 441
giving your full attention, 440
meeting basic needs, 437
one-year-olds, 14, 16
principles of, 439–40
realistic expectations for, 436
showing your child respect, 441
three-year-olds, 58, 60
two-year-olds, 36, 38
when to get help, 442
self-help skills
four-year-olds, 88–91
one-year-olds, 22–25
three-year-olds, 66–69
two-year-olds, 44–47
senses, exploring
activities for, 163–65
books to read with your child,
    166
sentences, speaking in
four-year-olds, 92, 94
three-year-olds, 70, 72
two-year-olds, 48, 50
    See also communication;
        conversation; language rules,
        understanding; phrases,
        speaking in; talking; words,
        understanding and using
separation anxiety and attachment
books for parents, 447
books to read with your child,
    446
creating separation and reuniting
    rituals, 445
dealing with strong feelings,
    445–46
dealing with your own feelings,
    446
definitions of, 443
developing secure attachments,
    444
easing the anxiety, 446
giving attention and love, 444
one-year-olds, 14
practicing separation, 445
realistic expectations for, 443
three-year-olds, 58
two-year-olds, 36
using comfort objects, 445
when to get help, 447